Agent Technologies and Web Engineering:
Applications and Systems

Ghazi Alkhatib
Applied Science University, Jordan

David Rine
George Mason University, USA

Information Science REFERENCE

INFORMATION SCIENCE REFERENCE
Hershey · New York

Director of Editorial Content: Kristin Klinger
Director of Production: Jennifer Neidig
Managing Editor: Jamie Snavely
Assistant Managing Editor: Carole Coulson
Typesetter: Larissa Vinci
Cover Design: Lisa Tosheff
Printed at: Yurchak Printing Inc.

Published in the United States of America by
Information Science Reference (an imprint of IGI Global)
701 E. Chocolate Avenue, Suite 200
Hershey PA 17033
Tel: 717-533-8845
Fax: 717-533-8661
E-mail: cust@igi-global.com
Web site: http://www.igi-global.com

and in the United Kingdom by
Information Science Reference (an imprint of IGI Global)
3 Henrietta Street
Covent Garden
London WC2E 8LU
Tel: 44 20 7240 0856
Fax: 44 20 7379 0609
Web site: http://www.eurospanbookstore.com

Library of Congress Cataloging-in-Publication Data

Agent technologies and web engineering : applications and systems / Ghazi Alkhatib and David Rine, editors.

p. cm.

Includes bibliographical references and index.

Summary: "This book presents various applications of the growing perspective of agent technologies as they apply the web engineering"--Provided by publisher.

ISBN 978-1-60566-618-1 (hardcover) -- ISBN 978-1-60566-619-8 (ebook) 1. Web site development. 2. Intelligent agents (Computer software) 3.

Web services. I. Alkhatib, Ghazi, 1947- II. Rine, David C

TK5105.888.A35 2009

006.7'6--dc22

2008044989

British Cataloguing in Publication Data
A Cataloguing in Publication record for this book is available from the British Library.

Advances in Information Technology and Web Engineering (AITWE) Series

ISBN: pending

Editor-in-Chief:
Ghazi I. Alkhatib, Applied Science University, Jordan
David C. Rine, George Mason University, USA

Integrated Approaches in Information Technology and Web Engineering: Advancing Organizational Knowledge Sharing
Ghazi I. Alkhatib, Applied Science University, Jordan & David C. Rine, George Mason University, USA
Information Science Reference * copyright 2009 * 361pp * H/C (ISBN: 978-1-60566-418-7) * US $195.00 (our price)

With the increasing proliferation of information technology and Web-based approaches to the implementation of systems and services, researchers, educators, and practitioners worldwide are experiencing a rising need for authoritative references to enhance their understanding of the most current and effective engineering practices leading to robust and successful solutions.

Integrated Approaches in Information Technology and Web Engineering: Advancing Organizational Knowledge Sharing presents comprehensive, research-driven insights into the field of Web engineering. This book collects over 30 authoritative articles from distinguished international researchers in information technology and Web engineering, creating an invaluable resource for library reference collections that will equip researchers and practitioners in academia and industry alike with the knowledge base to drive the next generation of innovations.

Agent Technologies and Web Engineering: Applications and Systems
Ghazi I. Alkhatib, Applied Science University, Jordan & David C. Rine, George Mason University, USA
Information Science Reference * copyright 2009 * 361pp * H/C (ISBN: 978-1-60566-618-1) * US $195.00 (our price)

In recent years, the emerging field of agent technologies has become mainstream in Web engineering. With constant field developments and updates, a reference source is needed that reflects the increased scope of agent technology application domains and development practices and tools.

Agent Technologies and Web Engineering: Applications and Systems presents the latest tools and applications addressing critical issues involved with information technology and Web engineering research. Covering topics such as next-generation networks, XML query processing, and Semantic Web services, this book provides cutting-edge research for practitioners and academicians involved in agent technology and Web engineering fields.

The Advances in Information Technology and Web Engineering (AITWE) Book Series aims to provide a platform for research in the area of Information Technology (IT) concepts, tools, methodologies, and ethnography, in the contexts of global communication systems and Web engineered applications. Organizations are continuously overwhelmed by a variety of new information technologies, many are Web based. These new technologies are capitalizing on the widespread use of network and communication technologies for seamless integration of various issues in information and knowledge sharing within and among organizations. This emphasis on integrated approaches is unique to this book series and dictates cross platform and multidisciplinary strategy to research and practice. The Advances in Information Technology and Web Engineering (AITWE) Book Series seeks to create a stage where comprehensive publications are distributed for the objective of bettering and expanding the field of web systems, knowledge capture, and communication technologies. The series will provide researchers and practitioners with solutions for improving how technology is utilized for the purpose of a growing awareness of the importance of web applications and engineering.

Table of Contents

Detailed Table of Contents

and by using any of its communication-enabled devices. Consequently, next-generation networks will require efficient mechanisms which can match consumers' demands (requested services) to network-operators' supplies (available services). The authors propose an agent approach for enabling autonomous coordination between all the entities across the telecom value chain, thus enabling automated context-aware service provisioning for the consumers. Furthermore, the authors hope that the proposed service discovery model will not only be interesting from a scientific point of view, but also amenable to real-world applications.

This chapter proposes a mobile, intelligent agent-based e-business architecture that allows buyers and sellers to perform business at remote locations. An e-business participant can generate a mobile, intelligent agent via some mobile devices (such as a personal digital assistant or mobile phone) and dispatch the agent to the Internet to do business on her behalf. This proposed architecture promises a number of benefits: First, it provides great convenience for traders as business can be conducted anytime and anywhere. Secondly, since the task of finding and negotiating with appropriate traders is handled by a mobile, intelligent agent, the user is freed from this time-consuming task. Thirdly, this architecture addresses the problem of limited and expensive connection time for mobile devices: A trader can disconnect her mobile device from its server after generating and launching a mobile, intelligent agent. Later on, she can reconnect and call back the agent for results, therefore minimizing the connection time. Finally, by complying with the standardization body FIPA, this flexible architecture increases the interoperability between agent systems and provides high scalability design for swiftly moving across the network.

Many real-world problems can be viewed and represented as a constraint satisfaction problem (CSP). In addition, many of these problems are distributed in nature. To this end, agents are combined with a special type of CSP called an Interval Algebra network (IA network). An IA network is a graph where each node represents an interval. Directed edges in the network are labelled with temporal interval relations. A probabilistic IA network has probabilities associated with the relations on the edges that can be used to capture preferences. A probabilistic IA agent (PIA-Agent) is assigned a probabilistic IA network. PIA-Agent's networks are connected via edges. The authors of this chapter present an algorithm which allows the PIA-Agents to collaboratively solve and recommend a temporal schedule. A natural application of this proposed system is a distributed scheduling system. The particular one chosen for this chapter is a university example involving a professor, student and secretary. Each has their own schedule and preferences which must be globally coordinated.

This chapter describes a multiagent approach that configures semantic Web services following a design problem solving method. For that, a propose-and-revise strategy was modeled and implemented in OWL-S. The other contribution of the approach is the extension of OWL-S for recording the service execution flow followed by the agent. The trace of the agent's reasoning is stored in node sets represented in a proof markup language which make up a framework for explanations on the Web. The proposed approach is shown to be useful in the context of e-business where the workflow definition of services is automatically performed by the agents in order to configure a computer from a customer order.

Researchers spend considerable time searching for relevant papers on the topic in which they are currently interested. Often, despite having similar interests, researchers in the same lab do not find it convenient to share results of bibliographic searches and thus conduct independent time-consuming searches. Research paper recommender systems can help the researcher avoid such time-consuming searches by allowing each researcher to automatically take advantage of previous searches performed by others in the lab. Existing recommender systems were developed for commercial domains to assist users by focusing towards products of their interests. Unlike those domains, the research paper domain has relatively few users when compared with the huge number of research papers. This chapter presents a novel system to recommend relevant research papers to a user based on the user's recent querying and browsing habits. The core of the system is a scalable subspace clustering algorithm, SCuBA (Subspace ClUstering Based Analysis) that performs well on the sparse, high-dimensional data collected in this domain. Both synthetic and benchmark datasets are used to evaluate the recommendation system and to demonstrate that it performs better than the traditional collaborative filtering approaches when recommending research papers.

a new algorithm for answering CKNN in SNDB where the important measure for the shortest path is network distances rather than Euclidean distances. DAR and eDAR algorithms are proposed to address CKNN queries based on the progressive incremental network expansion (PINE) technique. The authors' experiments show that the eDAR approach has better response time, and requires fewer shortest distance computations and KNN queries than approaches that are based on VN3 using IE.

This chapter reports the result of the author's recent work on XML query processing/optimization, which is a very important issue in XML data management. In this work, in order to more effectively and efficiently handle XML queries involving pure and/or negated containments, a previously proposed deterministic optimization approach is largely adapted. This approach resorts to heuristic-based deterministic transformations on algebraic query expressions in order to achieve the best possible optimization efficiency. Specialized transformation rules are thus developed, and efficient implementation algorithms for pure and negated containments are presented as well. Experimental study confirms the validity and effectiveness of the presented approach and algorithms in processing of XML queries involving pure and/or negated containments.

This chapter presents an original approach for text summarization using conceptual data classification. The authors show how a given text can be summarized without losing meaningful knowledge and without using any semantic or grammatical concepts. In fact, concept date classification is used to extract the most interacting sentences from the main text and ignoring the other meaningless sentences in order to generate the text summary. The approach is tested on Arabic and English texts with different sizes and different topics and the obtained results are satisfactory. The system may be incorporated with the indexers of search engines over the Internet in order to find key words and other pertinent information of the new deployed Web pages that would be stored in databases for quick search.

Web page classification is considered one of the most challenging research areas. Where the Web has a huge volume of unstructured and distributed documents that are related to a variety of domains; so, considering one base for the classification tasks will be extremely difficult. In addition, the Web is full of noise that will certainly harm the classifier performance especially if it is found in the classifier training data. Generally, it will be more valued to build domain-oriented classifiers (vertical classifiers) to classify pages related to a specific domain and compensate those classifiers with novel learning techniques to achieve better performance. The contribution of this chapter is three edged; firstly, a novel learning technique called Continuous Learning is introduced. Secondly, the chapter presents a new trend for Web page classification by presenting the domain-oriented classifiers (vertical classifiers). A new way of applying Bayes and K-Nearest Neighbor algorithms is introduced in order to build Domain Oriented Naïve Bayes (DONB) and Domain Oriented K-Nearest Neighbor (DOKNN) classifiers. The third contribution is combining both disciplines by introducing a novel classification strategy. Such strategy adds the continuous learning ability to Bayes theorem to build a Continuous learning domain oriented Naïve Bayes (CLNB) classifier. Where the overfitting problem has a great impact on most Web page classification techniques, continuous learning can be considered as a proposed solution. It allows the classifier to adapt itself continuously for achieving better performance. The proposed classifiers are tested; experimental results have shown that CLNB demonstrates significant performance improvement over both DONB and DOKNN where its accuracy goes beyond 94.1% after testing 1000 pages.

Service-orientation has emerged as a new promising paradigm for enterprise integration in the manufacturing sector. This chapter focuses on the approach and technologies for constructing a service oriented manufacturing environment. The service orientation is achieved via virtualization in which everything, including machines, equipments, devices, various data sources, applications, and processes, are virtualized as standard-based Web services. The virtualization approach is based on the emerging Web Services Resource Framework (WS-RF). A case study of virtualizing an AGV system using WS-RF is described. The use of Semantic Web Services technologies to enhance manufacturing Web services for a semantic-rich environment is discussed, focusing on OWL-S for semantic markup of manufacturing Web services and OWL for the development of ontologies in the manufacturing domain. An enterprise integration architecture enabled by Semantic Web service composition is also discussed.

Preface

The *International Journal of Technology and Web Engineering* (JITWE) outlines a critical dimension of integrating information technology and Web Engineering (WE) systems and tools. In an effort to facilitate and foster such dimensions and viewpoints about integrating the two areas, we selected articles published in the first two volumes of JITWE and organized them into three sections: agent, collaboration and access technologies.

The following provides an overview of the contents of each section in this book material:

- **Section I—Agent Technology:** Agents, multi-agents for Web services and e-commerce.
- **Section II—Collaboration:** Clustering research group collaboration, e-portfolio for virtual learning groups, email filtering.
- **Section III—Access:** Algorithm for continuous queries, text summarization, XML query processing, vertical Web page classification, service-oriented architectures.

Section I: Agent Technologies

Agent technologies are emerging as a mainstream technology in Web engineering. For example, the Web site (Whitestein, 2008) lists the following references extracted for only 2007 and 2008. The titles reflect the increasing scope of agent technologies application domains and development practices and tools.

- Defense Industry Applications of Autonomous Agents and Multi-Agent Systems
- Agent Technology and e-Health
- Issues in Multi-Agent Systems
- Emerging Web Services Technology
- The Agent Modeling Language – AML
- Adaptive Bidding in Single-Sided Auctions under Uncertainty.

Furthermore, the Web site (Magnet, 2008) reports applications of agent technologies in the areas of dynamic resource allocation, planning and scheduling.

Reflecting this important trend, chapters in this section of book material derived from previous issue articles contain research related to agents, multiagents, and mobile agents on Web services and e-business platforms. Chapters employ multiagents to address workflow management of semantic Web services and how to create satisfaction in systems using a specific approach: Allen's Interval Algebra and Probabilities. Follow on chapters handle service composition and provisioning, respectively. Finally, chapters present their research on how to deploy mobile agents in an e-business environment.

Sections II: Collaboration

This section contains chapters on creating collaborative Web based systems. The first two chapters are related to establishing collaborative environments. The first chapter presents an approach to cluster research group members' interests to enhance collaboration among them, while the second chapter presents the use of e-portfolios to enhance virtual learning groups. The last chapter explains how to develop a system to semi-automate emails filtering to help in reading emails more efficiently.

Sections II: Access

Chapters in this section address the issues of information access and retrieval using queries, Web page classification, text summarization technique, service oriented architectures and semantic Web features in a manufacturing setup, increased access through classification of Web services discovery systems, and finally enhanced access through performance analysis of Web site access.

Linking the three areas together may form one scenario for future research:

- From the user point of view, deploy software agents, intelligent and autonomous, to personalize access base of user profiling. These multiagents could be treated as a community of social agents, leading to incorporating social and behavioral factors in controlling the interaction and group dynamics of agents. These issues may include:
    - creative and innovative thinking patterns, such as Herrmann Brain Dominance Instrument (HBDI) (hbdi, 2008)
    - personal values and cultures, such as gender, religion, education, and family,
    - cyber social communities, such as Wikkipedia (Spinellis, and Louridas, 2008), Internet-based gaming (Waldo, 2008), and Open software communities, and
    - globalization issues in agents' communication, such as rules and regulations, country characteristics, economic and political stability of regions, and travel requirements,
- By having a harmonious teams (co-located or virtual) or cyber societies of multiagents, collaboration will increase in efficiency and effectiveness, leading to knowledge societies and personal satisfaction form work and life.
- At the third tier, agents and collaboration will alleviate the effects of information overload by retrieving only relevant information pulled from integrated multiple loosely coupled data sources in the Internet and economy in general, or internal and external sources at the enterprise level in particular.

The following figure demonstrates this scenario:

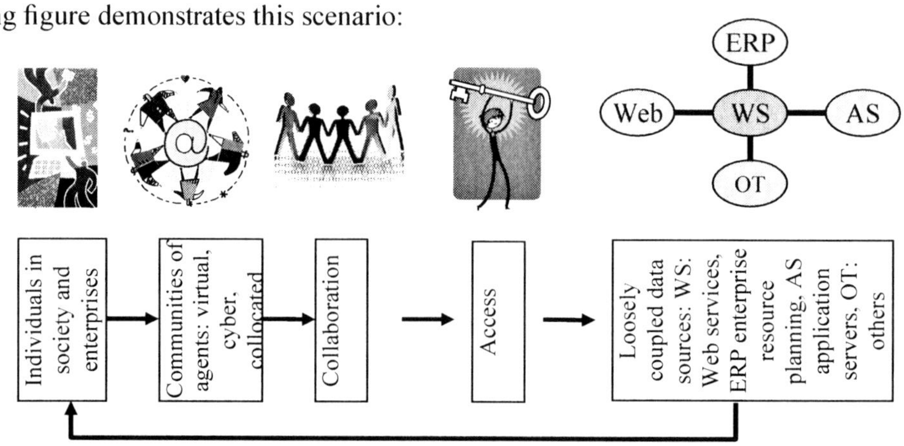

REFERENCES

hbdi.com, accessed September, 2008

Mmagenta-technology.com/en/ solutionsandservices/smartresource/ accessed September, 2008.

Spinellis, D. & Louridas, P. (2008). The collaborative organization of knowledge. *Communications of the ACM, 51*(8), 68-73.

Waldo, J. (2008). Scaling in games and virtual worlds. *Communications of the ACM, 51*(8), 38-44. See other articles on game theory in the same issue.

Wwhitestein.com/ library/whitestein-series-in-software-agent-technologies-and-autonomic-computing), accessed September, 2008.

About the Editors

Ghazi Alkhatib is an assistant professor of software engineering in the College of Computer Science and Information Technology, Applied Science University (Amman, Jordan). In 1984, he obtained his Doctor of Business Administration from Mississippi State University in information systems with minors in computer science and accounting. Since then, he has been engaged in teaching, consulting, training, and research in the area of computer information systems in the U.S. and Gulf countries. In addition to his research interests in databases and systems analysis and design, he has published several articles and presented many papers in regional and international conferences on software processes, knowledge management, e-business, Web services and agent software, workflow, and portal / grid computing integration with Web services.

David Rine is Professor Emeritus, Volgenau School of Information Technology and Engineering, George Mason University Virginia, USA. He has been practicing, teaching and researching engineered software development for over 30 years. Prior to joining George Mason University he served in various leadership roles in the IEEE Computer Society and co-founded two of the technical committees. He joined George Mason University in 1985 and was the founding chair of the Department of Computer Science and one of the founders of the (Volgenau) School of Information Technology and Engineering. Rine has received numerous research, teaching and service awards from computer science and engineering societies and associations, including the IEEE Centennial Award, the IEEE Pioneer Award, the IEEE Computer Society Meritorious Service Awards, the IEEE Computer Society Special Awards, and the IEEE Computer Society 50th anniversary Golden Core Award, the historical IEEE Computer Society Honor Roll and Distinguished Technical Services Awards. He has been a pioneer in graduate, undergraduate and high school education, producing computer science texts and leading establishment of the international Advanced Placement Computer Science program for the nation's high school students, co-designer the first computer science and engineering curriculum (1976) and the first masters in software engineering curriculum (1978). He has been an editor of a number of prestigious software-oriented journals. During his tenure he has authored over 300 published works and has directed many PhD students. Complementing his work at GMU, he has worked on many international technology and relief projects in various countries and made many life-long international friendships. His past students are the most important record of his technical achievements.

Section I
Agent Technologies

Chapter I
Employing Graph Network Analysis for Web Service Composition

John Gekas
University of Essex, UK

Maria Fasli
University of Essex, UK

ABSTRACT

The Web services paradigm has enabled an increasing number of providers to host remotely accessible services. However, the true potential of such a distributed infrastructure can only be reached when such autonomic services can be combined together as parts of a workflow, in order to collectively achieve combined functionality. In this paper we present our work in the area of automatic workflow composition among Web services with semantically described functionality capabilities. For this purpose, we use a set of heuristics derived from the connectivity structure of the service repository in order to effectively guide the composition process. The methodologies presented in this paper have been inspired by research in areas such as graph network analysis, social network analysis and bibliometrics. In addition, we present comparative experimentation results in order to evaluate the presented techniques.

INTRODUCTION

The increasing popularity the Web Service paradigm and the Semantic Web have gained recently shows clearly the overall need for unified access to semantically meaningful Web-based resources, whether these resources are data sources (such as Web sites) or functionality providers (in the form of Web applications and Web services). Numerous and valuable efforts have been presented in these research areas, coming both from industrial and academic colleagues. Furthermore, the notion of Service-Oriented Architecture (SOA) has arisen, referring to any decentralised software platform that allows the development, deployment, and integrated access to Web service applications. It has also been strongly argued that the full potential of such a service-oriented infrastructure can only be fulfilled if effective mechanisms for resource discovery and service composition exist as well (Berners-Lee, 2001).

It seems to be common practice that the process of service discovery and composition usually takes place within a predefined search space (often called service repository or service network), as opposed to the discovery of services over the Web on the fly. In industrial environments, many real world hosts (commercial or not) that offer service brokerage, query, discovery, and/or composition mechanisms seem to be following this approach as well: remote methods (http://www.remotemethods.com/), WSIndex (http://www.wsindex.org/), and Strike Iron Web Service Marketplace (http://www.strikeiron.com/default.aspx) all operate on predefined (but extensible) Web service networks. Noncommercial service discovery providers operate on given service networks as well, such as XMethods and SalCentral.

In this article, we examine the applicability of graph network analysis as a potential solution to the Web service composition problem domain. The presented approach involves the representation of the problem domain search space (Web service directory/composition network) as a graph network, and the use of specific graph network analysis metrics in order to "guide" the composition algorithm to successful solutions. The purpose of the network analysis metrics is to examine the link structure of the composition network (partly or as a whole) and use this information in order to assess which Web services are most likely to be useful with regards to a particular composition request.

We believe that the problem domain of Web service composition poses a number of restrictions, inherent to the nature of the research problem itself:

- The size of the Web service composition network may be extremely large. Most Web service directories are open, public communities where every developer is able to publish their Web services, thus network size may be increasing rapidly.
- Web service directories are dynamic and flexible communities by nature: new Web services are constantly added to existing Web service networks, whereas other services might be made obsolete. Programmable Web (http://www.programmableWeb.com/), a Web service listing directory that also produces daily estimates regarding the size of the Web service landscape, had observed a growth rate of 2.81 new composed services per day as of June 2006.

Due to the above restrictions, it may be difficult for a composition mechanism to possess complete knowledge of the search space it operates on. This could be either due to the prohibiting size of the composition network, which would make the information collection process time-consuming and computationally-intensive, or to the fact that constant updates would need to be performed so as the information remains up to date. Thus, we believe that composition mechanisms should be able to operate under conditions of incomplete knowledge on the Web service network they operate. Furthermore, even when complete information on the search space is readily available, the service composer should be able to provide successful solutions with only partial evaluation of the search space, so as not to be affected by the potentially very large size of the composition network.

In this context, we believe that graph network analysis is a promising candidate for the specific problem domain. The reasoning behind this choice is that graph network analysis has been successfully employed in the past in order to provide solutions to problems where partial evaluation of the search space was necessary, either due to the prohibiting size of the search space itself or the lack of extensive information.

This article is organised as follows: first, we review some background work that has inspired our research, both in the areas of Web service composition and graph network analysis. Next, we give a detailed presentation of our methodology and the experimental framework we have used for its evaluation. We then present some experimental results regarding the efficiency of the presented approach. Finally, we end the article by discussing some conclusions and directions for future work.

LITERATURE REVIEW

Web Service Composition

A number of approaches addressing the problem of automatic service composition have been presented in the literature, both academic and industrial. Peer (2004) suggests the use of existing AI planning systems, even though he does not present a solution prototype. Wu, Parsia, Sirin, Hendler, and Nau (2003) are also geared toward that direction, using SHOP2, an existing HTN (Hierarchical Task Networks) AI planning system.

Tut and Edmond (2002), on the other hand, propose the use of patterns in service composition. According to this approach, each composition request is matched against an appropriate abstract composition template, which is mapped to existing services at the implementation level. The approach followed by Limthanmaphon and Zhang (2003) is similar, where successful past composition requests are stored so that similar composition structures can be followed in future requests as well. Even though these approaches can be effective in many cases, they suffer from the restrictions posed by the patterns followed at composition time; in other words, effective solutions that do not follow the applied patterns are not likely to be found. Montebello and Abela (2003) follow a different approach: composition is performed with the use of a rule-based expert system, JTP (Java Theorem Prover). This is not the only approach where the use of expert systems is proposed for use with Semantic Web services: Kopena and Regli (2003) use Jess (Java Expert System Shell) in order to reason about Web services capabilities, and the composition approach followed by Ponnekanti and Fox (2002) is also rule-based.

Finally, we should also note that there are some approaches that view service composition as a semi-automatic and interactive process, where the system makes corrections and suggestions based on partially composed workflows. The approaches proposed by Sirin, Parsia, and Hendler (2004); Aggarwal, Verma, Miller, and Milnor (2004); and Kim, Spraragen, and Gil (2004) follow this logic.

However, we believe that the majority of the proposed approaches are not directly applicable in a real-world Web service composition framework, as they are bound by the same restriction: they require complete knowledge of the search space of the problem domain in order to operate. In the case of AI planning, for instance, all states and planning operators need to be known beforehand (similarly, rule-based systems, stemming from the AI planning research area, are bound by the same weakness). In the problem domain of automatic Web service composition, such a requirement might not always be feasible: as already mentioned, Web service directories can potentially be of very large size, with rather high growth rates (according to online sources, such as http://www.programmableWeb.com/). New functionality areas are becoming available, by new atomic and composite Web services that are being published on a daily basis. These conditions can cause two kinds of problems: (a) complete information on very large state spaces and planning operator sets may be hard and time-consuming to obtain, due to the size of the data involved, and (b) traditional AI planning problem domains (such as the blocks-world or the eight queens problems) are rather static; the states and operators involved do not change (both in number and in nature) over time, or only minor changes might occur. However, due to the nature of the Web service composition problem itself, the search space is dynamic and constantly evolving. This would mean that the planning domain would have to be downloaded or updated for every Web service composition request, which is inefficient.

Graph Network Analysis

Graph network link analysis is an area of research that has been applied to a wide range of information networks and has been very successful in a large number of test cases that can be represented as networks of interconnected resources: traditional examples are social network analysis (Breiger, 2004) and bibliometrics (Garfield, 1972). The term social network analysis refers to the analysis of connections and relationships among human actors and organisations within social networks. Any kind of relationship (friendly, business, commercial exchange, etc.) between members of a social network is regarded as a link between actors, and link analysis can help a researcher identify entities such as cliques, information channels, and degrees of influence within a social network. Bibliometrics, on the other hand, is the analysis of the citations network among research publications. A research paper citing another is regarded as a link (both between papers and between authors). The purpose of the analysis of the citations network is to identify which papers (or authors) are the most influential in particular scientific areas, or to identify co-citation cliques within the research community.

Network link analysis has also been applied to other information networks: e-mail communications networks (Ebel, Mielsch, & Bornholdt, 2002), protein structures (Qian & Luscombe, 2001), and the physical topology of the routers on the Internet (Faloutsos, Faloutsos, & Faloutsos, 1999) are some examples. As regards computer science research, link analysis has widely been applied in search engine technologies: the PageRank (Brin & Page, 1998) and HITS (Kleinberg, 1999) algorithms have been successfully used within major commercial search engines, in order to identify important documents on the World Wide Web. "Importance" in this case also refers to connectivity-based importance, rather than content importance. The notion behind this practice is that the more useful a Web site is, the heavier linked it will also be, since it is more possible that other Web sites will be linking to it.

The similarities that can be observed between the requirements of the Web service composition problem domain and those of social network analysis and bibliometrics have led us to believe that graph network link analysis is a promising candidate for this purpose.

METHODOLOGY OVERVIEW

Performing Web service composition when only partial information is available means that the Web service composer should be able to estimate whether including a particular Web service into a partial (and up to this point, only potential) solution can contribute to reaching the request goal or not. This requirement can be portrayed easier through a simple Web service composition example: let us assume a hypothetical service composition request where the provided data parameter is BookName and the required result data is BookPrice. We also assume that data types, like BookName and BookPrice, are defined in an ontological model used by the Web service composer. In this case, the user wishes to discover a composite Web service, which returns a book's price from Web-based e-commerce providers given its title. This is a rather simple composition request, which can be satisfied with the sequential execution of two (hypothetical) Web services: the first one accepts a book's title (BookName) and returns its ISBN code (BookISBN), whereas the second returns a book's price (BookPrice) given its ISBN code (BookISBN). During the composition process, the service composer will start forming partial solutions by adding these services that can accept the data type BookName—the provided data type from the user request. In a realistic Web service composition scenario, it is logical to expect that there will be a variety of Web services that can accept BookName: for instance, a service that returns the book's author (BookAuthor) given its title; a Web service that returns the year the book was published (PublicationDate); and, as mentioned earlier, a Web service that returns the book's ISBN code (BookISBN). Which one of these services will the Web service composer choose to add to the already existing workflow solution? One possible answer is that the composer will generate three different partial solutions, each of them containing one of the possible steps. From there on, the service composer would follow the same process until it reaches the goal specified in the composition request. However, such a process would potentially lead to exhaustive evaluation of the search domain, which is contrary to our research objectives. On the other hand, the service composer can estimate which of the three options is more "promising" to lead first to the request goal and examine this case first; if it fails, the composer can return and evaluate the remaining options.

A *Web service rank* is an estimate that is associated with each Web service and shows how "promising" that service is in order to retrieve successful solutions. Ranks can be based on a variety of link analysis metrics, so different ranks can be applied to the same Web service. A Web service directory can be formalised as a graph network that consists of interconnected online resources (Web services). Link analysis within the Web service network can help us identify which services are more prominent, important, or related to particular composition requests from a structural point of view. The importance of a Web service within a Web service network can be measured from different points of view (according to the exact network link analysis methodology that is being used); thus, we can apply different ranking measures to each Web service, each of them comprising a different estimation of how prominent a Web service is within a directory. Furthermore, we propose the use of a Web service composer that operates as a heuristic-based graph search algorithm, which attempts to retrieve the solutions to a particular request by following the shortest path navigating through the search space/graph network. In this sense, the service composer algorithm is based on the principles of A*, a generic heuristic-based graph search algorithm. The performance of such a service composition algorithm will depend heavily upon the quality of the problem-dependent heuristics that it uses. For this purpose, we are planning to use the Web service ranking metrics that can be derived through link analysis of the Web service network in order to guide the service composer and reach successful solutions with only partial evaluation of the search space. In other words, the general concept behind this methodology is that evaluating Web services of greater importance within the service network first, can help us reach the request goal faster.

FORMALISM

In this section, we will present in detail the elements of our experimental framework.

Composition Network

In our context, we assume that Web service composition takes place in a distributed Web service directory, where semantic information about all hosted Web services is centrally stored and available. The Web service directory is represented as a graph network. However, before we are able to formally define the concept of Web service network, we have to define the concept of a link between two given Web services:

Definition 1

Assume we have Web services W_i and W_j. We assume there is a link between W_i and W_j if and only if the output data provided by W_i are sufficient in order to call and execute W_j ($W_{iO} \subset W_{jI}$). In this case, Web services W_i and W_j can be considered compatible and can be consecutively placed in a composed workflow.

$$L_{W_i W_j} : W_i \rightarrow W_j \quad (1)$$

In addition, we can define the set of links W_L associated with each Web service W_a:

$$W_{aL} = \{L_{W_a W_j} : W_{aO} \subset W_{jI}\} \quad (2)$$

In this sense, a link has a source and a target Web service.

Having defined the concept of a link between two Web services, we can now represent a Web service network in terms of a graph network; it consists of a set of nodes (Web services) and a set of edges (links between Web services):

$$WSN = \{N, E\} \quad (3)$$

WSN represents the Web service network, *N* represents the set of Web services that belong to the Web service network, and *E* represents the set of all the links between the services of the network:

$$N = \{W_1, W_2, \ldots, W_n\} \quad (4)$$

$$E = \{L_{W_i W_{j1}}, L_{W_i W_{j2}}, \ldots, L_{W_i W_{jn}}\} \quad (5)$$

Web Service Composition Request

The composition request is the set of criteria that need to be satisfied by the resulting solution workflow. A universally agreed composition request format does not seem to exist across the Web service composition research community. However, real world Web service directories provide search facilities to their users based on functionality domain and/or keywords. Within our framework, the composition request is defined as the semantic description of the hypothetical composed Web service that is expected to be retrieved by the service composer. As such, the requests define the same attributes defined by Web service semantic descriptions. In addition, some attributes/criteria are required by the Web service composer in order to carry out the request, whereas some others are optional:

$$R = \{I, O, fd, QOS, length\} \quad (6)$$

where *I* refers to the set of input parameters provided by the user, *O* to the set of output data parameters expected by the solution, *fd* defines the overall functionality domain the expected solution will belong to, *QOS* refers to the set of nonfunctional requirements for the resulting solution (optional), and *length* is a maximum specified length of the solution. For example, we can consider that a user wishes to find a composite Web service that is able to return a complete bibliography of a specific book's author. However, only the book's name is known beforehand (and not the author's name). Furthermore, the user wishes that all the services that will be included in the solution should belong to the Informational Service functionality domain and that a successful solution should not include more than four Web services. This request can be represented as:

R = {{"BookName"}, {"AuthorBibliography"}," InformationalService", {}, 4}.

Web Service Composition Solution

In a generic form, the solution to a given request R is represented as the set of individual steps and the required order of execution that needs to be followed in order for R to be satisfied:

$$S = \{s_1, s_2, \ldots, s_{length}\} \tag{7}$$

S represents a solution to a given composition request R, s_1, s_2,..., s_{length} represent the parts the solution consists of, and *length* is the maximum allowed solution length specified in R.

Since the different steps that belong to a solution refer to Web services that belong to the service network, Equation 7 can be rewritten as:

$$S = W_1, W_2, \ldots, W_{length} \tag{8}$$

S represents a solution to a given composition request R, and W_1, W_2,..., W_{length} represent the Web service objects that are included in S. As before, *length* is the maximum allowed solution length specified in R.

Web Service Composition Algorithm

The Web service composer is the actual algorithm that retrieves successful solutions, if any, upon a given request. The purpose of the Web service composer is to discover the appropriate Web services that will be placed in a successful solution, along with the required sequence of execution. In this context, our approach addresses the problem of discovery of the appropriate Web services and order of execution. The composition of executable workflows in a formal workflow format (such as BPEL4WS) is not addressed. More detail on the representation of the composition solutions is given in the next section.

The Web service composer operates as a depth-limited heuristic graph search algorithm. When the service composition process starts, the service composer starts the search from the starting state, as specified in the request by the provided input parameters. The composer forms a (initially empty) partial solution at the starting state, and then adds steps to it by examining which Web services can be linked to the ones that are already part of the partial solution. The process is repeated until all the successful solutions are found.

The operation of the service composition algorithm is shown in Figure 1 as pseudocode.

The algorithm starts by generating a partial (initially empty) solution; the partial solution is gradually built, by having additional steps (services) added to it. The order with which potential new steps are evaluated (and added to the partial solution) depends on the ranking system that is being used: services with the highest rank are evaluated first, whereas the rest are placed in a Priority Queue in descending order. The process is repeated until all the successful solutions are retrieved. The available Web service ranking metrics and the way they are calculated are explained in more detail later.

Web Service Ranking

The term Web service ranking refers to the use of link analysis methods in order to reason on a Web service's "importance" or "usefulness" within the Web service composition network. The ranking metrics are used in order to guide the service composition. We believe that link analysis metrics that are based on local network information are better suited for our purpose so that Web service composition does not have to be dependent on global information on the search space, a sometimes unrealistic requirement. However, in this section, we will present link analysis ranks that are based on both local and global link structure

Figure 1. Web service composition algorithm, shown as pseudocode

```
MethodExpandPartialWorkflow (Workflow WF)
{
  Get WF PriorityQueue PQ
  for each p in PQ
  {
       add p to WF; PQ = new PQ
       Get nodes (n1, ..., nn) adjacent to p
       for each ni in (n1, ..., nn)
       {
           Calculate Rank
           Place in PQ
       }
       Sort PQ in Rank descending order
       ExpandPartialWorkflow
  }
{
```

so that we can compare their applicability and performance.

A variety of link analysis ranking metrics can be applied for our purpose. We have chosen to categorise these metrics according to two criteria:

- Local and Global: a ranking metric can be considered local when only local network knowledge is needed for its estimation; that is, only information on the associated node's immediate neighbourhood needs to be considered. Likewise, a rank can be considered to be global when information beyond a node's local neighbourhood is needed for its calculation. In this context, the term global might be a bit misleading: a global rank does not necessarily require complete knowledge of the whole network in order to be used; different ranks require different levels of global network knowledge. However, we use the term "global" to refer to any rank that needs anything beyond local neighbourhood information.
- Absolute and Relative: the terms "absolute" and "relative" refer to the rank's semantics, rather than to its method of calculation. A ranking metric can be considered absolute when its scope is general, irrelevant to the particular request that is being processed at the time. Similarly, a rank can be considered relative when its value is estimated in relation to a particular request.

The two options within each category (local-global and absolute-relative) are mutually exclusive: a rank cannot be both local and global at the same time. Similarly, a given rank will be either absolute or relative. However, options from different categories are not mutually exclusive: a local and a global ranking metric can be either absolute or relative. This way, we are presented with four separate subcategories of Web service ranks: local-absolute, local-relative, global-absolute, and global-relative. This categorisation scheme, along with the ranks that belong to each category, is shown in Table 1.

As can be inferred from the above categorisation scheme, ranking metrics are classified according to two factors: their calculation cost and their relation to a particular composition request. Local ranking metrics have in general lower cost than global ones (and thus are easier to estimate with the exception of the semantic similarity rank that is not purely link-based), whereas relative ranking metrics are more relevant to a particular request. The positioning of the ranking categories according to these criteria is illustrated in Figure 2.

We will present each ranking category separately.

Local-Absolute Ranking Metrics

Absolute Importance Rank

The absolute degree rank W_{ADR} of Web service W is a simple estimate of how well connected a particular Web service is within a service network. It simply shows the number of services a Web service can be connected to, as a normalised percentage of the overall size of the composition network.

Hubs-Authorities Rank

The hubs-authorities rank W_{HAR} presents a rather simple comparison of the in-degree and out-degree of a given Web service. The W_{HAR} rank is calculated as the ratio of a Web service's incoming links (the in-degree) to the outgoing ones (the out-degree). The terms Hubs and Authorities have been borrowed from John Kleinberg (1999) and his work in Web page ranking on the World Wide Web: a Hub is a Web page that points to many other Web pages, whereas an Authority is a page that is linked to by many other Web pages.

Local-Relative Ranking Metrics

Relative Importance Rank

As is the case with the absolute degree rank, the relative degree rank W_{RDR} presents how well connected a particular Web service is; however, the estimation of relative degree rank is biased towards a particular query. In this sense, instead of the absolute link degree of a Web service, we are instead interested in that part of the degree (also as a normalised percentage) that belongs to the semantic data type categories specified as the required output data in the request.

Semantic Similarity Rank

The Semantic Similarity rank W_{SSR} examines how semantically similar two different Web services are. In this context, the term similarity refers to the similarity of the data flows generated by their services, estimated as the semantic distance between the corresponding data types. The use of this rank, which in fact is the only one that is not directly related to link analysis of the search network, is based on the concept that the number of informational Web services connecting two different pieces of information (semantic data types) will be higher, when the pieces of information are more closely (semantically) related to each other. For instance, it is logical to expect that there will be more services connecting the semantic data types (SDTs) BookName and BookAuthor, rather than, for example, BookName and AirportLocation. Semantic distance between data types, as described in Roddick, Hornsby, and De Vries (2003) can be estimated within a single ontological background, in this case the ontologies used by our system. In essence, the semantic distance between two given data attributes within a common ontology is estimated as the minimum number of edges that need to be traversed when the ontology is viewed as a graph.

Definition 2

Assume data type ontology O_{SDT} represented by graph tree G, and SDTs sdt_i and sdt_j. Also let us assume that the sets of edges that need to be traversed from the G root node to the nodes sdt_i and sdt_j are $A = \{e_{i1}, e_{i2},...,e_{in}\}$ and $B = \{e_{j1}, e_{j2},...,e_{jn}\}$, respectively. The sizes of the sets are represented by |A| and |B|. The semantic distance sd between sdt_i and sdt_j is defined as the size of the set $(A / B) \cup B$, thus being:

Table 1. Ranking metrics Categorisation scheme

	Local	Global
Absolute	Absolute Degree, Hubs-Authorities	PageRank, Closeness
Relative	Relative Degree, SDT semantic similarity	Maximum Flow Rank, HITS

Figure 2. Web service ranking matrix

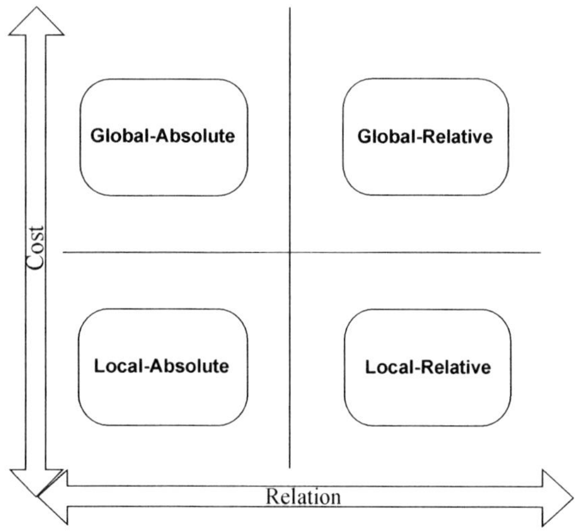

$$sd_{sdt_i, sdt_j} = |(A/B) \cup B| \quad (9)$$

Definition 3

Assume Web service W with output data types $W_O = \{sdt_{i1},..,sdt_{in}\}$ and request $R = \{I, O, fd, QOS, length\}$ with $O = \{sdt_{j1},..,sdt_{jn}\}$. The semantic similarity rank of W is given by

$$W_{SSR} = (sd_{sdt_{i1}, sdt_{j1}} + ... + sd_{sdt_{in}, sdt_{jn}})/n*m \quad (10)$$

Global-Absolute Ranking Metrics

PageRank

PageRank is also a direct adaptation of an already existing algorithm used in search engine Web page ranking: the PageRank algorithm was proposed by Larry Page and Sergey Brin (Google's founders) for the purpose of estimating how "important" a Web page is on the World Wide Web. As is the case with W_{ADR}, PageRank is also defined as a connectivity measure; however, it takes into account more than just direct links—that is, links that originated from a Web page but were found at a larger depth index. More details can be found in Brin and Page (1998).

Closeness Rank

The Closeness Rank W_{CR} shows the geodesic distance of a particular Web service from all the other services that belong to the Web service network. This distance can be measured either as the sum of all geodesic distances or as an average.

Global-Relative Ranking Metrics

Maximum Flow Rank

The maximum flow rank W_{FR} examines how many alternative routes exist between two given Web services within a service network. As is the case with the W_{CR} rank, the maximum flow rank is also easier to estimate as absolute figure, rather than a normalised one. The W_{FR} rank can be used in order to examine the overall reliability of the retrieved workflow solutions. In other words, this rank attempts to answer the question: if a part of the solution is unavailable, will the workflow solution fail?

HITS Rank

The HITS Rank W_{HITS} is a direct adaptation of Kleinberg's ranking algorithm for Web pages. The HITS algorithm was presented in Kleinberg (1999) and is a popular methodology used by search engines in order to determine link-based Web page popularity. The HITS algorithm is based on the same notion of in-degrees and out-degrees as W_{HAR}, but it does not simply take into consideration the direct in-degrees and out-degrees of a Web service: instead, it applies a hub weight and an authority weight to a Web service object, which are updated by examining the service's in-degrees and out-degrees at increasing depths.

Web Service Composition Performance

In order to estimate the performance of a specific composition simulation run, we first need to define the concepts of cost, benefit, and service composition performance with regard to a particular solution:

Definition 4

Assume solution S. The cost of S is defined as the total number of nodes en that were evaluated by the composition algorithm before the solution was found: $S^C = en$.

Definition 5

Assume solution S. The benefit of S is defined as the number of nodes sn that were part of the solution S: $S^B = sn$.

Definition 6

Assume solution S. The performance of the Web service composer with regards to S is defined as the ratio of the benefit to the cost: $S^P = S^B / S^C \Rightarrow S^P = sn/en$.

In other words, the performance of the service composition algorithm with regards to a specific solution is the ratio of the nodes that were successfully discovered as part of the solution to the total number of nodes that were evaluated. Similarly, we define the overall service composition performance with regards to a request (instead of a single solution):

Definition 7

Assume composition R with solutions S_1, S_2, ... , S_n. The performance of the Web service composer with regards to R is defined as the average performance of the composer with regards to the solutions S_1, S_2, ... , S_n:

$$R^P = (\sum_i^n S_i^P)/n \qquad (11)$$

R^P is measured as a normalised percentage that falls in the range [0...1]. A high R^P indicates a rather successful composition process; it shows that a large part of the expanded nodes were correctly evaluated, since they proved to be parts of successful solutions. Likewise, a low R^P indicates a rather unsuccessful service composition process.

EXPERIMENTAL EVALUATION

Experimental Setting

It is reasonable to expect that the performance of the Web service composer will vary, depending on the particular ranking metric that is in use every time. For this purpose, in order to examine the effect of each individual ranking metric on the efficiency of the composition algorithm, we have performed a series of simulation runs of the service composer featuring each ranking metric separately, against a set of randomly generated composition requests. The request set includes a large number of requests that have been randomly generated for different values of input and output parameters, according to the semantic data types defined in our ontologies. Finally, the experiments have taken place in an automatically generated, simulated Web service network that consists of approximately 2,450 Web services. The settings of the experiments are shown in Table 2.

Instead of examining the individual performance of each ranking metric, we can alternatively examine the average performance of the four ranking categories as defined in Table 1: absolute-local (AL), absolute-global (AG), relative-local (RL), and relative-global (RG). In this context, the experimental settings can be rewritten, as in Table 3.

Experimental Results

The curves in Figure 3 present the *cumulative distribution function* (CDF) of the recorded performance levels for each ranking metric within the featured composition network. The CDF of each result set shows what percentage of the whole result set is associated with a particular performance value. This way, the relative position of the CDF curve can show how effective each ranking metric was, in terms of successful guidance of the composition algorithm: the further to the right a CDF curve is, the more effective the guidance of the corresponding ranking metric has been. Figure 3 presents the CDF for the composition performance values of each individual ranking metric.

We can see that there is great diversity in the performance achieved by the different individual ranks. The ranking metric that achieved the lowest composition performance was the Hubs-Authorities Rank (the CDF curve that is the furthest to the left), whereas the metric that achieved the highest performance was the Closeness Rank (the furthest to the right). For instance, according to Figure 3, we can see that in the simulation run where the composition algorithm was operated under the Hubs-Authorities Rank, approximately 40% of the requests noted a performance level up to 25%, with the rest achieving higher performance levels. When the composition algorithm was operated under the Closeness Rank, however, the same 40% of the requests noted a performance level up to 52%. The performance of the Absolute Importance Rank is the second lowest after the Hubs-Authorities Rank, although a lot further to the right. The rest of the ranking metrics have reached considerably higher performance levels compared to the Hubs-Authorities and Absolute Importance Ranks, and they seem to be less diverse.

The rather similar performance levels achieved by most of the ranking metrics within this experiment do not allow us to form a clear view on which of the examined ranking metrics are indeed the most effective, apart from the distinct performance levels achieved by the Absolute Importance and Hubs-Authorities Ranks. In order to further distinguish among the examined ranking metrics, we can group the achieved performance levels per ranking category. The following comparisons will be presented:

- Absolute vs. Relative ranking metrics
- Local vs. Global ranking metrics
- Absolute-Local vs. Absolute-Global vs. Relative-Local vs. Relative-Global ranking metrics

According to this categorisation scheme, we can see that the Absolute ranking category consists of the Absolute Importance, the Page Rank, the Hubs-Authorities and the Closeness Ranks. Thus, the composition performance of

Table 2. Experiment settings: individual ranking metrics

Experiment Attribute	Value
Ranking Metric	ADR, RDR, HAR, HITS, PR, CLR, MFR, SD
Link Distribution	Uniform
No of Web Services	2450

Table 3. Experiment settings: ranking categories

Experiment Attribute	Value
Ranking Metric	AL, AG, RL, RG
Link Distribution	Uniform
No of Web Services	2450

Figure 3. CDF for each ranking metric performance, within a composition network with a uniform link distribution

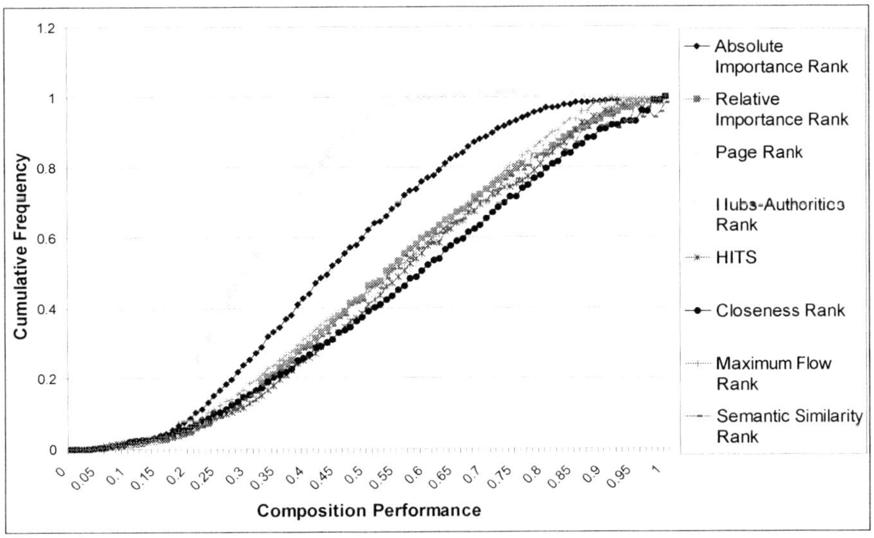

the Absolute ranking category can be estimated as the average composition performance of the ranks it consists of. The average composition performance of the other ranking categories can be estimated similarly. Figure 4 shows the CDF curves for the average composition performance levels achieved by Absolute and Relative ranking metrics; similarly, Figure 5 shows the CDF curves for the average composition performance levels achieved by Local and Global ranking metrics.

Figure 4 shows that there is a considerable difference between the performance achieved by the Absolute ranks and that of the Relative Ranks. For instance, the 40% of the requests that were satisfied with the use of Absolute ranking metrics achieved an average performance of up to 45%; the average performance of the same 40% of the requests that were satisfied with the use of Relative ranks was up to 62%. This difference in performance can be justified by taking into account the nature of the ranking metrics that form each ranking category: Absolute ranks present an absolute measurement, which would be the same within the given network, irrelevant to the request being evaluated; Relative ranks on the other hand present a relative measurement, which is in context only with regards to a specific composition request. The information provided by Relative ranks is "related" to the particular request that is being examined, and as such, it is reasonable to expect that they would achieve higher performance in the process of finding solutions for that request.

Table 4. Ranking metrics categorisation criteria

Categorisation Scheme	Ranking Metrics
Absolute	ADR, HAR, PR, CLR
Relative	RDR, HITS, MFR, SD
Local	ADR, HAR, SD, RDR
Global	HITS, PR, CLR, MFR
Absolute-Local	ADR, HAR
Absolute-Global	PR, CLR
Relative-Local	RDR, SD
Relative-Global	HITS, MFR

Figure 4. CDF for absolute and relative ranking metrics performance, within a composition network with a uniform link distribution

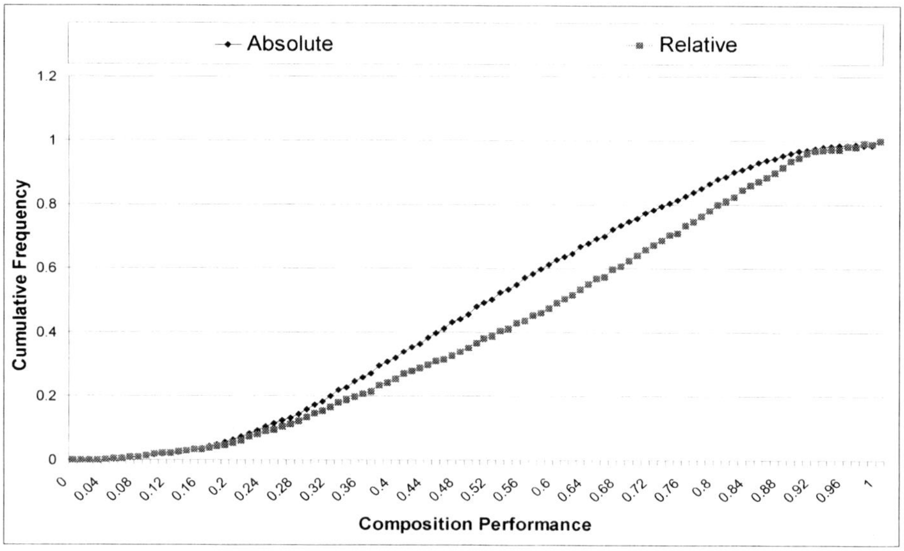

Figure 5. CDF for local and global ranking metrics performance, within a composition network with a uniform link distribution

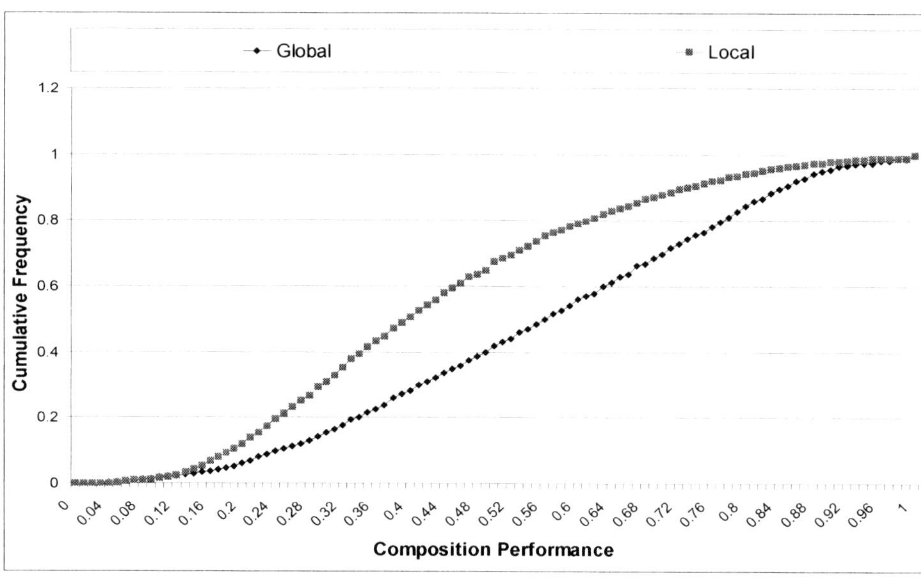

There also seems to be a considerable difference between the performance levels of the Local and Global ranking metrics, as seen in Figure 5. The performance gap also seems to be bigger than that between the Absolute and Relative ranks. As is the case with the comparison between the Absolute and Relative ranks, the noted difference can also be justified by taking into account the nature of the ranks that comprise the two examined ranking categories: Local ranking metrics are based solely on connectivity measures within the local neighbourhood of the network;

Figure 6. CDF for absolute-local, absolute-global, relative-local and relative-global ranking metrics performance, within a composition network with a uniform link distribution

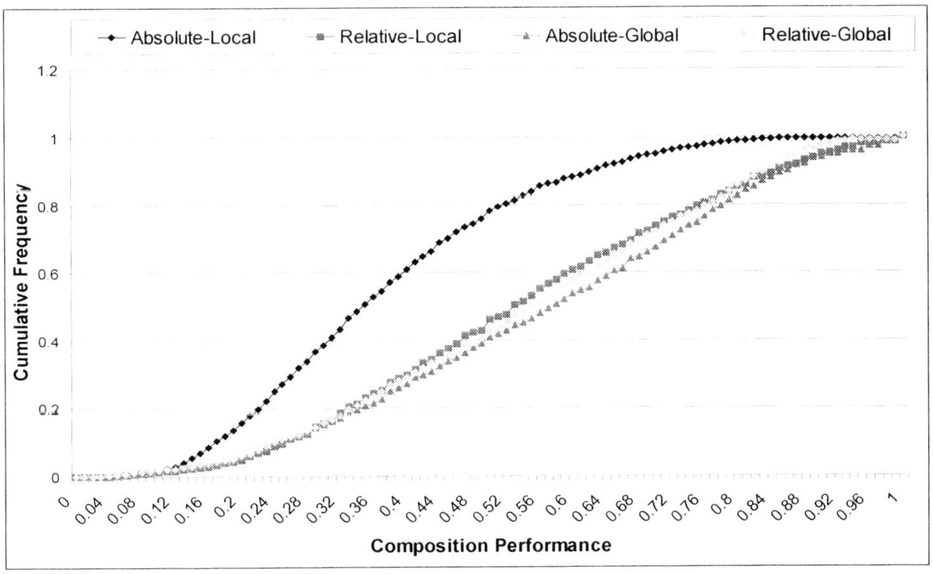

Global metrics, however, take into account connectivity measures regarding the structure of the whole network. Global ranking metrics provide a more reliable view on structural attributes of the composition network and, as such, are more efficient in leading to successful solutions for composition requests.

Finally, we can compare the average composition performance achieved by the four combined ranking categories: Absolute-Local, Absolute-Global, Relative-Local, and Relative-Global.

In Figure 6, we can see that the Absolute-Local ranking category shows the lowest composition performance (placed the furthest on the left), while the other three categories display considerably higher performance levels. Absolute-Global is the ranking category that displays the highest performance.

CONCLUSION

In this article, we have presented a methodology for Web service discovery and composition that is based on graph network analysis. This particular scientific methodology was chosen because we believe that it is capable of successfully addressing the objectives of our research. These objectives are to allow the Web service composition mechanism to retrieve valid solutions to a composition request:

- with only partial evaluation of the composition network/search space;
- when only incomplete information on the search space is available.

The methodology presented in this article is based on representing the composition network (search space) as a graph network, and then using specific graph network analysis metrics (ranks) to dynamically analyse its link structure in order to lead to solutions to a specific composition request. Our approach can be briefly summarised as follows:

- The Web service directory is represented as a graph network, where Web services are represented as nodes, and compatibility links between Web services are represented as edges.

- The Web service composer is implemented as a heuristic graph search algorithm.
- The composition algorithm is directed by a set of graph network analysis metrics (ranks) that dynamically examine how "important" or "relevant" each evaluated Web service is.
- The ranking metrics can be categorised according to their scope and the amount of information they require in order to be calculated. For experimental purposes, we distinguish between absolute and relative metrics, as well as local and global ones.

In the performed experiments, the performance of the composition mechanism when employing each ranking metric is recorded, in order to examine which ranking metrics are the ones that are more efficient, that is, can lead to the highest composition performance levels. Assessing the ranks has not been a very straightforward process due to the similar levels of composition performance achieved by many of the ranking metrics. However, more insight can be provided on the subject once we examine the results in an aggregated manner: instead of comparing the performance levels of each metric separately, we can compare the average performance levels that were observed for each ranking metric category, according to our categorisation scheme. This way, we can examine the average performance levels associated with the Absolute, Relative, Local, and Global ranking categories. Furthermore, the ranking categories are derived by combining the two categorisation criteria: Absolute-Local, Absolute-Global, Relative-Local, and Relative-Global.

During this process, the following observations were made:

- The Relative ranking metrics tend to lead to higher performance levels compared to the Absolute ones.
- The Global ranking metrics tend to lead to higher performance levels compared to the Local ones.
- The four combined categories appear in the following order, in terms of composition performance (from the lowest to the highest):
  1. Absolute-Local
  2. Absolute-Global
  3. Relative-Local
  4. Relative-Global

We believe that these results are intuitive if we take into account the nature of these ranking categories.

The research that is presented in this article is by no means complete: clearly, more experimental work needs to be carried out in order for the results and conclusions that have been produced to be further verified and extended. There are a number of directions for future work. We believe that an essential extension is to devise a more extensive evaluation process for the composition efficiency of the ranking metrics that can be used by the Web service composer. In the experiments that were presented in this article, the efficiency of a particular ranking metric has been assessed merely by the composition performance of the Web service composer when operated in combination with the ranking metric in question. However, other factors can be taken into account as well. Such an important factor is the computational cost these rankings entail: as it has been mentioned already, each ranking metric is of different scope within the Web service network, thus making some metrics more "expensive" to calculate than others. Finally, we intend to assess the performance of the presented ranking metrics and ranking categories under different experimental settings within composition networks that follow different link distributions (the composition network of the experiments presented in this article follows a uniform link distribution) and different link density levels.

REFERENCES

Aggarwal, R., Verma, K., Miller, J., & Milnor, W. (2004). Constraint driven Web service composition in METEOR-S. In *Proceedings of the 2004 IEEE International Conference on Services Computing* (pp. 23-30).

Berners-Lee, T. (2001). Keynote presentation on Web services and the future of the Web.

Breiger, R. (2004). The analysis of social networks. In *Handbook of data analysis* (pp. 505-526).

Brin, S., & Page, L. (1998). The anatomy of a large-scale hypertextual Web search engine. In *Proceedings of International Conference on the World Wide Web*, Amsterdam, The Netherlands (pp. 107-117). Elsevier Science Publishers.

Ebel, H., Mielsch, L.I., & Bornholdt, S. (2002). Scale-free topology of email networks. *Physical Review, E*(66), 035103.

Faloutsos, M., Faloutsos, P., & Faloutsos, C. (1999). On power-law relationships of the Internet topology. In *SIGCOMM '99: Proceedings of the Conference on Applications, Technologies, Architectures, and Protocols for Computer Communication* (pp. 251-262). New York: ACM Press.

Garfield, E. (1972). Citation analysis as a tool in journal evaluation. *Science, 178*(60), 471-479.

Kim, J., Spraragen, M., & Gil, Y. (2004). An intelligent assistant for interactive workflow composition. In *Proceedings of the 9th International Conference on Intelligent User Interfaces*, Funchal, Madeira, Portugal (pp.125-131). New York: ACM Press,.

Kleinberg, J. (1999). Authoritative sources in a hyperlinked environment. *Journal of the ACM, 46*, 604-632.

Kopena, J., & Regli, W. (2003). DAMLJessKB: A tool for reasoning with the Semantic Web. In *Proceedings of the 2nd International Semantic Web Conference (ISWC2003)*, Sanibel Island, Florida (pp. 628-643). Berlin: Springer-Verlag. Lecture Notes in Computer Science, 2870.

Limthanmaphon, B., & Zhang, Y. (2003). Web service composition with case-based reasoning. In *Proceedings of the 14th Australasian Database Conference on Database Technologies* (pp. 201-208). Darlinghurst, Australia: Australian Computer Society, Inc.

Milgram, S. (1967). The small world problem. *Psychology Today, 2*, 60-67.

Montebello, M., & Abela, C. (2003). DAML-enabled Web services and agents in the Semantic Web. In *Revised Papers from the NODe 2002 Web and Database-Related Workshops on Web, Web-Services, and Database Systems* (pp. 46-58). Berlin: Springer-Verlag.

Peer, J. (2004). A PDDL based tool for automatic Web service composition. In *Principles and Practice of Semantic Web Reasoning* (pp. 149-163). Berlin: Springer-Verlag.

Ponnekanti, S.R., & Fox, A. (2002). SWORD: A developer toolkit for Web service composition. In *Proceedings of the International Conference on the World Wide Web (WWW)*, Honolulu, Hawaii.

Qian, J., & Luscombe, N. (2001). Protein family and fold occurrence in genomes: Power-law behaviour and evolutionary model. *Journal of Molecular Biology, 313*(4), 673-681.

Roddick, J.F., Hornsby, K., & De Vries, D. (2003). A unifying semantic distance model for determining the similarity of attribute values. In *CRIPTS 03: Proceedings of the 26th Australasian Computer Science Conference in Research and Practice in Information Technology* (pp. 111-118). Darlinghurst, Australia: Australian Computer Society, Inc.

Sirin, E., Parsia, B., & Hendler, J. (2004). Filtering and selecting Semantic Web services with interactive composition techniques. *IEEE Intelligent Systems, 19*(4), 44-51.

Tut, M.T., & Edmond, D. (2002). The use of patterns in service composition. In *CAiSE 02/WES 02: Revised Papers from the International Workshop on Web Services, E-Business, and the Semantic Web* (pp. 28-40). Berlin: Springer-Verlag.

Wu, B., Parsia, B., Sirin, E., Hendler, J., & Nau, D. (2003). Automating DAML-S Web services composition using SHOP2. In *Proceedings of the International Semantic Web Conference* (pp. 195-210).

This work was previously published in Int. Journal of Information Technology and Web Engineering, Vol. 2, Issue 4, edited by G. Alkhatib, pp. 21-40, copyright 2007 by IGI Publishing (an imprint of IGI Global).

Chapter II
Context-Aware Service Provisioning in Next-Generation Networks: An Agent Approach

Vedran Podobnik
University of Zagreb, Croatia

Krunoslav Trzec
University of Zagreb, Croatia

Gordan Jezic
University of Zagreb, Croatia

ABSTRACT

This paper presents an application of multi-agent system in ubiquitous computing scenarios characteristic of next-generation networks. Next-generation networks will create environments populated with a vast number of consumers, which will possess diverse types of context-aware devices. In such environments the consumer should be able to access all the available services anytime, from any place, and by using any of its communication-enabled devices. Consequently, next-generation networks will require efficient mechanisms which can match consumers' demands (requested services) to network-operators' supplies (available services). The authors propose an agent approach for enabling autonomous coordination between all the entities across the telecom value chain, thus enabling automated context-aware service provisioning for the consumers. Furthermore, the authors hope that the proposed service discovery model will not only be interesting from a scientific point of view, but also amenable to real-world applications.

INTRODUCTION

We are entering a period when everything becomes digitized and when almost all software and devices are innately network-aware (Leuf, 2006). This induces an explosion of smart things, thus enabling the creation of pervasive smart spaces. When in the late 1980s Mark Weiser identified three main eras of computing (Weiser & Brown, 1997), he envisioned a transformation of physical spaces into computationally active and intelligent environments (Weiser, 1991). The first era was the era of mainframe computing, when large and powerful computers were shared by many people. The second era was the era of personal computing, when there was one computer per person. In the upcoming third era, we as humans will interact no longer with one computer at a time, but rather with a dynamic set of small networked computers, often invisible and embodied in everyday objects in the environment (Weiser, 1994). The third era is the era of *ubiquitous computing* (now also called *pervasive computing*), or the age of *calm technology*, when technology recedes into the background of our lives. "The most profound technologies are those that disappear", Weiser wrote. "They weave themselves into the fabric of everyday life until they are indistinguishable from it" (Weiser, 1991). The goal of ubiquitous computing is to create ambient intelligence where network devices embedded in the environment provide seamless connectivity and services all the time, thus improving human experience and quality of life without explicit awareness of the underlying communications and computing technologies. In the multi-agent system presented in this article, the pervasive computing concept is applied while creating such an environment which aims to minimize distractions on a consumer's attention and that adapts to the consumer's context and needs (Garlan, Siewiorek, Smailagic, & Steenkiste, 2002). In such an environment, diverse types of ubiquitous communication-enabled devices are used as a consumer's quiet and invisible servants, the enablers of calm technology.

Almost 20 years ago, at the time when Weiser tried to make his vision a reality, there were too many technological restraints for creating the real-world environment grounded on the ubiquitous computing concept. Meanwhile, tremendous developments in wireless technologies and mobile telecommunication systems, as well as rapid proliferation of various types of portable devices, have significantly amended computing lifestyles, thus advancing Weiser's vision toward technical and economic viability (Saha & Mukherjee, 2003). Weiser's ideas are becoming reality as the new generation of communication systems. The upcoming next-generation network (NGN) is characterized with evolution towards an all-IP (*Internet Protocol*) network, as well as with convergence of mobile and wireline networks into a single unified infrastructure. Figure 1 presents the key processes and the main actors which can be identified during the service provisioning in the NGN environment. Processes characteristic for the service provisioning life cycle are *discovery*, *fulfillment*, and *charging*. The main actors are *consumers* with their mobile/wireless terminals, *network operators*, and *content providers*. Usually, the network operator will offer services to the consumers, establishing a B2C (*Business-to-Consumer*) relationship with them. On the other hand, since the network operator very often does not possess the content needed for provisioning the service, it also has to establish B2B (*Business-to-Business*) relationships with the content providers. The essential step for the success of the NGN concept is creating a business model that produces added value for all the involved parties (consumers, network operators, content providers). Added value is created for the consumers if their level of satisfaction with the consumed service is more valuable than the money they have paid for the service provisioning. On the other hand, network operators and content providers

Figure 1. Service provisioning in next-generation networks

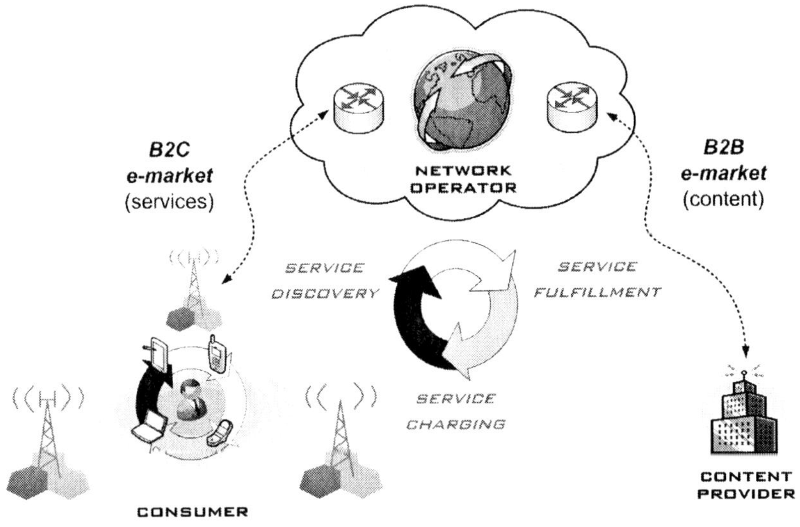

are business entities whose added value manifests only through their profits. In this article, it is going to be shown that the business model that stands behind the proposed agent-based service provisioning concept for the NGN can produce added value for all the involved parties.

The NGN will create heterogeneous and semantic-aware environments populated with diverse types of interconnected user devices that cooperatively and autonomously collect, share, and process information in order to adapt to the associated context, as well as provide the user with unobtrusive connectivity and services all the time. At the same time, a variety of content providers, while continuously competing with each other to improve market share and increase profit, will provide a remarkable selection of digital commodities (information/multimedia) through a set of services provisioned by network operators. In such an environment, consumers should access all the available services anytime, from anyplace, and by using any device, regardless of the type of access network. Consequently, a key challenge for the efficiency of service provisioning in the NGN environment is automation of the processes (especially the discovery process). The NGN will require efficient mechanisms which can match consumers' demands (requested services) to network-operators' supplies (available services).

In this article, we propose an agent approach for enabling autonomous coordination between all the entities across the telecom value chain, thus enabling context-aware service provisioning for the consumers. The proposed model also implements an automated mechanism for B2B digital commodities trading between content providers and network operators. The key element of the designed multi-agent system is a semantic-aware service discovery process which uses two-level filtration of available services before a final ranked set of eligible services is recommended to requesters in response to their needs. The filtration processes do not only consider the semantic information associated with available services, but also ratings regarding the actual performance of services (with respect to both price and quality). It is important to note that service discovery processes are completely automated by applying software agents. Software agents are consumer's personal assistants which act on their behalf, thus enabling seamless context-awareness, as well as the calm technology concept.

This article presents an agent-mediated semantic-aware environment developed from the multi-agent system, described in Podobnik, Jezic, and Trzec (2006) and Podobnik, Trzec, and Jezic, 2006) by upgrading and adapting its mechanisms for application in real-world ubiquitous computing scenarios characteristic for NGN environments. The proposed service discovery model is not only interesting from a scientific point of view, but is also very amenable to real-world applications. The organization of the article is as follows. In the second section, we present the related work in this field. The third section describes the NGN environment. The proposed multi-agent system is presented in the fourth section. The fifth section proposes directions for future work and concludes the article.

RELATED WORK

It has already been noted that efficient service discovery is essential for successful service provisioning. *Discovery* is the process of searching for possible matches between demands and supplies. However, the objective of this process is not simply to find all the available resources which match a requester's demand. Efficient discovery processes should identify all the supplies that can fulfill a given demand to some extent, and then propose just the most promising ones (Di Noia, Di Sciascio, Donini, & Mongiello, 2004).

Traditional discovery solutions, which are essentially based on the exact matching of syntactic patterns (e.g., keyword matching) cannot be flexible enough to effectively deal with the heterogeneity typical of mobile and pervasive environments (Bellavista, Corradi, Montanari, & Toninelli, 2006). Therefore, recent approaches to the discovery processes are increasingly grounded on mechanisms which exploit the semantics of resource descriptions ("intelligent discovery") (Colluci, Noia, Sciascio, Donini, & Mongiello, 2005; Keller, Lara, Lausen, Polleres, & Fensel, 2005; Klein & Bernstein, 2004; Sycara, Paolucci, Anolekar, & Srinivasan, 2004). In this work, we use an existing semantic-aware matching algorithm from Tang (2004) based on the available semantic information encoded in OWL-S.

All of the above mentioned mechanisms facilitate the discovery of adequate services solely through semantic matchmaking between descriptions of requested and available services. Thus, they either lack a mechanism for ranking matches, or they rank potentially suitable services only according to their semantic similarity. Such an approach to the discovery process can yield a large number of irrelevant search results since there is no assurance that information advertised by service providers is accurate (Lim & Tang, 2006). Furthermore, providers of services with identical descriptions may differ dramatically in performance levels (Luan, 2004). Therefore, we suggest automated service discovery based, not only on semantic service descriptions, but also on information regarding the actual performance of the specific services.

The performance of services is rated directly by the consumers with respect to both price and quality. Our performance model is founded on research regarding trust and reputation in electronic business (e-business) (Fan, Tan, & Whinston, 2005; Padovan, Sackmann, Eymann, & Pippow, 2002; Wishart, Robinson, Indulska, & Jøsang, 2005).

NEXT-GENERATION NETWORK ENVIRONMENT

The initial architecture of the Internet was geared towards delivering information visually to humans, while the initial purpose of mobile telecommunication systems was enabling people to communicate while they are in motion. The advent of NGN merges the Internet and telecom worlds into a single unified network infrastructure, which is based on the existing Internet infrastructure and emerging 3G (*Third Generation*) mobile networks. This network convergence creates a new telecom value chain, so it is essential to offer new business models to facilitate NGN proliferation, as well as gain the market approval. Therefore, this section will first present new telecom value chain and propose an adequate business model. Another great challenge for NGN environments is to adequately cope with the issues that are consequences of great heterogeneity of user devices and available access networks, as well as with the dynamic nature of available services and associated digital content. In order to achieve interoperability and common understanding across the entire NGN environment, we use Web Services enhanced with the Semantic Web idea. Also, we introduce software agents into an NGN environment, to enable users to consume context-aware ubiquitous services in a seamless manner. Therefore, this section will also present the Semantic Web services and software agents.

The New Telecom Value Chain

From a conceptual point of view, the NGN architecture evolves towards an "open" architecture, which is characterized with no limitations for when, where, and how services can be provisioned to the consumers. The ultimate goal is to create an environment where consumer-owned goal-directed applications could intelligibly and adaptively coordinate information exchanges and actions (Podobnik, Petric, & Jezic, 2006), thus enabling the calm technology concept for the consumers (Yoon, 2007). At the same time, computers physically "disappear" while being embedded into the environment, and they logically evolve from single isolated devices to entry points into a worldwide network of information exchange (Fensel, 2004). All this induces an advent of a new telecom value chain. Figure 2 presents the entities which compose such a value chain (*user, user terminals, network and servers, services,* and *content*) and relates them to the actors in the NGN environment (*consumers, network operators, content providers*). Consumers are users of network operators' services. They often own a variety of network-aware devices (i.e., user terminals) and should access all the available services anytime, from any place, and by using any terminal, regardless of the type of access network. Consumers are willing to pay the network operator for the provisioned services, but they demand a certain quality of service (QoS). Network operators own NGN infrastructure and servers needed to provide services. They offer consumers the ability to choose, free of charge, the services and associated content they want to utilize, but charges them for the service provisioning. Note that network operators define available services, but they do not own the required content for their provisioning. Therefore, they must purchase required content from the content providers.

In the traditional telecom value chains, the greatest value was comprised in the network infrastructure: hardware entities and technologies which enable the communication. Continual developments in both wireless and wired communications and networking have resulted in the price erosion of fixed and mobile telephony, as well as broadband Internet access. The trend is irreversible—there will be adequate fixed and wireless capacity everywhere for an affordable price. Consequently, the value distribution is shifting toward providing consumers with a remarkable selection of digital resources through a set of services. In so doing, the consumer-centric approach is applied, so that great care is taken to provide calm computing environment for the consumers.

Semantic Web Services

One of the driving forces behind the concept of the NGN is the ability to provide context-aware services across a wide range of user terminals over a heterogeneous network infrastructure. Context-awareness requires dynamic information

Figure 2. The new telecom value chain

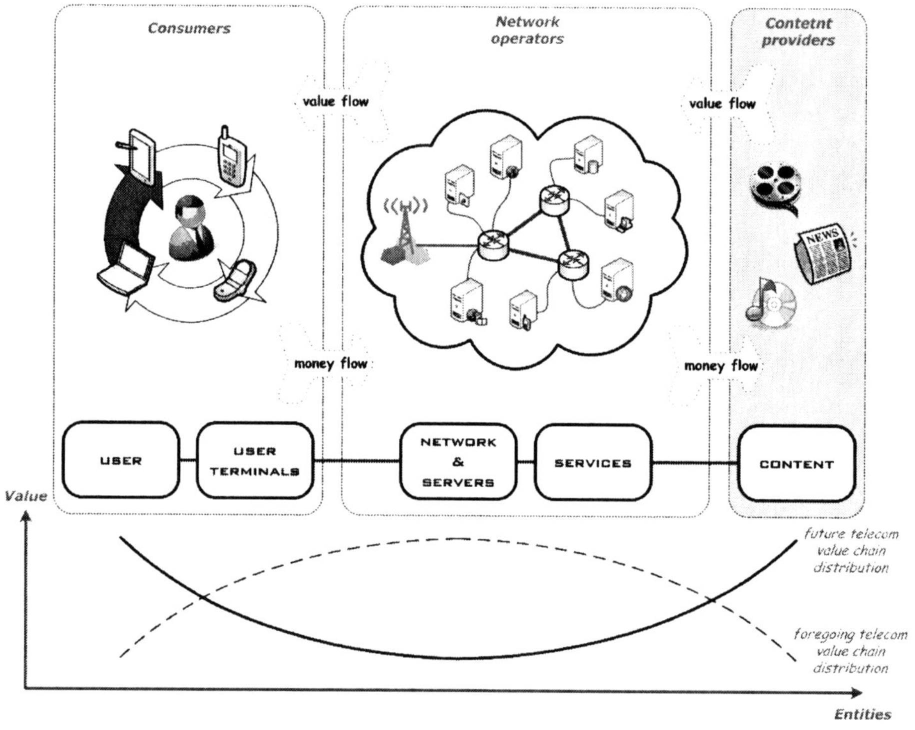

discovery, knowledge representation and sharing, context reasoning, and extendibility. Therefore, interoperability between a variety of different entities and actors in the NGN is needed. In the proposed multi-agent system, Semantic Web service technology is used to unambiguously represent both services provisioned by network providers and digital commodities offered by content providers.

Web Services

A Web Service (http://www.w3.org/2002/ws) is a software system designed to support interoperable machine-to-machine interaction over a network. It is identified by an URI (*Uniform Resource Identifier*, http://www.w3.org/Addressing) and has an interface described in a machine-processable format. Its interface can be discovered by other software systems. These systems can then interact with the Web service, using XML (*eXtensible Markup Language*, http://www.w3.org/xml) messages conveyed by Internet protocols. Figure 3 presents the classical Web service architecture.

WSDL (*Web Service Description Language*, http://www.w3.org/TR/wsdl) is a language that provides a communication level description for Web services. A WSDL document is basically an XML document specifying the location, operations, and methods of a Web service and instructions on how to access it. WSDL files are XML files with no semantics (Colluci et al., 2005). WSDL is the industry standard for Web service description.

A UDDI (*Universal Description, Discovery and Integration*, http://www.uddi.org) repository is a business registry which enables the discovery of services provided by external business partners. When a business registers a Web service, it typically stores a WSDL description of the service or a reference to the corresponding WSDL document, in addition to the usual information regarding the

Figure 3. The classical Web Service architecture

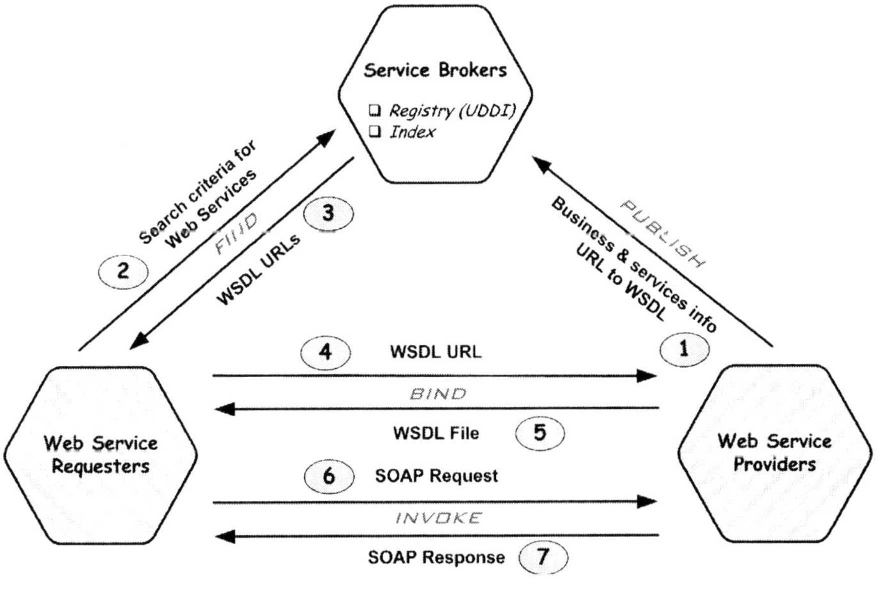

Web service. This specification then enables a user to easily connect to this Web service. There are also alternatives to UDDI, for example, SDEC (*Services and Data Exchange Catalogue*, http://sdec.reach.ie) or WSIL (*Web Services Inspection Language*, http://www.wsil.org).

The Semantic Web

The Semantic Web is an extension of the current Web in which information is given well-defined meaning, better enabling computers and people to work in cooperation. (Berners-Lee, Hendler, & Lassila, 2001)

This vision of the Semantic Web provides a foundation for the semantic architecture of Web Services (http://www.daml.org/services). By applying Semantic Web concepts, every Web service can be described using a set of ontologies.

Currently, Web accessible resources are mostly presented using HTML (*Hyper Text Markup Language*, http://www.w3.org/MarkUp), a language used to publish information by displaying it through a Web browser. While HTML helps us to visualize information on the Web, it does not describe Web resources in such a way that would enable software programs to find or interpret them. It is intended solely for human consumption. The Web can only reach its full potential if it becomes a place where data can be shared and processed by automated tools without human intervention. The idea is to enable programs to share and process data, even when they have been designed completely independently.

Ontologies represent a formal and explicit AI (*Artificial Intelligence*) tool for facilitating knowledge sharing and reuse (Fensel, 2004). An ontology refers to a description of concepts and relationships between these concepts in an area of interest. Therefore, an ontology is the terminology used for a given domain of interest. Predefined ontologies allow computer programs (i.e., software agents) to interpret the meaning of Web resources. Ontologies can refer to other ontologies, and thus create domain-dependent terminologies which describe certain concepts and relationships in more detail. As a result, intelligent software agents can interpret and exchange semantically enriched knowledge for their principals (Hendler, 2001). In the process of creating an ontology that describes a specific resource (e.g., network service or digital content), a variety of supporting technologies must be applied (Figure 4).

The HTTP (*Hypertext Transfer Protocol*, http://www.w3.org/Protocols), supported by URI mechanisms enabling worldwide unique identifying, provides assistance for sharing ontologies all over the Web. The XML, supported by Unicode standards (http://www.unicode.org), provides a surface syntax for structured documents, but imposes no semantic constraints on the meaning of these documents. The XML Schema (http://www.w3.org/XML/Schema) is a language used to restrict the structure of XML documents as well as extend XML with datatypes. The RDF (*Resource Description Framework*, http://www.w3.org/rdf) is a data model for objects ("resources") and relations between them. An RDF document describes knowledge in the form of triples called the subject-verb-object (SVO) form. Triples define relationships between concepts and thus provide simple semantics. The RDF Schema (http://www.w3.org/TR/rdf-schema) is a vocabulary used to describe the properties and classes of RDF resources. It includes semantics for generalization-hierarchies of such properties and classes. The OWL (http://www.w3.org/TR/owl-features) provides a larger vocabulary for describing properties and classes. This vocabulary can describe relations between classes (e.g., disjointness) along with their cardinality (e.g., exactly one) and equality. It can also provide richer descriptions of property characteristics (e.g., symmetry) and introduces enumerated classes. Therefore, OWL is a rich semantic language based on Description Logics (DL). DL is a formalism that can be used for knowledge representation and reasoning. It facilitates the quest for implicit consequences of explicitly represented knowledge. Figure 5 presents the OWL ontology describing *Multimedia Service* domain.

The OWL-S (http://www.daml.org/services/owl-s) is an OWL-based technology for describing the properties and capabilities of Web services in an unambiguous, computer interpretable markup language. Existing Web service description mechanisms, such as WSDL, provide a low-level communication layer for Web services. In other words, existing mechanisms only define *how* to access a Web service, while OWL-S defines *why* to utilize a certain Web service. By applying OWL-S, classical Web services can be transformed into Semantic Web services. The OWL-S architecture enables the execution of four basic tasks. Namely, OWL-S enables users and software agents to automatically discover, invoke, compose, and monitor Web resources

Figure 4. Technology stack that enables ontology creation

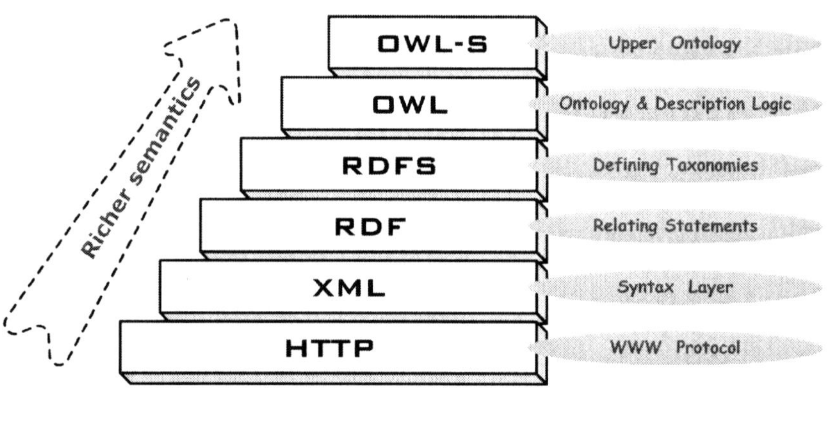

which offer services under specified constraints. The three main parts of an OWL-S ontology are (Figure 6): a service *profile* for advertising and discovering services; a *service model*, which gives a detailed description of a service's operation; and a service *grounding*, which provides details on how to interoperate with a service via messages. The existing *grounding* enables the alignment of the semantic specification with the implementation details described using WSDL.

Intelligent Software Agents

In vast and dynamic pervasive computing environments, it is hard for users to identify and activate services that match their needs (Lindberg, Pasman, Kranenborg, Stegeman, & Neerincx, 2007). In the designed multi-agent system, intelligent software agents, supported by AI mechanisms—semantic-aware matchmaking and negotiating mechanisms (Podobnik, Trzec, & Jezic, 2006; Tang, 2004—are used to impersonate consumers, network operators, and content providers in the volatile and heterogeneous environment of the NGN in order to enable automated interaction and coordination.

The dynamic and distributed nature of both data and applications in the NGN requires computer programs to not only respond to requests for resources but to intelligently anticipate and adapt to their environment while actively seeking ways to support their principals. Therefore, an intelligent software agent is an autonomous program which acts on behalf of its principal while conducting complex information and communication actions over the Internet. Intelligent software agents enable automated process execution and coordination, thus creating added value for its principal.

Figure 5. The OWL ontology describing Multimedia Service domain

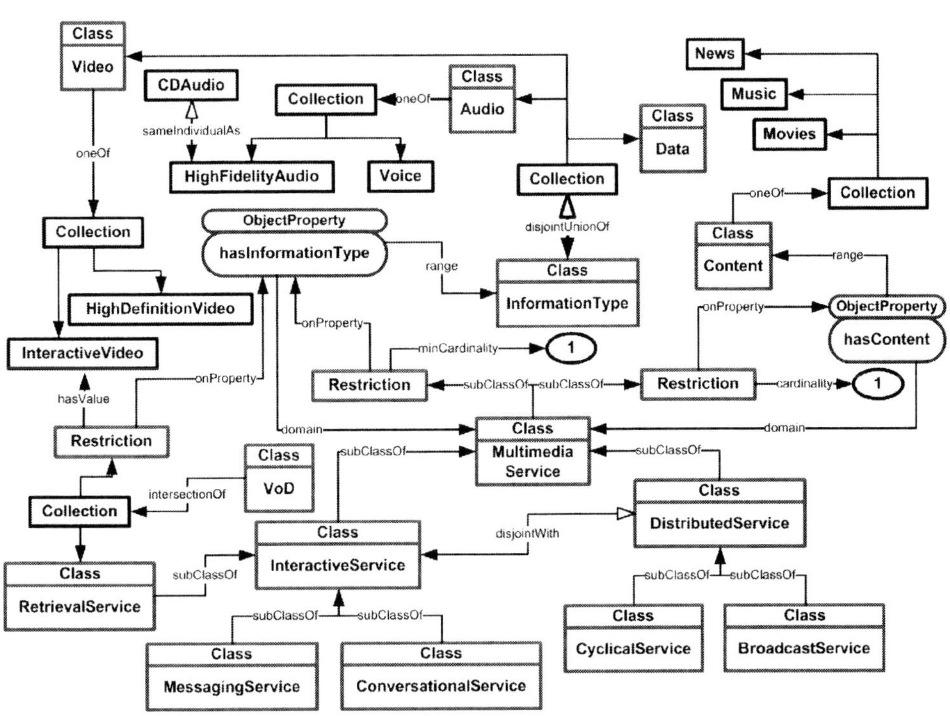

Figure 7 presents the relations between the main features of intelligent software agents (Bradshaw, 1997; Chorafas, 1998, Cockayne & Zyda, 1998, Jezic, Kusek, & Sinkovic, 2006; Kusek, Lovrek, & Sinkovic, 2005). An agent must possess some *intelligence* grounded on its *knowledge base*, *reasoning mechanisms*, and *learning capabilities*. Depending on an assignment of particular agent, there are differences in types of information contained in its knowledge base, but generally this information can be divided into two parts—*owner's profile* and agent's *knowledge about environment*. It is very important to notice that the agent's knowledge base does not contain static information. Adversely, the agent continuously updates its owner profile according to the latest owner needs, what allows the agent to efficiently represent its principal in the pervasive environment of NGN, thus realizing the calm technology concept. Additionally, the agent also updates knowledge about its environment with the latest events from its ambience and with the current state of observed parameters intrinsic to its surroundings, thus realizing context-awareness. *Context-awareness* describes the ability of the agent to provide results that depend on changing context information (Bellavista et al., 2006). In our model, we differentiate the *situation context* (e.g., user location and environment temperature) and the *capability context* (e.g., features of a device which offers agent-based service). An agent executes tasks autonomously without any interventions from its principal; this is what makes it an invisible servant, just as Weiser envisioned (Weiser & Brown, 1997). An agent must be *reactive*, so it can properly and in time respond on impacts from its environment. An agent does not just react on excitations from its environment but is also taking initiatives coherent to its tasks. A well-defined objective is an inevitable prerequisite for *proactivity*. An efficient software agent collaborates with other agents from its surroundings: it is *cooperative*. If an agent is capable of migrating between heterogeneous network nodes interconnected through ubiquitous NGN, this agent is called *mobile* software agent. An agent

Figure 6. The structure of OWL-S ontology

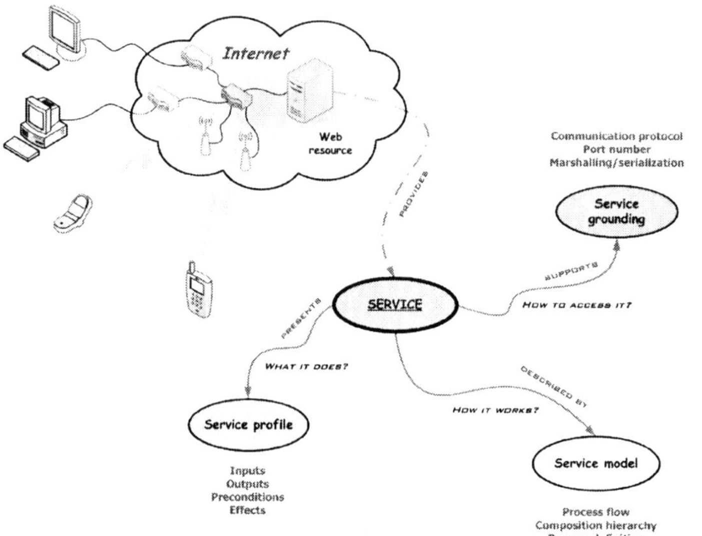

Figure 7. A model of an intelligent software agent

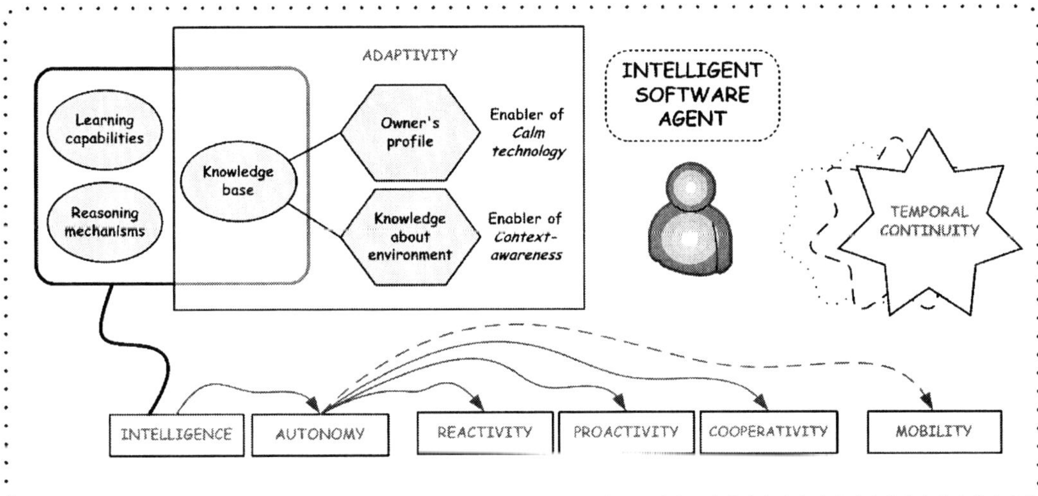

has a lifetime throughout which the persistency of its identity and its states should be retained, so it is characterized by *temporal continuity*.

The next-generation networks will be shaped by open, heterogeneous, and complex structures, consisting of diverse types of ubiquitous semantic-aware communication-enabled devices. Intelligent software agents will interact and negotiate on behalf of their principals, but OWL is not sufficient in providing software agents with semantic abilities. Software agents must implement adequate knowledge-based mechanisms which can extract knowledge from OWL documents and understand the corresponding semantic information. A matching algorithm is a mechanism which assists in the discovery of eligible resources given the owner's preferences. In this work, we use an existing matching algorithm from Tang (2004) based on the available semantic information encoded in OWL-S. More specifically, it matches (compares) available service parameters with the requested needs (i.e., parameters). This match obtains results with some degree of similarity; that is, the comparison is assigned a rank. Such a ranking will eventually become relevant since it is highly unlikely that there will always be a Web service available which offers the exact functionality requested. Consumers (or software agents that act on behalf of consumers) can make a decision based on these rankings on whether they want to use a certain service which does not exactly match the desired functionality. The matching algorithm compares both all input and all output parameters of the advertised service with all input and all output parameters of the requested service. Moreover, it also considers parameters classification and allows customization through plug-ins (Tang, 2004). All these parameters are defined through a semantic description in an OWL-S document, using a service *profile*. Matching procedure is logically divided into four stages, each independent of the other three. The final result (MATCH or FAIL) will be based on the results of each matching stage ("logical AND"). These stages are: *input matching*, *output matching*, *profile matching*, and *user-defined matching*. The implemented *Matching Agent* uses two components to realize the semantic match-making process of requested and advertised services. These components are *OWL Inference Engine* and *OWL-S Matchmaker* (Kopena & Regli, 2003) (Figure 8). They are necessary to accomplish complex reasoning tasks, including a Java understandable interpretation of service descriptions

Figure 8. Software components required for implementing a Matching Agent

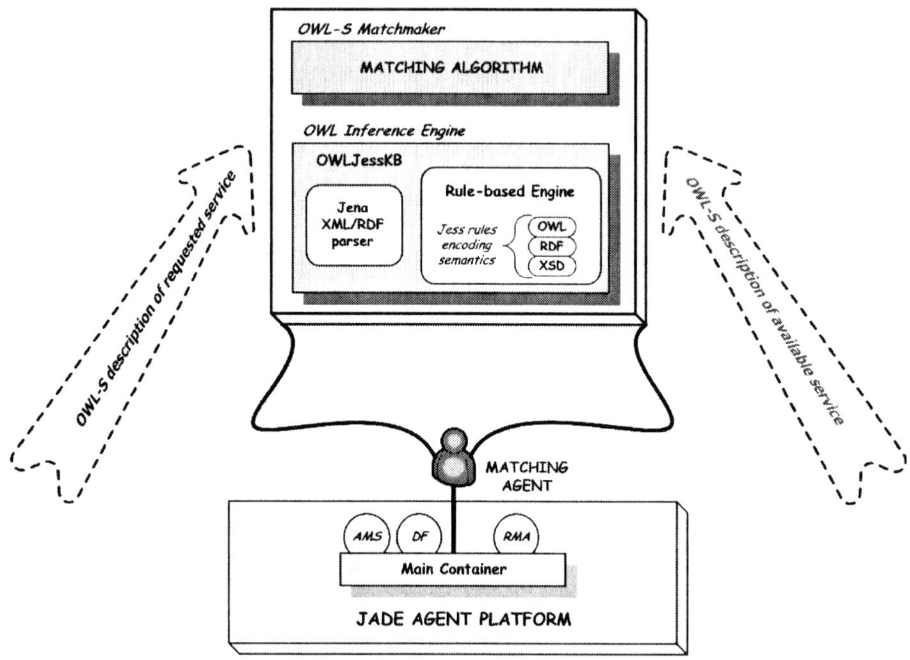

written in OWL-S. The OWL Inference Engine component is used to transform OWL files in the form appropriate for the OWL-S Matchmaker component that, applying the matching algorithm, semantically compares transformed OWL files and calculates the degree of similarity between services. The OWL Inference Engine represents off-the-shelf DL reasoner for ontologies written in OWL, named *OWLJessKB*, which uses the Jena API (*Application Programming Interface*) to parse OWL-S descriptions into SVO (*subject-verb-object*) triples. OWLJessKB also uses Jess (*Java Expert System Shell*) (Freidman-Hill, 2003), rule-based engine, and scripting environment, which can be used for the creation of agent KB (*Knowledge Base*) populated with facts and rules. Jess uses the Rete algorithm (pattern matching mechanism) to process facts and deduce new information according to rules. It is used to enable the Matching Agent to process SVO triples, represented as Jess facts, according to Jess rules that represent OWL axioms. Consequently, the *Matching Agents* can understand semantics of OWL-S descriptions using the OWLJessKB component and use the OWL-S Matchmaker component to semantically compare requested and advertised services. More detailed explanation of semantic matchmaking performed by *Matching Agent*, as well as a simple telecom case study, can be found in Podobnik, Jezic, and Trzec (2006).

A MULTI-AGENT SYSTEM FOR CONTEXT-AWARE SERVICE PROVISIONING

The classical Web Service mechanisms (already presented in Figure 3) require consumers to find an appropriate service manually and determine whether a particular service description provides the functionality they need. This is mostly done by browsing a registry, such as UDDI, or by directly obtaining a service description from a business partner. Since both consumers and businesses try to minimize the amount of time and effort put into maintaining and running their applications, we were motivated to extend the classical architecture of Web services with Semantic Web concepts and intelligent software agents. As a proof-of-concept application, we implemented a multi-agent system (Figure 9) for context-aware service provisioning in NGN environment. The proposed multi-agent system enables automated semantic-aware service discovery according to consumer context and its preferences. Representation of network operators' services and content providers' commodities in the NGN, as well as automation of discovery process, are facilitated through Semantic Web services and enabled by applying AI concepts—semantic-aware matchmaking and negotiating mechanisms (Podobnik, Trzec, & Jezic, 2006; Tang, 2004)—realized through intelligent software agents. We introduce three types of agents into the classical architecture of Web services. They are *Consumer Agents (CAs)*, *Provider Agents (PAs)*, and *Network Agents (NAs)*. These agents extend the classical architecture of Web services by upgrading it with the capabilities of automated service discovery and autonomous negotiation regarding the utilization of chosen services. A CA acts on behalf of its owner (consumer) in the discovery process of suitable services and subsequently negotiates the utilization of these services. A PA acts on behalf of a content provider in the process of digital commodities sale. A NA acts on behalf of a network operator while negotiating with PAs about purchasing their digital commodities, as well as while recommending ranked sets of eligible services to CAs in response to their requests.

The implemented multi-agent system integrates functionalities of both B2B electronic market (e-market) and B2C e-market. Figure 1 already presented the actors and main processes in these markets. First, in transactions conducted in a B2B e-market, network operators purchase digital commodities from the content providers. Afterwards, in a B2C e-market, network operators use purchased content to provide services to consumers.

Types of Agents

In Figure 9, which presents the designed multi-agent system, four different types of software agent can be identified. Three of them are *Consumer Agent (CA)*, *Provider Agent (PA)*, and *Network Agent (NA)*, which represent their principals in the transaction in B2B and B2C e-markets and whose role is already specified above. The fourth one is the *Matching Agent (MA)*, which does not participate in interactions on e-markets, but is "hidden" in the network operators' infrastructure. A brief description of all the agents follows.

The Network Agent (NA)

The NA is a representative of one network operator for PAs and CAs. When the NA is contacted by another agent, it must first determine whether the other agent is a PA or a CA (if it is neither of them, the NA ignores the contact message). If the other agent is a PA (interaction **1**), then the NA negotiates the possibility of purchasing the content that PA is selling. The content is semantically described with the use of OWL-S. If the other agent is a CA, then the NA provides that agent with a ranked list of all the available services which semantically match the one requested by the CA (interaction **2**), as well as negotiates the terms of service utilization by the CA's owner (interaction **3**). During all these actions, the NA interacts with its MA, either providing it with certain information or requesting certain information from it.

The Provider Agent (PA)

The PA is a representative of one content provider, which offers certain digital commodities (information/multimedia) in the B2B e-market. The PA interacts with the NAs of various network providers and negotiates the sales arrangements (interaction **1**).

Figure 9. The implemented multi-agent system

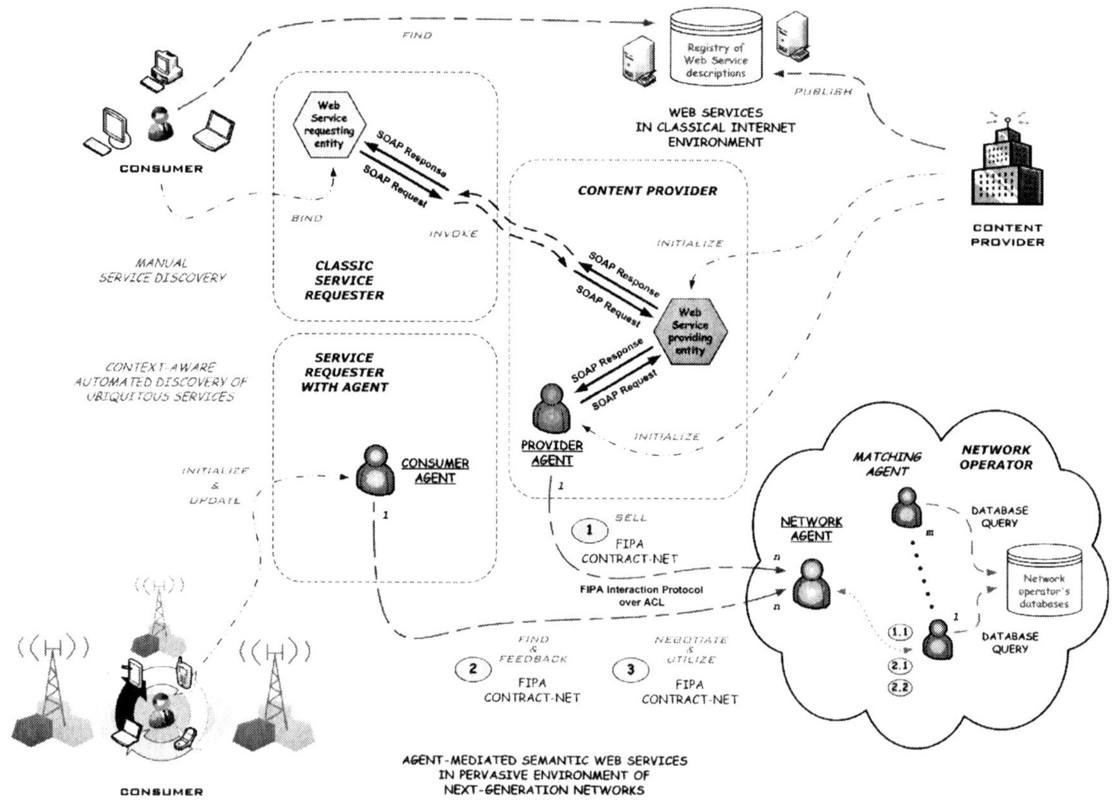

The Consumer Agent (CA)

The CA is a representative of one consumer, which requires a certain service in the B2C e-market. The CA contacts the NA requesting information regarding the services which semantically match its requirements (interaction **2**). Upon acquiring a ranked list of all the available services which semantically match the one requested, the CA negotiates the terms of service utilization and makes a deal for the most appropriate one, for example, the service that is characterized by the lowest cost (interaction **3**).

The Matching Agent (MA)

The MA is "hidden" in the network operators' infrastructure and enables the automation of service discovery. Every network operator, to enable concurrent task execution within its network, actually has more than one MA (note that there are *m* identical MAs in Figure 9). However, for an external observer, it seems there is only one MA per network operator. The MA first facilitates semantic matchmaking, which corresponds to the first level of filtration in the service discovery process. It receives OWL-S descriptions of requested services (interaction **2.1**), performs a semantic matchmaking, and generates a list of all semantically suitable services. The MA afterwards carries out second-level filtration, which produces a final ordered list of top-ranked available services. The second-level filtration is based on ratings regarding the actual performance of services (with respect to both price and quality). It is important to note that these ratings do not only serve in discovery processes to adjust the service proposal to the consumer preferences, but they are also an indirect indicator of quality of content providers whose digital commodities are utilized as a part of a specific service. Therefore, network operators also use these ratings while negotiating on the B2B e-market with content providers (interaction **1**). A service performance model tracks a service's past performance which can be used to estimate its performance with respect to future requests (Luan, 2004). Our model monitors two aspects of the service's performance—the service quality and the price of utilizing the service (Fan et al., 2005; Padovan et al., 2002; Wishart et al., 2005). A more detailed explanation of second-level filtration performed by the *Matching Agent*, as well as a simple case study, can be found in Podobnik, Trzec, and Jezic (2006). After the second-level filtration is over, an ordered list of top-ranked available services is generated. This list is then forwarded from the MA to the NA (conclusion of interaction **2.1**). At a later stage, the MA receives feedback information from the CA (through the NA) regarding the performance of the proposed services (interaction **2.2**).

Interactions on the E-Market

The multi-agent system was implemented using the JADE (*Java Agent Development Framework*, http://jade.tilab.com) agent platform (Bellifemine, Caire, & Greenwood, 2007). Agents communicate by exchanging ACL (*Agent Communication Language*, http://www.fipa.org/repository/aclspecs.html) messages. Efficient coordination between agents is achieved by applying IEEE (*Institute of Electrical and Electronics Engineers*) FIPA (*Foundation for Intelligent Physical Agents*, http://www.fipa.org) interaction protocols. Two types of predefined FIPA conversation protocols—FIPA Request and FIPA Contract-Net (Pitkäranta, 2004)—are used.

FIPA CONTRACT-NET (PA (Initiator) and NA (Responder)): Interaction *1*

A PA wishes to sell the digital commodities. It uses the FIPA Contract-Net interaction protocol because this protocol enables it to send *cfps* (*Call for Proposal*) to multiple NAs. After the PA receives proposals from all the contacted NAs, it chooses the one which offers the best transaction conditions (e.g., offers the highest price for buying the offered content).

FIPA REQUEST (NA (Initiator) and MA (Responder)): Interaction *1.1*

After a NA receives a message of acceptance for its proposal (from the PA), it requests its MA to update the database of available content adding this new one.

FIPA CONTRACT-NET (CA (Initiator) and NA (Responder)): Interaction *2*

A CA wishes to find the service most appropriate to its needs (a CA sends a *cfp* containing OWL-S information regarding the needed service to a multiple NAs). Interactions **2.1** and **2.2** are parts of this conversation. It is important to note that the process of service discovery does not result in an agreement between the consumer and the network operator—this is the purpose of the negotiation process which follows the service discovery procedure (interaction **3**).

FIPA REQUEST (NA (Initiator) and MA (Responder)): Interaction *2.1*

After a NA receives a *cfp* (from the CA), it requests from its MA to generate an ordered list of top-ranked available services. The MA performs the filtration (already described the two-level filtration) of all the available services from the

Figure 10. The communication between agents during the simulation of one transaction

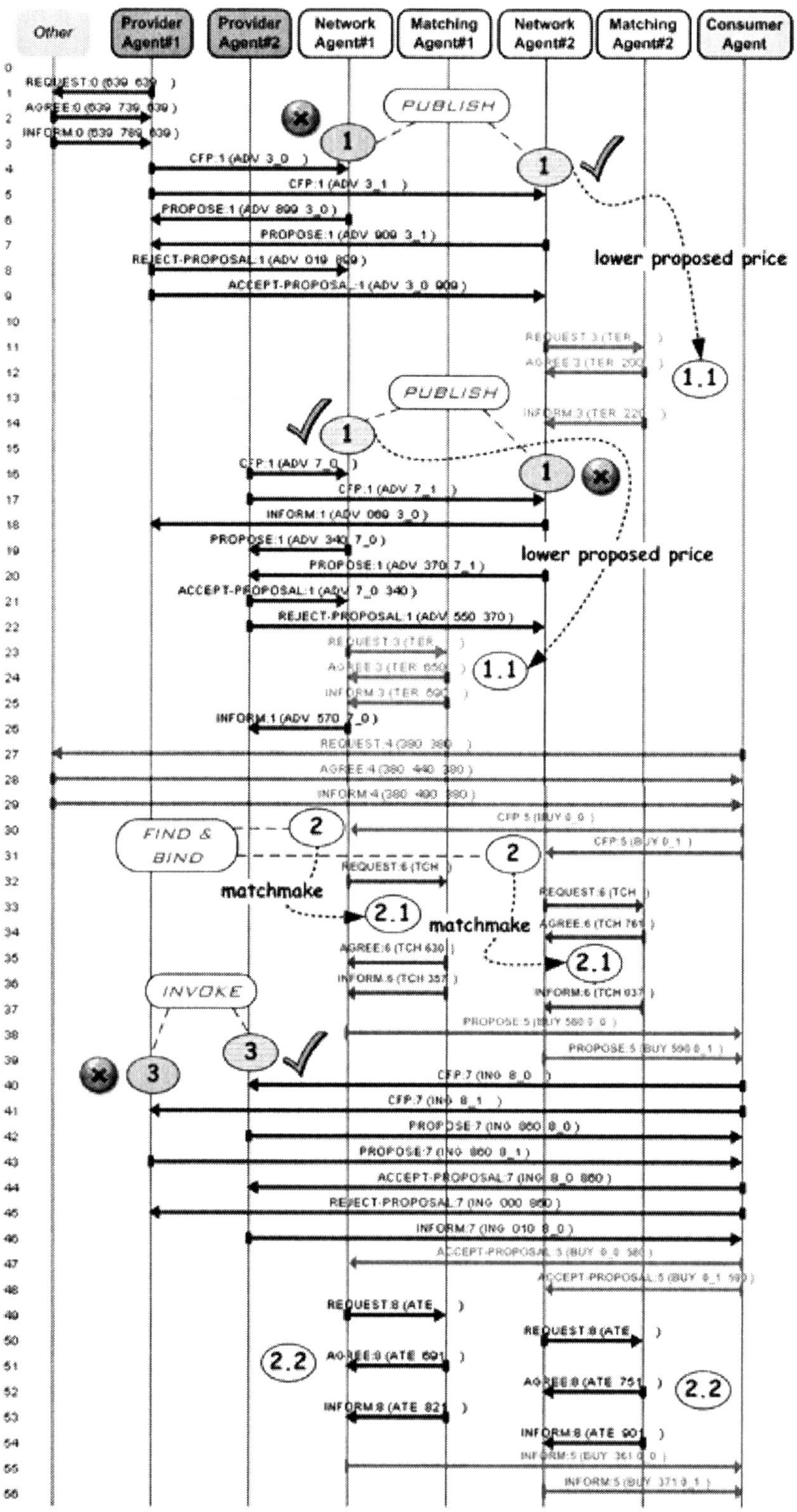

network operator's database with the required service. When the filtration is over, an ordered list of top-ranked available services is created. This list is then forwarded to the NA (conclusion of interaction **2.1**). This is also the list of services the NA is going to propose to the CA as the answer to its service discovery request.

FIPA REQUEST (NA (Initiator) and MA (Responder)): Interaction *2.2*

After a NA receives a message containing information regarding the CA's level of satisfaction with the proposed services, it sends a request to its MA. In that request, it asks the MA to update the ratings of the available services in its database.

FIPA CONTRACT-NET (CA (Initiator) and NA (Responder)): Interaction *3*

After a CA receives proposals from all the NAs to which it sent *cfps*, it tries to find the proposed service which offers the best utilizing conditions (e.g., charges the lowest price for utilization). A CA uses the FIPA Contract-Net interaction protocol because this protocol provides it with ability to send *cfps* for multiple services and to multiple NAs, thus enabling a CA to negotiate with network operators.

Figure 10 shows the communication which took place between the described agents during the simulation of one transaction and presents how the modeled e-market operates. Figure 10 is actually a screenshot of the agents' communication represented through JADE's Sniffer Agent. Although the developed e-market does not have a constraint on the number of agents participating, to enable straightforward presentation, we included only two content providers, two network operators, and one consumer. For a more detailed description of the agents' communication presented in Figure 10, refer to Figure 9 and the associated explanations.

CONCLUSION

New technological opportunities are emerging that provoke convergence of Internet and telecom worlds into a single unified network infrastructure. This new network concept is called next-generation network (NGN) and presents the architecture geared towards applications which intelligibly coordinate information exchange actions. In its first part, this article presents the NGN environment and the impact of this new network concept on the traditional telecom value chain. The creation of a business model that produces added value for all the involved parties (consumers, network operators, content providers) is identified as the essential step for the success of the NGN concept. Therefore, the second part of this article presents the multi-agent system for context-aware service provisioning in NGN, with a special emphasis put on the automated semantic-aware service discovery process. Implementation of the proof-of-concept prototype is grounded on the ubiquitous computing concept, enabled by the technologies of the Semantic Web Services and intelligent software agents, and supported by existing Internet infrastructure and emerging 3G mobile networks. In such a manner, we achieved the creation of a business model that enables a win-win-win situation for all three parties involved in the discovery process (Figure 11).

In the proof-of-concept application presented in this article, rather simple negotiating protocols are utilized, but we have also investigated much more complex protocols for enabling automated service advertising, negotiating, and provisioning in the NGN environment. We have analyzed agent behavior in B2B double auction electronic market for communication resources (Trzec & Lovrek, 2006; Trzec, Lovrek, & Mikac, 2006), as well as the design novel auction models—Semantic Pay-Per-Click Agent auction (Podobnik, Trzec, & Jezic, 2006). Our ultimate goal is to design economically and technically efficient protocols for

Figure 11. Business model resulting in win-win-win situation for all the actors

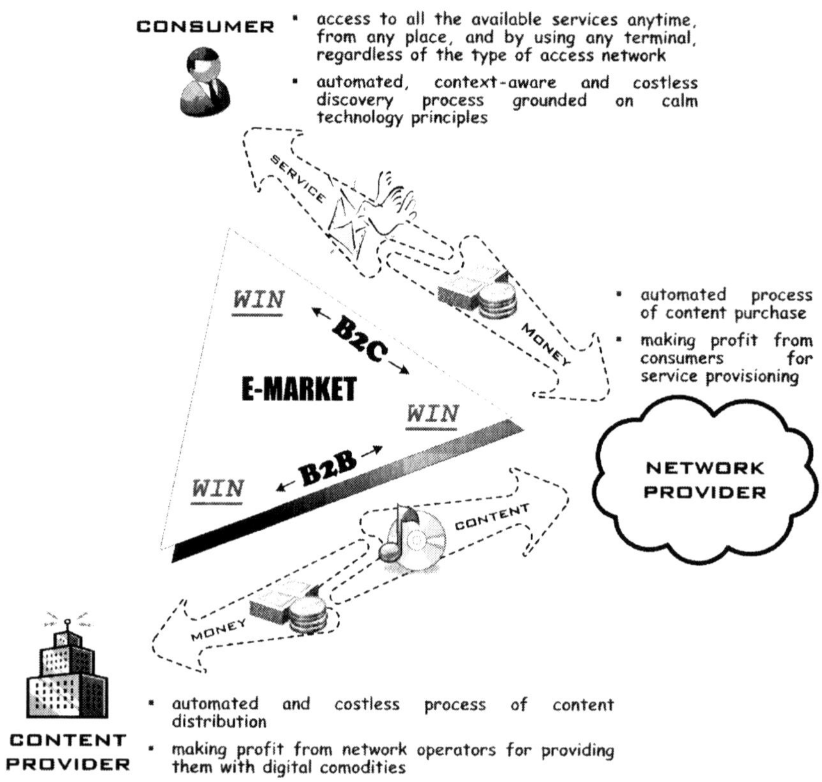

application in real-world scenarios characteristic for the NGN environment. While achieving that goal, we want to utilize the abilities of intelligent software agents to the maximum extent, as well. For future work, it is also planned to test the proposed discovery process in real-life scenarios, foremost to determine its behavior with respect to scalability and time performance.

ACKNOWLEDGMENT

This work was carried out within the research projects 036-0362027-1639 "Content Delivery and Mobility of Users and Services in New Generation Networks", supported by the Ministry of Science, Education and Sports of the Republic of Croatia, and "Agent-based Service and Telecom Operations Management", supported by Ericsson Nikola Tesla, Croatia

REFERENCES

Bellavista, P., Corradi, A., Montanari, R., & Toninelli, A. (2006). Context-aware semantic discovery for next generation mobile systems. *IEEE Communications, 44*(9), 62-71.

Bellifemine, F., Caire, G., & Greenwood, D. (2007). *Developing multi-agent systems with JADE.* West Sussex: John Wiley & Sons.

Berners-Lee, T., Hendler, J., & Lassila, O. (2001). The Semantic Web. *Scientific American, 284*(5), 34-43.

Bradshaw, J.M. (1997). *Software agents*. Cambridge, MA: MIT Press.

Chorafas, D.N. (1998). *Agent technology handbook*. New York: McGraw-Hill.

Cockayne, W.T., & Zyda, M. (1998). *Mobile agents*. Greenwich, CT: Manning Publications.

Colucci, S., Noia, T.D., Sciascio, E.D., Donini, F., & Mongiello, M. (2005). Concept abduction and contraction for semantic-based discovery of matches and negotiation spaces in an e-marketplace. *Electronic Commerce Research and Applications, 4*(3), 345-361.

Di Noia, T., Di Sciascio, E., Donini, F.M., & Mongiello, M. (2004). A system for principled matchmaking in an electronic marketplace. *International Journal of Electronic Commerce, 8*(4), 9-37.

Fan, M., Tan, Y., & Whinston, A.B. (2005). Evaluation and design of online cooperative feedback mechanisms for reputation management. *IEEE Transactions on Knowledge and Data Engineering, 17*(2), 244-254.

Fensel, D. (2004). *Ontologies: A silver bullet for knowledge management and electronic commerce*. Berlin: Springer-Verlag.

Freidman-Hill, E.J. (2003). *Jess in action: Java rule-based system*. Greenwich, CT: Manning Publications.

Garlan, D., Siewiorek, D., Smailagic, A., & Steenkiste, P. (2002). Project aura: Toward distraction-free pervasive computing. *IEEE Pervasive Computing, 1*(2), 22-31.

Hendler, J. (2001). Agents and the Semantic Web. *IEEE Intelligent Systems, 16*(2), 30-37.

Jezic, G., Kusek, M., & Sinkovic, V. (2006). Teamwork coordination in large-scale mobile agent network. *Lecture Notes in Artificial Intelligence, 4251*, 236-243.

Keller, U., Lara, R., Lausen, H., Polleres, A., & Fensel, D. (2005). Automatic location of services. *Lecture Notes in Computer Science, 3532*, 1-16.

Klein, M., & Bernstein, A. (2004). Toward high-precision service retrieval. *IEEE Internet Computing, 8*(1), 30-36.

Kopena, J., & Regli, W.C. (2003). DAMLJessKB: A tool for reasoning with the Semantic Web. *IEEE Intelligent Systems, 18*(3), 74-77.

Kusek, M., Lovrek, I., & Sinkovic, V. (2005). Agent team coordination in the mobile agent network. *Lecture Notes in Artificial Intelligence, 3053*, 240-246.

Leuf, B. (2006). *The Semantic Web: Crafting infrastructure for agency*. New York: Wiley.

Lim, W.S., & Tang, C.S. (2006). An auction model arising from an Internet search service provider. *European Journal of Operational Research, 172*(3), 956-970.

Lindberg, J., Pasman, W., Kranenborg, K.., Stegeman, J., & Neerincx, M.A. (2007). Improving service matching and selection in ubiquitous computing environments: A user study. *Personal and Ubiquitous Computing, 11*(1), 59-68.

Luan, X. (2004). *Adaptive middle agent for service matching in the Semantic Web: A quantitive approach*. Thesis, University of Maryland, Baltimore County.

Padovan, B., Sackmann, S., Eymann, T., & Pippow, I. (2002). A prototype for an agent-based secure electronic marketplace including reputation-tracking mechanisms. *International Journal of Electronic Commerce, 6*(4), 93-113.

Pitkäranta, T. (2004). *Software agents in Semantic Web environment*. Thesis, Helsinki University of Technology, Finland.

Podobnik, V., Jezic, G., & Trzec, K. (2006). An agent-mediated electronic market of Semantic Web services. In *Proceedings of the AAMAS Work-*

shop on Business Agents and the Semantic Web (BASeWEB '06), Hakodate, Japan (pp. 1-10).

Podobnik, V., Petric, A., & Jezic, G. (2006). The CrocodileAgent: Research for efficient agent-based cross-enterprise processes. (*LNCS, 4277*) 752-762.

Podobnik, V., Trzec, K., & Jezic, G. (2006). An auction-based semantic service discovery model for e-commerce applications. (*LNCS, 4277*), 97-106.

Saha, D., & Mukherjee, A. (2003). Pervasive computing: A paradigm for the 21st century. *IEEE Computer, 36*(3), 25-31.

Sycara, K., Paolucci, M., Anolekar, A., & Srinivasan, N. (2004). Automated discovery, interaction and composition of Semantic Web services. *Journal of Web Semantics, 1*(1), 27-46.

Tang, S. (2004). *Matching of Web services specifications using DAML-S descriptions.* Thesis, Technical University of Berlin, Germany.

Trzec, K., & Lovrek, I. (2006). Modelling behaviour of trading agents in electronic market for communication resources. In *Proceedings of the 2nd Conference on Networking and Electronic Commerce Research (NAEC '06)*, Riva Del Garda, Italy (pp. 171-186).

Trzec, K., Lovrek, I., & Mikac, B. (2006). Agent behaviour in double auction electronic market for communication resources. *Lecture Notes in Artificial Intelligence, 4251*, 318-325.

Weiser, M. (1991). The computer for the 21st century. *Scientific American, 265*(3), 94-104.

Weiser, M. (1994). The world is not a desktop. *ACM Interactions, 1*(1), 7-8.

Weiser, M., & Brown, J.S. (1997). The coming age of calm technology. In P.J. Dening, R.M. Metcalfe, & J. Burke (Eds.), *Beyond calculation: The next fifty years of computing* (pp. 75-86). New York: Springer-Verlag.

Wishart, R., Robinson, R., Indulska, J., & Jøsang, A. (2005). SuperstringRep: Reputation-enhanced service discovery. In *Proceedings of the 28th Australasian Conference on Computer Science (ACSC'05)*, Newcastle, Australia (pp. 49-57).

Yoon, J.-L. (2007). Telco 2.0: A new role and business model. *IEEE Communications Magazine, 45*(1), 10-12.

This work was previously published in Int. Journal of Information Technology and Web Engineering, Vol. 2, Issue 4, edited by G. Alkhatib, pp. 41-62, copyright 2007 by IGI Publishing (an imprint of IGI Global).

Chapter III
A Mobile, Intelligent Agent-Based Architecture for E-Business

Zhiyong Weng
University of Ottawa, Canada

Thomas Tran
University of Ottawa, Canada

ABSTRACT

This paper proposes a mobile, intelligent agent-based e-business architecture that allows buyers and sellers to perform business at remote locations. An e-business participant can generate a mobile, intelligent agent via some mobile devices (such as a personal digital assistant or mobile phone) and dispatch the agent to the Internet to do business on her behalf. This proposed architecture promises a number of benefits: First, it provides great convenience for traders as business can be conducted anytime and anywhere. Secondly, since the task of finding and negotiating with appropriate traders is handled by a mobile, intelligent agent, the user is freed from this time-consuming task. Thirdly, this architecture addresses the problem of limited and expensive connection time for mobile devices: A trader can disconnect her mobile device from its server after generating and launching a mobile, intelligent agent. Later on, she can reconnect and call back the agent for results, therefore minimizing the connection time. Finally, by complying with the standardization body FIPA, this flexible architecture increases the interoperability between agent systems and provides high scalability design for swiftly moving across the network.

INTRODUCTION

Many people nowadays use mobile devices such as personal digital assistants (PDA) or mobile phones to access information through the Internet. In addition, they desire to have the ability to participate in e-business anywhere and anytime via their mobile devices. Current e-business applications, such as business-to-consumer (B2C) or Internet-based shopping, are typically developed over the Web for human-computer interaction. These applications require that users must login the intended Web sites from their personal computers or public terminals. Also, users often need to visit lots of sites and are always involved in a time-consuming process. To address these challenges, several wired agent-based e-business systems have been proposed. Kasbah (Chavez & Maes, 1996), for example, is an electronic marketplace where buying and selling agents can carry out business on behalf of their owners. Nevertheless, these systems do not satisfy the users' mobile demand due to their lack of wireless channels.

This article proposes a feasible architecture that combines agent mobility and intelligence for consumer-oriented e-business applications. It allows a user to create a mobile, intelligent agent via a mobile device, and then launch the agent to the Internet to perform business on the user's behalf. The aspect of mobility enables our architecture to support the agent's migration and the user's mobility (the ability to conduct e-business via mobile devices anyplace and anytime). The mobile agent will migrate from market to market, communicating with different trading agents to find the most appropriate one. Once an appropriate agent is found, it will inform the user of the results. This architecture complements the current Web-based, Internet systems by adding the wireless channel of mobile agents. Our current work focuses on lightweight mobile agents which act on behalf of consumers and participate in consumer-to-consumer (C2C) e-business applications. However, the architecture can be extended to business-to-consumer (B2C) or business-to-business (B2B) applications, as discussed later in the article.

Since personal software agents essentially need to communicate with other agents (to accomplish their designated tasks), they have to comply with a set of standards concerning the agent communication language and the protocols to be used. Although there is currently no universally accepted set of standards for developing multi-agent systems, the Foundation for Intelligent Physical Agents (FIPA), which aims at providing one language commonly understood by most agent-based systems (FIPA, 2006), is obtaining a growing acceptance. With FIPA becoming a de facto standard in this field, the architectures such as JADE (Java Agent Development Environment) have become available to allow for the implementation of a FIPA-compliant multi-agent system such as our proposed architecture (Chiang & Liao, 2004).

It should be noted that mobile devices suffer not only from limited battery time, memory, and computing power, but also from small screen, cumbersome input, and limited network bandwidth and network connection (Wang, Sørensen, & Indal, 2003). The proposed architecture, by making use of mobile agent technology, offers a solution to those problems. That is, after creating and initializing a mobile agent to act on the user's behalf, a user can disconnect the mobile device from the server. The user only needs to reconnect later on to recall the agent for results, hence minimizing the use of resources. In addition, mobile agent technology also addresses such challenges as increased need for personalization, high latency, demand for large transfers, and disconnected operation (Kotz & Gray, 1999).

The remainder of this article is organized as follows: the second section introduces background knowledge and related work. The third section illustrates the proposed architecture. The fourth section shows an implementation of the proposed architecture. The fifth section discusses some existing problems and future works. The sixth section concludes the article.

BACKGROUND AND RELATED WORK

Mobile Agent Paradigm

An intelligent agent is a piece of software, which differs from the traditional one by having such features as being autonomous, proactive, social, and so on. One of these characteristics is mobility, that is, the agents' ability to migrate from host to host in a network. Mobile agents are defined as programs that travel autonomously through a computer network in order to fulfill a task specified by its owner, for example, gathering information or getting closer to the required resources to exploit them locally rather than remotely. A mobile agent is not bound to the system on which it begins execution, and hence can be delegated to various destinations. Created in one execution environment, it has the capability of transporting its state and code with it to another host and execute in the same execution environment in which it was originally created. Several mobile agent systems have been designed in recent years. Telescript (White, 1996) is the first commercial mobile agent system developed by General Magic. Telescript provides transparent agent migration and resource usage control. Aglets from IBM (Lang & Oshima, 1998) is also a mobile agent system based on the concept of creating special Java applets (named aglets that are capable of moving across the network). JADE (Bellifemine, Caire, Trucco, & Rimassa, 2006) is one of the agent development tools that can support efficient deployment of both agents' mobility and intelligence in e-business applications. As a middleware implemented in Java and compliant with the FIPA specifications, JADE can work and interoperate both in wired and wireless environments based on the agent paradigm. JADE supports weak mobility; that is, only program code can migrate while no state is carried with programs. NOMADS (Suri et al., 2000) supports strong mobility and secure execution; that is, the ability to preserve the full execution state of mobile agents and the ability to protect the host from attacks.

Recently, mobile agents have found enormous applications including electronic commerce, personal assistance, network management, real-time control, and parallel processing (Lange & Oshima, 1999). Kowalczyk et al. (2002) discuss the use of mobile agents for advanced e-commerce applications after surveying the existing research. There are many advantages of using the mobile agent paradigm rather than conventional paradigms such as client-server technology: reduces network usage, introduces concurrency, and assists operating in heterogeneous systems (Lange & Oshima, 1999).

Related Work

Mobile agents have been recognized as a promising technology for mobile e-business applications. The interest of developing mobile agent systems for mobile devices has increased in recent years. Telescript describes a scenario in which a personal agent is dispatched to search a number of electronic catalogs for specific products and returns best prices to a PDA from where it starts (Gray, 1997). An integrated mobile agent system called Nomad allows mobile agents to travel to the eAuctionHouse site (http://ecommerce.cs.wustl.edu) for automated bidding and auction monitoring on the user's behalf even when the user is disconnected from the network (Sandholm & Huai, 2000). They aim at reducing network traffic and latency.

Impulse (2006) explores a scenario in which e-business meets concrete business through a system of buying and selling agents representing individual buyers and sellers that carry out multiparameter negotiation and running on the wireless mobile devices. Impulse deploys personal agents on mobile devices to help users seek agreement on purchase terms. However, these personal agents are directed to move online to participate in negotiations, and hence resulting in potentially long-time connection with the Internet. We also think that the Impulse system was designed with a single communication protocol for all agents. This presents drawbacks due to the heterogeneity of exchanged information and leads to an inflexible environment, which can only accept those agents especially designed for it. Agora (Fonseca, Griss, & Letsinger, 2001) is a project conducted at HP Labs to develop a test-bed for the application of agent technology to a mobile shopping mall. A typical scenario consists of mobile shoppers with PDAs interacting with store services while in the mall, on the way to the store, or in the store itself. The Zeus agent toolkit, developed by British Telecommunications, was used to implement all agents in the Agora project. Only the infrastructure agents speak the FIPA Agent Communication Language (ACL), causing the architecture to conform partly to FIPA, although more effort in conformance is needed. The purpose of the Agora project is to gain experience in agents' communication protocols and to realize the significance of architectural standards.

It has been shown that modern agent environments such as JADE could be easily scaled to 1,500 agents and 300,000 messages (Chmiel et al., 2004). Thus, it is now possible to build and experiment with large-scaled agent systems. Moreno et al. (2005) use JADE-LEAP (JADE Lightweight Extensible Agent Platform) to implement a personal agent on a PDA. This agent belongs to a multi-agent system that allows the user to request a taxi in a city. The personal agent communicates wirelessly with the rest of the agents in the multi-agent system, in order to find the most appropriate taxi to serve the user. IMSAF (Chiang & Liao, 2004) is an architecture designed to fulfill the requirements of Impulse-introduced mobile shopping and implemented using JADE-LEAP tools. LEAP can also be used to deploy multi-agent systems spread across mobile devices and servers; however, it requires a permanent bidirectional connection between mobile devices and servers. Considering the current expensive connection fees for cell phones, such a required permanent connection is not affordable for consumers in practice.

In contrast to the above works, we are motivated to propose a mediator-based architecture that attempts to enable users' wireless participation in several e-marketplaces through their mobile devices. The mobile agents can move across the network and perform trading tasks on behalf of their users when the users are disconnected from the network. We believe that it is important to consider the limitations of mobile devices, such as low-battery, low bandwidth, high latency, limited computing ability, and expensive connection fees. The fact that consumers in our physical world may need to access the worldwide markets and distributed e-business environments requires the agents to operate in heterogeneous and dynamic environments as well as to talk a common language. By complying with the FIPA specifications, the proposed architecture provides an interoperable solution to allow users dynamically to connect to the network by means of their mobile devices only when needed. Also, the mobile devices will not suffer those limitations mentioned above. In addition, the benefit of using mobile agents to a user becomes more obvious in our architecture if the user has a mobile phone and is interested in minimizing expensive connection costs. The next section explains the architecture in more detail.

SYSTEM ARCHITECTURE

Overview

Figure 1 shows a distributed C2C wireless e-business environment and a traditional wired e-business one. A consumer can connect a mobile device, such as a PDA or mobile phone, to the mediator server through wireless connection and then send a request for creating a mobile buying

Figure 1. Distributed e-business environment

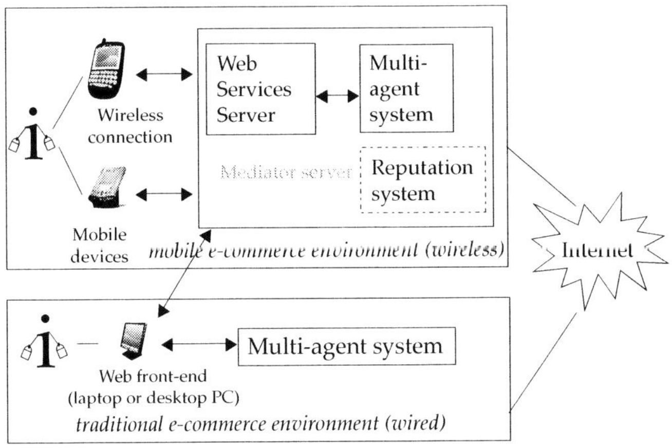

or selling agent to undertake a specific business task (e.g., auction bidding) on the user's behalf. A personal agent that resides on the mobile device is needed to interact directly with the consumer and to consider the consumer's personal preferences. Considered as a true representative of the consumer, the personal agent represents the consumer's interests and allows the consumer to have a choice of dispatching either a buying or a selling agent. The mediator server sits in the fixed network and provides services such as generating mobile agents according to consumers' requests. After being created, the mobile agents will autonomously travel to multiple agent-based servers on the Internet. The agent-based servers offer places for selling and buying agents to meet and negotiate with one another. The proposed mediator server contains two main components: the Web services server, which facilitates mobile agents to interface with other agents, and the multi-agent system, which manages the agents and plays the role of a marketplace similar to an agent-based server. An additional component, a reputation system, will be necessary in our architecture. Using this reputation system, agents could sign binding contracts and check user's credit histories and reputations. The trust problem will be further studied in future research (e.g., Jøsang & Ismail, 2002 present a Beta Reputation System). Also, the mediator server provides a Web-based interface, and as shown in Figure 1, a consumer can also connect a laptop or a desktop PC to the network and launch an agent to execute on the mediator server.[1] In this article, we focus on the electronic trading of second-hand products for owners of mobile devices.

The main idea is that a consumer will request the mediator server to create a buying or selling agent and then dispatch it to agent-based servers on the Internet. The main operation that occurs in an agent-based server is price negotiation where buying agents negotiate price with selling agents. According to the consumer's preferences, the buying agent may travel to different e-market sites known by the white-page agent[2] to seek goods, when the consumer desires to conduct a global multiple markets comparison. The W3C's XML schema specification (www.w3.org/XML/Schema) provides a standard language for defining the document structure and the XML structures' data types. The consumer's preferences can be represented in an XML format. In a real business situation, we would have to ensure that messages are reliably delivered to the mediator server from the personal agents. Although this communication protocol's reliability is not detailed in our architecture currently, we could use a reliable transport at the very least, such as Reliable HTTP

(HTTPR) (Todd, Parr, & Conner, 2005), for the communication between the personal agents and the mediator server. Another consideration is to encrypt the communication. Encryption technologies can also help ensure that even intercepted transmissions cannot be read easily.

A Scenario of Our Architecture

To understand the environment best, let us consider a typical scenario taken from daily life, where two hypothetical customers, named Mary and Tom, try to participate in an eBay-like auction. Mary wants to sell her used Sony MP3 player. At her office, she initiates a selling agent from a PDA, through a wireless LAN connection with the mediator server in the building. Then this selling agent lives in the server and waits for potential shoppers. Due to some unpredictable event, Mary may have to leave her office and cannot access the selling agent via her PDA (as there may be no available wireless LAN network coverage). However, she will be able to reconnect later on.

Haphazardly, Tom enters his buying preferences into his Java-enabled mobile phone, trying to buy a second-hand Sony MP3 player under a maximum price. The personal agent on his mobile phone establishes a connection with the mediator server and asks the server to launch a mobile buying agent according to his preferences. Then Tom disconnects his cell phone from the server. The mobile agent knows where and how to migrate, as instructed in the migration itinerary. As days pass, while this buying agent is roaming around the Internet, it enters into Mary's mediator server and searches for services provided. After the negotiation between the selling agent and buying agent, they reach an agreement on the item and price. With that, the buying agent will return to its host server and send a SMS (Short Message Service)-based notification to the personal agent running on Tom's mobile phone, about the potential seller gathered from the Internet. Also the selling agent sends an e-mail-based notification to the personal agent running on Mary's PDA. Finally, things left to Mary and Tom seem to be simple and easy since they could have either the cell phone number or the e-mail address from the information reported by their personal agents, respectively. As we have seen, mobile consumers only need a small bandwidth connection twice, once for initiating a migrating mobile agent and once for collecting the results when the task is finished.

Architecture Description

We explain how the whole system works in this section. Figure 2 illustrates the system architecture and the operation process. As shown in Figure 2, mobile devices are supported by personal agents and connected to the mediator server via a wireless connection. A personal agent is a static agent running on a mobile device and offers a graphical user interface (GUI) for its user to communicate with the system. The mediator server is connected to the Internet where other mediator servers or other FIPA-compliant systems exist. In the mediator server, a servlet answers any requests from the personal agent and is linked to the behavior of a proxy agent[3] in charge of handling the requests. The proxy-agent interfaces with the servlet and constructs a bridge between the Web service server and the multi-agent system. Each instance of the behavior[4] connects not only to the AMS agent (Agent Management Service as defined in FIPA, i.e., the white-page agent mentioned above), asking for the creation of a buying or selling mobile agent in the multi-agent system as well as providing a response, but also connects to the agent DF (Directory Facilitator as defined in FIPA, i.e., the yellow-page agent), retrieving the list of agents advertising services with the DF. In this architecture, the multithreaded-servlet server is mirrored by a multibehavior proxy agent to allow for handling multiple requests in parallel.

As illustrated in Figure 2, the procedures from (1) to (6) depict how a buying or selling mobile agent is created by a user according to preferences:

1. At the first step, the user configures the preferences via the personal agent (residing in the mobile device). The personal agent then sends an XML-based request to the mediator server.
2. An instance of the servlet accepts the request and communicates with the proxy agent.
3. The proxy agent cooperates with the AMS agent who lives in the main container of the JADE platform to create a buying or selling mobile agent.
4. If the buying or selling agent is created successfully in the container, it might be mobilized to other systems to undertake the user's task.
5. and (6) The personal agent receives a response from the proxy agent via the servlet and informs the user of the relevant mobile agent being created.

The above is an asynchronous process after which the user can disconnect from the network at will. Even if the user decides to disconnect from the network, the user will still receive an SMS-based notification from the mediator server via an interface with the wireless carrier, or an e-mail-based notification from the mediator server via an interface with a mail server, as long as the user reconnects to the network.

The mediator server provides the required support for the creation of mobile agents, messaging among agents, agent migration facility, collaboration, protection, destruction, and control of mobile agents. Mobile agent platforms such as JADE have been proposed to provide the supporting environment. Obviously, any multi-agent system can be used here as long as it provides the required support.

Different Types of Agents in Our Architecture

The following agents co-exist in our architecture: personal agents, proxy agents, buying or selling agents, yellow-page agents, and white-page agents. Among them, only buying or selling agents are mobile agents, while personal agents

Figure 2. System architecture and process

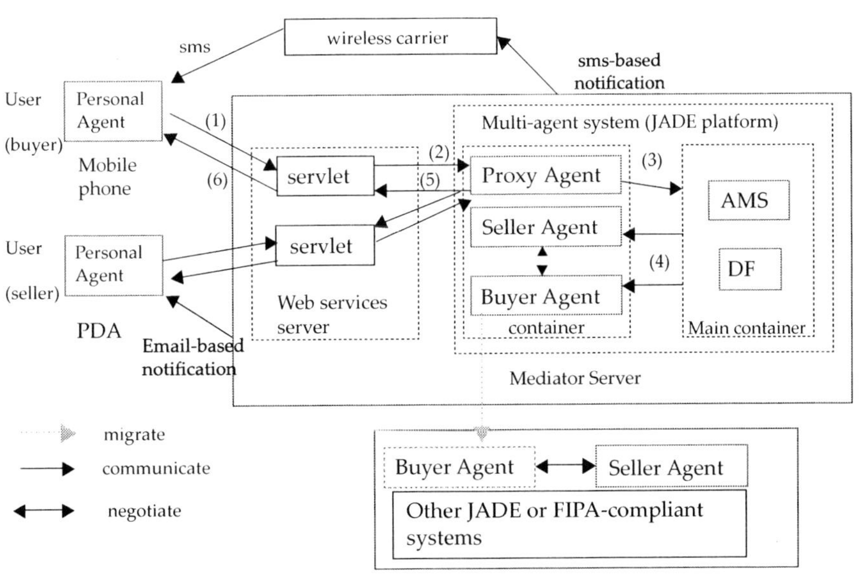

and proxy agents are stationary agents. Both the yellow-page and white-page agents are fixed on a component of the mediator server. Details of these agents are described as follows:

A personal agent is a stationary agent that runs on a user's mobile device and provides a graphical interface to allow the user to configure a mobile buying or selling agent (from the mobile device). When starting the personal agent on the mobile device, the user can choose either to initiate a new mobile agent or to recall a previous mobile agent. One may argue that such a personal agent is nothing more than an interface. From the agent's viewpoint, however, the personal agents are able to autonomously communicate with the proxy agent which is running in the mediator server.

A proxy agent is also a stationary agent which links the multi-agent system to the Web service server. It is one of the agents that is always up and running in the multi-agent system. The proxy agent cooperates with the AMS (white-page) agent to create a mobile buying or selling agent for each user. There is only one proxy agent per mediator server due to its unique multibehavior ability.

A yellow-page agent (such as the DF agent in the JADE platform) provides the service of yellow pages, by means of which an agent can receive information about available products or find other agents providing necessary services to achieve its goal. A white-page agent (like the AMS agent in the JADE platform) represents the authority and provides naming services. It stores information about addresses and identifiers of all agents in the system. In our architecture, sellers have permission to advertise their products; and buyers are allowed to query the sellers which post the products they are looking for. Selling agents update yellow pages by publishing their services via the yellow-page agent. Buying agents query relevant services from the yellow-page agent. Both buying and selling agents update white pages by registering in or deregistering from the system. They communicate with each other via querying agent's information from the white-page agent.

Both buying and selling agents are mobile agents, which are also called *service agents*. A service agent is the counter part of a personal agent and is involved in the migration from host to host on the Internet. A service agent first negotiates with other service agents in the same host mediator server before migrating among multiple Web sites to talk to other service agents, provided that they can talk a common language.

To demonstrate a useful mobile agent system, we present a prototype for buying and selling agents, with attributes depicted in Table 1. This means that a user will configure a mobile buying or selling agent on a mobile device, precisely according to the characteristics in Table 1.

Behaviors of Mobile Agents

As illustrated in Figure 3, a mobile (buying or selling) agent starts with its registration in the system and ends with a timeout of its lifetime. There are three time events that indicate the behaviors of a mobile agent: (1) the agent starts its negotiation process at a regular interval (e.g., every minute); (2) the agent starts its migration when activity time per server is reached; and (3) the agent ends its life cycle when its lifetime is exhausted. An argument may arise; how can one be sure that the mobile agent will be terminated according to the parameter and lifetime, as users prefer? This parameter may be changed by a third party (including the mediator server). The assumption we made is that the mobile agent can be protected from the attacks (e.g., from the host or other agents) once a future security mechanism is imposed on our architecture. (The security problem is discussed in the Discussion and Future Work section.)

Negotiation Process

The proposed interaction between agents complies with the FIPA-Contract-Net Protocol (FIPA, 2006). This protocol allows a buying agent

Table 1. Attributes of a mobile agent

Attribute	Description
Agent type	The agent type that a user can select, that is, either a buying agent or a selling agent
Agent server	The configuration of the mediator server address.
User id	The user identification which can be email address, cell phone number, or IMEI (International Mobile Equipment Identity).
Quantity	Quantity of the predefined product.
Price	For a buying agent, this is the maximum price that the agent can bid: for a selling agent, this is the minimum price that the agent can accept.
Current Price Inquired	For a buying agent, this is the best price offer colledted from the Internet.
Lifetime	The total time an agent can be away before being recalled or terminated.
Mobility	Specification of whether a user desires to enalbe the agent's migration ability (i.e., in the context of a local, single or global, multiple market comparison)
Server Activity Time	The time an agent can spend on each server before migrating ot another.

(initiator) to send a call for proposals (CFP) to a set of selling agents (responders), evaluate their proposals, and then accept the most preferred one (or even refuse all of them). Both initiators and responders should register in the system before they negotiate with each other.

In this article, we consider a classical situation in which a selling agent offers a single item to the highest bidder (similar to eBay), and the simplest type of bid is an offer to buy or sell one unit at a specified price. As shown in Figure 4, the buying agent sends a CFP to all the available selling agents (obtained from the yellow-pages service). After receiving the message, a selling agent can send the buying agent a proposal with the price for the product. If the product is not available or sold, it does not need to send any proposal. The buying agent will place a purchase order if the offer price is within the maximum price that the customer has specified. Results of price negotiations are sent back to the personal agent and showed in a graphical interface to the user. Since the system is fully asynchronous, an intention to make a purchase does not have to lead to a successful transaction. By the time the offer is made, other buying agents may have already purchased the last available item.

Agent Migration

The general process of migration is depicted in Figure 5. An agent starts its migration from its host server (i.e., the mediator server) with the itinerary list acquired from the host. We assume that there are n servers, which will be visited by the agent in sequence. In each server, two time events happen resulting in two actions respectively: if the agent reaches its lifetime, it will return to its host where it was created, and then end the migration process; if the agent exhausts its server activity time, it will migrate to the next server. Additionally, before the agent migrates to the next server, it should also make the decision if it has fulfilled the task at the current server. As we know, a task is finished when an agent receives an acceptable offer from another agent. The migration process actually describes a scenario of price comparison (finding a price less than a buyer's reservation price for buying, or searching for a price greater than a seller's reservation price for selling). The agent may access its host server repeatedly during its lifetime and updates its itinerary list every time when visiting its host server. One interesting problem here is how the mediator server maintains the itinerary list that

Figure 3. Activity diagram of mobile agent

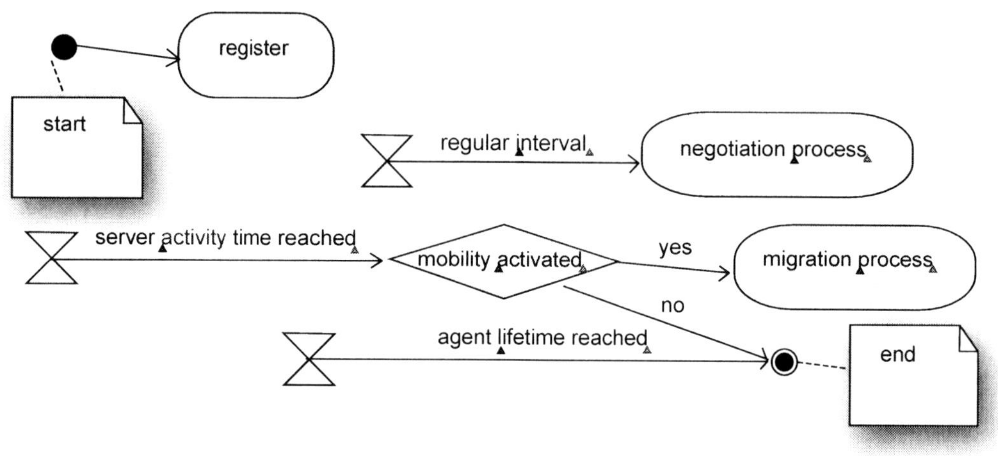

includes a series of service-providing servers to be visited by the agent. Curbera, Duftler, Khalaf, Nagy, Mukhi, and Weerawarana (2002) state that "several individual companies and industry groups are starting to use 'private' UDDI directories to integrate and streamline access to their internal services" (p. 90). UDDI (Universal Description, Discovery and Integration) (UDDI, 2006) enables businesses to publish service listings and to discover each other. We assume that the white-page agent can interact with the UDDI server to obtain other service-providing servers' addresses (the feasibility of this function will be further studied) and therefore mobile agents can update the itinerary list during their migration. Only the mobile agents, which are originally created in this mediator server, are allowed to access this resource (a list of servers).

System Implementation

We have implemented a simple prototype to evaluate the concepts proposed in our architecture, using the Java programming language. Figure 6 shows the screenshots of a personal agent and a JADE-based multi-agent system, respectively. The personal agent was developed as a J2ME MIDlet[5] application that offered a graphical interface for its user to initiate or recall the mobile agent, and to dialogue with the mediator server. The mediator server played an important role in our architecture, running a Tomcat Apache Servlet Engine on a JADE platform. JADE is an open-source with good scalability, one of the best modern agent environments compliant with FIPA. As shown in Figure 6, there are two containers on the JADE system, Main-container and Container-1. Main-container holds the basic management agents defined by FIPA (AMS, DF, and RMA, which manages the GUI of the JADE platform). The proxy agent, buying agents, and selling agents run in Container-1. We can deploy the mediator-based architecture in one or several PCs.

The Web services architecture communications are based on JSR172, J2ME Web services, which include two independent parts: the JAX-RPC and JAXP. XML is chosen as the standard way for clients to interact with backend servers so as to use the remote services. J2ME JAX-RPC APIs subset solves how to access the SOAP/XML Web services and JAXP APIs subset solves how to process the XML messages. Messages exchanged by agents in the multi-agent system have a format specified by the ACL language defined by FIPA for agent interoperability.

Figure 4. Negotiation process

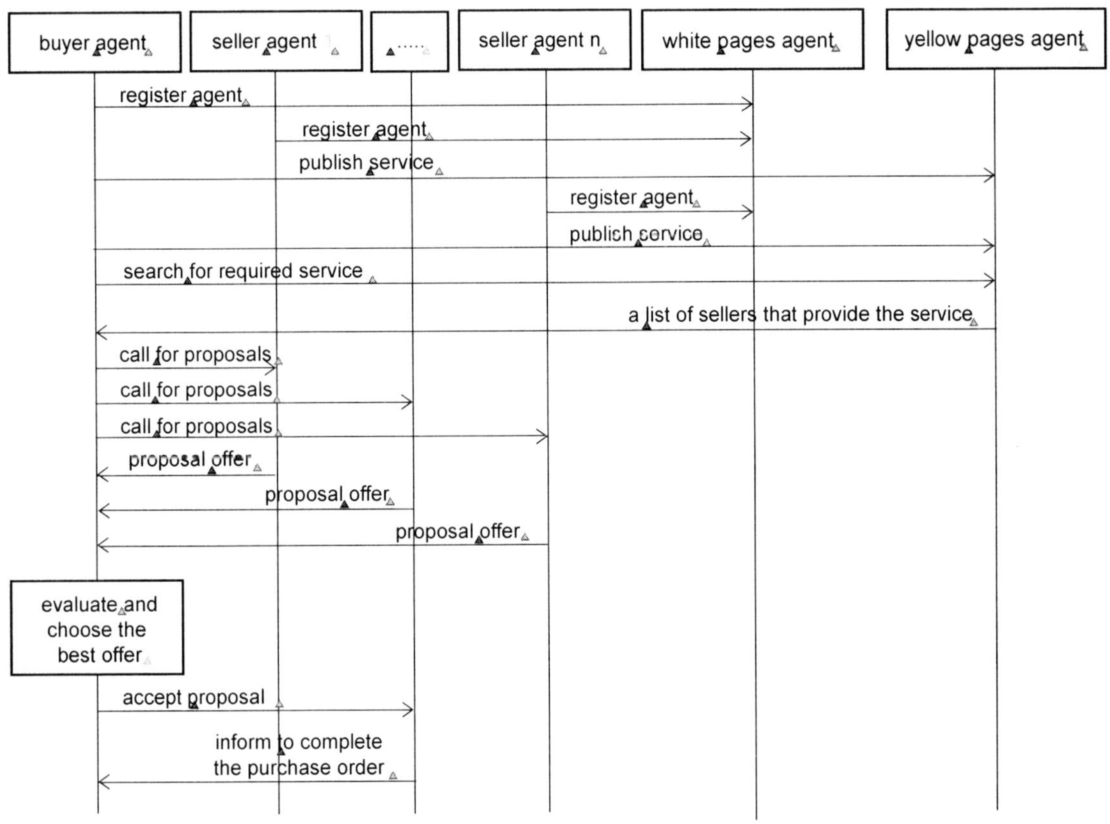

Figure 5. Agent migration process

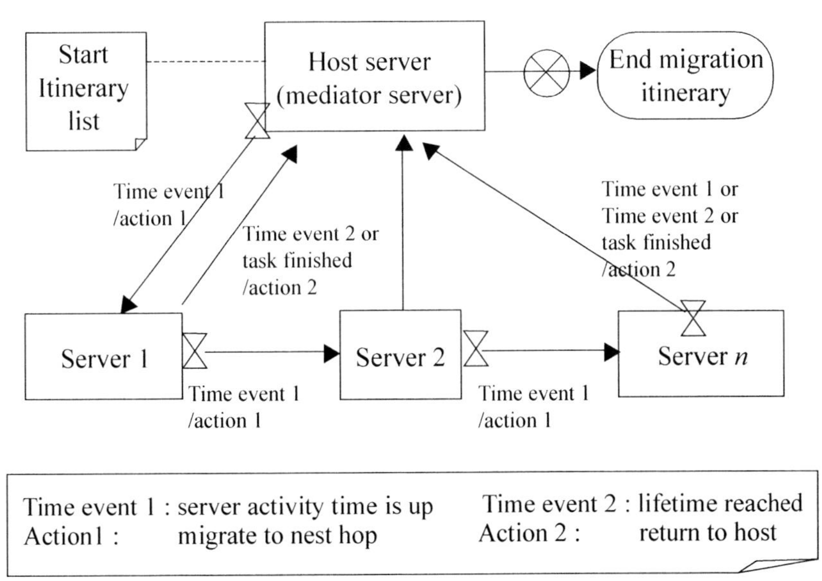

Figure 6. Screenshots of a personal agent and the JADE platform

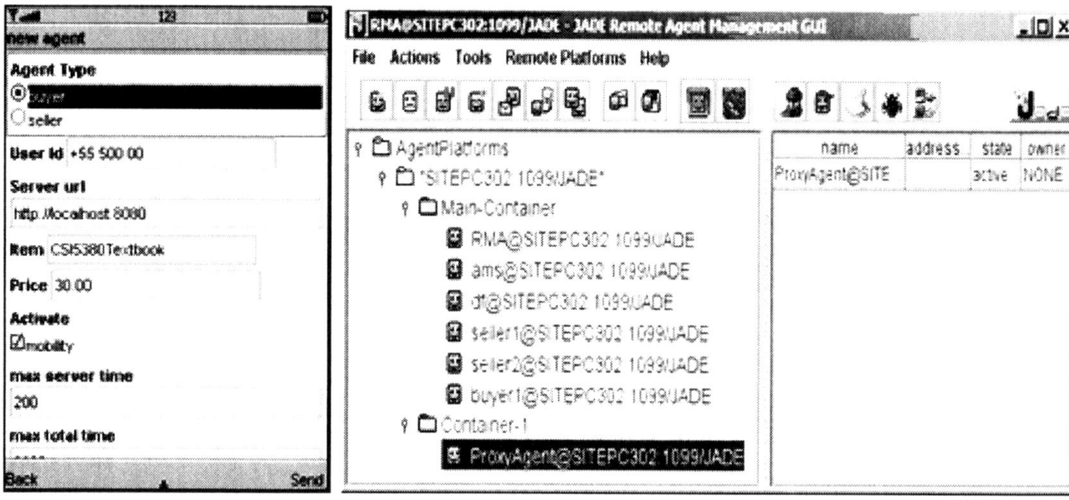

Figure 7. Experiment environment

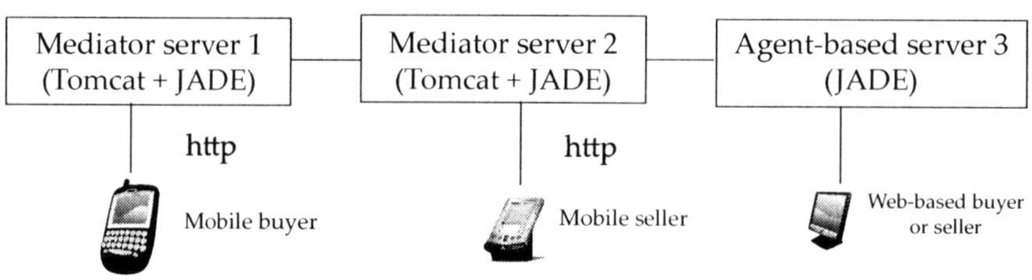

As shown in Figure 7, we deployed three servers in the Local Area Network, installed J2ME MIDlet in two mobile phone simulators, provided one GUI for the Web-based seller, and simulated a simple used-item electronic trading scenario similar to the one we described in A Scenario of Our Architecture section previously. The mobile phone emulator is a tool provided by the Sun J2ME wireless toolkit 2.2. Both mediator servers deployed the Tomcat server and the main container of JADE platform was initialized. The third computer played the role of an agent-based marketplace on the Internet. For the buyer's emulator, the user activated the mobility of the buying agent, but it was not the case for the seller's emulator. We observed the following results:

- Mobile users can connect to mediator servers via HTTP and initiate mobile buying or selling agents in the mediator server.
- Mobile users do not need to instruct their mobile agents of what to do after configuring their preferences.
- Mobile users can add new items anytime and relevant mobile agents will be created to handle the trading of these new items respectively.
- Mobile users can kill their mobile agents to cancel their tasks by sending instruction to their personal agents.
- Mobile agents are active in their servers within the specified server activity time and then migrate to other servers.

- Buying agents can reach agreements with selling agents when the required item and price are matched. Mobile users then receive text messages from their agents, displayed on the screen of the simulators.
- Mobile agents end their life cycles when finishing their tasks.

As confirmed by the experiments, mobile users connect to their servers only when they need to add new items or to cancel their tasks. This obviously results in such benefits as reduced bandwidth utilization, increased battery life for mobile devices, and no complicated computation conducted in mobile devices. Also, mobile agents can move to various servers to negotiate autonomously, and mediator servers can accept mobile agents from outside their systems. This feature enables users to participate in multiple markets on the Internet.

In particular, we observed the migration process of a mobile agent. Mobile agents should be active in their servers within a specified time and migrate among the servers. Thus, we developed a scenario where we supposed that a buying agent started from Serverl and continued searching for the required product or service in Server2 and Server3. We set up two parameters for this mobile agent: Maximum server active time was set to 100 seconds and total lifetime was set to 850 seconds. As expected, the buying agent contacted the other agents in Serverl and then migrated to Server2 after approximately 100 seconds. Similarly, the buying agent communicated with other agents in Server2 and then traveled to Server3. The same things happened in Server3. Because there were no more sites to be visited, the buying agent migrated back to Serverl, ending its first round of migration. The second round was started since the total lifetime was not reached. We assumed that no sellers offered the required product or service to this buying agent. With the time elapsed, the buying agent was in its third round and roamed into Server2. At this stage, the buying agent used up its lifetime of 850 seconds and predicted an ending of its life cycle. Therefore it migrated back to the host Serverl, even though the third round trip was not finished. In another scenario, we used the same parameters for the buying agent, except that the total lifetime was enlarged to 1,000 seconds. The difference was that we dispatched a selling agent in Server2 at the moment the buying agent was ready to launch its third round trip. This selling agent offered exactly the service that the buying agent needed. As we expected, the two agents met and reached an agreement after negotiating with each other. This experiment confirmed that after completing its task, the buying agent migrated back to Serverl, regardless of its remaining lifetime that had not yet been exhausted.

DISCUSSION AND FUTURE WORK

In this article, we propose a feasible mobile agent architecture that assists users in C2C e-business. It enriches the resources for users to perform comparison shopping activities at the point of purchase. Users' mobile devices connect to the network only when needed, thus making efficient use of limited bandwidth and reducing the network traffic. In addition, it helps cell phone users save money from their expensive bills. At any time, users may add items via their personal agents and specify their preferences such as time limit and preferred price for trading. Through the negotiation process between mobile buying and selling agents, users also gain valuable information for making trading decisions.

Our proposed architecture is extensible: On the one hand, XML-based communication is used to enhance extensibility; on the other hand, the architecture could be easily extended to B2C, or even B2B business models. That is, not only individuals but also business companies can be attached to the architecture. With mobile phones and PDAs already being used as extended enterprise tools, business companies, such as retailers and suppliers, can publish their products and/or services on their servers via mobile devices. As long as these businesses take part in our architecture parties, they could benefit from the automatic discovery of other business partners. Also, it is possible for businesses, especially for retailers, to sell their products to potential buyers in the manner described in the proposed architecture as an extra way to their traditional ones. In this sense, our architecture is an integration model of C2C, B2C, and B2B e-business. Nonetheless, using mobile devices for complex tasks can be quite frustrating (e.g., difficult to enter data), so probably people will not use it. An idea is to incorporate targeted messaging or advertising into our model, where businesses could send a message to users who are physically located in their vicinity. Agents could negotiate a transaction, and the buyer would already be located nearby to complete the purchase and pick up the item.

Currently, we present a conceptual framework that needs to be refined. Using this work as a starting point, we have outlined a number of future research directions:

(1) Negotiation protocols do not have to be hard-coded into the agents. Instead, mobile agents can adapt to any intelligent negotiation strategies when they arrive at a new remote location. Thus, our architecture paves the way for future research in which more general architectures can be explored to allow mobile agents to participate in a variety of negotiation protocols, such as factor negotiation (price, quality, delivery time, etc.), electronic contracting, and so on. Currently, the negotiation strategy module consists of only a purchase determined by price (agents seek a preferable price by a fixed amount). FIPA defines auction protocols (e.g., Dutch and English auctions) as well as simpler strategies such as fixed pricing, fixed pricing with a discount, and so on. We will add them into the negotiation protocols in our future research.

(2) Items are described only by their names. Obviously, other attributes, such as color, age, terms of warranty and delivery should also be considered. We believe that ontologies can help to solve this problem. It should be noted that the small screen of mobile devices will bring inconvenience to users when they specify many attributes of an item. A possible solution is to make use of the persistent memory of mobile devices to store the users' preferences.

(3) Mobile agent technology currently has some limitations, such as identity management, fault tolerance, protection of agents, and resource security. These limitations have brought up some concerns about the practical utilization of mobile agents. For example, in the area of security, e-business applications are often involved with money and thus users may hesitate to use mobile agents, unless mobile agents are secure enough to be trusted.

In the situation presented in this article, the mobile agents representing different buyers or sellers migrate over the Internet and then execute themselves on remote computers. These mobile agents are thus exposed to open environments and may become vulnerable. Since the mobile agents execute on unknown computers and interact with unknown agents, a reliable security infrastructure is vitally needed for the design of the system. The mobile agents must be able to deal with situations where they have been shipped off to the wrong address or to a hostile environment (Neuenhofen & Thompson, 1998). Listed below are some possible security concerns:

- Malicious mobile agents can try to access services and resources without adequate permissions. In addition, a malicious agent may assume the identity of another agent in order to gain access to platform resources and services, or to cause mischief or even serious damage to the platform.

- Mobile agents may suffer eavesdropping attack from other mobile agents. A malicious agent can sniff the conversations between other agents or monitor the behavior of a mobile agent in order to extract sensitive information from it.
- Mobile agents may suffer alteration attack from malicious hosts. To execute the agent and update its state, the host must definitely be capable of reading and writing the agent. A malicious host may steal private information from the agent or modify the agent to compute the wrong result or to misbehave when it jumps to another site.

Current research efforts in the area of mobile agent security adopt two different perspectives (Kotz, 2002): First, from the platform perspective, we need to protect the host from malicious mobile agents (such as viruses and Trojan horses) that are visiting it and consuming its resources. Second, from the mobile agent perspective, we need to protect the agent from malicious hosts. There are many mechanisms to protect a host against malicious agents. Digital signatures and trust management approaches may help identify the agent and evaluate how much it should be trusted. The malicious host problem, in which a malicious host attacks a visiting mobile agent, is the most difficult problem. We found in the literature some works on powerful techniques such as Sandboxing and Proof-Carrying Code (PCC). Sandboxing (Wahbe, Lucco, Anderson, & Graham, 1993) is a software technique used to protect a mobile agent platform from malicious mobile agents. PCC (Lee & Necula, 1997) introduces the technique in which the code producer is required to provide a formal proof that the code complies with the security policy of the code consumer. Therefore, we envisage that the security of mobile agents is an important issue that will encourage techniques and mechanisms for e-business in the future.

CONCLUSION

We propose in this article an e-business architecture that allows traders to do business at remote locations by means of mobile intelligent agents. Our architecture, which adheres to standardization efforts in the multi-agent field such as FIPA paves a possible way towards a near future when mobile buying (and selling) agents can smoothly travel among different agent-based marketplaces to carry out tasks on their users' behalves. Our purpose of presenting this idea is to improve our understanding of the value of mobility and to encourage the conceptual construction of a global community. We do not claim that buyers and sellers around the world would have to buy into this to make it work, and that worldwide C2B e-commerce would be revolutionized thereby. In practice, however, we hope that our work would be useful on a smaller scale and lead to new investigations that may result in new solutions to the problems we addressed. Our proposed architecture, aimed at providing new capabilities for advanced e-business solutions, employs an approach that integrates intelligent and mobile agents. Intelligent agents can provide automation support for decision-making tasks, while mobile agents can extend that support by allowing users to participate in several marketplaces in a networked e-business. We believe that intelligent and mobile agent technology is also a promising solution to the problems of low speed, high latency, and limited computing ability that the current wireless network is facing.

REFERENCES

Bellifemine, F., Caire, G., Trucco, T., & Rimassa, G. (2006). JADE programmer's guide. Retrieved July 7, 2007, from http://jade.cselt.it/docs

Chavez, A., & Maes, P. (1996). Kasbah: An agent marketplace for buying and selling goods. In *Proceedings of the 1st International Conference on the Practical Application of Intelligent Agents and Multi-Agent Technology*, London, United Kingdom.

Chiang, H., & Liao, Y. (2004). An agent-based architecture for impulse-induced mobile shopping, *Computer and Information Technology*.

Chmiel, K., et al. (2004). Testing the efficiency of JADE agent platform. In *Proceedings of the 3rd International Symposium on Parallel and Distributed Computing* (pp. 49-57). IEEE Computer Society Press.

Curbera, F., Duftler, M., Khalaf, R., Nagy, W., Mukhi, N., & Weerawarana, S. (2002, March-April). Unraveling the Web services Web: An introduction to SOAP, WSDL, and UDDI. *IEEE Internet Computing, 6*(2), 86-93

FIPA. (2006). Retrieved July 7, 2007, from http://www.fipa.org

Fonseca, S., Griss, M., & Letsinger, R. (2001). *An agent-mediator e-business environment for the mobile shopper* (HP Tech. Rep. No. HPL-20010157).

Gray, R.S. (1997). Agent Tcl. *Dr. Dobb's Journal*, pp. 18-26.

Impulse. (2006). Retrieved July 7, 2007, from http://agents.media.mit.edu/projects/impulse/

Jøsang, A., & Ismail, R. (2002, June). The Beta Reputation System. In *Proceedings of the 15th Bled Electronic Commerce Conference*, Bled, Slovenia.

Kotz, D. (2002). Future directions for mobile agent research. *IEEE Computer Science*.

Kotz, D., & Gray, R. (1999). Mobile code: The future of the Internet. In *Proceedings of Autonomous Agents'99: Workshop on Mobile Agents in the Context of Competition and Cooperation*.

Kowalczyk, R., et al. (2002). Integrating mobile and intelligent agents in advanced e-business: A survey. In *Proceedings of Agent Technologies, Infrastructures, Tools, and Applications for E-Services, NODe'2002 Agent-Related Workshops*, Erfurt, Germany.

Lange, B.D., & Oshima, M. (1998). *Programming and deploying Java mobile agents with aglets*. Addison-Wesley.

Lange, D.B., & Oshima, M. (1999). Seven good reasons for mobile agents. *Communications of the ACM*.

Lee, P., & Necula, G. (1997). Research on proof-carrying code on mobile-code security. In *Proceedings of the Workshop on Foundations of Mobile Code Security*.

Moreno, et al. (2005). Using JADE-LEAP to implement agents in mobile devices. Retrieved July 7, 2007, from http://www.zdnet.de/itmanager/whitepapers

Neuenhofen, K.A., & Thompson, M. (1998). Contemplations on a secure marketplace for mobile Java agents. In K.P. Sycara & M. Wooldridge (Eds.), *Proceedings of Autonomous Agents 98*, Minneapolis, Minnesota. New York: ACM Press.

Sandholm, T., & Huai, Q. (2000). Nomad: Mobile agent system for an Internet-based auction house. *IEEE Internet Computing*, pp. 80-86.

Sun. (2006). Java. Retrieved July 7, 2007, from http://java.sun.com/javame/

Suri, N., et al. (2000). NOMADS: Toward a strong and safe mobile system. In *Proceedings of the 4th International Conference on Autonomous Agents* (pp. 163-164). New York: ACM Press.

Todd, S., Parr, F., & Conner, M. (2005). An overview of the reliable HTTP protocol. Retrieved July 7, 2007, from http://www-128.ibm.com/developerworks/Webservices/library/ws-phtt/

UDDI. (2006). Retrieved July 7, 2007, from http://www.uddi.org/

Wahbe, R., Lucco, S., Anderson, T.E., & Graham, S.L. (1993). Efficient software-based fault isolation. In *Proceedings of the 14th ACM Symposium on Operating Systems Principles* (pp. 203-216).

Wang, A.I., Sørensen, C.F., & Indal, E. (2003). A mobile agent architecture for heterogeneous devices. *Wireless and Optical Communications.*

White, J.E. (1999). Telescript technology: Mobile agents. In Mobility: Processes, computers, and agents (pp. 460-493). New York: ACM Press/Addison-Wesley.

ENDNOTES

1 In the experiment, we developed a GUI in the mediator server for users to launch a buying or selling agent.

2 The white-page agent maintains different service provider sites. Section 3.4 will describe this agent in more detail.

3 Detailed description of the proxy agent is provided in Section 3.4.

4 In an object-oriented context, a behavior is an inner class of the proxy agent.

5 MIDlet is a Java program generally running on a cell phone, for embedded devices, more specifically the Java ME virtual machine.

This work was previously published in Int. Journal of Information Technology and Web Engineering, Vol. 2, Issue 4, edited by G. Alkhatib, pp. 63-80, copyright 2007 by IGI Publishing (an imprint of IGI Global).

Chapter IV
A Multi-Agent Temporal Constraint Satisfaction System Based on Allen's Interval Algebra and Probabilities

Elhadi Shakshuki
Acadia University, Canada

André Trudel
Acadia University, Canada

Yiqing Xu
Acadia University, Canada

ABSTRACT

Many real-world problems can be viewed and represented as a constraint satisfaction problem (CSP). In addition, many of these problems are distributed in nature. To this end, we combine agents with a special type of CSP called an Interval Algebra network (IA network). An IA network is a graph where each node represents an interval. Directed edges in the network are labelled with temporal interval relations. A probabilistic IA network has probabilities associated with the relations on the edges that can be used to capture preferences. A probabilistic IA agent (PIA-Agent) is assigned a probabilistic IA network. PIA-Agent's networks are connected via edges. The overall goal is to make each PIA-Agent's network consistent and optimal. Each PIA-Agent is independent and has sole control over its network. But, it must communicate and coordinate with other PIA-Agents when modifying or updating edges that are shared between two PIA-Agents. We present an algorithm which allows the PIA-Agents to collab-

oratively solve and recommend a temporal schedule. At the agent level, this schedule is optimal under the given local constraints. Although the global solution may not be optimal, we try to generate near optimal ones. Note that our distributed system is not centrally controlled. Our algorithm decides which PIA-Agent should be given an opportunity to update the solution next. Also, when a conflict is detected, the algorithm modifies the PIA-Agent execution order in order to deal with the inconsistency.

INTRODUCTION

Many real world problems such as scheduling, planning, and configuration can be viewed as constraint satisfaction problems (CSP). A CSP consists of variables and a domain of possible values is associated with each variable. It may not necessarily be the case that all the domains are equal. A binary constraint between two variables is a subset of the Cartesian product of their domains. A solution to a CSP is an assignment of a value to each variable from its domain such that all the constraints hold.

Another powerful tool for solving complex real world problems is intelligent agents (Chaib-draa et al., 1996). The intelligent agent paradigm has been successfully applied in many research areas, such as distributed databases and Artificial Intelligence. The agents are viewed as autonomous and goal-driven entities (Wooldridge and Jennings, 1995; Shakshuki et al., 2005). Autonomy refers to the ability of the agent to make decisions concerning its own actions without any external interference. Goal-driven refers to the ability of the agent to interact with other agents at the 'goal level'. Furthermore, this entity can interact with the user and other software systems (agent-based or non agent-based). Due to the dynamic and flexible characteristics of these agents, they are being used in an increasingly wide variety of applications.

Recently, researchers have combined the intelligent agent and CSP paradigms into single systems. For example, Calisti and Neagu (2004) analyzed and discussed possible ways of integrating CSP and agent techniques. Other researchers (e.g., Makoto et al., 1998) used agents to solve distributed versions of a CSP (DCSP). In a DCSP, constraints are shared between agents. In Bhaskar, et al. (2001), they used a DCSP to schedule access to nearby transmission nodes of an *ad hoc* network and presented experimental results to demonstrate the complexity of this problem. Liu and his co-workers (Liu et al., 2002) presented a multi-agent oriented method for solving CSPs. In their method, distributed agents represent variables and a two-dimensional grid-like environment in which the agents inhabit corresponds to the domains of the variables. Researchers in Jung et al. (2001) presented a DCSP as a computational model for investigating negotiation via argumentation. They modeled argumentation as constraint propagation in DCSPs to resolve conflicts, where agents provide explicit arguments or justifications for their proposals for resolving conflicts.

In this work, we combine agents with a special type of CSP called a Probabilistic Interval Algebra network (PIA network). A PIA network is a directed graph where each node represents a temporal interval, and the edges are labelled with constraints between intervals. A PIA-Agent is an agent which has ownership and control over a PIA network. A node in one PIA-Agent's network can be connected by an edge to a node in another PIA-Agent's network. PIA-Agents, who can only solve their local PIA networks, must collaborate in order to solve the global network.

The problem we consider has multiple connected PIA-Agent networks as input. The output is a consistent network where the product of the probabilities on the unique label assigned to each edge is near optimal. The proposed algorithm

Table 1. Allen's interval relations

Relation	Symbol	Example
A before B	b	AAA BBB
A meets B	m	AAABBB
A overlaps B	o	AAAAAA BBBBBB
A during B	d	AAA BBBBBBB
A starts B	s	AAA BBBBBBB
A finishes B	f	AAA BBBBBBB
A equals B	=	AAA BBB

makes each PIA-Agent network locally optimal subject to the constraints imposed by its neighbouring PIA-Agents, however global optimality cannot be guaranteed.

Note that a typical IA network is not being solved as in van Beek & Manchak (1996). The edge labels are augmented with probabilities. Also, since we have a distributed multi-agent system, we cannot use an algorithm which has global access to the network. Instead, PIA-Agents make local changes to the network, and collaborate to guarantee global consistency.

Our PIA-Agent system architecture has PIA-Agents that are adaptive, autonomous, goal driven, dynamic, collaborative, and act as mediators between the user(s) and problem domain (Shakshuki et al., 2003). The PIA-Agents are in a position to recommend a temporal schedule that based on the negotiation and constraints imposed by the other PIA-Agents, is locally optimal.

The remainder of this article is organized as follows. The second section formally describes the problem we solve. The third section discusses the main design issues. The fourth section provides a description of the agent architecture. The fifth section explains in detail the problem solver component of the proposed agent. The sixth section provides examples. The seventh section describes the implementation, and the eighth section presents the conclusions and future work.

FORMAL PROBLEM DESCRIPTION

Allen's (Allen, 1983) temporal representation approach, which is based on intervals and the 13 possible binary relations between them as shown in Table 1 is used. The relations are before (b), meets (m), overlaps (o), during (d), starts (s), finishes (f), and equals (=). Each relation has an inverse. The inverse symbol for b is bi and similarly for the others: mi, oi, di, si, and fi. The inverse of equals is equals. A relation between two intervals is restricted to a disjunction of the basic relations, which is represented as a set. For example, (A m B) V (A o B) is written as A {m,o} B. The relation between two intervals is allowed to be any subset of I = {b,bi,m,mi,o,oi,d,di,s,si,f,fi,=} including I itself.

An IA (Interval Algebra) network is a graph where each node represents an interval. Directed edges in the network are labelled with subsets of I. By convention, edges labelled with I are not shown. An IA network is consistent (or satisfiable) if each interval in the network can be mapped to a real interval such that all the constraints on the edges hold (i.e., one disjunct on each edge is true).

Figure 1. Professor-Student-Secretary PIA-Agent Network

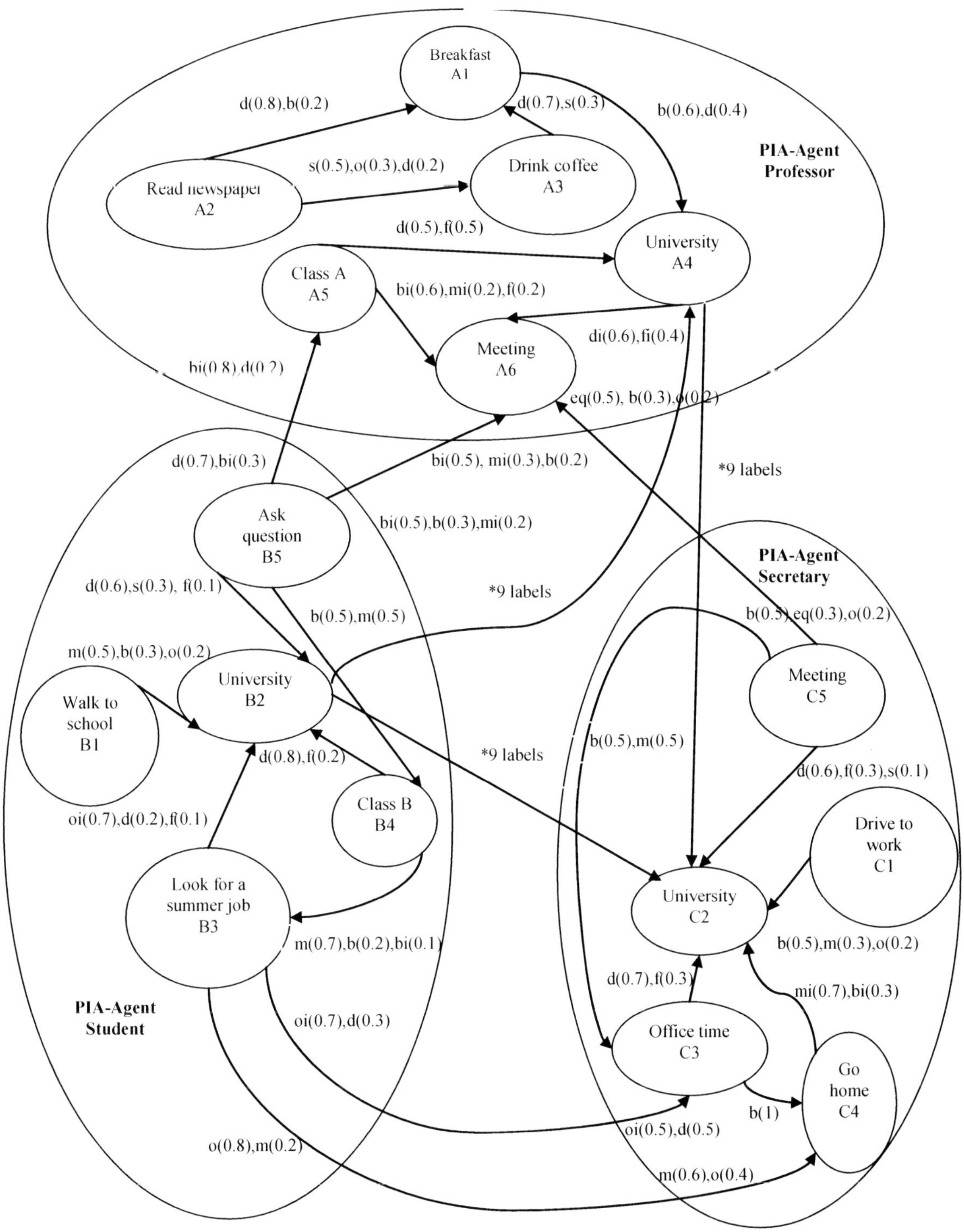

**9 labels: eq(0.2),o(0.1), oi(0.1), s(0.1), si(0.1), d(0.1), di(0.1), f(0.1), fi(0.1)*

Figure 2. Professor's internal network

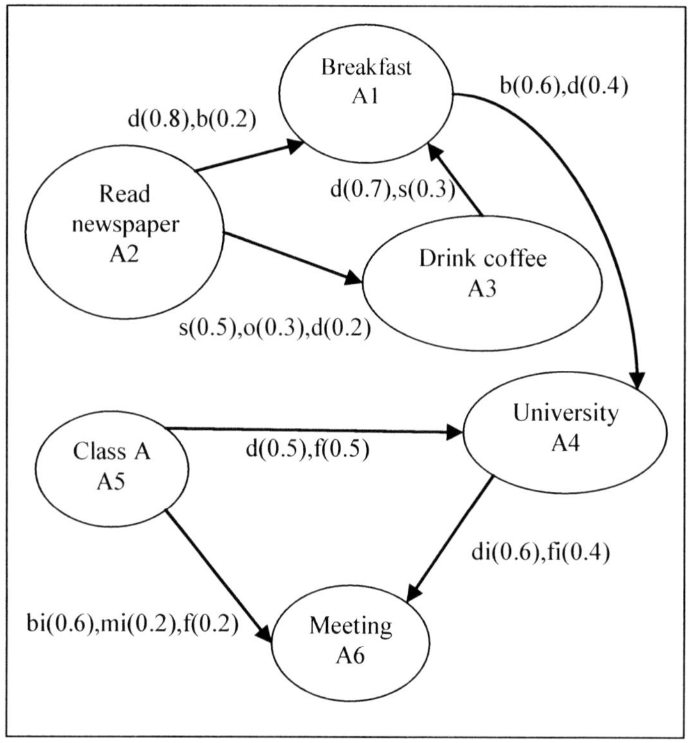

An IA network is a binary constraint satisfaction problem (CSP) with infinite domains. The intervals are the variables. The domain of each variable is the set of pairs of reals of the form (x,y) where x < y. The constraint between two variables i and j is the label on the edge (i,j) in the IA network.

A Probabilistic IA network (PIA network) is an IA network with probabilities associated with each interval relation. For example, if we prefer to read the newspaper during breakfast instead of before, we could have: "read newspaper" {d(0.9), b(0.1)} "breakfast".

Directed edges in the network are labelled with subsets of I, and each relation in the subset is assigned a probability. The probabilities on an edge sum to 1. By convention, the labels in a set are listed by decreasing order of probability. A PIA network is consistent (or satisfiable) if one disjunct on each edge is true. The probability of a solution is defined to be the product of the probability on each of its edges. Given two solutions, the one with higher probability is preferred. The proposed system attempts to generate a solution with maximum probability.

A *PIA-Agent* is an agent which has ownership and control over a PIA network. A node in one PIA-Agent's PIA network can be connected by an edge to a node in another PIA-Agent's network. The individual PIA-Agent networks along with their interconnecting edges, is called a *PIA-Agent network*. For example, Figure 1 shows a 3 PIA-Agent network that includes a professor, student, and secretary. Each node in the network represents a real world event in the PIA-Agent's daily life.

The PIA network completely contained within a PIA-Agent is called its *internal network*. A PIA-Agent's internal network along with the edges that connect the internal network to other networks is called its *external network*. Note that the external network contains the nodes at both ends of the edges that connect the internal network to other networks. For example, the Professor's internal network in Figure 1 is shown in Figure 2, and its external network is shown in Figure 3. Note that some inter-agent edges have two label sets associated with them. For example, the edge from node B5 to A5 in Figure 1 has the sets {bi(0.8), d(0.2)} and {d(0.7), bi(0.3)} (the sets do not necessarily have to contain the same labels). The reason for the dual sets is that the former is associated with the Professor and the latter with the Student (i.e., the Professor prefers that questions be asked after class, while the Student prefers to ask questions during class). When both agents have the same set of labels, it is only written once (e.g., edge B2, A4). Internal network edges will always have one set of labels.

A PIA-Agent has complete control and knowledge of its internal network. For example, in Figure 1, only the Professor can make its internal network consistent. The student and secretary do not know the structure of the Professor's internal network and cannot change any of its labels. An edge between two PIA-Agents is shared by the agents. For example, the edge from node B5 to A5 in Figure 1 is shared by the Student and Professor. They both locally store a personal copy of what they consider to be the label set on the edge. The Professor stores {bi(0.8),d(0.2)} and the Student {d(0.7),bi(0.3)}. The Professor cannot view or modify the label set stored by the Student, and vice versa. Each PIA-Agent can communicate with every other PIA-Agent.

The problem we consider in this article has a PIA-Agent network as input. The output is

Figure 3. Professor's external network

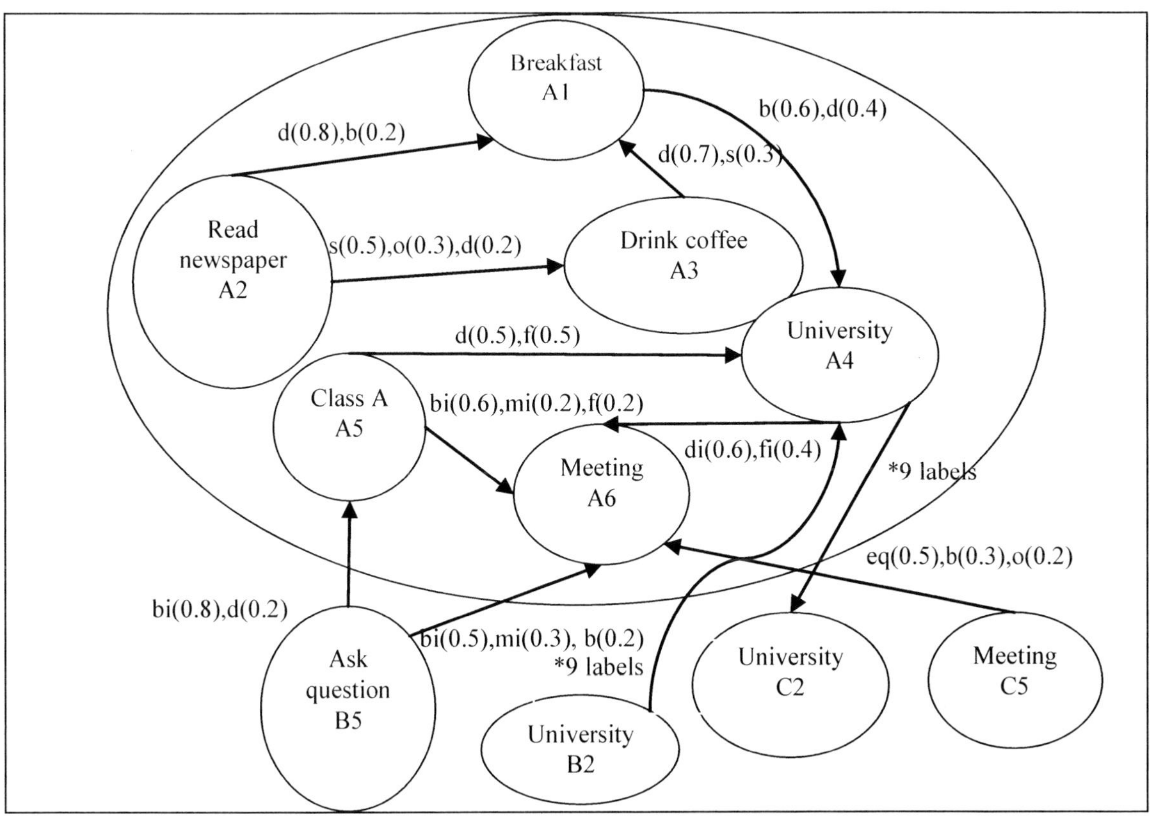

Figure 4. Global solution

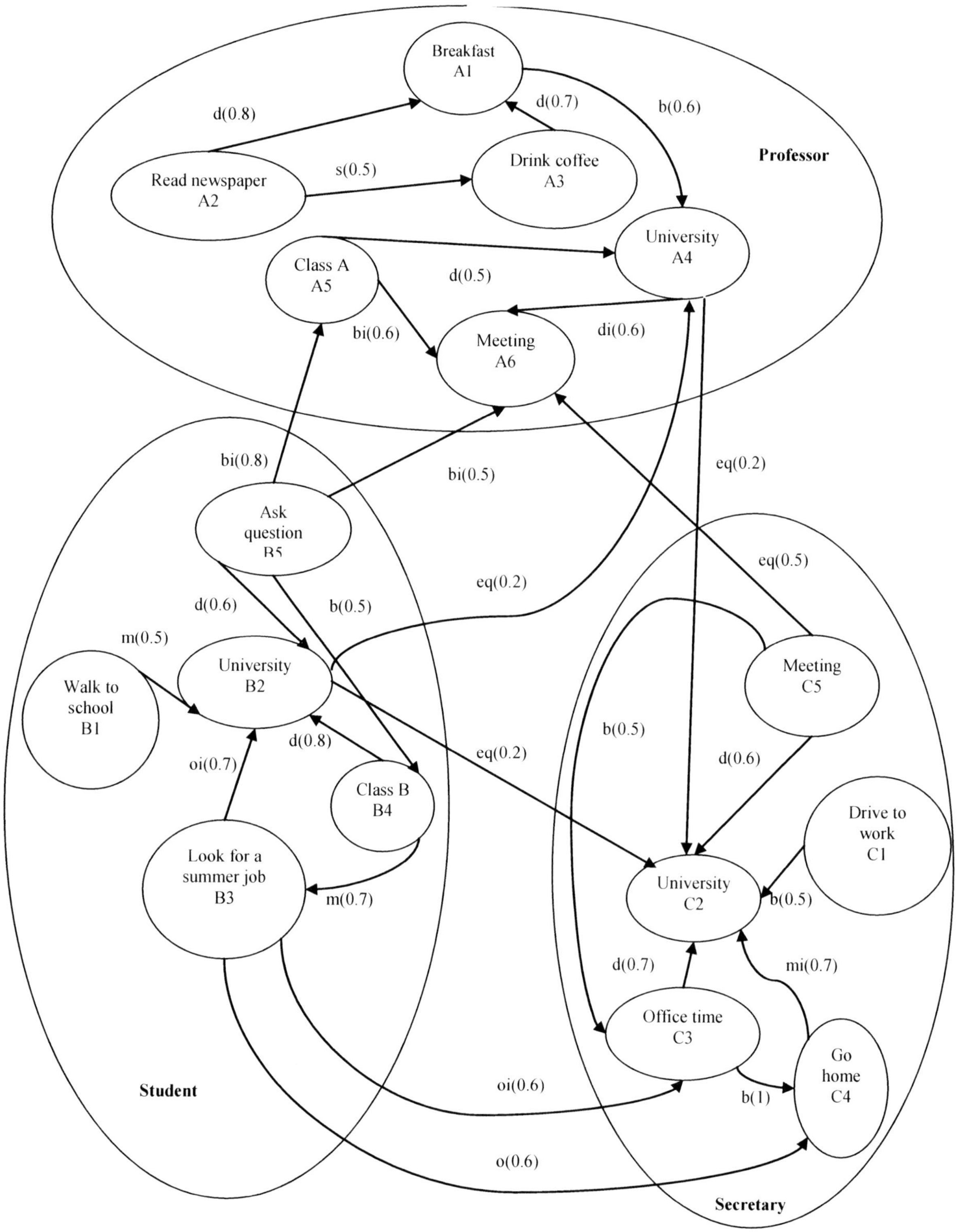

a consistent network where the product of the probabilities on the unique label assigned to each edge is near optimal. Our proposed algorithm makes each PIA-Agent external network locally optimal subject to the constraints imposed by its neighbouring PIA-Agents. Global optimality is desired, but cannot be guaranteed. For example, the solution to Figure 1 is shown in Figure 4.

DESIGN ISSUES

PIA-agents need to communicate with each other, coordinate their activities, and be allowed to exhibit different behaviours. Communication is the essential means by which the PIA-Agents cooperate and coordinate their activities in order to achieve their goals. The following are essential requirements for successful inter-agent interaction: a common protocol to establish the communication between the entities; a common understanding (i.e., the ontological commitments between them); and communication protocols and mechanisms to enable them to exchange information. The PIA-Agents communicate with each other using KQML Knowledge Query Manipulation Language (KQML) (Finin et al., 1997). We assume that the PIA-Agents share a common ontology.

A single PIA-Agent cannot solve the PIA-Agent network independently. PIA-Agents need to coordinate their activities. For example, they need to share labels, agree on changes to shared labels, and take turns working on the network. Coordination is achieved through communication and negotiation utilizing a contract net mechanism (Davis and Smith, 1983).

In general, agents may exhibit different types of behaviour when they interact with each other. For example, some domains require agents with benevolent behaviour, and always accept requests from other agents (Huhns & Mohamed, 1999). Other domains may need agents with selfish behaviour, where agents attempt to maximize

Figure 5. PIA-Agent architecture.

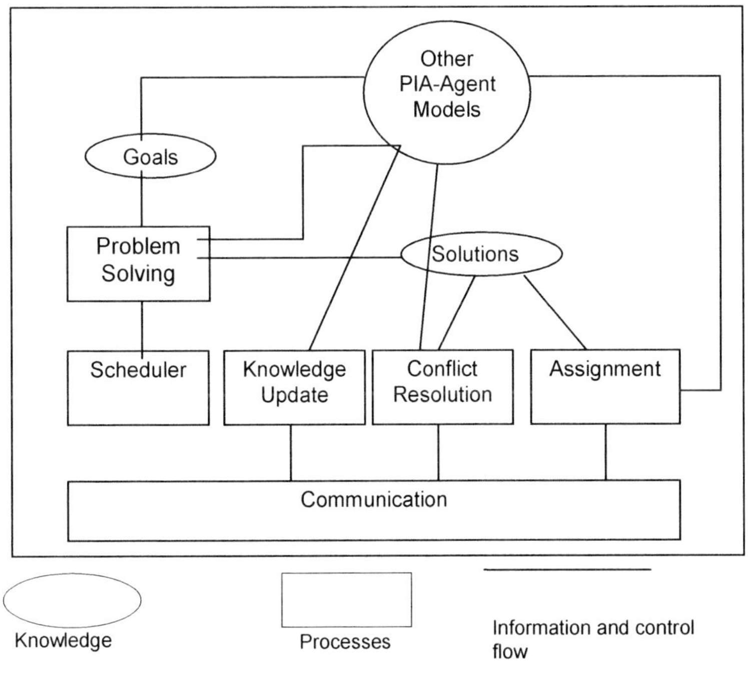

their individual benefits (Rosenschein & Zlotkin, 1994). In this approach, agents are characterized by cooperative behaviour (Shakshuki, 2002), where the agents help each other whenever it is possible and beneficial.

PIA-AGENT ARCHITECTURE

The PIA-Agent architecture is driven by its functionality and is described in terms of its knowledge and capabilities (Shakshuki et al., 2003), as shown in Figure 5. The architecture has six major processes:

1. The communication component allows the PIA-Agent to send, receive and interpret messages with the other elements of the environment, including users, PIA-Agents, and objects such as databases.
2. The problem solving component, the subject of the next section, provides the PIA-Agent with the capability to generate an appropriate solution to satisfy a goal.
3. The assignment component allows the PIA-Agent to delegate goals to be achieved by other PIA-Agents. When a PIA-Agent finds a solution to its external network, it consequently assigns the responsibility of achieving the global solution to another PIA-Agent if required.
4. The conflict resolution component allows the PIA-Agent to assign goals that generated conflicting labels to another PIA-Agent.
5. The knowledge-update component provides the PIA-Agent with the capability to have up-to-date knowledge about other PIA-Agents' goals, solutions, and changes in the values of the variables (labels).
6. The scheduler component is a time-indexed agenda for PIA-Agent goals, which provides the PIA-Agent with a mental processor that enables the PIA-Agent to assign or allocate times to goals to be achieved on a virtual-time line and produces a local schedule.

PROBLEM SOLVING COMPONENT

One major architecture process in Figure 5 is the problem solving component. This component consists primarily of an algorithm used by the PIA-Agent to solve its external network. Before presenting this algorithm, we describe in the following sub-section the pre-processing required by the algorithm.

Pre-Processing

At system initialization, each PIA-Agent must store information to be used by the algorithm in addition to its internal network. Each PIA-Agent is assigned a unique integer *ID*. *ID* is used by the algorithm to control the execution order and backtracking. If there are n PIA-Agents, then $1 \leq ID \leq n$. The *ID*s are assigned as follows. Choose one agent randomly and assign it *ID*=1; this will be the first PIA-Agent to execute. For example, choose the Professor in Figure 1. Instead of randomly choosing the first PIA-Agent, future work will involve investigating different heuristics including: pick the PIA-Agent with the largest

Figure 6. Connected graph G

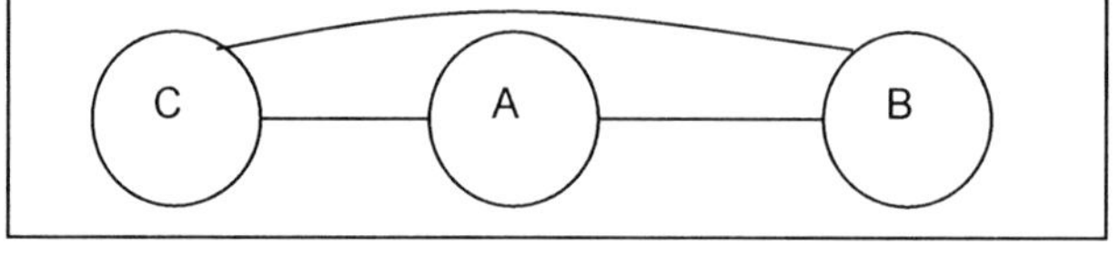

internal network, largest number of edges going to other PIA-Agents, or the largest total number of labels. We next construct a connected graph G from the original PIA-Agent network. Each internal network collapses to a single node. And multiple directed edges between two internal networks collapse to a single undirected edge. For example, the connected graph G for Figure 1 is shown in Figure 6, where A = Professor, B = Student, and C = Secretary.

In Figure 6, the node in the center A (Professor) is assigned *ID*=1. Perform a breadth first search starting at this node, and assign an increasing *ID* to each IA-Agent as it is visited during the traversal. For example, B (student) has *ID*=2, and C (Secretary) has *ID*=3. Note that the breadth first traversal guarantees that if a PIA-Agent's *ID* is not equal to 1, then it is connected to at least one other PIA-Agent with a smaller *ID* number.

After the IDs are assigned to all PIA-Agents, pairs of agents that share one or more edges need to negotiate to agree on a unique label set for each shared edge. For example, the Professor and Student in Figure 1 each store a different label set for edge B5, A5. There are many approaches that can be taken to reconcile the label sets:

- Randomly choose one over the other.
- Assign priorities to the PIA-Agents and choose the label set associated with the highest ranked agent. A tie breaking rule may be needed.
- Apply the principle of indifference and take the average of the individual labels.

For our example in Figure 1, we give the Professor priority over the other two. The Student and Secretary have equal priority and use the principle of indifference. If a shared edge has a unique label set, it is not changed. After negotiating, the shared label sets are:

- Edge (B5,A5): bi(0.8),d(0.2)
- Edge (B5,A6): bi(0.5),mi(0.3),b(0.2)
- Edge (B2,A4): 9 labels
- Edge (A4,C2): 9 labels
- Edge (C5,A6): eq(0.5),b(0.3),o(0.2)
- Edge (B2,C2): 9 labels
- Edge (B3,C3): oi(0.6),d(0.4)
- Edge (B3,C4): o(0.6),m(0.4)

It should be noted that each PIA-Agent stores a local copy of the label set assigned to a shared edge. In some cases, it is necessary to add new edges to the PIA-Agent network. For every pair of PIA-Agents K and J: let NJ be the set of nodes in J that are connected to a node in K. For every node y in K that is connected to a node in J, edges need to be added so that y is connected to every node in NJ. The added edges have the label "I". Each label in the set "I" is assigned a probability of 1/13. Note that the added edges do not affect the final solution. For example, between the Professor and Student in Figure 1, the following edges must be added: (B2,A5), (B2,A6), and (A4,B5). It does not matter which direction the arrow points.

If there is an edge between PIA-Agents i and j, then both agents store a copy of the set of labels assigned to the edge between them. Also, the current singleton label from the set that is assigned to the edge must be kept track of. This singleton label is called: *label*. Initially, *label* is set to the first label. For example, if after negotiation the labels on an edge between PIA-Agents i and j is {bi(0.8),mi(0.2)}, then both agents store a local copy of *label* = bi(0.8). If i changes its value for *label*, it does not affect j's copy. The PIA-Agents engage in the negotiation process to synchronize their local copies of *label*.

During the problem solving process, if a PIA-Agent discovers a labelling on its edges that are connected to other PIA-Agents that cannot lead to a consistent external network, this labelling is stored in a *bad* set of the agent self model. Initially *bad* is empty. Note that no edges from a PIA-Agent's internal network are stored in its *bad* set.

Whenever a PIA-Agent finds a consistent labelling for its external network, the labelling

Table 2. PIA-Agent initial knowledge

	Professor		Student		Secretary	
ID	1		2		3	
Bad set	Ø		ø		ø	
solutions	Ø		ø		ø	
Edge	**Set**	**Label**	**Set**	**Label**	**Set**	**Label**
(B5,A5)	{bi(0.8), d(0.2)}	bi(0.8)	{d(0.7), bi(0.3)}	d(0.7)		
(B5,A6)	{bi(0.5), mi(0.3), b(0.2)}	bi(0.5)	{bi(0.5), b(0.3), mi(0.2)}	bi(0.5)		
(B2,A4)	{eq(0.2), o(0.1), oi(0.1), s(0.1), si(0.1), d(0.1), di(0.1), f(0.1), fi(0.1)}	eq(0.2)	{eq(0.2), o(0.1), oi(0.1), s(0.1), si(0.1), d(0.1), di(0.1), f(0.1), fi(0.1)}	eq(0.2)		
(A4,C2)	{eq(0.2), o(0.1), oi(0.1), s(0.1), si(0.1), d(0.1), di(0.1), f(0.1), fi(0.1)}	eq(0.2)			{eq(0.2), o(0.1), oi(0.1), s(0.1), si(0.1), d(0.1), di(0.1), f(0.1), fi(0.1)}	eq(0.2)
(C5,A6)	{eq(0.5), b(0.3), o(0.2)}	eq(0.5)			{b(0.5), eq(0.3), o(0.2)}	b(0.5)
(B2,C2)			{eq(0.2), o(0.1), oi(0.1), s(0.1), si(0.1), d(0.1), di(0.1), f(0.1), fi(0.1)}	eq(0.2)	{eq(0.2), o(0.1), oi(0.1), s(0.1), si(0.1), d(0.1), di(0.1), f(0.1), fi(0.1)}	eq(0.2)
(B3,C3)			{oi(0.7), d(0.3)}	oi(0.7)	{oi(0.5), d(0.5)}	oi(0.5)
(B3,C4)			{o(0.8), m(0.2)}	o(0.8)	{m(0.6), o(0.4)}	m(0.6)
Added edges						
(B2,A5)	I	di(1/13)	I	di(1/13)		
(A4,B5)	I	di(1/13)	I	di(1/13)		
(A4,C5)	I	di(1/13)			I	di(1/13)
(B2,A6)	I	di(1/13)	I	di(1/13)		
(A6,C2)	I	d(1/13)			I	d(1/13)
(B2,C3)			I	eq(1/13)	I	eq(1/13)
(B2,C4)			I	m(1/13)	I	m(1/13)
(B3,C2)			I	oi(1/13)	I	oi(1/13)

is stored locally in the set *solutions*. This set is initially empty and can potentially allow old solutions to be re-used during backtracking. The first element of *solutions* always contains the PIA-Agent's most recent solution.

Table 2 shows the initial knowledge stored by each PIA-Agent in Figure 1. Each PIA-Agent's internal network representation is omitted. Note that the *label* chosen for each added edge differs. The liberty of initially choosing *labels* that lead to a solution in order to save space and limit the complexity of an example which appears later in the chapter was taken. The implementation would choose the same *label* for each added edge. The algorithm would then change the *labels* as required.

When the negotiation process is completed, the PIA-Agents knowledge is updated as in Table 3. Here, only the changed information is shown.

The Algorithm

The PIA-Agent problem solver is based on the proposed algorithm which appears in Figure 7. The algorithm is explained through examples in the next section.

Table 3. PIA-Agent knowledge after negotiation

	Professor		Student		Secretary	
Edge	**Set**	**Label**	**Set**	**Label**	**Set**	**Label**
(B5,A5)	{bi(0.8), d(0.2)}	bi(0.8)	**{bi(0.8), d(0.2)}**	**bi(0.8)**		
(B5,A6)	{bi(0.5), mi(0.3), b(0.2)}	bi(0.5)	**{bi(0.5), mi(0.3), b(0.2)}**	bi(0.5)		
(C5,A6)	{eq(0.5), b(0.3), o(0.2)}	eq(0.5)			**{eq(0.5), b(0.3), o(0.2)}**	**eq(0.5)**
(B3,C3)			**{oi(0.6), d(0.4)}**	**oi(0.6)**	**{oi(0.6), d(0.4)}**	**oi(0.6)**
(B3,C4)			**{o(0.6), m(0.4)}**	**o(0.6)**	**{o(0.6), m(0.4)}**	**o(0.6)**

Figure 7. Algorithm to solve PIA-Agents network

```
1.  current = 1
2.  PIA-Agent ID=current solves its external network.
3.  If a solution is found:
4.      If labels on edges between current and other PIA-Agents were modified:
5.          Set current to be the minimum of (current + 1) and
6.          the ID's of the PIA-Agents whose edge labels have been changed.
7.          Go to 2.
8.      Else
9.          If current=n then terminate in success.
10.         current = current +1
11.         Go to 2.
12. Else terminate in failure.
```

Figure 8. Inconsistent PIA-Agent network

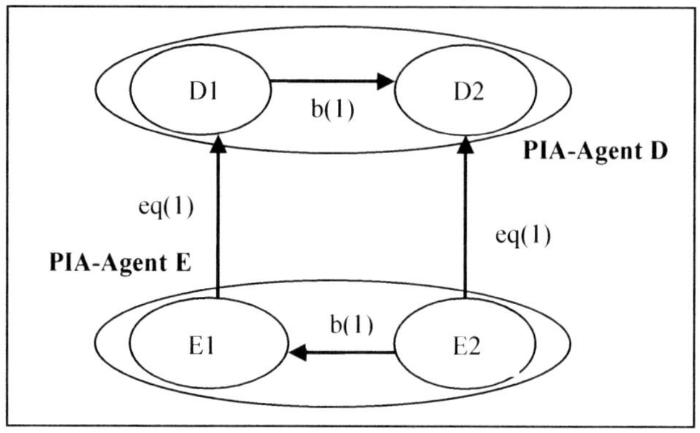

Table 4. Knowledge needed by PIA-Agents D and E

	PIA-Agent D		PIA-Agent E	
ID	1		2	
bad set	ø		ø	
solutions	ø		ø	
Edge	**Set**	**Label**	**Set**	**Label**
(E1,D1)	{eq(1)}	eq(1)	{eq(1)}	eq(1)
(E2,D2)	{eq(1)}	eq(1)	{eq(1)}	eq(1)
Added edges				
(E1,D2)	I	b(1/13)	I	b(1/13)
(E2,D1)	I	b(1/13)	I	b(1/13)

Table 5. PIA-Agents D and E knowledge after PIA-Agent D finds a solution

	PIA-Agent D		PIA-Agent E	
ID	1		2	
Bad set	**{{(E1,D1)=eq(1), (E2,D2)=eq(1), (E1,D2)=b(1/13), (E2,D1)=b(1/13)}}**		ø	
solutions	**{{(E1,D1)=eq(1), (E2,D2)=eq(1), (E1,D2)=b(1/13), (E2,D1)=bi(1/13), (D1,D2)=b(1)}}**		ø	
Edge	**Set**	**Label**	**Set**	**Label**
(E1,D1)	{eq(1)}	eq(1)	{eq(1)}	eq(1)
(E2,D2)	{eq(1)}	eq(1)	{eq(1)}	eq(1)
Added edges				
(E1,D2)	I	b(1/13)	I	b(1/13)
(E2,D1)	I	**bi(1/13)**	I	**bi(1/13)**

Notes on solving the external network in line 2 of the proposed algorithm:

- If the PIA-Agent discovers combinations of labels on the edges that connect it to other PIA-Agents that cannot lead to a solution, these combinations are recorded in its local *bad* set.
- The PIA-Agent does not change the labels on edges connected to another PIA-Agent without first receiving an approval message from the other PIA-Agent. When the other agent receives the approval request, it first checks its *bad* set. If the change does not violate its *bad* set, it updates its edge labels and returns an approval message. Otherwise, a message rejecting the change is returned.
- To minimize the impact on other PIA-Agents, the currently executing PIA-Agent should first try to change labels on its internal network before attempting to modify the labels on edges connected to other PIA-Agents.
- Any algorithm for solving a PIA network can be used.

ILLUSTRATIVE EXAMPLES

In this section, two different examples are used to demonstrate the execution of the algorithm. In the first example, there is a two PIA-Agent network that is not globally consistent. In the second example, the professor, student, and secretary scenario is utilized to demonstrate how the PIA-Agents interact locally to find a globally consistent solution.

Example 1: No Solution

It is possible to have a PIA-Agent network which is consistent at the local PIA-Agent level, but inconsistent at the global level. Figure 8 contains such a network. Note that each edge has a singleton label with probability 1.

A breadth first search is first performed where D is assigned an *ID* of 1 and E gets 2. It is also needed to add I labelled edges from node E1 to D2 and from E2 to D1. The knowledge stored by the two agents is identical at this point, and is shown in Table 4.

After PIA-Agent D solves its network (line 2 of the algorithm in Figure 7), the updated stored knowledge is shown in Table 5. The changes between Tables 4 and 5 are bolded.

After executing lines 3-7 in Figure 7, control is given to PIA-Agent E. E determines that the current labelling is inconsistent. Thus, PIA-Agent E updates its *bad* set, and a new solution is found. Table 6 shows the knowledge after E terminates, and before PIA-Agent D resumes.

PIA-Agent D attempts to solve its external network. In order to do so, the label on the edges (E1,D2) and (E2,D1) must be changed to b and bi respectively. Before such a change can be made, approval must be obtained from E. E first checks its *bad* set and sees that the proposed labelling is contained therein. E will refuse the proposed labelling because it knows it cannot lead to a solution. D then attempts to find an alternate solution and cannot. The algorithm terminates in failure at line 12 of Figure 7.

Example 2: Professor-Student-Secretary network from Figure 1

The algorithm in Figure 7 was used to solve the network in Figure 1. Assume the PIA-Agents have finished the pre-processing and negotiation phases of the algorithm and their stored knowledge is as shown in Table 3. The Professor executes line 2 of the algorithm in Figure 7 and finds a solution to its external network:

Table 6. PIA-Agents D and E knowledge after PIA-Agent E finds a solution

	PIA-Agent D		PIA-Agent E	
ID	1		2	
Bad set	{{(E1,D1)=eq(1), (E2,D2)=eq(1), (E1,D2)=b(1/13), (E2,D1)=b(1/13)}}		**{{(E1,D1)=eq(1), (E2,D2)=eq(1), (E1,D2)=b(1/13), (E2,D1)=bi(1/13)}}**	
solutions	{{(E1,D1)=eq(1), (E2,D2)=eq(1), (E1,D2)=b(1/13), (E2,D1)=bi(1/13), (D1,D2)=b(1)}}		**{{(E1,D1)=eq(1), (E2,D2)=eq(1), (E1,D2)=bi(1/13), (E2,D1)=b(1/13), (E2,E1)=b(1)}}**	
Edge	**Set**	**Label**	**Set**	**Label**
(E1,D1)	{eq(1)}	eq(1)	{eq(1)}	eq(1)
(E2,D2)	{eq(1)}	eq(1)	{eq(1)}	eq(1)
Added edges				
(E1,D2)	I	**bi(1/13)**	I	**bi(1/13)**
(E2,D1)	I	**b(1/13)**	I	**b(1/13)**

Solutions =

{{(B5,A5)=bi(0.8), (B5,A6)=bi(0.5), (B2,A4)=eq(0.2), (A4,C2)=eq(0.2), (C5,A6)=eq(0.5), (B2,A5)=di(1/13), (A4,B5)=di(1/13), (B2,A6)=di(1/13), (A6,C2)=d(1/13), (A4,C5)=di(1/13), (A2,A1)=d(0.8), (A2,A3)=s(0.5), (A3,A1)=d(0.7), (A1,A4)=b(0.6), (A5,A4)=d(0.5), (A5,A6)=bi(0.6), (A4,A6)=di(0.6)}}

Since the Professor did not change labels on edges to other PIA-Agents, lines 9-11 in Figure 7 sets *current*=2 (i.e., the Student). The Student then solves its external network:

Solutions =

{{(B5,A5)=bi(0.8), (B5,A6)=bi(0.5), (B2,A4)=eq(0.2), (B2,C2)=eq(0.2), (B3,C3)=oi(0.6), (B3,C4)=o(0.6), (B2,A5)=di(1/13), (B2,A6)=di(1/13), (A4,B5)=di(1/13), (B2,C3)=eq(1/13), (B2,C4)=m(1/13), (B3,C2)=oi(1/13), (B5,B2)=d(0.6), (B5,B4)=b(0.5), (B4,B2)=d(0.8), (B1,B2)=m(0.5), (B3,B2)=oi(0.7), (B4,B3)=m(0.7)}}

Fortunately, since the Student also does not change labels on the edges to the Professor and Secretary, lines 9-11 in Figure 7 sets *current*=3 (i.e., the Secretary). It is then the Secretary's turn to find a solution (i.e., line 2). The current labelling on the edges between the Student and Secretary cannot lead to a solution and the Secretary records this combination in its *bad* set:

Bad =

{{(A4,C2)=eq(0.2), (C5,A6)=eq(0.5), (B2,C2)=eq(0.2), (B3,C3)=oi(0.6), (B3,C4)=o(0.6), (A4,C5)=di(1/13), (A6,C2)=d(1/13), (B2,C3)=eq(1/13), (B2,C4)=m(1/13), (B3,C2)=oi(1/13)}}.

The Secretary then solves its external network and the solution involves changing the label on the edge (B2,C3) to di(1/13). Since the Student's *bad* set is currently empty, the Student approves the change. The Secretary's solution set becomes:

Solutions =

{{(A4,C2)=eq(0.2), (C5,A6)=eq(0.5), (B2,C2)=eq(0.2), (B3,C3)=oi(0.6), (B3,C4)=o(0.6), (A4,C5)=di(1/13), (A6,C2)=d(1/13), (B2,C3)=di(1/13), (B2,C4)=m(1/13), (B3,C2)=oi(1/13), (C1,C2)=b(0.5), (C3,C2)=d(0.7), (C3,C4)=b(1), (C4,C2)=mi(0.7), (C5,C2)=d(0.6), (C5,C3)=b(0.5)}}.

Since the Secretary changed labels on edges between itself and the Student, lines 5-6 of Figure 7 chooses the minimum of 2 and 4 which is 2 (i.e., the Student). Then go to line 2 and the Student attempts to find a solution. The Student easily finds a solution which does not involve changing labels on edges to other PIA-Agents. The Student's updated solution set becomes:

Solutions =

{{ (B5,A5)=bi(0.8), (B5,A6)=bi(0.5), (B2,A4)=eq(0.2), (B2,C2)=eq(0.2), (B3,C3)=oi(0.6), (B3,C4)=o(0.6), (B2,A5)=di(1/13), (B2,A6)=di(1/13), (A4,B5)=di(1/13), (B2,C3)=di(1/13), (B2,C4)=m(1/13), (B3,C2)=oi(1/13), (B5,B2)=d(0.6), (B5,B4)=b(0.5), (B4,B2)=d(0.8), (B1,B2)=m(0.5), (B3,B2)=oi(0.7), (B4,B3)=m(0.7) },
{(B5,A5)=bi(0.8), (B5,A6)=bi(0.5), (B2,A4)=eq(0.2), (B2,C2)=eq(0.2), (B3,C3)=oi(0.6), (B3,C4)=o(0.6), (B2,A5)=di(1/13), (B2,A6)=di(1/13), (A4,B5)=di(1/13), (B2,C3)=eq(1/13), (B2,C4)=m(1/13), (B3,C2)=oi(1/13), (B5,B2)=d(0.6), (B5,B4)=b(0.5), (B4,B2)=d(0.8), (B1,B2)=m(0.5), (B3,B2)=oi(0.7), (B4,B3)=m(0.7) }}.

It is then the Secretary's turn to find a solution. Since the Secretary's current solution is still valid and no labels have been modified, the algorithm terminates in success. The final solution is shown in Figure 4.

IMPLEMENTATION

The proposed system involves multiple agents which can potentially be residing and executing on different hardware platforms which are geographically isolated. The natural choice of implementation language is Java. We use JXTA (JXTA, 2006) to deal with the communication and networking issues. JXTA is an open-source industry leading Peer-to-Peer (P2P) platform, originally developed by Sun Microsystems Inc. JXTA allows users to establish a virtual network with peers on top of the Internet and non-IP networks. It also enables peers to directly communicate, collaborate, and share resources independently of their network connectivity. Each PIA-Agent is represented by one JXTA peer, which is able to find other peers on the network and build a pipe to communicate with each other. All network resources in the JXTA network, such as peers, pipes, and services are represented by advertisements. Advertisements are language-neutral metadata structures resource descriptors represented as XML documents. Peers can discover and find available network resources by searching for their associated advertisements. A JXTA pipe advertisement is used to find peers and create pipes in this system. Each PIA-Agent has its own unique pipe advertisement, which includes the corresponding pipe ID and pipe name. The pipe name of the PIA-Agents is composed of corresponding peer name and peer ID. This special format of pipe name is designed for extracting both the peer and pipe information from only one advertisement. An example of a pipe advertisement for PIA-Agent professor is shown in Figure 9.

Communication is the essential means by which the agents cooperate and coordinate their activities in order to solve their CSPs. In order for

Figure 9. Pipe advertisement


```
<jxta:PipeAdvertisement xmlns:jxta="http://jxta.org">
        <Id>

        urn:jxta:uuid-59616261646162614E504720503250337CDA2489269F4E74BB9688
AF56FEA1FA04
        </Id>
        <Type>

        JxtaUnicast
        </Type>
        <Name>

        pianetwork:professor-urn:jxta:uuid-59616261646162614A7874615032503326EB11
FDACBA4879B2BE85EB276A3DD503
        </Name>
</jxta:PipeAdvertisement>
```


a PIA-Agent to communicate with other agents, it needs to find the corresponding pipe advertisement by the pipe ID first, and then build a point-to-point pipe connection between each other with a unidirectional and asynchronous channel to send and receive messages. In this implementation, PIA-Agent joins the default JXTA peer group, named "NetPeerGroup", every time the system starts. The system automatically helps PIA-Agent to discovery other peers in the same group and prepares pipes for the communication.

The PIA-Agents exchange their messages using KQML message formats. A customized KQML parser in the PIA-Agents' communication component was implemented. When a PIA-Agent receives a message from other PIA-Agents, the parser extracts the desired information such as PIA-Agent ID, name, bad sets, shared edge sets, and so forth, from the incoming message. Figure 10 shows an example of a KQML message exchanged by PIA-Agents.

Figure 10. Example of messages between PIA-Agents

```
(ask-one
  :sender 1
  :receiver 2
  :language KIF
  :ontology CSP
  :replay-with 1-P1
  :address 1111
  :component conflict-Resolution
  :content (BadSet
             (b 1,5)
             (m 1,4)
           )
)
```

```
(tell
  :sender 2
  :receiver 1
  :language KIF
  :ontology CSP
  :in-replay-to 1-P1
  :address 2111
  :component conflict-Resolution
  :content (GoodSet
             (bi 2,3)
             (f 6,3)

           )
)
```

Figure 11. PIA-Agent Interface

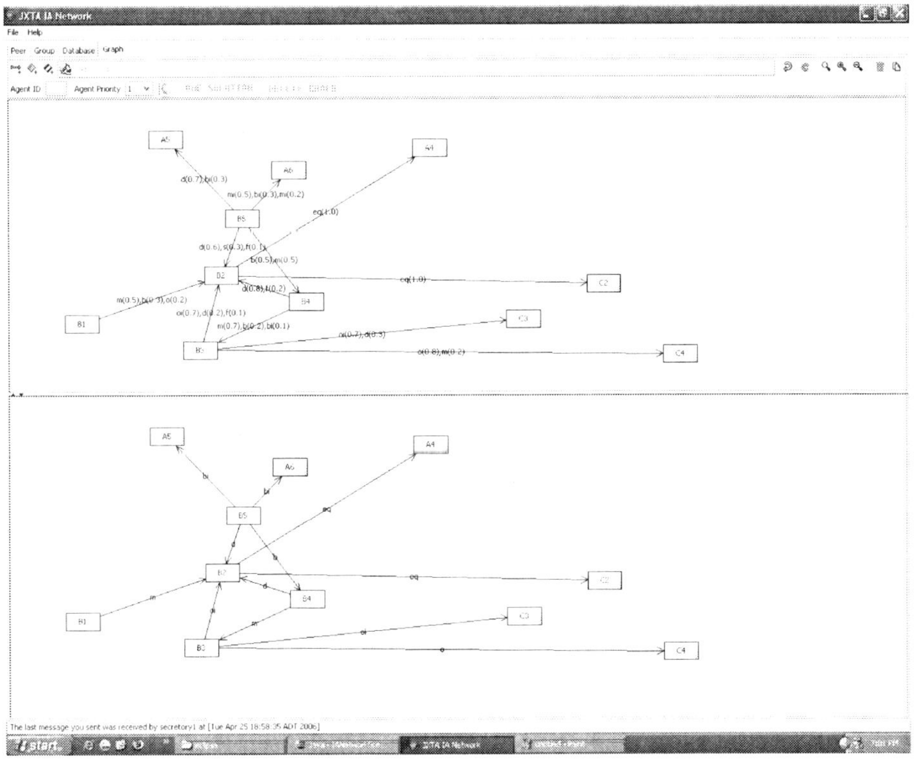

Figure 12. A rule that fires UpdateBadList action

=> (AND (AND (AND (AND (AND (EventName "UpdateBadList"))(EdgeA ?ea))(EdgeB ?eb))(label ?lab))(Prob ?pr))

Users interact with the PIA-Agents using graphical user interfaces (GUIs). The AWT and Swing classes handle all the interface events, such as menu selections or button clicks. An example of an interaction window is shown in Figure 11. Through this interface a user can construct the desired network by adding nodes, edges, and desired labels. A user can also establish a virtual network and display it during the whole process of the algorithm. In addition to constructing the network, a user is provided with additional features such as dragging, re-sizing, redo/undo, etc. The input and output of virtual PIA networks are implemented using JGraph. The main paint panel allows a user to draw nodes to represent one person's daily activities and edges to represent the relation between each pair of activities, and fill in the data on these nodes and edges. Figure 11 consists of two windows. In this figure, the upper window shows the PIA-Agent's external network for the student, and the lower window shows the proposed solution for the student which represents part of the global solution.

To draw a network, the user must first click the "NODE" button on the tool bar. Each click in the top window of the interface adds a new node. Second, a user selects the button "EDGE" to connect two nodes. Then, he or she is allowed to add labels with or without probability on each edge by double clicking on the corresponding edge. Third, the user can select "ONE SOLUTION" button to generate the possible solution. To provide a user friendly interface, we added several features such as zoom in and zoom out, delete node, redo, and undo functions.

The PIA-Agent knowledge that consists of the probabilistic interval algebra network, bad sets, and solution sets are represented in Knowledge Interchange Format (KIF) (Genesereth, et. al., 1998). The PIA-Agent's problem solver is implemented as a rule based system. The IA-Agents' problem solver uses the constraint programming language Eclipse (ECL^iPS^e, 2005). The code to solve a PIA network utilizes the implementation presented in (Trudel & Zhang, 2005). Figure 12 shows an example of a rule of *UpdateBadList* action with its pre-conditions and post-conditions.

As for performance, each example in this article can be solved in a few minutes. The most time consuming task is initializing, broadcasting, and finding the JXTA peers. Once the networking overhead has been dealt with, finding a solution is relatively fast. All the implementation effort to date has been to develop a working system. Thus, testing has consisted of the toy problems described in this article. Future work will involve extensive testing with both many agents and large networks. The plan is to then solve a real world problem with the system.

REAL WORLD APPLICATIONS

This article concentrated on a university example involving a professor, student, and secretary. The example can be generalized to any scheduling problem involving two or more schedules that are controlled by different people or agents. For example, before the registrar's office can schedule the final exams, they must consult and coordinate with the department heads, the university's time window for offering exams, individual professors that may be travelling for research purposes during the exam period, student course loads (e.g., no more than two exams in one day for each student), and so forth.

Another application is the execution of multi-agent plans. Assume the plans have been generated. Each agent must execute its own plan in an environment which may or may not require cooperation, but at least requires co-ordination between agents. Before execution begins, the system can be used to determine a deadlock free sequence of actions for each agent.

A similar application domain is the execution and monitoring of business processes in a large corporation. Individual employees or units are often responsible for many business processes that require information such as documents to be passed back and forth, and synchronization in the form of approvals (e.g., signing off).

Note that the system is not restricted to solving real world problems that explicitly involve quantitative probabilities or preferences. For example, if there is an edge labelled with five Allen interval relations and no probabilities, an equal probability to each (i.e., 1/5) can be asssigned. If one label is preferred over the others, it can be assigned 2/5, and the others each receive 3/20.

CONCLUSION AND FUTURE WORK

This article defined PIA-Agent networks, and presented an algorithm to solve them. The approach is independent of the particular algorithm chosen to make a local PIA network consistent. PIA-Agents are used to resolve conflicts between sub-graphs to find a global solution to the network. A university setting example was used to illustrate how the PIA-Agents find a globally consistent solution which attempts to maximize the desires of each individual involved in the problem domain. A prototype of a distributed time management system is implemented using Java, JXTA and JGraph.

In the future, there are plans to incorporate a learning component in the PIA-Agent architecture, using machine learning techniques and explore and develop different negotiation strategies. There are also plans to investigate the possibility of introducing concurrency in the algorithm. For example, while idle, an agent can search for and store alternative solutions which may be useful in the future.

ACKNOWLEDGMENT

This project is supported in part by grants from the Natural Sciences and Engineering Research Council of Canada (NSERC) and an internal grant from research and graduate studies of Acadia University. The authors would like to thank Kaur Singh and Mohammad Masum for developing the first single-agent version of the implementation.

REFERENCES

Allen, J.F. (1983). Maintaining Knowledge about Temporal Intervals. *Communications of the ACM, 26*, 832-843.

Bhaskar, K., & Ramon, B, & Stephen W. (2001). Distributed Constraint Satisfaction and the Bounds on Resource Allocation in Wireless Networks. Sixth International Symposium on Communications Theory & Application (ISCTA01), Ambleside, UK.

Calisti, M., & Neagu, N. (2004). Constraint Satisfaction Techniques and Software agents. Agents and Constraints Workshop, AIIA'04, Perugia, Italy.

Chaib-draa, B., & Moulin, B., & Mandiau, R., & Millot, P. (1996). Trends in Distributed Artificial Intelligence, Foundations of Distributed Artificial Intelligence. G.M.P.O' Hare and N. R. Jennings (Eds.), John Wiley & Sons Inc., 3-55.

Davis, R., & Smith, R. (1983). Negotiation as a Metaphor for Distributed Problem Solving. *Artificial Intelligence, 20*, 63-109.

ECL^iPS^e (2005). http://www.icparc.ic.ac.uk/eclipse/

Finin, T., & Labrou, Y., & Mayfield, J. (1997). KQML as an Agent Communication Language. In Bradshaw J.M. (Ed.), *Software Agents* (pp. 291-316), Cambridge, MA: AAA/MIT Press.

Genesereth, M. et al. (1998). Knowledge Interchange Format, draft proposed American National Standard (dpANS), NCITS.T2/98-004.

Huhns, M., & Mohamed, A. (1999). Benevolent Agents, *IEEE Internet Computing, 3*(2), 96-98.

JGraph (JGraph, 2006). http://www.jgraph.com/

Jung, H., & Tambe, M., & Kulkarni, S. (2001). Argumentation as Distributed Constraint Satisfaction: Applications and Results. Proceedings of the fifth international conference on Autonomous agents, Montreal, Quebec, Canada, 324-331.

JXTA (JXTA, 2006). http://www.jxta.org/

Liu, J., & Jing, H, & Tang, Y. (2002). Multi-agent Oriented Constraint Satisfaction. *Artificial Intelligence, 136*(1), 101-144.

Makoto Yokoo, M., & Durfee, E., & Ishida, T., & Kuwabara, K. (1998). The Distributed Constraint Satisfaction Problem: Formalization and Algorithms. *IEEE Transaction on Knowledge and Data Engineering, 10*(5), 673-685.

Rosenschein, J. S., & Zlotkin, G. (1994). Rules of Encounter, MIT Press.

Shakshuki, E. (2002). Intelligent Agents for Open Environments. The 6th IASTED International Conference on Artificial Intelligence & Soft Computing, Banff, Alberta, Canada, 37-41.

Shakshuki, E., & Ghenniwa, H., & Kamel, M. (2003). Agent-based System Architecture for

Dynamic and Open Environments. *International Journal of Information Technology and Decision Making, 2*(1), 105-133.

Shakshuki, E., & Luo, Z., & Gong, J. (2005). An Agent-based Approach to Security Service. *International Journal of Network and Computer Applications, 28*(3), Elsevier Science Journal, 183-208.

Trudel, A., & Zhang, H. (2005). Exploiting the Relationship between IA Networks and Finite Domain CSPs. 12th International Symposium on Temporal Representation and Reasoning (TIME'05), Burlington, Vermont, USA.

van Beek, P., & Manchak, D. (1996). The Design and Experimental Analysis of Algorithms for Temporal Reasoning. *Journal of Artificial Intelligence Research*, 1-18.

Wooldridge, M., & Jennings, N. (1995). Intelligent agents: theory and practice. *The Knowledge Engineering Review, 10*(2), 115-152.

This work was previously published in Int. Journal of Information Technology and Web Engineering, Vol. 2, Issue 2, edited by G. Alkhatib and D. Rine, pp. 45-64, copyright 2007 by IGI Publishing (an imprint of IGI Global).

Chapter V
A Multiagent Approach for Configuring and Explaining Workflow of Semantic Web Services

Vasco Furtado
University of Fortaleza, Brazil

Leonardo Ayres
University of Fortaleza, Brazil

Gustavo Fernandes
University of Fortaleza, Brazil

ABSTRACT

In this paper, we describe a multiagent approach that configures semantic Web services following a design problem solving method. For that, a propose-and-revise strategy was modeled and implemented in OWL-S. The other contribution of the approach is the extension of OWL-S for recording the service execution flow followed by the agent. The trace of the agent's reasoning is stored in node sets represented in a proof markup language which make up a framework for explanations on the Web. The proposed approach is shown to be useful in the context of e-business where the workflow definition of services is automatically performed by the agents in order to configure a computer from a customer order.

INTRODUCTION

In the Semantic Web context, the popular queries realized by the user in Web pages tend to evolve into an interactive process between a person and intelligent software agents (Berners-Lee, Hendler, & Lassila, 2001). From users' requirements and preferences, intelligent agents must be able to find services and, if necessary, compose them to produce the results which are expected by the users.

This automation process has led to the conception of the so-called "virtual organizations", where organizations are dynamically linked in a way as to meet a specific objective (or many). Several works have been proposed in the sense of automating or semi-automating the processes of discovery, composition, and execution of Web services (McIlraith, Son, & Zeng, 2001; Paolucci, Kawamura, Payne, & Sycara, 2002). The proposals presented are not concerned with a fundamental aspect in this context: how to explain to the users why a particular result was produced in the automatic process of Web service selection and execution.

In this article, we describe our multiagent system that is able, from users' goals and preferences, to automatically create a workflow of semantic Web services that, in turn, is able to design an artifact. During the distributed process of problem solving, the system generates justifications that will be used to provide explanations to the user. The generation of the final workflow of the Semantic Web services is driven by the agent's reasoning module which follows a design problem solving method, more specifically a configuration one. The basis for such modeling was the work in the area of Knowledge Engineering that defines Problem-Solving Methods (PSM) (Fensel & Benjamins, 1998) to assist in the representation and acquisition of knowledge from experts. PSM are patterns describing how to use reasoning steps to solve knowledge-intensive tasks such as planning, scheduling, diagnosis, design, and assessment.

User's preferences are modeled in OWL (McGuinness & van Harmelen, 2004) and are used by the agents for creating the Web service workflow. The agent's reasoning module implements the propose-and-revise PSM in OWL-S (OWL-S Java API, 2004), a set of ontologies written in OWL for describing Web services. The rationale behind the use of OWL-S is twofold. First, we aim at having an explicit conceptual representation of the tasks the agent must realize as well as the way to link this conceptual definition with Web services that implement the tasks. The second point is that we embedded in the OWL-S API, a service for generating an infrastructure of justifications which allow the production of explanations to the user. Thus, our solution presents a distributed way to solve a design problem via agents and Semantic Web services as well as providing an explanation of how the problem was solved by means of the different components involved.

OWL-S is one of most mature and well-developed solutions for modeling and implementation of Semantic Web services technology, allowing the representation of composite processes. Also, it has an API (OWL-S Java API, 2004) that interprets the ontologies allowing the execution of services that follow the flow described in the ontology. Its extension was necessary in the sense of propitiating the capacity for explanations of the service execution. As mentioned by Moore (1995), extensiveness is a prominent feature to be observed in explanation systems, which indicates that the explanation facilities must be easily extendable in order to be easily reused for the development of other applications, thereby reducing the effort of implementation. The extension of OWL-S that we are proposing constitutes an important contribution in that sense, and was done through modifications in the OWL-S API to record node sets in PML (Proof Markup Language), a language created with the objective of representing proofs and providing explanations on the Web (Pinheiro, McGuinness, & Fikes, 2004). In this way, our methodoloy is shown to be extensible to the generation of an infrastructure to support the explanation for other types of PSM—not just configuration—and for Web process workflows in general. The validation of our methodoloy is done through an example of e-business where we represented the process of designing a computer based on a demand effectuated by a customer on the Web.

THE PROPOSED ARCHITECTURE

Overview

The basic functioning of the multiagent application for designing a workflow of semantic Web services can be comprehended from the agents interactions depicted in Figure 1. The architecture is composed of agents, called PSM-agents, that attempt to reproduce the steps of reasoning for designing an artifact. From the user's goals and preferences, and from the domain ontology, the agent follows the design method in order to produce a workflow of Semantic Web services that will be executed to produce the final artifact. A special feature of the architecture is that a PSM-agent can interact with other agents to collaboratively solve the problem. We assume that each PSM-agent is inserted into a context that represents a particular area describing a set of sites with available Web services (see Horrocks et al., 2004 for an example of context-aware services to mobile devices). We also assume that, during the design process, the agent knows how to compute the cost of the design being built which will be useful for deciding the best solution to apply. When a PSM-agent asks others for assistance, it sends the problem to be solved (typically a conflict that must be solved and will drive the actions of the PSM-agent receiver), the current state of the design, and the constraints and preferences that must be taken into account during the resolution process. On the other hand, the receiver PSM-agents seek a solution to the problem and answer the solicitor agent by sending it back the action to be taken to solve the problem with a cost as-

Figure 1. Overview of the multiagent architecture

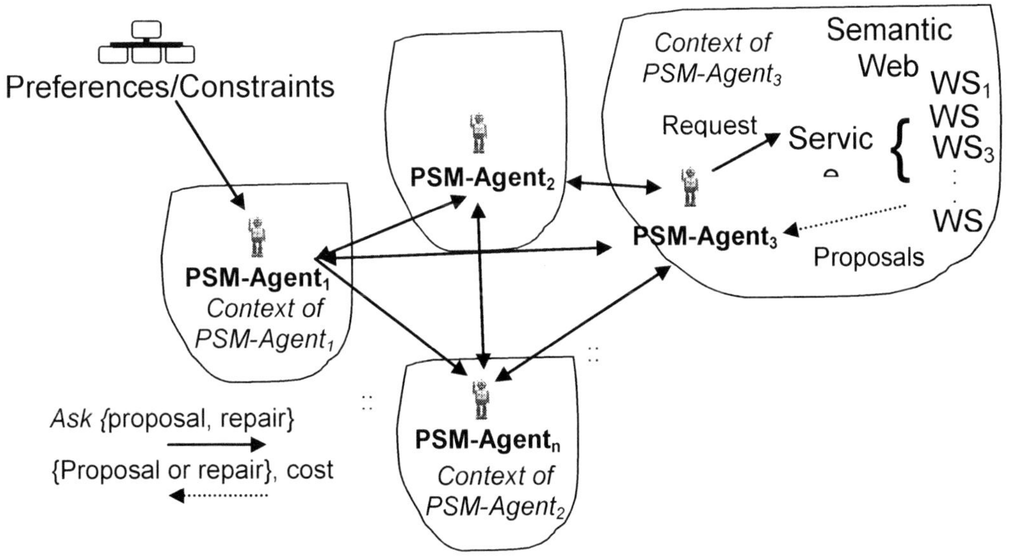

sociated. Then the solicitor PSM-agent selects the best solution based on the lowest cost among all the received solutions. For instance, suppose a process of computer configuration developed by an agent in a context of a plant P1. Let us assume that the design is already composed by a motherboard and a screen monitor, and that the user has specified a preference for computers cheaper than US$1,000.00. The next component to be part of the design would be a hard disk, but the available options to the agent would create a design with a price higher than the user's maximum preference. Then it decides to ask for assistance from others by requesting hard drive proposals for this particular design and passing along with the solicitation the design and the preferences of the user. Each PSM-agent that receives this requisition, in turn, executes its PSM method to propose a particular hard-disk with a particular cost. The solicitor PSM-agent chooses the best solution and continues the process of design.

We are modeling the agent behavior as a design PSM described in OWL-S. During the process of design, the agent interacts with a service discovery system that has the responsibility to find the appropriate Web services to execute each one of the steps necessary to produce the final artifact. The details of the internal modeling will be described further.

Another important feature of the architecture comes from the fact that, in the process of workflow preparation, an infrastructure of proofs describing such a process is recorded in order to provide explanations about the manner whereby the agent has decided to compose the service workflow as well as the manner whereby the final artifact was produced. In the following paragraphs, we will describe the main components of the architecture, focusing on the representation of the agents' inputs, the communication protocol they use, and the agents' internal behavior.

Representing Constraints and Preferences

Constraints must be defined in OWL via the ontologies representing the domain concepts. OWL provides mechanisms for constraint representation such as the *owl:restriction* class. For instance, the representation of the constraint stating that a computer can only have Pentium processors is done as seen in Box 1.

The representation above shows a class representing the intersection of the computer class with the restriction class. The restriction class defines that the processor must be a Pentium.

As for the representation of preferences, because OWL does not provide any special concept to treat this, we were obliged to define our own preference ontology. Doing so, we provide a declarative, domain-independent, and machine-interpretable way to represent preferences. The preference ontology will be useful for knowledge sharing by the agents, allowing the representation of partial order between attributes, classes, and value of attributes in OWL. The main concepts of the ontology, depicted in Figure 2, are inspired from the preference XPath proposal (Kießling, Hafenrichter, Fischer, & Holland, 2001) and from the work of Boutilier, Brafman, Domshlak, Hoos, and Poole (2004) on Augmented Conditional Networks. At a high level, the ontology possesses three kinds of concepts for representing simple, composite, and conditional preferences.

Simple preferences refer either to attributes (prefer price to color), classes (prefer notebook to desktop, meaning that all the instances of notebook are preferred over the instances of desktop), or values of attributes (prefer Seagate hard drive to ATA hard drive). Note that the ontology refers to OWL concepts, then classes refer to the *owl:class* concept, while attributes refer to properties of objects as well as data types (*owl:ObjectProperty* and *owl:DatatypeProperty*, respectively).

Box 1.

```
<owl:Class rdf:ID="RestrictedPC">
<rdfs:subClassOf rdf:resource="#Computer" />
  <rdfs:subClassOf>
    <owl:Restriction>
      <owl:onProperty>
        <owl:DatatypeProperty rdf:about="#hasProcessorName" />
      </owl:onProperty>
      <owl:hasValue rdf:datatype="&xsd;string>
        Pentium
      </owl:hasValue>
    </owl:Restriction>
  </rdfs:subClassOf>
</owl:Class>
```

Finally, preference of values of attributes are the possible values that *owl:ObjectProperty* and *owl:DatatypeProperty* can assume.

In the case of preferences for values of attributes, it is possible to represent concepts such as the following:

- **Maximum and Minimum Preference:** represents the preference for the maximization/minimization of a value of property. For instance: *prefer the most powerful processor* or *prefer the cheapest mouse*.
- **Around Preference:** represents the preference of a value that is closest of a reference value. For instance: prefer to change clock frequency as little as possible (considering a reference value of frequency).

It also allows the composition of these previous types for representing order (prefer desktop, tablet, handheld—in that order) disjunctions (prefer qwerty keyboard or three-button mouse) and pareto-optimal (prefer price and color as equally important). The representation of preferences that vary depending on a context is possible with conditional preferences such as *if location is Brazil, prefer Pentium processors*. Expressions of conditional preferences are represented in SWRL (Horrocks, Patel-Schneider, Boley, Tabet, Grosof, & Dean, 2004) (*swrl:expression*).

Figure 2. Piece of the preference ontology

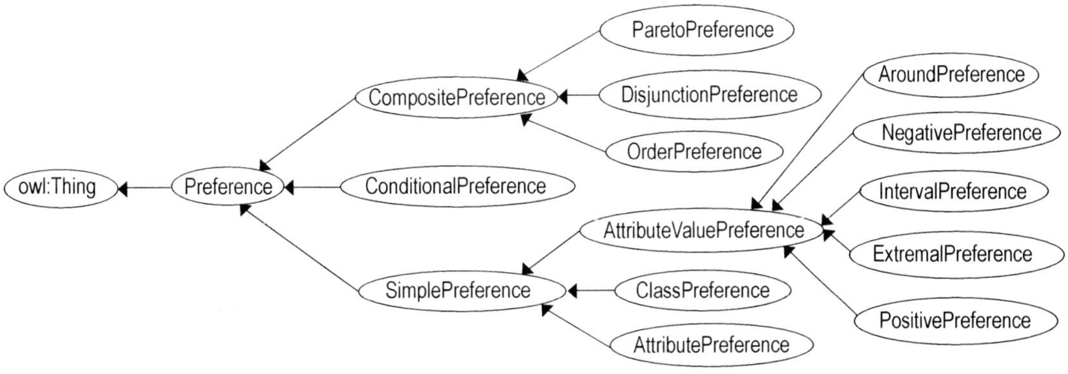

Communication Protocol

In our proposal, the PSM-agents interact at the level of "problem solving methods" rather than at lower levels of granularity. We have used the same strategy followed by Lopes and Botelho (2005) who have proposed an extension in the OWL-S grounding specification, called *AgentGrounding*. The idea behind this extension is to provide the necessary expressivity for representing the interaction between Semantic Web services and agents. The excerpt below exemplifies a request message from an OWL-S service to a PSM-agent following the AgentGrounding methodoloy (see Box 2).

The main content of the query is shown below. In this example the *personalAgent* (line 2) asks the *proposeAgent* (line 3) to realize the action *proposeProcess* (line 5) passing as parameters the type of component to be proposed and the preferences about it (lines 6 and 7). The configuration process is defined in the configuration ontology (line 9). Thus, when the agent receives a message, it is able to understand the content of the message.

The communication protocol follows the FIPA ACL (FIPA Agent Communication, 2004) standard. The assertives that we are using in the system are REQUEST, INFORM, AGREE, and REFUSE. The excerpt in Box 3 exemplifies an agent's answer with a result (line 9).

The Agent Reasoning Module

General Architecture

The agent's internal architecture is depicted in Figure 3 in three modules: perception, cognition, and performance. The agent initiates its activities starting from the receipt of information from the user. This receiving process occurs in the agent's Perception module (1), where messages are sent by other agents or directly by the user. In this case, it would be up to the user to define his/her personal preferences regarding a particular domain. Moreover, constraints will also be supplied to the agent, for example, constraints of computer parts (only Intel motherboard with Intel processor, etc.) and constraints of forms of payment (credit cards accepted only for purchases above a certain amount, etc.). Once in possession of this, the personal agent's actions during problem solving will be guided by the preferences and constraints.

In this stage, the agent evaluates its internal state as for its availability to solve the problem. An agent can accept or refuse the collaboration request. Requests for help from other agents have less priority than direct requests from the user.

Box 2.

```
1 (REQUEST
2 :sender (agent-identifier :name personalAgent@mia.unifor.br)
3 :receiver (set (agent-identifier :name proposeAgent@mia.unifor.br
4                             :addresses (sequence http://grid10:7778/acc)))
5 :content "(action (proposeProcess
6                             :propose http://mia.unifor.br/computer.owl#HardDisk
7                             :preferences http://mia.unifor.br/myPreferences.owl#PreferAboutHD))"
8 :language fipa-sl
9 :ontology configuration-ontology
10 :protocol fipa-request
11 :conversation-id PSMOWLS-MIA-1315817452067)
```

Box 3.

```
(INFORM
  :sender (agent-identifier :name proposeAgent@mia.unifor.br)
  :receiver (set (agent-identifier :name personalAgent@mia.unifor.br
                     :addresses (sequence http://grid10:7778/acc)))
  :content "(action (responseProcess
     :query (
                     :propose http://mia.unifor.br/computer.owl#HardDisk
                               :preferences http://mia.unifor.br/ myPreferences.
owl#PreferAboutHD)
                     :result http://mia.unifor.br/result.owl))"
  :language fipa-sl
  :ontology configuration-ontology
  :protocol fipa-request
  :conversation-id PSMOWLS-MIA-1217810292357)
```

Figure 3. Agent's internal architecture

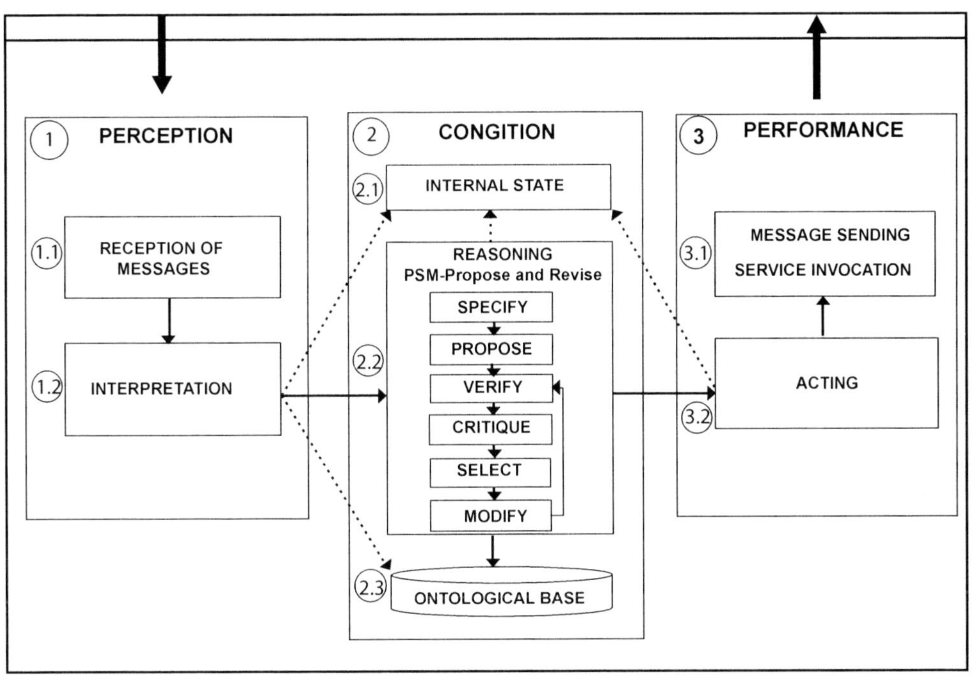

With its modified internal state containing the data referring to its objective, the cognition process is initiated (2), whereby the agent executes its reasoning process (2.2). The Cognition module is responsible for the agent's decision making. In this module, the agent executes a method for solving a particular problem that is based on the propose-and-revise PSM which is basically divided into the following phases:

1. Specify. It generates a list of typical components of the artifact to be produced.
2. Propose. It proposes to insert a component in the design.
   - 2.1 It searches for the components of one particular type and requests collaboration if necessary.
   - 2.2 It selects one component based on cost.
3. Verify. It verifies whether the inserted component violates any constraint. If a constraint was violated, go to 4 or else go to 2.
4. Critique. It produces a list of actions for fixing the problems identified in 3 and requests collaboration if necessary.
5. Select. It selects the repair action to be executed.
6. Modify. It executes the action modifying the design and goes to 5 until all the constraints are satisfied. Go to 2.

Finally, the Performance module is responsible for the actions of the agent. A decision (design) is made as a result of the reasoning process (design). This decision is implemented by the performance module (3) where the action-taking process occurs (3.2) and the rendering of the action by means of service invocation or message sending (3.1) to the user or other agent.

How the Agents Use Preferences and Constraints

Agent's exploration of a Knowledge Base (KB) is done by means of SPARQL queries. When a constraint is defined, no special mechanism is needed since SPARQL queries with their clauses such as order, group, and filter are enough to select a KB record, taking into account the specified constraints. However, when the agents need to query a KB taking into account the preferences, a special reasoning mechanism is needed. We leveraged the work of Siberski, Pan, and Thaden (2006) who have extended SPARQL to work with preferences. In their work, special statements such as *and, preferring,* and *cascade* were created for allowing filter KB records (instances of OWL/RDF) that fulfill only partially the user's requirements. We call their extension SPARQL Preference, which considers preferences. Our methodoloy consists of mapping the instances of preference ontology to SPARQL preference. The mapping between the preference defined in the ontology and the corresponding SPARQL Preference sentence is carried out according to each type of Preference. For each OWL concept, we have defined the corresponding sentence in SPARQL Preference. A correspondence table has been drawn up containing all possible transformations. Based on this table, we are able to generate SPARQL sentences.

In Figure 4, we have an example of a mapping of a positive preference to an equivalent SPARQL preference sentence. The highlighted items are the variables of properties, which will be mapped from the ontology representation of preference for SPARQL Preference sentence. In that case, the API verifies that *hasOWLClass* and its value (line 2 on the left side) are equivalent to an *rdf:type* clause in SPARQL. The same process is repeated with the other highlighted properties.

Figure 4. Example of OWLPref mapping for SPARQL preference

```
<PositiveDatatypePreference rdf:ID= Pref_Hotel_5Star >
    <hasOWLClass rdf:resource= #Hotel />
    <hasOWLProperty rdf:resource= #Stars />
    <hasOperator rdf:resource= swrl:#equal />
    <hasValueDatatypeProperty rdf:datatype="#int > 5
    </hasValueDatatypeProperty>
</PositiveObjectPreference>
```

```
PREFIX rdf: <http://www.w3.org/1999/02/22-rdf-syntax-ns#>
SELECT *
WHERE
{ ?var rdf:type Hotel .
  ?var Stars ?num
}
PREFERRING ( ?num = 5 )
```

MODELING THE CONFIGURATION PSM IN OWL-S

In order to adapt the configuration PSM for the Web, we had to consider each subtask of this as an independent Web service. This propitiates several advantages, for example:

- **Decoupling of Services**: Since each subtask is a service that is totally detached from the others, different implementations can arise from the same subtask for different developers. For example, each subtask of the PSM can be implemented in a different language.
- **Replication of Services:** If a particular subtask is unavailable, the agent can look for others and also make assessments on cost, availability, and performance.
- **Explanation:** The use of the tasks as services and the composition of such allows greater ease in the explanation of how they were "composed," since there are languages that describe the functioning of Web services (OWL-S, etc.).
- **Automation:** Describing these tasks as services facilitates not only the automation of the invocation but also the localization and even the composition.

The configuration PSM was modeled and implemented following a service-oriented architecture using OWL-S, since this offers elements for flow control. The OWL-S ontology is composed of the following parts: the service profile, process model, and grounding. The profile describes the inputs, outputs, preconditions, and effects of the service provided. The process model describes the way of interaction with the Web service, and grounding defines the execution to a Web Service Description Language (WSDL) operation. Moreover, it is important to note the distinction between atomic processes that do not have any internal structure and composite processes that can be constructed from other processes.

We address the Configuration PSM as a Composite Process of OWL-S. That is, each subprocess

Figure 5. Propose-and-Revise configuration method

```
specify (requirements -> skeletal-design);
while NEW-SOLUTION  do {
  propose (skeletal-design + design + preferences -> extension);
  verify (design + constraints -> truth-value + violation);
  IF (truth-value == false) THEN {
    critique(violation + design -> action-list);
    REPEAT
      select (action-list -> action);
      modify (design + action -> design);
       verify (design + constraints -> truth-value + violation);
     UNTIL truth-value == true;
  }
}
```

is a task of the PSM implemented as a Web service. A Web service described in OWL-S possesses the *ProposeAndRevise* service and its interlinking with its properties (what it is and how it works). Its definition is in the *ProposeAndRevise* Profile; its functioning is described in the *ProposeAndRevise* Process. Since the *ProposeAndRevise* Profile has advertisement and localization purposes, we will focus only on the *ProposeAndRevise* Process, where the entire functioning of the configuration PSM is detailed.

For the sake of understandability, Figure 5 describes a pseudocode of a propose-and-revise configuration PSM in a nonservice-oriented programming language. We modeled and implemented this PSM following a service-oriented architecture using OWL-S. For each subtask, we created a corresponding service with the same input and output parameters. Thus, we created the *SpecifyProcess*, *ProposeProcess*, *VerifyProcess*, *CritiqueProcess*, *SelectProcess*, and *ModifyProcess*; remember that by definition of OWL-S, a service is described by its process. Notice that the *ProposeProcess* invokes two other services. The first one is that of searching for components, which possesses two input parameters: the type and the properties of the component. The result of this Web service is a list of the components encountered for the type and parameters entered. Afterwards, it invokes the service of selection of components, which returns the chosen component according to the preferences specified.

Therefore, the configuration PSM in OWL-S is a composition of all these services or—to use a more appropriate term—all these OWL-S processes. For the purpose of providing an example of how to model the PSM in OWL-S, we describe (in Figures 3, 4, and 5) excerpts of such modeling.

In Figure 6, we show the modeling of the PSM conditional control of the Verify task whereby the constraint violation is tested (the conditional control of line 5 of Figure 6).

#Condition_1 in line 2 is the instance of the OWL-S process ifCondition. It represents the constraint violation condition that the agent must evaluate. In the case of true, the sequence of the rest of the PSM tasks (Sequence_1) is executed. One way we have to represent a sequence in OWL-S is by means of a list. In the example of Figure 6, CtrlConstructList_1 is a list with the header containing the Perform_Critique process and with the tail containing another list (CtrlConstructList_2) with the rest of the PSM tasks. The detailed description of the PSM modeling in OWL-S with more examples is done in Greenwood and Calisti (2004).

Figure 6. Use of if-then-else in the PSM in OWL-S

```
1 <process:If-Then-Else rdf:ID="If-Then-Else_1">
2 <process:ifCondition rdf:resource="#Condition_1"/>
3  <process:then>
4    <process:Sequence rdf:ID="Sequence_1">
5    <process:components>
6    <process:ControlConstructList rdf:ID="CtrlConstructList_1">
7        <list:first rdf:resource="#Perform_Critique"/>
8        <list:rest rdf:resource="#CrtlConstructList_2"/>
9    </process:ControlConstructList>
10   </process:components>
11   </process:Sequence>
12  </process:then>
13 </process:If-Then-Else>
```

GIVING OWL-S EXPLANATION CAPABILITIES

After modeling the PSM in OWL-S, we began to program functionalities that offer the possibility of the agent's providing explanations regarding its decisions. Our methodoloy consists of an extension of OWL-S and the API (Narayanan & McIlraith, 2002) that interprets it. This extension can be used by any type of problem modeled in OWL-S and not just in the Configuration PSM that we are using. The extension consists of the creation of an object called *ExplanationTracer*. It performs the interception of the calls made by the API during the interpretation to the elements of flow control of OWL-S. When these elements are used at the time of executing a process in OWL-S, the values of the input and output parameters used by these elements are recorded in a data structure that will be used in the explanation process. The order of recording these values determines the call sequence of each element within a process, and likewise allows it to identify the sequence of each process. The Inference Web framework (IW) (McGuinness & Pinheiro da Silva, 2004) provides a way to represent and annotate the steps and the inferences of a problem solver. IW data includes proofs and explanations published anywhere on the Web that are represented using IW format—PML. PML is the IW portable proof specification and includes two major components of proof trees: inference steps and node sets. A proof can then be defined as a tree of inference steps explaining the process of deducing the consequent sentence. The node set represents a statement and the last step in a deductive path that led a system to derive the statement. An inference step is a single application of an inference rule, whether the rule is atomic or derived.

The process of explanation of workflows can likewise be validated from this framework. The central idea is to define structures that allow the automation of process flow. We decided to represent the inputs and outputs of a control element. A list of node sets represents the execution of these elements. Figure 7 illustrates the implementation of the OWL-S API for a control element of the *if-then-else* type. In lines 2, 3, and 4, the three components of this control

Figure 7. Excerpt of the API of OWL-S for interpretation of the if-then-else element

```
protected void executeIfThenElse(IfThenElse ifThenElse) {
    Condition ifCondition = ifThenElse.getCondition();
    ControlConstruct thenCC = ifThenElse.getThen();
    ControlConstruct elseCC = ifThenElse.getElse();
    if (isTrue( ifCondition ))
        executeConstruct(thenCC);
    else if (elseCC != null)
        executeConstruct(elseCC);
}
protected boolean isTrue(Condition condition) {
    ValueMap binding = (ValueMap) performResults.get(OWLS.Process.TheParentPerform);
    boolean result = condition.isTrue(envKB, binding);
    ExplanationTracer.saveIfThenElse(condition, binding, result);
    return result;
}
```

Figure 8. Description of the ExecuteProcess process

```
protected ValueMap executeProcess(Process process, ValueMap values) {
    setCurrentExecuteService(process);
    explanation.saveProcessInput(process, values);
    if (checkPreconditions) checkPreconditions(process, values);
    if (process instanceof AtomicProcess) {
        ValueMap out = executeAtomicProcess((AtomicProcess) process, values);
        explanation.saveProcessOutput(process, out);
        return out;
    }
    else if (process instanceof CompositeProcess) {
        ValueMap out = executeCompositeProcess( (CompositeProcess) process, values);
        explanation.saveProcessOutput(process, out);
        return out;
    }
    else if (process instanceof SimpleProcess) {
        String message = "Executing simple processes is not implemented!";
        explanation.saveException(message);
        throw new NotImplementedException(message);
    }
    else {
        String message = "Unknown process type " + process;
        explanation.saveException(message);
        throw new ExecutionException(message);
    }
}
```

element are represented: the condition (If), the construction block to be executed if the condition is true (Then), and the construction block to be executed if the condition is false (Else). In line 5, the condition is verified through the *isTrue* call function (line 10). Within this function (line 13), the *ExplanationTracer* records one node set with the parameters used in the condition (binding), the condition itself (condition), and the result obtained (result). *ExplanationTracer* is inserted here because it is executed for *if-then-else*, but it is also used for *repeat-until* and *repeat-while*. The interpretation API in OWL-S continues its task and decides whether the *then* construction block (line 6) or the *else* construction block (line 8) should be executed.

Assuming that the construction block chosen in the *if-then-else* mentions the execution of a *Perform*, the *Perform* calls the *executeProcess* function informing the process to be executed and its inputs as a parameter. Figure 8 shows the *executeProcess* function. At the start of this function, the *ExplanationTracer* already stores the process input data (line 3). Afterwards, it checks whether the preconditions for executing this process have been satisfied (lines 4 and 5). If any precondition of the process has not been satisfied, the process is interrupted and the node set will be recorded informing that there was a violation of some precondition for the process in question. Otherwise, the process follows the normal flow of execution and will identify the type of process to be executed.

When dealing with the execution of a composite process—as such processes can be a composition of atomic processes or other composite processes or blocks of construction containing elements of control flow—the API of interpretation continues its activity and, consequently, the *ExplanationTracer* continues to record the list of node sets. In addressing an atomic process (line 7), the execution flow would be terminated and the list of node sets would be complete. The recording of node set (lines 8, 13, 18, and 23) is only performed after the actual execution of the process invoked.

SECTION PROOF OF CONCEPT EXAMPLE

Modeling the Computer Manufacturing Domain

To exemplify our methodoloy, we performed a modeling of a just-in-time computer configuration context based on what was described in Greenwood and Calisti (2004) regarding the manufacturing process for Dell computers. In this context, a customer places an order for a computer over the telephone or over the Web. The user's order contains information such as special features desired, user preferences, personal information of the buyer, ship-to address, bill-to address, credit card information, and so forth. After that, the order is analyzed by the Dell experts who prepare a configuration of the computer to be produced, taking into account information of the six assembly plants worldwide. Thus, the configuration of the computer depends on—in addition to the user's preferences—information from the suppliers. Once the plant and the computer parts have been selected, the configuration is shown to the user for order confirmation. Finally, the computer parts are ordered by the plant from its suppliers, and the computer is produced.

As previously explained, the problem of computer configuration is modeled in this article as a generation of a Web service workflow. The objective of the Configuration PSM is to combine predefined services that provide information for configuring a computer that meets the requirements and obeys the constraints. Each one of the computer parts is called a *Configuration* component.

A configuration PSM is made out of parameters, constraints, and preferences. The parameters are characteristics of a computer part such as brand, model, and price of a component. The constraints define the choice of a configuration component or the value of a parameter. For example, a supplier can only receive a maximum of 10 orders for parts per hour. The preferences steer the choice of the parts desired for the configuration of the computer whenever there is more than one option for parts from which to choose.

The problem of a computer configuration begins with the choice regarding which assembly plant to send the computer order. The agent must discover which plants are available and choose one to send the order according to the user's preferences and the assembly plant's constraints. For example, the user may have a preference to receive the computer as soon as possible. The enterprise user (i.e., a Dell employee) could have the preference that the order be sent to an assembly plant located in the same geographic region or the one that is closest in proximity to the user. On the other hand, the assembly plant may have a constraint as to the maximum number of orders that it can receive in a given period of time. The agent is responsible for attempting to meet the preferences and constraints of these different kinds of users. Once the assembly plant has been chosen, the configuration process gets under way in order to compose the services that will allow assembly of the computer.

The configuration components to be produced are processors, memories, video boards, keyboards, and so forth. The first phase of the PSM, the *Specify* phase, is where the assembly of a skeletal-design is done, containing information on all the types of components that a computer should have.

In the second phase of the PSM, the *Propose* phase, the configuration of the computer begins being produced, considering the preferences of the user, with the filling in of the skeletal-design with components that may be configuration options. In this phase, the agent searches for the components through Web services. We are assuming that each one of these suppliers presents its service described in OWL-S, thus making it possible for the agent to identify the parameters required to access the service. By accessing these services, the agent retrieves information on the desired component and composes the list of available components. If necessary, it requests proposals from other agents that could be in another context (other plants, for instance).The return is a list of components from various suppliers and with diverse features. The agent must sort them out according to the user's preferences, aiming to satisfy the highest possible number of preferences. After that, the configuration of the computer is extended with the addition of the best option at the moment from the list of components.

The third phase of the PSM, the *Verify* phase, receives—as input parameters—the extended configuration and the constraints of the domain and of the business. The PSM verifies whether the proposed component violates any constraint and carries this violation to the next phase. Otherwise, it returns to the *Propose* phase for a suggestion of a new type of component.

The fifth phase, the *Critique* phase, verifies the list of actions to be executed as a result of the violation. Here again an interaction is possible with other agents for receiving different suggestions of repair for the problem identified. The following phase, the *Select* phase, selects one of these actions to attempt to repair the violation. The next phase is the *Modify* phase, where the selected action is executed and the cycle of verification of the constraints is resumed.

Explaining to the User

Let us assume that a configuration of a computer is under way and a component of the type AMD motherboard has already been proposed. The next type of component to be proposed is that of processors. An Intel Pentium IV model processor was proposed because it meets the preference of being produced by an Asian supplier, but this

Figure 9. Explanations shown by the agent

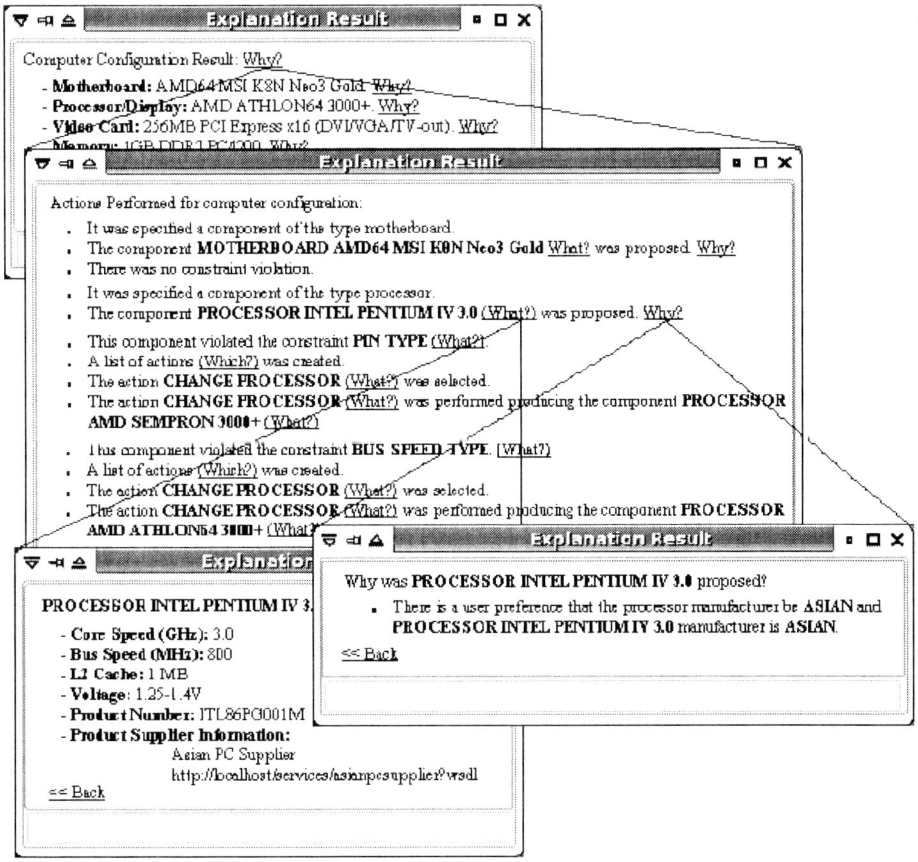

model possesses an incompatibility with the motherboard already selected and thus violates a constraint in the configuration. A proposal for repairing this problem suggests that it must be exchanged for another processor, a Sempron model which, in turn, had another constraint violated in function of bus incompatibility. A new repair is suggested and this processor also is exchanged for an Athlon64 processor, which violated no constraints. The process persists until the configuration is complete. The user then receives a reply describing the configuration of the computer to be produced.

It is normal for the users (whatever their types are) to request an explanation about the reasons that lead to the produced configuration. Particularly in this example, this happens due primarily to the fact that the result did not take into account one of the enterprise user's preliminary preferences: to have a processor produced by an Asian supplier. In this fashion, one may question why this occurred. The agent would then respond as specified in Figure 9; the Asian supplier had a Pentium IV but it was incompatible with the PIN type of the motherboard already chosen. The description of the PSM with the results and the sequence of the subtasks executed during the problem solving are displayed to the user. Questions *why* and *which* drive the explanation allowing for the follow-up about the domain concepts, preferences, and the inference step of the production rules.

RELATED WORKS

Explanations for Knowledge-Based Systems (KBS) have appeared as a significant and independent topic of study but in terms of extensiveness they have some shortcomings. The NEOMYCIN project (Clancey, 1986) contributed to explanation research in KBSs by using an explicit representation for problem resolution strategies and by using metarules in explanation planning. However, it was specific to MYCIN in terms of problem solving and domain representation.

The use of Ripple Down Rules (RDRs) (Richards, 2000) presents a new paradigm for KBS in which cases are used to explain an answer to a query. RDR provide only cases as representation for explanation which is very well suited to classification tasks. Therefore, it is not trivial to extend the RDR methodoloy to other knowledge-intensive tasks such as design.

WOZ (Shankar, Tu, & Musen, 1998) is a framework for explaining component-based decision-support systems. The framework is composed of functional components, which represent the reasoning process and the cooperative visualization agents associated, which are responsible for explanation presentation and user interaction, and application domain models such as user model, agent model, and explanation strategy. Although WOZ meets the extensiveness criterion, it is not easily scalable since a new explanation strategy must be developed for each application.

Some works extend OWL-S functionalities (Sirin, Hendler, & Parsia, 2003; Sirin, Parsia, & Hendler, 2005), which defines the concept of abstract processes that are not linked to any specific profile or grounding description or with any other existing process. None of these works are concerned with explanation capabilities.

Some methodoloyes have developed strategies to support (semi)automatic composition of Web services (McIlraith et al., 2001; Narayanan & McIlraith, 2002; Paolucci et al., 2002; Sirin et al., 2003; Sirin et al., 2005) but the main difference of our methodoloy is the modeling in a declarative way of a propose-and-revise PSM which brings reusability and extensiveness. An exception to this, and in a complementary manner of our work, is Gomez-Perez, Gonzalez-Cabero, and Lama (2004). It also uses the PSM methodoloy and defines a framework for design Web service composition on a conceptual level. Doing so, it allows for using OWL-S as any other modeling language for the implementation of the composition process.

Using the preference ontology (by means of class or attribute preferences) in conjunction with SPARQL preference it is possible to define preferences that are more important than others instead of addressing as many preferences as possible, similar to the work on utility theory proposed by Boutilier et al. (2004).

Finally, the integration of agents and Web services reported in this article is similar to that reported in WSIG (Greenwood & Calisti, 2004) within the JADE environment. However our methodoloy models this integration at a higher level of abstraction: the PSM level.

CONCLUSION

In this work, we have described a distributed multiagent system that uses PSMs whereby the agents cooperate with each other to configure a Web service workflow. In this model, different agents playing different roles would represent subtasks of PSMs. This means that we can have many agents proposing (in the case of the PSM Propose-and-Revise) and/or executing repair actions. The advantage of this methodoloy is the agents' ability to collaborate, making them more robust. Other characteristics of the agents are the fact that they follow a strategy of reasoning based on a propose-and-revise strategy, the fact that they have this strategy of reasoning modeled and implemented in OWL-S, and finally, the fact that they use an extension of OWL-S that records the execution trace of its reasoning with the objective of providing explanations regarding the decisions that they make. An example in e-commerce aided the understanding of the focus and the visualization of the way in which the agent performs its activities.

FUTURE WORK

We are evolving the methodoloy described in this article in order to improve the visualization of the explanations. Merely following the execution trace of a process—mainly when dealing with several components—is inefficient and scarcely informative to a user. We are studying the heuristics of visualizing the explanations at different levels of abstraction. Generic explanations are supplied in a first stage and, if necessary, the user can delve deeper into the detailing of the process flow. Another heuristic is to perform simplifications of structures that are repeated during the flow of execution. Our idea is to create an ontology of concepts for explanations that would replace repetitive patterns found in the execution trace. For example, the concept of sequence of repairs could replace a set of repairs done successively by the agent during the solving of a problem. Thus, instead of an explanation that enumerated them, a more succinct explanation could be given that would state only that a sequence of repairs was effected and that these repairs generated a particular result.

One important point worthy of further investigation relates to the difference between creating a workflow and executing it. This is a typical problem studied in the planning literature since one may be able to find a service that promises to deliver a component in time, but when the workflow is executed, the promise cannot be fulfilled. Even though we have focused on the functional aspects of a workflow execution, we consider that our explanation methodoloy can partially address this issue by means of an explanation of why the service was not executed at the run time (for instance, service not available). Further tests and investigations with real users by simulating these situations will be an object of our studies.

REFERENCES

Berners-Lee, T., Hendler, J., & Lassila, O. (2001, May). The Semantic Web. *Scientific American*.

Boutilier, C., Brafman, R., Domshlak, C., Hoos, H., & Poole, D. (2004). Preference-based constrained optimization with CP-nets [Special issue]. *Computational Intelligence, 20*(2), 137-157.

Clancey, W.J. (1986). From GUIDON to NEOMYCIN and HERACLES (Twenty Short Lessons: ORN Final Report 1979-1985). *AI Magazine, 7*(3), 40-60.

Fensel, D., & Benjamins, V.R. (1998). Key issues for automated problem-solving methods reuse. In *Proceedings of the 13th European Conference on Artificial Intelligence*. John Wiley & Sons.

FIPA Agent Communication. (2002). Retrieved July 3, 2007, from *http://www.fipa.org/repository/aclspecs.html*

Gomez-Perez, A., Gonzalez-Cabero, R., & Lama, M. (2004). A framework for design and composition of Semantic Web services. In *Proceedings of the AAAI Spring Simposyum on Semantic Web Services*. AAI Press.

Greenwood, D., & Calisti, M. (2004, October). **Engineering Web service: Agent integration.** *Proceedings of the IEEE International Conference on Systems, Man and Cybernetics, 2.*

Horrocks, I., Patel-Schneider, P.F., Boley, H., Tabet, S., Grosof, B., & Dean, M. (2004). SWRL: A Semantic Web rule language combining OWL and RULEML (W3C Member Submission). Retrieved July 3, 2007, from http://www.w3.org/Submission/SWRL/

Kieβling, W., Hafenrichter, B., Fischer, S., & Holland, S. (2001, September). Preference XPATH: A query language for e-commerce. *In Proceedings of the 5th International Tagung WirtschaftsInformatik*, Augsburg, Germany.

Lopes, A., & Botelho, L. (2005). *SEA: A Semantic Web services context-aware execution agent. In Proceedings of the AAAI Fall Symposium in Agents and the Semantic Web, Arlington, Virginia.*

McGuinness, D., & Pinheiro da Silva, P. (October 2004). Explaining answers from the Semantic Web: The inference Web approach. *Journal of Web Semantics, 1*(4), 397-413.

McGuinness, D., & van Harmelen, F. (2004). OWL Web ontology language overview (World Wide Web Consortium (W3C) Recommendation). Retrieved July 3, 2007, from http://www.w3.org/TR/owl-features

McIlraith, S., Son, T.C., & Zeng, H. (2001, March/April). Semantic Web services [Special issue]. *IEEE Intelligent Systems,* 16(2), 46-53.

Moore, J.D. (1995). *Participating in explanatory dialogues: Interpreting and responding to questions in context.* Cambridge, MA: MIT Press.

Narayanan, S., & McIlraith, S. (2002). Simulation, verification and automated composition of Web services. In *Proceedings of the 11th International World Wide Conference*, Hawaii (pp. 77-88).

OWL-S Java API. (2004). Retrieved July 3, 2007, from http://www.mindswap.org/2004/owl-s/api/

Paolucci, M., Kawamura, T., Payne, T., & Sycara, K. (2002). Semantic matching of Web services capabilities. In *Proceedings of the 1st International Semantic Web Conference (ISWC).* Berlin: Springer-Verlag.

Pinheiro, P., McGuinness, D., & Fikes, R. (2004). *A proof markup language for Semantic Web services* (Tech. Rep. KSL-04-01). Stanford University.

Richards, D. (2000). User-centred and driven knowledge-based systems for clinical support using ripple down rules. In *Proceedings of the 33rd Hawaii International Conference on System Sciences.*

Shankar, R.D., Tu, S.W., & Musen, M.A. (1998). *A declarative explanation framework that uses a collection of visualization agents.* Stanford Medical Institute, Stanford University School of Medicine, Stanford, California.

Siberski, W., Pan, J.Z., & Thaden, U. (2006). Querying the Semantic Web with Preferences. In *Proceedings of the 5th International Semantic Web Conference,* Athens, Greece.

Sirin, E., Hendler, J., & Parsia, B. (2003). Semi automatic composition of Web services using semantic descriptions. In *Proceedings of the Workshop on Web Services: Modeling, Architecture and Infrastructure.*

Sirin, E., Parsia, B., & Hendler, J. (2005, November). Template-based composition of Semantic Web services. In *Proceedings of the AAAI Fall Symposium on Agents and the Semantic Web*, Arlington, Virginia.

This work was previously published in Int. Journal of Information Technology and Web Engineering, Vol. 2, Issue 4, edited by G. Alkhatib, pp. 1-20, copyright 2007 by IGI Publishing (an imprint of IGI Global).

Section II
Collaboration

Chapter VI
A Subspace Clustering Framework for Research Group Collaboration

Nitin Agarwal
Arizona State University, USA

Ehtesham Haque
Arizona State University, USA

Huan Liu
Arizona State University, USA

Lance Parsons
Arizona State University, USA

ABSTRACT

Researchers spend considerable time searching for relevant papers on the topic in which they are currently interested. Often, despite having similar interests, researchers in the same lab do not find it convenient to share results of bibliographic searches and thus conduct independent time-consuming searches. Research paper recommender systems can help the researcher avoid such time-consuming searches by allowing each researcher to automatically take advantage of previous searches performed by others in the lab. Existing recommender systems were developed for commercial domains to assist users by focusing towards products of their interests. Unlike those domains, the research paper domain has relatively few users when compared with the huge number of research papers. In this paper we present a novel system to recommend relevant research papers to a user based on the user's recent querying and browsing habits. The core of the system is a scalable subspace clustering algorithm, SCuBA (Subspace ClUstering Based Analysis) that performs well on the sparse, high-dimensional data collected in this domain. Both synthetic and benchmark datasets are used to evaluate the recommendation system and to demonstrate that it performs better than the traditional collaborative filtering approaches when recommending research papers.

BACKGROUND AND MOTIVATION

The explosive growth of the world-wide Web and the emerging popularity of e-commerce has caused the collection of data to outpace the analysis necessary to extract useful information. Recommender systems were developed to help close the gap between information collection and analysis by filtering all of the available information to present what is most valuable to the user (Resnick and Varian, 1997).

One area of the Web that has seen continued growth is the online publication of research papers. The number of research papers published continues to increase, and new technology has allowed many older papers to be rapidly digitized. A typical researcher must sift through a large quantity of articles manually, relying on keyword-based searches or paper citations to guide him. The search results of researchers with similar interests can help direct a more effective search, but the process of sharing search results is often too cumbersome and time consuming to be feasible. A recommender system can help by augmenting existing search engines by recommending papers based on the preferences of other researchers with similar interests. We assume that the proposed system is localized in a typical lab setting which augments an existing search engine. Rather than performing search in some digital library, SCuBA tries to take advantage of the existing search results. It tries to find similar interest groups of users based on their browsing patterns and recommends research papers which might be interesting to them.

There are two main branches of recommender systems; content based filtering and collaborative filtering. Content based filtering (CBF) approaches create relationships between items by analyzing inherent characteristics of the items. Collaborative filtering (CF) systems do not analyze an items properties, but instead take advantage of information about users' habits to recommend potentially interesting items. The analysis of user behavior patterns, allows collaborative filtering systems to consider characteristics that would be very difficult for content based systems to determine such as the reputation of the author, conference, or journal. CF approaches are also well suited to handle semantic heterogeneity, when different research fields use the same word to mean different things.

In many domains, there is an ever increasing number of users while number of items remains relatively stable. However, in domains such as research paper recommendation (Singh et al., 2005), the number of users (researchers) is much less than the number of items (articles). Collaborative filtering systems face two major challenges in the research paper domain: scalability to high dimensional data and data sparsity. In a typical recommender system there are many items. For example, Amazon.com recommends specific books of interest from a large library of available books. Item-based approaches that determine similarity measures between items do not perform well since the item space is extremely large. A user based approach allows us to leverage the relatively small number of users. An intuitive solution used by early collaborative filtering algorithms is to find users with similar preferences to the current user and recommend other items that group of users rated highly. Even with a relatively small number users, however, this approach is computationally complex. The use of clustering algorithms to predetermine groups of similar users has been used to significantly increase performance (Ungar and Foster, 1998; Mobasher et al.,2000).

A particular user of the system will probably purchase a very small percentage of the available books. As a result, if we consider the data as a user-item matrix, a typical row will be extremely sparse, with only a few columns containing 1's, representing purchased books. Similarly, in the domain of research papers where a researcher will be interested in articles related only to a particular research area, the row representing the researcher will also be very sparse. Notice that the number of articles is ever increasing since there are many papers published each year which further compounds the degree of sparsity. Presence of sparsity poses a problem for user-based approaches because they often rely on nearest neighbor schemes to map a new user to the existing user groups. It has been demonstrated that the accuracy of nearest neighbor algorithms is very poor for sparse data (Sarwar et al., 2001; Demiriz, 2004).

We propose a new approach to collaborative filtering utilizing a novel subspace clustering algorithm suited to sparse, binary and high-dimensional data. Subspace clustering is a branch of clustering algorithms that is able to find low dimensional clusters in very high-dimensional datasets. This approach to clustering allows our system to find groups of users who share a common interest in a particular field or sub-field regardless of differences in other fields. Searching for similar users across all of the items leads to finding users who share many common interests. By finding groups based on subsets of items, subspace clustering find groups of users who share an interest in a particular area, regardless of their differences in other areas or fields.

The remainder of the paper is organized as follows. In the following section we present a formal definition of the problem we propose to solve. In the section on proposed algorithm we give a detailed description of our algorithm. Then experimental results are presented, including description of the dataset used, the evaluation metrics and discussion. Following the experimental section, related work in the area of subspace clustering and recommender systems is introduced. Finally, we conclude the paper with some directions for future research.

Problem Definitions

The proposed algorithm utilizes a binary user-item matrix, where a "*1*" in position i, j indicates that user i selected article j during a session. Each row is generated by anonymously recording the browsing pattern of users. The algorithm then finds clusters of users that are connected by subsets of papers they selected in common. The subsets of items are stored and used to make recommendations. The subsets of papers form groups of research articles that are connected by fields of interest. When a user selects a paper, the system recommends other papers that are in subsets containing the selected paper. This allows the system to respond to current, short-term interests of users that change from visit to visit.

We define the data space in the research paper domain as an $m \times n$ matrix such that there are m researchers $R = \{ r_1, r_2, ..., r_m \}$ and n articles $A = \{ a_1, a_2, ..., a_n \}$. The row r_i represents the interests of researcher i and consists of a list of articles A_{r_i} which indicates the user's interest in those articles. In the research paper domain, this could indicate that the user has read or accessed a certain article. For a given session there is an *active researcher* ($r_{active} \in R$) for which the collaborative filtering algorithm would like to recommend new articles that may be of interest to r_{active} based on the researcher's interest in the current session and the opinion of other like-minded researchers.

In order to predict which articles will be of high interest, we must have models of like-minded researchers. Given the $m \times n$ matrix, we can find like-minded researchers by finding groups of researchers $r \subseteq R$ who have expressed interest in similar articles $a \subseteq A$. The problem of finding such groups can be transformed into a problem of *subspace clustering* using the previously described binary matrix as input. The result of subspace clustering would be clusters, of researchers in corresponding subspaces of articles. Here, the underlying assumption is if a group of researchers have similar interests then they usually access similar sets of articles or vice-versa.

Problem Statement: Given a binary $m \times n$ matrix, where rows represent m researchers ($R = \{r_1, r_2, ..., r_m \}$) and columns represent n articles

Figure 1. Transformation: A row in the original matrix is transformed into a string containing the position of the non-zero columns

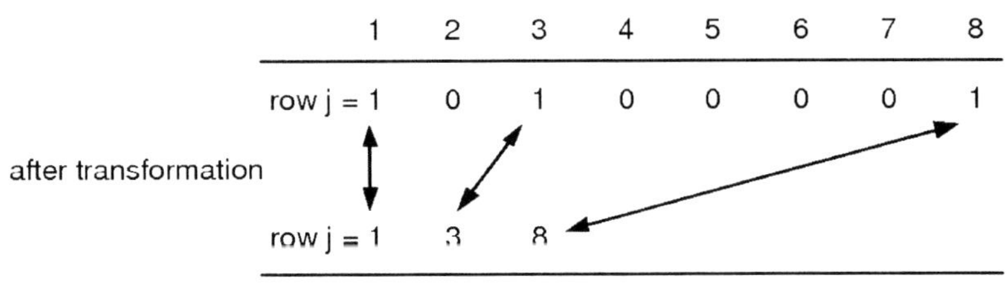

Figure 2. Transformed Data D after being compressed

row id					
1	1	2	3	17	
2	1	2	3		
3	2	3	4	50	
4	1	2	3		
5	2	3	4		
6	2	3			
7	5	6	7	8	21
8	6	7	40		
9	5	6	7	8	26

($A = \{a_1, a_2, \ldots, a_n\}$), find subspace clusters of researchers, $r \subseteq R$, defined in subspaces of articles, $a \subseteq A$.

Proposed Algorithm

Let us consider a large research lab setting with several researchers working on various topics. The access patterns of these researchers can be maintained by tracking the log of research papers they access. In order to preserve privacy, researchers could be assigned an encrypted form of identification for tracking purposes. From these access patterns, we can generate a researcher/article data space as defined in the previous section.

Each area of research has a group of people who are highly involved in the field, which we define as experts in the particular field. We believe that inferences about such experts can be drawn by analyzing the researcher article data space. More specifically, we infer that people accessing a similar set of articles are interested in the topics represented by the articles. Such a group is represented by a subspace cluster in the researcher/article data space. Finding these experts will ultimately help us achieve our goal of finding the groups of articles that form fields of interest. We adopt a subspace clustering approach to find groups of these experts.

Our proposed subspace clustering algorithm is a two-step process starting with finding subspaces that form clusters and then post-processing to remove redundancy. The outputs of these steps are sub-matrices of the original data matrix. Before discussing the above steps in detail, we will show how the proposed algorithm addresses the

Figure 3. Subspace clustering algorithm

```
Input: Tranformed data D with number of rows m and minimum density
count.
Output: A set S of subspaces.

hash_table_temp;
hash_table_global;

for j = 0; j < m; j++
        get row-j;
        for k=j+1; k < m; k++
                get row-k;
                find_intersection(row-j, row-k);
                put intersection in hash_table_temp;
                update count in hash_table_temp;

        if entries of hash_table_temp not in hash_table_global
        put in hash_table_global;

for j = 0; j < hash_table_global.size(); j++
        if count of an entry e >= minimum density
                S += e;
End
```

challenges associated with sparse, high-dimensional, binary-valued data in the research paper domain.

Challenges of the Domain – Addressed

Sparsity and Binary data. High sparsity means that for a given r_i, which is a vector in n dimensional space, most of the entries in the vector are zeros. Since we are only interested in the values which are not zeroes, we transform the original vector into a string containing positions of non-zero values. An example is shown in Figure 1. The result of the transformation is compact representation resulting in a reduced memory requirements and less processing overhead.

High-dimensional data. In high dimensional data, the number of possible subspaces is huge. For example, if there are N dimensions in the data, the number of possible subspaces is 2^N. Hence, subspace clustering algorithms must devise an efficient subspace search strategy (Parsons et al., 2004). Most existing algorithms will work well when the number of dimensions is relatively small. In the research paper domain there are thousands of dimensions and such approaches may become impractical. For example, based on our work in (Parsons et al., 2004), we chose an efficient representative subspace clustering algorithm, MAFIA (Goil et al., 1999), to run on a data set with 1000 dimensions. The program ran out of memory because the algorithm was designed to be very efficient for datasets with many rows but comparatively few dimensions. In the research paper domain, we have a unique property that the number of rows is significantly less than the number of dimensions. We overcome this challenge of high-dimensional data by devising an algorithm that exploits the row-enumeration space rather than the larger dimension space.

By combining our exploitation of the row-enumeration space and compact representation of binary sparse data, we convert the challenges into advantages in our subspace clustering algorithm. The next two sections discuss the major steps of our algorithm in more detail.

Find Subspaces that Form Clusters

The most straightforward way to find subspaces is to project the instance in all possible subspaces and find the ones in which clusters are formed. Such an approach is not feasible for data with a large number of dimensions since the number of possible subspaces is exponential, $O(2^N)$. Therefore, we propose a search strategy which explores the smaller row-enumeration space.

Subspace Search: The result of the transformation (as shown in Figure 1) of the high-dimensional data is a list of strings representing rows in the original data. We call the new, transformed dataset *D*. An example is shown in Figure 2.

The subspace search proceeds by comparing row_i with each successive row (row_{i+1}, row_{i+2}, row_{i+3}, ..., row_m). For example, if we start at row_1 in Figure 2, we first find the intersection between row_1 and row_2. The result of the intersection is *1 2 3* which represents a subspace in dimension *1, 2 and 3* with row_1 and row_2 as cluster members. *1 2 3* is stored as a key in a temporary hash table and the number of cluster members is stored as the value in the table. In addition, we also store the row-id as the values in the table in order to keep track of the cluster members for a given subspace. Next, row_1 is compared with row_3 and the intersection *2 3* is placed in the hash table. The intersection of row_1 and row_4, *1 2 3*, is already present in the table, so the count value is updated. At the end of the pass for row_1, the hash table will have two entries *1 2 3* and *2 3*. At this point, the entries in the temporary hash table are put in a global hash table which only accepts entries which are not already present in the global table and the temporary hash table is flushed. The rationale for having this rule is the following. When the search commences at row_2, it will find the intersection *1 2 3* and eventually it will update the global hash table with its local one. Notice here that the subspace *1 2 3* has already been found during the search commencing from row_1. Therefore, there is no requirement to update the global table. At the end of the search, the global hash table will have five entries, *5 6 7 8*, *1 2 3*, *2 3*, *2 3 4* and *6 7*. Notice that the subspace *2 3* is subsumed by the subspace *1 2 3* or *2 3 4*. This redundant subspace is removed in the next step. The formal description of the algorithm is shown in Figure 3.

Memory usage: The main sources of memory consumption are the temporary and global hash tables, and the transformed dataset. It should be noted that this dataset is a compressed version of the original data and thus uses significantly less memory. The hash table memory requirement grows slowly since the temporary hash table is flushed every time a new search commences and the global hash table only contains previously unfound entries. Although use of a hash table may lead to some overhead of space due to unmapped entries, the advantage of constant time lookup greatly outweighs such overhead. In our algorithm we make heavy use of lookups in the hash table to check whether a subspace has already been found and to maintain counts and cluster member-ids. Generally, it was noticed that the memory requirements grew linearly and were stable during our experiments.

Time Complexity: The algorithm takes advantage of the fact that the number of rows, *m*, is relatively small. As a result, the subspace search is performed on the row enumeration space which is $O(m^2)$. It should be noted that in our case, it is actually less than m^2 because if we are at row_i, we only look at row_{i+1}, row_{i+2}, ..., row_m. The algorithm also requires finding intersection of two strings which is performed in $O(k)$ time where the *k* is the length of the strings. Notice that *k* is usually very small due to the high sparsity of the data. In summary, the total complexity is $O(m^2k)$.

Figure 4. Set of Subspaces S with redundancy. Subspaces marked with arrows are pairs where one subspace is subsumed by another. For example, subspace 4 is subsumed by subspace 1.

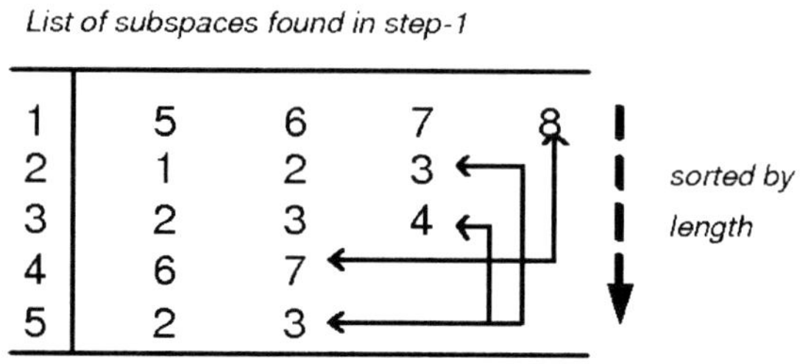

Post-Processing to Remove Redundancy

A larger subspace which contains several smaller subspaces covers more articles within the same field of interest. Removing smaller subspaces subsumed by larger ones helps in making recommendation process faster in the absence of redundant subspace clusters.

The result from the previous step is a collection of subspaces, *S*. An example of such a collection is shown in Figure 4. The subspaces connected with arrows indicate two subspaces, one of which subsumes another. We must remove the fourth subspace which is *6 7* since it is subsumed by subspace *5 6 7 8*. In general, to remove the redundant/subsumed subspaces in *S*, we perform the following steps:

1. Sort the set *S* according to the size of each subspace in descending order. The result of sorting is shown in Figure 4.
2. Take an element s_i from the set, *S*, and pass through s_{i+1}, s_{i+2}, ..., $s_{|S|}$ removing any element if it is a subset of s_i.

By performing step one, we place the largest subspace as the first element in *S*. Then performing step 2, starting with the first element of the set, we will remove all subsets of s_1, in the first pass. Since s_1 is the largest subspace, without loss of generality, we can assume that there will be a large number of subsets of s_1 in *S*. As a result, |S| will shrink considerably and the remaining passes through S will be shorter, resulting in reduced running time.

The time complexity is $O(|S|^2 p)$ where *p* is the size of the subspaces when computing subsumption between two subspaces. Notice that *p* is quite small due to sparsity and |S| is shrinking with each iteration. The time complexity for sorting is $O(|S|\lg|S|)$, so the overall complexity is still $O(|S|^2 p)$.

Finding Overlapping Subspaces

In real world data or data which is highly sparse, it might be possible that subspace clusters in the form of sub-matrices will not be significant in number and size. In that case, we relax our subspace search so that we can find clusters of irregular shape as opposed to strict sub-matrices. These irregularly shaped clusters are larger in size and cover more of the data. Overlapping of subspace clusters can represent extended or implicit relationships between both items and users which might be more interesting to the user.

An example is shown in Figure 5. Four subspace clusters are grouped together because they share common subspaces. We apply a simple clustering algorithm to cluster the subspaces. For each element in the list of subspaces, the overlap between the given element and the other subspace clusters are found. The degree of overlap is con-

Figure 5. The subspaces are grouped together in one cluster if there is overlap between subspaces

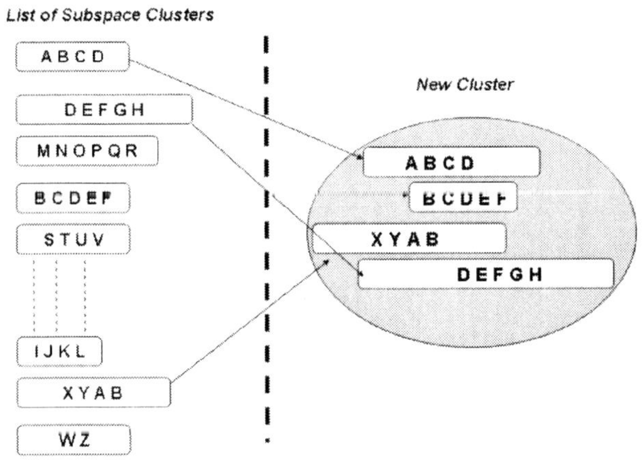

Figure 6. Using the subspace clustering model to generate recommendations

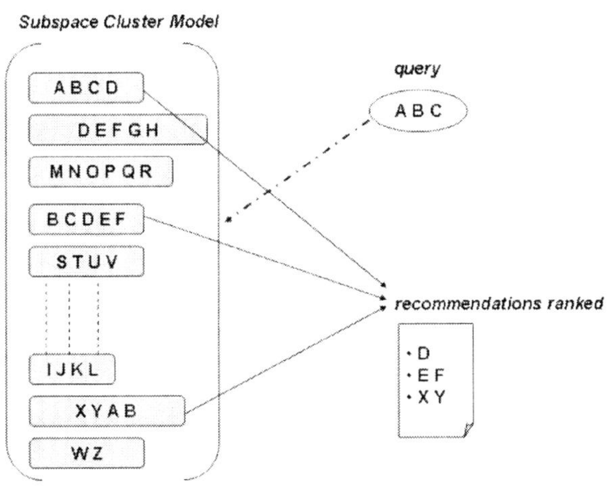

trolled by a threshold parameter. If the overlap exceeds the given threshold, the original subspace cluster is selected as a member of the cluster and is considered the *seed* of the cluster. For example in Figure 5, the seed of the new cluster found is the subspace *A B C D*. The other members of this cluster have some degree of overlap with *A B C D*. In this example, subspaces with at least one item in common with the seed, are put into the new cluster. This process is repeated for each element from the list of subspaces, resulting in large clusters of subspaces. A feature of this clustering process is that we allow a subspace to be member of several clusters as opposed to forming discrete partitions. This allows us to find all of the relationships that a subspace may participate in, instead of restricting it to one cluster membership.

Generating Recommendations

The process of generating recommendations illustrated in Figure 6 involves mapping a user's

Figure 9. Scalability with dimensionality of the embedded clusters. Size of the subspace (number of dimensions) is increased linearly keeping the number of dimensions in the data set fixed

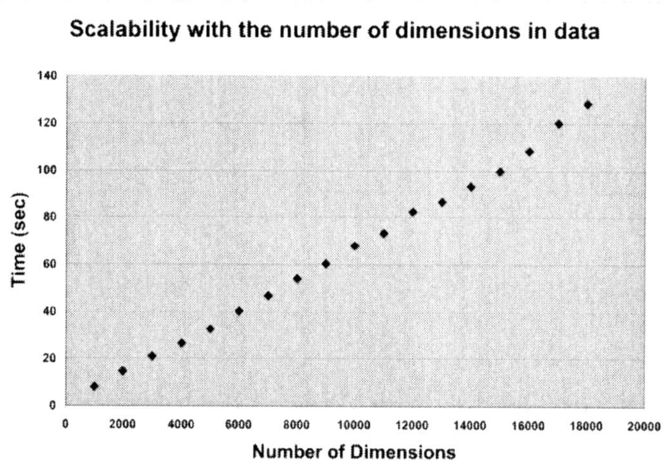

Figure 10. Scalability with dimensionality of the embedded clusters. Size of the subspace (number of dimensions) is increased linearly with the number of dimensions in the data set. Subspace size, indicated in curly braces, is set to be 1% of dimension size

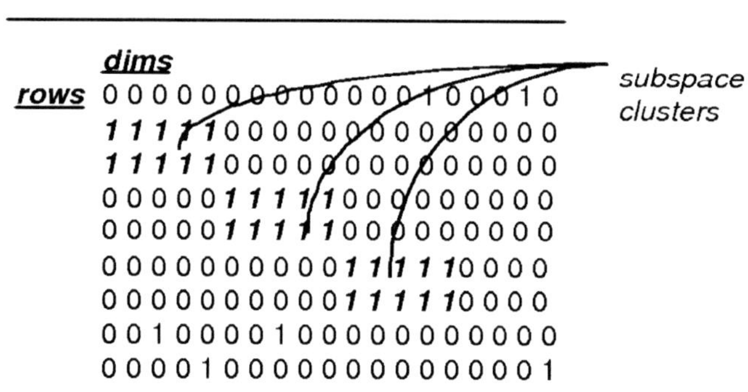

query to the subspaces and making recommendations based on the subspaces. The query represents the current selection of the active user. All of the subspaces containing the query item are collected and the matching subspaces are ranked based on the *coverage* of the query. Coverage is defined as the number of query items present in the subspace. The subspace with the highest coverage is ranked first and the ranked order of the subspaces determines the ranking of the recommendations. The recommendations are the elements in the subspace that are not part of the query. For example, in Figure 6 for the query *A B C*, the subspace *A B C D* has the highest coverage so the recommendation from that subspace, *D*, is ranked first. In the case of a tie while ranking, the subspace with the higher *strength* is picked first where the strength is defined as the number of cluster members present in the subspace. In Figure 6, subspaces *B C D E F* and *X Y A B* have equal coverage. In this case, their ranking is determined by their cluster strengths.

Fall-Back Model

Since the process of generating recommendations is dependent upon the successful mapping of a query to the subspace clustering model, we consider the scenario where a query is not covered by the subspace clustering model. Although this is a rare case (see subsection on Coverage Results), there must be a mechanism to handle such a scenario if it arises.

The subspace clustering approach finds relationships between articles in the researcher/article space. There will be a number of articles which do not form any significant relationship with other articles and hence will not form subspace clusters. If a query contains such articles, the subspace clustering model will not be able to cover the query. In this case, a *fall-back model* is provided which can be used to make recommendations for the query. Although the fall-back model provides no assurance on the quality of the recommendations, it does guarantee that a given query will be covered with minimal cost for maintaining and using the model.

The fall-back model utilizes the researcher/article matrix directly. For a given query, the articles in the query are indexed in the matrix and the corresponding rows (researchers) are found. The articles in the rows are ranked according to their global frequency and the recommendations are made in the ranked order. This approach is similar to the user-based approach where the items in the nearest user-vector are recommended to the active user. Notice that the computational requirements of the fall-back approach are minimal, consisting mainly of indexing the query articles and ranking according to the article frequency. Article frequency information can be maintained in a table enabling inexpensive look up cost.

Finally, recommender systems generally work under the principle that a queried item exists in the user/item matrix. An interesting scenario is, when a researcher selects an article that does not exist in the researcher/article matrix. The consequence will be that both the fall-back model and the subspace clustering model will not be able to cover the query. In this case, the top-N frequent (or popular) articles are returned to the researcher. Here, the quality of the recommendation will be poorer than the fall-back model but the goal of covering the query will be satisfied.

EXPERIMENTS

We first evaluate our subspace clustering algorithm using synthetic data and then evaluate the recommendation approach with the benchmark data. With synthetic data, we can embed clusters in specified subspaces. Since we know these locations, we can check whether the clustering algorithm is able to recover the clusters. For evaluating the quality of recommendations, *MovieLens* (Herlocker et al., 2004) benchmark dataset has been used. We compare our approach using SCuBA with the baseline approach defined in subsection on Recommendations from Benchmark data.

Clustering Evaluation on Synthetic Data

We have developed a synthetic data generator that allows us to embed clusters in subspaces. We can control the number and the size of such clusters and also size of the dataset. Apart from the clusters, the data space is filled with noise. For each row we place x noise values at random positions where $x = \alpha x$ the number of dimensions. We set $\alpha = 1\%$. An example of a synthetic data with three clusters is shown in Figure 7.

For scalability, we measure the running time as we increase the number of dimensions in increments of 1000. The number of rows is kept fixed at 1000. We embed 5 subspace clusters.

Figure 11. Running time comparison between SCuBA and MAFIA with increasing dataset dimensionality and increasing subspace size

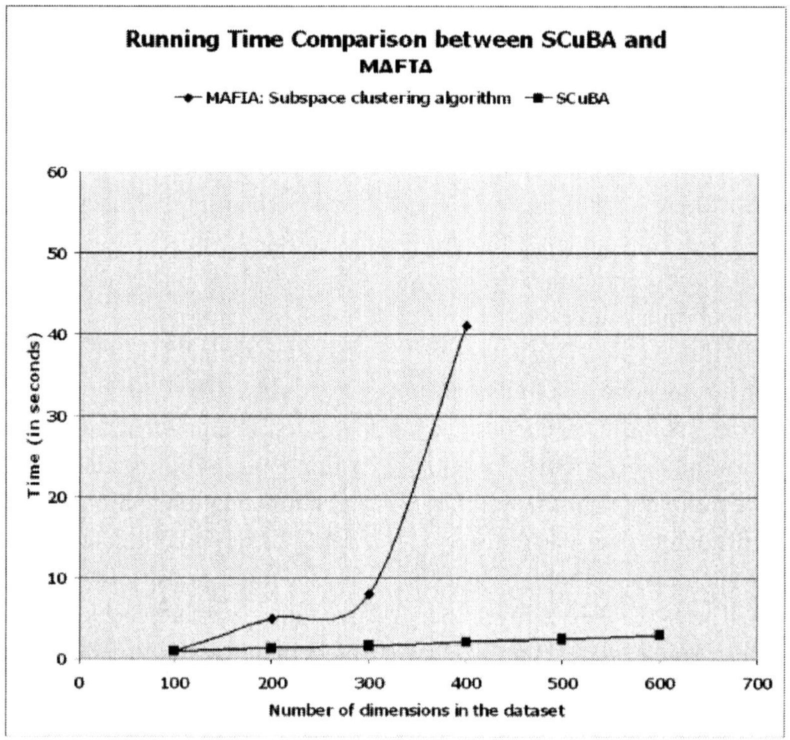

Figure 12. Running time comparison between SCuBA and MAFIA with increasing dataset dimensionality and increasing subspace size

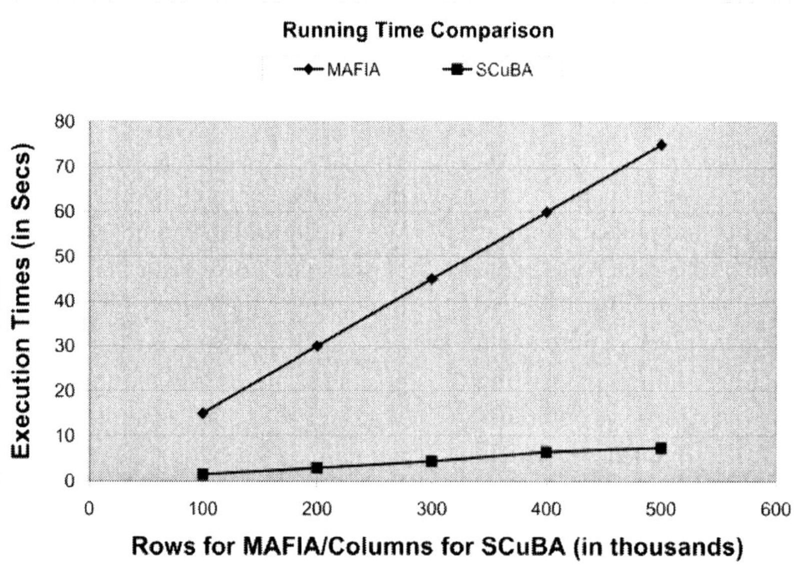

Each subspace cluster has 20 dimensions and 10 instances. Figure 8 shows the scalability of our algorithm as we increase the dimensions in the data. Notice that the curve is linear since our subspace search strategy is not dependent on the number of dimensions but rather it searches in the row-enumeration space.

In the second scalability graph, shown in Figure 9, size of the subspaces is linearly increased with the number of dimensions in the data. The size of the subspace is set to 1 percent of the number of dimensions. For example, when the number of dimensions is 5000, the size of the subspace is 50. Here the running time is negligibly higher than the previous case but the curve is still linear. The higher running time is due to the computation of intersection, *k*, between two strings to check for redundancy as mentioned in subsection on Post-processing to Remove Redundancy. As discussed previously, the size of *k* is generally very small due to the high sparsity of the data.

In the third scalability experiment as shown in Figure 10, we check the behavior of SCuBA as the density of the dataset increases. Dimensionality of the dataset is fixed to 2000 and the number of instances to 1000. We embed 5 subspace clusters each with 10 instances. The subspace size is increased from 20 to 200 in steps of 20. It can be observed that running time increases with the density of the dataset but the curve remains linear.

We present accuracy results of our subspace clustering algorithm in Table 1. Here, accuracy is defined by the number of true positives and true negatives w.r.t. the recovered clusters. In all cases, the embedded clusters were completely recovered as shown in Table-1. No extra clusters were reported even though α = 1% of noise is present in the data.

Finally we present a comparison between SCuBA and an existing subspace clustering algorithm, MAFIA (Goil et al., 1999). In the first experiment, as shown in Figure 11, we compare the running times of both the algorithms with increasing number of dimensions of the dataset from 100 to 600 in steps of 100. Again 5 subspace clusters were embedded with subspace size, 10% of the dimensionality of the dataset. Number of instances in the dataset is fixed to 500 and instances in subspace cluster is fixed to 10. As expected, SCuBA scales linearly with increasing number of dimensions whereas MAFIA shows exponential behavior till 400 dimensions, after which it runs out of memory. The second experiment compares the strength of both the algorithms. MAFIA is known to perform well for dataset with more number of instances as compared to the number of dimensions. SCuBA performs well for more number of dimensions as compared to the number of instances as mentioned in subsection on Challenges of the Domain - Addressed. So we transpose the high-dimensional low-instance data (for SCuBA) to get low-dimensional high-instance data (for MAFIA). Subspaces, thus generated for these datasets will be exactly the same. We compare the running times for both SCuBA and MAFIA. For MAFIA, the number of dimensions is fixed to 20 but number of instances change from 100K to 500K. Similarly, for SCuBA the number of dimensions is increased from 100K

Table 1. Accuracy in recovering the embedded subspace clusters. Five datasets with increasing number of dimensions. In all cases, the 5 embedded clusters are recovered.

Data Dimensions	1000	2000	3000	4000	5000
Recovery Accuracy	5/5 (100%)	5/5 (100%)	5/5 (100%)	5/5 (100%)	5/5 (100%)

Figure 14. Precision measurements as the percentage of query items is reduced

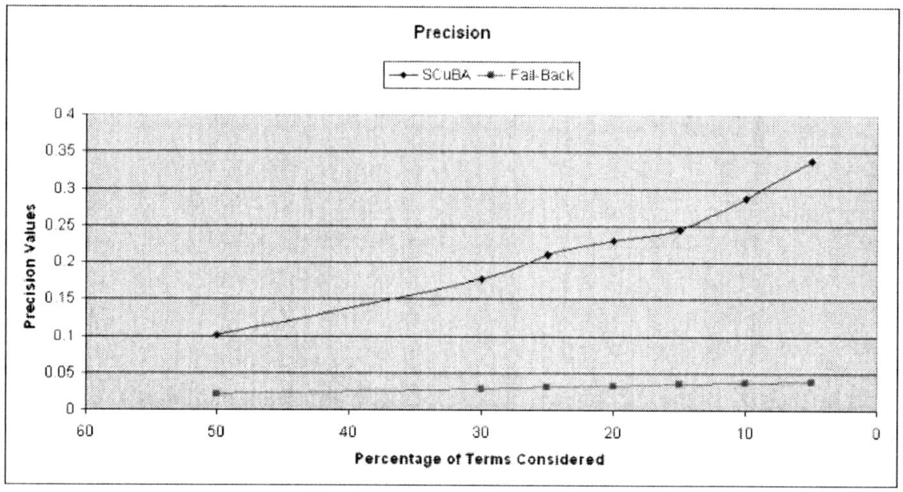

Figure 15. Time comparison of building models with two approaches on Biolog Dataset

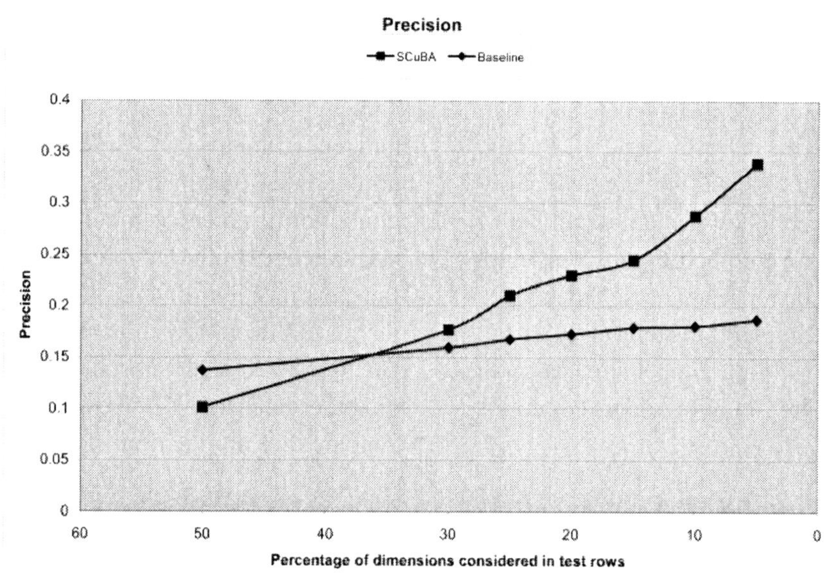

to 500K, keeping the number of instances fixed at 20. Although both algorithms scale linearly with increasing dimensionality (instances) for SCuBA (MAFIA), the time difference between SCuBA and MAFIA is near ten-folds, as shown in Figure 12.

Recommendations from Benchmark Data

In this part of the experiment we evaluate the quality of the recommendations made by the SCuBA approach on the *MovieLens* dataset.

In Background and Motivation section, we reviewed two approaches in CF and pointed out that memory-based approach produce high quality recommendations by finding the nearest neighbors of a target user. We use this as our baseline approach. It is quite practical to assume that users view or rate very few articles of the thousands of available. Since we want to make recommendations based on the few articles a user looks at, we show that when the number of selected terms is few, our approach produces higher quality recommendations than the baseline approach.

Precision and *recall* are widely used measures to evaluate the quality of information retrieval systems. In our experiments, we define quality using precision which is the ratio between number of relevant results returned and the total number of returned results. We choose this measure for the following reasons. The goal of a recommender system is to present a small amount of relevant information from a vast source of information. Therefore, it is more important to return a small number of recommendations that contains relevant items rather than giving the user a large number of recommendations that may contain more relevant recommendations but also requires the user to sift through many irrelevant results. The ratio between the number of relevant results returned and the number of true relevant results is defined as recall. Notice it is possible to have very high recall by making a lot of recommendations. In the research paper recommendation domain, a user will be more interested in reading papers that really qualify for his interests rather than going through a huge list of recommended papers and then selecting those which are of interest. Precision more accurately measures our ability to reach our goal than recall.

Experimental Setup: We divide the data into training and testing sets with 80% used for training and 20% for testing. For our subspace clustering approach, we build subspace clustering models from the training data and for the baseline approach we use the training data to find similar users and make recommendations based on those similar users. During the testing phase, for each user from the test set we take a certain percentage of the items from the test row. We call these *query items*. The rest of the items in the test row are called *hidden items*. We make recommendations (using both approaches) for the user, based on the query items. The list of recommended items is compared with the hidden items and the intersection gives the number of relevant recommendations (results) returned. This forms the basis of our precision measure.

Results and Discussion: The precision curve in Figure 13 shows that we perform better than the baseline approach as we reduce the percentage of query items. As the query items decrease, both relevant recommendations and total recommendations also decrease. In case of our approach using SCuBA, the decrease in relevant recommendations is less than the decrease in total recommendations which is not the case with the baseline approach. Therefore an increase in the precision value is observed. The results validates the discussion presented in Background and Motivation section where it was pointed out that al though the user comparison approach produces very high quality recommendations, it will not perform well in our domain where we would like to make recommendations based on very few query terms. Moreover, user comparison approach does not scale linearly with the number of dimensions as shown in Figure 16. These results also verify the fact that more focused relations are captured using our approach.

The user comparison approach treats users as vectors and computes the similarity between two vectors. The similarity calculations will be poor when there are only a few terms in the test row. In other words, this approach requires large user profiles (similar to e-commerce applications) to generate high quality recommendations which in turn warrants user-tracking and raises pri-

Figure 16. Time comparison of building models with two approaches on MovieLens Dataset

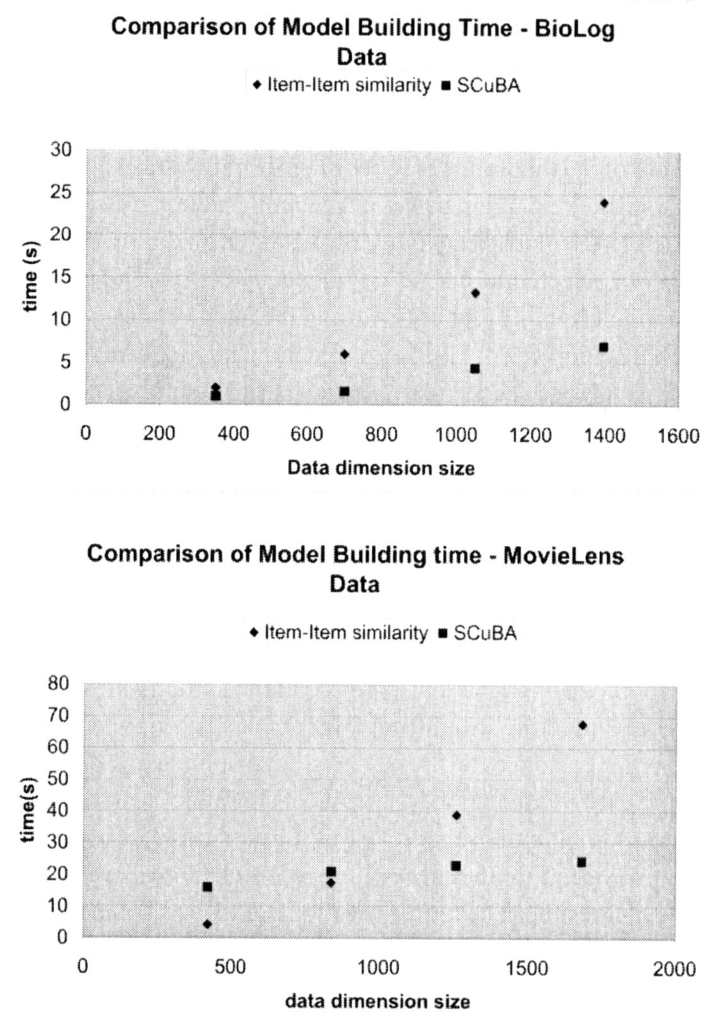

vacy issues. Since SCuBA performs better than the baseline approach for lesser query terms, as shown in the precision curve we can overcome this challenge in our approach. Hence, in our case we do not require user-profiles, which saves the overhead of user-tracking and preserves privacy as well. Moreover, at a given instant, a researcher may be interested in a new research topic(s), and if we use the researcher's previous profile or likings, we will not find relevant articles matching his/her current interest(s).

Model Building Times

In model-based approaches a model is created using item similarity (Deshpande and Karypis, 2004). Since, the complexity of building the similarity table is dependent on the number of items, this approach would be unnecessarily computationally expensive in the research paper domain where we have large number of articles but much smaller number of users. Our proposed solution takes advantage of the small number of users and avoids dependence on the number of items. Hence, we would expect that the time required to build models following the subspace clustering approach would be much less than the above approach in (Deshpande and Karypis, 2004).

Our claim is validated by the results shown in Figure 15 and Figure 16. Here, we measure the time taken to build models from the two data sets used in the experiments. The subspace clustering approach clearly outperforms the item-item similarity approach.

Coverage Results

In this section we present statistics on query coverage of the subspace clustering model. As was discussed earlier, we anticipated that the subspace clustering model will not be able to provide complete coverage of queries and hence we proposed a fall-back model. The results shown in Table 2 validate our hypothesis but more importantly they show that percentage of queries not covered by the subspace clustering model is very low. This means that the fall-back model is rarely used and hence the overall quality of the recommendation will not suffer too much.

The dataset used was the same benchmark dataset, *MovieLens*, used to evaluate the quality of recommendations in subsection on Recommendations from Benchmark data. Here the query length denotes the number of terms considered in the test row. The total number of test rows considered is 188 which is 20% of the complete dataset, 80% of which was used to construct the subspace cluster model. For queries of length 1, there were 16 test rows out of 188 for which no recommendation was made, or the miss percentage is 8.5%. For query lengths greater than 4, miss percentage become zero or some recommendation was made.

Comparing Subspace Cluster Model with Fall-Back Model

In subsection on Fall-Back Model, a fall-back model was introduced which is used when there is no mapping of query terms to the subspace cluster model. In these experiments we try to show that the fall-back model is not a replacement for subspace clustering model. The fall-back model avoids those situations when subspace cluster model fails to make recommendations and it should be used for that purpose only. The experimental setup is same as in subsection on Recommendations from Benchmark data. We compare *Precision* again for both the models, SCuBA as well as the fall-back. The precision curve in Figure 14 shows that SCuBA performs far better than the fall-back model for different values of query terms considered. These results also support the discussion in subsection on Fall-Back Model, the goal of the fall-back model, to provide coverage for query items even if the quality of recommendations is compromised.

RELATED WORK

Recommender systems can be grouped into two broad categories, content based and collaborative filtering. Research paper recommendation systems are mainly content based systems, utilizing a combination of text based analysis as well as the citations of each paper to generate recommendations. Collaborative filtering algorithms have been

Table 2. Percentage of queries that were not covered by the subspace cluster model

Query Length	1	2	3	4	5
Miss Percentage	8.5%	0.5%	0.5%	0.5%	0%

very successful in other domains, however, and their application to research paper recommendation has not been fully explored. Most collaborative filtering systems generate models in order to scale up massive numbers of users and items. We developed SCuBA, based on the principles of subspace clustering, to generate the collaborative filtering models to recommend research papers. This section explores related work in both recommender systems and subspace clustering.

Recommender Systems

In the research paper domain, the *CiteSeer* system utilizes the citation network between papers to find related papers (Bollacker et al., 1998; Giles et al., 1998; Bollacker et al., 1999). *CiteSeer* also utilizes text-based analysis, but as a separate list of recommendations. Bradshaw et. al. combined text based analysis by taking into account how the work was cited (Bradshaw et al., 2000). In *ClaiMaker*, Li et. al. propose a system that analyzes the claims made in a paper (Li et al., 2002). *ClaiMaker* utilizes ontologies to improve the accuracy of the analysis. *Quickstep* and *FoxTrot* both utilize ontologies of research topics to assist in recommending research papers (Middleton et al., 2004). McNee et. al. propose a method to combined the citation network with various existing CF algorithms (McNee et al., 2002).

Collaborative filtering approaches can be divided into user-based and model-based approaches. The nearest neighbor, user-based approaches make recommendations by examine the preferences of similar users. Model-based approaches attempt to improve performance by building models of user and item relationships and using those models to make recommendations.

Early CF systems compare the active user to all of the other users and found the *k* most similar users (Konstan et al., 1997; Sarwar et al., 2000; Shardanand and Maes, 1995). Weights are then assigned to items based on the preferences of the neighborhood of *k* users, using a cosine or correlation function to determine the similarity of users. Recommendations are made using the weighted list of items. The recommendations produced are high quality and the systems are easily able to incorporate new or updated information, but the approaches do not scale well (Schafer et al., 2001). Mobasher (Mobasher et al., 2000) and Ungar (Ungar and Foster, 1998) addressed the issue of performance by comparing the current user to pre-computed clusters of users. Performance was improved, however, the quality of the recommendations suffered.

To overcome the scalability issues, model based systems were developed. These systems pre-build a user or item based model that is used to make recommendations for an active user. There are two major categories of models, user based and item based. Billsus and Pazzani used a neural network approach to model building, which produce high quality recommendations, but was still rather slow (Billsus and Pazzani, 1998). Aggarwal et. al. introduced a graph-based approach where the nodes were users and the edges their similarity. Bayesian probability networks also proved to be useful in building models (Breese et al., 1998). Performance was further improved by using dependency networks (Heckerman et al., 2001).

Two issues of particular interest to research paper recommender systems, and addressed by SCuBA, are the sparsity of data the communities of researchers. Using a bipartite graph, Huang et. al. were able to find transitive associations and alleviate the sparsity problem found in many recommender system datasets (Huang et al., 2004). Hofmann was able to discover user communities and prototypical interest profiles using latent semantic analysis to create compact and accurate reduced-dimensionality model of a community preference space (Hofmann, 2004).

Sarwar et. al. used correlations between items to build models (Sarwar et al., 2001). Taking advantage of the categorical nature of the data, many item based models are based on association rules

(Lin et al., 2000; Mobasher et al., 2000; Demiriz, 2001; Demiriz, 2004). In the most recent, Demiriz borrows from clustering approaches and uses a similarity measure to find rules, instead of an exact match (Demiriz, 2004). Deshpande and Karypis used conditional probability models, used to find higher-order item correlations (Deshpande and Karypis, 2004).

Subspace Clustering Algorithms

Subspace clustering algorithms can be broadly categorized based on their search method, top-down or bottom-up (Parsons et al., 2004). Top down approaches search in the full dimensional space and refine the search through multiple iterations. Searching in all of the dimensions first means they are not well suited for sparse data such as that found with recommender systems. Bottom-up approaches first search for interesting areas in one dimension and build subspaces. This approach is much more suited to sparse datasets where clusters are likely to be found using fewer than 1% of the dimensions.

The prototypical bottom-up algorithm is based on the downward closure property of density. This states that a area that is dense in *n* dimensions must also be dense in all *n*-1 dimensional projections. By combining dense areas in lower dimensional spaces, bottom-up algorithms greatly reduce the higher dimensional search space. *CLIQUE* was the first such algorithm and follows the basic approach (Agrawal et al., 1998). Adaptations to the basic method include *ENCLUS* which uses entropy instead of measuring density directly (Cheng et al., 1999) and *MAFIA* which uses a data-driven adaptive method to form bins (Goil et al., 1999). *CLTree* uses a decision tree algorithm to determine the boundaries of the bins (Liu et al., 2000). *Cell Based Clustering* also attempted to optimize the binning procedure (Chang and Jin, 2002). Another algorithm, DOC, compares randomly selected bins to find those that best define clusters (Procopiuc et al., 2002). Each of these algorithms focuses on continuous valued data and do not perform well on categorical or binary data. Recently there have been subspace clustering algorithms developed for binary (Patrikainen and Manilla, 2004) and categorical data (Peters and Zaki, 2005). The few algorithms designed for both sparse and binary high-dimensional data do not cluster in subspaces of the dataset (Dhillon and Guan, 2003; Ordonez, 2003).

CONCLUSION AND FUTURE WORK

In this paper, we proposed a subspace clustering approach for recommender systems aimed at the research paper domain. A useful source of information when recommending research papers is the reading habits of other researchers who are interested in similar concepts. Thus, we adopted a collaborative filtering approach which allows us to use data collected from other researchers browsing patterns, and avoids issues with the interpretation of content. Such data consists of a small number of users (researchers) and a very large number of items (research papers). Our proposed approach takes advantage of the unique characteristics of the data in this domain and provides a solution which is fast, scalable and produces high quality recommendations. SCuBA has been successfully used in the BioLog project (Singh et al., 2005) as the recommendation component for sparse high-dimensional data.

Existing approaches for recommender systems were developed primarily for e-commerce domains and thus have to deal with a large and ever increasing user base. These approaches use models based on either item/item comparisons or based on finding users groups of similar users. Creating an item/item matrix is unnecessarily expensive, since the number of users is so small in comparison to the huge number of research papers, and thus must often be done o²ine. User/user models address this when the number of users is small. However, existing approaches use a nearest neighbor approach comparing users across the entire dimensionality of the dataset (all items). This requires that the target user be defined by extensive profile information. Our system finds similar users in subspaces of the dataset, each representing a particular area of interest. This allows us to make recommendations based on as few as a single query item. This has the advantage of allowing us to adapt our recommendations to the immediate, short-term interests of the user.

In order to improve the perceived quality and usefulness of the recommendations, a ranking scheme could be developed as an extension to the algorithm. This scheme could rank the recommendations in order of the likelihood they would be useful. The algorithm could also be extended to include the subjective user ratings rather than treating them as binary values and categorize recommendations under strong, mediocre and weak recommendations. A lot of work has been done in mixing the two models, content based filtering and collaborative filtering, to generate a hybrid model which tries to enhance the recommendation quality and also solve the Cold-Start problem for the case where there are no user preferences at all (Schein et al., 2002). This could be one of the future directions that can be pursued from the work in this paper.

REFERENCES

Agrawal, R., Gehrke, J., Gunopulos, D., and Raghavan, P. (1998). Automatic subspace clustering of high dimensional data for data mining applications. In *Proceedings of the 1998 ACM SIGMOD International Conference on Management of Data*, pages 94-105. ACM Press.

Billsus, D. and Pazzani, M. J. (1998). Learning collaborative information filters. In *Proceedings of the Fifteenth International Conference on Machine Learning*, pages 46-54. Morgan Kaufmann Publishers Inc.

Bollacker, K., Lawrence, S., and Giles, C. L. (1998). CiteSeer: An autonomous Web agent for automatic retrieval and identification of interesting publications. In Sycara, K. P. and Wooldridge, M., editors, *Proceedings of the Second International Conference on Autonomous Agents*, pages 116-123, New York. ACM Press.

Bollacker, K., Lawrence, S., and Giles, C. L. (1999). A system for automatic personalized tracking of scientific literature on the Web. In *Digital Libraries 99 - The Fourth ACM Conference on Digital Libraries*, pages 105-113, New York. ACM Press.

Bradshaw, S., Scheinkman, A., and Hammond, K. J. (2000). Guiding people to information: providing an interface to a digital library using reference as a basis for indexing. In *Intelligent User Interfaces*, pages 37-43.

Breese, J. S., Heckerman, D., and Kadie, C. (1998). Empirical analysis of predictive algorithms for collaborative filtering. In *In Proceedings of the 14th Conference on Uncertainty in Artificial Intelligence.*

Chang, J.-W. and Jin, D.-S. (2002). A new cell-based clustering method for large, high-dimensional data in data mining applications. In *Proceedings of the 2002 ACM symposium on Applied computing*, pages 503-507. ACM Press.

Cheng, C.-H., Fu, A. W., and Zhang, Y. (1999). Entropy-based subspace clustering for mining numericaldata. In *Proceedings of the fifth ACM SIGKDD International Conference on Knowledge discovery and data mining*, pages 84-93. ACM Press.

Demiriz, A. (2001). An association mining-based product recommender. In *In NFORMS Miami 2001 Annual Meeting Cluster: Data Mining.*

Demiriz, A. (2004). Enhancing product recommender systems on sparse binary data. *Data Min. Knowl. Discov.*, 9(2):147-170.

Deshpande, M. and Karypis, G. (2004). Item-based top-n recommendation algorithms. *ACM Trans. Inf. Syst.*, 22(1):143-177.

Dhillon, I. S. and Guan, Y. (2003). Information theoretic clustering of sparse co-occurrence data. In *Proceedings of the third International Conference on Data mining*. IEEE Press.

Giles, C. L., Bollacker, K. D., and Lawrence, S. (1998). CiteSeer: an automatic citation indexing system. In *Proceedings of the third ACM conference on Digital libraries*, pages 89-98. ACM Press.

Goil, S., Nagesh, H., and Choudhary, A. (1999). Mafia: E±cient and scalable subspace clustering for very large data sets. Technical Report CPDC-TR-9906-010, Northwestern University, 2145 Sheridan Road, Evanston IL 60208.

Heckerman, D., Chickering, D. M., Meek, C., Rounthwaite, R., and Kadie, C. (2001). Dependency networks for inference, collaborative filtering, and data visualization. *J. Mach. Learn. Res.*, 1:49-75.

Herlocker, J. L., Konstan, J. A., Terveen, L. G., and Riedl, J. T. (2004). Evaluating collaborative filtering recommender systems. *ACM Trans. Inf. Syst.*, 22(1):5-53.

Hofmann, T. (2004). Latent semantic models for collaborative filtering. *ACM Trans. Inf. Syst.*, 22(1):89-115.

Huang, Z., Chen, H., and Zeng, D. (2004). Applying associative retrieval techniques to alleviate the sparsity problem in collaborative filtering. *ACM Trans. Inf. Syst.*, 22(1):116-142.

Konstan, J. A., Miller, B. N., Maltz, D., Herlocker, J. L., Gordon, L. R., and Riedl, J. (1997). Grouplens: applying collaborative filtering to usenet news. *Commun. ACM*, 40(3):77-87.

Li, G., Uren, V., Motta, E., Buckingham-Shum, S., and Domingue, J. (2002). Claimaker: Weaving a semantic Web of research papers. In *Proceedings of the 1st International Semantic Web Conference, Sardinia, June 2002.*

Lin, C., Alvarez, S., and Ruiz, C. (2000). Collaborative recommendation via adaptive association rule

mining. In *In Proceedings of the International Workshop on Web Mining for E-Commerce (WEBKDD*

2000).

Liu, B., Xia, Y., and Yu, P. S. (2000). Clustering through decision tree construction. In *Proceedings of the ninth International Conference on Information and Knowledge Management*, pages 20-29. ACM Press.

McNee, S. M., Albert, I., Cosley, D., Gopalkrishnan, P., Lam, S. K., Rashid, A. M., Konstan, J. A., and Riedl, J. (2002). On the recommending of citations for research papers. In *Proceedings of the 2002 ACM Conference on Computer supported cooperative work*, pages 116-125. ACM Press.

Middleton, S. E., Shadbolt, N. R., and Roure, D. C. D. (2004). Ontological user profiling in recommender systems. *ACM Trans. Inf. Syst.*, 22(1):54-88.

Mobasher, B., Cooley, R., and Srivastava, J. (2000). Automatic personalization based on Web usage mining. *Commun. ACM*, 43(8):142-151.

Ordonez, C. (2003). Clustering binary data streams with k-means. In *Proceedings of the 8th ACM SIGMOD workshop on Research issues in data mining and knowledge discovery*, pages 12-19. ACM Press.

Parsons, L., Haque, E., and Liu, H. (2004). Subspace clustering for high dimensional data: a review. *SIGKDD Explorations.*, 6(1):90-105.

Patrikainen, A. and Manilla, H. (2004). Subspace clustering of high-dimensional binary data - a probabilistic approach. In *Workshop on*

Clustering High Dimensional Data and its Applications, SIAM International Conference on Data Mining.

Peters, M. and Zaki, M. J. (2005). Clicks: Clustering categorical data using k-partite maximal cliques. In *IEEE International Conference on Data Engineering*. IEEE.

Procopiuc, C. M., Jones, M., Agarwal, P. K., and Murali, T. M. (2002). A monte carlo algorithm for fast projective clustering. In *Proceedings of the 2002 ACM SIGMOD International Conference on Management of Data*, pages 418-427. ACM Press.

Resnick, P. and Varian, H. R. (1997). Recommender systems. *Commun. ACM*, 40(3):56-58.

Sarwar, B., Karypis, G., Konstan, J., and Reidl, J. (2001). Item-based collaborative filtering recommendation algorithms. In *Proceedings of the tenth International Conference on World Wide Web*, pages 285-295. ACM Press.

Sarwar, B., Karypis, G., Konstan, J., and Riedl, J. (2000). Analysis of recommendation algorithms for e-commerce. In *Proceedings of the 2nd ACM Conference on Electronic commerce*, pages 158-167. ACM Press.

Schafer, J. B., Konstan, J. A., and Riedl, J. (2001). E-commerce recommendation applications. *Data Mining and Knowledge Discovery*, 5(1/2):115-153.

Schein, A., Popescul, A., Ungar, L., and Penncok, D. (2002). Methods and metrics for cold-start recom mendations. In *Proceedings of the 25th Annual International ACM SIGIR Conference on Research and Development in Information Retrieval (SIGIR 2002).*

Shardanand, U. and Maes, P. (1995). Social information filtering: algorithms for automating word of mouth. In *Proceedings of the SIGCHI Conference on Human factors in computing systems*, pages 210-217. ACM Press/Addison-Wesley Publishing Co.

Singh, P., Bhimavarapu, R., Davalcu, H., Baral, C., Kim, S., Liu, H., Bittner, M., and Ramakrishnan, I. (2005). Biolog: A browser based collaboration and resource navigation assistant for biomedical researchers. In *Proceedings of 2nd International Workshop on Data Integration in the Life Sciences (DILS'05).*

Ungar, L. H. and Foster, D. P. (1998). Clustering methods for collaborative filtering. In *In Workshop on Recommendation Systems at the 15th National Conference on Artificial Intelligence.*

This work was previously published in Int. Journal of Information Technology and Web Engineering, Vol. 1, Issue 1, edited by G. Alkhatib and D. Rine, pp. 35-58, copyright 2006 by IGI Publishing (an imprint of IGI Global).

Chapter VII
E-Portfolio to Promote the Virtual Learning Group Communities on the Grid

Emilie Conté
Université de Pau et des Pays de l'Adour, France

Guy Gouardères
Université de Pau et des Pays de l'Adour, France

ABSTRACT

In Vocational and Educational Training, new trends are to social learning and more precisely to informal learning. In such settings, the article introduces a process - the e-Qualification - to manage informal learning on the "Learning Grid". It argues that this process must occur in a social context such as Virtual Communities. On the one hand, it describes their necessary characteristics and proprieties, which lead to the creation of a new kind of virtual community: the Virtual Learning Grid Community. On the other hand, e-qualification cannot occur without the help of a kind of user's profile, which is called e-Portfolio. Moreover, the e-Portfolio is also a process, which is used to manage the Virtual Learning Grid Communities. The e-Qualification and the Virtual Learning Grid Communities' management will probably rely on the co-operation of different distributed, autonomous, goal-oriented entities, which are Mobile Peer-to-Peer Agents. Furthermore, the authors hope that implementing these services will decrease the lacks of informal learning treatment on the Grid and will become the bases for new services on the Learning Grid.

INTRODUCTION

The continuous development of new technologies has brought new perspectives for more advanced and enhanced learning services. One example is the emerging of the Grid Computing.

According to Foster (2003), " Grid computing has emerged as an important new field, distinguished from conventional distributed computing by its focus on large-scale resource sharing, innovative applications, and, in some cases, high-performance orientation. (….) The "Grid problem," which we define as flexible, secure, co-ordinated resource sharing among dynamic collections of individuals, institutions, and resources-what we refer to as virtual organizations."

The Globus Alliance, which is a community of organizations and individuals developing fundamental technologies behind the «Grid», has defined the Open Grid Services Architecture (OGSA). This is a Service-Oriented architecture for the Grid Model of a computing system and is the current standard for the Grid middlewares and services.

The Semantic Grid is an extension of the current Grid in which information and services are given well-defined meaning, better enabling computers and people to work in co-operation. According to De Roure (2003), "the Semantic Grid is characterised as an open system in which users, software, components and computational resources (all owned by different stakeholders) come and go on a continual basis."

According to Allison & al. (2002), "From the perspective of good educational practice an online collaborative learning environment should provide certain features for learners, like group-work support, interactive, engaging, responsive, real-world input, student-centred, anytime/anywhere."

Those pedagogical goals imply a radical change of the technical requirements and bring forward a new design for the semantic Grid in which "social learning" will be of paramount importance.

In such settings, the European Learning Grid Infrastructure (ELeGI) project has the ambitious goal to develop software technologies for effective human learning (Dimitrakos & al., 2004). ELeGI has chosen a synergic approach, sometimes called "human centred design", to replace the classical, applicative approach to learning. In this approach, learning occurs as a side effect of interactions, conversations and enhanced presence in dynamic Virtual Communities. Two kinds of learning are pointed out: formal learning versus informal learning. According to Allison (2005), Informal learning groups are ad hoc temporary clusters of students within a single work session. Informal learning groups can be initiated, for example, by asking students to spend two minutes discussing a question or problem posed by the teacher. In this case some students gather in order to solve the question or problem. In this way, the informal learning groups form with the only purpose to solve the posed problematic situation and their life expectancy is limited to the work session. In Vocational and Educational Training – VET–, informal learning refers to what the user learns during the debriefings in groups.

Nowadays, there is a real lack of tools able to manage informal learning. Our major research objective is to define a process able to point out what the learner has acquired through an informal way and to guide the learner according to this new information. This process is called e-Qualification and cannot occur without introducing new suitable tools which are the e-Portfolio and the Virtual Learning Grid Community -VLGC.

In the context of the learning Grid, the e-Qualification process becomes mandatory to qualify users and the provided services.

E-qualification cannot occur without using the Peer-to-Peer communication mode. According to Schollmeier (2001), "a distributed network architecture may be called a Peer-to-Peer (P-to-P,

P2P,.) Network, if the participants share a part of their own hardware resources (processing power, storage capacity, network link capacity, printers,). These shared resources are necessary to provide the Service and content offered by the network (e.g. file sharing or shared workspaces for collaboration). They are accessible by other peers directly, without passing intermediary entities. The participants of such a network are thus resource (Service and content) providers as well as resource (Service and content) requestors (Servant-concept)."

Our purpose in this article is to argue that these new tools are mandatory to perform the e-Qualification process and so to manage informal learning. Note that our activities are specific to VET, where informal learning has a real importance in the learning process.

Agents possess attractive features including autonomy, proactiveness, intelligence; social ability and mentalist characterization can be used to build advanced distributed systems. So, Multi Agents System suits the best to the Grid and we will detail their use in our works on the Grid.

This paper is structured in five sections. The first one details the context in which e-Qualification occurs. The two following sections deal with VLGCs and e-Portfolio. Then, we focus on the agents' work. We end by an application of the e-Qualification process to the Use Case ASIMIL (Aero user friendly SIMulation based dIstant Learning) which is a training flight simulator.

CONTEXT

In the ELeGI learning vision, the learner is an active actor in the learning process and his knowledge construction occurs through conversations, collaboration and direct experience in a social context. Informal learning can only occurs in social cases (Eisenstadt & al., 2005). So, Virtual Communities are the best place to support discussions, "informal learning". Virtual communities are social aggregations that emerge from the net when enough people carry on these public discussions long enough, with sufficient human feeling, to form Webs of personal relationships in cyberspace (Rheingold, 1993).

We will take into consideration students who are working into virtual communities. Qualification is the passage from a knowledge state to another one, which occurs before assessment. e-Qualification is a mandatory process to continuously evaluate users during their learning process.

We can define the e-Qualification as a three-step process which (a) identifies the new knowledge, skills, etc. (learned by formal and informal ways), (b) updates the learner's "profile" and (c) places him into the virtual community that suits the best to its previous needs and upgraded skills. Note that in a learning process, each user has a profile to store its personal information, skills, knowledge, evolution, etc. Moreover, the e-Qualification process must continuously occur to be more efficient: a user who is always in a suitable Virtual Community learns faster that a user who "waits" an important change in his profile to be oriented toward the suitable Virtual Community. So e-Qualification is also a process that continuously identifies and qualifies the users' improvements.

The e-Qualification guiding principle is:

- Each user has a profile and must belong to at least a virtual community. (There is always a kind of "basic virtual community" in which every user is authorised to belong to.)
- Each user is continuously qualified: the process identifies his new skills and knowledge before, after and during exercises.
- When the Virtual Community does not well suit to the user's profile, the process looks for a new one and integrates the user into it.

Of course, users are not the sole actors of this process: he cannot continuously update its profile, check whether he matches with his virtual community, argue to enter in another virtual community. This is the agents' work. Therefore, a Multi Agents System is implemented to carry out e-Qualification and to manage virtual communities.

Regarding the previous statements, the user's profile is a major tool, which allows the user to integrate (or not) a community. Agents use this one to perform e-Qualification and manage virtual communities. It is no more just a profile. It is a real tool for working, the user workspace, which must be accessible and understood by the agents. We call it the e-Portfolio, which is described in section 4 and must not be mixed up with the general terms "portfolio" or "eportfolio".

Having introduced the context of e-Qualification, we can now focus on the heart of the article's topic: the creation of specific virtual communities on the Grid and of the e-Portfolio, which are two mandatory tools to manage informal learning.

VIRTUAL LEARNING GRID COMMUNITY

ELeGI project has defined its own definition of Virtual Learning Community –VLC. The § 3.1 deals with ELeGi projet's beliefs and their choices for VLC. Then, in § 3.2, we explain why this definition does not suit for e-Qualification. Therefore, we introduce the Virtual Learning Grid Community.

Virtual Learning Community (VLC)

According to Garber (2004): " To be a learning community, participants must be committed to the learning process, and responsive to the contributions of other participants through "reciprocity" based on trust between the community members. ".

According to Schwier (2004): "a virtual learning community is a particular type of virtual learning environment. Virtual learning environments happen when the process of learning takes place outside the boundaries of face-to-face contact, typically online. But environments are not necessarily communities. For a community to emerge, a learning environment must allow learners to engage each other intentionally and collectively in the transaction or transformation of knowledge".

In the rest of this paragraph, we refer to the ELeGI project's choices for VLGC with some quotations.

VLC are design in order to allow collaborative learning. "The term "collaborative learning" refers to an instruction method in which learners at various performance levels work together in small groups toward a common goal. The collaborative learning is a teaching strategy in which "both teachers and learners are active participants in the learning process; knowledge is not something that is delivered to students in this process, but something that emerges from active dialogue among those who seek to understand and apply concepts and techniques." (Burgstahler & Swift 1996). (...) The collaborative learning is also a democratic process, in which all the participants are equal and are treated like that, playing a role that is valued by everyone of them. "

ELeGi project treats the two kinds of learning: informal versus formal. It says that "the informal group is characterized by a specific task related to a single work session, on the contrary the formal group typologies are specific for task with longer duration. For this reason the informal groups can be constituted by a limited number of persons of same class that develop in the same moment, the same task. This group is only limited to the single session and it dissolves when the session finishes. (...) So is not necessary to define a specific structure within the group, they can be generated in random way and it is enough the presence of tutor, who support and facilitate the collaborative learning."

Regarding this last quotation, it is clear that ELeGI project 's VLCs are only designed for formal learning.

Virtual Learning Group Community (VLGC)

As quoted before, the collaborative learning is a democratic process, in which all the participants are equal and treated like that. But in ELeGI project's definition, a VLC contains several types of members such as visitor, reader, member, learner and a technical chief administrator. It is not convenient for pure informal learning, because users have not to ask the permission to freely discuss. Therefore, our VLC cannot have an administrator and the different members must not be categorised: they are just members.

Making reference to VET, informal debriefing groups are some « groups of qualification »: each trainee qualifies his work according to the discussions he has with others and the prerequisite in his e-Portfolio. These groups are more than VLCs, they are groups in which each member has the same « rights »; there is no longer any distinction between trainees, instructors or tutors.

So the ELeGI Project's VLC definition cannot be efficient to make informal collaborative learning. This process does not allow centralisation (e.g. even if a «virtual KapelMeister» acting as Super Peer will do it - Airlines' pilots don't accept). That explains why we must use the Peer-to-Peer communication mode, which is decentralised.

Training Centers do not work like schools. Informal and Formal Training are done alternatively with real life practice. And so, informal learning cannot be seen as a limited period. It is « life long » training.

Moreover, VLC are designed for formal learning. They are built to answer to precept objectives (e.g. succeed in exercise 1). We cannot define these objectives in the context of informal learning.

Finally we opt to define the Virtual Learning Group Community (VLGC) adapted to informal learning and more precisely, to informal learning in Vocational and Educational Training. A VLGC can be defined as a VLC in which all members are equal (implemented on a Peer-to-Peer way) and which have some global objectives and continuously evolve.

The User Representation

Each user has at least one representative agent and its Behaviour (past, present & future), knowledge, skills and goals are stored in an e-Portfolio.

More than a storage tool, the e-Portfolio is a real process that is not only used during the "regular learning process". It is made up of a personal part and a shared one. Sharing notion is really important: if the user learns with speaking with other users, he also learns with looking at their e-Portfolio.

The agents must be able to communicate together and to understand an e-portfolio. Regarding the ubiquity of the GRID, we must use a common « architecture » to allow communication between agents (that may be implemented in different languages).

One piece of solution is the use of Ontology, which consists of a set of concepts and relationships that describes an area of interest. "The role of an ontology, is considered as a set of logical axioms designed to account for the intended meaning of a vocabulary" (Guarino, 1998).

Let us assume a global ontology, which contains all the existing concepts (for a given area) and which is understood by all agents. Personal e-Portfolio contains a « functional ontology », which is a view of this global ontology and which depends on the user's category (a mechanic has not the same fontional ontology as a pilot; but their two functional ontologies are built according to the global one).

In informal learning, the notion of personalization is very important. So the e-portfolio's ontology is made up of two kinds of ontology: a User Modeling Ontology and a Goal Driven one. The user modeling ontology contains the skills, knowledge, personal information, results, etc. and really depends on the user (because the architecture of the ontology depends on the user's category). The Goal Driven one contains all the user's objectives and the process to attain these ones.

The Membership to a VLGC

Let us remind that the members of a VLGC must target some common goals. These goals are more important than the personal ones. The achievement of their group objectives must not be an hindrance to reach their personal objectives. A major principle is that each member has the same rights and all decisions are made according the group's thinking and the group 's objectives.

A VLGC is represented at two levels. The first level is a high one: users are grouped and work together (learning activity). We will take care on the second one: the representative agents that are managing VLGCs.

The multitude of activities that the learner can simultaneously perform implies that we have to give each learner the possibility to belong to several VLGCs. But we distinguish "Strong" membership to "weak" one. A user cannot "strongly" belong to several VLGCs. He "strongly" belongs to one VLGC, and "weakly" belongs to some others VLGCs (if he needs it).

To belong to a VLGC, the user must share some common knowledge, abilities, needs and goals with the VLGC's members. This common information defines the signature of the e-Portfolio. (Note that we can extract several signatures from an e-Portfolio).

So, the signature is an extract of e-Portfolio, which depends on the VLGC the user belongs to. It is a service provided by the e-Portfolio and stored in each user e-Portfolio. More precisely, each member's signature has the same "shared ontology" but of course, the content is personalised (e.g.: it is impossible that every member have succeeded in a same exercise with the same note). A basic level has to be defined too.

The signature of a VLGC determines in part who is allowed to integrate the community or not.

We define the VLGC signature as:

- the intersection of the members' ontology architecture (so a student cannot integrate a mechanics' VLGC, because he has not the same ontology architecture)
- Some common objectives and minimum level and skills that the user already has (we consider here the content of the ontology).

So, e-Portfolio contains a functional ontology and provides several signatures that are also stored into it.

It is an essential service to made e-qualification because it is the basic tool for agents to manage VLGC.

The VLGC's Life Cycle

The VLGC life cycle is made up of 4 phases: creation, operation, evolution and dissolution.

Creation

At the creation of a learning/training domain, there must exist at least one community: the beginning VLGC, which contains all the learners. Regarding the P2P communication model, a sole administrator cannot create a VLGC; it must emerge from the decision of a whole group. Each VLGC is a real entity and has a signature, which is regularly updated.

The creation of a new VLGC occurs when a user wants to reach a particular goal but is refused by all the VLGCs. Then, if another user accepts to work with him, they can decide to form a new VLGC. The VLGC's signature is established according to the needs and abilities of the two members.

As soon as the VLGC is created, its signature will change according either to the content of new members' e-Portfolio or to the evolution of the objectives of the VLGC's members.

Operation

There are three possible operations in a VLGC:

- Integration of a new member
- Work, communication
- Exit of a member.

The integration of a member is based on the use of signature. It results from a communication between agents. The representative agent of the learner who wants to integrate the community enters in communication with one member agent. This agent will give him the signature's ontology. Here, we can see the real utility of the ontology: the learner agent knows what he has to extract from his e-Portfolio to try an overlay. Then, they try it. If the overlay succeeds (with a predefined tolerance), the two agents will discuss the different conditions to enter into this community. As soon as he has integrated the community, the agent who has authorised this entrance informs the VLGC. This step is called "notification" (or "sonnet").

A member has to quit a community when his signature does not match anymore with the VLGC's one. His agent has to inform the whole members that he quits the community (sonnet).

As soon as the VLGC's signature is updated, the whole VLGC is informed. Each member agents has to regularly check if its signature matches with the VLGC's one. Some rules must be fixed to be sure that every member is always « right on mark » in his community. We impose that a comparison between the member agents' signatures occurs when:

- A change of the VLGC's signature occurs.
- the user has performed an exercise and has made progress (change of level). The contrary runs too: if the user 's level has decreased, he can be fired.
- the user has no more common goals with the group, he must quit the VLGC.
- the user has a new objective which can not be reached within this VLGC, he can search for a new one (with a new signature) and decide whether he leaves this one, according to his other objectives and needs. Do not forget that every user can belong to several VLGCs.

Evolution

The major difficulty is to determine if some members have to quit the VLGC or if the VLGC has to evolve. This situation can occur in two cases:

- When a sonnet indicates that a new member has integrated the VLGC. Agents discuss about what this member can bring to the VLGC and choose whether they update the signature (adding for example new objectives).
- When a member has progressed and if his signature does not match anymore with the VLGC's one. He can suppose that he is not the only one who has evolved and contact the other agents to speak about his new skills and knowledge. Then, if a great part of the VLGC has the same new skills, members can vote and decide to update the VLGC's signature.

Dissolution

A VLGC disappears when it contains only a member (or none). This last member must move in another VLGC.

E-Portfolio

A short definition of e-Portfolio has already been given in the §3.3 in order to detail the VLGC management. Let us remind what our e-Portfolio is composed of:

- A functional ontology, which contains the knowledge, skills, personal data, exercises, results, goals, etc., of the learner. This Ontology is made up of a User Modeling Ontology and a Goal Driven one. Note that the functional ontology infers from a global ontology, which is known and understood by all agents.
- Some signatures, which are extracts of the e-Portfolio's Ontology and allow the user to belong to one or several VLGC.

We will now study the dynamicity of our e-Portfolio. But first, we quote some generalities about portfolios.

The key concept of a virtual community usually involves the notion of shared knowledge, goals, and intentions that function as a common binding to team members. This can be achieved by a new design for the former portfolio or Electronic Portfolio. The e-Portfolio is a way of learning as a social activity and it is a tool for developing one's own knowledge and competencies and a kind of virtual representation of oneself. The student's ability to learn as well as his ability to share his knowledge with others and his ability to get feedback from others are also encountered.

The e-Portfolio is not just a tool but a service that helps the student to learn into a VLGC.

An e-portfolio is a repository of data and process (*e*lectronically stored) that facilitates reflective and critical thinking and may be used for collaboration or (self-) assessment and reflection by individuals and groups.

The My.Step.Stanford project (Vanides, 2002) develops special purpose softwares which provide a secure environment and structured as "ubiquitous, portable, electronic knowledge databases that are private, personalized and shareable, and are easily accessible via the Web"'. An electronic portfolio uses electronic or digital technologies that enable the portfolio developer to collect and organize portfolio artifacts in a variety of media: text, audio and graphic files, video clips, html files, hypermedia presentations and digitised photos.

The "Learning Grid" paradigm and the associate ELEGI infrastructure allow to go thoroughly by throwing the user into a Web learning workspace and a pervasive virtual learning world on the semantic grid (Allison & al., 2004)

The current my.Step prototype offers the following features (Vanides & al., 2002):

1. Ease of access both on campus and off campus.
2. Privacy is by default.
3. The data can be organized and cross-referenced according to multiple categories.
4. Supports for the sharing of learning artifacts with other members of the Learning Careers community.
5. As the content grows, a summary of the contents ("what's new") will give an overview of the E-Folio at a glance.
6. Different forms of storage media including audio files, digital pictures, video, and text in one virtual space.
7. The most recent entries are kept in a prominent location.
8. Supports for reflective activities.

Components can include a wide range of information: personal information, education history, recognition (awards and certificates), reflective comments, Coursework (assignment, projects), Instructor comments, previous employer comments, goals, plans, personal values and interests, presentations, papers, personal activities (volunteer work), professional development and all of the artifacts included shall have a purpose (demonstrating a skill, an attribute, and learning acquired from experience).

The introduction of Virtual Communities for Social Learning (i.e. Informal Learning in Vocational and Educational Training) needs very collaborative tools, which add an additional dimension to electronic portfolios. Allowing learners to interact with instructors, other learners, and mentors provides a more open social learning, based on virtual communities of practice (Zhang & al., 2005) designed by their proper class of portfolio.

This model is both individual and shared. It is shared because of the collaboration with the other members into the VLGC. And, at the same time, the e-portfolio reveals the user's abilities and skills by performing e-Qualification and so comparing him with other users.

Some have suggested that this Virtual Competency Group concept can be replaced by a concept of "lifetime personal Web page" (Cohn and Hibbitts, 2004): "The virtual structure could consist of multiple cells with flexible entrance points. It would allow connections between internal cells, as well as seamless connections to external entities (Web based courses, mentors, peer reviewers, libraries, and so forth)."

Our e-Portfolio offers the following features:

- The e-Portfolio is viewed as a real-time Process based on ontologies and managed by mobile P2P Agents. It is the main tool for both the formal and the informal learning and the e-Qualification process.
- Learners are introduced to formal learning sessions in VET (Virtual Lab, simulators,) by the Briefing stage. During this Briefing, instructors teach their know-how to trainees.
- Agents update e-Portfolios when the learners are completing their course work and assignments.
- Both the e-Portfolio and Teams of Agents are used for e-assessment of learning objectives and pedagogical issues and for updating the learner assignment to a new group of competence (VLGC). Instructor feedback can also be integrated back into the e-Portfolio by the Agent and treated as an artifact.
- The e-Qualification continuously occurs and so e-Portfolios are continuously used and evaluated.
- Learners continuously advising in VLGC evaluating their effective use of e-Portfolios (this is a meta-cognitive evaluation of portfolio use)

Dialogues, debates, discussions into VLGC are supported by mobile P2P agents to maintain the correct assignment of a user into his suited Group.

In the following paragraph we detail the mobile P2P agents ' work.

THE PEER TO PEER AGENTS

According to Ferber (1999), "an agent can be a physical or virtual entity that can act, perceive its environment (in a partial way) and communicate with others, is autonomous and has skills to achieve its goals and tendencies. It is in a multi-agent system (MAS) that contains an environment, objects and agents (the agents being the only ones to act), relations between all the entities, a set of operations that can be performed by the entities and the changes of the universe in time and due to these actions."

Agents communicate in a P2P mode in order to work in a decentralized way.

Usually, in a closed environment, some internal solutions are used to allow agents working in a P2P mode depending on the MAS they are working on. But in our case, programmer could not use his own solution (allowing agents to operate in a peer behaviour) because we have no guarantee that it will well work with other programmers solutions. So, we face two problems 1) we couldn't impose a common P2P mechanism for all the agents in our project, 2) we couldn't allow agents to use their own P2P mechanisms.

We propose to separate the two aspects (Agents and P2P) and to use a high level conceptual model for the P2P behaviour that shall be adopted by all the agents of our project. Our conceptual model is a set of conditions that shall be satisfied by agents in order to became PeerAgents (Agent that behaves in a P2P mode). Each agent could implement these requirements at a low level with any programming language. Separating the two parts (Agents, P2P) provides more flexibility and offers a work with a high level of abstraction that can be used on a large scale.

We distinguish two types of requirements. The first contains functional ones, including creating and sending a request message. The second type contains what we call "non functional requirement", including the way to use results found in the answers, and the possibility for agents to use the research tool even when they are in private networks. Let us enumerate all the requirements that must be satisfied by P2P agents to work in an open environment as the GRID (Gouarderes G., Mansour S. & al. 2005).

APPLICATION

The e-Qualification Process

E-Qualification is a way to determine the transition from a state of knowledge to another one. This process allows every learner to be « right on mark » in his VLGC. The goal is to « qualify » the level and needs of a learner and to replace him into the good community.

E-Qualification can occur in two cases:

- A student has made a specific error. The agent will assist the user to find a community that can help him.

Figure 1. Requirements for Agents

Requirement type	*Description of the requirement*
	Requirement for allowing agents to search in a P2P manner.
Functional	Creating and sending a research request.
Functional	Receiving an answer of the research request sent.
Non Functional	Using the information found in the answer.
Non Functional	Being able to send requests and receive messages even behind a firewall and in a secure private network.
	Requirement for agents to create and join VLGC
Functional	Creating a Virtual Community (VLGC).
Functional	Joining a VLGC.
Non Functional	Adding a security access mechanisms for created VLGC
Non Functional	Being able to join secure VLGC
	Requirement for agents to advertise their knowledge and services
Functional	Advertising capabilities, services and other information
Functional	Understanding
Non Functional	Being able to hide some private information, services ...
	Requirement for agents to communicate with other peers
Functional	Communicating with other peers (Agents or not).
Non Functional	Being able to communicate in "One to One" mode.
Non Functional	Being able to communicate in "One to Many" mode.

- A student wants to learn something specific.

In the two cases, the integration of a trainee into a community results from a communication between agents.

- Step 1: The user's representative agent broadcasts the trainee's signature to the whole communities (into the area of the training distributed software). It is not the currently signature, it is just a kind of "pre-signature" which indicates what kind of VLGC he searches.
- Step 2: If a Peer strongly guesses that this signature could match with his community's one, he will try to establish a conversation with him. To communicate, they have to use the same ontology. So, the peer who wants to enter in communication with the candidate must send him the ontology of his VLGC's signature. The candidate's representative peer extracts a new signature (according to the ontology he has received. This is the "real signature"). Then, when the conversation has been established, they will make an "overlay" of their two corresponding signatures which is called "the mirror effect". If the overlay is quite good, the trainee can integrate the community of the second one but this can not occur without a prerequisite negotiation. Note that the trainee can communicate with several peers and choose the best overlay.
- Step 3: During this step, the two peers are discussing the conditions for the trainee to integrate the community. If they come up to a trust, the student is accepted into this community.
- Step 4: An alarm indicating that someone has entered the community (Gap bridged successfully between two P2P communities) is sent.

e-Qualification in ASIMIL

Let us consider ASIMIL (Aero user friendly SIMulation based dIstant Learning, N° IST-1999-11286. FP5 http://www.cordis.lu/ist/projects.htmhttp://www.asimil.com) project as our Test Bed for e-

Qualification

ASIMIL, a networked distributed simulator training system is currently a Web-based application. In a first go, we will present the current version to reveal its shortcomings. Then we will focus on the new version, which integrates the e-Qualification process.

Description of ASIMIL

The experimental framework for the ASIMIL Training system is made up of 5 main components:

- A simulator : allows the trainee to performs exercises in "almost real" conditions,
- A Procedures Follow-up Component (PFC) : provides the text of the procedures (kind of "to-do list"),
- The Multi Agent System (MAS): helps the trainee and provides a suited evaluation of the session (with messages and advices at the end of the session). This MAS architecture is called ASITS (Actor Specification for Intelligent Tutoring Systems) (Gouardères, 2000) and is directly adapted from ACTORS (Frasson & al., 1996) by including a cognitive architecture based on ACT-R/PM that specify the role of the cognitive resources in the high level cognitive tasks and adopt proposals exchanged at the time of a conversation.
- Virtual Reality: improves the trainee's sensations,

- Online assistance: connects the trainee to the instructor (on the Web).

Each training session contains three phases: briefing, simulation and debriefing. Of course, each learner has a profile, which is updated according to its performances. This profile is divided into six categories: Trainee, Strategy, History, Curriculum, Exercise, Errors and Tolerance. This profile is stored into a database.

This trainee table contains trainee personal data: name, date of birth, address etc., but also information on course trainee recorded in (flight or maintenance), frequency of using system by trainee, information on pedagogical strategy to adopt (free or guided mode) focusing on number, gravity and frequency of errors.

Errors are classified into three categories: knowledge, ergonomic and psychology according to their origins in order to offer the best management as possible.

The use of this method is based on the analysis of the user's history. This does not occur during the debriefing but also in real time (to stop the trainee when he makes a too dangerous error, etc.) The MAS ensures the immediate and the delayed feedback on the trainee's actions. There is a real work of tracking. They have to constantly look for errors. There are 6 kinds of agents:

- An interface agent that is used as bridge between the MAS and the other components of Asimil
- An error detector agent that detects the errors made by the trainee
- Some error evaluator agents that make a quantitative evaluation of the trainee's errors.
- A pedagogical agent that realizes a qualitative evaluation of the trainee's errors formulates the teaching's intervention and stores the obtained trace in the curriculum agent's memory.
- A curriculum agent that stores all the messages (to use them again during the debriefing) and manages the trainee's profile.

The most important one is the Pedagogical agent because it is the one that "finds the solutions". It helps the trainee and the instructor. Its diagnostic depends on the training session in progress and the trainee's history. It is also based on the evaluation results provided by the error detector agent and the error evaluator one.

e-Qualification Services in ASIMIL: The EleGI Version

The scenario is the following one: after having some instructions during the briefing, the trainee performs the exercise/simulation. At the end of this simulation, his e-portfolio is updated according to his formal results, which leads to a change of VLGC, or not. Then debriefing occurs (in group so in VLGC) which is the informal part of the learning process. Agents monitor all. If at the end of this debriefing, the trainee has acquired (or not) some new skills. That can be checked only by the participation to a new test. If the test is successful, it means that the trainee has learned in an informal way. The e-Portfolio is updated and that is what we call « the informal learning treatment ».

The e-Portfolio's Ontology has been constructed from the user's profile and looks like:

The signature is an extract of the e-Portfolio's ontology as represented in figure 3:

The Signature's Extraction

We will now show in an example how the first signature (the one that will be extracted to be broadcast to find an adapted community) is extracted within an example. Let us consider first the current version. During the simulation, some errors are detected by the detectors agents and

Figure 2. e-Portfolio's Ontology

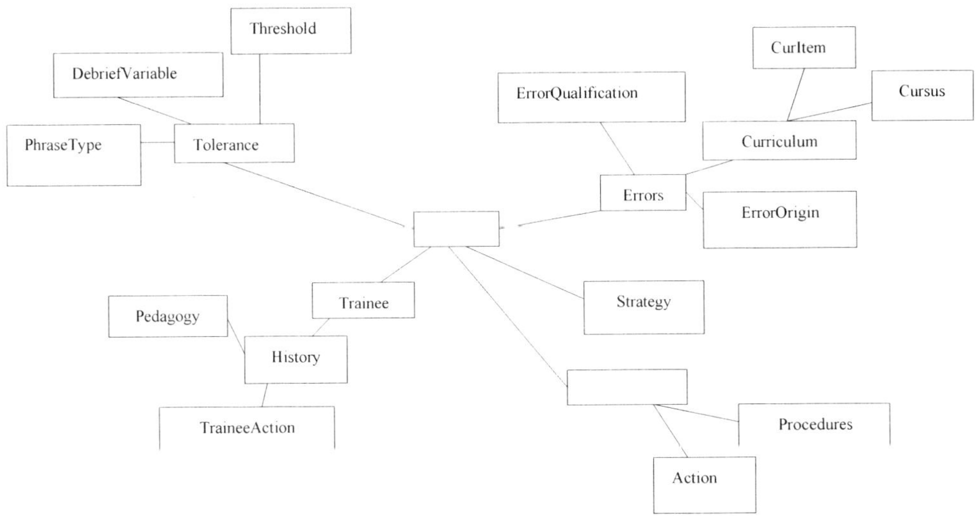

Figure 3. Signature

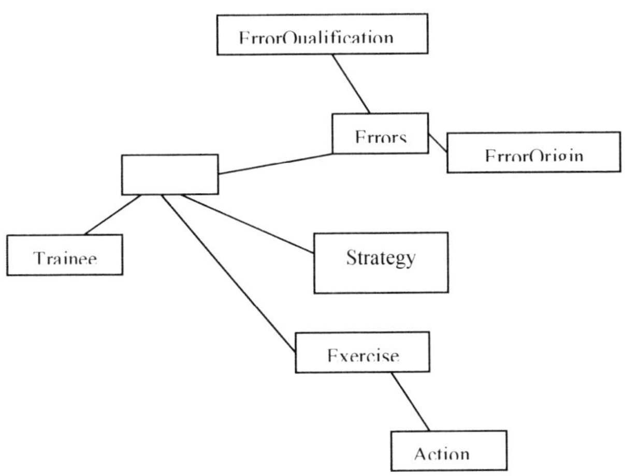

sent to the evaluator one (e.g. the ergonomical agent). He measures the gravity of the error and updates the errors history. If the same error occurs thrice, he sends a message to the pedagogical agent who takes a decision (stop the simulation/do nothing/send an alert message).

At the end of the simulation, the profile is updated according to the results.

In the ELeGI version, the pedagogical agent shares his work with some P2P agents. We can imagine that the ergonomical agent updates a kind of new signature simultaneously with the errors history. So, at the end of the simulation, the P2P agents just have to compare the new signature with the old one and to take a decision (beginning of e-qualification).

Example of Peer-to-Peer Review

In this paragraph, we will try to explain how agents will identify the origin of a detected error without the help of a centralized service or agent. We will take the example of a distributed environment working with VLGC and P2P agents, where an error has occurred and we will explain the agents' (Peer) reaction.

In this distributed environment, there are four agents from different platforms: two agents from Madkit platform (Madkit 4.0) and two agents from JADE Platform (JADE 3.2). We call the two Madkit agents, MadkitPeerAgent1 –MPA1– & MP2 and the JADE agents, JadePeerAgent3 –JPA3 – & JPA4.

The first time the agents MPA1, MPA2, JPA3 and JPA4 are launched, they implement some services required for any peer using the JXTA Platform (Project JXTA, 2003). Then, they can adopt a peer behaviour (i.e. communicate using a P2P mode).

The agents MPA1, MPA2, JPA3 and JPA4 join a VLGC of students, that we called AsimilVLGC in this example. Note that the first launched agent does not find the VLGC and so create it. After a certain time, several agents of the ASIMIL simulator have joined the VLGC.

Assume now that a user makes the error Error1, which is detected by the four agents MPA1, MPA2, JPA3 & JPA4.

Figure 4. Example's illustration

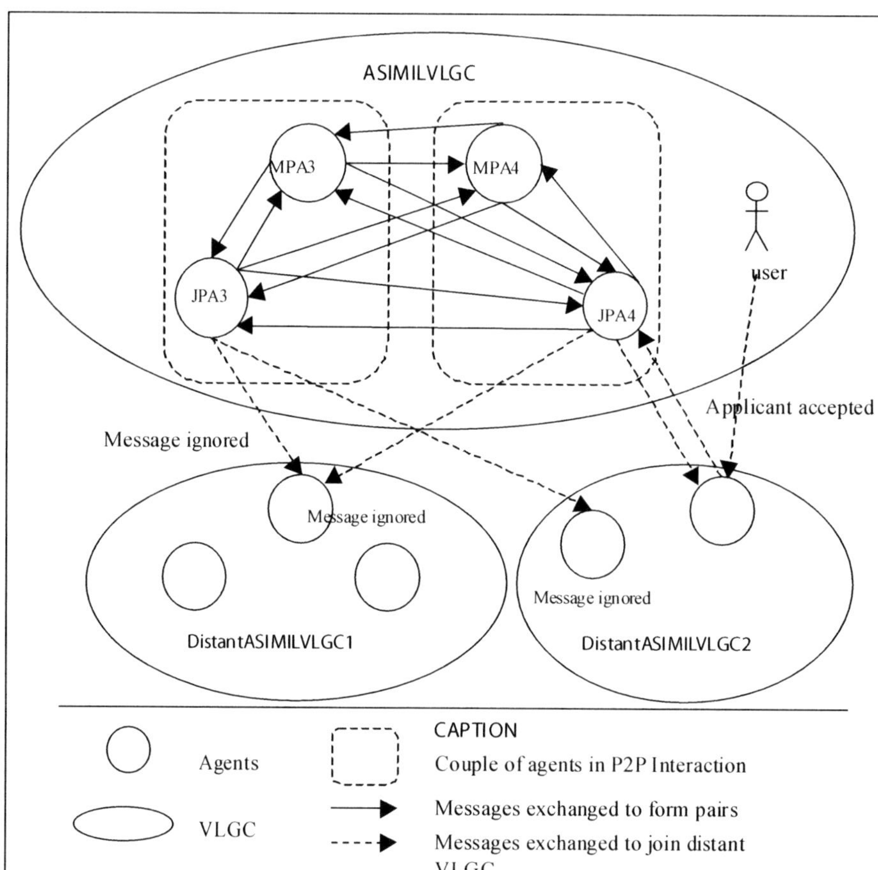

Each agent MPA1 and JPA3 proposes the origin1 's reason and broadcasts it. The agents MPA2 and JPA4 propose origin2's and broadcast it too.

An agent who receives the message and who has not proposed anything does not feel concerned by this message and ignores it.

MPA1 receives three messages. He ignores the message coming from MPA2 and JPA4 because each of their "reasons" does not match with his proposition. But the JPA3's reason matches with his one, so he decides to form a pair with him.

In the same way, MPA2 and JPA4 make a pair. The two pairs will modify locally a copy of the user's e-Porfolio with the proposed solution for this context. With this modification, they will try to found a VLGC that has a signature that matches with the user's one (according to the error and the pair proposition). Randomly one of the two peers of each pair will broadcast a message to the known distant VLGCs (called DistantA-simil VLGC1 & 2). In the distant VLGCs, one peerAgent will receive the message sent by the pairs, he compares the user's signature with his VLGC's one and decides whether he accepts the integration of the user in his VLGC.

At the end, the user joins the DistantASimil-VLGC1 as shown in figure 4.

Note that it is important that several agents (at least two, as MPA1 & JPA3) agree about the origin of the users' error. It shows that the solution is "reliable". If we do not process to this P2P review before searching a VLGC, it is possible that each agent searches a VLGC and so that the user is placed in several VLGC to solve a sole error. Note that in our example, agents are grouped in pair, but three, four or more agents can propose the same "reason" and group to search a VLGC for the user.

CONCLUSION

The paper has presented a set of core technologies that are ready to be applied for a new generation of learning services, exemplified by the e-Qualification grid learning services. The e-Portfolio associated with mobile P2P agents on the Grid are the most suitable methods and techniques to handle Virtual learning Group in Communities. On the one hand, the e-Portfolio requires a referential structure, which is the ontology, to contain the user's data & progress. On the other hand, tracking and monitoring the users in open learning situations (i.e., informal learning), must make maximum use of pervasive signatures extracted and maintained by agent by performing ubiquitous Peer-to-Peer reviews among VLGC

To sum up, in this paper, we have proposed to maintain and merge new technologies on the grid to promote:

- the collaboration in the VLGC as a basis for e-Qualification augments existing evaluation and certification in collaborative environments,
- The prominent role of e-portfolio equipped with ontology to exchange structure and with Mobile P2P agents to promote enhanced process tracking for reflections and agreements on the user performances in collective learning sessions supported by the VLGCs.
- The omnipresence of P2P agents that manage e-Qualification and VLGCs.

Finally, both the innovative process e-Portfolio and the new concept of Virtual Organization, which is the VLGC, allows the e-Qualification process as a Grid Learning Service to support continuous assessment of informal learning sessions on the Grid.

REFERENCES

Allison, C., Ruddle, A. & Michaelson, A. (2002): Systems Support for Collaborative Learning. In *1st LEGE-WG International Workshop on Educational Models for GRID Based Services*. Lausanne, Switzerland. 16 September.

Allison, C., Cerri, S. A., Ritrovato, P., Gaeta, A. & Gaeta, M. (2005) Services, Semantics, and Standards: Elements of a Learning Grid Infrastructure. *Applied Artificial Intelligence* 19(9-10): 861-879

Burgstahler, S. & Swift, C.(1996) Enhanced Learning Through Electronic Communities: A Research Review, http://164.116.18.39/research_report.html, February

Cohn, E. R. & Hibbitts, B. J., (2004). *Beyond the Electronic Portfolio: A Lifetime Personal Web Space*. Retrieved on December 10, from http://www.educause.edu/apps/eq/eqm04/eqm0441.asp.

Dimitrakos, T., Ritrovato, P. (2004) Progressing with a European Learning Grid. *4th International LeGE-WG Workshop - Towards a European Learning Grid Infrastructure*. Stuttgart, Germany. 27 - 28 April. BCS 2004

Eisenstadt, M. & Komzak, J. (2005) Peer Conversations for e-Learning in the Grid. Knowledge Media Institute, The Open University, UK & Stefano A. Cerri, LIRMM, CNRS & Université Montpellier II, France

Ferber, J. (1999) Multi-Agent System: An Introduction to Distributed Artificial Intelligence. Harlow: Addison Wesley Longman. ISBN 0-201-36048-9

Foster, I., Kesselman, K. & Tuecke, S. (2003) : The Anatomy of the Grid: Enabling Scalable Virtual Organizations. CCGRID 2001: 6-7

Garber, D.(2004). Growing Virtual Communities. International Review of Research in Open and Distance Learning, 3(4). August, 2004, ISSN: 1492-3831

Gouardères, G., Mansour, S. ,Yatchou, R. & Nkambo, R. (2005), The Grid-e-Card: Architecture for Collective Intelligence Sharing on the Grid

Guarino, N., (1998) Formal Ontology and Information Systems, In N. Guarino (ed.), *Formal Ontology in Information Systems, Proc. of the 1st International Conference*, Trento, Italy, http://www.ladseb.pd.cnr.it/infor/Ontology/Papers/FOIS98.pdf

JADE (Java Agent DEvelopment Framework) version 3.2

Project JXTA (2003) v2.0: Java™ Programmer's Guide *Sun Microsystems* May 2003

MadKit 4.0 (release 4.1) http://www.madkit.org/

Rheingold, H. (1993) The Virtual Community: Homesteading at the Electronic Frontier. A William Patrick Book Addison-Wesley, ISBN 0-201-60870-7

Roure D. de, Jennings, N. R. & Shadbolt, N. (2003) The Semantic Grid: A future eScience infrastructure. *Int. J. of Concurrency and Computation: Practice and Experience* 15 (11)

Schollmeier., R. (2001) A definition of peer-to-peer networking for the classification of peer-to-peer architectures and applications. In IEEE, editor, *2001 International Conference on Peer-to-Peer Computing (P2P2001)*, Departement of Computer and Information Science Linko ping Universität, Sweden, august 2001.

Schwier, R.A. (2004). Virtual learning communities. In G. Anglin (Ed.), *Critical issues in instructional technology*. Portsmouth, NH: Teacher Ideas Press.

Vanides, J. & Morgret, K. (2002) STEP ePortfolio Workspace : Supporting Pre-Service Teachers with Electronic Portfolio Creation, Reflection and Online Collaboration. ldt.stanford.edu/~**keri**/project/mySTEPstanford.doc

Vanides, J., (2002) A Personalized, Web-Based Learning Electronic ePortfolio Workspace, White paper. http://ldt.stanford.edu/~jvanides/eportfolio/STEP-eportfolio-workspace.pdf

Zhang, Y. & Tanniru, M. (2005) An Agent-based Approach to Study Virtual Learning Communities, *Proceedings of the 38th Annual Hawaii International Conference on System Sciences (HICSS'05)* - Track 1, January 03 - 06, 2005 Big Island, Hawaii.

This work was previously published in Int. Journal of Information Technology and Web Engineering, Vol. 1, Issue 2, edited by G. Alkhatib and D. Rine, pp. 25-42, copyright 2006 by IGI Publishing (an imprint of IGI Global).

Chapter VIII
Incremental Learning for Interactive E-Mail Filtering

Ding-Yi Chen
University of Queensland, Australia

Xue Li
University of Queensland, Australia

Zhao Yang Dong
University of Queensland, Australia

Xia Chen
University of Queensland, Australia

ABSTRACT

In this paper, we propose a framework namely, Prediction-Learning-Distillation (PLD) for interactive document classification and distilling the misclassified documents. Whenever a user points out misclassified documents, the PLD learns from the mistakes and identifies the same mistakes from all other classified documents. The PLD then enforces this learning for future classifications. If the classifier fails to accept relevant documents or reject irrelevant documents on certain categories, then PLD will assign those documents as new positive/negative training instances. The classifier can then strengthen its weakness by learning from these new training instances. Our experiments results have demonstrated that the proposed algorithm can learn from user identified misclassified documents, and then distil the rest successfully.

INTRODUCTION

Even after the dot-com bubble, the growth of the Internet does not stop. For example, according to the Australian bureau of statistics (Australian Bureau of Statistics, 2005), at the end of September 2004, total Internet subscribers in Australia numbered over 5.7 million. This was an increase of over 520,000 (10%) from the end of March 2004, and data downloaded by subscribers during the September quarter 2004 increased significantly (72%) to 11,004 million MBs from the 6,409 million MBs downloaded during the March quarter 2004. This data indicates that more and more people are joining the Internet, and they have shown that they were using the Internet as on of the primary sources to gain information.

One of the main reasons people want to be connected is the ability to use email. Email was originally designed for asynchronous communications, the same as traditional post mail. However, since email service is useful, easy to use, and cheap to send and receive, a great number of applications have been built upon the email service, such as document delivery and archiving, work task delegation and task tracking. It is also used for storing personal names and addresses, for sending reminders, handling customer services, scheduling appointments, and for handling technical support queries (Whittaker & Sidner, 1996). Email has become an essential field in contact address books.

As a low-cost, common used contact method, there is always drawback. Many email users start to realise themselves that they have been overloaded by the information from email. If the amount of email documents received each day by a user exceeds around 50, the time spent on analysing what are important and what is not, then replying to important ones, can take up a considerable amount of daily working hours. To many university academic staffs, a two-hour session of processing email has become a routine of a normal workday. The time wasted sifting through daily email is a time consuming, yet extremely important task. Consequently, document classifiers, especially email filters are put into practise to ensure that a user is not inundated with useless information, which in turn causes them to miss a critical email, file, or an announcement.

Problems with Email Filtering

Before applying filtering techniques, people would like to ask following questions:

- Can the filter guarantee effectiveness?
- Is the filter easy to use?
- Is the filter really a time saver?

An important assessment for the email filter is how many correct decisions the filter makes. People neither want junk mail to appear in their in-box folder, nor are they happy to see their legitimate mail to be dumped to the junk folder. Table 1 shows four filter decision types which are used to measure the quality of filter decision making (Sebastiani, 2002):

Positive means the email item is spam, while negative means the email is not spam. True positives (TP) and true negatives (TN) are right decisions, as user and filter agree each other; however, false negatives (FN) indicates that the filter considers the spam mail item is a legitimate mail item, while false positives (FP) denotes that the filter denotes the legitimate mail as junk.

If email filter users share the same preference, and they stick on their choice, then a fully automatic filter can be constructed by a knowledge engineering expert system such as TCS system (Hayes, Andersen, Nirenburg, & Schmandt, 1990). However, this is usually not the case. This general rule does not always apply to everyone. That is the reason why people do not put much credit on fully automatic filters because users doubt whether the general filtering rules can completely satisfy their preferences (Crawford, Kay, & McCreath,

2002). As Jiawei Han states in SIGKDD 2002 panel (Ankerst, 2002), different users may like to mine data for different kinds of knowledge, and with different requirements, and they prefer to refine the mining query interactively.

Another issue of email filtering is whether the email filter is easy to use. Most email clients, including Microsoft Outlook, provide functions for users to create folders in which they can place messages. Although the idea itself is good, it is often a time-consuming and difficult task for a user to perform. For each message the user must first decide which folder is appropriate. Then the user must inform the mail handler of their selection by moving that message into the desired folder through click and drag, or via menu functions. These undesirable tasks that must be performed by the user often discourage them from organising their email into folders, resulting in unmanageable in-boxes that contain hundreds or thousands of messages (R. Segal & Kephart, 1999). Moreover, many current filter implementations bundle in email clients require user to input filter rules to activate the email classify function. This might be painful for users with less computer operating skills, because they might not be able to figure out the meaning of each input field, nor can they know the usage of Boolean operators needed for defining the rules.

Since the performance of computer hardware grows dramatically, our focus is not on the program execution effectiveness. Instead, we are interested in how much effectiveness we can achieve within a given number of training instances. In this paper, we define the learning efficiency as (Tresch & Luniewski, 1995):

$$L = \frac{\rho}{\ell} \qquad (1)$$

where ρ is the filter effectiveness, and ℓ stands for the number of instances learnt by filter.

An efficient Interactive Email Filter (IEF) such as SwiftFile (R. B. Segal & Kephart, 2000) (formerly known as MailCat (R. Segal & Kephart, 1999) or interactive document classifier like PLD (Chen & Li, 2004) can fulfil the requirements of user. After reading documents, an IEF demonstrates its learning result by labelling the documents. Figure 1 explains how an IEF system treats the feedback of user. The category labels are defined before using the classifier. Unlabelled mail items are fed to IEF to be classified. User then reviews the work of classifier and gives judgement comments. IEF can use these comments to improve the future classification.

These systems provide incremental learning methods, which allow user:

- Be able to modify the filtering hypothesis toward the opinion of user.
- Easily trains the system by providing a few more examples.
- Reduces the effort of filing documents by hand.

Nevertheless, interactive email filter has some potential problems, which is discussed in next section.

Problems with Interactive Email Filtering

We observed that in interactive email filtering, a user tends to point out only the misclassified email items, not the correct ones. Moreover, it is unlikely that a user would be diligent enough to identify all misclassified email. In this case, a classifier is expected to deal with misclassified email. Among them, it is possible that only a small proportion has been identified by the user.

We use a scenario to illustrate how the classification tasks are accomplished in real-life. In a company, a manager asks a secretary to put documents into relevant folders. In the beginning, the secretary classifies documents on her/his own. To improve the performance of the classification task, the manager will make some comments on the decisions of the secretary.

The manager might make two kinds of comments, one is to approve the decisions by the secretary, and the other is to reveal mistakes to the secretary. In the former case, the secretary might continuously make the same mistakes which have not yet been spotted, for he/she cannot perceive the errors, nor does he/she have motivation to correct the mistakes. In the latter case, the secretary perceives the errors, so he/she can correct his/her works based on the mistakes he/she has learnt. A similar conclusion can also be seen in the work of Tresch and Luniewski (1995). They suggest that learning from mistakes is more effective than learning from correct answers directly. The detail discussion of their work is in the subsection Mistaken-Driven Learning subsection in the Related Work section.

Another problem appears in an improper document model. A *document model* determines how a computer recognises documents. Whenever a computer receives documents, it decomposes documents into vectors of features. Then these vectors are used for further computations of the classification tasks. If a document model is not good enough to express documents, then even the user does point out all the mistakes, the learning of filter is flawed. In this case, two documents may have the same features, but may need to be classified differently. This problem is identified as "incomplete model" (Chen, Li, Dong, & Chen, 2005), to indicate that relevant features are missing from the document model.

We propose an enhanced version of Prediction-Learning-Distillation (PLD) framework (Chen & Li, 2004) for distilling the misclassified email messages. Originally, PLD framework is designed as a mistaken-driven framework, it learns from user-corrected mistakes. However, mistaken-driven methods are ineffective if the document model is incomplete.

The rest of the paper is organised as follows: Section 2 introduce significant relevant researches. Section 3 shows our research aim, including preliminary definition and problem statements. Section 4 explains our proposed incremental learning approach to accomplish IEF. Section 5 illustrates the experiment results. Finally, section 6 provides the conclusions.

RELATED WORK

There have been many different attempts at implementing intelligent email filtering agent software. The email filtering process can be separated into two layers, as shown in Figure 2.

The lower layer shown in Figure 2 is a document modelling layer, and the upper layer is a classification layer. In the document modelling layer, a document is modelled as a vector of computable features. The modelling process is also called *document indexing*, because the text information needs to be indexed to be interpreted by a classifier (Sebastiani, 2002). In the classification layer, the filter utilises the output of modelling layer - vectors of computable features to induce hypotheses which is used to filter documents.

Mistaken-Driven Learning

Although there are many of classifiers for email filtering, we concentrate on mistaken-driven incremental classifiers, a.k.a. on-line classifiers, for they provide incremental learning methods which are able to refine the hypothesis immediately after user corrections inputted.

As described in (Vlastos, 1980), mistakes reveal the flaws in learning and can be used to improve the immature learning. The learning occurs when a classifier is told that it had made some mistakes on given instances, then the classifier uses the instances to improve its classification hypothesis (Blum & Mitchell, 1998). On the other hand, the hypothesis will not be updated when classifier make correct decisions.

Tresch and Luniewski (1995) have examined three learning strategies: positive learning (learning from correctly classified documents), negative learning (learning from misclassified documents), and all file learning (learning from a mixture of positive and negative examples). They concluded that the negative learning is the best way of the three. In the work (Tresch & Luniewski, 1995), all documents are reviewed by user. But in our case, uncommented filtered email documents are not necessarily reviewed by user, and there is no explicit rule to tell whether these email documents are correctly classified or not.

The classifier which implements reinforcement learning (Mitchell, 1997) utilises feedbacks of previous decisions to learn. However, in interactive email filtering, the classifier might obtain only a small proportion of feedbacks from users. Muggleton (1994) suggests that positive instances can be learnt if the distribution of instances is available; however, learning from mistakes involves not only positive instances but also negative ones, which provide additional information to facilitate the hypothesis induction.

Perceptron (Schutze, Hull, & Pedersen, 1995) is an example of mistake-driven learning method. If it makes correct decisions, nothing will happen; but if mistakes have been identified, the perceptron learns from new training instance by adjusting the weights of features with following formula:

$$w_{i_{new}} = w_{i_{old}} + (t - y) f_i \zeta \quad (2)$$

where t is the decision from training instances, y is the decision from classifier, w_i is the weight of i-th feature, f_i is the value of i-th feature, and ζ is a constant such that $\zeta \in \{0,1\}$.

As we can see, the weight will only be updated if and only if $t \neq y$.

Winnow (Dagan, Karov, & Roth, 1997; Littlestone, 1988, 1991; Yamazaki & Dagan, 1997) can also learns by modifying the weight of features. If a false positive is discovered, the weights of active features (features possessed by training instance) will be demoted, that is, multiplied by demote parameter ranged between 0 and 1; if a false negative is found, the weights of active features will be promoted by multiplying promote parameter which is greater than 1.

Document Modelling

The problem in document model can be described in two aspects: 1) the definition of features; 2) the definition of the weights of the features. Frequencies of words or phrases in documents are usually defined as features. Document models such as binary independence retrieval (BIR) (a.k.a. bag of words (BOW)) (Robertson & Jones, 1976) and Vector Space Model (VSM) (Salton, Wong, & Yang, 1975) use words or phrases counting as features; while Darmstadt Indexing Approach (DIA) (Fuhr, 1989) and the essay grading model by Larkey (1998) use some other properties such as the length of document. Latent Semantic Indexing (LSI) (Deerwester, Dumais, Furnas, Landauer, & Harshman, 1990) does not use words as features, instead, they apply the dimensional reduction technique to reduce the feature set, then use the reduced features to index documents. For HTML formatted email, implementation of Paul Graham includes the other interesting features such as colour. According to his research, occurrence of 'ff0000' (bright red colour in HTML) was as good as an indicator of Spam mail as the occurrence of the words "enter" or "free" (Graham, 2004).

The BIR model uses binary value {0, 1} to weight the features. If a certain feature appears, then 1 is assigned, otherwise 0 is assigned. VSM uses $tf(t_k, d_j) \times idf(t_k)$, where t_k is a feature in the available feature set. The $tf(t_k, d_j)$ is the frequency that t_k occurs in d_j, and $idf(t_k) = \log_2(N / N(t_k))$, where N is the total number of documents, and $N(t_k)$ denotes the number of documents with the term t_k. Chakrabarti et al. (1999; 1998; 2003) suggested the use of the Fisher's score (Duda & Hart, 1973) as a discriminative feature weight.

Fitness of a Model

Fitness of a model is a factor of classification effectiveness. If the model is insufficient to express the classification task, conflict instances will appear and weaken the effectiveness of classifier.

Conflict instances are actually the symptoms of insufficient document model. There are several ways to deal with conflict instances. In rule inducing classifier such as C4.5 (Quinlan, 1996), conflict examples are simply removed. In rough sets approach (Pawlak, Grzymala-Busse, Slowinski, & Ziarko, 1995), the lower approximation (non-conflict examples) can be used to build "certain rules", and the rules induced from upper approximation (conflict examples) can be used to build "possible rules". However, lower approximation completely discards conflict examples, while upper approximation only deals with the conflict examples which win the votes of labels.

Hashemi (1992) suggested to use Bayes theorem to deal with conflict examples. Also, Haruechaiyasak (2002) used fuzzy association to avoid the ambiguity of features, and Liu (2003) used fuzzy set to accomplish the classification task.

In those approaches, conflict instances are used to show the uncertainty of classification results. We, however, found a novel way to explain and utilise conflict instances: conflict examples show the weakness of document models, thus, the fitness of model is negatively related to the number of conflict instances. The details of our ideas of using conflict instances can be found in the work (Chen et al., 2005).

Please note that a complicated model does not always have the advantage over a simple one. According to the experimental results from Apte (1994), Dumais (1998), and Lewis (1992), sophisticated models do not lead to better classification effectiveness. It might be due to the over-fitting problem, that is, the classifier bind to less-informative features than relevant ones.

Fitness Measurement

Current comparative studies on the fitness of models choose specific classifiers to grade a model. Lewis (Lewis, 1992) uses the *Maxcat* text categorisation package which is based on the probability classifier to compare the word based model with the phrase indexing model. Apte et al (1994) applies the SWAP-1 (Weiss & Indurkhya, 1993) rule induction method to select features. Dumais (1998) uses similar (variant) (Rocchio, 1971), decision trees (Chickering, Heckerman, & Meek, 1997), naive Bayes (Good, 1965), Bayes net (Heckerman, 1994), and SVM (Joachims, 1998) to accomplish the feature selection. However, they are all limited by the learning capacities of classifiers. In order to avoid the influence of the classifier, we provide a classifier independent method to evaluate the fitness of document models.

PROBLEM STATEMENTS

The purpose of interactive email filtering system is to reduce the user effort, while minimising the cost of misclassification. The objectives can be reformed as following research problems: Given a collection of email and a set of decisions from user,

1. Find a hypothesis which minimising the cost of misclassification.
2. Find a minimal subset of decision set to generate the hypothesis mentioned in (1).

Preliminary Definitions

Email Documents and Folders

An email document *d* usually contains two parts, header fields and body text. Header fields contain several important fields, such as senders, receivers, the encoding and subjects. The body text is the content of the email, which is represented as a sequence of words, graph, or any other objects which may carry information and concepts. The symbol *D* denotes the collection of email documents *d*.

A feature *f* represents an informative attribute of email, such as the occurrence of a keyword, or a value which indicates whether the sender is in address book. To simply the filtering process, we usually organise features in vector format to represent documents. The translating process is referred as *modelling*, and the translation function is named *model*. Formula 3 formalises the relationship among document, features, and model:

$$M(d) = [f_1, f_2, \ldots, f_{|F|}] \tag{3}$$

where f_i is the *i*-th feature from feature collection *F*, whose size is $|F|$.

A folder (category) implies a topic of interest of user. Folders are identified by the *category labels*. In email filter application, one category label, "junk", is needed, for we can easily tell that the mail documents with junk label are junk mail, the others are legitimate mail.

Filtering

A filtering task is considered as assigning Boolean values to the email collection. The user classification preference can be described as the following function:

$$\Phi(d_i) = \begin{cases} 1 & , \quad d_i \text{ is junk} \\ 0 & , \quad \text{otherwise} \end{cases} \tag{4}$$

where $d_i \in D$, the number 1 stands for filing document to junk folder, and 0 stands for filing document to legitimate mail folder. Classification problem can be viewed as find a function Ψ, namely *hypothesis*, which fills a $D \times C$ table with either 1 or 0. The hypothesis Ψ can be expressed as follows:

$$\Psi : D \times C \rightarrow \{1,0\} \tag{5}$$

An algorithm which can generate the hypothesis from instances defines a *classifier*. The degree of the evidence that d_i should be filed to c_j is described as *probability of positive (POP)* (Chen et al., 2005), whose range is a real number between 0 and 1, that is, how much confidence does classifier have in making positive decision (file mail as junk).

A *classification decision* is the Boolean value of (d_i, c_j), which can be determined by *POP* and a threshold. If *POP* is greater or equal to threshold τ, then a positive decision is made; otherwise, the negative decision is made. The value of the threshold τ reflects the cost of misclassification. According to Cooper (1973) and Lewis (1995), the threshold should be set to:

$$\tau = \frac{\lambda_{FP} - \lambda_{TN}}{(\lambda_{FN} - \lambda_{TP}) + (\lambda_{FP} - \lambda_{TN})} \tag{6}$$

where λ_{TP}, λ_{FP}, λ_{TN}, λ_{FN} are the penalty for TP, FP, TN and FN. If we show no special interests among TP, TN, FP, and FN, which implies $\lambda_{FP} = \lambda_{FN}$, $\lambda_{TP} = \lambda_{TN} = 0$, thus $\tau = 0.5$. However, in email filing, the cost of FP is greater than FN. For example, the threshold τ should be set to 0.75 if the penalty of FP is three times higher than FN.

The classification decision process can be formalised as:

$$\Psi(d_i) = \begin{cases} 1 & , \quad \text{if } POP(d_i) \geq \tau \\ 0 & , \quad \text{if } POP(d_i) < \tau \end{cases} \tag{7}$$

This function can then be use to make classification decisions.

Problem Description

In the environment of mistaken-driven interactive email filtering, user does not do anything until he/she discovers mistakes. Thus, only a decision table subset $\Delta\Phi$ is fed to IEF as the corrections of user. In other words, $\Delta\Phi$ is treated as training set for IEF to refine its hypothesis. We then formularized the research problem as follow:

Given a set of user's correction $\Delta\Phi$ and a hypothesis Ψ_i at iteration *i*, find a hypothesis refining method $\Im$:

$$\Im(\Delta\Phi, \Psi_i) \rightarrow \Psi_{i+1} \quad (8)$$

which minimises the total cost λ, defined as:

$$\lambda = \lambda_{FP} \times \ell_{FP} + \lambda_{FN} \times \ell_{FN} \quad (9)$$

where ℓ_{FP}, ℓ_{FN} are the numbers of false positive and false negative decisions.

PROPOSED APPROACH: PLD FRAMEWORK

In the manager-secretary scenario, a qualified secretary should do three things to improve her/his performance:

1. Reviewing all past classified documents to check out those misclassified documents that are similar to the one that has just been pointed out by the manager;
2. Remembering the mistake that he/she has just made and never make the same/similar mistake in future;
3. Trying to recognise the conflict instances and ask the manager for further instruction.

Compared with an interactive classification process, as the example shown, the manager stands for the user, while the secretary stands for an email filter. The only feedback is a set of misclassified documents that are identified by user, which is relatively smaller than the whole training set.

Since we cannot expect that user is capable of revealing enough number of misclassified examples for conventional approaches, learning from the uncommented email documents becomes essential. For learning latent information from uncommented filtered email, we define four important types of email documents:

1. Identified Misclassified Documents (IMD): the misclassified email documents identified by user.
2. Uncommented Documents (UD): the documents without user comments.
3. Uncommented Misclassified Documents (UMD): the misclassified documents which are not revealed by user but are identified by our learning program.
4. Uncommented Correctly classified Documents (UCD): the uncommented email documents that are correctly classified. Our learning program will verify these.

These four terms are to be implemented as variable sets of email documents. Initially they are all empty. After user feedback is received, the classifier will put documents together with user comments into IMD and proceed with the learning. The others are in UD. Our framework will then extract UMD and UCD from UD. In other words, user points out some part of misclassified email, our proposed framework will reveal other misclassified email.

PLD Framework

The proposed framework, *Prediction-Learning-Distillation (PLD)*, discriminates uncommented misclassified documents (UMD) from uncommented documents (UD). In order to provide flexibility, PLD is designed to work with various incremental classification algorithms, as long as they provide following functions:

1. ***predict(d)***: Algorithm assigns category labels to an unlabelled document d.
2. ***train(D)***: Algorithm learns from a set of labelled documents *D*.

The "plugged-in" classification algorithm is referred as "core classifier" in later of this section.

The idea of our algorithm is based on following observations:

1. The hypothesis for email filtering should be changed after learning from the IMD.
2. Based on different 'version' of classification hypotheses, the classification decisions on a certain uncommented email might be different.

Should it happen, the email documents might be in set UMD, while the others are in set UCD.

Obviously, observation 1 is true because IMD indicates that the original hypothesis does not fit the training instances. Therefore, hypothesis should be updated to reflect the new training instances. Observation 2 is actually based on observation 1 - the newer hypothesis tends to be more accurate for it has been trained with more training instances. Therefore, if the newer classification decision on a given document is different from the older one, the email is likely to be misclassified by the older hypothesis.

The learning is triggered when the user submits his/her comments on misclassified documents. These identified misclassified documents (IMD) are then used as learning materials of PLD. Please note that $D_{UMD} = D_{UFN} \cup D_{UFP}$ and $D_{IMD} = D_{IFN} \cup D_{IFP}$.

The PLD framework has three components: predictor, learner, and distiller.

1. **Predictor:** The component which assigns category labels using previous learnt hypothesis. It will call the function *predict(d)* of core classifier to assign labels.
2. **Learner:** The component which learns from user correction and refines hypothesis. It is actually the function *train(D)* of core classifier.
3. **Distiller:** The component which distils UMD from UD. It will call the function *predict(d)* of core classifier to assign new labels.

The PLD framework works as follows (see Figure 3 for the data flow diagram (DFD)): Whenever the incoming documents are received, the predictor labels these documents. At beginning, if supervised algorithms such as SVM and Winnow are adopted as core classifiers, they do not have any "knowledge" (hypothesis) to classify the documents, hence predictor does not put any labels on them. User then spends some time to read the documents and points out the misclassified ones to be sent to (IMD).

According to the refined hypothesis, the distiller assigns new labels to each document of UD, and then compares the new labels with the old ones, if the labels are identical; the document is identified as in UCD, otherwise in UMD. The overall algorithm of PLD framework is given as follows.

After the new hypothesis is generated by the learner, the distiller filters out the unidentified misclassified documents by comparing the predicted labels (which are assigned by the predictor) to the new labels from the new hypothesis.

Please note that the PLD framework itself does not tell the details of learning. The one which actually takes care of learning and predicting is

Table 1.

PLD Framework
Input: Set of buffered documents *D*, category labels, IMD from user.
Output: Classification hypotheses, set of UMD, and set of UCD
Algorithm:
1. Initialise the hypotheses $\Psi(d)$. (Depending on core classifiers)
2. The predictor assigns the 'predicted' category labels to each document according to the hypothesis.
3. The user provides the some correct decisions for misclassified documents (IMD).
4. The learner learns from IMD and update hypothesis.
5. The distiller assigns the new labels to each uncommented document according to the updated hypothesis.
The distiller separates the UCD and UMD from UD by comparing the new labels and the labels which are originally assigned by the predictor.

the core classifier. However, PLD provides the way to maximise the usage of instances.

EXPERIMENTS AND RESULTS

One of the objectives of our experiments is to examine the accuracy of UMD detection. In order to simulate the behaviour of users, we define a diligence parameter δ, reflecting the percentage of misclassified email identified. The value δ=1 means all misclassified documents are pointed out by the user, while δ=0 means none of misclassified email items are identified, so there is nothing to learn from. Hence, δ=0 is not included in our experiments.

The effectiveness of the classification decisions and UMD detection can be measured by F_1 function provided by Rijsbergen in (1979). The parameters of F_1 function, namely precision P and recall R are defined as:

$$P = \frac{\ell_{TP}}{\ell_{TP} + \ell_{FP}}, \qquad (10)$$

where ℓ_{TP}, ℓ_{FP}, and ℓ_{FN} are the numbers of TP, FP, and FN decisions respectively.

Then the effectiveness of the classification decisions ρ is obtained by F_1 function:

$$\rho = \frac{2PR}{P + R} \qquad (11)$$

Similarly, the UMD detection effectiveness ρ_{UMD} is measured by:

$$\rho_{UMD} = \frac{2P_{UMD} R_{UMD}}{P_{UMD} + R_{UMD}} \qquad (12)$$

Note that if δ=0, recall will be zero, and precision P will not be available, for $\ell_{TP} + \ell_{FP} = 0$

In order to test our framework, we use online SVM (Tax & Laskov, 2003) and balanced Winnow (Littlestone, 1988) as examples of core classifiers.

Experiment Design

To our knowledge, currently available public email corpuses do not have standard training/test set splits. Therefore, we choose a standard text classification benchmark, the modified Apte ("ModApte") split on Reuters-21578 corpus (Lewis, 2000) to examine the effectiveness of our system. The ModApte split separates the whole corpus into a training set (with 9,603 documents) and a test set (with 3,299 documents). The Porter Algorithm (Porter, 1980) is applied for stemming the postfix of words in order to aggregate the relative words.

When processing the training set, PLD assigned category labels to the documents in the buffer. If the labels differed from the true labels (i.e., the labels assign by corpus itself), these documents were regarded as misclassified. The examiner (the program which examines classifier) separated the misclassified documents from UD into IMD and UMD according to a diligence value. IMD was learnt as described in the algorithm detailed in our paper (Chen & Li, 2004); while the UMD and correctly classified documents were merged together as uncommented documents. The distiller then split the uncommented documents into UCD and UMD. The precision and recall of UMD detection can be calculated after distillation.

When processing the test set, the learner ceased learning; only predictor assigned labels to test documents. The precision and recall of classification decision making can be scored after finishing the examination of the test set.

Results

In our experiments, online SVM and balanced Winnow are both used as core classifiers of PLD framework separately in order to test the effectiveness of PLD, and whether the algorithms are dependant on the PLD framework. Figure 4, Figure 5, and Figure 6 illustrate the differences of the effectiveness between each classifier. As it can be seen, the overall performance of online SVM is better than balanced Winnow.

Figure 7, Figure 8, and Figure 9 are used in particular to show the differences of effectiveness between online SVM and Balanced Winnow algorithms in the distillation of set UMD. Again, online SVM shows a better result than the balanced Winnow algorithm, especially when diligence is low. It also means that Online SVM works well in the PLD framework, even if the user only reveals a small amount of misclassified documents.

Another observation we have made on Figure 9 is that the PLD framework is algorithm dependent, which means that the selection of core classifiers does affect the distillation effectiveness of PLD.

Figure 10 and Figure 11 show the effectiveness comparison between PLD and non-PLD filtering. Dots shown in Figure 10 and Figure 11 stand for effectiveness on certain percentages of training instances revealed to classifier. For PLD, the dots stand for diligence = 20%, 40%, 60%, 80% and 100%, from left to right; and for non-PLD, they stands for 20%, 40%, 60%, 80% and 100% of training instances which have been seen by the classifier. In both figures, the curves of PLD are closer to y-axis (F_1 value) than the curves of non-PLD. It indicates that PLD requires less training instances than non-PLD in order to reach the same effectiveness.

CONCLUSION

Electronic mail has been proven to be one of the main communication means between people throughout the world. It is due to its diversity of use, popularity, and speed of delivery that users are now being inundated with email each day. Most filtering techniques do not enable the incremental learning to meet the various preferences of users and correct the past mistakes. This paper has described an approach for an intelligent email filtering system that extends the capabilities of the filter by allowing the users to browse folders with email placed in by an online classifier and then the users give feedbacks to the system. After that the system will learn from user-identified mistakes.

Incremental learning provides a reasonable way of appropriately inducing the preference of users. Whenever an incremental learning system receives users' feedbacks, it can process on the newly acquired data without re-process the historical data. As shown in the experiments on the PLD (Prediction-Learning-Distillation) framework, the results from incremental learning system are as good as the ones from conventional approaches. Moreover, the system based on PLD framework requires smaller training set than the system without PLD in order to reach the same effectiveness. This implies that the PLD have better learning efficiency.

Applying the PLD framework on email messages has a number of advantages over other email filtering agent programs. Firstly, it can boost the confidence of the users who uses the system by an incremental learning approach that can reflect users' feedbacks. Secondly, an interactive filtering process can keep up the changes of Spam after the users click on the misclassified email messages to inform the filter to realise the changes, therefore it is a dynamically evolving system. Thirdly, the training of the filter becomes much effective and faster, since the users are the best resources in the machine learning process. Finally the interactive filtering of email messages has provided a better way to personalise the email filtering services by adopting the users' intentions immediately through the core classifiers used in the PLD framework.

Currently, we are investigating the effectiveness of PLD in a real life email filtering application. Specifically, the Enron email corpus (Klimt & Yang, 2004) is chosen as the training/test set. Though Enron email corpus does not have the Spam label for email documents, its folder structure reveals how users organising their email. This enables the research on the user behaviour in email classification.

ACKNOWLEDGMENT

Support for SYOM Technology Pty Ltd is gratefully acknowledged by the authors. We also thank Paul Smith for providing valuable ideas and comments.

REFERENCES

Ankerst, M. (2002). Report on the SIGKDD-2002 Panel the Perfect Data Mining Tool: Interactive or Automated? *ACM SIGKDD Explorations Newsletter, 4*(2), 110-111.

Apte, C., Damerau, F., & Weiss, S. M. (1994). Automated Learning of Decision Rules for Text Categorization. *TOIS: ACM Transactions on Information Systems, 12*(3), 233-251.

Australian Bureau of Statistics. (2005). *8153.0 Internet Activity, Australia,* from http://www.abs.gov.au

Blum, A., & Mitchell, T. (1998). *Combining Labeled and Unlabeled Data with Co-Training.* Paper presented at the COLT 1998: Proceedings of the 11th Annual Conference on Computational Learning Theory, Madison, Wisconsin, United States.

Chakrabarti, S., Berg, M. v. d., & Dom, B. (1999). *Focused Crawling: A New Approach to Topic-Specific Web Resource Discovery.* Paper presented at the WWW 1999: In Proceedings of 8th International World Wide Web Conference, Amsterdam, Netherlands.

Chakrabarti, S., Dom, B., Agrawal, R., & Raghavan, P. (1998). Scalable Feature Selection, Classification and Signature Generation for Organizing Large Text Databases into Hierarchical Topic Taxonomies. *VLDB Journal: The International Journal on Very Large Data Bases, 7*(3), 163-178.

Chakrabarti, S., Roy, S., & Soundalgekar, M. (2003). Fast and Accurate Text Classification via Multiple Linear Discriminant Projections. *VLDB Journal: The International Journal on Very Large Data Bases, 12*(2), 170-185.

Chen, D.-Y., & Li, X. (2004). *PLD: A Distillation Algorithm of Misclassified Documents.* Paper presented at the WAIM 2004: Advances in Web-

Age Information Management: 5th International Conference, Dalien, China.

Chen, D.-Y., Li, X., Dong, Z. Y., & Chen, X. (2005). *Determining the Fitness of a Document Model by Using Conflict Instances.* Paper presented at the ADC 2005: The 16th Australasian Database Conference, Newcastle, Australia.

Chickering, D. M., Heckerman, D., & Meek, C. (1997). *A Bayesian Approach to Learning Bayesian Networks with Local Structure.* Paper presented at the UAI 1997:Proceedings of 13th Conference on Uncertainty in Artificial Intelligence.

Cooper, W. S. (1973). On Selecting a Measure of Retrieval Effectiveness. *JASIS: Journal of the American Society for Information Science, 24*, 87-100.

Crawford, E., Kay, J., & McCreath, E. (2002). *An Intelligent Interface for Sorting Electronic Mail.* Paper presented at the IUI 2002: Proceedings of the 7th International Conference on Intelligent User Interfaces, San Francisco, California, USA.

Dagan, I., Karov, Y., & Roth, D. (1997). *Mistake-Driven Learning in Text Categorization.* Paper presented at the EMNLP 1997: Proceedings of 2nd Conference on Empirical Methods in Natural Language Processing, Providence, US.

Deerwester, S., Dumais, S. T., Furnas, G. W., Landauer, T. K., & Harshman, R. (1990). Indexing by Latent Semantic Analysis. *JASIST: Journal of the American Society for Information Science and Technology, 41*(6), 391-407.

Duda, R., & Hart, P. (1973). *Pattern Classification and Scene Analysis.* New York: Wiley.

Dumais, S. T., Platt, J., Heckerman, D., & Sahami, M. (1998). *Inductive Learning Algorithms and Representations for Text Categorization.* Paper presented at the CIKM 1998: Proceedings of the 7th International Conference on Information and Knowledge Management, Bethesda, Maryland, United States.

Fuhr, N. (1989). Models for Retrieval with Probabilistic Indexing. *Information Processing and Management, 25*(1), 55-72.

Good, I. J. (1965). *The Estimation of Probabilities: An Essay on Modern Bayesian Methods*: Cambridge, Mass., M.I.T. Press.

Graham, P. (2004). *A Plan for Spam*, from http://www.paulgraham.com/spam.html

Haruechaiyasak, C., Shyu, M.-L., Chen, S.-C., & Li, X. (2002). *Web Document Classification Based on Fuzzy Association.* Paper presented at the COMPSAC 2002: Proceedings of the 26th IEEE Computer Society International Computer Software and Applications Conference, Oxford, England.

Hashemi, R. R., Razzaghi, M., Jelovsek, F. R., & Talburt, J. R. (1992). *Conflict Resolution in Inductive Learning from Examples.* Paper presented at the SAC 1992: Proceedings of the 1992 ACM/SIGAPP Symposium on Applied computing, Kansas City, Missouri, United States.

Hayes, P. J., Andersen, P. M., Nirenburg, I. B., & Schmandt, L. M. (1990). *TCS: A Shell for Content-Based Text Categorization.* Paper presented at the CAIA 1990: Proceedings of the 6th Conference on Artificial Intelligence for Applications, Santa Barbara, California, United States.

Heckerman, D. G., Dan & Chickering, David Maxwell. (1994). *Learning Bayesian Networks: The Combination of Knowledge and Statistical Data.* Paper presented at the KDD Workshop.

Joachims, T. (1998). *Text Categorization with Support Vector Machines: Learning with Many Relevant Features.* Paper presented at the ECML 1998: Proceedings of 10th European Conference on Machine Learning, Chemnitz, DE.

Klimt, B., & Yang, Y. (2004). *Introducing the Enron Corpus.* Paper presented at the CEAS 2004: The 1st Conference on Email and Anti-Spam, Mountain View, CA, U.S.A.

Larkey, L. S. (1998). *Automatic Essay Grading Using Text Categorization Techniques.* Paper presented at the SIGIR 1998: Proceedings of the 21st Annual international ACM SIGIR Conference on Research and Development in Information Retrieval, Melbourne, Australia.

Lewis, D. D. (1992). *An Evaluation of Phrasal and Clustered Representations on a Text Categorization Task.* Paper presented at the SIGIR 1992: Proceedings of the 15th Annual International ACM SIGIR Conference on Research and Development in Information Retrieval, Copenhagen, Denmark.

Lewis, D. D. (1995). *Evaluating and Optimizing Autonomous Text Classification Systems.* Paper presented at the SIGIR 1995: Proceedings of the 18th Annual International ACM SIGIR Conference on Research and Development in Information Retrieval, Seattle, Washington, United States.

Lewis, D. D. (2000). *Reuters Corpus (21578)*, from http://www.daviddlewis.com/resources/testcollections/reuters21578/

Littlestone, N. (1988). Learning Quickly When Irrelevant Attributes Abound: A New Linear-Threshold Algorithm. *Machine Learning, 2*(4), 285--318.

Littlestone, N. (1991). *Redundant Noisy Attributes, Attribute Errors, and Linear-Threshold Learning Using Winnow.* Paper presented at the Proceedings of the fourth annual workshop on Computational learning theory, Santa Cruz, California, United States.

Liu, W. Y., & Song, N. (2003). A Fuzzy Approach to Classification of Text Documents. *JCST: Journal of Computer Science and Technology, 18*(5), 640-647.

Mitchell, T. M. (1997). *Machine Learning*: McGraw Hill.

Muggleton, S. (1994). *Bayesian Inductive Logic Programming.* Paper presented at the COLT 1994: Proceedings of the 7th Annual ACM Conference on Computational Learning Theory, New York.

Pawlak, Z., Grzymala-Busse, J., Slowinski, R., & Ziarko, W. (1995). Rough Sets. *CACM: Communications of the ACM, 38*(11), 88-95.

Porter, M. F. (1980). An Algorithm for Suffix Stripping. *Program, 14*(3), 130-137.

Quinlan, J. R. (1996). Improved Use of Continuous Attributes in C4.5. *JAIR: Journal of Artificial Intelligence Research, 4*, 77-90.

Robertson, S. E., & Jones, K. S. (1976). Relevance Weighting of Search Terms. *JASIS: Journal of the American Society for Information Science, 27*, 129-146.

Rocchio, J. J. (1971). Relevance feedback in information retrieval. In G. Salton (Ed.), *The SMART Retrieval System: Experiments in Automatic Document Processing* (pp. 313-323): Prentice-Hall.

Salton, G., Wong, A., & Yang, C. S. (1975). A Vector Space Model for Automatic Indexing. *CACM: Communications of the ACM, 18*(11), 613-620.

Schutze, H., Hull, D. A., & Pedersen, J. O. (1995). *A Comparison of Classifiers and Document Representations for the Routing Problem.* Paper presented at the SIGIR 1995: Proceedings of the 18th annual international ACM SIGIR conference on Research and development in information retrieval, Seattle, Washington, United States.

Sebastiani, F. (2002). Machine learning in automated text categorization. *CSUR: ACM Computing Surveys, 34*(1), 1-47.

Segal, R., & Kephart, J. O. (1999). *MailCat: An Intelligent Assistant for Organizing E-Mail.* Paper presented at the AGENTS 1999: Proceedings of the 3rd International Conference on Autonomous Agents.

Segal, R. B., & Kephart, J. O. (2000). *Incremental Learning in SwiftFile.* Paper presented at the

ICML 2000:Proceedings of the 7th International Conference on Machine Learning, Stanford, CA, USA.

Tax, D. M. J., & Laskov, P. (2003). *Online SVM Learning: From Classification To Data Description And Back.* Paper presented at the NNSP: IEEE International Workshop on Neural Networks for Signal Processing, Toulouse France.

Tresch, M., & Luniewski, A. (1995). *An Extensible Classifier for Semi-Structured Documents.* Paper presented at the CIKM 1995: Proceedings of the 4th International Conference on Information and Knowledge Management, Baltimore, Maryland, United States.

Van Rijsbergen, C. J. (1979). Evaluation. In *Dept. of Computer Science, University of Glasgow*: Department of Computer Science, University of Glasgow.

Vlastos, G. (1980). The Socratic Elenchus. *Oxford Studies in Ancient Philosophy, 1*, 27-58.

Weiss, S. M., & Indurkhya, N. (1993). Optimized Rule Induction. *IEEE Expert, 8*(6), 61-69.

Whittaker, S., & Sidner, C. (1996). *Email Overload: Exploring Personal Information Management of Email.* Paper presented at the CHI 1996: Proceedings of the SIGCHI conference on Human factors in computing systems, Vancouver, British Columbia, Canada.

Yamazaki, T., & Dagan, I. (1997). *Mistake-Driven Learning with Thesaurus for Text Categorization.* Paper presented at the NLPRS 1997: Proceedings of the Natural Language Processing Pacific Rim Symposium, Phuket, TH.

APPENDIX 1

Table 1. The contingency table of user judgements and filter decisions

Is email item *d* a spam?		User Judgements	
		Positive	Negative
Classifier Decisions	Positive	True Positive	False Positive
	Negative	False Negative	True Negative

Figure 1. An interactive email filter process

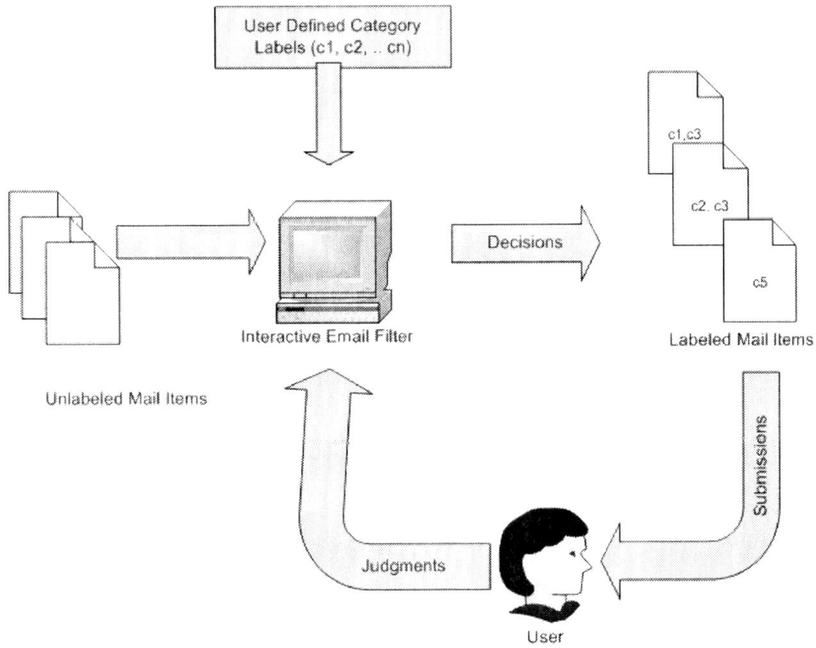

Figure 2. The layers of interactive email filtering processing

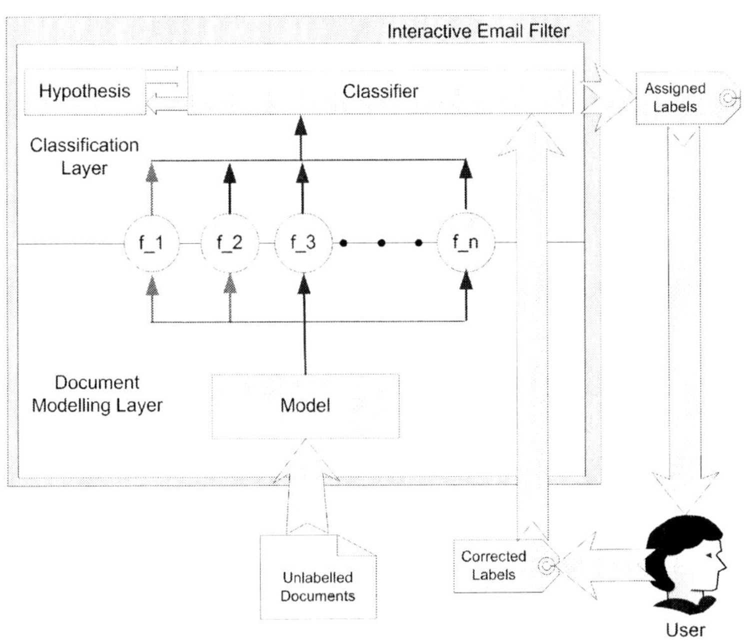

Figure 3. DFD diagram of PLD framework

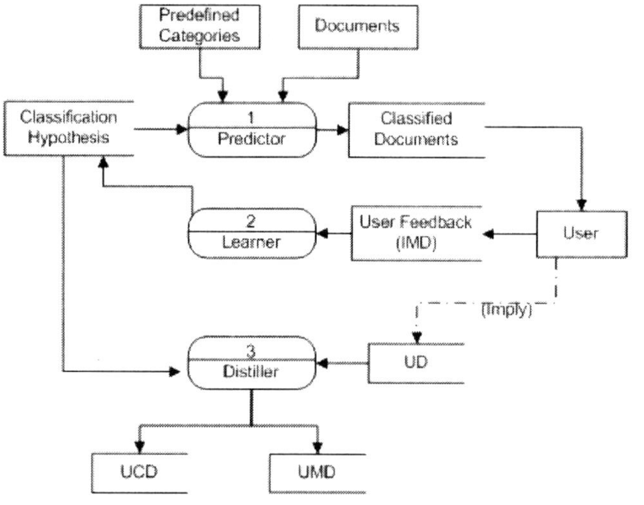

Figure 4. Classifier comparison of precisions between online SVM and balanced Winnow

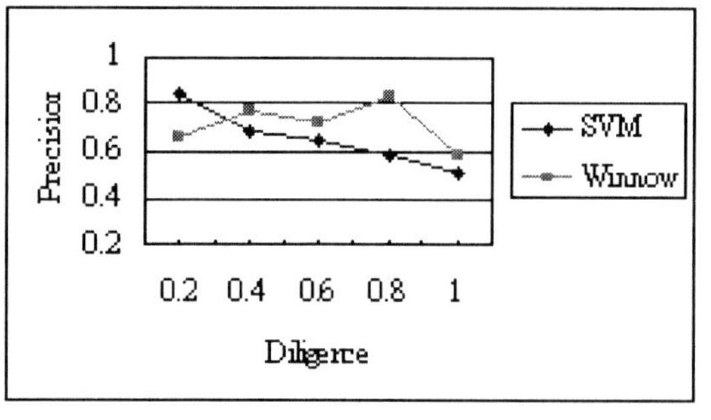

Figure 5. Classifier comparison of recalls between online SVM and balanced Winnow

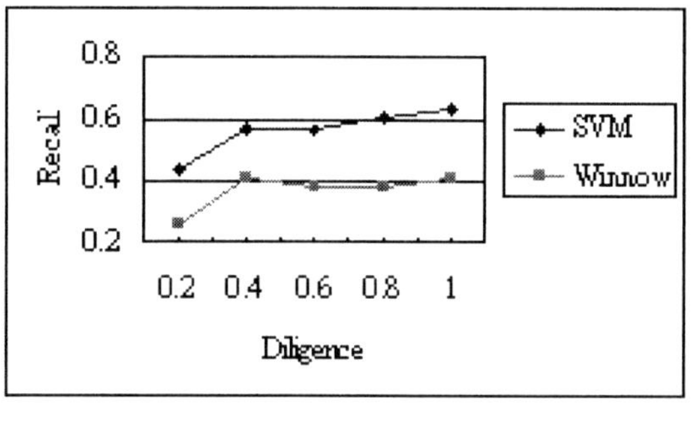

Figure 6. Comparison of overall effectiveness of online SVM and balanced Winnow.

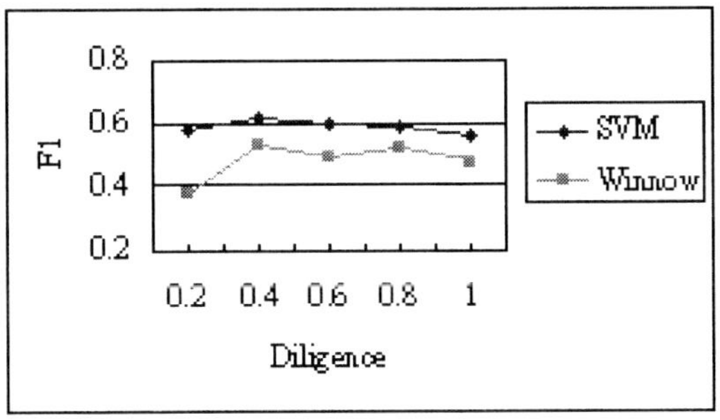

Figure 7. UMD distillation comparison of precisions between online SVM and balanced Winnow

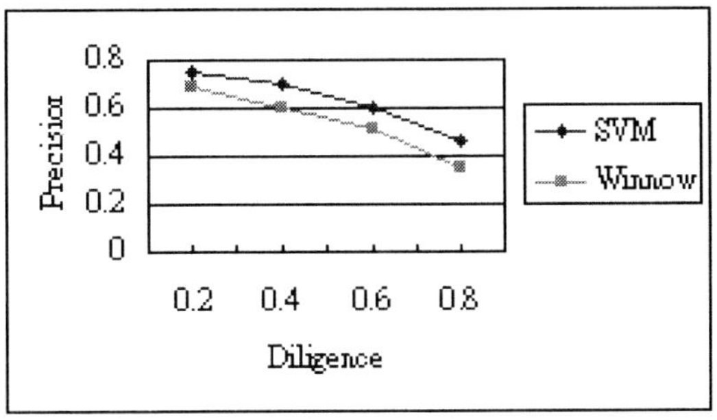

Figure 8. UMD distillation comparison of recalls between online SVM and balanced Winnow

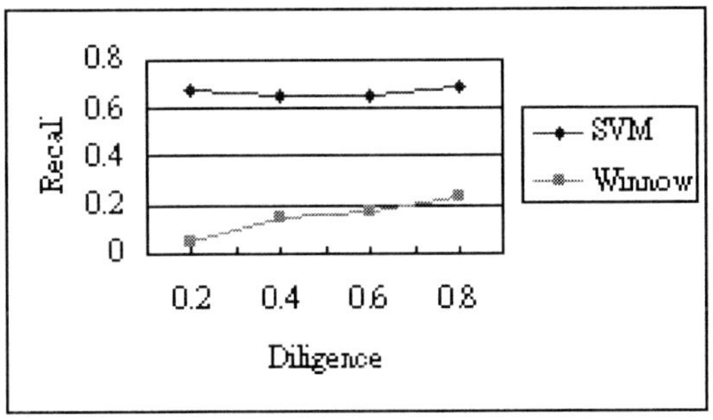

Figure 9. UMD distillation comparison of overall effectiveness of online SVM and balanced Winnow

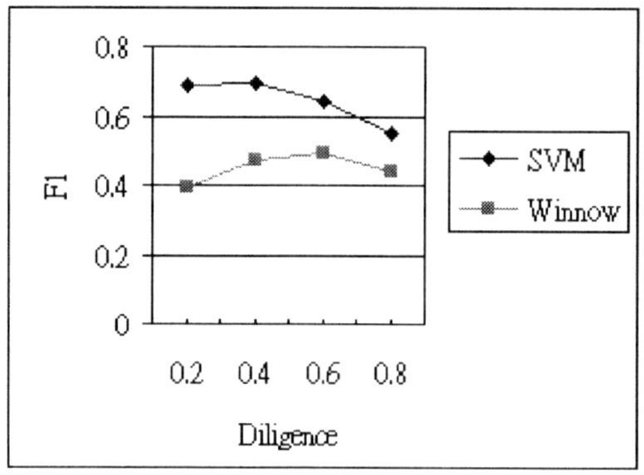

Figure 10. Effectiveness of SVM without/with PLD

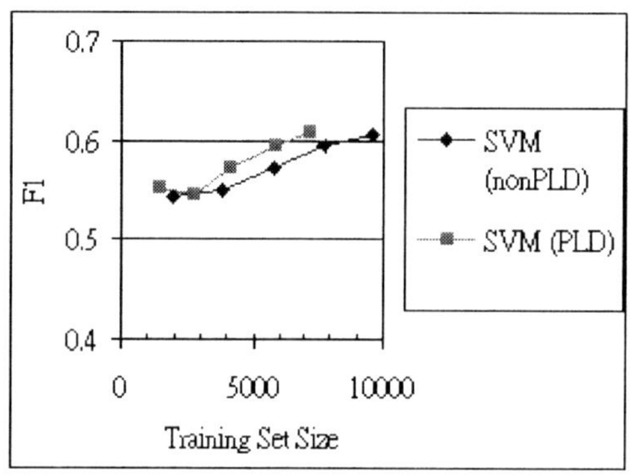

Figure 11. Effectiveness of Winnow without/with PLD

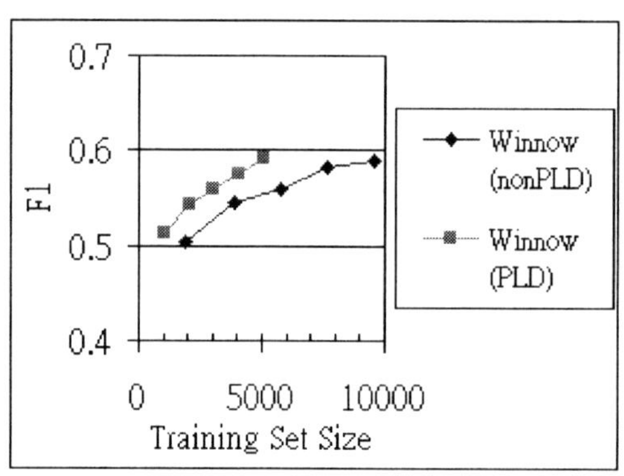

This work was previously published in Int. Journal of Information Technology and Web Engineering, Vol. 1, Issue 2, edited by G. Alkhatib and D. Rine, pp. 60-78, copyright 2006 by IGI Publishing (an imprint of IGI Global).

Section III
Access

Chapter IX
eDAR Algorithm for Continuous KNN Queries Based on Pine

Maytham Safar
Kuwait University, Kuwait

Dariush Ebrahimi
Kuwait University, Kuwait

ABSTRACT

The continuous K nearest neighbor (CKNN) query is an important type of query that finds continuously the KNN to a query point on a given path. We focus on moving queries issued on stationary objects in Spatial Network Database (SNDB) The result of this type of query is a set of intervals (defined by split points) and their corresponding KNNs. This means that the KNN of an object traveling on one interval of the path remains the same all through that interval, until it reaches a split point where its KNNs change. Existing methods for CKNN are based on Euclidean distances. In this paper we propose a new algorithm for answering CKNN in SNDB where the important measure for the shortest path is network distances rather than Euclidean distances. We propose DAR and eDAR algorithms to address CKNN queries based on the progressive incremental network expansion (PINE) technique. Our experiments show that the eDAR approach has better response time, and requires fewer shortest distance computations and KNN queries than approaches that are based on VN3 using IE.

INTRODUCTION

Several types of nearest neighbor (NN) search algorithms have been proposed and studied in the context of spatial databases. The most common type is the point KNN query, which is defined as: given a set of spatial objects (or points of interest), and an input query point, retrieve the (K) nearest neighbors to that query point. The NN is the target object with the shortest path from the query point on the route. The efficient implementation of KNN query is of a particular interest in geographical information systems (GIS). For example, a GPS device in a vehicle gives information of an object's location, which, once located onto a map, serves as a basis to find the K closest restaurants or gas stations with the shortest path to them.

Different variations of KNN queries have been introduced. One variation is the continuous KNNs of any point on a given path. As an example, when the GPS device of the vehicle initiates a query to continuously find the three nearest gas stations to the vehicle at any point of a path from source to destination. The result is a set of intervals or split points where the KNNs of a moving object on a path will be the same up to these points. The versatility of K nearest neighbors search increases substantially if we consider other variations of it such as the continuous KNN (CKNN). CKNN query is defined as the K nearest point of interest to every point on a path, and has found applications in the GISs (e.g., find my nearest three gas stations at *any* point during my route from city *A* to city *B*). The result of this type of query is a set of tuples <*result, interval*> such that *result* is the KNN of all points in the corresponding interval ordered by distances to the query point. The *interval* is defined by two end-points called *split points*, which specify where on the path the KNNs of a moving object will change. This means that the KNNs of an object traveling in one interval of the path remain the same all through that interval until it reaches a split point where its KNNs change.

In spatial network databases, as well as in practice, objects are restricted to move only on a predefined set of paths as specified by the underlying network (road, railroad, river, etc.) Thus, the network distance (i.e., the length of the shortest path connecting two objects is what represents the real distance between objects and *not* the objects' relative position in space). Surprisingly, most of the existing work considers only the Cartesian (Euclidean) spaces where the path between two objects is the straight line connecting them, which renders the distance computation impractical for spatial network databases (SNDBs.)

Our objects are restricted to move on pre-defined paths (e.g., road) that are specified by an underlying network. This means that the shortest network path (distance) between the objects (e.g., the vehicle and the gas station) depends on the connectivity of the network rather than the objects locations. In Safar (2005), we proposed a Voronoi-based progressive incremental network expansion (PINE) technique to solve the KNN queries. The main idea behind PINE is to first partition a large network into smaller regions by generating a network Voronoi diagram over the points of interest. Each cell of this Voronoi diagram is centered by one object (e.g., restaurant) and contains the nodes that are closest to that object in network distance. Next, we pre-compute the inter distances for each cell (i.e., distances across the border points of the adjacent cells). This would later reduce the pre-computation time and space to answer KNN queries. To find the first nearest neighbours of a query object, we find the first nearest neighbour by simply locating the Voronoi cell that contains the query object, then starting from the query point, we perform network expansion by computing the distance from our query to its first nearest neighbour (its Voronoi cell center point) and exploring the objects that are close to the query object then computing their distances to the query object during the expansion. In PINE, at the first scale inside the Voronoi cell, which contains the query object, the network expansion is similar to INE (incremental network expansion) (Papadias, Zhang, Mamoulis, & Tao, 2003) but when we reach the border point of a Voronoi cell, the second expansion is similar to VN^3 (Voronoi-based network nearest neighbour) (Kolahdouzan & Shahabi, 2004b).

In this article, we use our previous work (PINE) to address CKNN queries in SNDBs. Developing an efficient algorithm to solve such type of query is important for real time applications. It is important to note that issuing a traditional nearest neighbor query at every point of the line segment is infeasible due to the large number of queries generated and the large overhead. The challenge for this type of query is to efficiently find the location of the split point(s) on the path. Or in other words, where in the path do the KNNs change. The main idea behind our approach is that the KNNs of any object on a path between two adjacent nodes (e.g., intersection in road network) can be a subset of any points of interest (e.g., gas stations) on the path. Hence, the solution is based on breaking the entire path into smaller segments (sub-paths), where each segment is surrounded by two adjacent nodes. Our approach is then based on finding the minimum distances between two subsequent nearest neighbours of an object, only when the two neighbours can have a split point between them. This distance specifies the minimum distance that the object can move without requiring a new KNN query to be issued.

We first propose the DAR algorithm to solve CKNN based on PINE. To do that, first we find the KNNs of two end nodes. If there is no difference in KNNs between these two nodes, then there will be no split points between them. Otherwise, as we move from one end point to the other, the order of the KNNs of the first node would change until it becomes similar to KNNs of the second node. The order of the KNNs is always changed at a split point. Therefore, given the KNNs of the start point, we change the places of its ordered KNNs until we reach an order of KNNs similar to the end point. According to the number of changes that we do, there will be split points between the two nodes. In addition, we propose an enhanced variation of DAR named eDAR approach that is more efficient and reduces the number of required KNN queries. Furthermore, contrary to DAR, it requires no shortest path computations and requires fewer queues (hence memory) to find the answer to the CKNN query. We compare our algorithms with CKNN based on VN^3 using IE (intersection examination).

The remainder of this article is organized as follows. The second section provides a related work study, then we provide a review of the Voronoi diagram, network Voronoi diagram, IE, and PINE in the third section. In the fourth and fifth sections, we discuss our approaches to DAR and enhanced DAR (eDAR), respectively. Then in the sixth section, we provide our experimental results. Finally, we conclude our work in the seventh section.

RELATED WORK

The most common type of query encountered in spatial databases is the *point k* nearest neighbor (KNN) query, which is defined as: given a point query in a multidimensional space, find the *k* closest objects in the database to the query point. This type of query is extensively used in geographical information systems (GIS) and thus was the focus of many researches. There are two groups of algorithms proposed to address the KNN query. Some of the algorithms are based on utilizing the Euclidean distances; others are based on network distances. The regular KNN queries are the basis for several variations such as the Continuous KNN. In this section, we overview previous work related to KNN query, and its variation CKNN query.

The existing work on the first group considers Cartesian (typically, Euclidean) spaces, where the distance between two objects is determined by their relative position in space. The major disadvantage with the approaches in Korn, Sidiropoulos, Faloutsos, Siegel, and Protopapas (1996), Roussopoulos, Kelley, and Vincent (1995), and Seidl and Kriegel (1998) is that the shortest path calculations are performed based on Euclidean distances while in practice, objects usually move only on pre-defined roads. This makes the distance calculations depend on the connectivity among these objects. Here, the important measure is the network distance, which renders the algorithms in the first group impractical for SNDB.

The other group of research focuses on solving the KNN for spatial network databases. In these databases, the underlying network connections are captured and the distance between two objects is the length of the shortest path connecting them. The approaches in Kolahdouzan et al. (2004b), Papadias et al. (2003), and Safar, 2005) support the exact KNN queries on spatial network databases.

The solution in Papadias et al. (2003), called the incremental network expansion (INE), introduces an architecture that integrates network and Euclidean information. It is based on creating a search region for the query point that expands from the query which is similar to Dijkstra's algorithm. The advantages of this approach are: (1) it offers a method for finding the exact distance in networks, and (2) the architecture can support other spatial queries like range search and closest pairs. However, this approach suffers from poor performance when the objects (e.g., restaurants) are not densely distributed in the network because this will lead to large portions of the database to be retrieved. This problem happens for large values of *k* as well.

The Voronoi-based network nearest neighbor (VN^3) approach proposed in Kolahdouzan et al. (2004b) is based on the properties of the network Voronoi diagrams (NVD). It uses localized precomputations of the network distances for a very small percentage of neighboring nodes in the network to enhance query response time and reduce disk accesses. In addition, network Voronoi polygons (NVPs) of a NVD can directly be used to find the first nearest neighbor *q*. Subsequently, NVP's adjacency information provides a candidate set for other nearest neighbors of q. Finally the pre-computed distances are used to refine the set. The filter/refinement process in VN^3 is iterative: at each step, first a new set of candidates is generated from the NVPs, then the pre-computed distances are used to select "only the next" nearest neighbor of q. The advantages of this approach are: (1) it offers a method that finds the exact distances in networks, (2) fast query response time, and (3) progressively returns the k nearest neighbors and their distances from the query point. The main disadvantage of this approach is its need for pre-computing and maintaining two different sets of data: (1) query to border computation: computing the network distances from q to the border points of its enclosing network Voronoi polygon, and (2) border to border computation: computing the network distances from the border points of NVP of *q* to the border points of any of the other NVPs. Furthermore, this approach suffers in performance with lower density data sets.

We proposed in Safar (2005), a novel approach termed PINE to efficiently address KNN queries in SNDBs. The main idea behind this approach is to first partition a large network into smaller more manageable regions, then pre-compute distances across the regions. Those two steps can be easily and efficiently implemented using a first order Voronoi diagram, then a computation similar to the INE can be used for the computation of intra-distances. The advantage of PINE is that it has less disk access time and less CPU time than VN^3. In addition, PINE's performance is independent of the density and distribution of the points of interest and the location of the query object. By performing across-the-network computation for only the border points of the neighboring regions, we avoid global computations later on.

The solutions proposed for regular KNN queries are either directly used or have been adapted to address the variations of KNN queries such as

CKNN queries. Given a predefined route, a continuous query retrieves tuples of the form <*result, interval*> where each result is accompanied by a future interval, during which it is valid. Despite the importance of continuous queries in SNDBs, the scarce studies in the literature are designed for Euclidean spaces (e.g., Tao, Papadias, & Shen, 2002), which are not applicable to SNDBs.

For example, the approach proposed in Tao et al. (2002) uses the R-tree as the underlying data-partition access method. Their algorithm traverses the tree and prunes unnecessary node accesses based on some heuristics that uses Euclidean distances. Their goal is to perform one single query of the entire path. The algorithm starts with an initial list of split points (SL) containing only the path starting and ending nodes, and an empty initial list of NNs, and then it incrementally updates the *SL* during query processing. After each step, the *SL* contains the current result with respect to all the data points processed so far. The final result contains each split point that *remains* in *SL* after the termination together with its nearest neighbor. The advantage of Tao et al. (2002) is the avoidance of multiple database scans by reporting the result with a single traversal of the database. Yet, it still has the major disadvantage of using Euclidean distances that are not applicable to network distances.

Finally, Kolahdouzan and Shahabi (2004a) address the problem of CKNN queries in road networks. They proposed two techniques termed intersection examination (IE) and upper bound algorithm (UBA) to find the location and KNN of split point(s) on the path. The first solution, IE, finds KNNs of all the nodes on a path by breaking the path into segments and only examining the KNNs of intersection nodes. There is a split point on the shortest path between two adjacent nodes with different KNNs and the location of that point is calculated. The second approach, UBA, improves the performance of IE by reducing the number of KNN computations by eliminating the computation of KNNs for the nodes that cannot have any split points in between. The intuition of UBA is that when a query object is moved slightly, it is very likely that its KNNs remain the same. UBA proposes a method to find the minimum distance that the object can move without requiring a new KNN to be issued.

There are three shortcomings of Kolahdouzan et al. (2004a): (1) the total number of split points computed using this algorithm is sometimes redundant or useless for some kinds of applications as we explained in the first section, (2) The distance to all the KNN of both end nodes (i.e., the distance to the candidate list of each segment) is updated and ordered at each split point which incurs unnecessary overhead, and (3) The PINE algorithm is more efficient than VN^3 in finding the KNN of a point. (For experimental results see Safar, 2005). To the best of our knowledge, Kolahdouzan et al. (2004a) is the only approach that uses network distances to find CKNN.

BACKGROUND

Our proposed approach to address the nearest neighbor queries is based on both the *Voronoi diagram* and *Dijkstra's* algorithm. A Voronoi diagram divides a space into disjoint polygons where the nearest neighbor of any point inside a polygon is the generator of the polygon. Dijkstra's algorithm provides one of the most efficient algorithms that finds the shortest paths from the source node to all the other nodes. In this section, we review the principles of the Voronoi diagrams. We start with the Voronoi diagram for *2-dimensional* Euclidean space and present only the properties that are used in our approach. We then discuss the *network Voronoi diagram* where the distance between two objects in space is their shortest path in the network rather than their Euclidean distance and hence can be used for spatial networks. Then, we talk about two different approaches for solving

KNN queries (i.e., IE and PINE) that our proposed DAR and eDAR algorithms depend on. A thorough discussion on Voronoi diagrams is presented in Okabe, Boots, Sugihara, and Chiu (2000) and Safar (2005).

Voronoi Diagrams

Imagine you are looking for a school for your kid. Among the criteria to be considered will be the length of the way to school. If you formulate this as a spatial analysis problem, you are looking for the school that is closest to your home, among all schools in your city. The classical approach to solve this spatial analysis problem is the Voronoi diagram. The Voronoi diagram isolates the area that is closest to each school. The Voronoi diagram of a point set *P*, *VD(P)*, is a unique diagram that consists of a set of collectively exhaustive and mutually exclusive *Voronoi polygons* (*Voronoi cells*), *VPs*. Each Voronoi polygon is associated with a point in *P* (called *generator point*) and contains all the locations in the Euclidean plane that are closer to the generator point of the Voronoi cell than any other generator point in *P*. The boundaries of the polygons, called *Voronoi edges*, are the set of locations that can be assigned to more than one generator. The Voronoi polygons that share the same edges are called *adjacent polygons* and their generators are called *adjacent generators*. The following property holds for any Voronoi diagram and is used to answer KNN queries:

The nearest generator point of p_i *(e.g.,* p_j*) is among the generator points whose Voronoi polygons share similar Voronoi edges with* $VP(p_i)$. (Kolahdouzan et al., 2004b; Okabe et al., 2000)

In genereal, a Voronoi diagram of a set of "sites" (points) is a collection of regions that divide up the plane. Each region corresponds to one of the sites, and all the points in one region are closer to the corresponding site than to any other site.

Network Voronoi Diagrams

Sometimes the approach is of limited value, especially if the possibilities to move in space are limited to one or several networks. In this case, the previously described method gives only rough estimates and might even be significantly wrong. Several assumptions of the Voronoi diagram are violated in urban areas; distances between two addresses are not Euclidean; they have to be measured along the travel network(s). If your son has to walk around a block of buildings, the way to school can be significantly longer than the Euclidean distance. Thus, we use the network Voronoi diagram (Okabe et al., 2000):

A network Voronoi diagram, termed NVD, is defined for graphs and is a specialization of Voronoi diagrams where the location of objects is restricted to the links that connect the nodes of the graph and the distance between objects is defined as their shortest path in the network rather than their Euclidean distance. (Kolahdouzan et al., 2004a; Roussopoulos et al., 1995)

Spatial networks (e.g., road networks) can be modeled as weighted planar graphs where nodes of the graph represent the intersections and roads are represented by the links connecting the nodes.

The network Voronoi diagram considers distances only in networks, not in the plane. It divides the network, not the space, into Voronoi cells. A Voronoi cell in a network is the set of nodes and edges that are closer to one Voronoi generator (here, a school) than to any other. For the construction of the network Voronoi diagram, an algorithm is used based on the shortest path algorithm of Dijkstra. Dijkstra's algorithm calculates in a connected network the shortest path from a selected start node to any other node in the network (Kolahdouzan et al., 2004a; Roussopoulos et al., 1995).

Intersection Examination: IE

IE (Kolahdouzan et al., 2004a) is one of the techniques used to address CKNN queries in a spatial network database. It is based on examining the KNNs of the intersections on the path. In IE, in order to find the continuous KNN of any point on a path, we can first break the path into smaller segments, then we find the continuous KNN for each segment, and finally, the union of the results for all segments generates the result set for the entire path. The K nearest points of interest to any object on a path is a subset of K nearest points of interest to both adjacent nodes. If two adjacent nodes have similar KNNs, then every object on the path between the nodes will have similar KNNs as the nodes (i.e., there will be no split points). Once the KNNs of the nodes in the network are specified, we need to find the locations and the KNNs of the split points on each segment (i.e., path between two adjacent nodes). We divide the KNNs of a node to two increasing and decreasing groups. As a definition a point of interest o is called increasing for the direction, $n_i \rightarrow n_j$ if the shortest path from n_i to o does not pass through n_j, and it is called decreasing otherwise.

Voronoi-Based Progressive Incremental Network Expansion: PINE

PINE (Safar, 2005) is similar to incremental network expansion (INE) (Papadias et al., 2003), which performs network expansion starting from the query point q and examines the interest points in the order they are encountered. PINE is also based on the properties of the network Voronoi diagrams and pre-computation of the network distances for a very small percentage of the nodes in the network. In PINE, to reduce the computation time, all the distances between the border to border and border to interest node of the network Voronoi polygons (NVP) are pre-computed before.

PINE works as follows: First it locates the network Voronoi polygon (NVP(q)) that the query point q belongs to. Hence, the first nearest neighbor (the generator point of NVP(q)) will be retrieved and placed in priority queue PQ. Then, the links that cover q are located and the nodes of those links are placed in a queue called priority node queue (PNQ) according to their network distance to q and are explored later. Next, the node closest to q (i.e., the node on top of PNQ), for example, c, is removed from PNQ and nodes that are connected to c are retrieved from the database. Subsequently, the minimum possible network distances (d_{mnp}), distances from q to these nodes are computed and the nodes are placed in PNQ (if they are already in PNQ, their locations on the queue are updated based on their new distances to q). During the progressive process when we reach a n_{Net} (node inside the NVP(q)), we expand from it as INE algorithm using the original network edges/nodes of NVP(q). However, when we reach a n_{NVP} (node on a border of NVP(q)) connecting to a new polygon (NVP(j)) adjacent to NVP(q), then we do not need the original network edges/nodes of NVP(j). This is because, for any polygon we know how to reach (shortest path) from any border point to any other border point and how much it costs. Therefore, we consider that all other border points of NVP(j) as the links that we can reach from n_{NVP} and we add them to PNQ to be explored later. In addition, we know the distance from any border point of NVP(j) (including n_{NVP}) to its generator point (interest point). Therefore, we compute the d_{mnp} to that generator (not the actual shortest distance) and add the generator point for NVP(j) to our k interest points queue PQ. At any point during the algorithm execution, the nodes inside the PQ are only candidate neighbors that we can reach so far and their order in the queue is ordered ascendingly according to distance. The order of the nodes in the queue may change at each execution step, if we are able to find a shortest path to reach the same node that is ready in PQ.

Nodes can also be added or dropped depending on their updated d_{mnp}. This is because our algorithm depends on Dijkstra's algorithm that updates the distance estimates to all vertices adjacent to the currently selected vertex. Only at the end of the progressive process, PQ would have the K interest points of q ordered from top to bottom. We recursively apply the previous algorithm and terminate it when we have the queue PQ filled with K interest points and the distances from q to any element of PNQ is greater than the distance to reach any node in PQ. This means, from any point in PNQ, we cannot reach another neighbor with a distance shorter than any of the K interest points already discovered.

DAR ALGORITHM

DAR algorithm is used to find continuous K nearest neighbor (CKNN), which is defined as the nearest points of interest to all the points on a path (e.g., continuously finding the three nearest gas stations to a moving car). The result of this algorithm is a set of split points and their corresponding K nearest neighbors (KNNs), such that the KNNs of all objects within each interval of two points are the same.

DAR algorithm works as follows: First, we divide the path P into sub-paths according to the number of nodes (intersection points) in its way. Let's say there are m nodes on path P that start from node N_1 and end with node N_m. P= $\{N_1, N_2, \ldots, N_m\}$. Start with the first sub-path (interval) between nodes N_1 & N_2 and find their KNNs using PINE algorithm (Safar, 2005) then arrange the KNNs according to their order in two priority-queues PQ_1 & PQ_2 with distances, respectively. Compare the KNNs in both PQ_1 and PQ_2, if there is an interest point in PQ_1 that is not in PQ_2, put that point at ready-in queue of

Figure 1. Path P

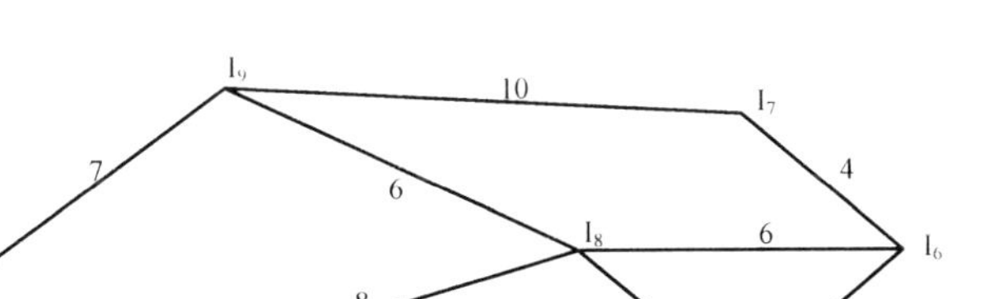

Figure 2. Example on path AB

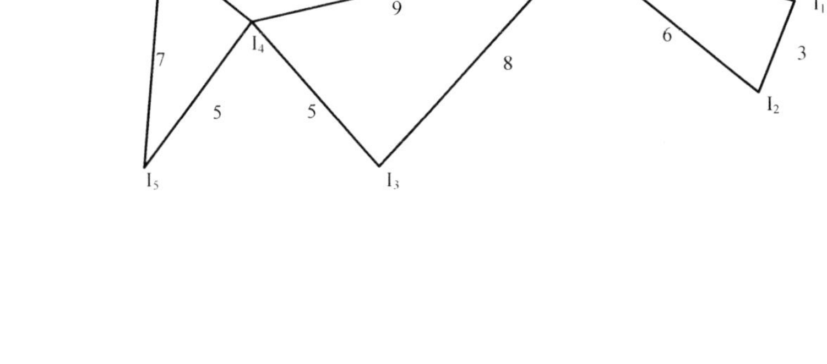

N_1 (RQ_1) and do the same for node N_2, because we need to compare between the two queues later and the number of KNNs in both queues should be the same. Compare the order of KNNs in both PQ_1 & PQ_2, if there is no difference, there will be no split point(s) between the two nodes; otherwise, check the KNNs in PQ_1, one by one from top to bottom, if the position of one of the KNNs in PQ_1 did not match the position of the same KNN in PQ_2, then the KNN should change place up or down to get to the same position in PQ_2. As one step change happenes in the order of PQ, there will be one split point. So the number of changes needed to be done on PQ_1 to match with PQ_2 will be the number of split points on the interval between N_1 & N_2.

Let $PQ_1 = \{ I_1, I_2, \ldots, I_k \}$ and $PQ_2 = \{ I'_1, I'_2, \ldots, I'_k \}$ be the K nearest points of interest to N_1 and N_2, respectively. Start from the top of PQ_1 ($I_i = I_1$) and go down through all KNNs (up to $I_i = I_k$), if the position of one of the interest points in PQ_1 is not the same as its position in PQ_2 (i.e., $I_i \neq I'_i$), we compute

$$\lambda_{I_i, I_{i+1}} = \frac{d(A,B) + d(B, I'_i) + d(A, I_i)}{2} - d(A, I_i) = \frac{d(A,B) + d(B, I'_i) - d(A, I_i)}{2}$$

λ represents the distance from the start node (i.e., A) to the split point, where this point is on the path between the two interest points (A and B), and at this point the order of the nearest neighbor will change. When we are at the bottom of PQ_1, compute λ of that interest point with all the interest points in RQ_1. Compare between all λs and take the minimum λ to be the split point. According to λ we make the changes in the order of PQ_1 queue. If the changes have to be done between last interest point in Priority-Queue and Ready-In-Queue, pop out the interest point in PQ and bring in the interest point from RQ queue to PQ queue. Note that if the last interest point in PQ_1 has come from the Ready-In queue (RQ_1), then there is no need to compute λ for it, since

Figure 3. DAR 3NNs of nodes A & B

PQ_1		PQ_2	
I_6	4	I_4	3
I_8	4	I_{10}	4
I_1	5	I_5	7

Figure 4. DAR after updating with RQ

	PQ_1		PQ_2		
	I_6	4	I_4	3	
	I_8	4	I_{10}	4	
	I_1	5	I_5	7	
RQ_1	I_4	9	I_8	8	RQ_2
	I_5	14	I_6	14	
	I_{10}	15	I_1	16	

Figure 5. DAR PQ_1 after finding first split point

I_6	4
I_8	4
I_4	9
I_5	14
I_{10}	15

recently it has come from the RQ_1 and it will not go back to RQ_1 again.

To make our algorithm more clear, we will explain it with an example. Consider Figure 1. In our example, we want to find three nearest neighbors through the path P. We divided path P into sub-paths according to the number of nodes (intersection points) in its way. In our example, A and B are two intersection points (nodes), so the path AB is a sub-path of path P. To illustrate our technique, we focus on the AB segment. The other consequent segments can be treated similarly.

In Figure 2, the path AB, interest points $I = \{I_1, I_2, \ldots, I_{10}\}$, and their distances are shown. To find the continuous 3-NN through path AB, we have to find the break points, where the 3-nearest neighbors on the path are the same up to the break point. The break points on path AB will be found as follows. First we find 3NN of both end points of path AB by using PINE algorithm and we store the result in PQ_1 and PQ_2 with their shortest path to A & B respectively (see Figure 3).

As it is clear the KNN nodes in PQ_1 will change to KNN nodes in PQ_2 since as the car moves from starting point A to B, the order of nearest neighbors will change through the path and for each change there will be one split point.

At the second step, after comparing PQ_1 with PQ_2, we see that all the interest points in PQ_2 are not in PQ_1, so we put all the interest points I_4, I_{10} & I_5 in RQ_1 with their shortest path to A, and we do the same for B (see Figure 4). PQs are shown with solid lines in the table and RQs with dashed lines.

At the third step, we calculate λ as mentioned before. We see that none of the interest points in PQ_1 are aligned with other respective interest points in PQ_2, I_6 is aligned with I_4, I_8 aligned with I_{10} and I_1 aligned with I_5. So we calculate the following λs.

$\lambda_{I_6 \& I_8} = (11+8-4)/2 = 7.5$, $\lambda_{I_8 \& I_1} = 7$

$\lambda_{I_1 \& I_4} = 4.5$ ← split-point #1

$\lambda_{I_1 \& I_{10}} = 5$, $\lambda_{I_1 \& I_5} = 6.5$

Note that if one of the interest points is aligned, then we are not going to calculate λ for it, since it is in the right position and does not need to change its place. As seen above, we calculate λ for all interest points which are next to each other in PQ_1. Also we calculate λ of I_1, which is at the bottom of PQ_1 with all interest points at RQ_1. For example $\lambda_{I_6 \& I_8}$ is obtained by adding the distance of path AB with the shortest path of B to I_8 and subtracting the shortest path of B to I_6 and dividing the answer by 2. We take the smallest $\lambda_{I_1 \& I_4}$=4.5 to be our first split point (distance

Figure 6. DAR PQ_1 after finding second split point

I_6	4
I_4	9
I_8	4
I_5	14
I_{10}	15

Figure 7. DAR PQ_1 after changing places of I_4 & I_6

I_4	9
I_6	4
I_8	4
I_5	14
I_{10}	15

Figure 8. DAR PQ_1 after finding split point #3

I_4	9
I_6	4
I_{10}	15
I_5	14

Figure 9. DAR PQ_1 after changing places of I_6 & I_{10}

I_4	9
I_{10}	15
I_6	4
I_5	14

from node A), and we conclude that at that point I_1 will change place with I_4. So PQ_1 will change as shown in Figure 5.

Since I_1 has to change place with I_4 that is in RQ_1, we pop out I_1 from RQ_1. Since if we insert I_1 into RQ_1, it will not come back to PQ_1 again, therefore we remove I_1 here.

At the fourth step, since PQ_1 is still not aligned with PQ_2, we continue calculating λ as in step three. The λs that we have to calculate are:

$\lambda_{I_6\&I_8} = 7.5$ been computed before

$\lambda_{I_8\&I_4} = 5$ ←split-point #2

~~$\lambda_{I_4\&I_{10}} = 3$~~ I_4 has just came in from Ready-queue

~~$\lambda_{I_4\&I_5} = 4.5$~~

Since I_4 has been brought in from RQ_1, there is no need to compute its λ with all other interest points in RQ_1, because it will not go back to RQ_1 again and it will not create a new split point. The smallest λ is $\lambda_{I_8\&I_4}$=5 and it is our split point #2. So I_8 will change place with I_4 (see Figure 6).

Figure 10. DAR PQ_1 after finding split point #4

I_4	9
I_{10}	15
I_5	14

At the fifth step, the λs have been calculated as follows:

$\lambda_{I_6\&I_4} = 5$

~~$\lambda_{I_4\&I_8} = 5$~~ The order of I_4& I_8 has been changed before

$\lambda_{I_8\&I_{10}} = 5.5$

$\lambda_{I_8\&I_5} = 7$

The order of I_4 & I_8 has been changed before, so they are not going to be changed again, therefore there is no need to calculate its λ. Here the smallest λ is $\lambda_{I_6\&I_4}$=5 and I_6 is going to change place with I_4. Notice that at this step, we do not have any new split points, because at λ=5 we already had a split point.

At the sixth step, there is no need to calculate λ for I_4 since it is at the right place by comparing with PQ_2 and the λs are as follows:

$\lambda_{I_6\&I_8} = 7.5$

$\lambda_{I_8\&I_{10}} = 5.5$ ←split-point #3

$\lambda_{I_8\&I_5} = 7$

At $\lambda_{I_8\&I_{10}}$=5.5 we have a split point and I_8 is going to pop out and I_{10} will replace it (see Figure 8).

At the seventh step, we have to calculate only $\lambda_{I_6\&I_{10}}$=5.5 and places of I_6 and I_{10} are going to be changed. There is no new split point because already at this point we had a split point. At this

Figure 11. DAR step changes on PQ_1

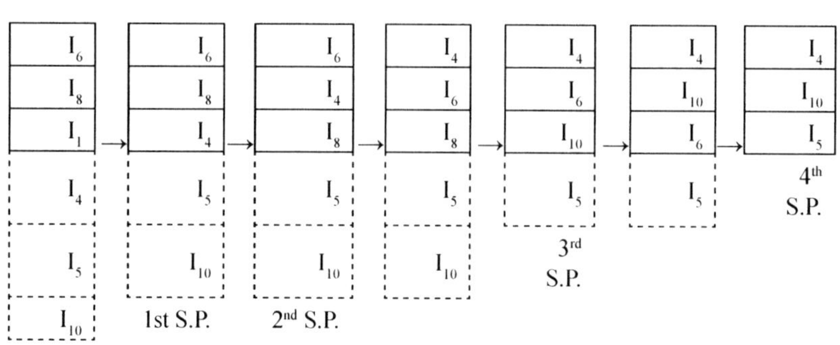

Figure 12. eDAR after updating with RQ

	PQ_1		PQ_2	
	I_6	4	I_4	3
	I_8	4	I_{10}	4
	I_1	5	I_5	7
RQ_1	I_4	3		
	I_{10}	4		
	I_5	7		

Figure 13. eDAR PQ_1 after finding the first split point

	PQ_1	
	I_6	4
	I_8	4
	I_4	3
RQ_1	I_{10}	4
RQ1	I_5	7

step we are not going to calculate λ for I_{10} and I_5, because I_{10} was at RQ_1 before (see Figure 9).

At the last step, we will have split point #4 at $\lambda_{I_6\&I_5}=7$ and PQ_1 after changing I_6 with I_5 will look like PQ_2 (see Figure 10).

Hence the total number of split points on path AB is 4 and all the step changes of PQ_1 are shown in Figure 11.

Algorithm: DAR (P,k)

1. Divide the path P into subsets according to the number of nodes in its way. $P=\{n_0,n_1,\ldots,n_m\}$, where ni's are intersections or interest points.
2. Start from $n_i = n_0$, if $n_i \neq n_m$:-

a. Find KNN for n_i & n_{i+1} and put them in PQ_i & PQ_{i+1} respectively.

b. Compare the order of KNN in both PQ of n_i & n_{i+1} , if there is an interest-point in PQi that is not in PQ_{i+1}, put that point in the RQ of n_i (RQ_i) with distance (shortest path) to n_i and do the same for n_{i+1}.

c. While the order of KNN in PQ_i & PQ_{i+1} is not the same:-

i. Start from the top of PQ_i ($PQ_i[j]$,j=0,1,…,h) as $j \neq h$ (j is/not at the end of PQ_i):-
1. If $PQ_i[j] \neq PQ_{i+1}[j]$, compute λ_j.

$$\lambda_j = \frac{d(n_i,n_{i+1}) + d(n_{i+1},PQ_{i+1}[j+1]) - d(n_i,PQ_i[j])}{2}$$

2. When j=h (h is the last interest-point of PQ_i), if the last interest-point did not come from the RQi, compute λ_j of n_i[j=h] with all interest-points which are in RQ_i.

ii. Compare all the λ_js and take the minimum λ_j to be the split-point (if it is not included yet). If the value of λ_j equals the previous λ, then we ignore the last λ.

iii. According to λ_j we make the changes in order of PQ_i. If the changes have to be done between the last interest-point in PQ_i and RQ_i, pop out the last interest-point in PQ_i and bring in the interest-point from RQ_i to PQ_i.

END

EDAR ALGORITHM

eDar algorithm is an enhanced variation of the DAR algorithm. With DAR we maintain two priority queues (PQ_1 and PQ_2) to store the KNNs of each sub-path endpoints (A and B), and two ready-in-queues (RQ_1 and RQ_2). RQ_1 stores all KNNs of B (in PQ_2) but not KNNs of A (in PQ_1) with their shortest path to A, and we do the same for B and RQ_2. Then, if the KNNs in both PQs do not match node names or positions in the PQs, we start from the top of PQ_1 and compute λ (shortest path) for every two consecutive KNNs in PQ_1

Figure 14. eDAR PQ_1 after finding second split point

PQ_1

I_4	3
I_6	4
I_8	4

RQ1

I_{10}	4
I_5	7

Figure 15. eDAR PQ1 after finding split point #3

PQ_1

I_4	3
I_{10}	4
I_6	4

RQ1

I_5	7

Figure 16. eDAR PQ_1 after finding split point #4

PQ_1

I_4	3
I_{10}	4
I_5	7

and compute λ for the last KNN in PQ_1 and every entry in RQ_1. λs represent the distances from the start node (i.e., A) to the candidate split points, where this point is on the path between the two interest points (A and B), and at this point the order of the nearest neighbor will change. Finally, we compare all λs and take the minimum λ to be the split point. According to λ we make the changes in the order of PQ_1 queue. If the changes have to be done between the last interest point in priority-queue and ready-in-queue, we pop out the interest point in PQ and bring in the interest point from RQ queue to PQ queue. The computation of λs continues at each step of the algorithm (requiring the use of expensive shortest path algorithm) until PQ_1 matches PQ_2 (i.e., all split points are found).

With eDar, we strive to reduce the number and size of the required queues, and in addition we try to reduce the number/complexity of distance computations (λs). In eDAR, we still maintain two priority queues (PQ_1 and PQ_2) as in DAR. However, we maintain only one ready-in-queue (RQ_1) that stores all KNNs of B (in PQ_2) but not KNNs of A (in PQ_1). For the entries in RQ_1, we store their distances to B (and not to A as in DAR). Note that, by this, we do not need to compute the actual shortest path distances from the KNNs to the entries in RQ_1 as in DAR, we only copy the entries from PQ_2 into RQ_1. Hence we reduce the complexity of our algorithm. To find the split points on the sub-path we compute λs for all interest points in PQ_1 with all the interest points in PQ_2, regardless of the position of those interest points inside the priorities queues PQ_1 and PQ_2. Note that, in contrary to DAR, eDAR λs are computed only at this step of the algorithm, and the subsequent steps will not require computing any more λs. In addition, we do not need to use the shortest path algorithm to compute such λs.

The next step in eDAR is to reduce/delete some redundant and unnecessary λs, in the sense that they will not produce any real split points. Towards this end, we check if a λ value is negative or greater than the distance of the sub-path (i.e., *d(A, B)*), then it is deleted. This is because they would represent split points that are outside the sub-path; hence they cannot be considered as real split points for the sub-path. In addition, we delete λs which have been computed by the same two interest points, one in PQ_1 and the other in PQ_2 (i.e., $\lambda_{Ii,I'j}$, where I_i is the same as I'_j), since a split point can only exist between two different interest points. Finally, we delete duplicate λs (e.g., $\lambda_{Ii,I'j}$ is the same as $\lambda_{I'j,Ii}$), since a split point can appear only once between two different interest points.

Figure 17. eDAR PQ1 after finding split point #4

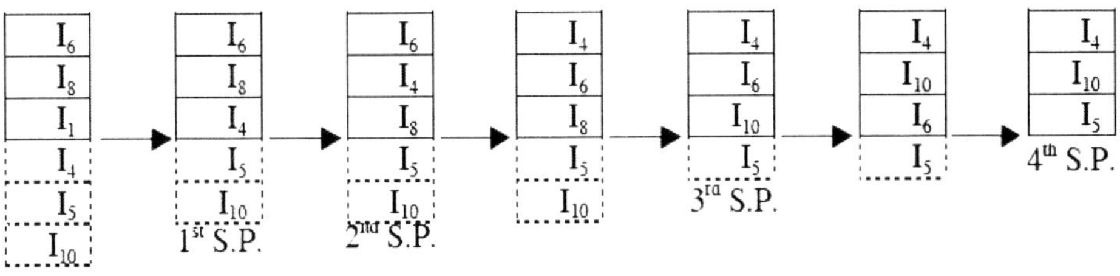

We arrange the remaining λs in ascending order from smallest to biggest in a queue (LQ). All λs are going to represent split points on the sub-path. However, some of them are not real split points (i.e., no change in the order of the interest points would occur). Hence, in the next step we want to identify such λs and remove them from LQ. The remaining λs in LQ would be the real set of split points on the sub-path. If one of the interest points in PQ_1 changes place with one of the interest points in RQ_1, then it will never go back to PQ_1 again (as explained in section 4). Hence, this interest point will not make any further split points on the path. Therefore, once an interest point moves from PQ_1 to RQ_1, we need to remove all the λs computed from that interest point from LQ.

To make our algorithm more clear, we will explain it with an example. We will use the exact same network and query as the example in the fourth section. To find the break points on path AB, first we find 3NN of both end points of path AB by using PINE algorithm and we store the result in PQ_1 and PQ_2 with their shortest path to A & B respectively (see Figure 3). At the Second step, after comparing PQ_1 with PQ_2, we see that all the interest points in PQ_2 are not in PQ_1, so we put all the interest points I_4, I_{10} & I_5 in RQ_1 with their distances to B (see Figure 12). PQs are shown with solid lines in the table and RQs with dashed lines.

At the third step, we calculate λ for all points in PQ_1 with all points in PQ_2 as follows:

$$\lambda_{I_6\&I_4} = (11 + 3 - 4) / 2 = 5$$
$$\lambda_{I_6\&I_{10}} = (11 + 4 - 4) / 2 = 5.5$$
$$\lambda_{I_6\&I_5} = (11 + 7 - 4) / 2 = 7$$
$$\lambda_{I_8\&I_4} = (11 + 3 - 4) / 2 = 5$$
$$\lambda_{I_8\&I_{10}} = (11 + 4 - 4) / 2 = 5.5$$
$$\lambda_{I_8\&I_5} = (11 + 7 - 4) / 2 = 7$$
$$\lambda_{I_1\&I_4} = (11 + 3 - 5) / 2 = 4.5$$
$$\lambda_{I_1\&I_{10}} = (11 + 4 - 5) / 2 = 5$$
$$\lambda_{I_1\&I_5} = (11 + 7 - 5) / 2 = 6.5$$

For example $\lambda_{I_6\&I_4}$ is obtained by adding the distance of path AB with the shortest path of B to I_4 and subtracting the shortest path of A to I_6 and dividing the answer by 2.

At the fourth step, we arrange the λs according to their values from smallest to largest.

$$\lambda_{I_1\&I_4} = 4.5$$
$$\lambda_{I_6\&I_4} = 5 \quad \lambda_{I_8\&I_4} = 5 \quad \lambda_{I_1\&I_{10}} = 5$$
$$\lambda_{I_6\&I_{10}} = 5.5 \quad \lambda_{I_8\&I_{10}} = 5.5$$
$$\lambda_{I_1\&I_5} = 6.5$$
$$\lambda_{I_6\&I_5} = 7 \quad \lambda_{I_8\&I_5} = 7$$

We take the smallest $\lambda_{I_1\&I_4} = 4.5$ to be our first split point (distance from node A), and we conclude that at that point I_1 will change place with I_4. So PQ_1 will change as shown in Figure 13.

Since I_1 has to change place with I_4, that is in the RQ_1, we pop out I_1 from RQ_1. Since if we insert I_1 into RQ_1, it will not come back to PQ_1 again, therefore we remove I_1 here and all the λs which have been computed by I_1. We remove $\lambda_{I_1\&I_{10}} = 5$ and $\lambda_{I_1\&I_5} = 6.5$. The remaining λs are as follows:

$\lambda_{I_1\&I_4} = 4.5$

$\lambda_{I_6\&I_4} = 5 \quad \lambda_{I_1\&I_{10}} = 5$

$\lambda_{I_6\&I_{10}} = 5.5$

$\lambda_{I_1\&I_5} = 6.5$

$\lambda_{I_6\&I_5} = 7 \quad \lambda_{I_8\&I_5} = 7$

Now, the second smallest λ is $\lambda_{I_8\&I_4}=5$ & $\lambda_{I_6\&I_4}=5$ and it is our second split point. Hence, I_8 will change place with I_4 and at the same time I_4 will change place with I_6 (see Figure 14).

The third split point is $\lambda_{I_8\&I_{10}}=5.5$ & $\lambda_{I_6\&I_{10}}=5.5$, where at distance 5.5 from node A, I_8 will change place with I_{10} and at the same time I6 with I_{10} (see Figure 15).

Since I_8 has to change place with one of the points in RQ_1, we remove all the λs which have been computed by I_8. We remove $\lambda_{I_8\&I_5}=7$. The remaining λs are as follows:

$\lambda_{I_1\&I_4} = 4.5$

$\lambda_{I_6\&I_4} = 5 \quad \lambda_{I_1\&I_{10}} = 5$

$\lambda_{I_6\&I_{10}} = 5.5$

$\lambda_{I_1\&I_5} = 6.5$

$\lambda_{I_8\&I_5} = 7$

At the last step we will have the fourth split point at $\lambda_{I_6\&I_5}=7$ and PQ_1 after changing I_6 with I_5 will look like PQ_2 (see Figure 16).

Hence the total number of split points on path AB is 4 and all the step changes of PQ_1 are shown in Figure 17.

Algorithm: eDAR (P,k)

1. Divide the path P into subsets according to the number of nodes in its way. P = $\{n_0, n_1, \ldots, n_m\}$, where n_i's are intersections or interest points.
2. Start from $n_i = n_0$, while $n_i \neq n_m$ do :- Find KNNs for n_i & n_{i+1} and put them in PQ_i & PQ_{i+1} with their distances (shortest path) to n_i & n_{i+1}, respectively.

a. Compare the order of KNNs in both PQ of n_i & n_{i+1}, if there is an interest-point in PQ_i that is not in PQ_{i+1}, put that point in the RQ of n_i (RQ_i) with its distance to n_{i+1}.

b. While the order of KNNs in PQi & PQ_{i+1} are not the same:-

i. For all nodes in PQ_i [x=1,2,…,h] & PQ_{i+1}[y=1,2,…,q]

Compute λ=

$$\frac{d(n_i, n_{i+1}) + d(n_{i+1}, PQ_{i+1}[y]) - d(n_i, PQ_i[x])}{2}$$

ii. If $PQ_i[x] \neq PQ_{i+1}[y]$ & the λ for the two nodes has not been computed before and $\lambda < d(n_i, n_{i+1})$ & $\lambda>0$, put λ in LQ.

c. Remove the unneeded Split-points from LQ with the following properties: (1) λ value is negative, (2) λ value is greater than the distance of the sub-path, (3) λs which have been computed by the same two interest points one in PQ_i and the other in PQ_{i+1}, (4) duplicate λs (e.g., $\lambda_{I_i\&I_j}$ is the same as $\lambda_{I_j\&I_i}$), and (5) λs of interest points that move from PQ_i to RQ_i.

END

PERFORMANCE EVALUATION

We conducted several experiments to compare the performance of DAR and eDAR algorithms on PINE to solve continuous KNN queries to that of continuous KNN on VN^3 (IE). We used real-world data sets obtained from NavTech Inc., used for navigation and GPS devices installed in cars, and represent a network of approximately 110,000 links and 79,800 nodes of the road system in downtown Los Angeles. The experiments were using Oracle 9 as the database server. We present the average results of 100 runs of continuous K nearest neighbor queries where K varied from 1 to 20.

Continuous KNN using PINE (DAR and eDAR)

We conducted several experiments to evaluate the performance of the continuous KNN queries with PINE structure (DAR and eDAR) using different sets of points of interest (e.g., restaurants, shopping centers, …, etc.). We calculated the number of times that the KNN query must be issued and the execution time in seconds for different values of K and assumed that the length of the traveling paths are equal to 4 km. The traveling paths were generated randomly, however, we made sure that we did not visit any node more than once (to avoid cycles).

In Table 1, we present the average results of 5 runs of continuous K nearest neighbor queries using DAR. For example, in Table 1 we show the query response time for DAR when the length of the traveling path is 4 km and the value of K varies from 1 to 4. The first and second columns specify the entities (or points of interest) and their population and cardinality ratio (i.e., the number of entities over the number of links in the network), respectively. From the third column and forward, each table entry has two values (averaged over five runs): (1) number of KNN queries that were issued and (2) execution time in seconds. Due to the slow response time of DAR algorithm, we decided to only average the results of five experiments and to use four as the largest value for K.

In the next experiment, we used eDAR algorithm on PINE structure to solve continuous K nearest neighbor queries. In Table 2, we present the average results of 100 runs (except for the case of K = 20 using Hospitals were we ran only 10 queries) of eDAR algorithm for different values of K varying from 1 to 20.

Continuous KNN using VN^3 (IE)

We conducted several experiments to evaluate the performance of the continuous KNN queries with VN^3 structure (IE) using different sets of points of interest (e.g., restaurants, shopping centers, …, etc.) and for different values of K (values of {1, 3, 5, 10, 20}). We used traveling paths of length 4 km. In Table 3, we present the average results of 100 runs of IE for different values of K varying from 1 to 20.

ANALYSIS

From Table 1, Table 2, and Figure 18, we conclude that the total query response time of eDAR is better than the query response time of DAR. On average eDAR is 30 times faster than DAR algorithm. This is because eDAR requires to compute fewer and requires no expensive shortest path computations. However, as the number of K increases the difference in performance marginally reduces. In general, as the density (number of of interest points compared to total number of links in the network) of the data increases, more intersection points are created. Hence, more split points are expected to appear on the path. From Figure 18 we conclude that as the density of the data increases the performance of DAR degrades more relative to eDAR for the same reasons mentioned before.

Table 1. Performance of DAR algorithm on PINE to solve continuous KNN queries

Travelling Path = 4Km Averaged over 5 queries		K=1	K=2	K=3	K=4
Entities	Qty (density)	#KNN Queries / Excecution Time	#KNN Queries / Excecution Time	#KNN Queries / Excecution Time	#KNN Queries / Excecution Time
Hospital	46 (0.0004)	31.2	33.6	28	-
		38.17	59.3	62.49	-
Shopping Centre	173 (0.0016)	31	36	40.4	38.8
		16.06	31.98	53.82	63.12
Parks	561 (0.0053)	30.4	35.6	35.6	40.4
		3.86	9.25	12.31	20.05
Schools	1230 (0.015)	39.6	41	50.6	42.8
		16.34	26.13	40.35	43.82
Auto Services	2093 (0.0326)	43.8	50.2	59.2	60.4
		38.3	50.74	60.18	61.94
Restaurants	2944 (0.0580)	46.8	48	59.6	63.2
		32.77	50.86	66.01	69.79

Table 2. Performance of eDAR algorithm on PINE to solve continuous KNN queries

Travelling Path = 4Km Averaged over 100 queries		K=1	K=3	K=5	K=10	K=20
Entities	Qty (density)	#KNN Queries / Excecution Time	#KNN Queries / Excecution Time	#KNN Queries / Excecution Time	#KNN Queries / Excecution Time	#KNN Queries / Excecution Time
Hospital	46 (0.0004)	24.12	22.96	23.9	22.97	22.5
		29.51	48.23	74.86	148.97	636.7
Shopping Centre	173 (0.0016)	23.88	22.87	23.22	22.71	23.02
		9.28	18.17	24.12	38.12	90.87
Parks	561 (0.0053)	23.15	22.74	22.58	22.31	23.56
		1.56	5.62	10.52	17.03	32.84
Schools	1230 (0.015)	23.06	23.15	22.98	23.31	23.27
		.78	2.47	3.96	8.51	15.55
Auto Services	2093 (0.0326)	23.71	23.6	23.33	23.2	23.35
		.33	1.08	1.85	3.61	8.02
Restaurants	2944 (0.0580)	22.34	22.66	22.51	22.69	22.06
		0.36	0.83	1.3	2.62	5.47

Table 3. Performance of IE to compute continuous KNN queries using VN³

Travelling Path = 4Km Averaged over 100 queries			K=1	K=3	K=5	K=10	K=20
Entities	Qty (density)	#KNN Queries	#KNN Queries	#KNN Queries	#KNN Queries	#KNN Queries	
		Excecution Time	Excecution Time	Excecution Time	Excecution Time	Excecution Time	
Hospital	46 (0.0004)	#KNN Queries	25.9	31.95	33.03	43.0	-
		Excecution Time	2.26834	197.72453	595.34759	1939.87747	-
Shopping Centre	173 (0.0016)	#KNN Queries	26.51	32.47	42.22	51.93	61.54
		Excecution Time	2.00076	26.92842	77.16223	418.76657	1729.38662
Parks	561 (0.0053)	#KNN Queries	29.44	39.75	48.16	60.39	70.06
		Excecution Time	2.36323	16.69154	32.5062	87.47607	226.11334
Schools	1230 (0.015)	#KNN Queries	30.96	44.58	50.18	64.61	64.73
		Excecution Time	3.55226	14.43126	26.33117	66.72495	161.87087
Auto Services	2093 (0.0326)	#KNN Queries	34.64	45.72	50.54	64.99	65.7
		Excecution Time	6.56426	36.73133	73.98197	182.22826	386.11334
Restaurants	2944 (0.0580)	#KNN Queries	35.44	47.19	54.2	58.9	-
		Excecution Time	11.57722	54.57086	106.13824	241.58423	-

Figure 18. Relative execution time of DAR vs. eDAR

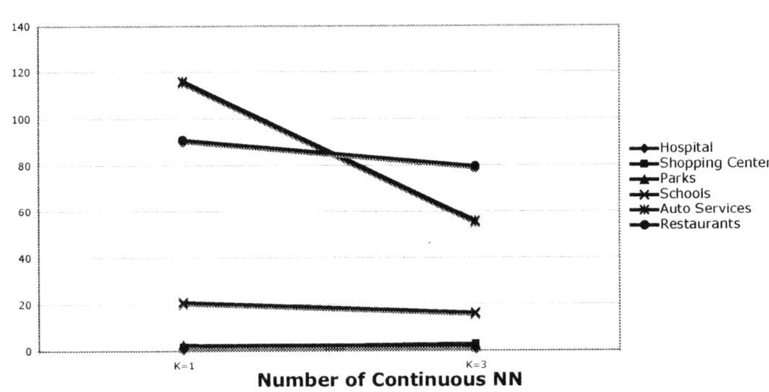

One thing to note in Figure 18 is the outlier data for auto services data at K = 1, it is because of the small number of queries that were averaged (only five), however, the general trend is clear in the Figure. From Figure 19, we conclude that the number of KNN queries issued by DAR and eDAR are almost the same (slightly increased by increasing K), and that as the density increases, the number of K queries increase also but by a small factor (on average by 1.5 times).

From Table 2, Table 3, and Figure 20, we conclude that the total query response time of eDAR (based on PINE) is better than the query response time of IE (based on VN³). On average eDAR is 20 times faster than IE. This is because eDAR requires no expensive shortest path computations, and as shown in (Safar, 2005) VN³ requires 8.5 times the number of computations required by PINE to compute any required KNN. As the number of K increases the difference in performance

Figure 19. Relative number of KNN queries of DAR vs. eDAR

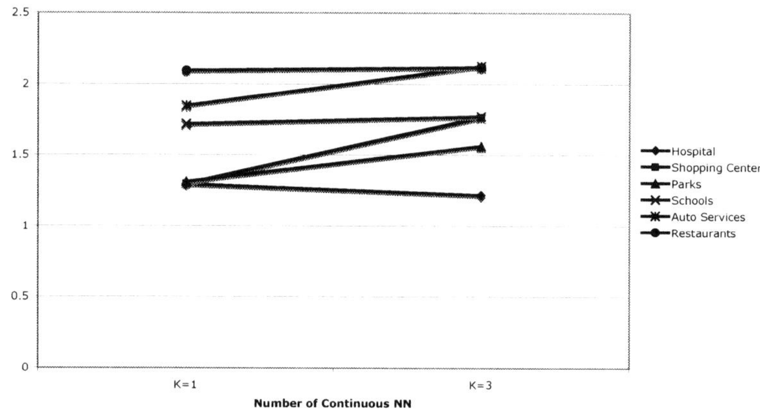

Figure 20. Relative execution time of IE vs. eDAR

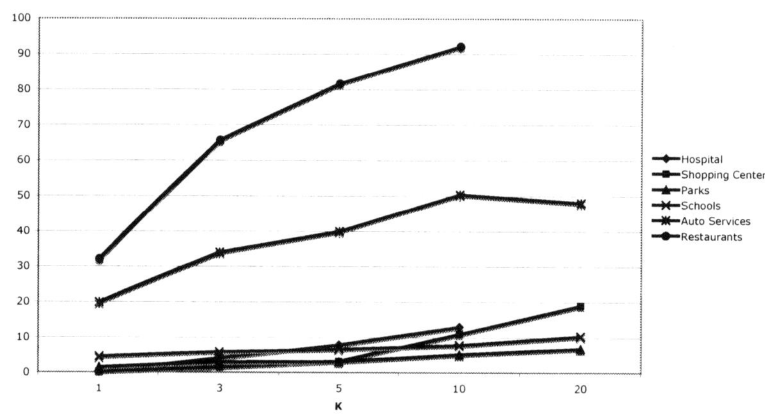

Figure 21. Relative number of KNN queries VN³ vs. eDAR

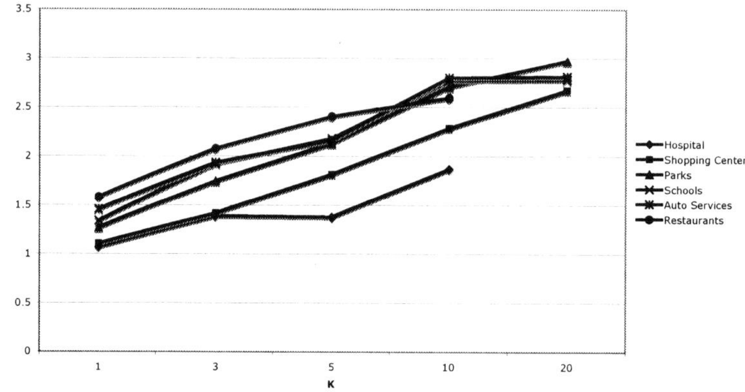

gets even larger. For example, for K = 10, CKNN using IE is almost 100 times slower than CKNN using eDAR. In general, as the density increases, the performance of IE degrades more relative to eDAR for the same reasons mentioned before (see Figure 20). From Figure 21, we conclude that the number of KNN queries issued by IE is on average twice that of eDAR (slightly increased by increasing K), and that as the density increases, the number of K queries increase also but by a small factor.

CONCLUSION

In this article, we presented DAR and eDAR algorithms as alternative solutions for continuous K nearest neighbor queries in spatial network databases based on a progressive incremental network expansion algorithm (PINE). Both algorithms find the location of split points and the corresponding KNNs on a path. In DAR approach, we showed that the location of split points on a path can be determined by first computing the KNNs using PINE structure for all the nodes on the path, and then examining the differences of shortest paths between the adjacent nodes using four queues (two PQs and two RQs). Then we described an enhanced DAR algorithm (eDAR) that does not require the expensive shortest path computations and reduces the overall distance computations. In addition, it requires only three queues (two PQs and one RQ). The main features of eDAR are as follows: (1) eDAR CPU time outperforms both DAR and IE, one of the few and recently proposed algorithms for CKNN queries in spatial network databases. It outperforms DAR with a factor of 30, and IE with a factor of 20 depending on the value of K and the density of the points of interest, (2) eDAR requires fewer KNN computations as compared to both DAR and IE. DAR requires a factor of 1.5 more computations, and IE requires a factor of two more computations depending on the value of K and the density of the points of interest.

We plan to extend eDAR to address similar KNN queries such as group KNN, constraint KNN, reverse KNN, and finding the actual shortest path between a query and its closest neighbors, as our future work.

ACKNOWLEDGMENT

This research was funded by Research Administration at Kuwait University (Project No EO02/04).

REFERENCES

Berchtold, S., Ertl, B., Keim, D. A., & Kriegel, H. P. (1998). Fast nearest neighbor search in high-dimensional space. In *Proceedings of the 14th IEEE Conference on Data Engineering (ICDE)* (pp. 209-218).

Bozkaya, T., & Ozsoyoglu, M. (1997). Distance-based indexing for high-dimensional metric spaces. In *Proceedings of ACM Special Interest Group on Management of Data (SIGMOD)* (pp. 357-368).

Chiueh, T. (1994). Content-based image indexing. In *Proceedings of the 20th International Conference on Very Large Data Bases (VLDB)* (pp. 582-593).

Ciaccia, P., Patella, M., & Zezula, P. (1997). M-tree: An efficient access method for similarity search in metric spaces. In *Proceedings of the 23rd International Conference on Very Large Data Bases (VLDB)* (pp. 426-435).

Corral, A., Manolopoulos, Y., Theodoridis, Y., & Vassilakopoulos, M. (2000). Closest pair queries in spatial databases. In *Proceedings of the 2000 ACM International Conference on Management of Data (SIGMOD)* (pp. 189-200).

Hjaltason, G. R., & Samet, H. (1999). Distance browsing in spatial databases. In *Proceedings of*

ACM Transactions on Database Systems, 24(2), 265-318.

Jung, S., & Pramanik, S. (2002). An efficient path computation model for hierarchically structured topological road maps. In *Proceedings of IEEE Transaction on Knowledge and Data Engineering (TKDE), 14(1),* 1029-1046.

Kolahdouzan, M., & Shahabi, C. (2004a). Continuous K nearest neighbor queries in spatial network database. In P*roceedings of the 2nd Workshop on Spatio-Temporal Database Management (STDBM)*.

Kolahdouzan, M., & Shahabi, C. (2004b). Voronoi-based K nearest neighbor search for spatial network database. In *Proceedings of the 30th International Conference on Very Large Data Bases (VLDB)* (pp. 840-851).

Kollios, G., Gunopulos, D., & Tsotras, V. J. (1999). Nearest neighbor queries in a mobile environment. In *Proceedings of the International Workshop on Spatio-Temporal Database Management* (pp. 119-134).

Korn, F., Sidiropoulos, N., Faloutsos, C., Siegel, E., & Protopapas, Z. (1996). Fast nearest neighbor search in medical image databases. In *Proceedings of 22nd International Conference on Very Large Data Bases (VLDB)* (pp. 215-226).

Okabe, A., Boots, B., Sugihara, K., & Chiu, S. N. (2000). *Spatial tessellations: Concepts and applications of Voronoi diagrams* (2nd ed.). John Wiley & Sons.

Papadias, D., Zhang, J., Mamoulis, N., & Tao, Y. (2003). Query processing in spatial network databases. In *Proceedings of 29th International Conference on Very Large Data Bases* (pp. 802-813).

Rigaux, P., Scholl, M., & Vorsard, A. (2001). *Spatial databases with applications to GIS.* Morgan Kaufmann, Inc.: San Francisco.

Roussopoulos, N., Kelley, S., & Vincent, F. (1995). Nearest neighbor queries. In *Proceedings of the ACM International Conference on Management of Data (SIGMOD), 24(2)*, 71-79.

Safar, M. (2005). K nearest neighbor search in navigation systems. *Journal of Mobile Information Systems (MIS), 1(3)*, 1-18.

Saltenis, S., Jensen, C. S., Leutenegger, S. T., & Lopez, M. A. (2000). Indexing the positions of continuously moving objects. In *Proceedings of the ACM International Conference on Management of Data (SIGMOD)* (pp. 331-342).

Seidl, T., & Kriegel, H.P. (1998). Optimal multi-step k-nearest neighbor search. In *Proceedings ACM International Conference on Management of Data (SIGMOD)* (pp. 154-165).

Shahabi, C., Kolahdouzan, M., & Sharifzadeh, M. (2002). A road network embedding technique for k-nearest neighbor search in moving object databases. In *Proceedings of the 10th ACM International Symposium on Advances in Geographic Information Systems (ACMGIS)* (pp. 94-100).

Song, Z., & Roussopoulos, N. (2001). K-nearest neighbor search for moving query point. In *Proceedings of the 7th International Symposium on Advances in Spatial and Temporal Databases* (pp. 79-96).

Tao, Y., Papadias, D., & Shen, Q. (2002). Continuous nearest neighbor search. In *Proceedings of the 28th International Conference on Very Large Data Bases (VLDB)* (pp. 287-298).

Yu, C., Ooi, B. C., Tan, K. L., & Jagadish, H. V. (2001). Indexing the distance: An efficient method to KNN processing. In *Proceedings of the 27th International Conference on Very Large Data Bases* (pp. 421-430).

This work was previously published in Int. Journal of Information Technology and Web Engineering, Vol. 1, Issue 4, edited by G. Alkhatib and D. Rine, pp. 1-21, copyright 2006 by IGI Publishing (an imprint of IGI Global).

Chapter X
A Deterministic Approach to XML Query Processing with Efficient Support for Pure and Negated Containments

Dunren Che
Southern Illinois University Carbondale, USA

ABSTRACT

This article reports the result of the author's recent work on XML query processing/optimization, which is a very important issue in XML data management. In this work, in order to more effectively and efficiently handle XML queries involving pure and/or negated containments, a previously proposed deterministic optimization approach is largely adapted. This approach resorts to heuristic-based deterministic transformations on algebraic query expressions in order to achieve the best possible optimization efficiency. Specialized transformation rules are thus developed, and efficient implementation algorithms for pure and negated containments are presented as well. Experimental study confirms the validity and effectiveness of the presented approach and algorithms in processing of XML queries involving pure and/or negated containments.

INTRODUCTION

XML has become the de facto standard for information, data exchange, and representation on the Internet and elsewhere. As a result, more and more data sources have been adopting the XML standard. The rapid accumulation of XML data calls for specialized solutions for managing and querying XML data resources. Among the many challenges related to the XML database management technology, XML query optimization is very interesting because it not only is a critical issue for XML DBMS but it also provides a key infrastructure for the future semantic Web and applications (especially, the semantic-based Web search engines).

Query optimization typically applies the cost-based approach (Selinger, Astrahan, Chamberlin, Lorie, & Price, 1979) and aims at obtaining the least expensive—the optimal—evaluation plan for each input query. Heuristic knowledge may be exploited in addition so that a reduced number of (only highly potential) candidate plans need to be examined and from which the best plan is to be identified.

XML data has the semi-structured nature and XML queries needed to check not only the *contents* but also the *structural patterns* of the source XML data. Comparing to relational data, XML data has higher complexity (as it has to additionally deal with the structural part), and this complexity trivially translates to an enlarged search space for the "optimal" plan during query optimization (assuming the cost-based approach is adopted). Consequently, a plain application of the cost-based optimization approach does not usually yield the same good efficiency for XML queries as it does for relational queries. On the other hand, apart from adding extra complexity and causing inefficient (cost-based) query optimization, the structural part of XML data implies a rich resource of knowledge that can be used in favor of efficient optimization of XML queries. We are thus motivated to develop a comprehensive optimization framework for XML queries. This framework consists of two separate yet collaborative optimization stages. The first stage performs logical-level optimization. This stage is unique to XML as it explores the specific features (e.g., semantic knowledge) of XML data for query optimization. By its nature, this stage is strongly heuristic-based because it does not rely on any particular knowledge about the underlying storage structure. The second stage—physical optimization—typically applies specialized cost-based optimization techniques. In such an optimization framework, these two stages need to collaborate in a way that the first stage provides a reduced (or pre-screened) set of logical plans to the second stage and the latter shall conduct specialized techniques for cost-based optimization by adequately considering the optimization that has already been exerted at the first stage.

In previous research (Che, 2003, 2005, 2006), we studied the query equivalence issue in the context of XML, which forms the basis of our transformation-based optimization approach to XML queries. A comprehensive methodology for fast XML query optimization at the logic level was proposed (Che, Aberer, & Özsu, 2006) based on exclusive application of deterministic transformations on XML queries represented as PAT algebraic expressions (Böhm, Aberer, Özsu, & Gayer, 1998; Salminen & Tompa, 1994). The utmost benefit of this unique approach is the great potential for superb optimization efficiency. More recently, we substantially extended the PAT algebra, which leads to ePAT (extended PAT), endowed with more expressive power. Based on ePAT, we redefined the query equivalences and the deterministic transformation rules, and adapted the prior optimization strategy in order to efficiently support XML queries with pure and/or negated containments. Containment is a core operation in XML queries, and negated containment is as important as the regular containment for XML queries (for example, "find all employees who do *not* have a homepage," though simple, can be a common (sub-)query pattern). However, little result on efficient support for pure and negated containments has been reported.

In this article, we make the following important contributions:

- An adapted deterministic optimization approach for XML queries with pure and/or negated containments is presented.
- A group of specialized join algorithms dedicated for pure and negated containment operations are proposed (realizing the known structural join algorithms (Srivastava et al., 2002; Zhang, Naughton, DeWitt, Luo, & Lohman, 2001) cannot provide efficient support for these special containment operations).
- An experimental study is conducted, and the obtained result confirms the validity and effectiveness of this new approach and the specialized supporting algorithms.

The remainder of this article is set forth as follows: the second section provides necessary background knowledge and a sketchy overview of the new approach. The third section illustrates the new approach by presenting sample deterministic transformation rules that are later on applied to a running example (query). The fourth section presents a number of specialized join algorithms intended for pure and negated containments. The fifth section addresses the experimental study and result. The sixth section reviews related work before the article is finally concluded in the seventh section.

BACKGROUND KNOWLEDGE

The main theme of this work is to carry out deterministic transformations on algebraic query expressions for optimization. This section first reviews a few important notions, then the ePAT algebra adopted in this work; after that, sample XML query equivalences are provided, and lastly, an overview of the adapted approach is furnished.

Basis Notions

In XML documents/data, elements are identified by means of "tags." For a given class of documents, the legal markup tags are defined in a DTD/XSD (XML Schema Definition). DTD and XSD basically serve the same kind of function, but the latter is more powerful. The presentation in this article is based on DTD, but the approach presented shall straightforwardly extend to the situations when XSD is used instead.

Figure 1. A portion of the XMark benchmark DTD-graph annotated with index info

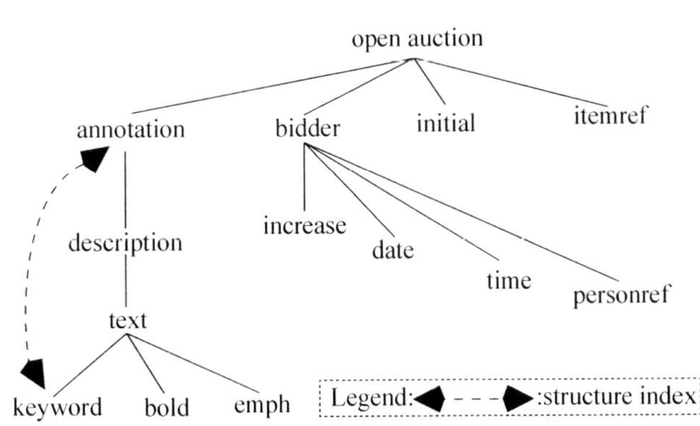

A tag (with a distinct name) defined in a DTD corresponds to a type of XML data element, which may comprise some other tags in its content model. The constructional relationships among the element types are an important source of knowledge that will be utilized by our approach for efficiently pursuing XML query optimization. We introduce the *DTD-graph* mechanism to help envision important structural relationships among the element types. Instead of providing a formal definition for this notion, we use an example to illustrate it. Figure 1 shows part of the structural relationships existing among the elements (types) about open auctions, which was adopted by the XMark benchmark project (Schmidt et al., 2002). In Figure 1, a dashed arrowed line (which is not a necessary part in a DTD-graph) indicates a structure index is available. A *structure index* is formally defined as a map from the extent of one element type to the extent of another element type (Che et al., 2006). A structure index may be intuitively considered as a "shortcut" between the two related extents (of two different element types). In our test-bed, structure indices are implemented as materialized (or pre-computed) structural join results (Srivastava et al., 2002; Zhang et al., 2001).

Containment is the dominant structural relationship in XML and is at the core of both the query languages, XPath (Clark & DeRose, 1999) and XQuery (Boag et al., 2003). Containments can be differentiated between direct containments (i.e., parent-child relations) and indirect containments (i.e., ancestor-descendent relations). A *path* in a DTD-graph is a sequence of edges. Paths are the primary means used in both XQuery (Boag et al., 2003) and XPath (Clark et al., 1999) to capture the structural relationships among the data elements.

In addition to the DTD-graph and the path notions, we adopt three other important notions for capturing particularly interesting structural relationships in XML data. These notions were initially introduced by Böhm et al. (1998) and is extensively exploited in Che et al. (2006). We review the three notions below.

1. **Definition (Exclusivity):** *Element type ETj is exclusively contained in element type ETi if each path (ej,...,ek) with ej being an element of type ETj and ek the document root contains an element of type ETi.*
2. **Definition (Obligation):** *Element type ETi obligatorily contains element type ETj if each element of type ETi in any document complying with the DTD has to contain an element of type ETj.*
3. **Definition (Entrance location):** *Element type EL is an entrance location for* $\tau(E1)$ *and* $\tau(E2)$ *given in a DTD if in any document complying with the DTD, all paths from an element e1 of* $\tau(E1)$ *to an element e2 of* $\tau(E2)$ *toward the document root pass through an element el of* $\tau(EL)$.

The ePAT Algebra for XML Query Optimization

It is typical in a query optimizer to represent queries as algebraic expressions for expediently exploring alternate evaluation plans based on equivalent transformations. ePAT is the algebra adopted in this work, which is extended from PAT (Böhm et al., 1998; Salminen et al., 1994).

In ePAT, an expression is generated according to the following grammar:

$$
\begin{aligned}
E ::= &\ \texttt{etn} \mid (E) \mid E1 \cup E2 \mid E1 \cap E2 \mid E1 - E2 \\
&\mid \sigma_r(E) \mid \sigma_{a,r}(E) \mid E1 \subset E2 \mid E1 \supset E2 \\
&\mid E1 \times_c E2 \mid \pi_{pl}(E) \mid I(E) \mid -E
\end{aligned}
$$

"E" (as well "E1" and "E2") stands for an ePAT expression, and `etn`, as the only atomic expression, retrieves the whole extent (i.e., all the instances) of the element type named `etn`. The expression (E) produces the same result as E and is needed mainly for composition purpose. $\cup$, $\cap$, and – are the three standard set operations.

ePAT requests type compatibility for its set operations. σ_r (E) and $\sigma_{a,r}$ (E) are the two basic selection operators applied to the textual contents and attribute values of elements, respectively. The "r" parameter in the two selection operators introduces a regular expression specifying a matching condition on the textual contents or attribute values of elements, and the "a" in $\sigma_{a,r}$(E) designates a particular attribute name. $\subset$ returns elements of the first argument that are contained in an element decided by the second argument, and $\supset$ returns elements of the first argument that contain an element of the second argument. $\times_c$ is a "power" join operation that can be tailored to almost any specific form of joins such as structural joins (Srivastava et al., 2002; Zhang et al., 2001), *unstructural joins* (i.e., joins not based on any structural relationship), and Cartesian products based on the nature of the join predicate specified by the parameter c. π_{pl} is the projection operator that carries a projection list specified by the parameter pl. I is a generic operation that connotes the application of a relevant index of any type (such as content indices of elements, value indices of attributes, and structure indices). Finally, –E stands for the "negated" form of E and here the E subexpression is limited to only a selection or a containment operation. When it is a selection, the negation is logically applied to the filtering condition of the selection operation; when it is a containment (e.g., E 1 $\supset$ E 2), the negation is applied to the containment operation.

It is helpful to point out that in the ePAT algebra, the containment operations, $\supset$ and $\subset$, are redundant (analogous to the natural join operation in the relational algebra), considering that they can be represented as a general structural join followed by a leftward projection. Yet, there are advantages of retaining this redundancy: considering the dominant role of containment operations in XML data and XML queries, dedicated containment operations greatly facilitate exploiting the structural relationships in XML data for query optimization.

We use the following query as a running example. First, we show how the query is formulated as an ePAT expression. Later on, we show how (logical) optimization can be achieved through consecutive deterministic transformations performed on ePAT expressions.

Example. Find the keyword from the annotation of an `open _ auction` that has received a bid from the person (an instance of `bidder`) whose reference is `123`.

A partial DTD-graph of the XML data source is shown in Figure 1. The corresponding XPath expression and ePAT expression are respectively formulated as follows (our query optimization and processing will be solely based on ePAT expressions).

XPath: //open_auction[./bidder[@personref="123"]]/annotation//keyword

ePAT: (keyword$\subset$(description$\subset$(open_auction $\supset \sigma_{a=\text{'personref'},\ r=\text{'123'}}$ (Bidder))))

Sample XML Query Equivalences

Our approach to XML query optimization is based on equivalent algebraic transformations, which are accomplished via deterministic transformation rules derived from equivalences in cooperation with relevant heuristics for query optimization in the context of XML. While these deterministic rules embody our optimization methodology, the equivalences form the basis of this work. In the following, sample equivalences are provided for illustration purpose.

We identify three knowledge sources from which equivalences can be derived: set-theory properties, explicit constraints imposed by DTD/XSD, and hidden constraints representing knowledge about the structure of XML data (often implied in DTD/XSD). Accordingly, our equivalences are classified into three categories.

It is worth noting that we would have obtained a (very) large number of equivalences including less-useful or even useless ones, if we do not limit our choice to only those potential ones from which profitable transformations can be derived. For instance, am equivalence must not imply transformations that merely complicate/expand a query without improving the query's evaluation efficiency (from a heuristic point of view).

In our work, equivalences take the form of "E1 $\Leftrightarrow$ E2" and transformation rules take the form of "E1 $\Rightarrow$ E2." For compactness, we will use "σ" to simply represent both σ_r and $\sigma_{a,r,}$ and use EL as a short hand notation for "entrance location."

In the following, we present sample equivalences from each category.

Set-Oriented Equivalences

As ePAT is a set based algebra, a group of equivalences were directly derived from the set-theoretic properties of relevant ePAT operators. A couple of these equivalences are given next (A complete list can be found in Che et al., 2006).

ε1. (E1 $\supset$ E2) $\cap$ E3 $\Leftrightarrow$ (E1 $\cap$ E3) $\supset$ E2
ε2. (E1 $\supset$ E2) $\supset$ E3 $\Leftrightarrow$ (E1 $\supset$ E3) $\supset$ E2

Equivalence ε2 is called the commutativity law of the containment operations.

Equivalences Based on Explicit DTD Constraints

There are equivalences based on checking the explicit constraints as given by the DTD/XSD. Two such examples are given next (symbol τ is used to denote the resultant type of a query expression):

ε3. $\sigma_{a,r}$(E) $\Leftrightarrow$ ϕ if 'a' isn't an attribute of τ(E)
ε4. E1 $\subset$ E2 $\Leftrightarrow$ ϕ if τ(E1) isn't contained in τ(E2)

Equivalences Based on Derived Constraints About XML Document Structure

This is a far more interesting class of equivalences as they bear the potential of rendering significant improvement on input query expressions. Following are a few samples of these types of equivalences:

ε5. (E1 $\supset$ E2) $\supset$ E3 $\Leftrightarrow$ E1 $\supset$ (E2 $\supset$ E3) if τ(E2) is an EL for τ(E1) and τ(E 3)
ε6. (E1 $\supset$ E2) $\supset$ E3 $\Leftrightarrow$ E1 $\supset$ (E3 $\supset$ E2) if τ(E3) is an EL for τ(E1) and τ(E2)
ε7. E1 $\subset$ E2 $\Leftrightarrow$ E1 $\subset$ (E3 $\subset$ E2) if E3 is an EL for τ(E1) and τ(E2)

ε5 is referred to as the *associativity* of the containment operations. ε6 embodies both the properties of commutativity and associativity in a single equivalence, thus we coined a new name, *cossociativity*, to characterize this specific algebraic law in the context of XML. ε7 directly connotes the meaning of the entrance location concept. Similar equivalences hold when all occurrences of $\supset$ in ε1, ε2, ε5, and ε6 are substituted by $\subset$. Combined application of these algebraic laws with the concepts exclusivity, obligation, and entrance location introduced at the beginning of this section yields more equivalences, which form the basis of our deterministic optimization approach as detailed in (Che et al., 2006).

Strategy Overview

We identify a large set of potential equivalences as the basis for XML query optimization; these equivalences are centered around the containment operations. However, equivalences are not directly used in our approach for query optimization (this is in contrast to the traditional way such as in Graefe & DeWitt, 1987) where equivalences are directly used for plan enumeration). Instead, we recognize the potential of XML document structure in query optimization and the specific feature of XML queries (i.e., always carrying a structure pattern). We are prompted to focus our attention on the logic-level optimization of XML queries as the first step toward thorough optimization. As such, optimized queries may need be further complemented by a succeeding physical optimizer (cost-based) in case highly optimized query plans are expected (e.g., by those repeatedly running and complex queries). Otherwise, the logical optimizer alone can be used.

Therefore, our emphasis is on logical optimization and our approach is designed to extensively explore the rich structure knowledge of XML data to achieve fast XML query optimization.

To obtain the previous goal, we derive heuristic-based, deterministic transformation rules based on the identified equivalence in collaboration with relevant heuristics and the availability of structure indices built in an XML database. These transformation rules are applied to each query (expression) step-by-step, and each performed transformation solidly improves the input query (in terms of evaluation efficiently) until no more transformations can be performed.

During this process, transformation rules are arranged in a certain order according to well-established optimization heuristics. When there are multiple rules applicable to an input expression, the precedence is always given to the first applicable rule. The details of our rule control strategy and the transformation algorithms can be found in Che (2005) and Che et al. (2006).

In this article, we limit our discussion to the optimization issue of query expressions involving only the main ePAT operators: `etn`, $\cap$, $\cup$, $-$, σ, $\supset$, $\subset$. Logical optimization in this work consists of three consecutive transformation phases: *normalization*, *semantic optimization*, and *simplification* (clean up). The normalization phase enforces straightforward DTD/XSD constraints, performs straightforward simplification, and reorders operators in the following order (from bottom up): `etn`, $\cap$, $-$, σ, $\supset$, $\subset$, $\cup$. It is interesting to note that, after this phase, all $\cap$ and $-$ operations sediment to the bottom on the operation tree and get ultimately eliminated from the query expressions after applying dedicated transformation rules.

The second phase, semantic optimization, starts with a normalized ePAT expression, explores deep structure knowledge of XML data in order to render an application of a potential structure index into the query. Due to the particular pattern that a query expression may be in, structure indices, although available, may not be applicable to the query. The central goal of the second phase is to reveal such opportunities.

The third phase performs a thorough cleaning-up. For this purpose, an intensive set of simplification rules are needed, including rules specially added for handling the possible redundancy that might be rendered by the second (main) phase.

A key feature of our approach is that deterministic transformations are exclusively applied to all queries at all three phases to achieve quick optimization. Consequently, a typical problem of all rule-based systems—uncontrollable run-time behavior—is expediently circumvented. A second important feature is that after thorough transformation of an input query for optimization, the $\cap$ and $-$ operations eventually get eliminated. This once again brings enhanced performance to the optimization itself and to the optimized queries.

DETERMINISTIC XML QUERY OPTIMIZATION

This section presents selected transformation rules and addresses the heuristics behind these rules.

Normalization

The normalization phase has three main tasks: enforcing simple DTD-constraints, reordering the operators (to facilitate semantic optimization at the second phase), and performing straightforward simplification.

Enforcing Explicit DTD-Constraints

We do not assign this task to the query parser because we do not generally assume the existence of database schemas in the contest of XML due to the semi-structured nature of XML data. This group of rules checks the queries' consistency with the explicit constraints induced by a given DTD/XSD (if anny). A couple of example rules are given below:

R1. $\sigma_{a,r}(E) \Rightarrow \phi$ if 'a' is not an attribute of $\tau(E)$
R2. $E1 \subset E2 \Rightarrow \phi$ if $\tau(E1)$ is not contained in $\tau(E2)$

Operator Reordering

The goal of this group of rules is to completely eliminate the $\cap$ and – operations from a query, and re-permute the remaining operators in the following order: `etn` and σ at the bottom, $\supset$ and $\subset$ in the middle, $\cup$ on the top, in order to facilitate the subsequent semantic optimization phase to achieve the primary goal – bringing a beneficial structure index into a query if possible. Several example rules are given next:

R3. $\sigma(E1 \cup E2) \Rightarrow \sigma(E1) \cup \sigma(E2)$
R4. $E1 - (E2 \supset E3) \Rightarrow E1 \cap (E2 \not\supset E3)$
R5. $(E1 \supset E2) \cap E3 \Rightarrow (E1 \cap E3) \supset E2$
R6. $E \cap E \Rightarrow E$
R7. $\sigma(E1 \supset E2) \Rightarrow \sigma(E1) \supset E2$
R8. $(E1 \supset E2) \supset E2 \Rightarrow E1 \supset E2$
R9. $-\sigma(E) \Rightarrow \not\sigma(E)$
R10. $-(E1 \supset E2) \Rightarrow E1 \not\supset E2$

Successful application of R5 makes it possible for R6 to eliminate an occurrence of the $\cap$ operator. The binary "–" operator is dealt in a similar way. The unary "–" operation (which negates a selection or a containment) is eliminated in a different way: R9 and R10 absorb the negation into the subsequent selection or containment operation (for convenience presentation, in these rules "$\not\supset$" is used to denote the directly negated form of $\supset$, and "$\not\sigma$" represents the negated form of σ). Ideally, specialized join algorithms for $\not\supset$ will be provided for direct and efficient implementation of the operation, while σ is easily handled by simply interpreting the negation as negating the selection operator's filtering predicate. The above discussion similarly applies to the $\in$ operator (i.e., by working with the counterparts of rule R4, R5, R7, R8, and R10 after $\not\supset$ is replaced by $\in$ in these rules).

Straightforward Simplification

We observe that most of the simplification carried out at an early stage are beneficial, e.g., $E \subset E \Rightarrow E$, while some less straightforward simplification if hastily done at a too early stage may cause the whole optimization process to be quickly captured at a local optimal. For example, while a leftward application of ε7 eliminates E3, it takes away the opportunity of applying the structure index between $\tau(E3)$ and $\tau(E2)$ if such a structure index is indeed available, or later on, a reverse transformation has to be called upon to restore the lost opportunity. Therefore, at the normalization phase we only pursue straightforward simplification, and the simplification rules mostly are only related to the set operations. We furnish a couple of such rules for simplification in the following.

R11. $\sigma(E) \cup E \Rightarrow E$
R12. $(E1 \supset E2 \cup E1) \Rightarrow E1$

A counterpart of R12 analogously works with the $\subset$ operation.

Semantic Optimization

The second phase, semantic optimization, is the core in our optimization approach. The primary goal of this phase is to discover potential opportunities of applying structure indices to a query. Three situations have been identified for this purpose:

- A structure index is available for a $\supset$ or $\subset$ operation in an input expression and the index is then simply applied. This is by far the most favorable situation.
- A structure index is available but is not superficially applicable because of an unfavorable pattern that the query expression is in. However, after desired transformations are performed, the index becomes applicable and used.
- No relevant structure index is available, but a after introducing a third element type as an entrance location into a query, a previously irrelevant index becomes relevant and eventually gets applied.

In summary, the first situation applies a structure index effortlessly, the second situation makes an "inapplicable" index applicable, and the third situation makes an "irrelevant" index relevant and applied. In the following, we present sample rules that exploit the usage of structure indexes corresponding to each of these situations:

1. **Applying readily available structure indices:** For an input (sub)query of form "E1 $\supset$ E2", if a structure index between the two involved element types, τ(E1) and τ(E2), happens to be available, our strategy firmly grasp this opportunity and applies the index by invoking the following transformation rule (where the parameter τ(E1), appearing as a subscript of the index operator I , indicates the resultant type of the index operation; a similar rule holds for $\subset$).

R13. (E1 $\supset$ E2) $\Rightarrow$ ($I_{\tau(E1)}$(E2) $\cap$ E1) if a structure index is available between τ(E1) and τ(E2)

2. **Making an "inapplicable" structure index applicable:** There are chances that a relevant structure index is available but not applicable because of the particular pattern that a query expression is in. Nevertheless, the applicability of the structure index to the query can enabled by desired transformations rendered by the commutativity and/or associativity laws w.r.t. $\supset$ and $\subset$ in the ePAT algebra. Specifically, the following transformation rules can be used (note the counterparts of R14 and R15 analogously work for $\subset$):

R14. (E1 $\supset$ (E2 $\supset$ E3)) $\Rightarrow$ ((E1 $\supset$ E2) $\supset$ E3) if there exists a structure index between τ(E1) and τ(E2), and τ(E2) is an EL for τ(E1) and τ(E3)

R15. (E1 $\supset$ (E2 $\supset$ E3)) $\Rightarrow$ ((E1 $\supset$ E3) $\supset$ E2) if there exists a structure index between τ(E1) and τ(E3), and τ(E2) is an EL for τ(E1) and τ(E3)

R16. (E1 $\subset$ (E2 $\supset$ E3)) $\Rightarrow$ ((E1 $\subset$ E2) $\supset$ E3) if there exists a structure index between τ(E1) and τ(E2), and τ(E1) is an EL for τ(E2) and τ(E3)

R17. (E1 $\supset$ (E2 $\subset$ E3)) $\Rightarrow$ ((E1 $\supset$ E2) $\subset$ E3) if there exists a structure index between τ(E1) and τ(E2), and τ(E1) is an EL for τ(E2) and τ(E3)

These rules are a result of a guided application of the equivalences that relate to the entrance location notion. A comprehensive list of the rules can be found in Che et al. (2006).

3. **Making "irrelevant" structure indexes relevant and applicable:** For an input query, if there is no structure index found relevant, our approach checks whether it is possible to

make a related index relevant by introducing an entrance location (a new element type) into the query (a related index is one that relates to just one of the involved element types, and thus is not quite relevant). To explore this kind of opportunities, we need specialized (and more complex) transformation rules that check specific structural properties (e.g., those connoted by the exclusivity and/or obligation notions, in addition). Our approach examines numerous cases, from most beneficial to least favorable in a heuristic point of view, in order to achieve the previous goal. In many of these cases, element type substitution is performed so that an opportunity of bringing a potential structure index into a query is discovered. After a desired transformation is performed, R13 is then called during the next iteration to secure the application of an identified potential structure index. The transformation rules corresponding to the four most favorable cases were identified in our prior work (Che et al., 2006) are presented next:

R18. $(E1 \subset E2) \Rightarrow (E1 \subset E3)$ if E3 is an EL for $\tau(E1)$ and $\tau(E2)$ and is exclusively contained in $\tau(E2)$, free(E2), and a structure index between $\tau(E3)$ and $\tau(E1)$ is available

R19. $(E1 \supset E2) \Rightarrow (E1 \supset E3)$ if E3 is an EL for $\tau(E1)$ and $\tau(E2)$ and obligatorily contains $\tau(E2)$, free(E2), and a structure index between $\tau(E3)$ and $\tau(E1)$ is available

R20. $(E1 \subset E2) \Rightarrow (E1 \subset E3)$ if $\tau(E2)$ is an EL for $\tau(E1)$ and $\tau(E3)$ and is exclusively contained in $\tau(E3)$, free(E2), and a structure index between $\tau(E3)$ and $\tau(E1)$ is available

R21. $(E1 \supset E2) \Rightarrow (E1 \supset E3)$ if $\tau(E2)$ is an EL for $\tau(E1)$ and $\tau(E3)$ and obligatorily contains $\tau(E3)$, free(E2), and a structure index between $\tau(E3)$ and $\tau(E1)$ is available

In the previous rules, the *free(E)* condition is used to denote that the evaluation of the expression E is required to return the *full extent* of type $\tau(E)$. free(E) trivially holds for every `etn`, which is the primary intended use of this predicate. With nontrivial expression E (i.e., a non `etn` expression), database statistics can be used to quickly determine whether the predicate holds without physically accessing the database.

If introducing a structure index into a query is impossible, our approach switches to a less favorite choice—that is, merely reducing the navigation paths required by a query. This kind of rules are relatively less interesting, especially when efficient structural join algorithms (e.g., Chien, Vagena, Zhang, Tsotras, & Zaniolo, 2002; Srivastava et al., 2002) are available for implementing the general containment operations.

It is worth to mention that there may exist alternatives to the new element type E3 interpolated by the previous rules into a query (as an entrance location). In order to retain our framework deterministic under all circumstances, we developed an algorithm that searches the optimal entrance location for these rules. This algorithm is discussed in detail in Che et al. (2006).

Simplification

The third phase, simplification, re-invokes most of the simplification rules covered by Phase 1. This is necessary because, after major transformations being performed for semantic optimization (the second phase), new redundancies may be introduced, especially when new element types (as entrance locations) are interpolated. The rules that enforce DTD-constraints and reorder operators do not need to be called again as semantic optimization does not introduce new inconsistencies with the DTD-constraints nor causes major structural changes in the queries. Besides, at this point we expect a thorough clean up on the optimized queries, and for this purpose, we add two new types of rules to the third phase.

Firstly, the following rules are added to remove the $\cap$ operations that may be reintroduced together with a structure index operation:

R22. $(I_{\tau(E1)}(E2) \cap E1) \Rightarrow (I_{\tau(E1)}(E2))$ if free(E1)

R23. $(I_{\tau(E1)}(E2) \cap \sigma(E1)) \Rightarrow \sigma(I_{\tau(E1)}(E2))$ if free(E1)

Secondly, toward thorough clean up, we add the following rules that carry out deep clean up by exploiting relevant structure knowledge (as characterized by the three notions: exclusivity, obligation, and entrance location). A few such rules as examples are given next:

R24. $E1 \subset E2 \Rightarrow E1$ if $\tau(E1)$ is exclusively contained in $\tau(E2)$

R25. $(E1 \subset (E3 \subset E2)) \Rightarrow (E1 \subset E2)$ if $\tau(E3)$ is an EL for $\tau(E1)$ and $\tau(E2)$, and free(E3)

R26. $(E1 \subset (E3 \supset E2)) \Rightarrow (E1 \supset E2)$ if $\tau(E1)$ is an EL for $\tau(E3)$ and $\tau(E2)$ and obligatorily contained in $\tau(E3)$, and free(E3)

An Optimization Example

In the following, we show the transformations applied to the example query introduced in the third section:

(keyword $\subset$ (description $\subset$ (open_auction $\supset$ $\sigma_{a=\text{'personref'}, r=\text{'123'}}$ (bidder))))

$\Rightarrow$ (by R14, i.e., $\subset$ associativity)

((keyword $\subset$ description) $\subset$ (open_auction $\supset$ $\sigma_{a=\text{'personref'}, r=\text{'123'}}$ (bidder)))

$\Rightarrow$ (by R15, i.e., $\subset$ commutativity) ((keyword $\subset$ (open_auction $\supset$ $\sigma_{a=\text{'personref'}, r=\text{'123'}}$ (bidder))) $\subset$ description)

$\Rightarrow$ (by R13, i.e., index introduction)

(($I_{keyword}$(open_auction $\supset$ $\sigma_{a=\text{'personref'}, r=\text{'123'}}$ (bidder)) $\cap$ keyword) $\subset$ description)

$\Rightarrow$ (by R22: $\cap$ deletion)

(($I_{keyword}$(open_auction $\supset$ $\sigma_{a=\text{'personref'}, r=\text{'123'}}$ (bidder))) $\subset$ description)

$\Rightarrow$ (by R23: simplification based on exclusivity)

($I_{keyword}$(open_auction $\supset$ $\sigma_{a=\text{'personref'}, r=\text{'123'}}$ (bidder)))

The performed transformations eventually make the structure index `Ikeyword(open _ auction)` interpolated and applied, and have the element type `description` completely removed from the query because of the identified exclusive containment property between `keyword` and `description`. As a result, the query expression (a logical plan)

Figure 2. The ICJoin algorithm calculating "D⊂A"

```
Algorithm ICJoin (DList, AList)
/* the algorithm computes the result of "D⊂A" */
input: DList of type D, and AList of type A; both in sorted order of startPos and
    all elements having the same docId
output: OList holding a sub list of DList that satisfy "D⊂A"
begin
a = AList->firstNode; OList = NULL;
for (d = DList -> firstNode; d != NULL; d =d -> nextNode) {
    while (a.end < d.end && a->hasNextNode()) a = a->nextNode;
    /* Now find the first possible descendant d of node a: */
    if (a.begin < d.begin && a.end > d.end) add d to OList
} /* end of for loop */
end
```

Figure 3. The CJoin algorithm calculating "A⊃D"

```
Algorithm CJoin (AList, DList)
/* the algorithm computes the result of "A⊃D" */
input: AList of type A, and DList of type D; both in sorted order of startPos
    and all
     elements having the same docId
output: OList holding a sub list of AList that satisfy "A⊃D"
begin
1. d = DList->firstNode; OList = NULL;
2. for (a = AList -> firstNode; a != NULL; a = a -> nextNode) {
3.     while (d.begin < a.begin && d->hasNextNode()) d = d->nextNode;
4.     /* find the first possible descendant d of node a */
5.     if (a.end > d.end && a.begin < d.begin) add a to OList
6. } /* end of for loop */
end
```

is considerably improved because the original form involves three containment operations, while the optimized one has only one containment operation plus a structure index. Without first performing the accomplished transformations, the structure index between `open _ auction` and `keyword`, although available and relevant, would not be eventually applied to this query.

SUPPORT FOR PURE AND NEGATED CONTAINMENTS

While structural joins (Srivastava et al., 2002; Zhang et al., 2001) have been widely recognized as important primitives for evaluating the containment operations that are at the core of XML queries, there are aspects of containment operations that necessitate specialized algorithms. This important issue however, does not seem to receive sufficient attentions from other researchers. Pure and negated containments represent two special but important cases of containment operations.

Structural joins are proper for the situation when both operands are required for output or for serving a subsequent operation during query evaluation. Nevertheless, this does not cover all the cases that the structural relationships (typically via containment operations) need to be involved in an XML query.

A rather common situation is when a query (or a sub-query) simply asks for qualified elements from one operand, for example, "find all the `items` listed in `Australia`," assuming the XMark dataset (Schmidt et al., 2002) is used. This query can be formatted as the following ePAT expression: `item` ⊂ `Australia`. This query involves a pure containment operation that needs to return only the elements from the first operand, while the second operand in this query is used only to help screen the elements from the first operand. This query, as consisting of a pure containment operation, is thus referred to as a *pure containment query*. If, instead, a general structural join as defined in Srivastava et al. (2002) and Zhang et al. (2001) is used for answering this query, the query plan shall consist of the following three nontrivial steps: performing the structural join, projecting the result to the left operand, and eliminating duplicates from result set.

Figure 4. The NICJoin algorithm calculating "D ⋐ A"

```
Algorithm NICJoin (DList, AList)
/* the algorithm computes the result of "D ⋐ A" */
input: DList of type D, and AList of type A; both in sorted order of startPos and
    all elements having the same docId
output: OList holding a sub list of DList that satisfy "D ⋐ A"
begin
OList = DList;
a = AList->firstNode; OList = NULL;
for (d = DList -> firstNode; d != NULL; d =d -> nextNode) {
    while (a.end < d.end && a->hasNextNode()) a = a->nextNode;
    /* Now find the first possible descendant d of node a: */
    if (a.begin < d.begin && a.end > d.end) remove d from OList
} /* end of for loop */
end
```

Figure 5. The NCJoin algorithm calculating "A ⋑ D"

```
Algorithm NCJoin (AList, DList)
/* the algorithm computes the result of "A ⋑ D" */
input: AList of type A, and DList of type D; both in sorted order of startPos
    and
    all elements having the same docId
output: OList holding a sub list of AList that satisfy "A ⋑ D"
begin
OList = AList;
d = DList->firstNode; OList = NULL;
for (a = AList -> firstNode; a != NULL; a = a -> nextNode) {
    while (d.begin < a.begin && d->hasNextNode()) d = d->nextNode;
    /* find the first possible descendant d of node a */
    If (a.end > d.end && a.begin < d.begin) remove a from OList
} /* end of for loop */
end
```

Alternatively, if the query engine calls for a specialized algorithm that directly computes the pure containment semantics of ⊂ as defined in ePAT (see the last section), the evaluation plan of this query then comprises just a single evaluation step (i.e., the invocation of this specialized containment algorithm, which may also be called a *pure containment join* or *containment join* for short). Now, an arising question is will this single algorithm be more efficient than the previous three-step evaluation plan? The answer is an absolute yes, in fact, this pure containment join

Figure 6. ANMPMJIN: A straightforward counterpart of MPMGIN for negated containments

```
Algorithm ANMPMJIN (list1, list2)
begin
copy list1 to list3
set cursor1 at beginning of list1
set cursor2 at beginning of list2
set cursor3 at beginning of list3
while (cursor1 != end of list1 and
          cursor2 != end of list2) do
    if (cursor1.docno < cursor2.docno) then
        cursor1++; cursor3++
    else if (cursor2.docno < cursor1.docno) then
        cursor2++
    else
        mark = cursor2
        while (cursor2.position < cursor1.position   and
                            cursor2 != end of list2) do
            cursor2++
            if (cursor2 == end of list2) then
                cursor1++; cursor3++
                cursor2 = mark
            else if (cursor1.val (directly)contains   cursor2.val)   then
                remove cursor0.val
                cursor1++
            endif
        endwhile
    endif
endwhile
output list3
end
```

is much cheaper than a corresponding structural join alone, not to mention the other two extra steps required by the first plan that uses a general structural join.

Containment joins come in two different forms. In our work, the one that computes $\subset$ is called ICJoin (the "Is-Contained" Join), and the one that computes $\supset$ is called CJoin (the "Contains" Join). The pseudo code of the two algorithms are respectively given in Figures 2 and 3. In these algorithms, we adopt the same numbering scheme for elements as in Srivastava et al. (2002) (i.e., `DocId, StartPos : EndPos, LevelNum`), which uniquely encodes the doc-id, the start and end position of an element, and the nesting level of the element in the DOM tree of the source document. With both algorithms, the AList (a list of potential ancestors) and DList (a list of potential descendents) are scanned just once, and there is no need to use any stacks or queues (this is in contrast to the tree-merge and stack-tree algorithms presented in Srivastava et al. (2002).

Both algorithms have the time complexity of $\Theta(|\text{AList}| + |\text{DList}|)$, while all the structural join algorithms proposed in the papers (Srivastava et al., 2002; Zhang et al., 2001) have the complexity of O(|AList| + |DList| + |OutputList|), where |OutputList| alone can be the scale of |AList| * |DList|, which is far larger than |AList| + |DList|. The performance advantage of the pure containment joins over general structural joins thus becomes obvious. This superiority gets further amplified when the extra operations (which may be required if a general structural join is used instead) are taken into account, as illustrated by the example given at the beginning of this section.

From our specialized containment join algorithms (see Figures 2 and 3), we further derive the negated counterparts for the operations $\in$ and $\ni$, respectively. These two algorithms are shown in Figures 4 and 5, correspondingly.

As can be seen, NICJoin and NCJoin both reverse the logic of their non-negated counterparts. That is, for example, whenever a qualified descendant is identified by ICJoin, it is excluded from output by NICJoin. NICJoin and NCJoin share the same time complexity as their counterparts. Applying negated containment joins to negated containment queries (i.e., queries involving negated containments like the example that is to be addressed at the end of this section) is yet another persuasive case demonstrating the advantage of resorting to specialized containment joins.

In Che (2005), two alternative algorithms (i.e., NMPMJIN and NSTD) for computing negated containments were presented that are based on direct modification on the two well-known structural join algorithms, MPMJIN in Zhang et al. (2001) and Stack-Tree-Desc in Srivastava et al. (2002), respectively. NMPMJIN and NSTD were aligned to the same style and numbering scheme adopted by Stack-Tree-Desc. In the following, we present an alternated version of NMPMJIN (Che, 2005), which is straightforwardly revised from MPMJIN for ease of comparison. We refer to this algorithm as ANMPMJIN.

ANMPMJIN is the algorithm that we implemented in our test-bed and for the experimental study to be reported in Section 6 (and MPMJIN is the counterpart structural join algorithm adopted

Table 1. Characteristics of database 1 at scale 1, 5, and 10 (cardn. stands for cardinality)

Scale	Size (MB)	#Docs	#Elements	Max degree	Min degree	Depth	Max cardn.	Min cardn.
1	28.93	100	1,206,221	20	1	6	421,681	100
5	138.80	500	5,763,581	20	1	6	2,125,564	500
10	252.40	1000	11, 546, 873	20	1	6	3, 695,219	1000

Table 2. Database 1 benchmark queries and properties (the select column indicates the selectivity of queries and the optimize column records the optimization time in seconds)

	Queries (formatted in XPath)	Select	Optimize
Q1	// Article[./ Title ft contains "Data Warehouseing" or ./ Keywords ft contaions "Data Warehousing"]	2.0%	0.192
Q2	// Article[./Title ft contaions "Data Warehousing"]/Abstract	1.1%	0.153
Q3	// Article[./ Title ft contains "Data Warehouseing"]/ Sections/ Section [@title= "Introduction"]/ Paragraph	6.4%	0.769
Q4	//Article[.// Surname ft contains "Aberer"]	2.3%	0.737
Q5	//Section/Paragraph [@title = "Summary"]	1.8%	0.841
Q6	// (article Short Paper)// Paragraph[.ftcontains "Multidimension" or .ftcontain "OLAP"]	1.1%	2.221

by our test-bed). ANMPMJIN follows exactly the same logic as MPMGIN (Zhang et al., 2001). It accepts two sorted lists of items as input and outputs a list of items (usually a sub list of the first input list) that do not have a containment relationship with any item from the second input list. ANMPMJIN has two levels of nested loops (while MPMGIN has three). The worst-case time complexity of ANMPMJIN is $O(n^2)$ (comparing with $O(n^3)$ of the original MPMGIN).

Finally, we look at an example query that has a negated containment operation – a so-called negated containment query. Assume this query asks for `open_auctions` that have not received a `bid`, which is formatted as "`open_auction` – (`open_auction` $\sqsupset$ `bidder`)." A reasonable plan (an ePAT expression) for this query is "`open_auction` $-\pi_{open\_auction}$(`open_auction` $\times_{\sqsupset}$ `bidder`)," which means a structural join algorithm (e.g., MPMGIN, is to be called first for computing the operation $\times_{\sqsupset}$;) then a leftward projection is invoked for computing $\pi_{open\_auction}$; after that, duplicates are eliminated, and finally the difference is computed. This plan consists of four steps. A much better alternative plan is "`open_auction` $\not\sqsupset$ `bidder`," assuming dedicated algorithm like ANMPMJIN for computing the "$\not\sqsupset$" operation is implemented. The superiority of the second plan is obvious if we consider that $\not\sqsupset$ is the only operation needs and its implementation (e.g., ANMPMJIN) is more efficient than MPMGIN alone ($O(n^2)$ vs. $O(n^3)$), not to mention the other three extra operations remained in the first evaluation plan, which all come with a nontrivial cost.

EXPERIMENTS

In order to evaluate our new optimization approach that has integrated support for pure and negated containments, we conducted an experimental study. As our new approach is adapted from the deterministic optimization approach, we presented previously in Che et al. (2006), and the effectiveness, efficiency, and scalability of the general approach has been inherited. Herein, we only show the performance advantage of this newly adapted approach as compared with the prior version of the approach (Che et al., 2006).

Our prototype system is implemented in the Java programming language and the Oracle RDBMS is used as a fast platform for storage management (however, our optimization approach is platform independent per se). Query processing in our test-bed consists of the following steps: translation from XQuery to ePAT expressions, logical optimization performed on ePAT expressions, translation from optimized ePAT expressions to Oracle SQL, and SQL query execution by Oracle query engine.

Our test-bed is set in a typical client/server database environment. The client side runs Oracle SQL*Plus (Release 8.1.6.0.0) on Window XP Pro, and the CPU is a Celeron processor of 500MHZ with 192MB RAM. The server side runs an Oracle8i Enterprise Edition (Release 8.1.6.0.0) database server, installed on Sun Ultra 5 with an UltraSparc-II CPU of 333MHZ and a RAM of 512MB.

For this test, the benchmark databases and queries are the same as in Che et al. (2006). Here we present the result of our test with only Database 1, which is a synthesized one based on a rather practical DTD (Che et al., 2006) for conference proceedings. The characteristics of this database are shown in Table 1 (The database was populated at different scales; Table 1 shows the statistics at the representative scales, 1, 5, and 10). The benchmark queries and their selectivities are shown in Table 2.

The performance data (obtained when the database was populated at scale 10) are illustrated in Figure 7. From Figure 7, one can see that the new approach with dedicated support for pure and negated containments outperform the old approach by several times. This is true

Figure 7. Performance comparison: new approach with special containment join support vs. previous approach without special support (Opt, Non-opt, OptN, and Non-optN stand for optimized and non-optimized queries in regard to our previous and new adapted approach, respectively)

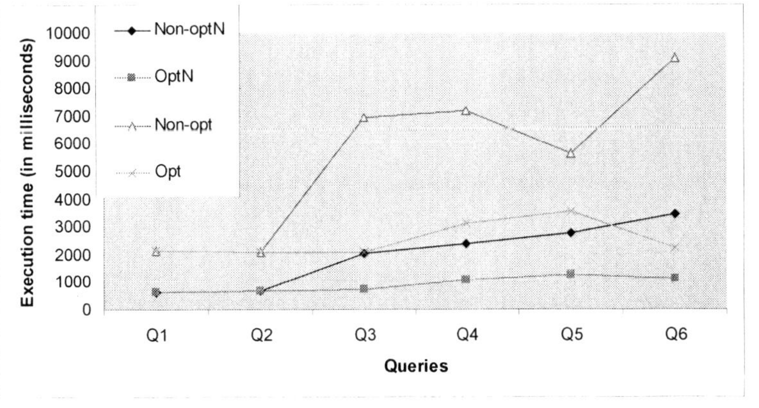

for both optimized and non-optimized queries. This observation further means that the performance gain of the new approach is mainly from the contribution of the specialized containment join algorithms integrated within the new approach; these specialized algorithms (as additional primitives) can be broadly and separately applied to other XML querying systems.

Finally, before concluding this section, we would like to point out: analytically, we believe ICJoin and CJoin (and their negated counterparts, NICJoin and CJoin) shall bring more improvement on the query performance because they all have a linear time complexity as shown in the last section (at this time our experiment is based on ANMPMJIN and NMPMJIN only).

RELATED WORK

Now we briefly review some related work. Lore (McHugh, Abiteboul, Goldman, Quass, & Widom, 1997; McHugh & Widom, 1999) is a DBMS originally designed for semi-structured data and later migrated to XML-based data model. The Lore optimizer is cost-based and does not perform logic-level optimization. The work in Consens and Milo (1994) is one of the early works reported on using the DTD knowledge on query transformations. The DTDs considered there are much simpler than that of XML. In Fernandez and Suciu (1998), a comparable strategy for exploiting a grammar specification for query optimization over semi-structured data is studied. In that study, efforts were made on how to make a complete use of the available grammar to expand a query. Our focus is different—we identify transformations that introduce "guaranteed" improvements on query expressions from a heuristic point of view. In Chung and Kim (2002), a fresh idea about using the DTD of XML documents to guide the query processor's behavior was proposed, where, the same type of elements (corresponding to the same node in the DTD-graph) is further classified according to the diverging paths from the type node. Query processing is then guided to a more specific class of the elements of this type to prune the search space. This classification information can effectively guide the query engine to narrow the search space and speed up query evaluation. But with relatively complex DTD, too many classes may be produced. In Wang and Liu (2003), based on the notion of rooted paths, two types of optimization were proposed: path complementing (i.e., if the path in a path query has a complement and its evaluation is cheaper, then the complement substitutes for the original path) and path shortening (i.e., if the head segment of a path is the unique one that reaches the ending point of the segment, then this segment is removed). The path shortening idea is similar to ours (Che, 2005; Che et al., 2006). However, our algorithm is more general and may identify more opportunities of reducing a path (which in our approach does not need to be rooted). In Buneman, Fan, and Weinstein (1999), path constraints were used to convey the semantics of semi-structured data and applied to query optimization. It is worth noticing that there are two types of semantics with regard to XML data: *data semantics* (i.e., the meanings of the data) and *structure semantics* (i.e., the knowledge about the general structure or structural relationships among the data elements). The path constraints investigated in Buneman et al. (1999) is restricted to only data semantics. Our approach exploits structural semantics. Path and tree pattern matching build the core of XML query processing. A bundle of approaches (Bremer & Gertz, 2003; Grust, 2002; Li & Moon, 2001; Srivastava et al., 2002; Zhang et al., 2001) have been proposed for supporting path and tree pattern matching, commonly known as structural joins. These approaches focus on composing the path/tree query patterns node-by-node through pair-wise matching of ancestor and descendant or parent and child nodes. These approaches have performance advantages over the simple path navigation method and have been integrated with our deterministic optimization approach in our prototype implementation.

Distinctively, we provide direct support for pure and negated containments (which are common in XML queries), and developed a family of specialized supporting algorithms, which showed performance potential.

To the best of our knowledge, our work as reported in Che et al. (2006) and in this article is the only one that uses algebraic transformations extensively to exploit structural properties and other important optimization heuristics for XML query optimization, and our work is the only one that integrates special containment join algorithms with a deterministic optimization approach.

SUMMARY

In this article, we presented an innovative, logic-level optimization approach, which is particularly adapted for dealing with XML queries that may contain special containments such as pure and negated containments. Regular structural join algorithms cannot be efficiently applied to these kind of queries. The uniqueness of our work lies in, first, we applied a deterministic approach for XML query optimization, which shows great potential for improved optimization performance; second, we proposed dedicated algorithms for special containment operations (i.e., pure and negated containments) in the context of XML query processing. Our experimental study confirmed the validness and performance advantage of the presented new approach and the proposed special containment join algorithms.

REFERENCES

Böhm, K., Aberer, K., Özsu, T. M., & Gayer, K. (1998). Query optimization for structured documents based on knowledge on the document type definition. In *Proceedings of IEEE International Forum on Research and Technology Advances in Digital Libraries (ADL'98)* (pp. 196-205), Santa Barbara, California, April 22-24, 1998.

Böhm, K., Aberer, K., Neuhold, E. J., & Yang, X. (1997). Structured document storage and re?ned declarative and navigational access mechanisms in HyperStorM. *The VLDB Journal*, *6*(4), 296-311.

Boag, S., Chamberlin, D., Fernandez, M. F., Florescu, D., Robie, J., & Simeon, J. (2006). *XQuery*

1.0: An XML query language. Retrieved from http://www.w3.org/TR/xquery/

Bremer, J. M., & Gertz, M. (2003). *An efficient XML node identification and indexing scheme.* University of California at Davis. Technical Report, 2003 (http://www.db.cs.ucdavis.edu/papers/TR CSE-2003-04 BremerGertz.pdf).

Buneman, P., Fan, W., & Weinstein, S. (1999). Query optimization for semistructured data using path constraints in a deterministic data model. In *Proceedings of DBPL Conference* (pp. 208-223).

Chan, C. Y., Felber, P., Garofalakis, M., & Rastogi, R. (2002). Efficient filtering of XML documents with XPath expressions. In *Proceedings of the International Conference on Data Engineering* (pp. 235-244), San Jose, California, February 2002.

Chan, C. Y., Garofalakis, M. N., & Rastogi, R. (2002). RE-Tree: An efficient index structure for regular expressions. In *Proceedings of VLDB Conference* (pp. 263-274), Hong Kong, China, 2002.

Che, D. Accomplishing deterministic XML query optimization. *Journal of Computer Science and Technology, 20*(3), 357-366.

Che, D. Efficiently processing XML queries with support for negated containments. *International Journal of Computer & Information Science, 6*(2), 119-120.

Che, D. Implementation issues of a deterministic transformation system for structured document query optimization. In *Proceedings of the 7th International Database Engineering and Applications Symposium* (pp. 268-277), Hong Kong, July 16-18, 2003.

Che, D., Aberer, K., & Özsu, M. T. (2006). Query optimization in XML structured-document databases. *The VLDB Journal, 15*(3), 263-289.

Chien, S. Y., Vagena, Z., Zhang, D., Tsotras, V. J., & Zaniolo, C. (2002). Efficient structural joins on indexed XML documents. In *Proceedings of VLDB Conference* (pp. 263-274), Hong Kong, August 20-23, 2002.

Chung, T. S., & Kim, H. J. (2002). XML query processing using document type definitions. *Journal of Systems and Software, 64*(3), 195-205.

Clark, J., & DeRose, S. (1999). *XML path language (XPath) Version 1.0.* Retrieved from http://www.w3.org/TR/1999/REC-xpath-19991116

Consens, M., & Milo, T. (1994). Optimizing queries on files. In *Proceedings of ACM SIGMOD International Conference on Management of Data* (pp. 301-312), Minneapolis, Minnesota, May 1994.

Fernandez, M. F., & Suciu, D. (1998). Optimizing regular path expressions using graph schemas. In *Proceedings of the 14th International Conference on Data Engineering* (pp. 14-23), Orlando, Florida, USA, February 23-27, 1998.

Frasincar, F., Houben, G. J., & Pau, C. (2002). XAL: An algebra for XML query optimization. In *Proceedings of the 13th Australasian Database Conference, (ADC2002)* (pp. 49-56).

Gottlob, G., Koch, C., & Pichler, R. (2002). Efficient algorithms for processing XPath queries. In *Proceedings of VLDB Conference* (pp. 95-106), Hong Kong, China, 2002.

Graefe, G., & DeWitt, D. (1987). The EXODUS optimizer generator. In *Proceedings of ACM SIGMOD International Conference on Management of Data* (pp. 160-172), May 1987.

Grust, T. (2002). Accelerating XPath location steps. In *Proceedings of ACM SIGMOD Conference* (pp. 109-120), 2002.

Guha, S., Jagadish, H. V., Koudas, N., Srivastava, D., & Yu, T. (2002). Approximate XML joins. In *Proceedings of the ACM SIGMOD Conference* (pp. 287-298), 2002.

Jagadish, H. V., Lakshmanan, L. V. S., Srivastava, D., & Thompson, K. (2001). TAX: A tree algebra for XML. In *Proceedings of DBPL Conference* (pp. 149-164), Rome, Italy, 2001.

Li, Q., & Moon, B. (2001). Indexing and querying XML data for regular path expressions. In *Proceedings of VLDB Conference* (pp. 361-370), Rome, Italy, September 2001.

McHugh, J., & Widom, J. (1999). Query optimization for XML. In *Proceedings of VLDB Conference* (pp. 315-326), Edinburgh, Scotland, September 1999.

McHugh, J., Abiteboul, S., Goldman, R., Quass, D., & Widom, J. (1997). Lore: A database management system for semistructured data. *ACM SIGMOD Record, 26*(3), 54-66.

Milo, T., & Suciu, D. (1999). Index structures for path expressions. In *Proceedings of ICDT* (pp. 277-295).

Salminen, A., & Tompa, F. W. (1994). PAT expressions: An algebra for text search. *Acta Linguistica Hungarica, 41*(1), 277-306.

Schmidt, A. R., Waas, F., Kersten, M. L., Carey, M. J., Manolescu, I., & Busse, R. (2002). XMark: A benchmark for XML data management. In *Proceedings of VLDB* (pp. 974-985), Hong Kong, China, August 2002.

Selinger, P. G., Astrahan, M. M., Chamberlin, D., Lorie, R., & Price, T. (1979). Access path selection in a relational database management system. In *Proceedings of ACM SIGMOD Conference* (pp. 23-34), 1979.

Srivastava, D., Al-Khalifa, S., Jagadish, H. V., Koudas, N., Patel, J. M., & Wu, Y. (2002). Structural joins: A primitive for efficient XML query pattern matching. In *Proceedings of ICDE Conference* (pp. 141-152), San Jose, CA, February 26-March 1, 2002.

Wang, G., & Liu, M. (2003). Query processing and optimization for regular path expressions. In *Proceedings of CAiSE Conference* (pp. 30-45), Klagenfurt, Austria, June16-18, 2003.

Zhang, C., Naughton, J. F., DeWitt, D. J., Luo, Q., & Lohman, G. M. (2001). On supporting containment queries in relational database management systems. In *Proceedings of ACM SIGMOD Conference* (pp. 425-436), Santa Barbara, CA, USA, 2001.

This work was previously published in Int. Journal of Information Technology and Web Engineering, Vol. 1, Issue 4, edited by G. Alkhatib and D. Rine, pp. 49-67, copyright 2006 by IGI Publishing (an imprint of IGI Global).

Chapter XI
Text Summarization Based on Conceptual Data Classification

Jihad M. ALJa'am
University of Qatar, Qatar

Ali M. Jaoua
University of Qatar, Qatar

Ahmad M. Hasnah
University of Qatar, Qatar

F. Hassan
University of Qatar, Qatar

H. Mohamed
University of Qatar, Qatar

T. Mosaid
University of Qatar, Qatar

H. Saleh
University of Qatar, Qatar

F. Abdullah
University of Qatar, Qatar

H. Cherif
University of Qatar, Qatar

ABSTRACT

In this paper, we present an original approach for text summarization using conceptual data classification. We show how a given text can be summarized without losing meaningful knowledge and without using any semantic or grammatical concepts. In fact, concept date classification is used to extract the most interacting sentences from the main text and ignoring the other meaningless sentences in order to generate the text summary. The approach is tested on Arabic and English texts with different sizes and different topics and the obtained results are satisfactory. The system may be incorporated with the indexers of search engines over the Internet in order to find key words and other pertinent information of the new deployed Web pages that would be stored in databases for quick search.

INTRODUCTION

Most of intelligent information retrieval methods need to realize data classification and make minimization of their representation in the memory. The word *classification* means pattern generation and recognition. Formal concept analysis offers simple, original, uniform, and mathematically well-defined methods for data clustering. In fact, we can easily associate a pattern with a formal concept (i.e., a set of objects sharing the maximum of properties). In this article, we are interested in text summarization using conceptual data classification. This new approach allows us to extract the most significant and interacting sentences in a given text in order to generate its summary. It can be applied on any text of any language—Arabic, English, French, etc.—as it doesn't use any semantic or grammatical concepts. The idea consists of minimizing the information representation by selecting only "optimal concepts." We assume that data may be converted into a binary relation as a subset of the product of a set of objects and a set of properties. Due to the huge amount of data contained in most existing documents and databases, it becomes important to find a priority order for concept selections to enable the users to find pertinent information from a given document. A search engine over the Internet can be extended with such a system in order to select the most appropriate documents and Web pages that match with the user's queries. In fact, the system can be used as an indexer of the search engine in order to select key words and other pertinent information from the new deployed Web pages, which will be stored in databases for quick and efficient search. We mention that we have used this approach in our previous works to supervise learning and we obtained defendable results in terms of error rate comparing with other well known methods (for more details you can see Al-Rashdi, Al-Muraikhi, Al-Subaiey, Al-Ghanim, & Al-Misaifri, 2001; Ben Yahia, Arour, Slimani, & Jaoua, 2000; Ben Yahia & Jaoua, 2001; Jaoua & Elloumi, 2002; Maddouri, Elloumi, & Jaoua, 1998; Mineau & Godin, 1995).

The article is organized as follows: in the second section, we present the mathematical foundation of concept analysis. In the third section, we give a polynomial approximate algorithm to the NP-complete problem of the coverage of a binary context with a minimal number of optimal concepts. In the fourth section, we explain how to apply the idea of optimal concept (called also optimal rectangle) on text summarization for English and Arabic texts. In the fifth section, we show the obtained results of our experiments, while in the sixth section we conclude the article.

MATHEMATICAL FOUNDATIONS

Among the mathematical theories found recently with important applications in computer science, lattice theory has a specific place for data organization, information engineering, data mining, and reasoning. It may be considered as the mathematical tool that unifies data and knowledge, as well as information retrieval and reasoning (Davey & Priestley, 1990; Ganter & Wille, 1999; Jaoua, Bsaies, & Consmtini, 1999; Jaoua, Boudriga, Durieux, & Mili, 1991; Schmidt & Ströhlein, 1989). We will define the binary context, the formal concept, and the lattice of concepts associated with a binary context.

Definition 1 (Binary Context): A *binary context* (or *binary relation*) is a subset of the product of two sets O (the set of objects) and P (the set of properties).

Example: Let O = {*Leech, Bream, Frog, Dog, Spike-weed, Reed, Bean, Maize*}, and let

$P = \{a, b, c, d, e, f, g, h, i\}$.

where O is a set of some animals, and P is a set of properties displayed in Table 1.

Let f be a function from the powerset of the set of objects O (i.e., 2^O) into the powerset of the set of properties P (i.e., 2^P), such that:

$$f(A) = \{m \mid \forall\, g \in A \rightarrow (g,m) \in R\}$$

f(A) is the set of all properties shared by all objects of A (subset of O) with respect to the context R. Let g be a function from 2^P to 2^O, such that:

$$g(B) = \{g \mid \forall\, m \in B \rightarrow (g,m) \in R\}$$

$g(B)$ is the set of objects sharing all the properties B (subset of P) with respect to the binary context R. We define the closure function as follows:

$closure(A) = g(f(A)) = A'$, and
$closure(B) = f(g(B)) = B'$.

The meaning of A' is that a set of objects A is sharing the same set of properties $f(A)$ with other objects (A'- A), relatively to the context R. A' is the maximal set of objects sharing the same properties as objects A. In the previous example, if A = {*Leech, Bream, Frog, Spike-weed*}, then A' = {*Leech, Bream, Frog, Spike-weed, Reed*}. This means that the shared properties a and b of the animals in A, are also shared by a *Reed*, the only element in A'- A. The meaning of B' is that if an object x of the context R verifies properties B, then x verifies also some number of additional properties (B'-B). B' is the maximal set of properties shared by all objects verifying properties B. In the previous example, if $B = \{a,h\}$, then $B' = \{a,h,g\}$. This means that any animal that needs water (a) and has lambs (h), can move around (g). For each subset B, we may create an association rule as follows: $B \rightarrow B'$- B. The number of these rules depends on the binary context R. In Ganter et al. (1999), we can find different algorithms to extract the minimal set of such association rules.

Definition 2 (Formal Concept): A *formal concept* of binary context is a pair (A, B), such that $f(A) = B$, and $g(B) = A$. We call A the *extent* and B the *intent* of the concept (A, B). If (A_1, B_1) and (A_2, B_2) are two concepts, (A_1, B_1) is called a *sub-concept* of (A_2, B_2), provided that $A_1 \subseteq A_2$, and $B_2 \subseteq B_1$. In this case, (A_2, B_2) is a *super-concept* (A_1, B_1) and it is written as follows: $(A_1, B_1) < (A_2, B_2)$. The relation "<" is called the *hierarchical order relation* of the concepts. The set of all concepts of (G, M, I) ordered in this way is called the *concept lattice* of the context (G, M, I).

Formal concept analysis is used for deriving conceptual structures out of data. These structures can be graphically represented as conceptual hierarchies allowing the analysis of complex structures and the discovery of dependencies within the data. Formal concept analysis is increasingly applied in conceptual clustering, data analysis, information retrieval, and knowledge discovery. It is based on the philosophical understanding that a concept

Table 1.

a = needs water	*b = lives in water*
c = lives on land	*d = needs chlorophyll to produce food*
e = is two seed leaves	*f = one seed leaf*
g = can move around	*h = has limbs*
i = suckles its offspring	

Figure 1. An example of a binary context R

		A	B	C	d	e	f	g	H	i
1	Leech	1	1	0	0	0	0	1	0	0
2	Bream	1	1	0	0	0	0	1	1	0
3	Frog	1	1	1	0	0	0	1	1	0
4	Dog	1	0	1	0	0	0	1	1	1
5	Spike-Weed	1	1	0	1	0	1	0	0	0
6	Reed	1	1	1	1	0	1	0	0	0
7	Bean	1	0	1	1	1	0	0	0	0
8	Maize	1	0	1	1	0	1	0	0	0

Table 2.

	A	B	C	D
G1	1	1	0	0
G2	1	1	0	0
G3	0	1	1	0
G4	0	1	1	1
G5	0	0	1	1

Figure 2. Concept lattice of the context K

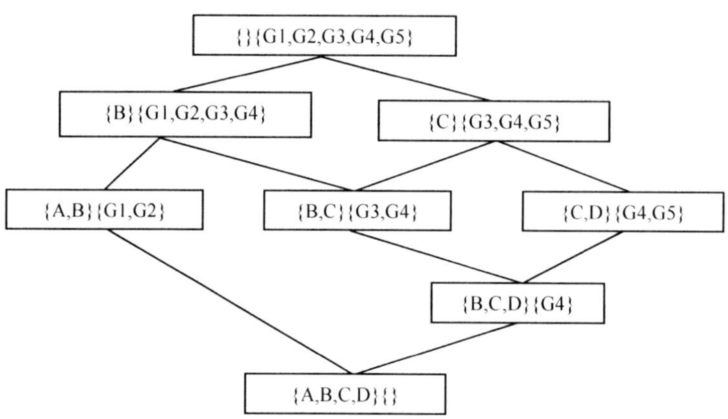

is constituted by two parts: its extension, which consists of all objects belonging to the concept, and its intension, which comprises all attributes shared by those objects. One of the main objectives of this method is to visualize the data in the form of concept lattices. Let *K* be the formal context in Table 2.

The formal concept has been introduced by different scientific communities in the world starting from 1945 by Riguet (1948) under the name of *maximal rectangle*, and in graph theory as a

Figure 3. Galois connection

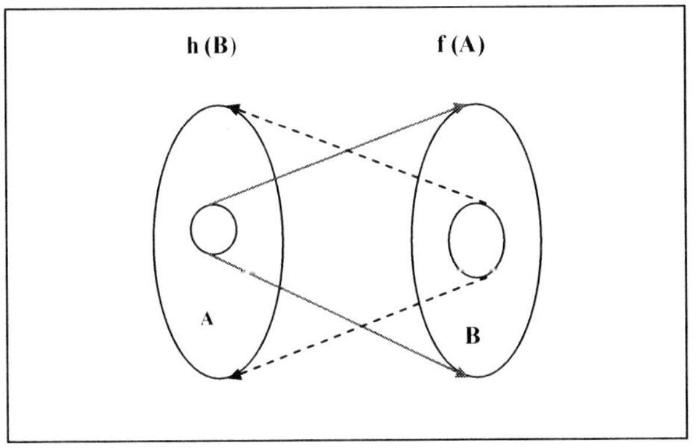

maximal bipartite graph. In addition, it has been exploited in 1986 in the thesis of *N. Le Than* (2) in database concepts to introduce a new kind of dependencies called *iso-dependencies*. Independently Jaoua, Belkhiter, Desharnais, and Moukam (1992) have introduced in Khcherif, Gammoudi, & Jaoua (2000) the *difunctional dependencies* as the most suitable name for iso-dependencies in database. The most recent mathematical studies about formal concept analysis are done by Ganter et al. (See Davey et al., 1990; Ganter et al., 1999; and Schmidt et al., 1989 for more details). What is remarkable is that concepts are used more and more in several areas of computer science as text analysis, machine learning, database, data mining, software decomposition, reasoning, and pattern recognition. A complete conjunctive query and its associated answer in a database is no more no less than a concept (i.e., an element in a lattice of concepts). We can almost find a bridge between any computer science application and concepts. Its generality and simplicity is very attractive. Combined with other methods for mapping any kind of data into a binary context, it gives an elegant base for data mining.

Galois Connection

Galois connection is a conceptual learning structure used to extract new knowledge from existing context (i.e., database) where a *context* is represented by a binary relation. We can decompose the context into a set of concepts and we can build a hierarchy of concepts known also as "*Galois Lattice*."

A pair ($f(A)$, $h(B)$) of maps is called a *Galois connection* if and only if we have the following equivalence:

$$A \subseteq h(B) \Leftrightarrow B \subseteq f(A)$$

It is also known that:

$$f(A) = fhf(A) \text{ and } h(B) = hfh(B).$$

Optimal Concept or Rectangle

A binary relation can be decomposed into a minimal set of optimal concepts (or optimal rectangles).

Definition 3 (Rectangle): Let R be a binary relation defined from E to F. A *rectangle* of R is a pair of sets (A, B) such that $A \subseteq E$, $B \subseteq F$, and $A \times B \subseteq R$. A is the *domain* of the rectangle where B is the *co-domain*. A rectangle is *maximal* if and only if it is a concept. A *binary relation* can be represented by different sets of rectangles.

In order to save in storage space, a gain function $W(R)$ will be defined in the next section, which is important for the selection of a minimal and significant set of maximal rectangles representing the relation. We will use indifferently the word "concept" and "maximal rectangle." Our conviction is that intelligence does not keep in mind all the lattice structure of concepts, but only few concepts covering all the data context. As a matter of fact, the thinking process might be efficient because it optimizes the quantity of data to keep in memory.

Definition 4 (Gain in storage space—Economy): The *gain* in storage space $W(R)$ of a binary relation R is given by the following equation:

$$W(R) = (r / dc)(r - (d + c))$$

where r is the cardinal of R (i.e., the number of pairs in R)

- d is the cardinal of the domain of R.
- *c is the cardinal of the range of R.*

Remark: The quantity (r / dc) provides a measure of the density of the relation R. The quantity $(r - (d + c))$ is a measure of the economy of information.

Definition 5 (Optimal Concept): A rectangle $RE \subseteq R$ containing an element (x, y) of a relation R is called *optimal* if it produces a maximal gain $W(RE(x, y))$ with respect to other concepts containing (x, y). Figure 4(a) presents an example of a relation R, and Figures 4(b), 4(c), and 4(d) represent three different rectangles containing the element $(y, 3)$. The corresponding gains are 1, 0, -1. Therefore, the optimal rectangle containing the pair $(y, 3)$ of R is the rectangle of Figure 4(b). It is easy to prove that it must always be a concept (maximal rectangle).

$W(RE_1(y, 3)) = (6 / 6)(6 - (2 + 3)) = 1$.
Here $r = 6$, $d = 2$, and $c = 3$.

$W(RE_2(y, 3)) = (4 / 4)(4 - (2 + 2)) = 0$.
Here $r = 4$, $d = 2$, and $c = 2$.

$W(RE_3(y, 3)) = (5 / 5)(5 - (1 + 5)) = -1$.
Here $r = 5$, $d = 1$, and $c = 5$.

We can notice that the function W, when applied on the concept RE, is always greater than - 1. The minimal value -1 is reached if $r = 1$ or $d = 1$. W is equal to 0 only whenever $r = d = 2$.

Definition 6 (Elementary Relation - PR): If R is a finite binary relation (i.e., subset of $E \times F$, where E is a set of objects and F a set of properties) and $(a, b) \in R$, then the union of rectangles containing (a, b) is the elementary relation PR (i.e., subset of R) given by the following equation:

$$PR = \Phi_R(a,b) = I(b.R^{-1}) \text{ o } R \text{ o } I(a.R)$$

where:

- I is the identity relation.
- R-1 is the inverse relation of R (i.e., set of inversed pairs of R).
- "o" refers to the relative product operator, where:

$$R \text{ o } R' = \{(x, y) \mid \exists z: (x, z) \in R \wedge (z, y) \in R'.$$

Let $A \subseteq E$, then $I(A) = \{(a, a) \mid a \in A\}$.

PR is the sub-relation of R, pre-restricted by the antecedents of b (i.e., $b.R^{-1}$), and post-restricted by the set of images of a (i.e., $a.R$).

In the next section, we use such elementary relations PR to find the coverage of a relation by some "minimal" number of optimal concepts. Note that this problem is known to be NP-complete. For that reason, we propose an approximate

Figure 4.

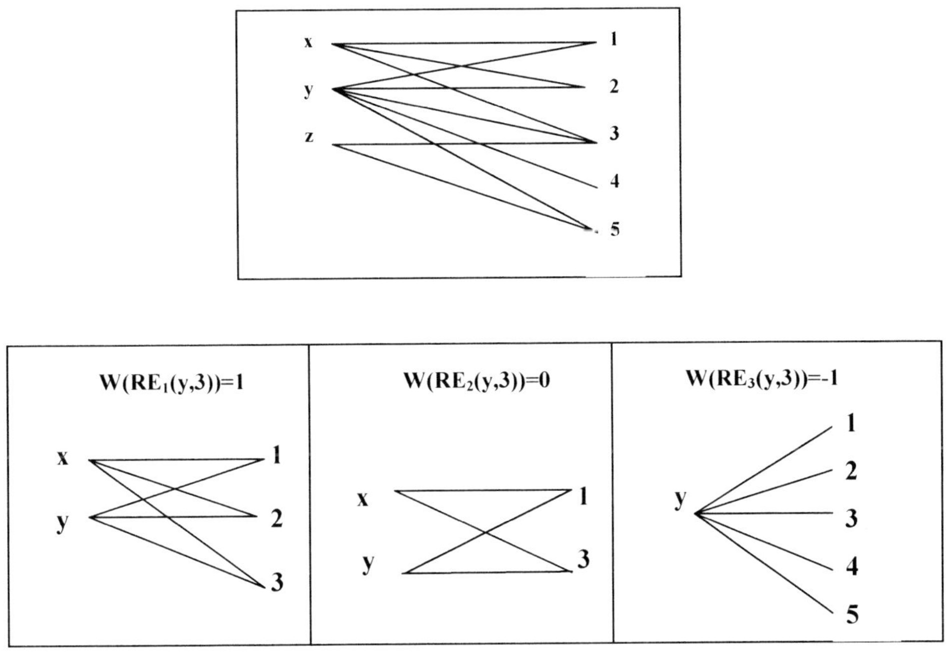

algorithm based on a greedy technique and using the gain function W.

APPROXIMATE ALGORITHM FOR MINIMAL COVERAGE OF BINARY CONTEXT

The research of a set of optimal rectangles that provides a coverage of a given relation R can be done through the following steps:

Let R be a finite binary relation between two sets as in Illustration 1.

Step 1: Divide the relation R into disjoint elementary relations $PR_1, PR_2, \ldots, PR_m$.

Step 2: For each elementary relation PR_i, search the optimal rectangle, which includes an element of PR_i.

If PR_i is a Rectangle, then it is an optimal rectangle containing (a, b), otherwise, check if PR contains other elements (x, y) in the form of (a, y) or (x, b) by trying all the images of a and all the antecedents of b.

The elementary relation of (1,7) is the following:

$$PR(1,7) = \Phi_{R(1,7)} = I(7.R^{-1}) \text{ o } R \text{ o } I(1.R)$$

So we search with an iterative way the optimal rectangles of $PR(1,7)$, which successively contains the elements (1,8), (1,9), (1,11), (2,7) and (3,7).

- **First Iteration:** From the five elementary relations of the previously mentioned elements select the first that gives a maximal gain:

1. $PR'_{1,8} = \Phi_{PR1,7}(1,8); W(PR'_{1,8}) = 0$
2. $PR'_{1,9} = \Phi_{PR1,7}(1,9); W(PR'_{1,9}) = 7/8$ ⇑**Selected**
3. $PR'_{1,11} - \Phi_{PR1,7}(1,11); W(PR'_{1,11}) = 7/8$
4. $PR'_{2,7} = \Phi_{PR1,7}(2,7); W(PR'_{2,7}) = 0$
5. $PR'_{3,7} = \Phi_{PR1,7}(3,7); W(PR'_{3,7}) = 7/9$

The selected elementary relation $PR'_{1,9}$ is not a rectangle, so the algorithm continues on the previous selected elements namely (1,7) and (1,9) (see Illustration 3).

- **Second Iteration:** Search now the optimal rectangles of $PR'_{1,9}$ that successively contain the elements (1,8), (1,11), and (3,9). This step provides three elementary relations:

1. $PR''_{1,8} = \Phi_{PR'_{1,9}}(1,8)$; $W(PR''_{1,8}) = -1$
2. $PR''_{1,11} = \Phi_{PR'_{1,9}}(1,11)$; $W(PR''_{1,11}) = 7/8$
3. $PR''_{3,9} = \Phi_{PR'_{1,9}}(3,9)$; $W(PR''_{3,9}) = 1$
   ⇑ **selected**

$PR''_{3,9}$ is a rectangle, so it is optimal and contains the element (1,7) of R (see Illustration 4).

Figure 5 illustrates the iterations searching steps to find the optimal rectangle. In bold you can see the selected elementary relation at each level of the search tree. Each level is associated with an iteration in the proposed polynomial algorithm. When we find an optimal rectangle, we continue to search for a next optimal one containing another pair not already selected. For instance, if we select the pair (6,12), we get at the first iteration the concept: $PR_{6,12} = \{5,6\} \times \{11,12\}$. Then if we select the pair (4,10), we obtain the concept: $PR_{4,10} = \{3,4\} \times \{9,10\}$. Finally, if we select the pair (2,8), we get the concept: $PR_{2,8} = \{2,1\} \times \{7,8\}$.

The selected coverage is composed of the following:

$\{PR''_{3,9}, PR_{6,12,} PR_{4,10,} PR_{2,8}\}$.

In the following sections, we explain how to apply the optimal concepts on text summarization.

SUMMARIZATION OF TEXTS WITH EXTRACTION RULES

The idea is to extract a summary from a given document, along with some association rules between the keywords contained in the document. For that purpose, we should first decide how to decompose the main text into chapters, sections, or sentences. Then we may ask the user if he or she wants either to automatically get the summary or to extract the association rules. Assume that the user decides to consider a sentence as the atomic structure of the text, which we cannot change or reduce. So, the system will first create a binary context R where objects are sentence numbers (recognized by their position in the text) and properties are words (each word is also recognized by a position in a hash table structure). By definition, (i, j) belongs to R if and only if the word number j belongs to the sentence number i or it is very similar to another word in the sentence number i. The crucial question about how to recognize that two words are similar has been resolved with an approximate algorithm. We

Illustration 1.

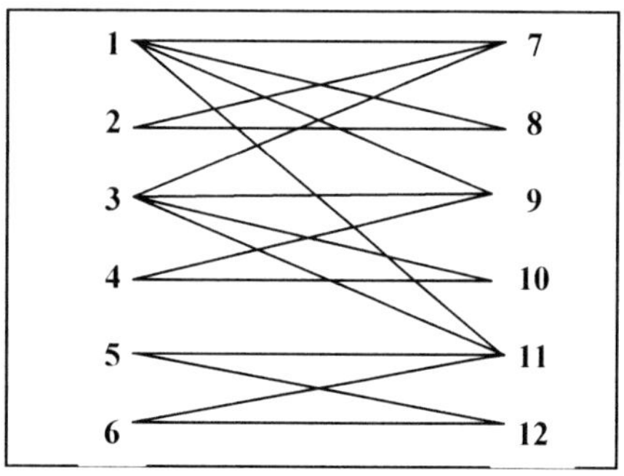

Illustration 2.

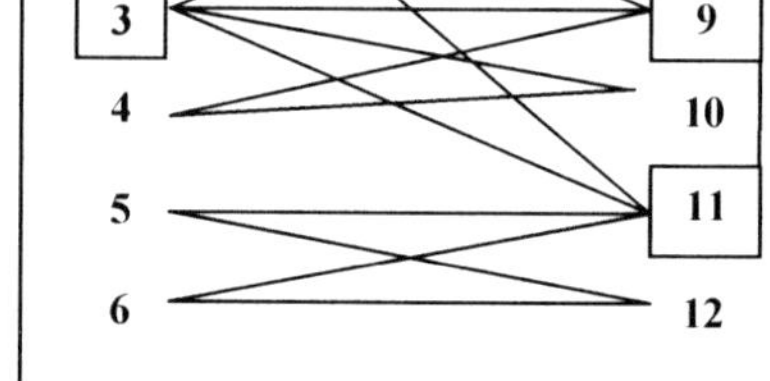

assume that two words are similar if they contain a longest common sub-sequence with some relative size greater than some value p near to 1. Here, when we decrease the value of p, we obtain words that are more similar and of course, this has some impact on the quality of the summary. As a next step, starting from the binary context R, we use the method proposed in the previous section to find the optimal concept. Then we select all sentences in the domain of this concept to generate the summary. If the user would like more precision about the document, he or she may ask about the next optimal concept, and obtain by the same way, a complement of information. We can repeat this process until covering the entire document. We tested the system on different documents with different sizes and topics and we are satisfied by the automatic selection of the sentences. In Figure 6, we give an algorithm that finds the longest common subsequence length belonging to two keywords, while in Figure 7, we give an algorithm for calculating the optimal concept containing a pair in the context R.

ILLUSTRATIVE EXAMPLE FOR TEXT SUMMARIZATION

Assume that we have the following text T about the United Nations:

Illustration 3.

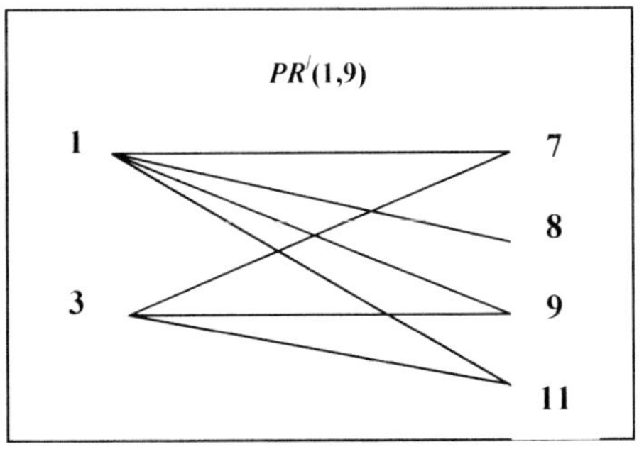

The United Nations

The United Nations was formed at the end of the Second World War on October 24, 1945. It was formed to try to make sure that future generations would not suffer from horrible damage caused by wars. It was also intended to develop friendly relations between countries around the world and to help with any problems countries might have. The most important part of the United Nations has always been the Security Council.

The Security Council

The Security Council was formed to try to keep peace and security around the world. In the beginning, the council consisted of 11 countries; now it has 15. Five of these are permanent members. Today they are Russia, China, France, the USA, and the UK. The other 10 member countries are elected for a period of two years. When decisions have to be made, each member of the council has one vote. The decision is only agreed upon if at least 9 of the 15 members vote for it. Even then, any one of the five permanent members can block or stop the decision by using its veto. Only the permanent members have a veto. This makes them very powerful.

The General Assembly

Another important part of the United Nations is the General Assembly where all member countries

Illustration 4.

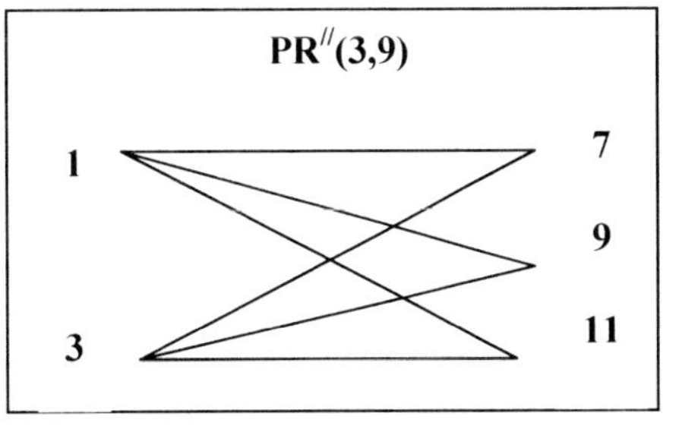

Figure 5. Iterations of searching for the optimal rectangle contained in R

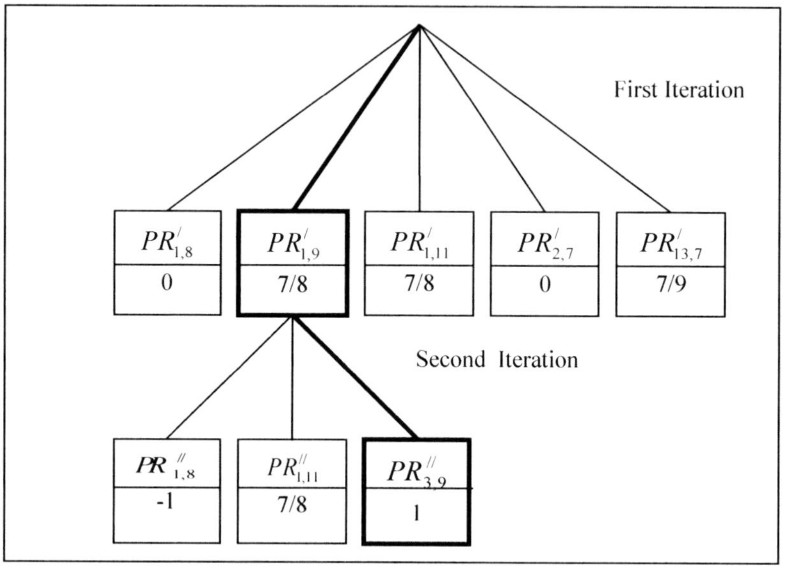

discuss world problems. When the United Nations was formed, there were 51 member countries. In 1982, there were a 155. Qatar joined in September 1971. Today, the number is still increasing. One reason for this is that some states are breaking up into separate countries. For example, the different countries that used to make up the single member state known as the Soviet Union have their own membership now. The main job of the assembly is to suggest what might be done in different countries as problems appear. It cannot make governments do what it would like them to do, but, because it is an international group, it gives a voice to world opinion.

The International Court of Justice

A third important part of the United Nations is the International Court of Justice. Countries and international organizations can take their problems to the court that will give advice on these problems. Like the general assembly, it cannot make countries follow its advice. However, it still has power because none of the countries want to see the court advise against it in the eyes of the rest of the world.

The Future of the United Nations

How effective is the United Nations? We have already seen that it cannot make countries do what they do not want to do. Another problem is that the United Nations was formed to try to stop countries from fighting each other. However, a new problem has arisen in the last few years. The United Nations has been asked to act in civil wars-situations where fighting occurs inside countries instead of between different countries. Examples are Somalia, Rwanda, and Yugoslavia. What can United Nations do in these situations? It can only send in observers or peacekeepers. Should there be a United Nations army with power to make people do what the general assembly wants them to do? This is a question now being asked. It is a question that has not been answered yet.

Figure 6. Algorithm to find the length of the longest common subsequence between two words

```
Problem: Determine the length of the longest common subsequence between two
   words.
Inputs:   Two strings A and B of length n and m respectively over the alphabet ∑
Outputs: A non-negative number, which is the maximum length of the longest
         common subsequence.

Begin
 // L[h][g] should contain the length of the longest subsequence of the prefix
 // of A between position 1 and h; and the prefix of B between position 1 and g.

   For i=0 to n Do L[i][0]= 0; //initialization of the first column of L to 0.
   For j=0 to m Do L[0][j]=0;  //initialization of the first row of L to 0.
   For i=0 to n Do

    // Using a dynamic programming method, we calculate L[i, j] following
    // the recurrence relation defined in I and II embedded in the following code

    For j=0 to m Do
     If A [i] = B [j]
      Then L [I] = L [i-1, j-1]+1                    // I
     Else    L [I] = max (L [i, j-1], Li-1, j])       // II
     End if
    End for
  End for
  Return L[n, m]  // L [n, m] contains the length of the longest subsequence
End (Algorithm).
```

The proposed system associates a given order number with each sentence and a given order number with each word. Then it builds a binary relation R associating sentences to their indexing words. Depending on a given precision level, two words are compared in terms of a longest common subsequence and are assumed to be similar or synonymous. By applying the previous algorithms, we select an optimal concept C. The domain of the concept C is composed of a set S of sentences' numbers in the text. The text of S is selected as a summary of the initial text T. For the given text T, our system generates the following summary S:

Figure 7. Algorithm to find an optimal rectangle in a binary relation R

```
Optimal_Rectangle (Relation R, s, w)
Problem: Determine the optimal rectangle of a binary relation R.
Inputs: A binary relation R[][] with a pair (s,w).
Outputs: The pair (s, w) containing an optimal rectangle in R.

Begin
  Let R [m][n] be the binary relation of n keywords and m sentences.
  Emax = 0;   // The maximum searched gain in R (W(R)) initialized to 0
  For s = 0 to n-1 Do
    For w = 0 to m-1 Do
      If R[s, w]! =0
       Then PR=I(R.w) o R o I(s.R); // calculating the elementary relation of
       (s,w)
       E = economy (PR);
       If (E > Emax)
         Then { Emax = E;
                  Highest = PR; // Highest is the concept of maximal gain
                  s'= s;
                  w'= w;}
         End if
      End if
    End for
    End for
  If Highest is not rectangle                    // r != cd
   Then Optimal_Rectangle (Highest ,s',w')     //Recursive call to function
                                               //Optimal_Rectangle starting from
                                               //relation Highest corresponding to the
                                               //next level in the search tree
  Else return the pair(s',w')
  End if
End (Algorithm).
```

The United Nations

The United Nations was formed at the end of the Second World War on October 24, 1945. The most important part of the United Nations has always been the Security Council. Another important part of the United Nations is the general assembly, where all member countries discuss world problems. When the United Nations was formed, there were 51 member countries. A third important

Figure 8. Algorithm to calculate the economy of a binary relation R

Problem: *Determine the economy of a binary relation.*

Inputs: *A binary relation R.*

Outputs: *The economy.*

Begin

Let R [m][n] be the binary relation of n keywords and m sentences.

Let r be the number of pairs in R.

Let c be the cardinality of domains of R.

Let d be the cardinality of co-domain of R.

Return *(r / (c * d)) * (r- (c + d))*

End.

part of the United Nations is the International Court of Justice.

The Future of the United Nations

How effective is the United Nations? We have already seen that it cannot make countries do what they do not want to do. Another problem is that the United Nations was formed to try to stop countries from fighting each other. The United Nations has been asked to act in civil war situations where fighting occurs inside countries instead of between different countries. What can the United Nations do in these situations? It can only send in observers or peacekeepers. Should there be a United Nations army with power to make people do what the general assembly wants to do? This is a question now being asked.

The user can ask for a more specific detail in the text. In that case, the system generates the next optimal concept. From the domain, of this concept, it generates the next sentences selection. The system may continue with the same way until the coverage of all the text is done. It also generates the list of 19 association rules between the words of the text as for example:

united → nations, nations → united
war → united, nations, countries
world → countries
future→united, nations
problems → countries, security → council
peace → countries, years
years → countries, years
decisions → council, members, vote, veto
veto → council, members, decisions, vote
justice→ international, court
advice → court, countries, power → countries,
… etc.

These rules have been extracted by using the two operators of Galois connections namely *f* and *g*. Using the relation *R*, for each word by the function *g*, we build all sentences indexed by some word *w*, and then by the function *f*, we extract all other words indexing all these sentences. These rules may be used to realize query expansion. Used in the context of a huge documentary database, it should minimize noise and silence, and improve the quality of the selected answers.

Other Experimental Results

Several experiments have been carried out on texts of different sizes and topics, and the obtained results are satisfactory. However, we need to improve the time complexity of the algorithms to make the system usable in the real life context, for instance, in search engines over the Internet. We also have to improve the semantic quality of the summary by introducing some relation order between the words of the text by using for example a thesaurus. Some results of the system are shown in Table 3.

Here we have a sample of six documents in English and Arabic of different sizes and topics. Our experimental results show that the system generates meaningful summaries of texts of acceptable sizes. However, when the size of the texts becomes large enough, we obtained moderate summaries, which are not fully precise. In fact, they help to understand approximately the main ideas of the original text. Thus, our approach will not provide all times optimal summaries and definitely, it should be improved by introducing new concepts.

CONCLUSION

In this article, we proposed a new approach to generate the summary of a given text using the optimal concept where the main text is considered as coverage of concepts. The text can be given in any languages as no semantic or grammatical concepts are used. Each concept represents a cluster of sentences sharing common indexing words. Depending on the user request, the system can generate different concepts in decreasing the order of importance that we measured by a gain function. The system extracts from each concept different parts of the text. The quality of the obtained summaries is satisfactory. This system may be integrated into search engines over the Internet to filter the Web pages belonging to the optimal concept associated with the binary relations, linking Web pages to their indexing words. It is even interesting to use the system to filter successive concepts from search engines to deliver only Web pages belonging to the main concepts from the global Web pages extracted from the usual search engines. We think that we may improve the quality of the optimal selected concept by using a better heuristics. One important aspect of these algorithms is that they may find concepts with an incremental way. So, even if the initial concepts extraction is expensive in terms of time, updating these concepts is not time consuming. It is important to mention that we found a summary *S'* of the summary *S* of the text *T* is fully identical to the summary *S*. Consequently, the system works correctly and generates a unique summary of the main text. However, we need to improve

Table 3.

	Documents	D1	D2	D3	D4	D5	D6
	A/E	E	E	E	E	A	A
Original Text	Pages	6	15	2	1	9	3
	Paragraphs	66	66	21	13	39	35
	Words	3318	7091	885	549	4710	1581
Summary Text	Pages	1	3	1	1	2	1
	Parapraphs	8	12	2	2	4	15
	Words	282	1099	243	188	706	727
	Quality	G	G	M	G	M	G

E: English
A: Arabic
G: Good
M: Moderate

the time complexity of the used algorithms in order to make the system efficient in real context. We have also to improve the semantic quality of the summary by introducing some order relation between the words of the text, which can be done by using a thesaurus.

REFERENCES

Al-Rashdi, A., Al-Muraikhi, H., Al-Subaiey M., Al-Ghanim, N., & Al-Misaifri, S. (2001). *Knowledge extraction and reduction system.* Senior Project, Computer Science Department, University of Qatar.

Belkhiter, N., Bourhfir, C., Gammoudi, M., Jaoua, A., Le Thanh, N., & Reguig, M. (1994). Decomposition Rectangulaire Optimale d'une Relation Binaire: Application aux Bases de Donnees Documentaires. *Canadian Journal: INFOR, 32*(1), 33-54.

Ben Yahia, S., & Jaoua, A. (2001). Discovering knowledge from fuzzy concept lattice. In A. Kandel, M. Last, & H. Bunke (Eds.), *Data mining and computational intelligence, studies in fuzziness and soft computing* (Vol. 68, pp. 167-190), Heidelberg: Physica Verlag.

Ben Yahia, S., Arour, K., Slimani, A., & Jaoua, A. (2000). Discovery of compact rules in relational databases. *Information Journal, 3*(4), 497-511.

Davey, B. A., & Priestley, H. A. (1990). *Introduction to lattices and order.* Cambridge Mathematical Textbooks.

Ganter B., & Wille, F. (1999). *Formal concept analysis.* Springer-Verlag.

Jaoua A., & Elloumi S. (2002). Galois connection: Formal concepts and Galois lattice in real relations: Application in a real classifier. *The Journal of Systems and Software, 60,* 149-163.

Jaoua, A., Belkhiter, N., Desharnais J., & Moukam, T. (1992). Properties of difunctional dependencies in relational database. *Canadian Journal INFOR, 30*(1), 297-315.

Jaoua A., Boudriga, N., Durieux, J. L., & Mili, A. (1991). Regularity of relations a measure of uniformity. *Theoretical Computer Science, 79,* 323-339.

Jaoua A., Bsaies, K., & Consmtini, W. (1999). May reasoning be reduced to an information retrieval problem. *International Seminar in Relational Methods in Computer Science,* Quebec, Canada.

Khcherif, R., Gammoudi, M. N., & Jaoua, A. (2000). Using difunctional relations in information organization. *Journal of Information Sciences, 125,* 153-166, Elsevier N.H.

Maddouri, M., Elloumi, S., & Jaoua, A. (1998). An incremental learning system for imprecise and uncertain knowledge discovery. *Information Science Journal, 109,* 149-164.

Mineau G. W., & Godin, R. (1995). Automatic structuring of knowledge bases by conceptual clustering. *IEEE Transactions on Knowledge and Data Engineering, 7*(5), 824-829.

Riguet, J. (1948). Relations Binaries, Fermetures et Correspondences de Galois. *Bulletin de la Societe Mathematique de France,* 114-155.

Schmidt, G., & Ströhlein, S. (1989). *Relations and graphs.* Springer-Verlag.

This work was previously published in Int. Journal of Information Technology and Web Engineering, Vol. 1, Issue 4, edited by G. Alkhatib and D. Rine, pp. 22-36, copyright 2006 by IGI Publishing (an imprint of IGI Global).

Chapter XII
Studying and Analysis of a Vertical Web Page Classifier Based on Continuous Learning Naïve Bayes (CLNB) Algorithm

H. A. Ali
Mansoura University, Egypt

Ali I. El Desouky
Mansoura University, Egypt

Ahmed I. Saleh
Mansoura University, Egypt

ABSTRACT

Web page classification is considered one of the most challenging research areas. Where the Web has a huge volume of unstructured and distributed documents that are related to a variety of domains; so, considering one base for the classification tasks will be extremely difficult. In addition, the Web is full of noise that will certainly harm the classifier performance especially if it is found in the classifier training data. Generally, it will be more valued to build domain-oriented classifiers (vertical classifiers) to classify pages related to a specific domain and compensate those classifiers with novel learning techniques to achieve better performance. The contribution of this paper is three edged; firstly, a novel learning technique called .Continuous Learning. is introduced. Secondly, the paper presents a new trend for Web page classification by presenting the domain-oriented classifiers (vertical classifiers). A new way of applying Bayes and K-Nearest Neighbor algorithms is introduced in order to build Domain

Oriented Naïve Bayes (DONB) and Domain Oriented K-Nearest Neighbor (DOKNN) classifiers. The third contribution is combining both disciplines by introducing a novel classification strategy. Such strategy adds the continuous learning ability to Bayes theorem to build a Continuous learning domain oriented Naïve Bayes (CLNB) classifier. Where the overfitting problem has a great impact on most Web page classification techniques, continuous learning can be considered as a proposed solution. It allows the classifier to adapt itself continuously for achieving better performance. The proposed classifiers are tested; experimental results have shown that CLNB demonstrates significant performance improvement over both DONB and DOKNN where its accuracy goes beyond 94.1% after testing 1000 pages.

INTRODUCTION

Recently, due to information overload, the most mind-engaging problem for everyone is how to achieve accurately the required information both easily and rapidly. The World Wide Web (WWW) can be viewed as a huge repository of accessible information in a variety of domains. However, searching WWW for the required information is not a trivial task due to the enormous amount of data available. Assistance in searching WWW can be achieved using either search engines or Web directories (*also called portals or catalogues*). Search engines rely on keyword-based queries that usually result in a long list of retrieved documents with low precision. In contrast, directories organize documents into a number of pre-defined categories. According to Chen (2000), WWW users prefer to use directories rather than navigation through long lists retrieved by traditional search engines.

Many directories are available on WWW today such as Yahoo and LookSmart. They classify Web pages according to a set of pre-defined categories usually organized in a hierarchical manner. Earlier, classifying Web pages was maintained by a set of domain experts. They read and analyze newly incoming pages, then classify them to the most suitable categories. However, due to the sheer amount of material on the Web with the exponentially increase in size, it is becoming increasingly difficult to maintain catalogues manually. Manual classification is too slow to keep track with the recent evolution of Web contents. According to Pieere (2000), over than 1.5 million of Web pages are daily added to the Web. Two logical solutions are suggested to overcome WWW scaling problems. The first is to build domain oriented classifiers or vertical classifiers (VCs). A VC is concerned with classifying documents related to a specific domain. In other words, it is interested in one slice of the Web. Cutting off the Web into a number of slices will certainly minimize such scaling problems and boost the classification accuracy dramatically. The second solution is to automate the classification process.

Automatic Web classification began using machine learning techniques that are applied efficiently to text classification (TC) (Lam, 2003), like support vector machines (SVM) (Sun, 2003; Yu, 2002), k-nearest Neighbor (KNN) (Kwon, 2003), decision trees (Apte, 1998), rule induction (Fabio, 2001), neural networks (Ruiz, 2002; Selemat 2002), and Bayesian classifier (Rennie, 2003). However, classifying Web pages is much more difficult than classifying pure text for different reasons. One reason is that: Web documents belong to a variety of domains, which means, considering one base for the classification task is extremely difficult. In addition, the Web is full of noise usually embedded in Web pages like advertisements and navigation bars. This noise will certainly harm the classifier performance; it may result in discarding main topics or important contents especially if it is found in the classifier training data. If traditional TC techniques are applied to the Web directly, they will certainly suffer from overfitting problem. Such problem occurs when the classifier is trained to fit a set of training examples with a quite small classification error, while the error is very large when classifying new documents during testing phase. Overfitting will logically hamper the automatic classification process. One solution to avoid overfitting is to use a very large training set; however, this approach is neither practical nor efficient due to the huge amount of human effort needed to prepare the training set. Hence, it is becoming necessary to resort to novel strategies that improve traditional classification techniques.

TRADITIONAL WEB PAGE CLASSIFIER VS. VERTICAL CLASSIFIER

Web page classification (WPC) (Yu, 2004) is the task of targeting an incoming Web page to a set of pre-defined classes. Classification may be *hard*, so that the page will be targeted to one (*and only one*) class, or it may be *soft*, so that the page may be targeted to any number of classes.

Figure 1. A block diagram representing traditional classifiers

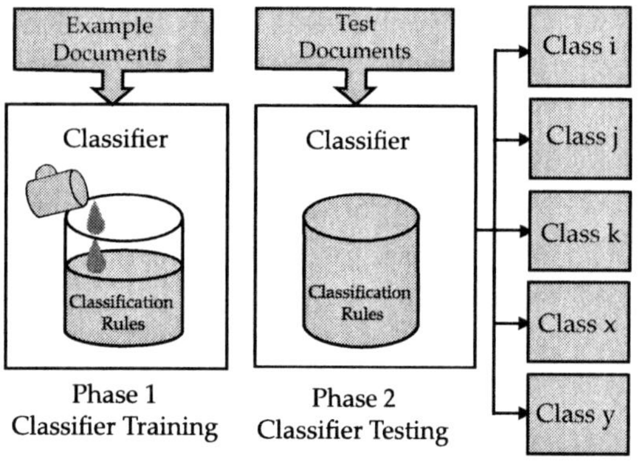

Most traditional Web page classifiers depend on machine learning concepts (Heb, 2005; Fung, 2005). The classifier (*as modeled in Figure 1*) operates in two different phases, namely training and testing. During the training, the classifier extracts as much classification rules as possible using a set of pre-classified examples (*training data*). The extracted rules vary according to the technique used for classification. For example, in neural network based classifiers, the rules are the exact weights for different network layers. While rules for Bayesian classifiers, are sets of probabilities. In contrast, classifying the newly incoming pages takes place during the testing phase according to the pre-extracted rules. Considering the Web as a whole will make the classification task so troublesome, while the Web can be viewed as a set of isolated (*or may be inter-connected*) domains (*like sports, computers, animals, etc.*) Considering one domain will certainly make classification easier and more valued.

When trying to incorporate traditional classification techniques with the knowledge of the domain of interest, a new generation of classifiers called domain oriented classifiers or vertical classifiers (VCs) will arise. This type of classifiers can be integrated with focused crawlers to build domain specific catalogues. A VC should be learned with the domain knowledge in order to set its classification rules, and then used to classify newly incoming pages during the testing phase. As proposed in Figure 2, a VC contains two basic functional modules, namely, distiller and classifier. The distiller can be considered as a filtration stage that discards pages related to other domains. On the contrary, the classifier module is used to classify pages according to a set of pre-defined domain classes.

TRADITIONAL LEARNING VERSUS CONTINUOUS LEARNING

In general, traditional learning techniques (Raqule, 2005; Hu, 2005) are classified into passive or active. Passive learning (PL) techniques (Xu, 2005; Solan, 2005; Getz, 2005), as illustrated in teacher-learner (T-L) model in Figure 3(A), assume that the learner is unwilling to learn. Neither the teacher nor the surrounding environment interacts with that lazy learner, but simply the learner learns from the data given to him from his teacher. Hence, the teacher is active, while the learner is passive.

Three different learning techniques lie in PL category, which are, supervised learning (Xu, 2005), unsupervised learning (Solan, 2005), and semi-supervised learning (Getz, 2005). In supervised learning, initially sets of training examples are labeled (often manually), and then learning algorithm is applied to build the classifier. A supervised system allows the user to control the building of the training sets and to correctly tune the classification process. However, such approach requires the training examples to be both manually collected and accurately labeled. Manual labeling is time consuming, expensive, and requires much effort of experienced human annotators especially for large dataset. Further, in some cases it may not be possible to provide accurate labels (*or cannot provide labels at all*); accordingly, supervised methods cannot provide solutions to these problems. Finally, supervised methods may sometimes suffer from overfitting (Aik, 2003). In order to go around supervised learning problems, semi-supervised learning is studied, which applies learning from a small set of labeled examples and a large set of unlabeled examples. It tries to reduce the human labeling effort; however, utilizing unlabeled examples may lead to degradation in system performance. The major drawback of unsupervised learning is the possibility of false estimation, which results in falsely structured clusters as there are no assured rules to guide the cluster generation. It may also result in too many or too few clusters (Bazzel, 2003).

Figure 2. A block diagram for a vertical classifier

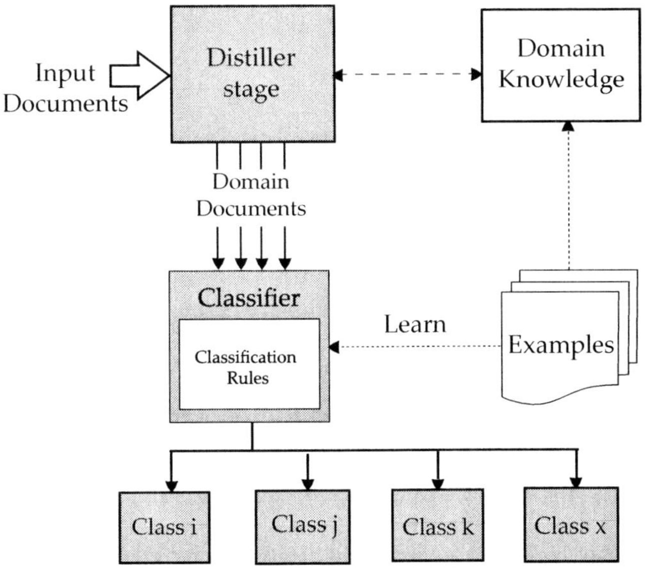

Figure 3. The teacher-learner model for various learning techniques

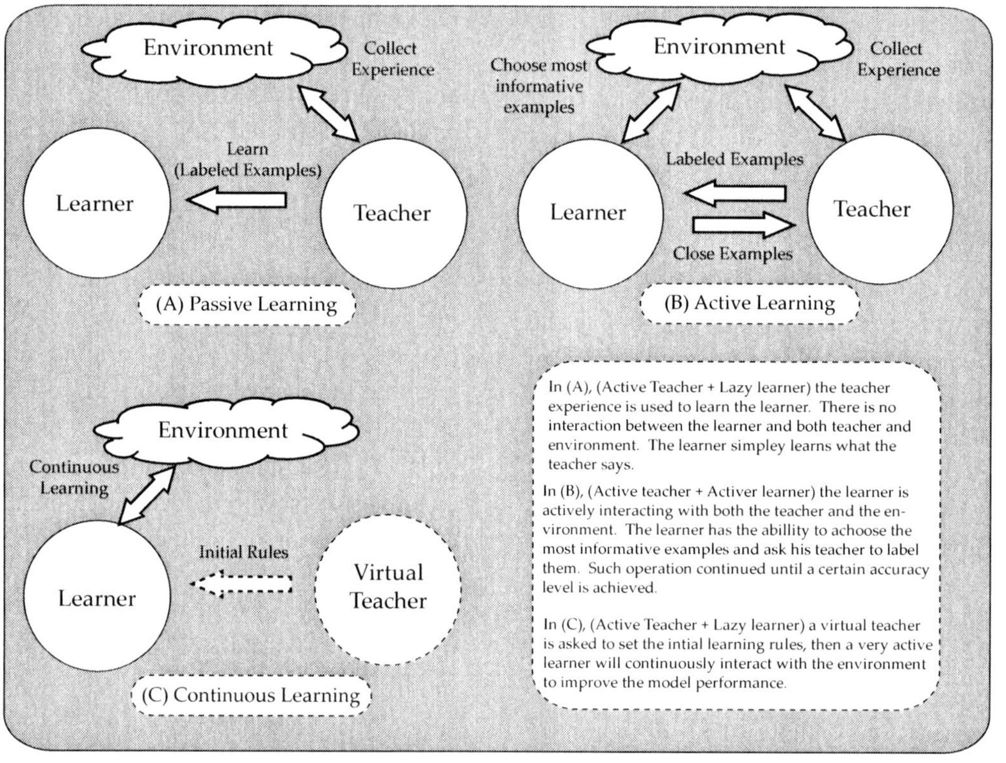

The goal of active learning (AL) (Brigham, 2005) is to precisely select the training examples to quickly improve the classifier's overall accuracy with minimum human effort. It assumes the existence of a small number of labeled examples and large number of unlabeled ones. As shown in Figure 4, the training phase is sub-divided into two different steps, *initial* and *extended*. In the initial training step, the model is trained using the existing labeled examples to generate an initial model. During the extended training, a long pool of unlabeled examples is available. The learner tries to select the *m*-most informative examples (*m* is an arbitrary number). Those examples are introduced to the teacher for labeling, and then added to the model training set. Finally, the model is re-trained again using the new training set. The loop is repeated until a specific level of accuracy is obtained. Shortly, the learner tries to get the best performance from the fewest number of labeled examples (human effort) as possible. As illustrated in T-L model in Figure 3(B), both the teacher and the learner can interact with each other and with the environment.

Recent work in the area of AL has emphasized two basic approaches, *certainty-based* (Aron, 2005) and *committee-based* (Becker, 2005). Both approaches rely on the principle that examples that can be easily classified by the model will not add new classification rules if they are added to the model training set. The most ambiguous examples for the system will certainly be the most informative and add more effective classification rules if they are added to the training set. So, a fewer highly informative examples provide much more information than many random ones. Although AL techniques provide significant savings in data-labeling effort in many situations, the ac-

Figure 4. The learning phase in the active learning technique

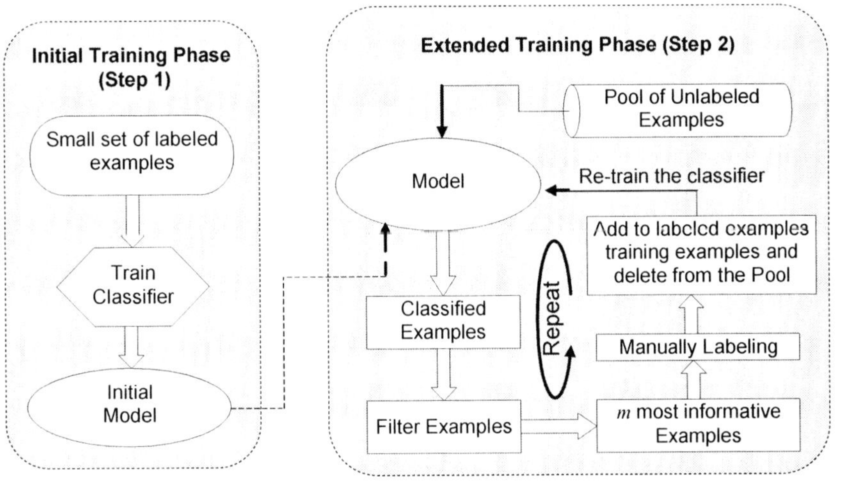

Figure 5. The automation: Human control spectrum for various learning techniques

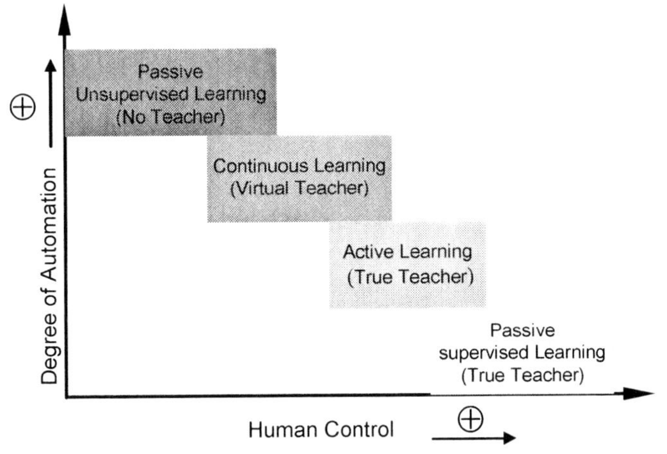

curacy level may fail to converge. In addition, there are still human efforts required for data labeling. Successful applications of AL include text classification (Tur, 2005), image classification (Huan, 2003), speech recognition (Tur, 2003), and software testing (Gang, 2005).

In this article, we introduce a novel learning strategy called continuous learning (CL). The continuous learning is obtained by utilising the testing phase rather than being limited to one phase of the model operation. CL as illustrated in Figure 3(C), depends on a virtual teacher to provide the initial to guide the learner. No training examples are provided and the learner continues to learn in order to improve his performance. A comparison between the proposed CL technique and traditional learning techniques is illustrated in Table 1. Through the experimental results, substantial empirical evidence has shown that continuous learning can dramatically expedite the learning process and assures system performance promotion with time.

As illustrated in 'Automation—Human Control' spectrum shown in Figure 5, all learning

Table 1. A comparison between the proposed continuous learning and traditional learning techniques

	Passive Learning		Active Learning	Continuous Learning
	Supervised	Unsupervised		
Used when	A large number of labeled examples are available for the algorithm to learn from.	No labeled examples are available	A large training pool of unlabeled examples is available and getting labels for them is time-consuming or difficult. (29)	No labeled examples are available, or getting labels is expensive.
Learning Strategy	Passive learning, no interaction between the learner and the teacher. The algorithm is able to train itself to generate the correct responses, according to the labeled examples. The experience gained during training phase is used to drive the model during testing phase.	Passive learning, no interaction between the learner and the teacher. Training is based on the features of examples and the goal is clustering the data according to similarity measures among them, so that all data within a cluster being similar to each other.	The learner actively interacts with the teacher during the training phase. It selects the most informative examples from a pool of unlabeled examples, and then asks the teacher to label them. The operation continued until a predefined level of accuracy achieved. Hence, the best performance can be achieved with the fewest number of labeled examples.	A Virtual .or No. teacher is provided to initiate the model. The learner continuously interacts with the environment to achieve better performance. No training examples are required at all (neither labeled nor unlabeled).
Human Efforts	Maximum	Minimum	Medium	Very Low
Labeled Examples	Required	Not Required	Required	Not Required
Unlabeled examples	Not Required	Required	Required	Not Required

continued on following page

Table 1. continued

Disadvantages	▪ Requires a large number of labeled examples to learn accurately. Which is time-consuming, expensive, and, tedious process? Further, in some cases it may not be possible to provide labels at all. ▪ It is generally not possible to add incrementally to the training data while training the classifier. If the training data are changed in any way, the entire training data set must be used to retrain the model. ▪ Supervised algorithms are limited by the quality of the labeled examples they are given. Hence, they may suffer from overfitting. ▪ Supervised learning is an all-or-nothing technique; it cannot make use of any unlabeled data. ▪ ▪ ▪	▪ The possibility of false estimation, hence falsely structured clusters. ▪ No heuristic rules are available to guide the cluster generation, and finding too many or too few clusters. ▪ They have difficulty determining whether their results are useful because they lack predetermined benchmarks of accuracy. ▪ ▪	▪ The tedious human efforts required for labeling have not been eliminated but they have been reduced since active learning costs a user's additional efforts in reading .uncertain documents.. ▪ Active learning does not successful in all situations. ▪ Although active learning technique provides significant savings in data-labeling effort in many situations, the accuracy level may fail to converge. ▪	▪ The continuous learning technique is a novel learning approach. We hope that it can be used to boost the accuracy of applications that employ learning algorithms.

techniques fail along a diagonal, illustrating the trade-off between automation and human control over the learning process. At the bottom right, passive supervised learning offers the greatest amount of control but offers little automation. At the top left, passive unsupervised learning offers the greatest automation with little control. Otherwise, the continuous learning tries to minimize the human effort (*provide high automation as possible*) with a reasonable human control to assure performance promotion during learning process.

Finally, it is important to mention that, choosing one learning technique to be the universal best approach is not possible since all techniques serve different learning goals. For example, supervised, active and continuous techniques are appropriate when the goal is to build a predictive model for the problem. While, unsupervised techniques are used when the goal is to analyze the input data to discover interesting structures and inter-relations among them (Costa, 2004).

ALTERNATIVE CLASSIFICATION STRATEGIES

In the following sub-sections, we will briefly explore some of the most commonly used classification strategies, namely artificial neural networks (ANNs), k-nearest neighbors (KNN), support vector machines (SVM), and naïve bayes (NB) classifier. The description of various classification strategies is followed by a decision to choose both NB and KNN as starting points for our proposed work.

Artifical Neural Networks (ANNs)

In order to build a Web page classifier based on ANNs, it is required primary to formulate a neural network classification model (NNCM). NNCM is a computational model consisting of the following parts: (1) a graphical structure of the ANN, which usually consists of three cascaded layers (*input, hidden, and output*) of interconnected nodes.

Figure 6. NNCM consists of three cascaded layers, n input attributes and m output classes

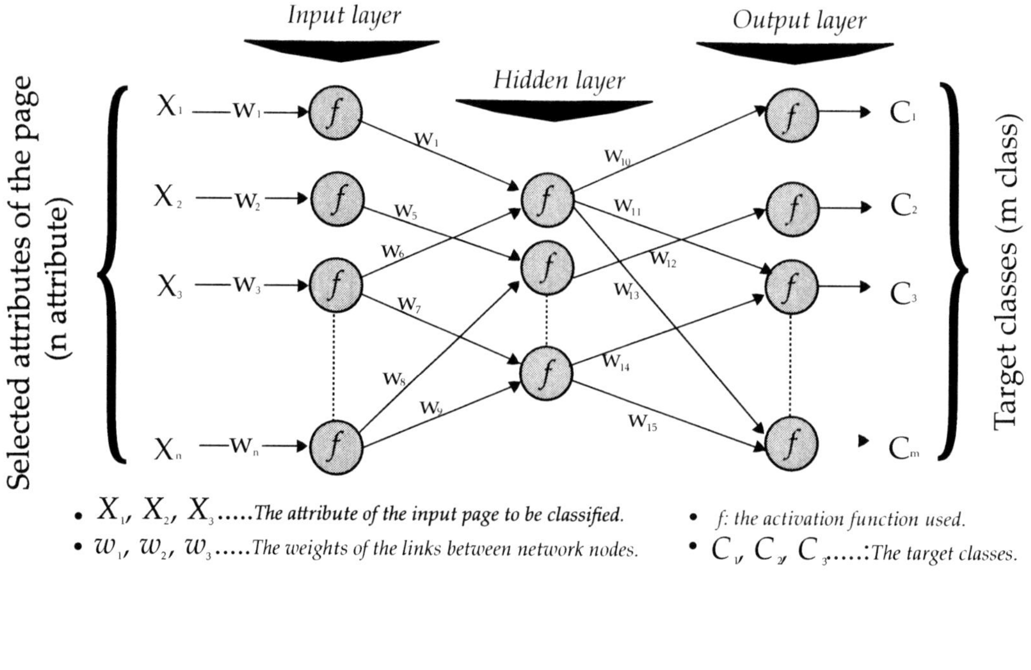

Each connection between any two nodes has a weight that is set initially by the domain expert and modified continuously during the training phase for better classification. The structure has one input for each attribute value of the examined page, and one output sink for each target class. The output value that is generated indicates the probability that the corresponding input page belongs to that class. The page will then be assigned to the class with the highest probability of membership. (2) A transformation technique that converts a given page attribute to a corresponding numerical value (input attribute for NNCM must be numeric). (3) A learning algorithm to indicate how learning takes place (setting up the exact weights). (4) An appropriate activation function f (also called squashing function or firing rule). (5) Recall techniques that determine how information is obtained from the network. Figure 6 represents a NNCM that consists of three cascaded layers, n input attributes and m output classes.

K-Nearest Neighbor Algorithm (KNN)

One of the most commonly used distance-based algorithms is KNN, which relies on distance measures as the only classification criteria. It assumes three basic principles: (1) any page can be represented by a single point in a proposed n-dimensional space, (2) pages related to the same class will be much closer (*similar*) to each other in the proposed space than pages related to any other class, and (3) when a classification is to be made for a new page, its distance to each item (page) in the training examples must be determined. Only the k closest examples (KCE) in the training examples is considered. The new page is then targeted to the class that contains the most items in KCE set.

Many distance measures can be used; one of the most commonly used ones are Euclidean (Costa, 2003) and cosine distances (Qian, 2004). To explain how it works, let an arbitrary page p_x be described by the following attribute vector in the proposed n-dimensional space; p_x=<$a_1(p_x)$,$a_2(p_x)$, ..., $a_n(p_x)$>, where $a_i(p_x)$ denotes the value of the ith attribute of p_x. Then, the distance between p_x and any other page p_y in the training examples is defined as $dis\ (p_x, p_y)$, where:

$$dis_{Euc}(p_x, p_y) = \sqrt{\sum_{k=1}^{n}\left(a_k(p_x)-a_k(p_y)\right)^2}$$

Euclidean distance

Figure 7. Classify two pages p_x and p_y using 5-earest Neighbor among three classes A, B, and C

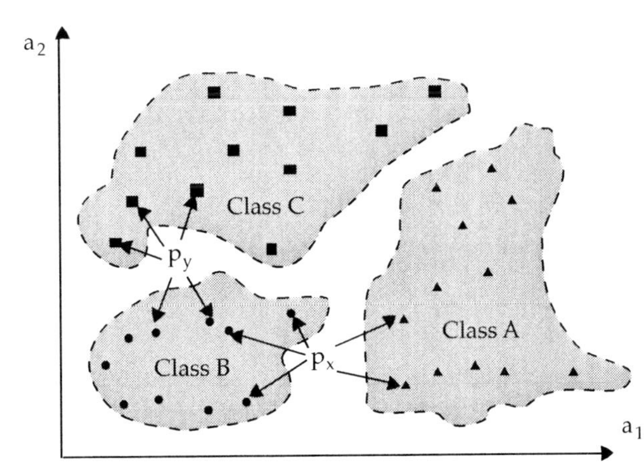

$$dis_{Cos}(p_x,p_y) = \frac{\sum_{k\in(p_x \cap p_y)} (a_k(p_x)\cdot a_k(p_y))}{\sqrt{\sum_{k=1}^{n}(a_k(p_x))^2 \cdot \sum_{k=1}^{n}(a_k(p_y))^2}}$$

Cosine distance

The page p_x will be targeted to the class that contains the maximum number of items in KCE. Consider a set of z pre-defined hypotheses (classes) $H=\{h_1, h_2, \ldots, h_z\}$, $KCE=\{CE(1), CE(2), \ldots\ldots, CE(K)\}$, where $CE(i)$ is the ith item (*Example*) in KCE set. All items in KCE will be targeted to a set of Probable Target Classes $PTC \subset H$, $PTC=\{PTC_1, PTC_2, \ldots, PTC_m\}$, where $m \le z$ (since some of the closest items may belongs to the same target class). Then, p_x will be targeted to $PTC_j \in PTC$ as expressed by the following equation:

$$\text{target}(p_x) = \text{argmax}_{PTCj\in PTC}\left[\sum_{i=1}^{K}\Theta(\text{Target}(CE(i)\,,\,PTCj)\right]$$

where Target($CE(i)$) is the target class of the ith closest item in KCE, and the function $\Theta(x,y)$ is defined as following:

$$\Theta(x,y) = \begin{cases} 1 \; if \; x = y \\ 0 \; if \; x \neq y \end{cases}$$

An illustration, shown in Figure 7, considers three classes A, B and C in a two-dimensional space. It is required to classify two pages p_x and p_y using 5-nearest neighbor algorithm. Then, p_x and p_y will be targeted to classes B, C respectively.

Support Vector Machines (SVM)

(Vapnik, 1999) proposed SVMs, which were primarily introduced to solve two-class pattern recognition problems using the structural risk minimization principle (Vapnik, 1998). Setting up a Web page classifier with SVMs involves expressing each page in the Training Set (TS) by a single point in an n-dimensional input space, then try to define a set of discriminative planes (also called hyperplanes) that defines the boundaries among various classes. A hyperplane is a separator that lies between a set of pages having different class membership. During the classifier training, two basic tasks must be performed. Initially, each page $p_x \in TS$ must be labeled (manually classified to a target class) and expressed by n-dimensional attribute vector $p_x = \langle a_1(p_x), a_2(p_x), \ldots, a_n(p_x)\rangle$,

Figure 8. The proposed hyperplane which separates between positive and negative examples with maximum margins

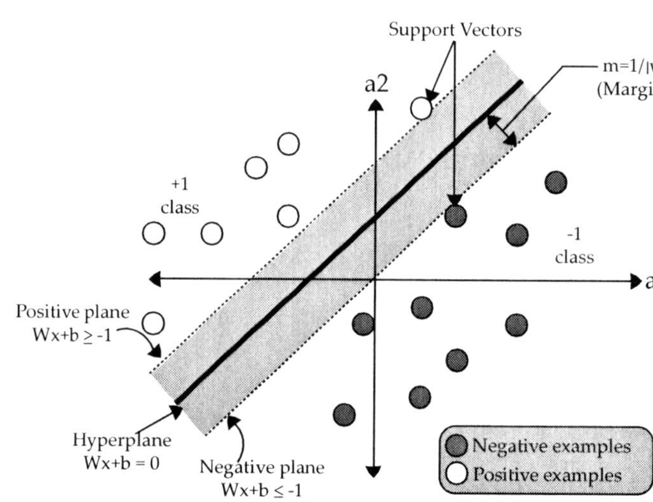

where $a_i(p_x)$ is the ith attribute of page p_x. Then, a set of hyperplanes with maximum margins and minimum number of misclassified patterns should be defined. During the testing phase, it will be easy to classify new unlabeled pages to the most suitable class based on the predefined hyperplanes.

For illustration purpose, consider the simplest case, a linear SVM (LSVM). LSVM tries to define a hyperplane that separates a set of positive pages (pages related to the class) from a set of negative ones (*unrelated pages*) with the maximum margin (*m*). The margin *m* indicates the distance from the proposed hyperplane to the nearest positive or negative page (*both distances are identical*). For further simplification, consider a two-dimensional, linearly separable problem (*each page represented by a two-attribute vector in the input space*) shown in Figure 8. Any page $p_x = <a_1(p_x), a_2(p_x)>$ *TS can be classified to one of two classes* {*+1 or –1*}. LSVM *tries to* separate the two kinds of points using the linear function *Y* defined as shown below:

$$Y = \langle w, p \rangle + b = \sum_{i=1}^{2} w_i \cdot x_i + b$$

Where, *w* is a two-dimensional vector, *b* is a scalar value and <*x,y*> indicates the dot product among vectors *x* and *y*. Two other imaginary planes should be defined besides to the proposed hyperplane, which are positive plane and negative plane (*see Figure 8*). All points lie on both planes are called support vectors. Equations of all proposed planes are expressed in Table 2.

So, any tested page will be classified to class .+1. if $w.x + b \geq 1$, otherwise it will be classified to .–1. if $w.x + b \leq -1$. The margin from positive or negative planes to the hyperplane can be easily calculated as $m=1/|w|$. An important criterion is that SVMs are linear classifiers, which limits their separating ability. Figure 9(a) shows a non-linear separable problem. To compensate for this limitation, a new representation of data is proposed by combining the kernel method with SVMs (Vapnik, 1999). By using a variety of kernel

Table 2. Equations of all proposed planes

Plane	Equation
Hyperplane	w.x+b = 0
Positive-plane	w.x+b=+1
Negative-plane	w.x+b=–1

Figure 9. Transformation from input space to high dimensionality feature space

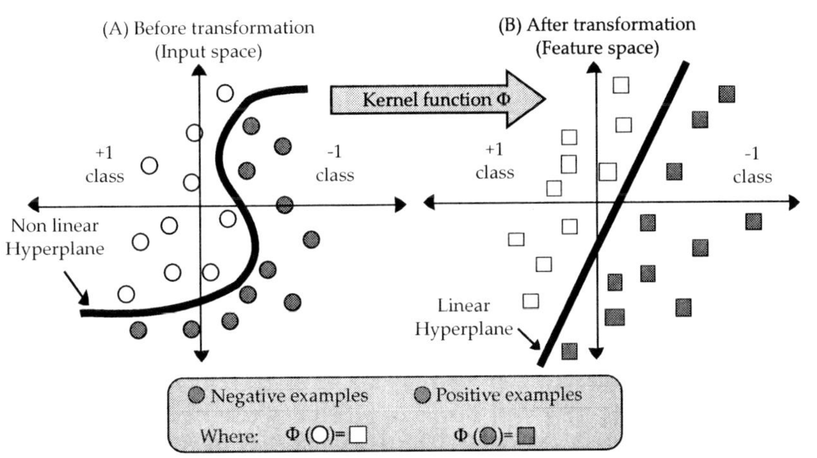

functions, feature vectors representing Web pages are mapped into a (higher dimensional) space and linearly separated there, see Figure 9 (a, b).

NAÏVE BAYES CLASSIFIER

Naïve bayes classifier is one of the most important probabilistic classifiers that are based on Bays' theorem. It considers a set of pre-defined hypotheses (classes or categories) $H=\{h_1, h_2, \ldots, h_x\}$ and its function is to find the most probable hypothesis $h \in H$ for a given input data D. Naïve bayes classifier operates in two different phases, training and testing. In the *training phase*, the classifier is allowed to set its classification rules and estimates the required parameters using a set of pre-classified data items (*examples*). When it is needed to classify a new data item D during testing phase, each hypothesis $h \in H$ will be assigned a probability given the data item D. This probability is called *posterior probability* (*probability that hypothesis h generated the data item D*) and denoted by $P(h|D)$. Calculating $P(h|D)$ can be carried out by firstly estimating the conditional probability $P(D|h)$ (*probability that data item D is generated using hypothesis h*) using rules established during the training phase. $P(D|h)$ can be calculated as following:

$$P(h \mid D) = \frac{P(D \mid h) * P(h)}{P(D)} = \frac{P(D \mid h) * P(h)}{\sum_{k=1}^{x} P(D \mid h_k) * P(h_k)}$$

Where: $P(h|D)$ is the posterior probability of hypothesis h, $P(D|h)$ is the conditional probability of data item D given the hypothesis h and $P(h)$ is the prior probability of hypothesis h. All $P(h_j|D)$ $\forall h_j \in H$ should be calculated, then D will be targeted to the hypothesis with the maximum posterior probability. Thus:

$$Target(D) = \arg\max_{h \in H} P(h \mid D) = \arg\max_{h \in H} \left[\frac{P(D \mid h) * P(h)}{P(D)} \right]$$

Since $P(D)$ is independent of h, it can be considered as constant. So:

$$Target(D) = \arg\max_{h \in H} \left[P(D \mid h) * P(h) \right] \qquad \text{(A)}$$

When the input data item D can be expressed by a set of attribute values, $D=\{t1, t2, \ldots, ty\}$. Substitute in eq(A), yields:

$$Target(D) = \arg\max_{h \in H} \left[P(t_1, t_2, \ldots, t_n \mid h) * P(h) \right]$$

Assuming independent attributes, then:

$$Target(D) = \arg\max_{h \in H} \left[\prod_{k=1}^{y} P(t_k \mid h) * P(h) \right] \qquad \text{(B)}$$

The probabilities $P(tk|h)$ is the fraction of times the attribute t_k is observed to occur n_c over the total number of chances n (i.e., n_c/n). However, when $n_c=0$ (*the attribute value does not exist in the training data*), this causes $P(tk|h)=0$. This *zero* will be multiplied by other conditional probabilities in eq(B). This difficulty can be avoided using the *m-estimate* as following:

$$P(t_k \mid h) = \frac{n_c + m * P}{n + m}$$

Where: p the prior estimate of the probability we wish to determine, assuming uniform priors. So, if the attribute has k possible values then $p=1/k$. m is the equivalent sample size (*it is assumed that m additional virtual samples are added to enhance the actual n observations, these samples are distributed according to p*).

Selected Classifiers for Our Work

NB and KNN classifiers are selected to be the starting points for our proposed work. These classifiers are used because of their simplicity and computational efficiency that make them an attractive choice. We believe that NB tends to be a top competitor in some text domains. On the contrary, KNN has shown to be very effective because of the availability of perfect similarity measures such as cosine measure (Salton, 1989). Another simplicity of KNN is that no computations are involved during training (*lazy learner*) (Duda, 1973); all the decisions are performed during the testing phase.

Although ANNs provide salient properties that many other AI techniques do not have, such as, the ability to improve performance by learning and the robustness in noisy environments, they may suffer from various problems when classifying Web pages such as: (1) NNCMs usually have complicated structures. Accordingly, they require long processing time to generate the decision. Moreover, it is difficult to decide an appropriate network structure accurately for a given problem (Kurino, 2004). (2) While the input data may be in any form, input attribute values for ANNs must be numeric. As a result, formulating data transformation technique is necessary. (3) Choosing the appropriate activation function is not an easy task. (4) The learning phase may fail to converge (Blum, 1992). (5) Different challenges must be considered during building the ANN structure, like, number of hidden layers, number of hidden nodes, interconnections between nodes, and the initial value of the weights. (6) The most commonly used algorithm for training multilayer ANNs is back propagation which is very slow (Starita, 1993); thousands of iterations may be required to solve simple problems, consuming hours of computer time (Koller, 1995). (7) The overfitting may occur, so the constructed NNCM becomes tuned to features specific to the training set. (8) In practice, as the dimensionality of the input data space increases (*inputs into neural network*), the complexity of neural networks become unmanageable and it becomes more difficult to converge during training phase.

On the contrary, SVMs exhibit good classification performance in many situations; however, they have a number of drawbacks. The first lies in the choice of the kernel (Brug, 1998; Shawe, 2001); the best choice of kernel for a give problem is still a research issue (Lodhi, 2002). A second limitation is that since SVM is an instance of binary classifiers, handling multi-class problem is not so easy (Weston, 1996). From a practical point of view, SVMs can be abysmally slow in test phase (Brug, 1996; Osuna, 1998). Training for very large datasets (*millions of support vectors*) is an unsolved problem That is because the formulization of SVMs is based on quadric programming (Vapnik, 1998), which requires at least $O(N^2)$ computation with a data set of size N (Burge 98).

PROPOSED DOMAIN ORIENTED NAÏVE BAYES (DONB) CLASSIFIER

Probabilistic classifiers such as NB are among the most effective classifiers currently known for classifying text documents (Rennie, 2003). One of the most challenges that must be considered when classifying Web pages is, the Web has numerous volume of data related to different domains with a high percentage of noise. Such challenges usually hamper the classification task and make finding one base for automatic Web page classification to be extremely difficult.

The proposed DONB (*domain oriented naïve bayes*) has the ability to classify only documents related to a specific domain given a set of x target hypotheses (*categories or classes*) $H=\{h_1, h_2, \ldots, h_x\}$. Setting of the classification rules can be carried out by providing the system with the domain knowledge during its training phase. Such knowledge is usually materialized in a set of pre-classified Web pages as training examples. These rules will be used during the testing phase to classify new pages. The used algorithm to implement DONB is stated in Figure 10. In this algorithm, a domain thesauri that contains all domain concepts $C=\{c_1, c_2, c_3, \ldots, c_n\}$ as well as

Figure 10. Domain oriented naïve bayes (DONB) algorithm

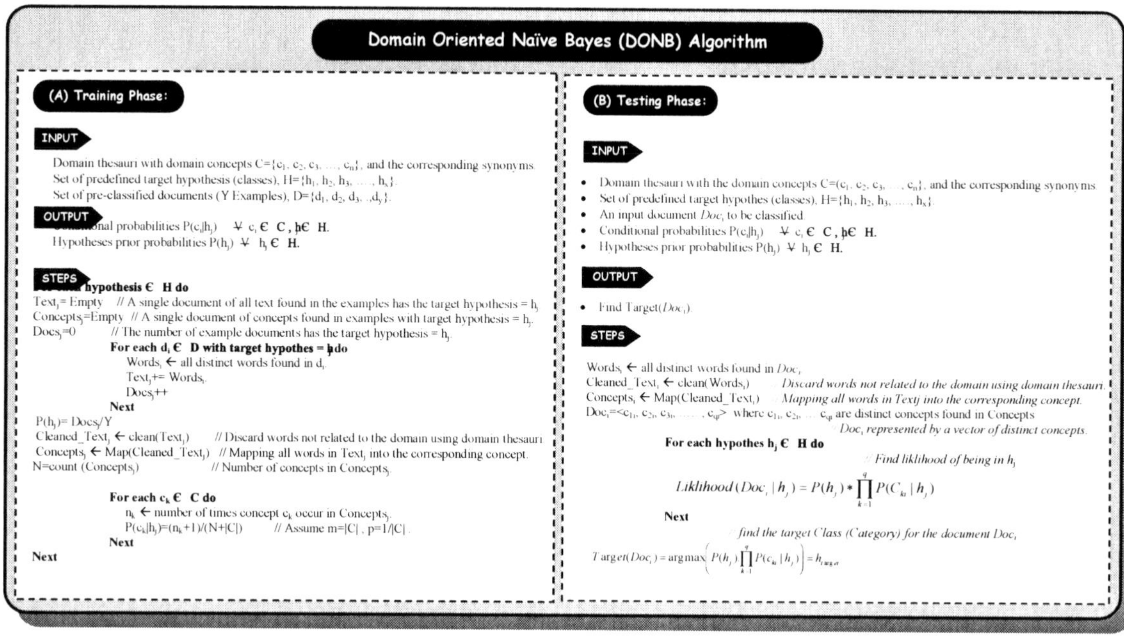

the corresponding synonyms (each concept $c_i \in C$ may have a set of synonyms) was employed to manage a conceptualization process (*convert domain keywords to domain concepts*). A domain concept can be defined as a common domain keyword that can be used to express a set of other uncommon ones (*its synonyms*). The main objective of conceptualization is *dimensionality reduction*. Hence, each input page can be expressed by a smaller set of domain concepts rather than using keyword vector that will certainly have a very large dimensionality.

DONB operates in two different phases, namely *training* and *testing*. In the training phase, given a set of pre-classified training examples (*such examples are a set of Web pages*), the main objectives are to find the conditional probabilities $P(c_i|h_j)$. $\forall c_i \in C$, $h_j \in H$, and also, hypotheses (*domain categories*) prior probabilities $P(h_j) \forall h_j \in H$. Otherwise, when a new page Doc_i need to be classified during testing phase, the probability that Doc_i related to each hypothesis is calculated (*which is also called the likelihood of being in the hypothesis*) based on the domain concepts extracted from Doc_i. If Doc_i contains q domain concepts, the likelihood of being in hypothesis h_j can be calculated as:

$$Liklihood(Doc_i \mid h_j) = P(h_j) * \prod_{k=1}^{q} P(C_{ki} \mid h_j)$$

Then, Doc_i will be targeted to the hypothesis (h_{target}) with the maximum calculated likelihood:

$$Target(Doc_i) = \arg\max\left(P(h_j).\prod_{k=1}^{q} P(c_{ki} \mid h_j) \right) = h_{target}$$

PROPOSED DOMAIN ORIENTED K-NEAREST NEIGHBORS CLASSIFIER (DOKNN)

One of the advantages of KNN is that being a lazy learner where there is no computation involved with training, all the decisions are performed during the categorization process. Hence, the classifier only needs to store the feature vectors that correspond to the training documents; no additional data structures have to be created, as with the other classification algorithms (e.g., *naïve bayes*). The disadvantage of KNN is the classification time being linear to the amount of training documents. This is due to the complete training set requiring to be ranked against the instance to be classified. The algorithm used to implement DOKNN is shown in Figure 11.

As shown in Figure 11, DOKNN also operates in two different phases (*training and testing*). During the training phase, given a set of pre-classified training examples, the main objective is to find the corresponding vector space model for each page in the training examples. No classification rules are collected since all computations take place during the testing phase. On the other hand, when a new page *Doc* needs to be classified during testing phase, initially *Doc* is also represented in the vector space model. Then the cosine similarity is used to find the similarity between *Doc* and all other training examples based on the vector space model of *Doc* and all examples. The *K* closest examples (KCE) was considered. *Doc* is then classified to the category that has the maximum number of items in the KCE collection.

A FRAMEWORK FOR THE PROPOSED VERTICAL CLASSIFIER

Figure 12 depicts a proposed framework for a vertical classifier which is established for evaluating the proposed DONB and DOKNN algorithms as will as the continuous learning naïve bayes (CLNB) that will be discussed later. The input for the proposed framework is the Web page to be classified. The framework analyzes that page, extracts existing domain keywords, maps keywords to the corresponding concepts, and then, determines whether that the page is related to the domain of interest or not. If the page is related to the domain of interest, such page will be clas-

Figure 11. Domain oriented K nearest neighbor (DOKNN) algorithm

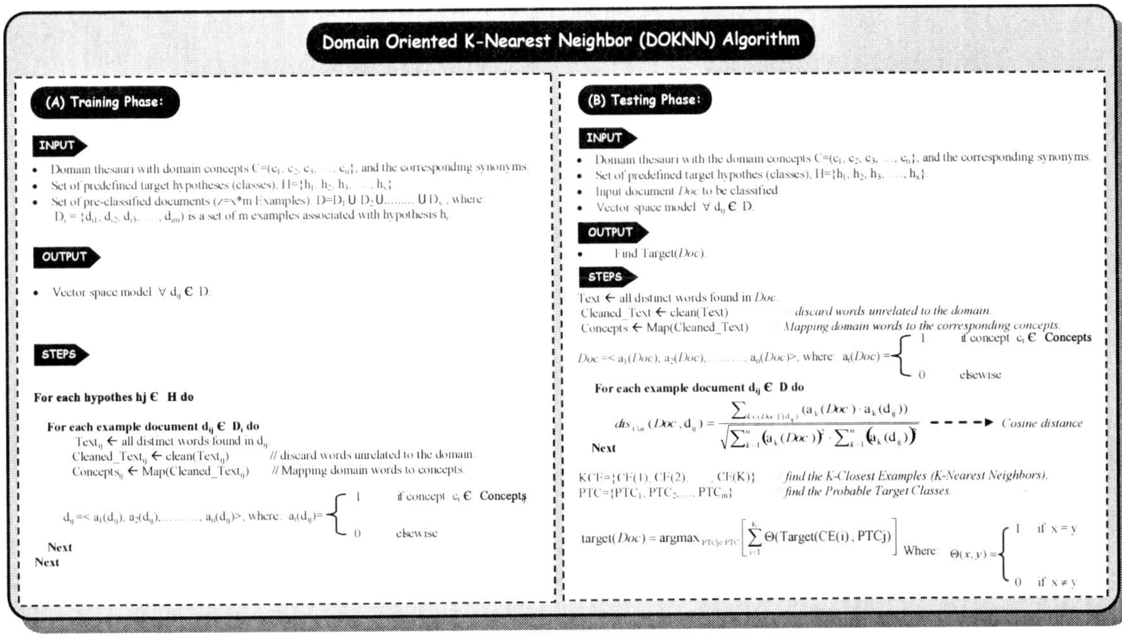

Figure 12. A proposed framework for a vertical classifier

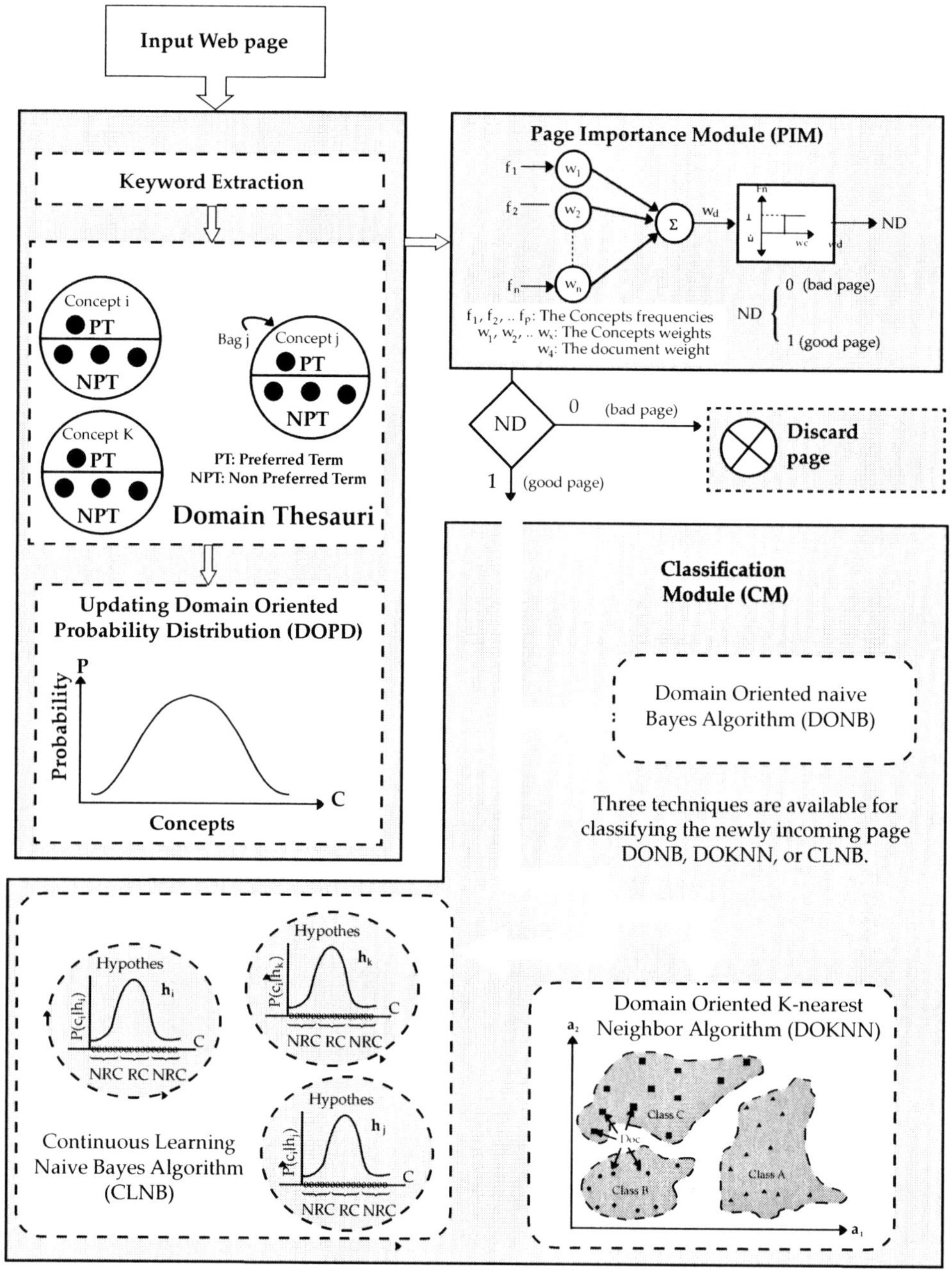

sified (targeted to the most suitable hypothesis) using one of the proposed classifiers; otherwise, it will be discarded.

As shown in Figure 12, the proposed framework consists of three basic modules, (1) page analysis module (PAM), (2) page importance module (PIM), and (3) classification module (CM).

Page Analysis Module (PAM)

The objective of this module is to extract the main features of the page. Domain thesauri will be employed for mapping the domain keywords found in the input page to the corresponding domain concepts. Thesauri is a classification system that combines a set of technical terms with a few basic relations, this makes thesauri a perfect way for knowledge mapping and conceptualization process (ISO 2788, 1986). Keyword-concept mapping allows better document description for two different reasons where: (1) The probability of two persons using the same term in describing the same thing is less than 20% (Btes, 1986) (*i.e., several keywords might be mapped to a single concept*). As a result, describing documents using concepts rather that set of keywords leads to more accurate description. (2) Mapping keywords to concepts simplify document understanding and analysis since the document keywords could be aggregated into a smaller number of concepts (*dimensionality reduction*).

The proposed domain thesauri divide the domain terms into a set of *Bags*, each bag consists of a set of synonyms and represents a specific concept. For each set, one *preferred term* (PT) is chosen to represent the underlying concept; the other terms are *non-preferred terms* (NPT) (instances of the concept). The only considered relation in the proposed Thesauri is the *Synonym* relation, which determines terms express the same concept. It is also noted that, any other domain oriented thesauri (related to the domain of interest) can be used as well, but we prefer to manually construct such simple and controllable thesauri since it will be more suitable to collected data set and has a simplified structure. Using such thesauri will certainly simply the idea validation as well as assuring the effectiveness of the proposed technique compared with traditional techniques when operate in the same working environment. Using other types of treasuries will certainly affect the classification efficiency of the system but will not has a great impact in the relative performance difference among tested classifiers. This is simply because such thesaurus will be used for all tested classifiers. Further extensions for the work can employ other treasuries with more complicated relations and large number of domain concepts; those thesauruses will be more suitable for large dada sets.

At the end of this stage, an input page d_i can be expressed as $d_i=\{(c_{i1},f_{i1}), (c_{i2},f_{i2}), \ldots\ldots,$ $(c_{im},f_{im})\}$. Where c_{ij}: is the jth concept in d_i, f_{ij}: is the frequency of c_{ij} in d_i, and m: is the number of domain concepts in d_i.

According to information theory, information is strictly defined in terms of the probabilities of events. Therefore, suppose that we have n domain concepts $C=\{c_1, c_2, c_3, \ldots c_n\}$ and a set of probabilities for these concepts (a probability distribution) $P=\{p_1, p_2, p_3, \ldots.. p_n\}$. The information gained by the occurrence of concept c_i is calculated as: $I(c_i) = \log(1/p_i)$. Where, $I(c_i)$: is the information gained by the occurrence of concept c_i, and p_i: is the occurrence probability of concept c_i. We propose a domain oriented probability distribution (DOPD) that serves as a source for the probabilities of all domain concepts. In DOPD, concepts are located in the horizontal axes and the corresponding probabilities in the vertical axes as shown in Figure 12. Again, if our domain of interest contains n concepts $C=\{c_1, c_2, c_3, \ldots c_n\}$, initially DOPD will be a flat curve with all concepts having the same probability $P_i=1/n$. With time, the probability of each concept will change as a new page is processed (*The probability of popular concepts will increase while the probability of rare concepts will decrease*). At the end of this stage, the input page di will be expressed as $d_i=\{(c_{i1},f_{i1},p_{i1}), (c_{i2},f_{i2},$ $p_{i2}), \ldots\ldots, (c_{im},f_{im}, p_{im})\}$. Where, P_{ij}: is the probability of the jth concept found inside the body of d_i obtained from DOPD.

Page Importance Module (PIM)

This module serves as a distiller that discards pages related to other domains. At this point, the processed page may relate to our domain (*labeled as a .good page.*), or it may not (*labeled as a .bad page.*). Bad pages must be discarded, while good pages will continue to higher processing stages for classification purpose. The decision will be taken according to the page importance w.r.t the domain of interest or it will be called as the document weight W_d.

As illustrated in Figure 12, a new way of implementing neural network is proposed for document weight (W_d) calculation. Calculating whether the page is relevant to the domain or not can be represented by a simple Boolean function. For example, we can assume Boolean values of 1 (*relevant*) and 0 (*irrelevant*). A single perceptron can be used to represent such function since it can be considered as a hyperplane decision surface in the n-dimensional space of features (*domain concepts*). Each page can be considered as a point in that space and located in one side of such surface. The proposed perceptron has an input sink for each domain concept and only one output sink to provide its output. Hence, in our case it has 215 input sinks. However, not all of these sinks are used. The only used are the ones that their corresponding concepts have been found inside the body of the tested page. In this situation, we consider that: Wd is affected by two different factors: (1) the importance of the domain concepts extracted from the page, so that more importance of the extracted concepts more page importance, (2) the frequency of the domain concepts extracted from the processed page.

Table 3. All Page Sets used to construct the Estimation_Set

Sub-Set	Number of Selected Pages
High Quality Pages	X
Medium Quality Pages	Y
Low Quality Pages	Z

The values of X, Y, and Z can be changed according to the opinion of the domain expert. For example, we can use X=Y=Z.

Figure 13. Critical weight initialization algorithm

Critical Weight Initialization Algorithm

INPUT

Domain thesauri with the domain concepts $C=\{c_1, c_2, c_3, \ldots, c_n\}$, and the corresponding synonyms.

- A Set of manually selected documents (Estimation_Set), $D=\{d_1, d_2, d_3, \ldots, d_N\}$. where, N=X+Y+Z, and, X: number of high quality pages, Y: number of medium quality pages, Z: number of low quality pages w.r.t the domain of interest

DOPD (Domain Oriented Probability Distribution) as a source of domain concepts probabilities.

OUTPUT

The proper initial (tunable) value of Wc [i.e. W_c(initial)].

STEPS

```
For each document dj Є Estimation_Set do
   Wordsi ← all distinct words found in di              Discard words not related to the domain using domain thesauri.
   Cleaned_Texti ← clean(Wordsi)                        Mapping all words in Textj into the corresponding concept.
   Conceptsi ← Map(Cleaned_Texti)                       add new concepts to Estimaion_Concepts set.
   Estimaion_Concepts += Conceptsi
Next

For each concept Cj Є Estimation_Concepts do            find the weight of all found domain concepts
W(Cj )=log (1/Pi)
Total_Weight += W(Cj )
Next
Wc(initial)= Total_Weight / N.                          find the initial value of the critical weight.
```

For example, assume a document d_i that contains m domain concepts c_{i1}, c_{i2}, c_{i3}, ... c_{im} that occur with frequencies f_{i1}, f_{i2}, f_{i3}, ... f_{im}. Hence, d_i can be expressed as d_i={(c_{i1},f_{i1}), (c_{i2},f_{i2}), ... , (c_{im},f_{im})}. Then, document weight calculation can be achieved by the following steps:

1. The importance of each domain concept (concept weight) found in the processed document di is calculated with the aid of DOPD as w_{ij}= log (1/p_j). Where, w_{ij} :is the weight of concept c_{ij}, and p_j: the probability of concept c_{ij} in DOPD. An updated expression of d_i (after adding the concepts weights) will be d_i={(c_{i1},f_{i1}, w_{i1}), (c_{i2},f_{i2} , w_{i2}), ..., (c_{im},f_{im} ,w_{im})}.
2. The document weight can be calculated using the neural network shown in Figure 12 (inside PIM module). The inputs of the neural network are the concepts frequencies f_{i1},f_{i2},f_{i3}, ... f_{im}. Each neural network input is multiplied by the corresponding concept weight w_{i1}, w_{i2}, w_{i3}, ... w_{im}. Hence, The document weight Wd_i can be calculated by the following equation:

$$W_{di} = \sum_{j=1}^{m} f_{ij} * w_{ij}$$

Using a modeling function F_n, the neural network can detect whether the processed page related to the domain of interest or not. Fn is a simple step function that has zero value before a critical weight *Wc* and has a *one-value* elsewise. The output signal *ND* is the neural network decision, which can be expressed as:

$$ND = Fn(W_{di}) = \begin{cases} 0 \ (Bad\ Page)\ Wd_i < Wc \\ 1 \ (Good\ Page)\ Elsewise \end{cases}$$

If the processed page is a bad one (*when ND*=0), it will be discarded by the classifier. Otherwise (*when ND*=1), the page is labeled as a good one, then, it will be allowed to continue to the higher processing stages for classification according to a set of predefined domain classes.

Although PIM module seems to be simple and attractive, two different issues must be addressed. The first is how to estimate the optimal value of W_c, while the second is to measure the impact of such module on the overall system efficiency. Smaller values of W_c will result in passing many pages that are not relevant to the domain of interest, and accordingly in lower classification performance since some non-relevant pages will be classified to one of the four proposed categories. This drawback is because any page that can successfully pass through PIM will certainly be classified. On the other hand, higher values of W_c will discard many pages that may be relevant. The task now is to estimate the proper value of Wc in order to; (1) Maximize the number of passed and relevant pages, and, (2) Minimize the number of passed and irrelevant pages. The efficiency of PIM must be measured to assure that it operates properly

Table 4. All possible outcomes of a binary classifier

Classifier outcome	Description
A	Number of documents that are assigned correctly
B	Number of documents that are assigned in-correctly
C	Number of documents that are rejected correctly
D	Number of documents that are rejected in-correctly

(*the efficiency of the system is hardly affected by the performance of PIM*). In the following sub-sections, the two issues will be addressed.

Estimating the Proper Value of W_c

It is believed that, the value of W_c must be balanced (*tuned*) so that relevant pages are passed while non-relevant are discarded. The value of W_c is dependent on the domain of interest (*change in value from domain to domain*) and can be set practically by initially set W_c to an arbitrary (*initial*) value. This value is changed to calculate the corresponding efficiency of PIM. Such process will be continued until a satisfactory efficiency value is achieved. In this section, a proper way to estimate the initial value that can be attached to W_c by following the next steps.

1. From the collected dataset, an *Estimation_Set* of (N=X+Y+Z) pages are selected where such set is manually classified into three different sub-sets according to the relevancy to the domain as shown in Table 3.
2. All domain terms are extracted from all pages in the *Estimation_Set* and mapped to the corresponding concepts. The weight of each concept is calculated with the aid of DOPD (*at its steady state case*) as well as the concept frequency.
3. The estimated initial value of Wc will be (*assuming m extracted concepts*):

$$W_c(initial) = \frac{\left(\sum_{k=1}^{m} w_k * f_k\right)}{N}$$

Hence, following those steps, it is predicted that the value of W_c will cause PIM to pass high quality pages as well as medium quality pages and reject the low quality ones. The algorithm used to estimate the initial value of W_c is shown in Figure 13. Validation of the proposed estimation technique is performed in the next sub-sections.

Evaluation Parameters

The most common way to measure the performance of multi-class classifiers is to divide the task into multiple binary classification tasks (Aas, 1999). All possible outcomes of a binary classifier are illustrated in Table 4.

The parameters, which can be calculated to measure the classifier performance are:

$$Precision = P = \frac{\text{Correct Classes Found}}{\text{Total Classes Found}} = \frac{A}{A+B}$$

$$Accuracy = Acc = \frac{\text{Total Correct Decisions}}{\text{Total Number of Documents}} = \frac{A+C}{A+B+C+D}$$

$$Recall = R = \frac{\text{Correct Classes Found}}{\text{Total Correct Found}} = \frac{A}{A+D}$$

$$\text{Error} = E = \frac{\text{Total Incorrect Decisions}}{\text{Total Number of Documents}} = \frac{B+D}{A+B+C+D}$$

Another evaluation parameter that combines both precision and recall is the *F-measure* (Yang & Liu, 1999), which can be expressed as following:

$$F_\mu = \frac{(\mu^2+1) * P * R}{\mu^2 * P + R}$$

Where μ: is the weighting factor that allows assigning different weights, for *precision* and *recall*. The most commonly used F-measure in text classification is F_1 (i.e., μ =1) which weights equally both precision and recall:

$$F_1 = \frac{2 * P * R}{P + R}$$

In order to evaluate the total classifier performance, the previously mentioned parameters must be averaged. Two methods of averaging are available, namely, *macro-averaging* and *micro-averaging*. In macro-averaging, the previously mentioned evaluation parameters (*P, R, Acc, and E*) are calculated for each class then averaged to compute the global means. Therefore, each class has a table similar to Table 4. However, micro-averaging performance scores are determined by first computing the total of A, B, C, and D for all categories and then use these totals to compute the various evaluation parameters. Hence, only one table (*like Table 4*) is constructed for all classes. This table contains the totals of values *A*, *B*, *C*, and *D* across all classes. As an example, if three different classes are available, the micro and macro average of the precision can be represented mathematically as:

$$\text{Precision}(\mathit{MicroAverage}) = \frac{A_1 + A_2 + A_3}{(A_1 + A_2 + A_3) + (B_1 + B_2 + B_3)}$$

$$\text{Precision}(\mathit{MacroAverage}) = \frac{\frac{A_1}{A_1 + B_1} + \frac{A_2}{A_2 + B_2} + \frac{A_3}{A_3 + B_3}}{3}$$

As illustrated in (Tsong, 2004), macro-averaging gives an equal weight to the performance on every category regardless of how rare or how common a category is. Micro-averaging, conversely, gives an equal weight to the performance on every tested page thus favoring the performance of common categories.

Performance Analysis of the Proposed PIM Module

PIM module can be considered as a simple binary classifier. It distinguishes (*separates*) between relevant and irrelevant pages (the output is one of two classes). Hence, The classification efficiency of such classifier can be measured by using the same parameters described in the previous section (*P, R, Acc, E, and F-measure*).

We assume that the optimal value of Wc is one that gives the highest classification accuracy is considered. A number of 2000 pages are used to measure the efficiency of PIM module. Those pages are divided into two sets. The first set is the relevant pages (1000 pages) and the other set is the irrelevant pages (1000 pages). The initial value of the critical weight Wc(initial) was estimated using algorithm in figure 13. The estimated value

Figure 14. PIM accuracy against the critical weight

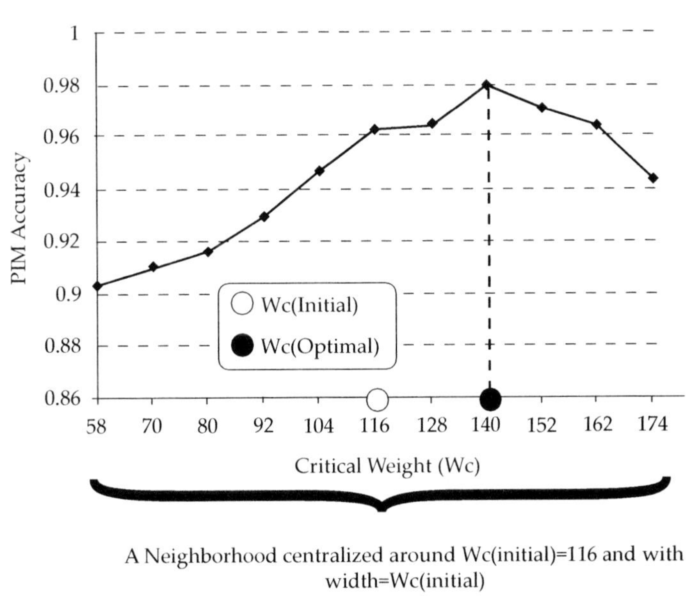

of Wc(initial) was 116 (assuming X=Y=Z=100 pages). In order to calculate the optimal value of Wc, a set of different values of Wc must be used and the optimal critical value is the one, which gives the higher accuracy. To establish such task, a neighborhood centralized around Wc(initial) was considered. The width of that neighborhood was also taken equal to Wc(initial) (i.e., =116). We search for the optimal value for the critical weight within that neighborhood. As shown in figure 14, the optimal value of Wc was found to be 140, which is the value considered in all the next experiments.

Classification Module

The various proposed classification algorithms (*DONB, DOKNN, as well as CLNB*) are embedded in this module for classifying good pages. More details about implementation and evaluation of such classification algorithms will be discussed in the following sections.

DONB PERFORMANCE, IMPLEMENTATION, AND EVALUATION

For implementing DONB, the University domain is selected to be the domain of interest (as a case study). In other words, DONB is concerned with only those pages related to university; any other pages will be discarded. Four different categories (*hypotheses*) are assumed to represent the university domain, namely, (1) academic and research, (2) university building and sites tools, (3) university management and routinism, and (4) tools, equipments and assistance technology. It is believed that, those proposed categories express almost

Figure 15. Data structure used in implementing DONB algorithm

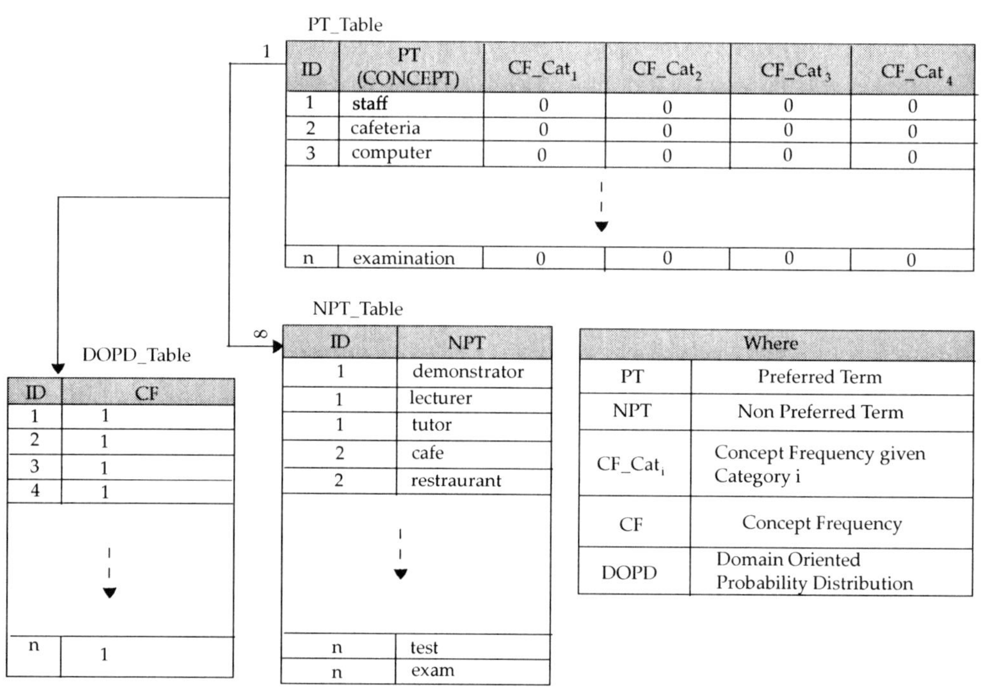

all contents, subjects, and activities of University domain. In contrast, the collected data set (using Google and Yahoo) and the constructed domain thesauri are closely related to those categories. For any other domains, another number of categories may be used according to the opinion of a domain expert. A number of 1100 terms (*domain keywords*) are collected to represent such domain (stored in the proposed domain thesauri). These terms are manually mapped to about 215 different concepts (*domain concepts*). For simplicity, the very specialized concepts related to university are not included (*for example, equipments used in medicine and engineering purposes*). However, the proposed algorithm is a scalable one. The chosen terms as well as concepts to express the domain of interest can be extended to be more suitable for large datasets.

Implementing Domain Thesauri and DOPD in DONB Classifier

In the case of DONB, the domain thesauri (*containing n concepts with the corresponding synonyms*) as well as DOPD are implemented in one structure as shown below in Figure 15.

As illustrated in Figure 15, each concept frequency was initialized with one. The frequency of each concept given each hypothesis (*category*) is calculated during the training phase, and then is used to calculate $P(c_i|h_j)$ during the testing phase using the following equation:

$$P(c_i \mid h_j) = \left[\frac{Freq(c_i) + 1}{\sum_{k=1}^{|C|} Freq(c_k) + |C|} \right]_{h=h_j}$$

Where, $|C|$: is the total number of domain concepts ($|C|=n=215$) and $(Freq(c_i))_{h=hj}$ is the frequency of concept ci given hypothesis h_j. DOPD is represented by a table called *DOPD_ Table*. Such table contains the frequency of each domain concept regardless of any category. When a concept appears in a new processed document, its frequency will increase in DOPD_Table to reflect the concept popularity. This means that the frequency of each concept may be updated after processing each page. The frequency of each domain concept found in the processed page will be used to calculate the processed page weight (*document weight W_d*) using the following equation:

$$W_d = \sum_{k=1}^{m} f_k w_k = -\sum_{k=1}^{m} f_k * \log \left[\frac{Freq(c_k)}{\sum_{i=1}^{|C|} Freq(c_i)} \right]$$

Where m is the number of domain concepts found in the processed document, $freq(c_i)$: is the frequency of concept c_i in *DOPD_Table*, f_i: is the frequency of concept c_i in the processed page. Moreover, and w_i: is the weight of concept c_i.

Collecting Dataset

For validating the effectiveness of DONB algorithm, a self-made benchmark data was constructed. Such test data consists of a set of HTML

Table 5. Yahoo categories used to retrieve a set of our collection

Category	URL
Higher Education	http://dir.yahoo.com/Education/Higher_Education/
Distance Learning	http://dir.yahoo.com/education/distance_learning/
Teaching	http://dir.yahoo.com/education/teaching/
Graduation	http://dir.yahoo.com/education/graduation/
Adults and Continuing Education	http://dir.yahoo.com/education/adult_and_continuing_education/

Figure 16. Probabilities of each category in the training examples

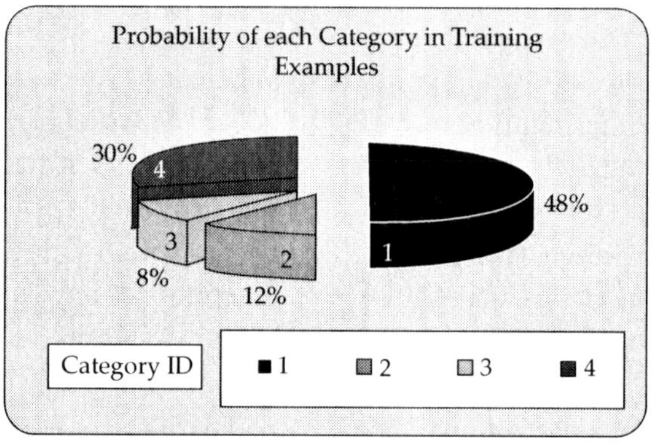

pages collected from different resources, namely Web directories and Web search engines. As illustrated in Table 5, some of Yahoo categories are chosen to retrieve a set of our collection. The other set was collected by querying Google for pages related to University domain.

We have noticed that it is preferred to use a self-made benchmark data for different reasons; (1) Such dataset is more controllable (we can simply calculate precision and recall), (2) It is suitable for the proposed domain thesauri with limited number of domain concepts, (3) it is simple in the validation of the idea rather than using more complicated structures where there is no guarantee of the accuracy of the obtained results, (4) Using any other testing data sets will not affect the relative performance difference between the tested classifier (which is the research target) since both testing data and domain thesauri used were fixed to all tested classifiers. However, any other general dataset can be used, but it must be insured that the used thesauri contains almost all domain concepts.

The collected pages were passed to the distiller (PIM) to choose those pages that were related to the university domain. DOPD is initialized (by setting all the domain concepts to the same probability). 2642 pages were passed to PIM to obtain a set of 2000 pages related to the domain using W_c=140 as proven before. The related pages were manually classified to destination categories, then, divided into two sets. The first 1000 pages will be used for the training purpose, while the others will be used to test the classifier performance. The probability of each category in the training examples is illustrated in Figure 16.

Analyzing Web Pages

The first challenge when building DONB is how to perfectly process the input page in order to extract the found domain concepts. Since HTML pages may be mal-formed, (many authors opening tags without closing them), many problems may arise when parsing these pages. To minimize the impact of such problem, the proposed framework relies on Tidy1, which is a perfect tool to fix the mal-formed html pages. We use HtmlAgilityPack2 as an HTML parser. Such parser transforms the page into a navigational DOM tree and allows navigating through the tree nodes in order to extract the inner text of each text node.

The obtained text within page is fragmented into tokens based on white spaces and some special characters like {..., .-., ./.,.:.}. These tokens are converted into lowercase, then compared with the domain thesauri in order to extract the found domain terms (*no need to apply stop-word filter*). The other tokens are ignored. The extracted domain terms are mapped to the corresponding

Figure 17. Start window of DONB classifier

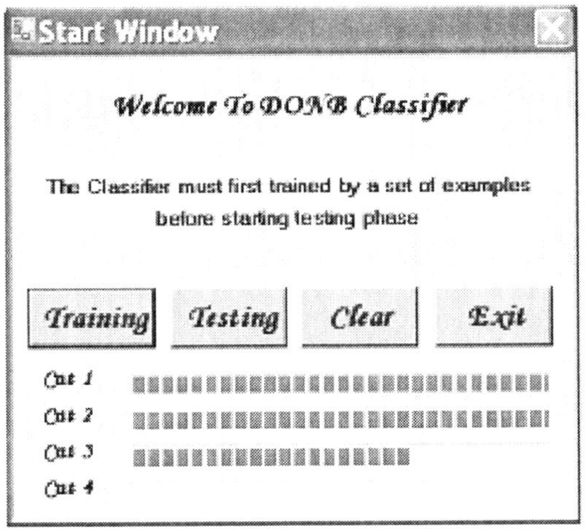

Figure 18. Testing phase of BONB

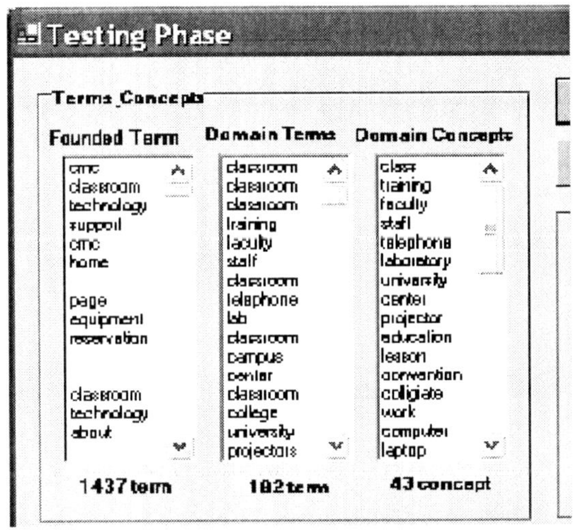

Table 6. Evaluation parameters for each category using DONB

Examples	Category 1				Category 2				Category 3				Category 4			
	P	R	Acc	E	P	R	Acc	E	P	R	Acc	E	P	R	Acc	E
400	0.447	0.536	0.578	0.442	0.889	0.635	0.944	0.056	0.872	0.787	0.933	0.067	0.777	0.771	0.876	0.124
600	0.575	0.617	0.671	0.329	0.863	0.698	0.948	0.052	0.946	0.841	0.957	0.043	0.666	0.709	0.822	0.178
800	0.590	0.645	0.685	0.315	0.893	0.730	0.955	0.045	0.867	0.816	0.936	0.064	0.739	0.760	0.860	0.140
1000	0.630	0.663	0.715	0.285	0.914	0.762	0.961	0.039	0.941	0.850	0.958	0.042	0.692	0.742	0.838	0.162

concepts. The page concepts as well as concepts frequencies are passed to PIM to pass only pages related to the domain. If PIM decides that the page related to the domain ($Wd > W_c$), the page will be passed to the classifier. Otherwise, it will be ignored.

DONB System

Firstly, the DONB must be trained to prepare the database for testing operations. When starting the DONB, the window shown in Figure 17 will appear.

When clicking the .Training. Button in the starting window of DONB shown in Figure 17, the pre-classified training examples are processed one by one to find the frequency of each concept w.r.t each category. More precisely, the four fields CF_Cat_1, CF_Cat_2, CF_Cat_3, and CF_Cat_4 that are shown in Figure 15 will be filled. The field CF_Cat_i represents the frequency of the domain concepts for category i. Hence, conditional probabilities $P(ci|hj)$ $\forall ci \in C$ (*Domain concepts collection*) and $hj \in H$ Domain Hypotheses collection can be easily calculated by substituting in equation (A). The hypotheses (domain categories) prior probabilities $P(hj)$ $\forall hj \in H$ are also calculated. The button .Clear. is used when it is required to initialize the concepts frequencies w.r.t domain categories with zeros. Clicking the .Clear. button will clear all data stored in fields CF_Cat_1, CF_Cat_2, CF_Cat_3, and CF_Cat_4 in *CF_Table* shown in Figure 15. Such button is used when it is needed to train the classifier with new data set.

During the testing phase, as shown in Figure 18, a new page can be loaded to the application by pressing .Load Page. button. Then, the page is analyzed to extract all domain terms (if PIM decides that it is related to university domain). Such terms are mapped to domain concepts, the likelihood that the page in each of the domain categories is found, and the input page will be classified to the category with the maximum likelihood.

DONB Results

As mentioned before, a set of 2000 related pages were collected. The first 1000 were used for training, while the second are used for the testing purpose. The most important parameter that affects the performance of DONB is the number of trained examples. By increasing the number of examples, the classifier will be trained well and collects enough amount of domain knowledge. Evaluation parameters for each category were measured using a set of 400, 600, 800, and 1000 Web pages (*training examples*). Results are reported in Table 6.

From Table 6, two important facts can be concluded; (1) the highest error occurs with category 1, which is the most popular category in university domain, while the error is quite small in rarely used categories (*categories 2 and 3*). The reason is that category 1 is the most common category; it has the highest probability when analyzing training examples. It also contains the most famous concepts related to the domain and shares many of its concepts with other categories. This causes DONB to be trapped. DONB classifies many pages to category 1 although they are related to other categories. This makes category 1 has a large number of assigned incorrectly pages and then a large error.

On the other hand, categories 2, 3 have most of their concepts that belong to them only (*do not share many of their concepts*). Therefore, when the classifier targets a page to one of these categories, the decision will have a high percentage of success. This what makes categories 2 and 3 have small amount of assigned incorrectly pages and a small amount of rejected incorrectly since they are rare categories. (2) most commonly used categories like category 1 and 4 have precision < recall, while rare categories (*like category 2, 3*) have precision > recall. This occurs for the same reason, which is the largest number of assigned incorrectly pages for the most popular categories compared to rare categories. For evaluating performance average across categories, the *micro-average* and *macro-average* scores are evaluated as reported in Table 7.

From Table 7, it is noticed that precision, recall, and F1-measure scores increase as the training examples (TE) increases. This insures that the performance of DONB increases when it is trained with a higher number of TE. Figures 19 and 20 illustrate micro and macro-averaged scores for precision and recall, while Figure 21 mixes both precision and recall measures to obtain the F1-measure. It can be concluded, in general, that the macro-average scores are higher than the micro-average scores. This was expected because DONB performs better in rarely used categories.

Figure 22 shows the accuracy as well as the error of DONB. It is noted that the classifier accuracy increases as it trained with higher TE. Classifier accuracy starts with *82.7%* when *TE=400* and reaches *86.8%* when *TE=1000.*

DOKNN PERFORMANCE, IMPLEMENTATION, AND EVALUATION

To test the performance of DOKNN, the algorithm is embedded into the classification module shown in Figure 12.

Implementing Domain Thesauri and DOPD in DOKNN Classifier

In the case of DOKNN, the domain thesauri as well as DOPD were implemented in a unified structure as shown in Figure 23. The structure of the domain thesauri used in implementing DOKNN is the same as the one used in DONB. The thesauri is represented by two tables: *PT_Table* which stores the various domain concepts (*215 concepts that sometimes called the preferred terms*) and *NPT_Table* which stores the synonyms of those domain concepts stored in *PT_Table*. DOPD is also simulated by the *DOPD_Table* that stores the IDs of the domain concepts with the corresponding frequencies regardless of any domain category. Domain frequencies were updated after processing new pages.

DOKNN Results

In the case of DOKNN, two important parameters must be considered, namely, the number of training examples and the *K* parameter. Controlling both parameters is more difficult than controlling just one (*number of training examples*) as in the case of DONB. Evaluation parameters for each category are measured using a set of 400, 600, 800, and 1000 Web pages (*training examples*) considering different values of *K* starting from 10 to 30 with increment of 2. The best efficiency level was obtained when *K=24*. A set of the obtained results are reported in Table 8.

By inspecting results in Tables 7 and 9, it can be concluded that the behavior of both DONB and DOKNN is almost the same. DONB outperforms DOKNN in precision, recall, accuracy levels for all values of K. In contrast, when inspecting the performance measures of DOKNN stored in Table 8, the following notations are concluded. Initially, it is noted that, the highest error is found in the most popular categories (categories 1 and 4) as in DONB. The reason behind that is similar to the one explained in DONB.

In general, due to the same pre-mentioned reason, the most popular categories have *Precision < Recall* while in rarely used ones *Precision > Recall*. For evaluating the average performance across all categories, both micro and macro average scores must be calculated. Table 9 shows such results.

From Table 9, it is obvious that the performance of DOKNN increases as the number of training examples increases. It is noted that the maximum Precision, Recall, and Accuracy are obtained at the maximum number of examples used (1000 example). The reason is quite simple. As the number of examples increases, the amount of domain knowledge and collected classification rules will certainly increase. This insures that, as in DONB, performance promotion of DOKNN can be accomplished by training the classifier with the higher number of training examples.

Figures 24 and 25 respectively, show the accuracy and error for DOKNN against the number of training examples using three different values of

Table 7. micro-average and macro-average scores using DONB

Examples	Precision		Recall		F1 measure		Accuracy	Error
	mic	mac	mic	mac	Mic	mac		
400	0.652	0.746	0.665	0.682	0.658	0.713	0.833	0.167
600	0.699	0.763	0.699	0.716	0.699	0.739	0.849	0.151
800	0.716	0.772	0.723	0.738	0.719	0.755	0.859	0.141
1000	0.736	0.794	0.736	0.754	0.736	0.773	0.868	0.132

Figure 19. micro average and macro average Precision in DONB

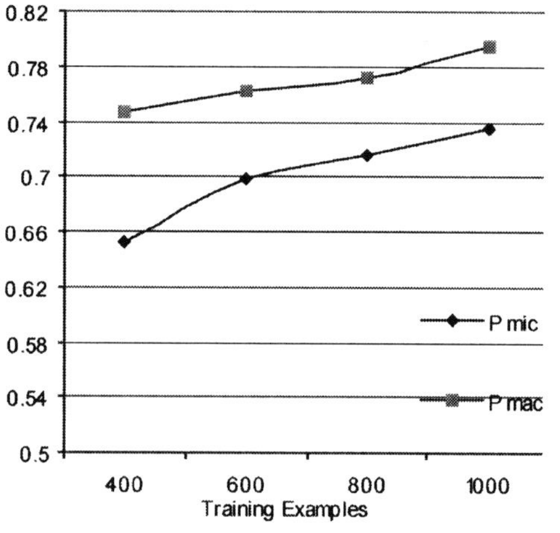

Figure 20. micro average and macro average Recall n DONB

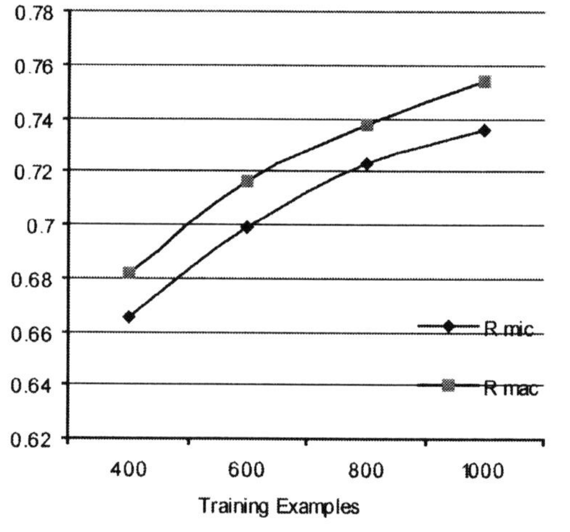

Figure 21. Macro average and micro average F1 in DONB

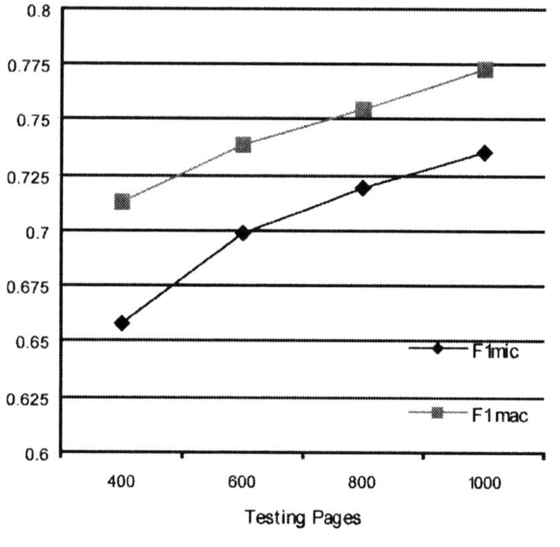

Figure 22. Accuracy and Error in DONB

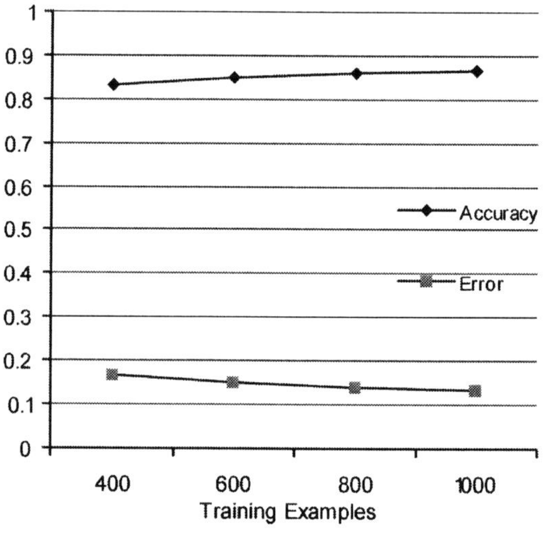

K (10, 24, and 30). The highest accuracy and lowest classification error are accomplished at K=24. Figures 26, 27, 28, and 29 show the micro and macro-average precision and recall for DOKNN against the number of training examples using different values of K. While Figures 30 and 31 combine precision and recall to evaluate the F1-measure. From these figures, it can be concluded that, as in the case of DONB, macro-average scores are higher than micro-average scores.

Figure 23. Data Structure used in implementing DOKNN algorithm

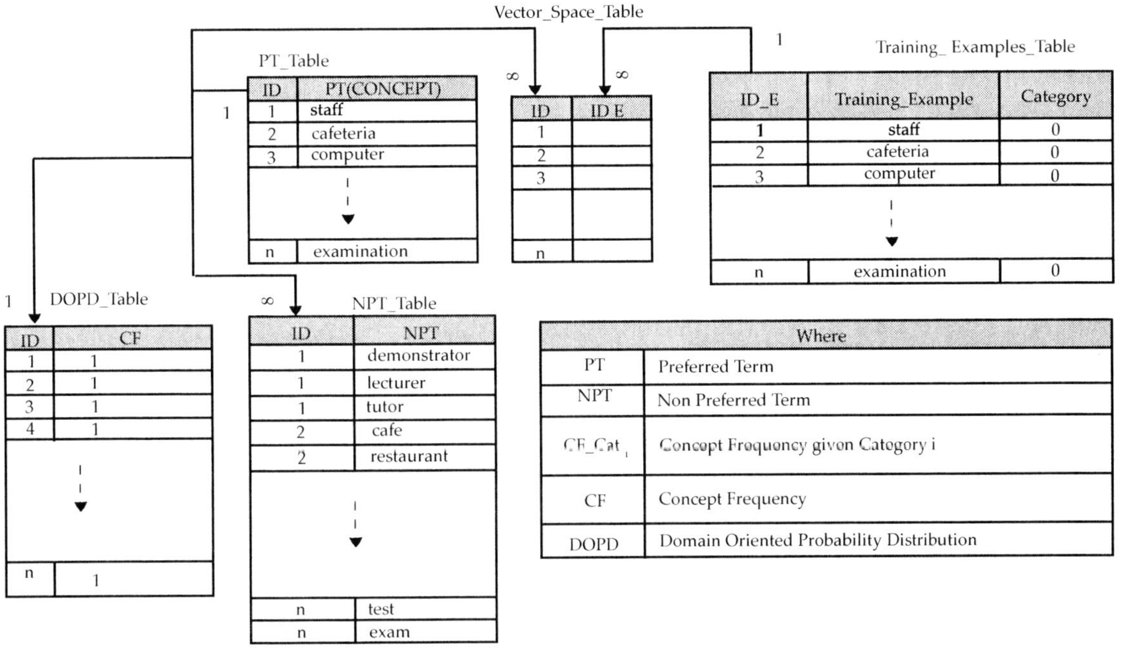

THE PROPOSED CLASSIFIERS AND OVERFITTING

As illustrated in the previous section, k-nearest neighbor and naïve bayes techniques seem to be quite simple and effective when applied to build domain-oriented classifiers. The proposed DONB algorithm presents an extremely high accuracy, 86.8% when trained with 1000 examples. Conversely, DOKNN algorithm introduces satisfactory level of accuracy, 83.6% when using 1000 training examples.

Generally, the accuracy of both DONB and DOKNN depends mainly on the chosen training examples. These examples are the only way for building classification rules used to classify new documents during testing phase. If the chosen examples are insufficient to build perfect classification rules during training phase, the classifier will be trapped during test phase since it will be driven by wrong or insufficient classification rules. Both classifiers will then suffer from overfitting.

DONB and Overfitting

In this sub-section, it will be proved that DONB may suffer from overfitting and need to be protected from such problem. Overfitting will cause the classifier to give inaccurate decisions since it has not been trained well (trained with sufficient examples). To clarify this problem, we assume; (1) two hypotheses (*classes*) *h*1, *h*2 are available in the domain of interest. (2) It is required to find the target hypothesis for an input *document* $d_i=\{c1, c2, c3, \ldots, cm\}$. Where, *c*1, *c*2, *c*3, ... etc are the domain concepts found in di. Our claim will be proved in two steps:

Step 1:

Purpose: Prove that the classification efficiency of DONB classifier during test phase depends on values of $P(c_i \mid h_j)$ and $P(h_k)$ $\forall c_i \in C$ and $h_i, h_k \in H$.

Proof:

Table 8. Evaluation parameters for each category using DONB

K=10																
Examples	Category 1				Category 2				Category 3				Category 4			
	P	R	Acc	E	P	R	Acc	E	P	R	Acc	E	P	R	Acc	E
400	0.422	0.485	0.538	0.462	0.856	0.611	0.938	0.062	0.826	0.744	0.914	0.086	0.736	0.731	0.854	0.146
600	0.492	0.528	0.601	0.399	0.775	0.627	0.930	0.070	0.875	0.778	0.931	0.069	0.666	0.720	0.828	0.172
800	0.503	0.551	0.611	0.389	0.796	0.651	0.891	0.109	0.841	0.792	0.926	0.074	0.703	0.724	0.840	0.160
1000	0.549	0.579	0.649	0.351	0.829	0.690	0.943	0.057	0.872	0.787	0.932	0.068	0.685	0.735	0.834	0.166

K=24																
Examples	Category 1				Category 2				Category 3				Category 4			
	P	R	Acc	E	P	R	Acc	E	P	R	Acc	E	P	R	Acc	E
400	0.423	0.464	0.542	0.458	0.861	0.690	0.947	0.053	0.762	0.744	0.899	0.101	0.835	0.811	0.904	0.096
600	0.508	0.538	0.615	0.385	0.757	0.643	0.929	0.071	0.832	0.768	0.920	0.080	0.697	0.727	0.838	0.162
800	0.537	0.571	0.639	0.361	0.785	0.667	0.935	0.065	0.865	0.802	0.933	0.067	0.708	0.731	0.843	0.157
1000	0.568	0.589	0.663	0.377	0.794	0.675	0.937	0.063	0.859	0.797	0.931	0.069	0.690	0.738	0.837	0.163

K=30																
Examples	Category 1				Category 2				Category 3				Category 4			
	P	R	Acc	E	P	R	Acc	E	P	R	Acc	E	P	R	Acc	E
400	0.498	0.523	0.606	0.394	0.856	0.659	0.943	0.057	0.767	0.778	0.905	0.095	0.722	0.738	0.850	0.150
600	0.543	0.569	0.643	0.357	0.741	0.659	0.928	0.072	0.839	0.783	0.924	0.076	0.694	0.694	0.835	0.165
800	0.565	0.589	0.661	0.339	0.754	0.651	0.928	0.072	0.874	0.807	0.936	0.064	0.686	0.724	0.833	0.167
1000	0.593	0.612	0.683	0.317	0.827	0.722	0.946	0.054	0.889	0.816	0.941	0.059	0.681	0.731	0.832	0.168

Table 9. Micro-average and macro-average scores using DOKNN

K=10								
Examples	Precision		Recall		F1 measure		Accuracy	Error
	mic	mac	mic	mac	Mic	mac		
400	0.622	0.710	0.622	0.643	0.622	0.675	0.811	0.189
600	0.645	0.702	0.641	0.663	0.643	0.682	0.823	0.177
800	0.651	0.711	0.661	0.680	0.657	0.695	0.817	0.183
1000	0.679	0.734	0.679	0.698	0.679	0.716	0.839	0.161

K=24								
Examples	Precision		Recall		F1 measure		Accuracy	Error
	mic	mac	mic	mac	Mic	mac		
400	0.652	0.711	0.652	0.675	0.652	0.693	0.826	0.174
600	0.665	0.704	0.665	0.676	0.665	0.69	0.833	0.167
800	0.679	0.718	0.679	0.693	0.679	0.705	0.84	0.16
1000	0.701	0.748	0.701	0.72	0.701	0.734	0.851	0.149

K=30								
Examples	Precision		Recall		F1 measure		Accuracy	Error
	mic	mac	mic	mac	Mic	mac		
400	0.646	0.720	0.646	0.677	0.646	0.698	0.823	0.177
600	0.651	0.699	0.651	0.698	0.651	0.698	0.826	0.174
800	0.675	0.724	0.675	0.693	0.675	0.708	0.838	0.162
1000	0.684	0.728	0.684	0.700	0.684	0.714	0.842	0.158

Figure 24. Accuracy level in DOKNN

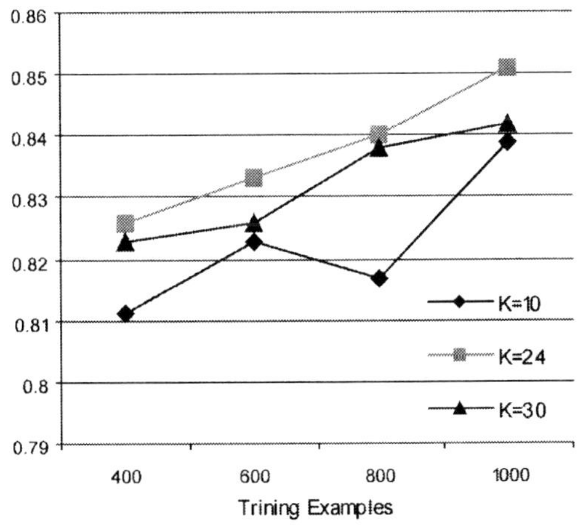

Figure 25. Error level in DOKNN

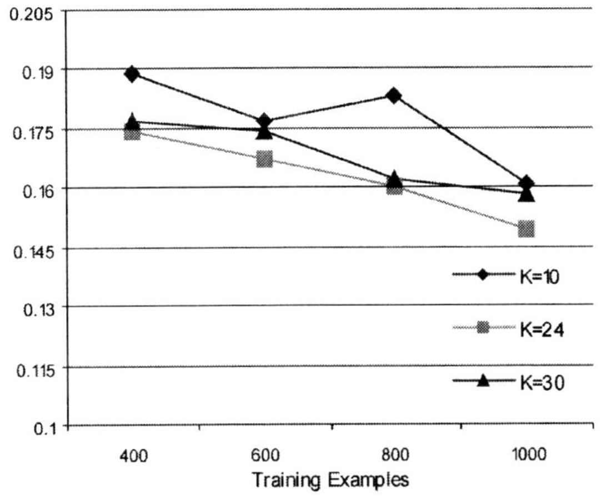

Figure 26. Micro-average precision in DOKNN

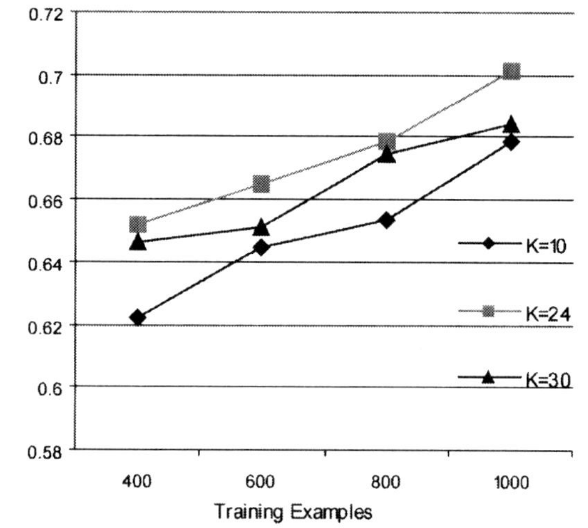

Figure 27. Macro-average precision in DOKNN

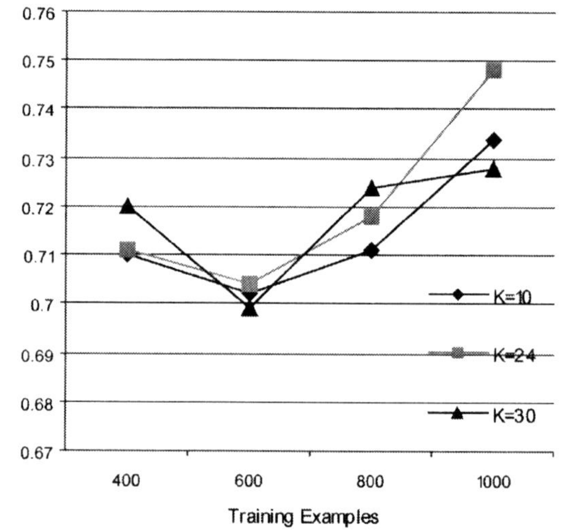

Figure 28. Micro-average recall in DOKNN

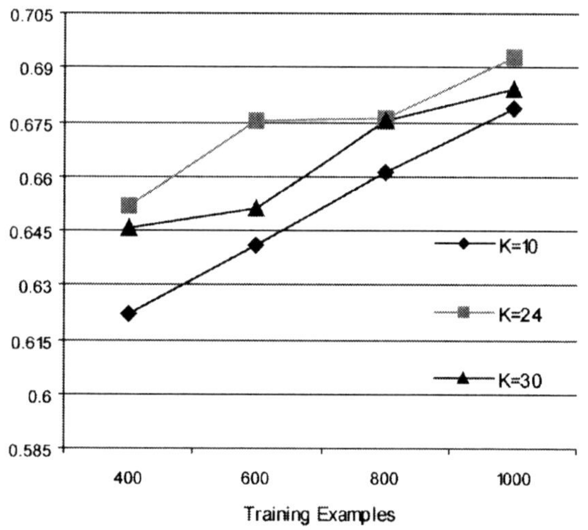

Figure 29. Macro-average recall in DOKNN

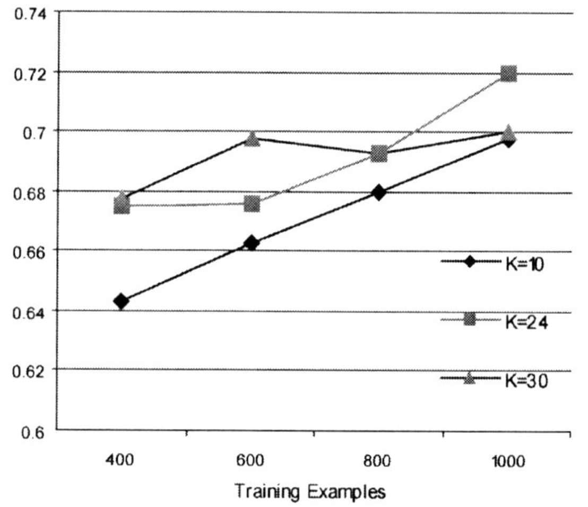

Where,

$$P(h_1 \mid d_i) = \frac{P(d_i \mid h_1) * P(h_1)}{P(d_i)} = \frac{P(d_i \mid h_1) * P(h_1)}{P(d_i \mid h_1) * P(h_1) + P(d_i \mid h_2) * P(h_2)}$$

So,

$$P(h_1 \mid d_i) = \frac{\prod_{k=1}^{m} P(c_k \mid h_1) * P(h_1)}{\prod_{k=1}^{m} P(c_k \mid h_1) * P(h_1) + \prod_{k=1}^{m} P(c_k \mid h_2) * P(h2)} \quad (1)$$

Also,

$$P(h_2 \mid d_i) = \frac{\prod_{k=1}^{m} P(c_k \mid h_2) * P(h_2)}{\prod_{k=1}^{m} P(c_k \mid h_1) * P(h_1) + \prod_{k=1}^{m} P(c_k \mid h_2) * P(h2)} \quad (2)$$

Comparing the two posterior probabilities calculated by equations 1and 2 . DONB can decide to which hypothesis document di will be targeted. The decision can be taken according to the posterior ratio R:

Figure 30. Micro average F1 measure in DOKNN

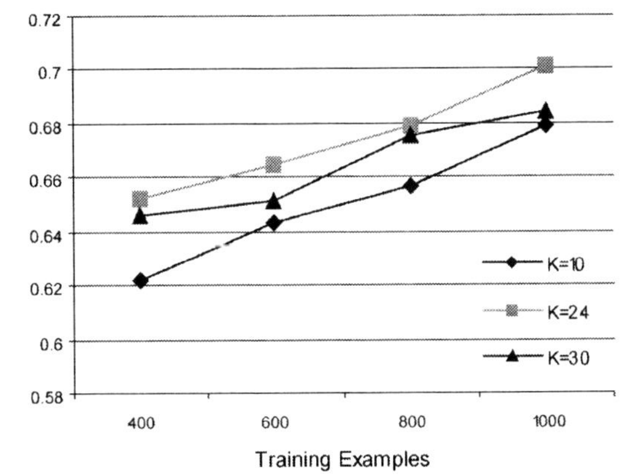

$$R(d_i) = \frac{P(h_1 \mid d_i)}{P(h_1 \mid d_i)} = \frac{P(h_1) * \prod_{k=1}^{m} P(c_k \mid h_1)}{P(h_2) * \prod_{k=1}^{m} P(c_k \mid h_2)} \quad (3)$$

According to R, DONB can take its decision by employing Rule 1.

Fact A: According to equation 3, the decision of the classifier in the test phase depends values of $P(c_i \mid h_j)$ and $P(h_k)$ $\forall c_i \in C$ and h_j, $h_k \in H$.

Step2

Purpose: prove that the values $P(c_i \mid h_j)$ and $P(h_k)$ $\forall c_i \in C$ and h_j, $h_k \in H$, calculated in the training phase may be inaccurate if the classifier is insufficiently trained.

Note: In the following proof, *Import*$(x \mid y)$ will be used to indicate the importance of object x given object y, *Count*$(x \mid y)$ is also used to indicate the count of object x given object y.

Proof: Considering the training set of example pages, some problems may arise while analyzing such examples like:

- **Problem 1:** Not all domain concepts are included, while; *Import(un_included_concepts | domain)* is very high. Moreover (or), *Import(included_concepts | domain)<<<Import(un_included_concepts | domain)*.
- **Problem 2:** *Count*$(c_i \mid h_k)$ >>> *Count*$(c_j \mid h_k)$ while *Import*$(c_i \mid h_k)$ <<< *Import*$(c_j \mid h_k)$ $\forall c_i$, $c_j \in C$ and $h_k \in H$.

From problems 1, 2: classification of the training examples will be held by rare or unimportant domain concepts, which results in: $P(c_i \mid h_k)$ >>> $P(c_j \mid h_k)$ while *Import*$(c_i \mid h_k)$ <<< *Import*$(c_j \mid h_k)$ $\forall c_i$, $c_j \in C$ and $h_k \in H$.

- **Problem 3:** *Count*$(examples \mid h_i)$ >>> *Count*$(examples \mid h_j)$ while *Import*$(h_i \mid domain)$ <<< *Import*$(h_j \mid domain)$ $\forall h_i$, $h_j \in H$.

From problem 3: many examples are targeted to unimportant domain hypothesis (classes) which results in: $P(h_i)$ >>> $P(h_j)$ while *Import*$(h_i \mid domain)$ <<< *Import*$(h_j \mid domain)$ $\forall h_i$, $h_j \in H$.

Rule 1.

<u>Rule 1:</u>
If $R(d_i) > 1$ then *target_hypothes*$(d_i) = h_1$
Else if $R(d_i) < 1$ then *target_hypothes*$(d_i) = h_2$
Else *target_hypothes*$(d_i) = h_1$? h_2

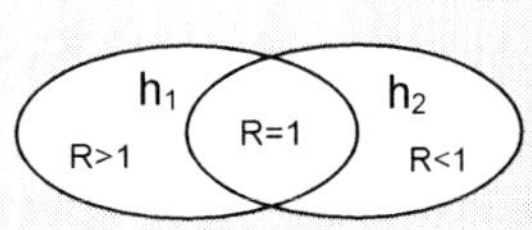

Fact B: From the above proof, we conclude that: wrongly chosen examples will lead to inaccurate values of $P(c_i \mid h_j)$ and $P(h_k)$ $\forall c_i \in C$ and $h_i, h_k \in H$.

Fact C: From facts A and B: it was proven that DONB performance depends on values $P(c_i \mid h_j)$ and $P(h_k)$ $\forall c_i \in C$ and $h_i, h_k \in H$. which may not be calculated perfectly during the training phase. This causes the classifier to suffer from overfitting which results in poor classification efficiency.

DOKNN and Overfitting

DOKNN performance depends mainly on the accuracy of measuring the similarity among vectors of the training examples and the page needed to be classified. A vector corresponds to a training example stores the set of domain concepts extracted from such example. To assure consistent classification decisions, the vectors of examples related to the same category must be close to each other compared to vectors for examples outside that category. Such condition is not always satisfied. Consider the following situations that may arise when using insufficient training examples:

(Note: In the following discussion, E1, E2, …… will be used to represent the training examples, Target(E) to indicate the target hypothesis, for example E, Vector(E) to represent the vector space model for example E, and, Simcos(X, Y) to indicate the cosine similarity among vectors X and Y).

- $Target(E_x) = Category_i$, while $Vector(E_x)$ stores many Concepts that are closely related to Categoryj.
- $Sim_{cos}(Vector(E_i), Vector(E_j))=1$ (*this means that vectors are identical*), while $Target(E_i) \neq Target(E_j)$.
- Consider the three examples E_x, E_y, and E_z, where: $Target(E_x) = Target(E_y) = Category_i$ and $Target(E_z)=Category_j$. However, $Sim_{cos}(Vector(E_x), Vector(E_y)) < Sim_{cos}(Vector(E_x), Vector(E_z))$.

Fact D: Such situations will certainly cause the classifier to be trapped. It may then classify newly incoming page to wrong categories. This causes the classifier to suffer from overfitting.

From facts C and D; lemma 1 is concluded.

A Proposed Solution for Overfitting Problem

Overfitting problem arises when the chosen examples are insufficient to express the domain of interest, which results in wrong or unsuitable classification rules (i.e., the classifier will be easily trapped during the testing phase). The innovation of our proposed solution is to adapt the classification rules even if those rules are initialized badly based on CL technique (i.e., add continuous learning ability (CLA) to the proposed classifiers). This is already done by extending the classifier learning during test phase. Classifica-

Lemma 1.

Lemma 1:

DONB and DOKNN perform well if they are trained with sufficient examples w.r.t the domain of interes., Otherwise, they will suffer from overfitting.

Figure 32. The accuracy of DOKNN and DONB against training examples

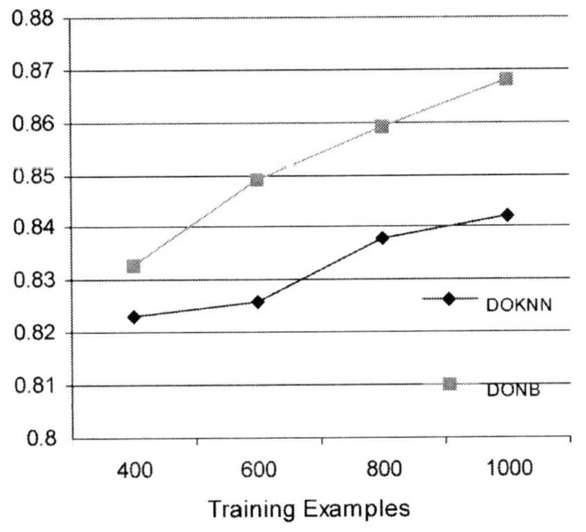

Figure 33. The error of DOKNN and DONB against training examples

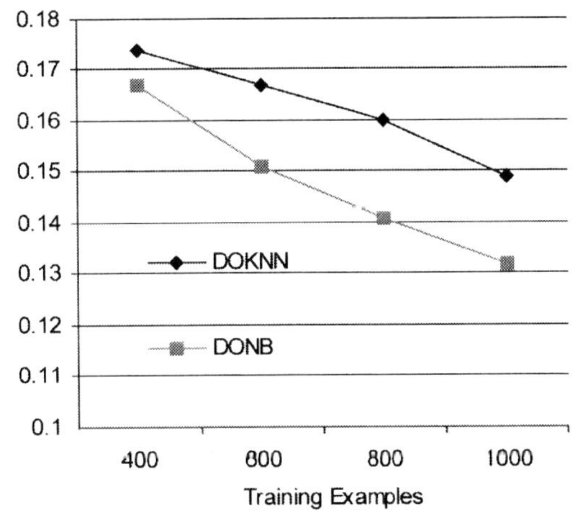

Figure 34. Two hypotheses sharing recommended concepts

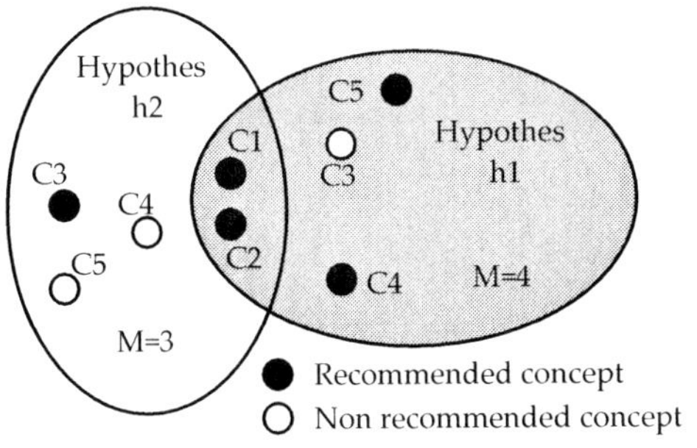

tion rules will be enhanced continuously rather than being limited to rules collected during the training phase.

Although applying KNN algorithm to build the proposed DOKNN classifier provides satisfactory classification accuracy, it is also important to mention that KNN suffers from various drawbacks. (1) the difficulty in deciding the optimal value of k. KNN performance is extremely sensitive to the value of k, which is determined empirically by conducting a series of experiments using different values. (2) high cost must be considered when classifying a new page. This is because KNN performs all the computations at testing phase. (3) in the presence of large feature space, it will become a problem to manage the classification, as the size of the training set increases as it requires large memory.

To evaluate the impact of adding CLA to Web page classifiers, DONB is chosen rather than DOKNN for different reasons. One reason is the simplicity. DONB is easy to program than DOKNN. In addition, experimental results have also shown that DONB outperforms DOKNN. As illustrated in Figures 32 and 33, DONB provides higher accuracy and lower classification error respectively when compared with DOKNN (K=24) with different values of the training examples.

Where, DOKNN is a lazy learner so it consumes long time to classify newly incoming pages since its similarity against all examples must be calculated. Hence, adding CLA to DOKNN will certainly add much damping to the classifier. Finally, an important problem is its sensitivity to the value of K, which is not easy to be determined accurately in all situations. Hence, DONB is the selected technique to add the continuous learning ability since it provides better results and less tuning variables.

CONTINUOUS LEARNING NAÏVE BAYES (CLNB) CLASSIFIER

Assuming that the domain of interest has X target hypothesis, $H=\{h_1, h_2, \ldots, h_x\}$ and n concepts, $C=\{c_1, c_2, c_3, \ldots, c_n\}$. For each hypothesis $h_i \in H$, a set of domain concepts are chosen (*by domain expert*) to represent h_i (*for example m concepts are chosen for* h_i). These concepts are called *recommended concepts* (*RC*) for h_i and denoted by the set $RC(h_i)=\{Rc_{i1}, Rc_{i2}, \ldots Rc_{im}\}$. The remaining is *not recommended concepts* (*NRC*) for h_i and denoted by the set $NRC(h_i)=\{NRc_{i1}, NRc_{i2}, \ldots NRc_{i\,n-m}\}$. For illustration, consider a domain with $C=\{c_1, c_2, \ldots, c_5\}$ and $H=\{h_1, h_2\}$. The domain concepts can be distributed as shown in Figure 34.

This idea allows hypothesis to interfere with each other (*share recommended concepts*) since a single concept may belong to multiple hypotheses. This idea agrees with the fuzziness nature of Web classification problem.

Each hypothesis $h_j \in H$ has a private *hypothesis probability distribution* (*HPD*) that represents each concept conditional probability $P(c_i|h_j)\ \forall c_i \in C$. All HPDs will be initialized during the training phase and will be updated continuously during classifier testing phase. Figure 37 summarizes the two phases required for Continuous Learning Naïve Bayes algorithm when applied to domain-oriented classifiers.

During the training phase, the task is to initialize:

- $P(Rc_i|h_j)\ \forall Rc_i \in RC,\ h_j \in H$. It is assumed that: all RCs for hypothesis h_j have equal initial probability.
- $P(NRc_i|h_j)\ \forall NRc_i \in NRC,\ h_j \in H$. All NRCs for hypothesis h_j will also have an equal initial probability.
- $P(h_j)\ \forall h_j \in H$.

For illustration, consider a hypothesis space H with X target hypothesis. Consider $h_j \in H$ with m recommended concepts. It is assumed that: each $Rc_i \in RC(h_j)$ gains an *initial vote* = β, each $NRc_i \in NRC(h_j)$ gains an *initial vote*=1 while $\beta > 1$. This yields the following initial assumptions:

$$P(Rc_i \mid h_j) = \beta\, P(NRc_i \mid h_j)$$

Since:

$$m * P(Rc_i \mid h_j) + (n - m) * P(NRc_i \mid h_j) = 1$$

$$m * \beta\, P(NRc_i \mid h_j) + (n - m) * P(NRc_i \mid h_j) = 1$$

$$P(NRc_i \mid h_j) = \frac{1}{n + (\beta - 1) * m} \qquad (4)$$

Figure 35. (a) Represents hypothes h_j at training phase, (b) represents h_j at steady state

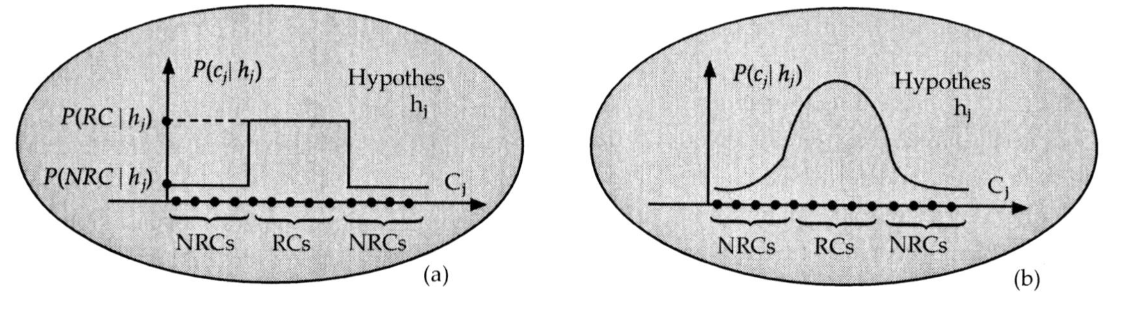

Table 10. The proposed categories with the corresponding recommended concepts

Category_ID	Category_Name	Category_Concepts
1	Academic and research	83
2	University building and sites	37
3	University management and routinism	62
4	Tools, equipments and assistance technology	49

Figure 36. Initial data structure used in implementing CLNB algorithm

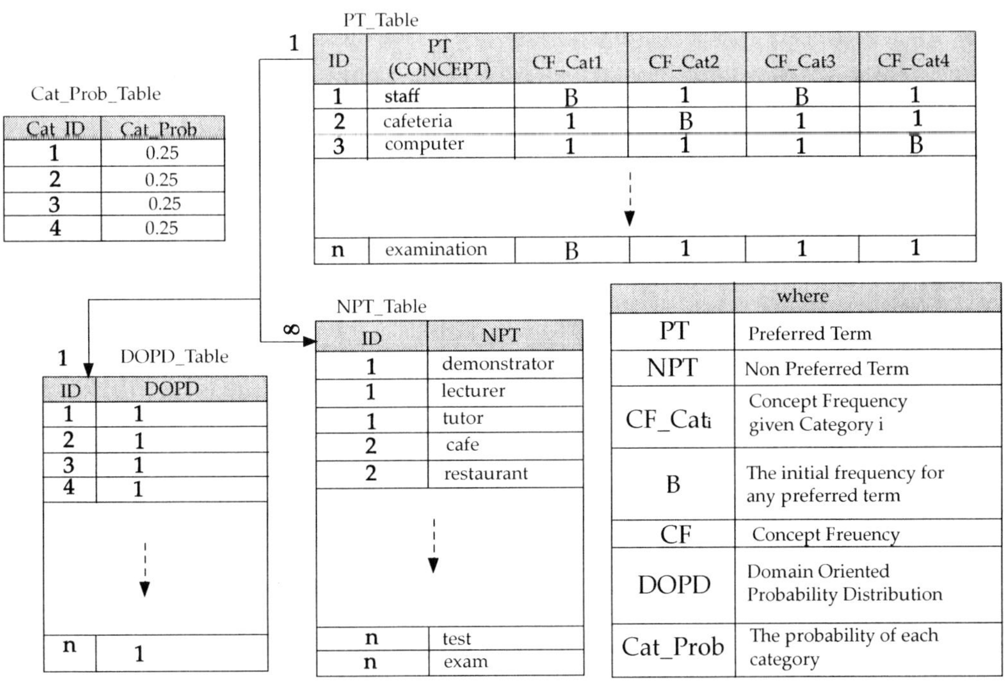

Similarly:

$$P(NRc_i \mid h_j) = \frac{\beta}{n + (\beta - 1) * m} \quad (5)$$

It is also assumed that all hypotheses have the same initial prior probability. So,

$$P(h_j) = \frac{1}{|H|} = \frac{1}{x} \qquad \forall h_j \in H \quad (6)$$

Using equations 6, 7, and 8 the initial conditional probabilities $P(NRc_i|h_j)$, $P(Rc_i|h_j)$, and the prior hypothesis probabilities $P(h_j)$ for hypothesis h_j can be calculated $Rc_i \in RC(h_j)$, $NRc_i \in NRC(h_j)$, and $h_j \in H$. The initial shape of $HPD(h_j)$ is shown in Figure 35a.

On the contrary, when an input Web document Doc_i is being classified *during testing phase*, the domain concepts found in Doc_i are extracted firstly. Then, the posterior probability for each hypothesis will be calculated based on *HPDs* and hypotheses prior probabilities. Doc_i will be targeted (*classified*) to the hypothesis with the maximum posterior. If Doc_i is targeted to h_j, two important issues must be performed to achieve

Figure 37. Continuous learning naïve bayes (CLNB) algorithm

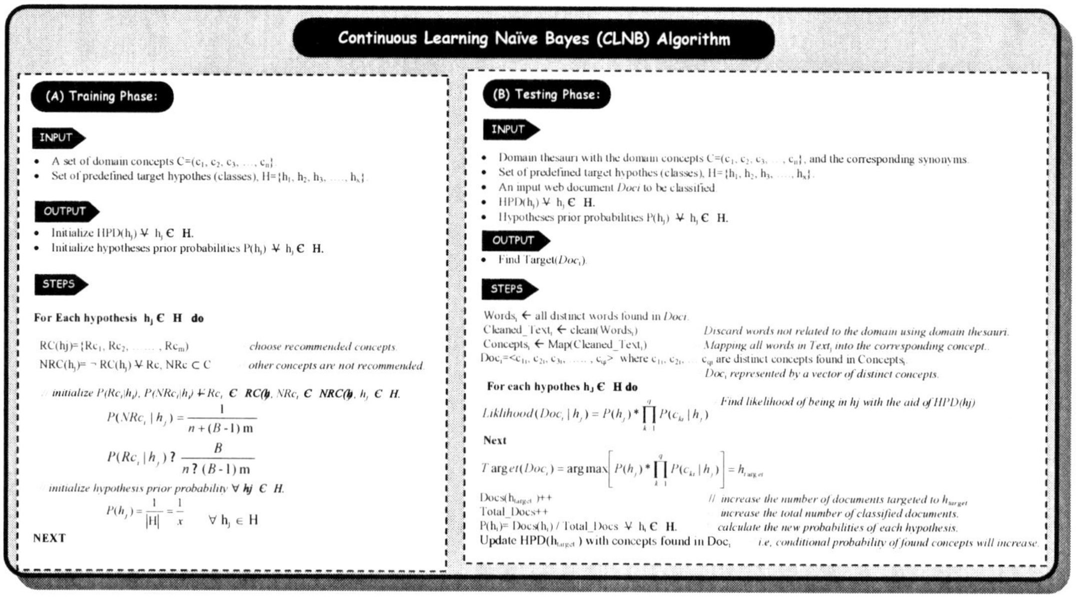

Table 11. Evaluation parameters for each category using CLNB

Testing Pages	Category 1				Category 2				Category 3				Category 4			
	P	R	Acc	E	P	R	Acc	E	P	R	Acc	E	P	R	Acc	E
400	0.821	0.879	0.878	0.122	0.910	0.784	0.963	0.037	0.907	0.829	0.955	0.045	0.871	0.918	0.940	0.060
600	0.851	0.898	0.915	0.085	0.952	0.800	0.970	0.030	0.929	0.839	0.953	0.047	0.852	0.909	0.932	0.068
800	0.864	0.962	0.915	0.085	0.908	0.775	0.961	0.039	0.899	0.816	0.944	0.056	0.888	0.920	0.938	0.062
1000	0.877	0.928	0.921	0.079	0.945	0.817	0.971	0.029	0.957	0.865	0.964	0.036	0.817	0.858	0.908	0.092

the continuous learning behavior. (1) Updating $HPD(h_j)$ according to the concepts found in Doc_i (*increase the probability of the found concepts*). The shape of $HPD(h_j)$ at steady state will be as shown in Figure 35b. (2) Updating $P(h_j)$ with respect to other hypotheses prior probabilities, since targeting a new document to h_j causes $P(h_j)$ to increase compared to other hypotheses.

For implementing CLNB, university domain with its four proposed categories will be considered again. Domain concepts will be distributed among the four categories. In other words, for each category, some concepts are chosen to represent the category (*category recommended concept*) as illustrated in Table 10.

Implementing Domain Thesauri and DOPD in CLNB Classifier

When implementing the CLNB algorithm, the same structure for domain thesauri and DOPD was used as in DONB classifier except that, the initial frequencies of each category recommended concepts were assigned to *B* (*w.r.t that category*). Otherwise, its frequency will be assigned to *one*. Another table *.Cat_Prob_Table.* is added to reflect the probability of each category (*as illustrated in Figure 36*). The structure has also a dynamic

Table 12. Micro-average and macro-average scores using CLNB

Testing Pages	Precision		Recall		F measure		Accuracy	Error
	mic	mac	mic	mac	Mic	mac		
400	0.865	0.877	0.865	0.853	0.865	0.865	0.936	0.064
600	0.877	0.896	0.877	0.862	0.877	0.878	0.938	0.062
800	0.879	0.890	0.879	0.859	0.879	0.874	0.939	0.061
1000	0.882	0.899	0.882	0.867	0.882	0.883	0.941	0.059

Figure 38. Accuracy and error in CLNB

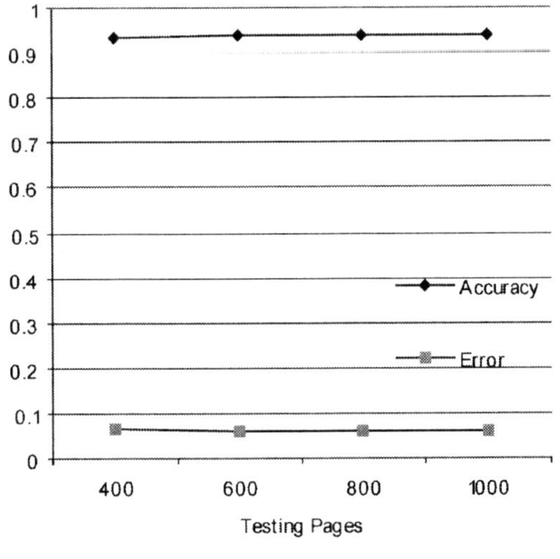

Figure 39. Micro average and macro average precision in CLNB

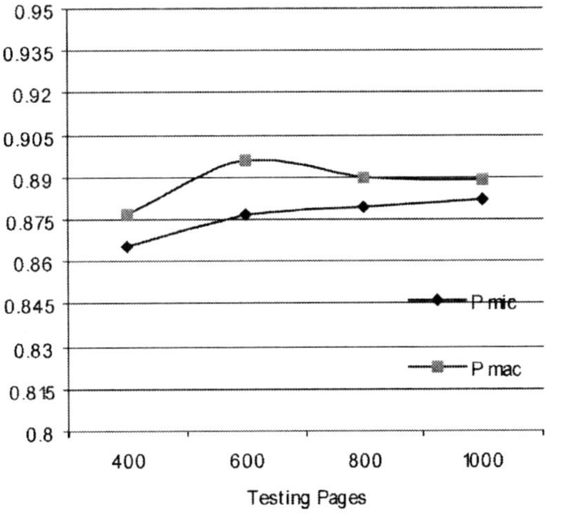

Figure 40. F1 measure in CLNB

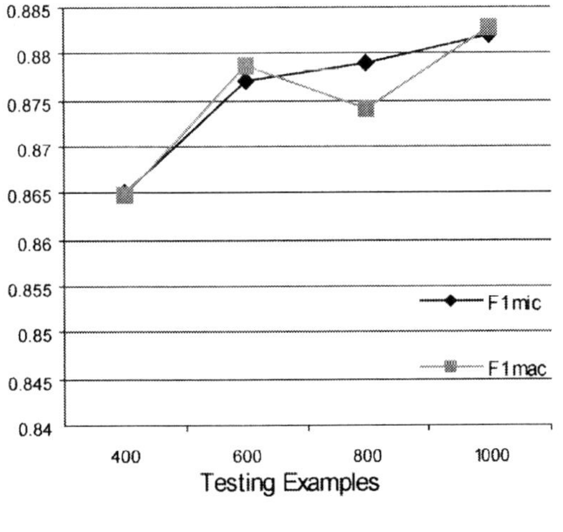

Figure 41. Micro average and macro average Recall in CLNB

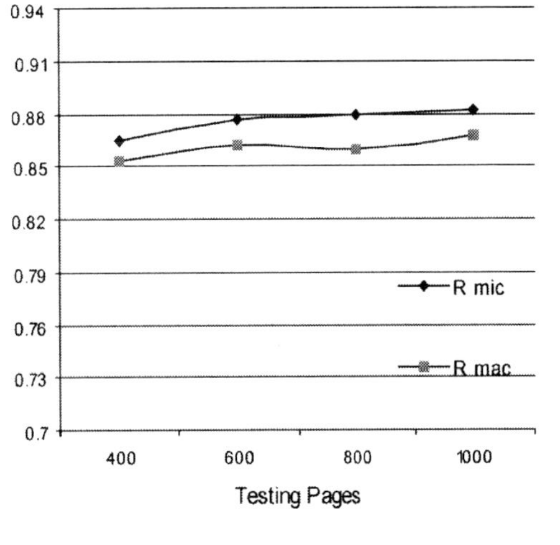

property, so the concepts frequencies (*w.r.t each category*) as well as each category probability will be updated after classifying each page.

CLNB Results

In CLNB, the initial domain knowledge will be set by domain expert in the training phase *(no need to any training examples*), and then it is allowed to classify new pages. The classifier has the ability to adapt its performance continuously since more domain knowledge will be added after processing each page. Thus, the basic parameter that affects CLNB performance is the number of processed pages. The same collected 1000 pages used to test DONB will be used again to test CLNB. Evaluation parameters for each category were measured after processing 400, 600, 800, and 1000 pages. Results are reported in Table 11.

From Table 11, it is obvious that the classifier introduces a good precision, recall, and accuracy in all categories. For evaluating performance average across categories, the *micro-average* and *macro-average* scores must be evaluated as reported in Table 12.

From Table 12, it is noted that; (1) precision, recall, and F1-measure scores increase as the testing pages (TP) increase. This insures that the performance of CLNB increases as it is tested with higher number TP. (2) $F_{mic} \approx F_{mac}$. This is simply because, in CLNB each category is described by a set of recommended concepts that are initialized with equal weights (*in both popular and rare categories*) w.r.t the category. In this case, the performance in popular and rare categories to be closed to each other, which leads to micro-averaged scores closed to macro-averaged (see Figures 39, 40, and 41).

Figure 38 shows the accuracy as well as the error of CLNB. Classifier accuracy was 93.6% when TP=400 and reaches 94.1% when TP=1000. Figures 39, 40, and 41 show the macro and micro averaged scores for CLNB. They show that both scores are close to each other.

COMPARING THE PROPOSED CLASSIFICATION ALGORITHMS

From previous results, it is clear that CLNB outperforms both DONB and DOKNN. CLNB has the highest precision and recall than DONB and DOKNN, which are the basic targets for any information retrieval systems. CLNB also has two salient properties that DONB and DOKNN do not have. The first is the ability to perform a continuous learning. This ability insures performance promotion during future tests. The other is the protection from overfitting. A comparison between DONB, DOKNN and CLNB algorithms is illustrated in Table 13.

Table 13. A comparison between DONB, DOKNN, and CLNB

Criteria	DONB	DOKNN	CLNB
Training Examples	Required	Required	Not Required
Domain Expert	Required	Required	Required
Learning Type	Supervised learning	Supervised learning	Continuous Learning
Accuracy	In between	Lower	Higher
Precision	In between	Lower	Higher
Recall	In between	Lower	Higher
Overfitting	Not Protected	Not Protected	Protected

Finally, it is important to mention that expressing each category by a set of concepts in both DONB and CLNB may cause a problem that we will call the *classifier trap* (*CT*). CT will happen when a tested page contains many concepts related to category X, while its actual classification is to category Y. This causes the classifier to be trapped and classifies the tested page to a wrong category. *Practically*, this drawback has no great impact on the overall system performance.

CONCLUSION

Naïve bayes classifier is one of the most important classifiers that are applied to the problem of Web page classification. Overfitting can be considered as the main problem that dramatically attacks the performance of such a classifier when trying to classify pages related to a specific domain. In order to overcome this problem two enhancement are provided. The first is to try to restrict the classifier to a specific domain. Managing the classification task in one domain will be much easier. The new generation of classifiers is called vertical or domain oriented classifiers. The second enhancement is to provide vertical classifiers with new learning technique that assures performance promotion.

The article introduced a new implementation of naïve bayes and k-nearest neighbor classifiers called DONB and DOKNN respectively, which are able to classify pages related to a specific domain, then the continuous learning technique was added to DONB to produce a novel classifier called CLNB. The proposed classifiers are tested and analyzed. From the results, it is concluded that, to insure better classification performance, it will be better to apply classification algorithms in their continuous learning version (whenever possible) for building domain oriented classifiers.

FUTURE WORK

The idea of expressing each domain by a set of candidate concepts (see Figure 42) permits to generalize the idea of continuous learning ability to obtain a scalable version of CLNB (build a general purpose CLNB classifier). The result is a generalized continuous learning naïve bayes (GCLNB) classifier.

In GCLNB, classification process will be performed in two steps. In the first, the probability that the processed page lies in each domain will be calculated, and then, the page will be targeted to the domain with the height priority. The page will be classified according to the pre-defined categories of the target domain.

Figure 42. Using CLNB as a multi-purpose Web page classifier

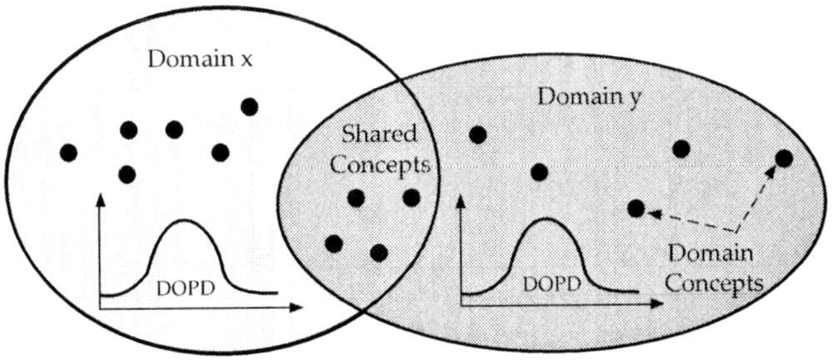

REFERENCES

Aas, K., & Eikvil, L. (1999). *Text categorization: A survey* (Tech. Rep.) Norwegian Computing Centre.

Anderson, B., & Moore, A. (2005). Active learning for hidden Markov models: Objective functions and algorithms. In *Proceedings of the ICML 2005 Conference*, Bonn, Germany.

Apte, C., Damerau, F., & Weiss, S. M. (1998). Text mining with decision trees and decision rules. In *Proceedings of the Conference on Automated Learning and Discovery*, Carnegie-Mellon University (pp. 72-79).

Bates, M. (1986). Subject access in online catalogs: A design model. *American Society for Information Science Journal, 37*(6), 357-376.

Bazell, D., Miller, D. J., & Borne, K. (2003). Novel approaches to semi-supervised and unsupervised learning. In *Proceedings of the ASP Conference Series, Astronomical Data Analysis Software and Systems XII* (Vol. 295).

Becker, M., Hachey, B., Alex, B., & Grover, C. (2005). Optimising selective sampling for bootstrapping named entity recognition. In *Proceedings of the ICML-2005 Workshop on Learning with Multiple Views*, Bonn, Germany.

Blum, A.L., & Rivest, R.L. (1992). Training a 3-node neural network is NP- complete. *Neural Networks, 5*(1), 117-127.

Burges, C. J. C., (1996). Simplified support vector decision rules. In *Proceedings of the 13th International Conference on Machine Learning* (pp. 71-77).

Burges, C.J.C. (1998). A tutorial on support vector machines for pattern recognition. In *Proceedings of the Data Mining and knowledge discovery* (Vol. 2, pp. 121-167).

Chen, H., & Dumais, S. T. (2000, April 1-6). Bringing order to the Web: automatically categorizing search results. In *Procceedings of the ACM SIGCHI 2000 conference on Human factors in computing systems*, The Netherlands, (pp.145-152).

Chen, T. Y., Kuo, F., & Merkel, R. G. (2004, September 8-10). On the statistical properties of the f-measure. In *Proceedings of the Fourth International Conference on (QSIC'04)* (pp. 146-153). Braunshweig, Germany.

Costa, J., & Hero, A. O. (2004, May). Manifold learning using Euclidean k-nearest neighbor graphs. In *Proceedings of the IEEE International Conference on Acoustic Speech and Signal Processing*. Montreal.

Ciravegna, F. (2001, August 4th-10th). Adaptive information extraction from text by rule induction and generalization. In *Proceedings of the 17th International Joint Conference on Artificial Intelligence*, Seattle, WA (pp. 133-139).

Cristianini, N., Shawe-Taylor, J., Elisseeff, A., & Kandola, J. (2001). On kernel-target alignment. In *Proceedings of the Neural Information Processing Systems (NIPS 2001)* (pp. 367-373).

Culotta, A., & McCallum, A. (2005). Reducing labeling effort for structured prediction tasks. In *Proceedings of the American Association of Artificial Intelligence (AAAI05)* (pp. 746-751).

Dasgupta, S., Tauman Kalai, A., & Monteleoni, C. (2005, June). *Analysis of perceptron-based active learning.*

Duda, R.O., & Hart, P. (1973). *Pattern classification and scene analysis.* New York: John Wiley & Sons.

Fernandez, R., Ginzburg, J., & Lappin, S. (2005). Using machine learning for non-sentential utterance classification. In *Proceedings of the SIGdial 6*, Lisbon, Portugal (pp. 77-86).

Fung, P., & Roth, D. (2005). Guest Editors Introduction: Machine learning in speech and language technologies. In *Proceedings of the ACM*, Numbers 1-3 (Vol. 60, pp. 5-9). The Netherlands: Springer.

Getz, G., Shental, N., & Domany, E. (2005). Semi-supervised learning—A statistical physics approach. In *Proceedings of the 22nd ICML Workshop on Learning with Partially Classified Training Data*, Bonn, Germany.

Heb, A., Johnston, E., & Kushmerick, N. (2005, February 13-18).Machine learning techniques for annotating semantic Web services. In *Proceedings of the Dagstuhl Seminar on Machine Learning for the Semantic Web*, (pp. 77-83).

Hu, Y., Li, H., Cao, Y., Meyerzon, D., & Zheng, Q. (2005, June 7-11). Automatic extraction of titles from general documents using machine learning. In *Proceedings of the 14th Joint Conference on Digital Library (ACM-JCDL'05)* Denver, CO (pp. 145-154).

ISO 2788. (1986). *Documentation-Guidelines for the establishment and Development of monolingual Thesauri* (2nd ed.).

Koller, R. D., & Wilamowski, B. M. (1995, July 17-21). A relaxation/regression algorithm for efficient training of multilayer neural networks. In *Proceedings of the World Congress of Neural Networks* Washington DC (Vol. 1, pp. 683-686).

Kurino, R., Sugisaka, M. & Shibata, K. (2004). Growing neural network with hidden neurons. In *Proceedings of the 9th International Symposium on Artificial Life and Robotics* (AROB) (Vol. 1, pp. 144-147).

Kwon, O. W., & Lee, J. H. (2003). Text categorization based on k-nearest neighbor approach for Web site classification. *Information Processing &Management, 39*(1), 25-44.

Lam, W., & Han, Y.Q. (2003). Automatic textual document categorization based on generalized instance sets and a meta-model. *IEEE Transactions on Pattern Analysis and Machine Intelligence, 25*(5), 628-633.

Liu, H., Mandvikar, A., Foschi, P., & Torkkola, K. (2003, August 9-15). Active learning with ensembles for image classification. In *Proceedings of the 18th International Joint Conference on Artificial Intelligence*, Acapulco, Mexico (pp. 1435-1436).

Lodhi, H., Saunders, C., Shawe-Taylor, J., Cristianini, N., & Watkins, C. (2002). text classification using string kernels. *Machine Learning Research Journal, 2*, 419-444.

Osuna, E., & Girosi, F.. (1998). Reducing the runtime complexity of support vector machines. In *Proceedings of the International Conference on Pattern Recognition.*

Pierre J. M. (2000, 21 September). Practical issues for automatic categorization of Web sites. In *Procceedings of ECDL 2000 Workshop on the Semantic Web*, Lisbon Portugal (pp. 83-88).

Qian, G., Sural, S., Gu, Y., & Pramanik, S. (2004). Similarity between Euclidean and Cosine angle distance for nearest neighbor queries. In *Proceedings of the ASM Symposium on Applied Computing.*

Rennie, J., et. al. (2003, August 21-24) .Tackling the poor assumptions of naive bayes text classifiers. In *Proceedings of the Twentieth International Conference on Machine Learning*, Washington (pp. 199-205).

Riccardi, G., & Tur, D. (2003). Active and unsupervised learning for automatic speech recognition. In *Proceedings of the Eurospeech.*

Ruiz, M. E., & Srinivasan, P. (2002). Hierarchical text categorization using neural networks. *Information Retrieval*, 5(1), 87-118. Kluwer Academic Publishers.

Salton, G. (1989). Automatic text processing: The transformation, analysis, and retrieval of information by computer. Addison-Wesley.

Selamat A., Omatu, S., & Yanagimoto, H.. (2002, August 5-7). Web news classification using neural networks based on PCA. In *Proceedings of the of SICE*, Osaka, Japan. (pp. 2388-2393).

Solan, Z., Horn, D., Ruppin, E., & Edelman, S. (2005, August 16). Unsupervised learning of natural languages. In *Proceedings of the National Academy of Sciences* (Vol. 102, No. 33, pp. 11629-11634).

Sperduti, A., & Starita, A. (1993). Speed up learning and network optimization with extended back-propagation. *Neural Networks, 6*, 365-383.

Sun A., Lim, E., & Ng, W. (2002). Web classification using support vector machine. In *Proceedings of ACM Workshop on Web Information and Data Management (WIDM'02)*, VA. (pp. 96-99).

Tan, A. C., Gilbert, D., & Deville, Y. (2003). Integrative machine learning approach for multi-class SCOP protein fold classification. In *Proceedings of the German Conference on Bioinformatics* (pp. 153-159).

Tur, G., Hakkani-Tür, D., & E.Schapire, R. (2005). Combining active and semi-supervised learning for spoken language understanding. *Speech Communication, 45*(2), 171-186.

Vapnik, V. (1998). *Statistical learning theory*. New York: John Wiley & Sons.

Vapnik, V. (1999). *The nature of statistical learning theory* (2nd ed.). New York: Springer-Verlag.

Weston, J., & Watkins, C. (1999). Multi-class support vector machines. In *Proceedings of the ESANN99* Brussels (pp. 219-224).

Xiao, G., Southey, F., Holte, R. C. & Wilkinson, D. (2005, July). Software testing by active learning for commercial games. In *Proceedings of the 20th National Conference on Artificial Intelligence (AAAI-2005)* (pp. 898-903).

Xu, J., Cao, Y., Li, H., & Zhao, M. (2005, May 10-14). Ranking definitions with supervised learning methods. *Special interest tracks and posters of the 14th international conference on World Wide Web*, Chiba, Japan (pp. 811-819).

Yang & Liu, X. (1999). A re-examination of text categorization methods. In *Proceedings of the 22nd Annual International ACM SIGIR Conference on Research and Development in Information Retrieval (SIGIR'99)* (pp. 42-49).

Yu, H., Han, J., & Chang, K. C. C. (2004, January). PEBL: Web page classification without negative examples. *IEEE Transactions on Knowledge and Data Engineering, 16*(1), 70-81.

Yu, H., Yang, J., & Han, J. (2003, August).Classifying large data sets using SVM with hierarchical clusters. In *Proceedings of the Ninth ACM SIGKDD '03 International Conference on Knowledge Discovery and Data Mining*, WA.

This work was previously published in Int. Journal of Information Technology and Web Engineering, Vol. 2, Issue 2, edited by G. Alkhatib and D. Rine, pp. 1-44, copyright 2007 by IGI Publishing (an imprint of IGI Global).

Chapter XIII
Building a Semantic-Rich Service-Oriented Manufacturing Environment

Zhonghua Yang
Nanyang Technological University, Singapore

Jing Bing Zhang
Singapore Institute of Manufacturing Technology (SIMTech), Singapore

Robert Gay
Nanyang Technological University, Singapore

Liqun Zhuang
Singapore Institute of Manufacturing Technology (SIMTech), Singapore

Hui Mien Lee
Nanyang Technological University, Singapore

ABSTRACT

Service-orientation has emerged as a new promising paradigm for enterprise integration in the manufacturing sector. In this paper, we focus on the approach and technologies for constructing a service oriented manufacturing environment. The service orientation is achieved via virtualization in which every thing, including machines, equipments, devices, various data sources, applications, and processes, are virtualized as standard-based Web services. The virtualization approach is based on the emerging Web Services Resource Framework (WS-RF). A case study of virtualizing an AGV system using WS-RF is described. The use of Semantic Web Services technologies to enhance manufacturing Web services for a semantic-rich environment is discussed, focusing on OWL-S for semantic markup of manufacturing Web services and OWL for the development of ontologies in the manufacturing domain. An enterprise integration architecture enabled by Semantic Web service composition is also discussed.

INTRODUCTION

Service-oriented architecture (SOA) has emerged as a new promising paradigm for building loosely coupled, standard-based and Web-enabled distributed applications and systems. SOA is an architectural style for building software applications that use services available in a network such as the Web, and the concept of services refers to as network-enabled entity delivered over the Web using XML-based technologies. *Services* provide the highest level of abstraction and support the right kind of programming model for open distributed systems in the following ways:

- Services are network-enabled components with well-defined interfaces that are implementation independent.
- Services are self-contained to offer functionality as defined in interfaces. Services can be dynamically discovered and their consumptions are by message exchange; Consumers are not concerned with how these services will execute their requests.
- Services are loosely coupled, only thin message-level connection exists, and thus more independent.
- Composite services can be built from aggregates of other services, providing the ability to choreography their behaviors so that the local policies can be applied autonomously and yet creates a coherent cross enterprise processes.

SOA provides a new opportunity for solving long-standing problems in industry and enterprises, for example, the notorious integration problem. In a nutshell, the integration problem can be viewed as a problem of service integration or service composition. This in turn imposes a new challenge of building a service-oriented environment. In this article, we focus on the approach and technologies for constructing a service-oriented manufacturing environment. The service orientation is achieved via *virtualization* in which every thing, including machines, equipments, devices, various data sources, applications, and processes, are virtualized as standard-based Web services. The virtualization approach is based on the emerging Web Services Resource Framework (WS-RF). We illustrate how WS-RF is used to virtualize an AGV system as Web services.

The full potentials of service-oriented environment can be fulfilled by enhancing it with semantics, creating a semantic-rich environment. We leverage Semantic Web technologies for this purpose, and use OWL-S for semantic markup of manufacturing Web services and OWL for the development of ontologies in the manufacturing domain.

SERVICE-ORIENTED ARCHITECTURE FOR MANUFACTURING

The overall semantic-enhanced service-oriented architecture is shown in Figure 1. Fundamental to the service orientation is the *virtualization layer*. Via a virtualization, all manufacturing systems to be integrated are exposed as Web services, and they can offer their services and functionality in a standard Web service environment. The emerging WS Resource Framework provides a standardized way for the virtualization (Graham, Karmarkar, Mischkinsky, Robinson, & Sedukhin, 2004). Using WS-RF, each manufacturing resource will be modeled as a WS-Resource, which is the combination of the Web Service and the stateful resource. The ultimate objective of virtualization is the construction of a service-oriented manufacturing environment, and all services are hosted in a standard Web service platform. The basic Web service infrastructure (SOAP, WSDL, UDDI) is augmented with Business Process Execution Service to support automated business process execution. This is the *Web services infrastructure layer*.

All the Web services, newly developed manufacturing services or those from the virtualization, will be enhanced with domain specific semantic information. The emerging Semantic Web standards provide the Web services infrastructure with the semantic interoperability that integration needs. They provide formal languages and ontologies, most notably OWL (McGuinness & van Harmelen, 2004) and OWL-S (Martin, Burstein, & *et al*, 2004) to reason about service description and capability. A Semantic Web service is a Web Service whose description is in a language that has well-defined semantics. The description is therefore unambiguously computer interpretable and facilitates maximal automation and dynamism in Web service discovery, selection, composition, negotiation, and invocation. This feature provides the sound technical foundation for achieving automated integration. In a way, Semantic Web transforms the Web service infrastructure into repository of computer manipulatable data with rich semantics (*Semantic-enhanced Web services layer*). The significance of this architectural design is that we obtain a semantic rich Web services environment and the semantics marked up in OWL-S are readily processable by autonomous agents.

Within a semantic-rich environment, we must develop *service-oriented requirements* ready for service realization. This is a process of transforming business processes into *service processes*. As shown in Figure 2, first, the requirements of enterprise are modeled as business processes. The essence of business process modeling is to create a *virtualized enterprise* (VE) which represents a coherent, integrated (and interoperated) business process for achieving enterprise's ultimate strategic business goals. Those parts of business processes that are IT-enabled will be realized using Web services processes. When leveraging OWL-S based approach for service composition, business process is transformed into OWL-S service process with Input, Output, Precondition and Effects (IOPE) being specified. A Semantic Web services composer will take OWL-S files as input and generate a set of Web services that realize the business process (Yang, Zhang, Tao, & Gay, 2005).

In a service-oriented approach to enterprise integration, Web services become an integral part of the enterprise IT landscape, and, as such, they are vital resources to enterprises. Managing such a service-oriented environment is critical for enterprises that use Web services to automate and integrate various internal functions, and deal with partners and clients electronically. We adopt the OASIS service management standards (i.e., WSDM) including two aspects: (1) management using Web Services and (2) management of the Web services resources via the former (Sedukhin, 2005). In addition, the emerging Web standard technologies can be used for security and Quality of Services (QoS). These two aspects are functionally orthogonal (Figure 1).

In the following sections of the article, we focus on how to create a semantic-rich service-oriented environment. The Semantic Web services based composition to achieve automated enterprise integration is discussed elsewhere (Yang, Gay, Miao, Zhang, & Shen, 2005).

SERVICE-ORIENTATION VIA VIRTUALIZATION

As emphasized previously, fundamental to realizing service-oriented enterprise integration is *virtualization*, hence creating a service-oriented environment. Every resource in a considered environment (machine, devices, equipments, data sources, processes and applications) is required to be virtualized as Web services offering its services and functionality in a standard Web service environment.

The benefits and advantages of service virtualization is well-documented (Foster, Kesselman, Nick, & Tuecke, 2002). Virtualization enables consistent resource access across mul-

Figure 1. A service oriented architecture for manufacturing

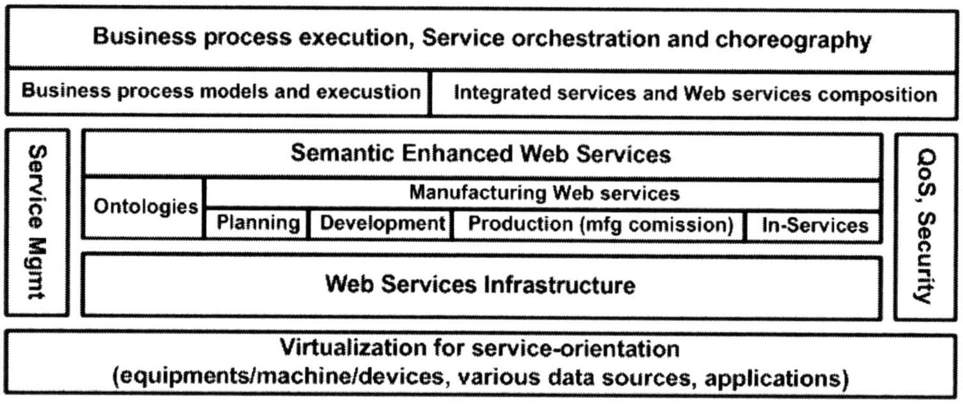

tiple manufacturing systems and environments. Virtualization also enables mapping of multiple logical resource instances onto the same physical resource and facilitates management of resources within/across enterprises based on composition from lower-level resources. Furthermore, virtualization allows us to compose basic services to form more sophisticated services, regardless of how these services are implemented. Virtualizing services also underpins the ability to map common service semantic behavior seamlessly onto native systems and facilities.

It is argued that although Web service's behavior is defined solely by the message exchanges through the interface description supported by the service, the external observable behavior implies the existence of *stateful resources* that are used and manipulated in the processing of a Web service request message. Particularly in manufacturing setting, many resources (machine and equipment, inventory state, process state) have a strong notion of *state* that they are in. Nonetheless, Web services are generally *stateless*. It is important to identify and standardize the patterns by which state is represented and manipulated, so as to facilitate the construction and use of interoperable services. Web Service Resource Framework (WS-RF), currently under standardization by OASIS, defines a generic and open framework for modeling and accessing stateful resources using Web services (WSRF TC, 2004). It provides a standard based approach for creation, addressing, inspection, and lifetime management of stateful resources. WSRF is a promising approach to virtualization. A WS-Resource is the combination of a Web service and a stateful resource on which it acts, and thus a WS-Resource is a virtualized representation of a stateful resource accessible using Web services. A WS-Resource has various properties. The values of these properties define the state of the resource. A change in the property values would indicate a state change of the resources. WS-RF relies on WS-Addressing, especially, *EndpointReference*, to specify the location of a particular WS-Resource using URI. EndpointReference is a pointer to the Web service associated with the WS-Resource.

As an illustration of virtualization based on WSRF, we consider a physical AGV (Automatic Guided Vehicle) system. An Automated Guided Vehicle system is a material handling system in which driverless, battery-powered carts are moved by means of Laser, Optical or Electronic guidance. The vehicles themselves may be towing vehicles, fork lifts, pallet trucks, or unit load carriers.

When virtualized as Web services, they can offer different views of the AGV, such as Physical, Operational, Performance, and Financial view (Dempsey, 1986). The view represents an abstraction of the physical system (Figure 3). The views of an AGV are defined in WS-ResourceProperty (Graham & Treadwell, 2004). The resource properties document type is associated with the WSDL 1.1 portType definition of a Web service, and thus provides the declaration of the exposed resource properties of the WS-Resource(Graham & Treadwell, 2004). In fact, the declaration of the WS-Resource's property represents a particular view or projection on the WS-Resource's state.

The virtualization takes the following steps.

Step 1. Defining the resource properties

The properties of the AGV system are defined using XML schema. A change in state requires a change in one or more of these property values, and vice-versa (see Box 1).

Step 2. Adding the resource property declaration to WSDL of the Web services

After we've created the representation of the stateful resource (the AGV system in a physical view), we have to tie it to the service using the WSDL file thus to actually create the WS-Resource. Here, the actual stateful resource is added to the WSDL file and associated it with the Web service (see Box 2).

Step 3. Defining the type of the WS-Resource

Next, we then establish the association of the resource properties document with the portType as defined in the WSDL. This association defines the type of the WS-Resource added to the WSDL file (see Box 3).

Notice that the important part of the portType is the wsrp:ResourceProperties attribute. That attribute specifies that any operations that the Web service performs are actually performed on a particular type of AGVsystem resource, as defined by a PhysicalAGVViewProperties element which is defined in the schema. The combination of that stateful resource and that Web service is the *WS-Resource*. As seen from above, this combination actually merged the Web service and (resource) properties into a WSDL file.

Step 4. Create a reference to an actual WS-Resource instance

In order to operate or manipulate on the WS-Resource, we must create a reference to an actual WS-Resource instance in the WSDL file (see Box 4).

Notice the difference of this WSDL file from those WSDL file with no WSResource in that the service returns an *EndpointReference* that points to the newly created WS-Resource.

Step 5. Defining the messages and operations for the Web services

The WSDL description of *message* and *operation* is done similarly to what is done with no WS-Resource.

Step 6. Manipulating the property values

Requesting the value of a property is a simple matter of constructing the appropriate SOAP message. The following shows an example of a basic SOAP message to request the value of the MaximumLoad property (see Box 6)

When the AGVsystem is created, the Web services will return an endpoint reference that point to the newly created WS-Resource. We can take that information and add to the Header of the SOAP message (see Box 7).

The **wsa:Action** element is not part of the original endpoint reference; it changes depending on how it is used. In this case, we're using the

Figure 2. Business process realization via Semantic Web services composition

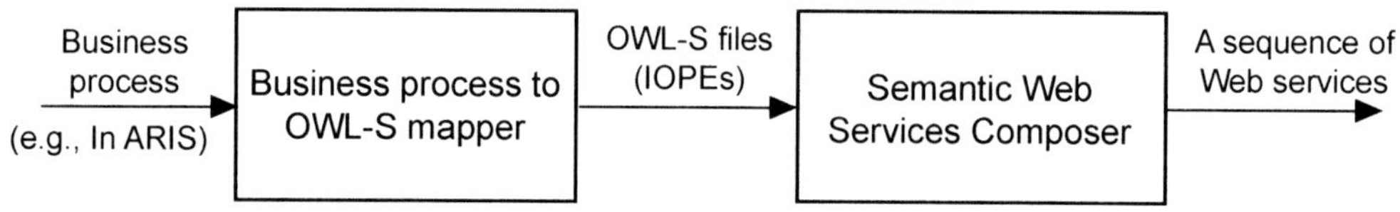

Figure 3. AGV as a WS-Resource

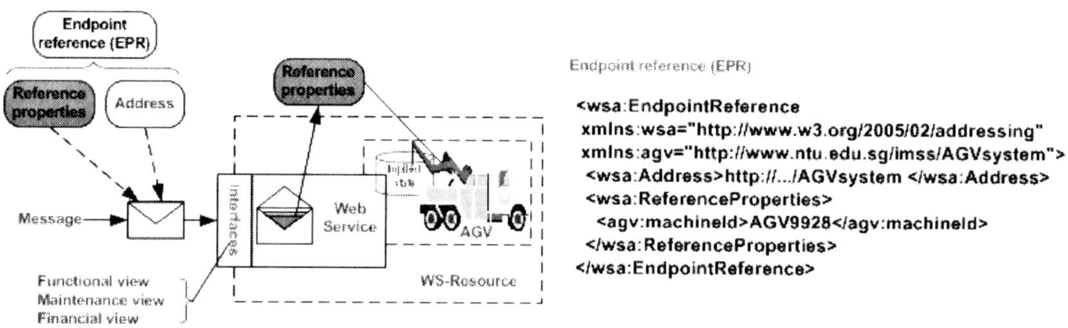

Box 1.

```
<xsd:schema targetNamespace="http://www.ntu.edu.sg/agvviews" ...>
  <!-- Resource properties doc declaration -->
  <xsd:element name="PhysicalAGVViewProperties">
     <xsd:complexType>
            <xsd:sequence>
                   <xsd:element ref="tns:AGVID" />
                   <xsd:element ref="tns:AGVType" />
                   <xsd:element ref="tns:GuidanceType" />
                   <xsd:element ref="tns:LoadHeight" />
                   <xsd:element ref="tns:LoadDiameter" />
                   <xsd:element ref="tns:MaximumLoad" />
                   <xsd:element ref="tns:MinimumLoad" />
                   ...
            </xsd:sequence>
     <xsd:complexType>
```

Box 2.

```
<!-- WSDL for AGV Web services -->
<?xml version="1.0" encoding="UTF-8"?>
<definitions name="AGVsystem" xmlns:tns="http://www.ntu.edu.sg/agvviews"
  xmlns:wsa="http://.../ws/2004/03/addressing"
  xmlns:wsrp="http://.../wsrf-WS-ResourceProperties.xsd" ...>
  <types>
     <xsd:schema
           <!-- property representation above added here-->
           ...
```

Box 3.

```
<!-- Association of resource properties document
  to a portType -->
           <wsdl:portType name="PhysicalAGVView"
                  wsrp:ResourceProperties="tns:PhysicalAGVViewProperties">
                  ...
           </wsdl:portType>
```

GetResourceProperty action. The wsa:To element takes the value from the wsa:Address in the endpoint reference, and any wsa:ReferenceProperty values are included directly in the Header.

WS-RF defines operations that allow you to get and set various resource properties using Web service operations: SetResourceProperties, Update, or remove a property completely, delete, among others.

Once a stateful resource is virtualized as a WS-Resource, we can manipulate the resource using the Web services associated with that resource. Very often, WS-Notification is used to obtain notifications of various events (e.g., state changes). WS-Notification is a family of specifications that define a standard way for Web service clients to *subscribe* to a particular topic and receive notification of various events.

In addition to equipments and machines, other logical resources such as data sources, workflow, applications, and systems can be virtualized in a similar way. Furthermore, we can develop the sophisticated stateful Web services by the sensible use of technologies in these specifications (WS-RF).

A SEMANTIC-RICH ENVIRONMENT

The service-oriented environment can be enhanced with rich semantics using Semantic Web technologies. Two core technologies are crucial for creating semantic rich environments: ontologies (upper ontologies and domain ontologies) and standard languages for developing ontologies.

Manufacturing knowledge exists in all aspects of manufacturing and can be captured at the different levels of generality. The corresponding ontologies typically include *domain ontology, value chain ontology*, and *product life cycle*

Box 4.

```
<types>
     <xsd:schema targetNamespace="..."
     xmlns:xsd="http://www.w3.org/2001/XMLSchema">
     <xsd:import
            namespace = "http://
                     schemas.xmlsoap.org/ws/2004/03/addressing"
            schemaLocation="WS-Addressing.xsd" />
     <xsd:element name="createAGV">
            <xsd:complexType />
     </xsd:element>
     <xsd:element name="createAGVResponse">
            <xsd:complexType>
                   <xsd:sequence>
                          <xsd:element ref=
                                     "wsa:EndpointReference" />
                   </xsd:sequence>
            </xsd:complexType>
     </xsd:element>
     ... ...
```

Box 5.

```
... ...
    <message name="CreateAGVRequest">
           <part name="request" element="tns:createAGV" />
    </message>
    <message name="CreateAGVResponse">
           <part name="response" element="tns:createAGVResponse" />
    </message>
    ... ...

    <portType name="PhysicalAGVView"
           wsrp:ResourceProperties="tns:PhysicalAGVViewProperties">
           <operation name="createAGV">
                  <input message="tns:CreateAGVRequest"
                         wsa:Action="http://.../CreateAGV" />
                  <output message="tns:CreateAGVResponse"
                         wsa:Action="http://.../CreateAGVResponse" />
           </operation>
    </portType>
    ... ...
```

Box 6.

```
<SOAP-ENV:Envelope xmlns:SOAP-ENV="http://.../soap/envelope/"
    xmlns:wsrp="" http://docs.oasis-open.org/wsrf/.../
    wsrf-WSResourceProperties..-01.xsd ">
    <SOAP-ENV:Header>...</SOAP-ENV:Header>
    <SOAP-ENV:Body>
            <wsrp:GetResourceProperty
                    xmlns:agvProp="http://.../AGVsystem">
                    agvProp:MaximumLoad
            </wsrp:GetResourceProperty>
    </SOAP-ENV:Body>
 </SOAP-ENV:Envelope>
```

Box 7.

```
<SOAP-ENV:Envelope xmlns:SOAP-ENV="http://.../soap/envelope/"
    xmlns:wsrp="" http://docs.oasis-open.org/wsrf/.../
                    wsrf-WSResourceProperties..-01.xsd ">
    <SOAP-ENV:Header>
            <wsa:Action>
                    http://..oasis../.../WS-
                            ResourceProperties/GetResourceProperty
            </wsa:Action>
            <wsa:To SOAP-ENV:mustUnderstand="1">
                    http://.../AGVsystem
            </wsa:To>
            <AGVId>
                    SAT9928
                    </AGVIdId>
    </SOAP-ENV:Header>
    <SOAP-ENV:Body>...</SOAP-ENV:Body>
 </SOAP-ENV:Envelope>
```

ontology. A domain ontology classifies the most general information that characterizes an entire domain. For example, a domain ontology would include general information about products, manufacturing techniques and tools, and so forth, applicable across the entire manufacturing domain. A value chain ontology include the general information about entire value chain involved in a certain manufacturing sector (semiconductor, for example). A product life cycle ontology has

Figure 4. OWL-S: an upper ontology for Semantic Markup for Web services

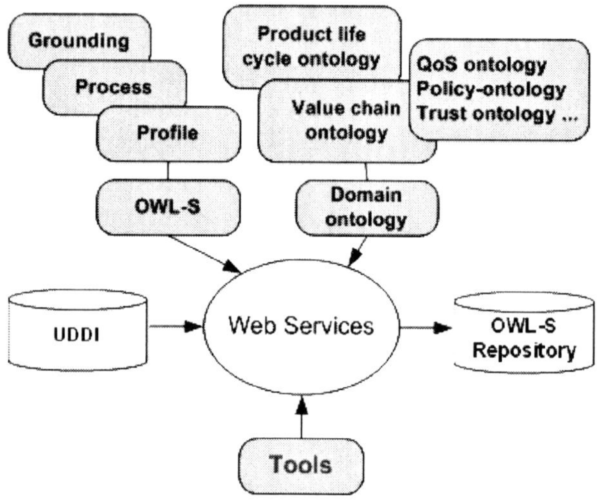

more specific information for a life cycle of a product and covers activities for implementation of production planning and control (product design, process design, layout design, production plan and scheduling plan), including information about all relevant kinds of objects, properties, and relationships for that product.

These manufacturing ontologies are developed using OWL. In order to bring semantics to Web services, a standard approach is to use OWL-S, an OWL-based Web service upper ontology, and domain ontologies (also in OWL) as shown in Figure 4.

CONCLUSION

In this article, we discussed the Web standard-based approach and technologies for constructing a service-oriented manufacturing environment. The service orientation is achieved via *virtualization* using the emerging Web Services Resource Framework (WS-RF). A practical AGV system was used as an illustration example.

We emphasize that the full potential of a service-oriented environment can be further fulfilled if it is enhanced with semantics. The Semantic Web standard based techniques for adding Semantics to Web services and thus creating a semantic rich environment were discussed in the article.

This work is part of ongoing project of enterprise integration which adopts a Semantic Web Services approach (Yang et al., 2005). The key notions of the project are constructing a service-orientation environment via virtualization which is further semantically enhanced using OWL-based domain ontologies and OWL-S service ontology and achieving automated service integration via software agents.

ACKNOWLEDGMENT

This work was supported in part by the Agency for Science, Technology, and Research (A*STAR) of Singapore under SERC TSRP on IMSS Project 0521160070.

REFERENCES

Dempsey, M. C. (1986). *Automated guided vehicle control systems: Design application and selection.* Society of Manufacturing Engineers Publication.

Foster, I., Kesselman, C., Nick, J. M., & Tuecke, S. (2002). Grid services for distributed system integration. *IEEE Computer, 35*(6), 37-46.

Graham, S., Karmarkar, A., Mischkinsky, J., Robinson, I., & Sedukhin, I. (2004).

Web services resource (WS-Resource) V1.2. OASIS.

Graham, S., & Treadwell, J. (Eds.) (2004, 10 June). *Web Services Resource Properties (WS-ResourceProperties) v1.2.* OASIS WSRF TC.

Martin, D., Burstein, M., & *et al.* (2004). *OWL-S: Semantic markup for Web services.* W3C Member Submission by the OWL-S (formerly DAML-S) Coalition.

McGuinness, D. L., & van Harmelen, F. (Eds.). (2004, February 10). *OWL Web ontology language overview* . W3C Recommendation.

Sedukhin, I. (Ed.). (2005, March 9). *Web services distributed management: Management of Web services.* OASIS Standard.

WSRF TC. (2004). *OASIS Web services resource framework (WSRF).* Retrieved from http://www.oasis-open.org/committees/tc home.php?wg abbrev=wsrf

Yang, Z., Gay, R., Miao, C., Zhang, J.-B., & Shen, Z. (2005). Automating integration of manufacturing systems and services. A semantic Web services approach. In *Proceedings of the 31st Annual Conference of the IEEE Industrial Electronics Society.*

Yang, Z., Zhang, J. B., Tao, J., & Gay, R. (2005). Characterizing Services Composeability and OWL-S based services composition. In H. Zhuge & G. Fox (Eds.), *The 4th international conference on grid and cooperative computing (GCC 2005),* Beijing, China (LNCS 3795, pp. 244-249).

This work was previously published in Int. Journal of Information Technology and Web Engineering, Vol. 2, Issue 3, edited by L. Zhang, pp. 53-64, copyright 2007 by IGI Publishing (an imprint of IGI Global).

Chapter XIV
A Survey of Web Service Discovery Systems

Le Duy Ngane
Nanyang Technological University, Singapore

Angela Goh
Nanyang Technological University, Singapore

Cao Hoang Tru
Ho Chi Minh City University of Technology, Viet Nam

ABSTRACT

Web services form the core of e-business and hence, have experienced a rapid development in the past few years. This has led to a demand for a discovery mechanism for Web services. Discovery is the most important task in the Web service model because Web services are useless if they cannot be discovered. A large number of Web service discovery systems have been developed. Universal Description, Discovery and Integration (UDDI) is a typical mechanism that stores indexes to Web services but it does not support semantics. Semantic Web service discovery systems that have been developed include systems that support matching Web services using the same ontology, systems that support matching Web services using different ontologies, and systems that support limitations of UDDI. This paper presents a survey of Web service discovery systems, focusing on systems that support semantics. The paper also elaborates on open issues relating to such discovery systems.

INTRODUCTION

Web service technology enables e-business and e-commerce to become a reality. It has become a competitive tool of companies by reducing cost through fast, effective, and reliable services to customers, suppliers, and partners over the Internet. It enables more efficient business operations via the Web and enhances business opportunities to companies. These are achieved through its support of *discovery, composition, invocation, monitoring,* and so on. A Web service is a software component representing a specific business function that can be described, published, and invoked over the network (typically Internet) using open-standards.

A Web service based on Web Service Description Language (WSDL) (Walsh, 2002) can be termed "non-semantic Web services". However, using WSDL to describe the services only allows them to be accessed by keyword. This limitation prevents fully automatic *discovery, composition, invocation,* and *monitoring.* The reason for this shortcoming is the lack of semantic understanding. To overcome this problem, Web services require a method to incorporate semantics. Just as the Semantic Web is an extension of the current World Wide Web, a semantic Web service is an extension of Web services. It overcomes Web service limitations by using knowledge representation technology from the semantic Web. Specifically, it uses ontologies to describe its service instead of using WSDL. Such ontologies can be understood by machines and can be reasoned upon. This allows a fully automatic *discovery, composition, invocation,* and *monitoring* in Web services.

In a Web service model, a *service provider* offers Web services which provide functions or business operations which can be deployed over the Internet, in the hope that they will be invoked by partners or customers; a Web *service requester* describes requirements in order to locate *service providers.* Publishing, binding, and discovering Web services are three major tasks in the model. Discovery is the process of finding Web services provider locations which satisfy specific requirements. Web services are useless if they cannot be discovered. So, discovery is the most important task in the Web service model.

The greatest difficulty in a Web service discovery mechanism is *heterogeneity* between services (Garofalakis et al., 2004). Heterogeneities include different platforms, different data formats, as well as heterogeneities of ontologies. Regarding ontology heterogeneities, semantic Web services may use different ontologies or different ontologies description language such as OWL, DAML, RDF, and so forth to describe the services. There is also heterogeneity between semantic Web services and non-semantic Web services. Therefore, when developing a discovery system, these heterogeneities should be borne in mind.

A survey of Web service discovery system is needed to explore existing techniques and to highlight the advantages and disadvantages of each system. (Garofalakis et al., 2004) presented a survey on these systems but their work mainly focused on aspects and approaches of Web service architecture and has not paid adequate attention to the usage of semantics. In semantic Web services, the usage of semantics is the most important factor. This article presents a survey of Web service discovery systems which focuses mainly on the use of semantics. In this article, we use the term "non-semantic Web services" to refer to Web services without semantics, whereas the term "Web services" is used in a generic manner to cover both semantic Web services and non-semantic Web services.

The rest of the article is as follows. The second section introduces the background of Web service description languages and the Web services model. The third section introduces a taxonomy of Web services discovery systems. In this section, advantages and disadvantages of each system are highlighted. The fourth section presents the issues related to Web services discovery, followed by the conclusion in the fifth section.

WEB SERVICES DISCOVERY

Web service discovery is widely used in workflow, e-learning, and e-business systems such as e-supply chain, e-manufacturing, and so forth. Non-semantic Web services can be discovered using UDDI (Walsh, 2002). UDDI is an industry specification for describing, publishing, and finding Web services. It allows developers to describe and classify their services, and the technical details about the interfaces of the Web services which are exposed. UDDI also enables developers to consistently discover services, or interfaces of a particular type, classification, or function. It also defines a set of Application Programming Interfaces (APIs) that developers can use in order to interact with UDDI data directly. The UDDI scheme uses *White, Yellow,* and *Green pages* as data categories. *White pages* store basic contact information about an advertised company. *Yellow pages* store industry classification. *Green pages* provide technical information on the behavior and supported functions of a business service hosted by a business.

Semantic Web service discovery systems have been developed to discover semantic Web services. To be discovered, Web services must be described by Web service description languages. This section introduces Web service description languages, followed by the Web service model and several categories of discovery systems.

Web Service Description Languages

WSDL is used to describe non-semantic Web services. Ontologies and features such as service name, service description in text, and so forth, are used to describe semantic Web service. The following is an introduction to WSDL and semantic Web description languages.

WSDL: A Non Semantic Web Description Language

Web Service Description Language (WSDL) (Walsh, 2002) is a standard to describe how to access a non-Web service and what operations (methods) it performs. It is also used to locate Web services when a service requester and provider use WSDL to describe the service. A WSDL document defines a Web service using four major elements, namely, port, message, types, and binding. An elaboration of these elements is as follows:

1. **WSDL Ports:** The <portType> is the most important element in WSDL. It defines a Web service with operations that can be performed and messages that are involved. The <portType> element is similar to a function library (or a module, or a class) in a traditional programming language.
2. **WSDL Messages:** The <message> element defines an abstract, typed definition of the data being communicated. Each message can consist of one or more logical parts like parameters of a function call in a traditional programming language.
3. **WSDL Types:** The <types> element defines a container for data type definitions that are relevant for the exchanged messages. For maximum interoperability and platform neutrality, WSDL uses XML Schema syntax to define data types.
4. **WSDL Bindings:** The <binding> element defines a concrete protocol and data format specification for a particular port type.

Semantic Web Service Description Languages

Semantic Web services use ontologies to describe their services. OWL-S, DAML-S, and RDFS are examples of semantic Web services description languages which use OWL, DAML, and RDF

Figure 1. Top level of the service ontology

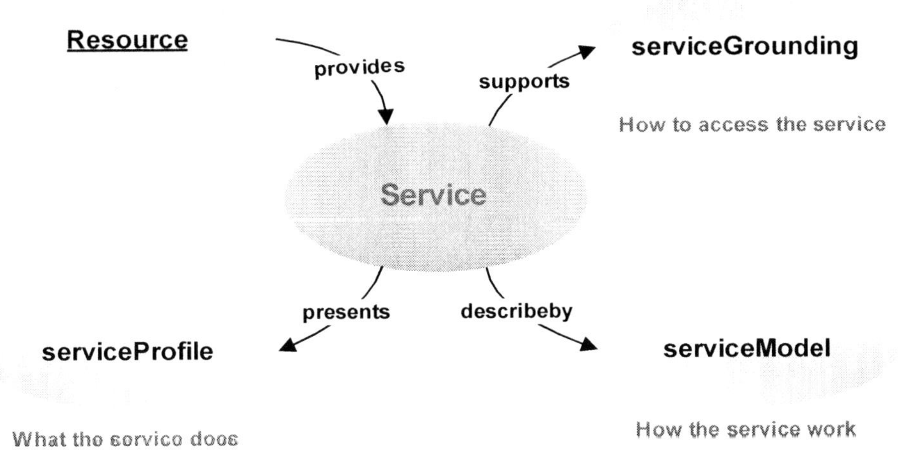

ontology respectively to describe their services. DAML-S and OWL-S which are widely used Web service description languages include *Service* class and three sub-classes, namely, *serviceProfile*, *serviceModel*, and *serviceGrounding* (Figure 1).

Matching uses only *ServiceProfile* because it contains the description of the service to be discovered. The *ServiceProfile* represents the service through class *Profile*. A class *Profile* has three basic types of information, namely, contact information, functional description of the service, and additional properties.

The contact information is meant for human users. It includes *serviceName* which is the name of the service, and *contactInformation* which shows the address, telephone number, and so forth, of the owner of the service. The *textDescription* provides a brief description of the service. It summarizes what the service offers, or describes what service is requested. In discovery, *textDescription* of the Web service provider and requester is checked to determine if two services have a common description. If such a commonality exists, it implies that the provider is able to meet the requester's need.

The functional description of the service is the most important declaration in the *Profile* that is used for matching. It specifies the parameters comprising the *inputs, outputs, preconditions,* and *effects* of the service. The *inputs* are parameters required by the service and the *outputs* are the parameters which are generated by the service. The *precondition* indicates the condition necessary before execution of the service and the *effect* is the condition after execution of the service. For example, to invoke a Web service to buy a computer and pay via credit card, the input is price, the output is the computer configuration, the precondition is that the credit card must be valid, and the effect is that the credit card must be charged. Additional properties which describe features of the service are *serviceParameter, qualityRating, serviceCategory,* and so forth. The Profile also declares an operation of the Web service.

Web Service Model

The Web service model in figure 2 shows the interaction between a service requester, service providers, and a service discovery system.

Figure2. Web service model

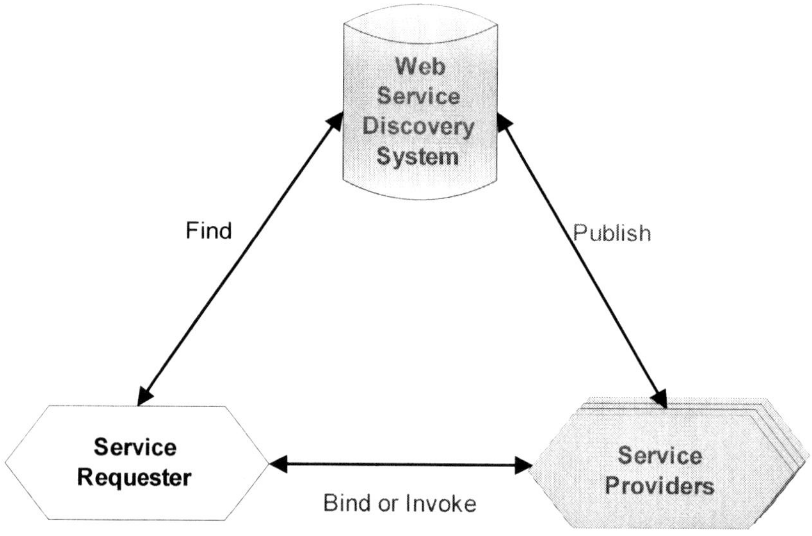

- The service providers offer Web services which provide functions or business operations. They are created by companies or organizations. In order to be invoked, the Web services must be described. This will facilitate discovery and composition. WSDL or service profile of semantic Web service is used to carry out this function.
- The Web service requester describes requirements in order to locate service providers. Service requesters usually contain a description of the Web service, though it is not a Web service which can run on the Internet. The requirements are usually described by WSDL, service template or service profile.
- The Web service discovery or service registry is a broker that provides registry and search functions. The service providers advertise their service information in the discovery system. This information will be stored in the registry and will be searched when there is a request from service requester. UDDI is used as a registry standard for non-semantic Web service. Semantic Web service discovery systems are developed for semantic Web services.

The above three components interact with each other via publishing, discovery, and binding operations. These operations are elaborated upon as follows:

1. **Publish:** the Web service providers publish their service information through the discovery system for requesters to discover. Through the publishing operation, the Web service provider stores the service description in the discovery system.
2. **Discovery:** the Web service requesters retrieve service providers from the service registry. Based on service descriptions, which describes the requirements of the Web service requesters, the discovery system will output a list of Web service providers which satisfy the requirements.
3. **Bind:** After discovering, the discovery system provides a number of Web service providers. The Web service requester invokes these Web service providers. The binding

occurs at runtime. The Web service requesters and Web service providers will communicate via SOAP protocol (W3C; Walsh, 2002) which is an XML based protocol for Web service exchange information.

Category of Web Service Discovery Systems

There are many ways to categorize Web services discovery systems. Depending on various view points, they can be categorized as follows: distributed systems, supporting QoS systems, or applying fuzzy logic to the systems. Details of each category are given in the following subsections.

Distributed Discovery Systems

While Web services have provided distributed operation execution, most discovery systems are still based on centralized registries. However, as the number of Web services grows rapidly, a single point failure and performance bottleneck result in centralized registries becoming impractical. To overcome the disadvantages of the centralized systems, a large number of decentralized solutions based on P2P technologies have been proposed. Most of the systems build on P2P network use ontologies to publish and discover the Web services descriptions. Some typical systems are found in (Gagnes et al., 2006; Y. Li et al., 2006; Wu et al., 2005; Yu et al., 2004a, 2004b). These systems present approaches for distributed Web services organization by combining the capabilities of semantic Web services with the dynamics and real-time search capabilities of peer to peer (P2P) networks. They use category ontology to organize services based on semantic classification of domains.

QoS Discovery Systems

Web service discovery can be divided into two phases. The first phase is matching functional aspects of the Web service such as input, output, precondition, effect, operation … and so forth. The output of the first phase may be many advertised Web service that satisfy the requirement. To reduce the number of advertised Web service providers and to find the most appropriate service, the second phase uses QoS. QoS refers to *Quality of Service* which considers availability,

Figure 3. Taxonomy of Web service discovery systems

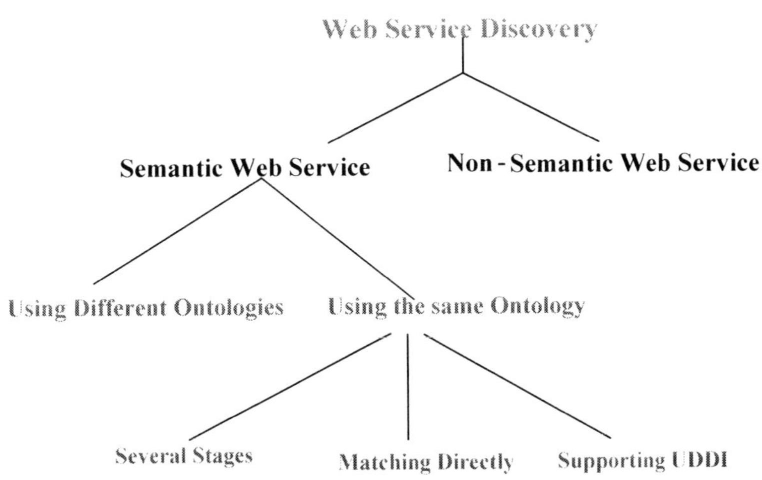

accessibility, integrity, performance, reliability, regulatory, and security. Several discovery systems supporting QoS have been developed such as (Frolund & Koistinen, 1998; Hondo & Kaler, 2002; Ludwig, 2003; Sahai et al., 2002; Zhou et al., 2005a, 2005b; Zinky et al., 1997).

Applying Fuzzy Logic to Discovery

Since the model-theoretic semantics of the languages used in the Semantic Web are crisp, the need to extend them to represent fuzzy data arises, (Chao et al., 2005; Huang et al., 2005; Recuerda & Robertson, 2005) (Mazzieri & Dragoni, 2005; Stoilos et al., 2005). As ontology languages are based on Description Logics which lack the ability to encode and reason with imprecise knowledge, (Stoilos et al., 2005) extended the DL language with fuzzy set theory and provided sound and complete reasoning algorithms for the extended language.

In semantic Web service, the method of using semantics is the most important factor. Therefore, the survey of discovery systems focuses on the use of semantics in Web service discovery systems.

A TAXONOMY OF WEB SERVICES DISCOVERY SYSTEMS

This section contains a survey of Web service discovery systems which focuses on methods using semantics. A taxonomy of Web service discovery systems is introduced. The survey also compares different systems to highlight the advantages and disadvantages of each system.

Introduction to the Taxonomy

Figure 3 presents a taxonomy of Web service discovery systems, which can be divided into systems for matching semantic Web services and systems for matching non-semantic Web services. The semantic Web service discovery systems include systems that support matching Web services using different ontologies and systems that support matching Web services using the same ontology. There are three main approaches for matching semantic Web services using the same ontology, namely, dividing matching process into several stages, matching two profiles directly and supporting UDDI.

The system described by (Liang et al.) is an example of non-semantic Web service discovery system. The authors introduced a system that can provide semi-automatic discovery and composition by indexing service advertisements. Currently, most systems use UDDI for discovering such services which are usually described in WSDL. Furthermore, these services use WSDL to register in UDDI. UDDI finds the service providers based on WSDL. The shortcoming of this system is a lack of semantic understanding. This shortcoming has been explained in earlier sections.

Semantic Web services overcome the mismatch of Web services. This is done by adding more information to the Web service descriptions.

Discovery of Semantic Web Services Using the Same Ontology

Almost all Web service discovery systems that support matching Web services assume the same ontology is used. Some systems divide the matching into several stages; others match two service profiles directly, while some support UDDI.

Direct Matching

This category of semantic Web services discovery systems matches two service description "profiles" directly instead of dividing the matching into several stages. As mentioned in the second section, the service profile consists of information about the services for matching purpose. In these systems, users are not permitted to manage the degree of similarity of matching. Direct matching systems are accurate but are time-consuming. Furthermore, they do not allow users to manage the trade-off between performance and quality of matching which is the most important characteristic of internet application.

InfoSleuth (Bayardo et al., 1997; Helal, 1997) is one of the earliest matching agent system. The matching agent enables the querying agent to locate all available agents that provide appropriate services. It supports syntactic and semantic matchmaking. In InfoSleuth, the service capability information is written in LDL++ (Hsu & Zaniolo, 1993; Shaw et al., 1993), a logic deduction language. Agents use a set of LDL++ deductive rules to support inferences about whether an expression of requirements matches a set of advertised capabilities. The system provides syntactic and semantic matching. However, LDL++ is outdated and limited in its expressivity. LDL++ is not a standard supported by W3C. At the point of its development, OWL-S and DAML-S which are currently emergent Web services description language were unavailable. Therefore, InfoSleuth does not support matching Web services using OWL-S and DAML-S.

Similarly, (Trastour et al., 2001) did not use DAML-S or OWL-S for describing Web services because their work was carried out before the existence of these languages. Therefore, they developed their own specification for Web services description by converting services to RDF graph. Services are nodes of the graph. Two nodes are considered matched if one node is a subtype of the other. Trastour et al. extended this work by using DAML+OIL as the Web description language (Castillo et al., 2001). The matching is based on the subsumption relationship to find matches between concepts. DL (Description Logic) reasoner is used to determine the similarity between concepts. The system has the drawback that it only considers the relationship between direct sub-concepts and super-concepts. It does not consider the relationship between concepts that are more distantly related.

Benatallah et al. (2005) present an approach for Web service discovery based on Description Logic. They formalized service discovery based on rewriting concepts using terminologies. This is called the *best covering problem*. They presented a formalization of the *best covering problem* in the framework of DL-based ontologies and proposed a hypergraph-based algorithm to effectively compute best covers of a given request. In this system, matchmaking is based on DAML-S. Similarly, Li and Horrocks (2003) developed a framework for matching Web service based on DAML-S. Their Matchmaker uses Racer (Haarslev & Möller, 2001) as DL (Description Logic) reasoner to determine the semantic match between services. It tries to match two profiles of the requested service and advertised service, instead of dividing the matching into several stages. As mentioned in the second section, the service profile is part of any Web service description language and includes information such as input, output, precondition, effect, user information, and so forth. Therefore, without dividing the matching into several stages, it will be difficult for these systems to automate reasoning techniques to compute semantic matching and the matching will be inefficient.

Web service modeling ontology (WSMO) provides a conceptual model for service discovery that exploits WSMO formal descriptions of goals and Web services. WSMO Discovery Engine (Roman et al., 2004) can match WSMO goals, and hence, Web services requester description against Web service provider's description. The advantages are that WSMO can be described semantically. However, WSMO is not a standard of W3C and the current version only supports goal matching.

Dividing the Matching Process into Several Stages

The challenge of dynamic matchmaking in the Internet is to optimize the trade-off between performance and quality of matching. Complex matching has to be restricted to allow meaningful semantic matches of requests and advertisements in a reasonable time. Direct matching systems are accurate but time-consuming. They do not allow users to manage the trade-off between performance and quality of matching. To overcome this, some systems divide the matching process into several stages. Systems that divide the matching process into stages include TU-Berlin (Jaeger et al.), LARKS (Sycara et al., 1999a, 1999b; Sycara et al., 2002), and the Matchmaker from the collaboration between Toshiba and Carnegie Mellon University (Kawamura et al., 2003, 2004).

As heterogeneous Web services use different description languages to describe the services and do not understand each other across distributed networks, the LARKS (Language for Advertisement and Request for Knowledge Sharing) project (Sycara et al., 1999a, 1999b; Sycara et al., 2002) defined an expressive common language called ACDL (Agent Capability Description Language). The LARKS matching agent uses this language to match Web services requesters with Web service providers. It includes five different filters, namely, context matching, word frequency profile comparison, similarity matching, signature matching, and constraint matching. Each filter has different functions. LARKS is expressive and capable of supporting inferences. Its knowledge is specified as local ontologies in the concept language ITL. It supports matching syntactical and semantic similarity among Web services by using techniques from information retrieval and AI. It also allows users to restrict the result of matching. However, all services in LARKS must be described in ACDL which is not a standard and is quite difficult to write. Furthermore, LARKS does not support other commonly used Web service description languages such as DAML-S and OWL-S.

(Paolucci et al., 2002) have developed an algorithm for matching semantic Web services using DAML-S. Their work considers only input and output matching. Input and output are concepts based on an ontology. Therefore, the similarity of input, output matching is treated as the similarity of concepts from the same ontology. Paolucci et al. defined four levels of similarity: exact, plug in, subsumes, and fail. This definition is based on concepts that have a direct relationship: sub-concept or super-concept. Matching two concepts should also include the properties of the two concepts. It should consider general and specific concepts when these concepts are not related directly as sub-concept or super-concept. It also should consider syntactic matching which is based on service name and description of the service.

The semantic Web service matching system from the collaboration between Toshiba and Carnegie Mellon University (Kawamura et al., 2003, 2004) is based on LARKS and the algorithm from (Paolucci et al., 2002). To overcome the drawback that requires ADCL, the system supports semantic Web services which are described in RDFS, DAML-S, and OWL-S. Similar to LARKS, the system provides a set of filters and allows users to configure these filters to achieve the desired tradeoff between performance and matching quality. There are four filters which are independent of each other. These are Namespace Filter, Text Filter, I/O Type Filter, and Constraint Filter. The system can be installed as an add-on to UDDI; therefore, it supports matching of both semantic Web services and non-semantic Web services. When it receives a request for a service, it performs the matching process. If it receives a non-semantic Web service request, it redirects the request to UDDI to perform the matching process.

The Matchmaker from TU-Berlin (Jaeger et al.) is a good example of a matching algorithm which is divided into four stages. The four stages are input matching, output matching, profile matching, and user-defined matching. By dividing the matching algorithm, the Matchmaker not only avoids the drawback in the system by (L. Li & Horrocks, 2003) but also helps users to choose the degree of matching from each stage in order to control the number of results and accuracy. An earlier version supported matching DAML-S semantic Web services while the current version supports matching OWL-S semantic Web services. The user-defined matching stage allows users to describe more constraints to restrict the number of results and to increase the accuracy of the results. However, the system is too simplistic. It only presents a demonstration of matching two Web services; it is not really a discovery system since it does not store the advertisement into a database. It is also very difficult for users to utilize user-defined matching. With user-defined matching, the user must define their rules and constraints without user-friendly graphical user-interfaces.

Supporting UDDI

Using UDDI for discovery has limitations. UDDI uses XML to describe its data model. XML's lack of explicit semantics proves to be an additional barrier to the UDDI's discovery mechanism. To overcome this problem, some projects add semantics to UDDI, for example, by including semantic Web service profile. The project from Carnegie Mellon (Srinivasan et al., 2004) is a typical example. It has added OWL-S profile to UDDI. Kawamura et al. (Kawamura et al., 2003, 2004) added advertising WSDL to UDDI and advertising DAML-S profile to its Matchmaker. If the requested Web services use WSDL, the discovery system will access UDDI to look for suitable service providers. Otherwise, the discovery system will revert to the Matchmaker. By combining the Matchmaker and UDDI, the system can support matching both semantic and non-semantic Web services, but in a separate manner. In other words, the two types of Web services are not considered as alternatives to each other. Matches are to either semantic or non-semantic Web services. Another example is from (Sivashanmugam et al., 2003) who have added semantics to WSDL using DAML+OIL ontologies. It also uses UDDI to store these semantics and searches for Web services based on these semantics. By adding semantics to WSDL and UDDI, the project in (Sivashanmugam et al., 2003) achieves sufficient expressiveness to automate the discovery process.

The registration and discovery with UDDI is based on a centralized design whereas Web service providers developed their own stores called private registries. As Web services support distributed operation execution, this has led to a demand to combine UDDI registry with private registries. (Thaden et al., 2003) have developed a distributed peer-to-peer infrastructure. They created a virtual global registry by connecting all private registries in a P2P network. Furthermore, they also used DAML-S to enhance semantic search capabilities.

The advantages and disadvantages of the three methods that use the same ontology are summarized in Table 1.

Discovery of Web Services Using Different Ontologies

The above mentioned Web service discovery systems only support matching Web services requesters and Web services providers who use the same ontology. This assumption implies that if different ontologies are used, matching cannot be carried out. This is a major limitation since Web services are heterogeneous, autonomous, and developed independently. It is necessary to discover Web services that are based on different ontologies.

Cardoso and Sheth in "Semantic e-Workflow Composition" (Cardoso & Sheth, 2003) have addressed this problem. The system supports syntactic matching, quality of service (QoS) match-

Table 1. Advantages and disadvantages of three approaches to semantic Web discovery based on the same ontology

Systems	Advantages	Disadvantages
Matching Directly	+ Matches all information of the two Web services.	- Consumes much time to match all information of the two Web services. - Does not support user-definition in each part of matching (e.g. input, output matching, etc).
Divide the matching process into several stages	+ Can specify the degree of the similarity. + Can define more constraints to enhance the result.	- Some information of Web service may not be matched; therefore, the accuracy may be lower than direct matching.
Supporting UDDI	+ Can support both semantic matching and non-semantic matching.	- Enhancing semantics to UDDI but not to a full extent.

ing, and semantic matching. Syntactic matching involves computing the syntactic similarity of Web services requesters and Web services providers based on their service names and service descriptions. They use "string-matching" as a way to calculate how closely service names and service descriptions of the two semantic Web services resemble each other. QoS is used to match Web services requesters and Web services providers based on three important QoS factors, namely, time, cost and reliability. Semantic matching is computed relying on concepts and their properties. Property matching is based on domain, name, and range of properties.

However, the system is a part of a work-flow project (Cardoso & Sheth, 2003). Therefore, this discovery system has been developed mainly to support the project. So, it is limited as a discovery system. It supports user defined degree of similarity but it does not allow users to declare more rules or constraints to restrict the matching result. Semantic matching based on only concepts, and their properties is insufficient. It must also include the sub-concept, super-concept, and properties of these concepts. The context of concepts also should be considered. Moreover, it is unclear how to determine whether two ontologies are the same or different.

Oundhankar et al. (2005) presented an extension of the algorithm in (Cardoso & Sheth, 2003) with two new measures: context and coverage similarity. The discovery technique is based on METEOR-S (Patil et al., 2004) which is a Web service discovery infrastructure. This infrastructure provides a facility to access registries that are divided based on business domains and grouped into federations. The discovery algorithm used input, output of Web services for matching. The matching is divided into *syntactic* and *semantic* matching. The syntactic matching is similar to Cardoso's work which uses n-gram (Angell & Freund, 1983; Salton, 1988; Zamora et al., 1981) technology. But in semantic matching, the algorithm improved Cardoso's work by considering the context and the coverage information of concepts.

By considering the concept and the coverage information of the matched concepts, the algorithm is able to find good matches and eliminate false matches. Moreover, based on METEOR-S, indexing and retrieving information in the registries is facilitated. However, the system does not allow users to intervene during the matching process. It also does not allow users to define more rules or constraints to restrict the matching result. This will be a significant problem since the number of Web services from matching arising is huge. Furthermore, the approach to measure coverage similarity is incomplete since it is only based on similarity and disjointness relationship.

Similarly, (Le & Goh, 2005; Le et al., 2005; Le et al., 2006) proposed an algorithm to support matching Web services that use both the same ontology as well as different ontologies. The system improves previous work by checking the relationship between ontologies before the matching process. If the two ontologies are related, the concept similarity is computed as they are in the same ontology. The two ontologies are related if they are formed from an original ontology. Otherwise, they are computed as in different ontologies. For different ontologies, the concept similarity is computed based on five similarity dimensions, namely, syntactic, properties, neighborhood, domain, and equivalent similarity. With the five dimensions, the system improves matching and avoids mismatch.

WEB SERVICES DISCOVERY ISSUES

This section introduces three Web service discovery issues. They are: matching semantic Web services against non-semantic Web services, matching semantic Web services using different description languages, and matching semantic Web services using different ontologies.

Matching Semantic Web Services Against Non-Semantic Web Services

As mentioned in earlier sections, UDDI and some systems have been developed for matching non-semantic Web services. They support searching by service names and service categories. They also support matching by inputs and outputs but are not based on semantics. The development of semantic Web services has led to discovery mechanisms for semantic Web services. Some semantic Web services discovery systems have been developed to meet this need. However, these systems only search for semantic Web services, and not non-semantic Web services. In short, we lack systems which can support matching both semantic Web services and non-semantic Web services.

For example, company A, developed Web services to sell computers online. At that time, semantic Web service technology was not available. Hence, WSDL was employed to describe the services. Another company B, which is interested in purchasing computers, started recently. It developed an ontology in OWL and uses OWL-S to describe their request services. Company A is able to provide services to company B. However, with the current Web service discovery, company A cannot be found to match the requirement of the company B because they use different Web service discovery languages: company A uses non-semantic Web services description language while company B uses semantic Web services description language.

Matching Semantic Web Services that Use Different Description Languages

Semantic Web services have developed very rapidly because of their contribution to e-business and e-commerce applications. There are a large number of semantic Web services based on different description languages, including DAML-S, OWL-S, WSMO, and so forth. Existing semantic Web services discovery mechanisms support matching based on specific description languages but they cannot perform matching on different description languages.

Suppose a Web service uses OWL-S to describe the service. Another service uses DAML-S to describe the service. OWL-S uses OWLJessKB as a reasoner while DAML-S uses DAMLJessKB as a reasoner. The service provider which is described by OWL-S can meet the requirements of a Web service requester which is described by DAML-S. However, these two services cannot be matched using current semantic Web services discovery systems because the two different reasoners do not interact with each other.

Matching Web Services Using Different Ontologies

Current discovery systems are adequate when the Web service requester and provider use the same ontology and reasoner to determine the relationship between two services. Unfortunately, most of them do not support the situation where a Web service requester and provider use different ontologies. Only one group from University of Georgia (Cardoso & Sheth, 2003; Oundhankar et al., 2005) has addressed this problem. However, there are short-comings which were mentioned in the third section. These drawbacks should be addressed. In the real world where the Web service requester and provider operate independently, each defines their own ontologies to describe their services. However, a Web service provider can provide an exact service to the requester even though both services use different ontologies. Therefore, a discovery system that supports Web services using distinct ontologies is necessary. This is an emergent research issue that has yet to be addressed.

Consider the following scenario: Some companies in Singapore provide computer solution services. They define their own ontology in the computer domain to describe their services. A company in Vietnam wishes to buy a computer and it defines its own ontology in the same computer domain to describe its services. There are no global ontologies in the domain and the provider and the requester do not know each other. So, though the two ontologies are within the same domain, they are basically different. Current discovery systems are unable to match the Web service requester and provider in such a situation, but obviously, the providers can provide an exact fit to the requester's demands.

CONCLUSION

The chapter presented a survey of Web services discovery systems which focuses on methods of using semantics. A taxonomy of discovery systems was introduced. The advantages and disadvantages of various systems were highlighted. There are two categories of the discovery systems that cater to semantic Web services and non-semantic Web services respectively. UDDI is a typical registry and discovery system for non-semantic Web services. For semantic Web services, the systems can be categorized as systems that support matching based on the same ontology or on different ontololgies. In systems supporting the same ontology, we can further classify them as systems that divide matching process into several stages, matching directly two Web service profiles, or supporting UDDI.

Three open issues arising from current Web service discovery systems have been introduced, namely, matching semantic Web services against non-semantic Web services, matching semantic Web services using different description languages, and matching semantic Web services using distinct ontologies. A new Web services discovery mechanism is required to overcome the three shortcomings. When designing a Web service discovery system, the main problem of dynamic matchmaking in the Internet, namely the trade-off between performance and quality of matching should be borne in mind. The heterogeneities of Web service also should be considered.

REFERENCES

Angell, R., & Freund, G. (1983). Automatic spelling correction using a trigram similarity measure. *Information Processing and Management, 19*(4), 255-161.

Bayardo, R., W, B., R, B., A, C., G, F., A, H., et al. (1997). *Semantic integration of information in open and dynamic environments.* Paper presented at the Proceedings of the 1997 ACM International Conference on the Management of Data (SIGMOD).

Benatallah, B., Hacid, M.-S., Leger, A., Rey, C., & Toumani, F. (2005). On automating Web services discovery. *The VLDB Journal—The International Journal on Very Large Data Bases, 14*(1), 84-96. Springer-Verlag New York.

Cardoso, J., & Sheth, A. (2003). Semantic e-Workflow Composition. *Journal of Intelligent Information Systems, 21*(3), 191-225. Kluwer Academic Publishers

Castillo, J. G., Trastour, D., & Bartolini, C. (2001). *Desctiption Logics for Matchmaking of Services.* Paper presented at the Paper presented at the Workshop on Application of Description Logic.

Chao, K.-M., Younas, M., Lo, C.-C., & Tan, T.-H. (2005). *Fuzzy Matchmaking for Web Services.* Paper presented at the WAMIS Workshop, Tamkang University, Taiwan.

Frolund, S., & Koistinen, J. (1998). QML: A Language for Quality of Service Specification. *Technical report HPL on HP Laboratories.*

Gagnes, T., Plagemann, T., & Munthe-Kaas, E. (2006). *A Conceptual Service Discovery Architecture for Semantic Web Services in Dynamic Environments.* Paper presented at the The 22nd International Conference on Data Engineering, Georgia, USA.

Garofalakis, J., Panagis, Y., Sakkopoulos, E., & Tsakalidis, A. (2004). *Web Service Discovery Mechanisms: Looking for a Needle in a Haystack?* Paper presented at the International Workshop on Web Engineering.

Haarslev, V., & Möller, R. (2001). *RACER System Description.* Paper presented at the the First International Joint Conference on Automated Reasoning.

Helal, A. (1997). InfoSleuth: Agent-based Semantic Integration of Information in Open and Dynamic Environments. In M. Huhns & M. Singh (Eds.), *Readings in Agents*: Morgan Kaufman.

Hondo, M., & Kaler, C. (2002). Web Services Policy Framework (WSPolicy) Version 1.0. Available at http://www.verisign.com/wss/WS-Policy.pdf

Hsu, P.-Y., & Zaniolo, C. (1993). *A new User's Impressions on LDL++ and CORAL.* Paper presented at the Workshop on Programming with Logic Databases (Informal Proceedings).

Huang, C.-L., Chao, K.-M., & Lo, C.-C. (2005). *A Moderated Fuzzy Matchmaking for Web Services.* Paper presented at the The 5th International Conference on Computer and Information Technology (CIT2005), Shanghai, China.

Jaeger, M. C., Tang, S., & Liebetruth, C., *The TUB OWL-S Matcher.*

Kawamura, T., Blasio, J. D., Hasegawa, T., Paolucci, M., & Sycara, K. (2003). *Preliminary Report of Public Experiment of Semantic Service Matchmaker with UDDI Business Register.* Paper presented at the 1st International Conference on Service Oriented Computing (ICSOC 2003), Trento, Italy.

Kawamura, T., Blasio, J. D., Hasegawa, T., Paolucci, M., & Sycara, K. (2004). *Public Deployment of Semantic Service Matchmaker with UDDI Business Registry.* Paper presented at the 3rd International Semantic Web Conference (ISWC 2004).

Le, D. N., & Goh, A. (2005). *Matching Semantic Web Services Using Different Ontologies.* Paper presented at the ICWE 2005, Sydney, Australia.

Le, D. N., Goh, A., & Tru, C. H. (2005). *Multi-Ontology Matchmaker.* Paper presented at the 7th International conference on Information Integration and Web Based Applications and Services (iiWAS2005), Malaysia.

Le, D. N., Hang, T. M., & Goh, A. (2006). *MOD-A Multi Ontology Discovery system.* Paper presented at the International Workshop on Semantic Matchmaking and Resource Retrieval, Seoul, Korea.

Li, L., & Horrocks, I. (2003). *A software framework for matchmaking based on semantic Web technology.* Paper presented at the 12th International World Wide Web Conference, Budapest, Hungary.

Li, Y., Su, S., & Yang, F. (2006). *A Peer-to-Peer Approach to Semantic Web Services Discovery.* Paper presented at the Computational Science – ICCS 2006: 6th International Conference, Reading, UK.

Liang, Q., Chakarapani, L. N., Su, S. Y. W., Chikkamagalur, R. N., & Lamr, H. (2004). A Semi-automatic approach to composite Web services discovery, description and invocation. *International Journal of Web Services Research, 1*(4), 64–89. Idea Group Publishing.

Ludwig, H. (2003). Web Service Level Agreement (WSLA) Language Specification Version 1.0. *Techincal report in IBM.*

Mazzieri, M., & Dragoni, A. F. (2005). *A Fuzzy Semantics for Semantic Web Languages.* Paper presented at the Proceedings of the ISWC Workshop on Uncertainty Reasoning for the Semantic Web, Galway, Ireland.

Oundhankar, S., Verma, K., Sivashanugam, K., Sheth, A., & Miller, J. (2005). Discovery of Web serivces in a Muti-Ontologies and Federated Registry Environment. *International Journal of Web Services Research, 1*(3).

Paolucci, M., Kawamura, T., Payne, T. R., & Sycara, K. (2002). *Semantic Matching of Web services Capabilities.* Paper presented at the 1st International Semantic Web Conference (ISWC 2002), Sardinia, Italy.

Patil, A., Oundhakar, S., Sheth, A., & Verma, K. (2004). *METEOR-S Web service Annotation Framework.* Paper presented at the Proceeding of the World Wide Web Conference.

Recuerda, F. M., & Robertson, D. (2005). *Discovery and Uncertainty in Semantic Web Services.* Paper presented at the Proceedings of the International Semantic Web Conference (ISWC 2005), Workshop 3: Uncertainty Reasoning for the Semantic Web, Galway, Ireland.

Roman, D., Lausen, H., & Keller, U. (2004). *Web Service Modeling Ontology - Standard (WSMO - Standard), WSMO deliverable D2 version 1.1.*

Sahai, A., Durante, A., & Machiraju, V. (2002). Towards Automated SLA Management for Web Services. *Technical report HPL-2001-310 (R.1) on HP Laboratories*

Salton, G. (1988). *Automatic Text Processing: The Transformation, Analysis and Retrieval of Information by Computer*: Massachusetts.

Shaw, S., Foggiato-Bish, L., Garcia, I., Tillman, G., Tryon, D., Wood, W., et al. (1993). *Improving Data Quality Via LDL++.* Paper presented at the Workshop on Programming with Logic Databases (Informal Proceedings).

Sivashanmugam, K., Verma, K., Sheth, A., & Miller, J. (2003). *Adding Semantics to Web Services Standards.* Paper presented at the The 2003 International Conference on Web Services (ICWS'03), Erfurt, Germany.

Srinivasan, N., Paolucci, M., & Sycara, K. (2004, 6-9). *Adding OWL-S to UDDI, implementation and throughput.* Paper presented at the First International Workshop on Semantic Web Services and Web Process Composition (SWSWPC 2004), San Diego, California, USA.

Stoilos, G., Stamou, G., Tzouvaras, V., Pan, J., & Horrocks, I. (2005). *The Fuzzy Description Logic f-SHIN.* Paper presented at the Proceedings of the ISWC Workshop on Uncertainty Reasoning for the Semantic Web, Galway, Ireland.

Sycara, K., J. Lu, M. K., & Widoff, S. (1999a). Dynamic service matchmaking among agents in open information environments. *ACM SIGMOD Record (Special Issue on Semantic Interoperability in Global Information Systems), 28*(1), 47-53.

Sycara, K., J. Lu, M. K., & Widoff, S. (1999b). *Matchmaking among heterogeneous agents on the internet.* Paper presented at the AAAI Spring Symposium on Intelligent Agents in Cyberspace.

Sycara, K., Widoff, S., & M. Klusch, J. L. (2002). *LARKS: Dynamic Matchmaking Among Heterogeneous Software Agents in Cyberspace.* Paper presented at the Autonomous Agents and Multi-Agent Systems.

Thaden, U., Siberski, W., & Nejdl, W. (2003). *A Semantic Web based Peer-to-Peer Service Registry Network* (Technical Report): Learning Lab Lower Saxony.

Trastour, D., Bartolini, C., & Gonzalez-Castillo, J. (2001). *A Semantic Web Approach to Service Description for Matchmaking of Service.* Paper presented at the 1st Semantic Web Working Symposium, CA.

W3C. Organization, *SOAP - Simple Object Access Protocol.*

Walsh, A. E. (2002). *UDDI, SOAP, and WSDL: The Web Services Specification Reference Book* (1st edition ed.) 0130857262: Pearson Education.

Wu, H., Jin, H., Li, Y., & Chen, H. (2005). *An Approach for Service Discovery Based on Semantic Peer-to-Peer.* Paper presented at the Advances in Computer Science – ASIAN 2005: 10th Asian Computing Science Conference, Kunming, China.

Yu, S., Liu, J., & Le, J. (2004a). *Decentralized Web Service Organization Combining Semantic Web and Peer to Peer Computing.* Paper presented at the Web Services: European Conference, ECOWS 2004, Erfurt, Germany.

Yu, S., Liu, J., & Le, J. (2004b). *Intelligent Web Service Discovery in Large Distributed System.* Paper presented at the Intelligent Data Engineering and Automated Learning – IDEAL 2004, Exeter, UK.

Zamora, E., Pollock, J., & al, e. (1981). The Use of Trigram Analysis for Spelling Error Detection. *Information Processing and Management, 6*(17), 305-316.

Zhou, C., Chia, L.-T., & Lee, B.-S. (2005a). Semantics in Service Discovery and QoS Measurement. *IEEE IT Professional Magazine, 7*(2), 29-34.

Zhou, C., Chia, L.-T., & Lee, B.-S. (2005b). Web Services Discovery with DAML-QoS Ontology. *International Journal of Web Services Research(JWSR), 2*(2), 44-67.

Zinky, J. A., Bakken, D. E., & Schantz, R. E. (1997). Architectural Support for Quality of Service for CORBA Objects. *Theory and Practice of Object Systems, 3*(1), John Wiley & Son.

This work was previously published in Int. Journal of Information Technology and Web Engineering, Vol. 2, Issue 2, edited by G. Alkhatib and D. Rine, pp. 65-80, copyright 2007 by IGI Publishing (an imprint of IGI Global).

Chapter XV
Web Site Performance Analysis Success Assessment of Information Driven Web Site on User Traces

Carsten Stolz
University Eichstaett-Ingolstadt, Germany

Michael Barth
Ludwig-Maximilian-University, Germany

ABSTRACT

With growing importance of the internet, Web sites have to be continuously improved. Web metrics help to identify improvement potentials. Particularly success metrics for e-commerce sites based on transaction analysis are commonly available and well understood. In contrast to transaction based sites, the success of Web sites geared toward information delivery is harder to quantify since there is no direct feedback of the user. We propose a generic success measure for information driven Web sites. The idea of the measure is based on the observation of user behaviour in context of the Web site semantics. In particular we observe users on their way through the Web site and assign positive and negative scores to their actions. The value of the score depends on the transitions between page types and their contribution to the Web site's objectives. To derive a generic view on the metric construction, we introduce a formal meta environment deriving success measures upon the relations and dependencies of usage, content and structure of a Web site. In a case study we got aware that in single cases unsatisfied users had been evaluated positively. This divergence could be explained by not having considered the user's intentions. We propose in this approach to integrate search queries carried within referrer information as freely available information about the user's intentions. We integrate this new source of information into our meta model of Web site structure, content and author intention. Hence we apply well understood techniques such as PLSA. Based on the latent semantic we construct a new indicator evaluating the Web site with respect to the user intention. In a case study we can show that this indicator evaluates the quality and usability of a Web site more accurately by taking the user's goals under consideration. We can also show, that the initially mentioned diverging user sessions, can now be assessed according to the user's perception.

INTRODUCTION

Apart from privately owned and maintained Web presences, professionally organized Web sites have become a natural part of everyday life and work. Companies adopt private initiatives and expand these ideas to a large number of internet users. Hao and Mendes (2006) see it as essential for a company's success. With ceased euphoria and growing realistic judgment about the possibilities of internet based business, companies focus on the profit generated by their Web sites. After more than ten years after creation of the World Wide Web, Jacoby and Luqi (2007) still ask in their work for measurable success indicators to evaluate and improve Web sites and their business models.

The assessment of success for a Web site can be approached from two sides, by direct enquiry or by observation of the Web site's users. Both techniques differ in their field of application. Enquiries provide very detailed information of a sample of all users which can be extrapolated to the whole user population. Ongoing, long-term evaluation of large, corporate Web sites can not be accomplished by user enquiry. Thus, our work concentrates on the continuous observation of user actions. Beside cost advantages, this approach covers all users and can be conducted over long time periods allowing to take dynamically built content into consideration.

The observation of user actions can be performed from server or client side. Like shown in the work of Cheung and Lee (2005), the client side allows to track all actions and even mouse movements of the users within his browser whether there is a data exchange with the Web server or not. Similar to a direct enquiry the scalability of this approach is questionable, since the approval of all users would be mandatory. Therefore, we rely on server side observation of user behaviour, although the observable actions are limited to the facts, shown in section \ref{domain}.

It depends on the business model of a Web site whether actions exist, that allow a direct determination of success.

The business models for a Web presence can follow one or more out of the following categories: **e-commerce** Web sites sell products and services, **content**-based Web sites aim to deliver and provide potentially useful information to their users, **communication**-based Web sites enable their users to contact and exchange each other or communicate with the company. Especially the so called Web 2.0 Web sites are based on this business variant. Finally, **context**-based Web sites organize and rearrange content within a new context to improve the entropy for their users, like search engines do.

Depending on the business model, it is possible to distinguish between user actions that contribute to the Web site's objectives and those actions without effect on the success.

Transaction Based Success Measures

Most e-commerce Web sites can evaluate their success by analyzing successfully completed transactions. Within these transactions users provide a direct feedback about the utility and the monetary value the Web site created for them.

Thus the success is easily measurable and allows deeper analysis of the whole purchasing process. Cutler and Sterne (2000) show how a chain of linked measures can describe the whole customer life cycle, starting from measures such as **reach**, acquisition, to **conversion** and **retention** of a customer, who can finally reach **loyalty** status. Other metrics like **abandonment**, **attrition**, and **churn** describe the migration of users. Applications of those measures can be found at Zviran, Glezer, and Avni (2005) and Yeung and Lu (2004), who all have described how to assess the success of transaction-based Web sites.

Web sites without transactions lack this evaluation possibility. In this approach we will concentrate on nontransactional Web sites. We subsume them under the term *information-driven Web sites* and describe in the following paragraph how other publications approached this challenge.

Information Provision Based Success Measures

Success measures for information-driven Web sites are rare. The problem to identify user intention is described by Pather, Erwin and Remenyi (2003) in a conceptual study to evaluate user satisfaction by gap measurement. The main reason why there are no satisfactory success measures is the lack of explicit user feedback about the successfulness of their sessions.

In a recent work about the success of companies' intranet portals, Jacoby and Luqi (2007) provide an overview of metrics of transactional Web sites and bring them into the context of general business requirements, but they did not explain how to measure the described metrics.

Many approaches combine structural, content and usage data to uncover the user intention, like Heer and Chi (2002) propose in order to discover user interest by clustering usage and content data. Any further applications towards success measuring by analysis of the user interests are not described their work.

Spiliopoulou and Pohle (2001) described an approach to evaluate the success of nontransactional Web sites by distinguishing between target and action pages with respect to the Web site's goals. According to this concept, a user accessing an action page is pursuing the site's goal while an access to a target page shows that the user has achieved the site's goal. Barth, Stolz, Viermetz, and Wilde (2005) evaluate non-sale-centric Web sites extending the concept of Spiliopoulou and Pohle by regarding a more general approach for assessing a user's attainment of the Web site's objectives. The following section \ref{sec:gpi} builds upon these approaches.

Developing Metrics for Information-Driven Web Sites

To overcome the problem of the missing user feedback, we propose to approximate an implicit user feedback. In our approach described in section 3 we estimate the user feedback by analysing his behaviour on the Web site under consideration of the Web site semantics. Having the clickstreams within the semantics of the Web site at hand, we evaluate each click of a user in respect to its contribution to fulfilling the Web site's objectives.

In later sections we demonstrate the applicability of our metric to a corporate Web site.

As one of the results we deem it necessary to describe the approach with a formal model in section 4. This model of a metaenvironment characterizes the relations of usage, content and structure within a Web site. Furthermore, since expectations and objectives of users and Web site owners are not necessarily the same, the resulting judgment about a successful Web site will consider both perspectives.

Figure 1. Grammatical perspective

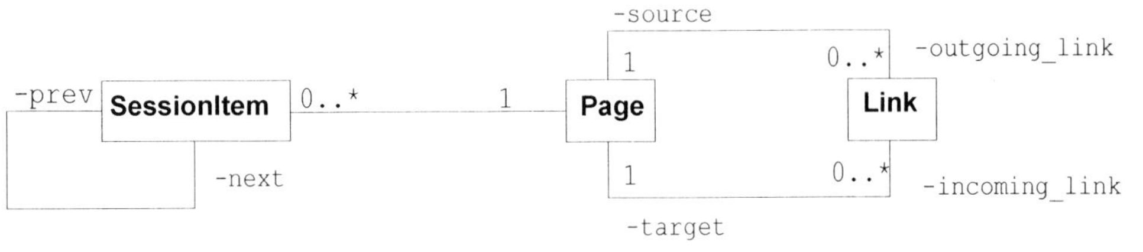

WEB SITE AND VISITS

A user of a Web site visits page's of a site one at a time. If one assumes a user takes notice of a page's content immediately after visiting it through a link, a visit of a site can be understood as a sequence of pages. The site's set of pages and the set of interconnecting links represent a transition system schematically depicted in Figure 1.

The potentially infinite set of page sequences generated by the site structure is equivalent to the set defined by a regular expression; for example, or a (Chomsky) type 3 grammar, if we prefer a linguistic analogue. Only these syntactical elements are accessible.

Intuitive Domain Analysis

Even if former approaches do not point out this difference: If we circumstantiate a Web sites success with a user's navigational behaviour, we talk about the site's semantics. And we inevitably have to make assumptions about the user's intentions and his interests, which represent his semantic domain. In Figure 2 the dependency of these terms is depicted.

At one hand the author ties pages with content; at the other hand a users session is driven by his or her intention and interests. The author creates a site as a set of pages. A page consists of a set of content items. A content item can be either a text token (words), a picture, or any media item. Then several words might be identified as keywords, if they carry semantic importance. Keywords can be grouped to topics. Now a page can be characterized by its participation in several topics. One may try to obtain these information directly from the author. Especially for huge Web sites this remains difficult. Thus, algorithmic techniques to derive keywords and clustering methodologies to identify topics will be discussed in the following.

The user remains as the most problematic part of any approach. Several assumptions have to be made, even if they are hardly ever mentioned explicitly. The duration, a time period that expires between calling a page and calling the immediate following one, can be determined unambiguously. One might interpret this as a time of mindful contribution to the pages content, but this implies assumptions such as the browser that caused the page's access has focus or the tab carrying the content is at the top, and so on. And even if the user is reading attentively, one can only assume he is engaged with interest and not reading a single part repeatedly, because of its poor presentation.

Perspectives on Measurable Artifacts

On part of the author, one can analyse the Web site. On part of the user, one can observe the click sequence of a session, if only server-side accessible information is available. The clickstream, as list of *SessionItems* defined in package *SessionStructure*, can be tracked on the server side. A concrete session resembles a path through the Web site graph. Artefacts arising from bookmarks, direct prompting of the URL, use of the back button in the browser or tabbed browsing, have

Figure 2. Semantic level

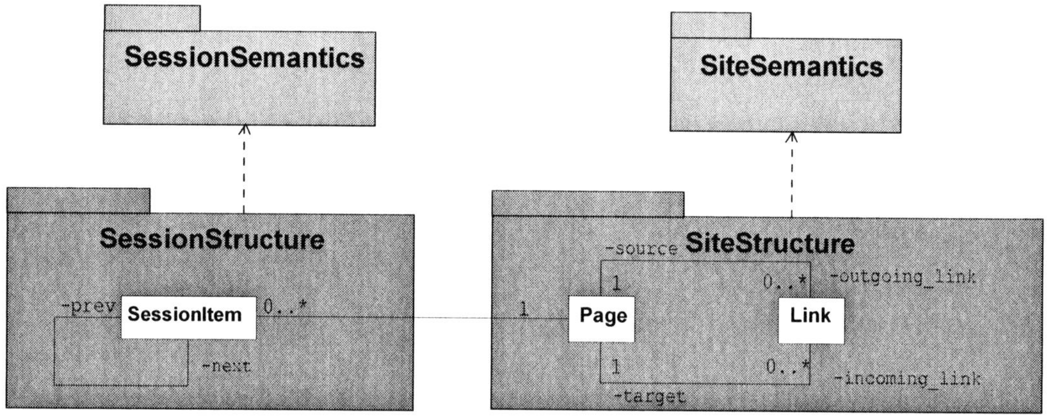

the effect, that all pages within a site can be the successor of each page.

Therefor we regard a complete graph and use the physical character of a link to distinguish between *internal*, *external*, and *virtual* links.

Describing the page view by a link with literal character *z* and a Web site as set of all reachable pages Σ, within the site, we get the *Clickstream* as string out of the set of all strings over this alphabet $\omega \in \Sigma^*$. We now can principally define measures on this alphabet, a single literal character, strings and substrings, that are calculable directly on the set or inductively by ω.

This approach retrieves an assessment of a distinct session relatively to a fixed estimation from an author's perspective. This broaches some topics: Such as obviation of sessions, where the user's interest does not match the author's intention or to achieve certainty whether an author's errors concerning content and structure caused either an undesired user behaviour or a misinterpretation in the calculation of the site's measures.

The smartness of the approaches presented here is basically substantiated in the restriction to server side accessible information. Therefore, only few additional information allow improvements interpreting a user's behaviour. One of these information is a search string, which is available for most sessions, that were initiated through a search engine. These terms are depicted in Figure 3. This search string consists mainly of text tokens that directly match content items of a page. Thereby one can assume, qualified on a higher level, that the semantics of these content items would describe a user's interest. Later we present a promising approach calibrating a semantic assessment of a site, based on a user's own search query. Thus we look at a Web site's performance through a user's glasses.

SUCCESS MEASURE FOR INFORMATION-DRIVEN WEB SITES

Having assessed the measurable facts on a Web site and their interpretation in the section above, we can now proceed and propose a generic success measure for information driven Web sites. The idea of the measure is based on the observation of user behavior in the context of Web site semantics regarding the objectives of the Web site.

Barnard and Wesson (2003) outline three measurements to evaluate the usability of a Web site in **effectiveness** for the users determining

Figure 3. Metaenvironment

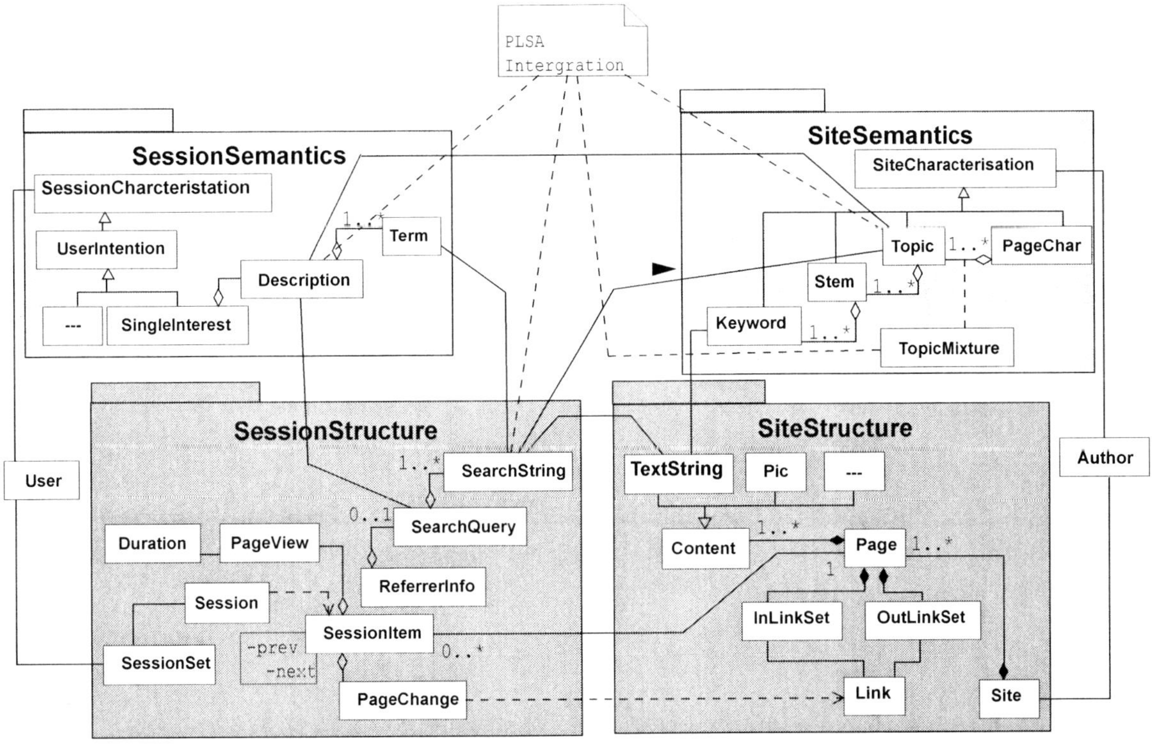

their tasks, **efficiency** measures the time it took the users to complete their tasks, and **satisfaction**, inquired from the user by questionnaire. According to Barnard and Wesson, we assume a generic objective of information driven Web sites comprehends the provision information to the user by leading him or her to a target Web page in an intuitive and fast way. We refer to this part of the Web site objective as **effectiveness**. Keeping the user on the page or on the whole Web site as long as possible is referred to as **efficiency**.

Following the approach of Spiliopoulou and Pohle (2001), we distinguish between **content** pages as target and **navigational** pages on the other side. By analysis of a user click resulting in a transition between both page categories, we derive a measure for the effectiveness of this transition.

Transition Type

We characterize the transition between certain categories of pages by the utility which the author assigned with respect to guiding the user to the target pages of a Web site. As can be seen in Table 1, the success of a transition towards content is seen as a positive step reflecting the focus of a Web site in delivering information.

Since navigational pages do not provide content, the transition between them or towards them is undesired resulting in negative values.

If a session ends on a navigation page, no more content could be distributed. Consequently, a negative value is assigned to this kind of transition.

Only transitions leading the user to content are evaluated positively. With the Transition Weight we want to assess more precisely to which degree the target has been achieved. Thereby we focus on

Table 1. Page category transition rating

		Destination				
		Home	Sitemap	Search	Content	Session End
Start	Home	-	-	-	+	-
	Sitemap	-	-	-	+	-
	Search	-	-	-	+	-
	Content	-	-	-	+	0

transitions between content pages, since content is the central matter of concern of this approach.

Transition Weight

To incorporate the content of the Web pages for our success measure, we use Probabilistic Latent Semantic Analysis (PLSA) as described by Hofmann (1999) and Baldi, Frasconi, and Smyth (2003) in conjunction with a crawler which extracts text from Web pages and calculates text length, removes stop words and applies stemming to reduce dimensionality of the word space. The following explanations refer to the remaining word stems as key words.

Topic Identification Algorithm

PLSA assigns topic vectors to words and documents. We create a matrix of Web pages and their key words. Afterwards we consider word classes as topics $\{z_j\}_{j=1}^{L}$, and model the likelihood of a document d (Web pages) as follows,

$$p(w_d) = \prod_w \left(\sum_z p(w \mid z, \beta) p(z \mid \theta_d) \right)^{n_{d,w}}$$

where β are parameters specifying the probability of words given topics, θd are document-specific parameters that indicate the topic mixture for document d, w_d is the word list of this document and $n_{d,w}$ is the number of occurrences of word w in w_d.

Then given a corpus of documents $d = 1, ..., n$, we have the following EM algorithm to estimate the parameters:

- E-step: for each document d, we estimate the posterior distribution of topics given each word w in it:

$$p(z \mid w, d) = \frac{p(w \mid z, \beta) p(z \mid \theta_d)}{\sum_z p(w \mid z, \beta) p(z \mid \theta_d)}$$

- M-step: we maximise the log-likelihood of "complete data" for the whole corpus:

$$\sum_d \sum_z \left(\prod_w p(z \mid w, d) \log \prod_w (p(w \mid z, \beta) p(z \mid \theta_d))^{n_{d,w}} \right)$$

We perform the E-step and M-step iteratively and at the convergence obtain the final estimate of $p(w \mid z)$ and $p(z \mid d)$. The meaning of these two parameters can be explained as follows:

- $p(w \mid z)$ indicates the probability of occurrence of word w given topic z. The algorithm groups semantically related words into topics and thus explores the semantic relations between words. Intuitively, if several words often occur together, these words are likely to be associated with one topic.
- $p(z \mid d)$ indicates the probability of topic z for document d.

As a result we obtain a topic vector for each content Web page. The transition between two content pages can be evaluated by measuring the distance between both topic vectors. For the whole user session we build an average topic vector indicating the content of the user session.

Let τ be a transition between content pages. The effectiveness of a transition is captured by an assigned weight factor μ_τ. We determine the overall topic mixture of a user session and contrast every click to the general nature of a session. Greater discrepancies indicate the user veering from his goal, which is now accounted by generating a lower score.

$$\mu_\tau = \begin{cases} \text{negligible topic shift} \Rightarrow 1 < \mu_\tau \\ \text{significant topic shift} \Rightarrow 0 < \mu_\tau < 1 \end{cases}$$

The effectiveness of a click and transition respectively is assessed by the **Transition Type** and **Weight**. The efficiency of a click expresses the extent to which the user's and Web site's objectives have been met.

Duration-Efficiency Factor

Let τ be a transition within the Web site. We have the duration d_τ which we compare with the average duration of all users $avg\left(d_\tau^{all}\right)$ having visited the specific Web page. Comparing d_τ with $avg\left(d_\tau^{all}\right)$ we consider long durations on content pages as desired user behavior, whereas navigational Web pages should guide the user quickly to the desired content. Therefore we assign greater values to short stays on navigation and long stays on content pages (as detailed in Table 2).

Guidance Performance Indicator

Having effectiveness and efficiency of a single click measurable, we determine the success of a session σ with $\sigma = (\tau_1, \tau_2, ...\tau_m)$ by combining transition type χ_{τ_i}, transition weight μ_{τ_i} and transition efficiency ϕ_{τ_i} for each transition $\tau \in \sigma$:

Table 2. Web page duration rating

	short duration	long duration
Navigation	+	-
Content	-	+

$$GPI_\sigma = \sum_{i=1,\tau_i \in \sigma}^{|\sigma|} \chi_{\tau_i} * \mu_{\tau_i} * \phi_{\tau_i}$$

This constitutes our server side centric view of session performance of an information driven Web site. As can be clearly seen, the measure only utilizes information freely available on server side. The user's intention is only implicitly captured by his browsing behaviour.

Evaluation of the GPI

For evaluation purposes, we analyse usage data from a corporate Web site dealing with financial products and services. Out of all Web pages, we regard two navigation pages and one content page as comparison. Both navigation pages are search pages, namely the simple search and the advanced search offering more selection possibilities.

Table 3 shows the absolute GPI values. In order to compare the GPI values of pages with different traffic density, we contrast their average GPIs per click.

The negative average GPI per click for the Simple Search page can have several reasons. Users need more time to find a relevant search result within all search results or the search leads to information not of interest to the user, whereas the Advanced Search reached a positive GPI by leading users faster to desired information. This is a reasonable result, since more selection criteria allow better search results—but 443 times the Simple Search was used compared to 75 times usage of Advanced Search. A recommendation could be to replace the Simple Search with the Advanced Search.

Table 3. GPI evaluated example pages

	GPI	no. of clicks	GPI per click
Simple Search	-350,5	443	-0,79
Advanced Search	14,9	75	0,20
Product A	775,5	1193	0,65

FORMAL PERSPECTIVE

Introduced in the second section, we argued a Web site being analogous to a transition system or a regular language. A single page and a sequence of visited pages are treated as elements of an alphabet $z \in \Sigma$ and expressions of a language $\omega \in \Sigma^*$.

Approach to Fixed Measurements

Evaluation of Structural Elements

On the highest level of abstraction, we consider a structural element and its characterisations, being interested in the measure they apply to. Thus with:

Measure	$M \in \mathcal{M}$
Charcterisation	$C \in \mathcal{C}$
Structural Element	$s \in \mathcal{S}$

for each structural domain $\mathcal{S}$, in respect of a distinct characterisation $\mathcal{C}$ out of the set of characterisations $\mathcal{C}_{Set}$, we are looking for a function β, that evaluates each element with:

$$[[s]]_{\mathcal{C}_x} = \beta(s,c)\, and\, \beta : \mathcal{S} \times \mathcal{C}_x \rightarrow M$$

β can be considered as weight function of the relation of domain $\mathcal{S}$ and co-domain $\mathcal{C}$. Exemplary, we regard the following application:

Example

Taking the categories of the third section as example for a characterisation $\mathcal{C}_{Cat}$, the set is explicitly determined by

$$C_{Cat} = \{Home, Sitemap, Search, Content, \bot\}$$

We assign ⊥ to the start and end of a session, since their source and destination is located outside of the regarded Web site.

Assigning each page to exactly one category requires the function β_{Cat}. We expect the predicate function:

$$\beta_{Cat} : \mathcal{S} \times \mathcal{C}_x \rightarrow M_{bool}$$

with: $M_{bool} = \{true, false\}$

which is unique, so:

$$\forall s \in \mathcal{S} : |\{c \in \mathcal{C}_{Cat} : \beta_{Cat}(s, c)\}| = 1$$

In the fourth section we determined the page categories manually.

The *Transition Rating* defined in Table 1 is a deliberate predefinition. Formally considered, this would be a complex process, including miscellaneous definitions and assumptions.

Transition Rating is an additional characterisation (by a single element set) evaluating a *Link* $\ell \in \mathcal{L} \subset \mathcal{S}$ of a Web site. The codomain of the monadic function $\beta_{tr}: \mathcal{L} \rightarrow M_{tr}$ is determined deliberately by $M_{tr} = \{-1, 0, 1\}$. We only know the clicked Link, but we need the categorisation of start and target page for the evaluation. Therefore, we introduce a navigational function to get access to the site structure:

Link:	$\ell \in \mathcal{L} \subset \mathcal{S}$
Page:	$p \in \mathcal{P} \subset \mathcal{S}$
Predecessor Page:	$pred : \mathcal{L} \to \mathcal{P}$
Successor Page:	$succ : \mathcal{L} \to \mathcal{P}$

By means of this function we can determine the start and target page of a link. For a particular page the related category has to be determined by β_{Cat}.

determine category:

$$\kappa : \Pi \times (\Pi \times C_{Cat} \to bool) \to C_{Cat}$$

with:

$$\kappa(\Pi, \beta_{Cat}) = \bigcup_{\beta_{Cat}(p,c)} c \times C_{Cat}$$

The table structure becomes directly apparent in the last auxiliary ν, used for the definition of β_{tr}:

$$\beta_{tr}(\ell) v(\kappa(pred(\ell), \beta_{Cat}), \kappa(succ\,(\ell), \beta_{Cat}))$$

with ν: $C_{Cat} \times C_{Cat} \to M_{tr}$ (defined by Table 1)

Insight Into the User's Goals by Search String Analysis

Beyond the case study in section 3.2 the GPI showed its applicability in daily use. Referring to the idea in section \ref{domain} of using search strings to adjust the GPI to the user perspective, we propose to use the referrer information as additional source of information. In case of users accessing the analyzed Web site from a search engine, the referrer information can carry the user's search string.

Search strings have been object of recent research, such as by Lee, Liu, and Cho (2005), focusing on the optimization of search engine results. Like them we assume, that search strings reflect the user's goals. Broder (2002) distinguishes different search goals. Navigational searches aim to find a certain Web site. Since all of our tracked users coming from search engines have reached our Web site, we can exclude those search strings, like the companies name, from further analysis. Likewise transactional searches are irrelevant for information driven Web sites. Finally, Content searches correspond to our analysis objectives, since users are interested in special pieces of information. Their intention should be expressed in the search string they have used on the search engine.

Out of 10,997 sessions we have found 15% with search strings. The focus on content searches narrows the number of sessions to 11.4 % of all sessions. Web site internal search engines were not analyzed in this work.

Formal Approach to an Enhanced GPI

In the following we introduce an approach to an analysis based on the user perspective at an abstract formal level. As a first improvement a page assessment is not longer based on a fixed or predefined order. We assume a user's intention to be accessible through a query's search strings. Thereon we state the construction of an enhanced intention based GPI. A site's set of pages is arranged as a space, ordered by a set of topic vectors. The search query's position itself can now be calculated. One can assume this position as a kind of fingerpost pointing to a user's goals. A session success indicator (*SSI*), introduced later, allows to judge whether a user's movement in this space is towards his desired direction. Finally, we close with a case study of an *ibGPI*- and *SSI*-application.

Table 4. Comparison of GPI and ibGPI

Sequence No.	Web page	GPI	Rank	ibGPI	SSI
		Session 1			
1	Home	-1,2	23	0,50	0,63
2	Search	-1,2	64	-0,50	0,63
3	Search	-1,2	64	0	0,63
4	advanced Search	0,75	56	0,01	0,63
5	1171	0,1	4	0,41	0,93
Total		-2,75		0,42	0,93
		Session 2			
1	Home	2,25	3	1,49	0,99
2	2578	0,91	62	-0,13	0,99
3	1067	0,27	58	0,002	0,99
4	1067	1,25	4	0,18	0,99
5	1042	0,25	55	-0,06	0,99
6	1302	1,54	39	0,05	0,99
7	2579	1,31	65	-0,04	0,99
8	1053	0,06	303	0,26	0,99
Total		7,83		1,23	0,99

Keyword Based Search Query Analysis

Depending on the number of occurrences of a search string s_q out of a query $q \in Q$ of a session σ in the bag of words s_ϕ on Web page ϕ we calculate rank ρ for all Web pages $\phi \in \Phi$ with a function

$$\rho: Q \times \Phi \rightarrow \mathbb{N}^+.$$

For each query q we now have a ranking of all Web pages $\phi \in \Phi$with $1 \leq \rho\ (q, \phi) \leq |\ \Phi\ |$.

The ranking of the entry page ϕ_{entry_σ} of session σ when compared to the other pages ϕ_{other_σ} of the same session allows the judgment whether Web pages exist, which would be a better match regarding the search query q, if the rank increases and $\rho\ (q, \phi_{other_\sigma}) < (q, \phi_{entry_\sigma})$.

Enhanced Intention-Based GPI

We consider each transition $\tau \in T^1$ with respect to the corresponding search query $q \in Q$. Let there be for each transition an initial query of the session, it is located in. Let this query be accessible by a function:

$$query : T \rightarrow Q.$$

We use the search strings, derived from the query, to calculate a query related topic vector $\vec{z} \in Z$. Here $\vec{z}$ corresponds to the definition of $\{z_j\}_{j=1}^{L}$ in section 3.1 and we claim $\vec{z}$ to be calculated on base of the same classes, which is used to calculate the site's topic vectors respectively. The derivation of a topic vector we denote with a function:

$$\zeta: Q \rightarrow Z.$$

Now we consider each transition τ to be successful if the rank ρ of the target page ϕ_{target}, introduced in the previous section, is higher than the source page ϕ_{Source}. We calculate this by the difference $\rho_{\phi_{Source}} - \rho_{\phi_{target}}$. If a transition leads to a page with a lower rank, we will retrieve a negative value. This results in an implicit consideration of a transition type. Thus we no longer need to consider different page categories and their changes like in Table 1. We aim to replace the μ_τ of the classic GPI by a function $\delta : T \rightarrow \mathbb{R}$. Whereas μ_τ of the classic GPI was only dependent on site metrics. Now we receive different functions δ, each depending on topic vector $\vec{z}$ corresponding to the initial query, which belongs to the session the transition is located in. We introduce a higher order function γ to generate these functions δ:

$$\delta : Z \rightarrow (T \rightarrow \mathbb{R}).$$

Due to lack of space we abstract from technical details (e.g., scaling) and can define the intention based GPI like

$$ibGPI_\sigma = \sum_{i=1, \tau_i \in \sigma}^{|\sigma|} \gamma\left(\xi\left(query(\tau_i)\right)\right)(\tau_i).$$

This definition of the function δ retrieves the weight of each distinct transition τ. The function itself is derived in dependency to τ via the query of the session in which τ is located and the related topic vector $\vec{z}$ which could be assigned to the set of search strings of the query.

A set of differing user interests is regarded correctly, if corresponding search strings can be found in the initial query. Thus they influence the calculation of $\vec{z}$. But we have to assume the user does not change his intention during the session as we are not able to identify these changes of interest. It has to be mentioned that strings, when used in both domains are assumed to have the same basic semantics.

Session Success Indicator

The additional source of information from search strings allows us to judge a session to be successful with respect to a user's intention. Since the click-based score of the GPI can hide the fact, that a user reached his goal by aggregation of the click-wise scores. Therefore we introduce as an additional measure a **S**ession **S**uccess **I**ndicator measuring the degree to which the user reached his intended area of interest.

The SSI uses the ranking function based on the relevance of Web pages in comparison to search string topics. The highest rank within a session indicates the proximity to his area of interest the user reached during his traversal of the Web site.

If we regard two pages ϕ_{Source}, ϕ_{target}, a transition $\tau = (\phi_{Source}, \phi_{target})$, we denote the source page of a transition with $\tau^- = \phi_{Source}$ and the rank of a page according to the function r, defined at the beginning of this section, we can define the SSI as follows:

$$SSI = 1 - \frac{\min\left\{\rho\left(query(\tau), \tau^-\right) : \tau \in \sigma\right\}}{|\Phi|}.$$

Due to value of 1 as the best rank, we search for the minimum of the set. According to this definition, the range of *SSI* may reach from $0 \leq SSI \leq 1$. The distribution of sessions according to this indicator allows for further interesting insights. Further enhancements of the *ibGPI* may result from weighted interpretation regarding their overall success. This is part of our current work and we will present results in the near future.

Validation by Case Study

Apart from the following application of both approaches for measuring the success of two corporate Web sites offering information to their users, we have conducted a parallel enquiry of 39 users. We gathered their feedback on a given task they had to perform on the Web sites. In order to make the sessions of the user study compatible to the search-query-based new ibGPI, we convert the given tasks into search strings identifying the target page. Similarly as with search queries we have now sessions with known user intentions and explicit user feedback.

The first example session is evaluated with a very negative score by the GPI, whereas the user deems his session to be successful since he reached his target page. The ibGPI on the other hand indicates that the user successfully heads towards his or her target page *1171*.

By reaching this page, the user's session receives a high score from the ibGPI as well as by the SSI. For this type of session, the ibGPI performed much better in modeling the user session in the same way the user perceived his or her Web site visit .

The second clickstream in table \ref{tab:casestudy_ibGPI2} does not diverge as much as the first session, but the GPI indicates a successful session in contrast to the user's judgment, since he or she was not sure to have reached all valuable Web pages. The user reached the relevant Web pages, which is correctly reflected by a very high SSI. But he or she did need several additional clicks which lead around the Web site; this can be seen from the slightly negative ibGPI. The combination of both resembles the user's feeling: having found all information, but under bad usability and navigational conditions.

Concluding the results from the application of GPI and ibGPI in comparison to the enquired user feedback, both measures improve the understanding of user behaviour on information driven Web sites, where no direct user feedback is available. The combination of the Web owner's perspective by the GPI and the user's perspective through the ibGPI provides better means to evaluate diverging objectives and varieties of user types.

CONCLUSION

It remains challenging for non-sale-centric but information-driven Web sites to optimize structure and content in accordance to the user's needs. Direct feedback such as purchases on transactional Web sites are not available. Before the development of a success measure a clarification of the nomenclature about the syntax and semantics of a Web site and its usage has been necessary. We presented to approaches to our objectives, both building upon user actions observable on server side. With our first approach we assessed the interaction of users with a Web site by evaluating each click with respect to the site's objectives. The click effectivity has been measured by analysing transitions between Web page categories. Either manually provided transition weights or the calculatorily derived degrees of change between topics have been assigned to single clicks. The topics of content pages have been analyzed by applying Probabilistic Latent Semantic Analysis. The efficiency of a click has been seen best represented by the duration a user remained on a Web page. By combining effectivity weight and efficiency weight we created a Guidance Performance Indicator. Its applicability to assess the success of information driven Web sites from the perspective of the Web site owner has been shown by applying the GPI on a corporate Web site.

With the GPI as a starting point, we have investigated how to incorporate the user's perspective. By formal derivation that analyses referrer information of a click the user's intention have been made accessible for analysis. We applied this new piece of information to enhance the GPI and make it more accurate not only to represent the site owner's perspective but also the user's view. The gain in accuracy has been demonstrated by comparing both measures with an explicitly raised user feedback in an enquiry.

Application: Search Engine Analysis

Beside the integration into a scoring model for static optimization of a Web site, we propose means to use search string queries from referrer information in combination with user behavior to improve search results of search engines. This approach is particularly valuable for an assessment of the Web site's internal search engine since one can influence its algorithms and results directly. Regarding external search engines and their potential for improvement, the ranking algorithms of search engines have to be analyzed and be understood. Additionally the recency of the last visit of a search engine's indexation bot has to be taken into consideration.

Application: Personalization

This approach is not only applicable for search engine analysis and optimization, but also for personalizing a Web site to the goals of users coming from external or internal search engines.

This approach adds a new perspective to traditional recommendation engines. It is not limited to the derivation of user intentions implicitly based on their behavior, but considers the users interests directly, since said interest is provided freely within the referrer information. This proceeding outmatches common recommendations by allowing to personalize a Web site on the first click. Analyzing the history of the user's behaviour, formerly the first and foremost source of information, may now potentiate further improvements as a second step.

REFERENCES

Baldi, P., Frasconi, P., & Smyth, P.(2003). *Modeling the Internet and the Web—Probabillistic methods and algorithms.* Wiley.

Barnard, L., & Wesson, J. L. (2003). Usability issues for e-commerce in South Africa: An empirical investigation. In *Proceedings of SAICSIT 2003* (pp. 258-267).

Barth, M., Skubacz, M., & Stolz, C. (2005). Web performance indicator by implicit user feedback—Application and formal approach. *Proceedings from the LNCS International Conference (WISE 2005).* New York: Springer.

Barth, M., Stolz, C., Viermetz, M., & Wilde, K. D. (2006). *Searchstrings revealing user intent—A better understanding of user perception.* Stanford: ICWE.

Broder, A. (2002). A taxonomy of Web search. *SIGIR Forum, 36*(2).

Cheung, C. M. K., & Lee, M. K. O. (2005). Consumer satisfaction with Internet shopping: A research framework and propositions for future research. *Proceedings of the ICEC 2005.* ACM Press.

Cutler, M., & Sterne, J. (2000). *E-metrics business metrics for the new economy.* Retrieved from www.netgen.com/emetrics

Eirinaki, M., & Vazirgiannis, M. (2003). Web mining for Web personalization. *ACM Transactions on Internet Technology, 3,* 1-27.

Hao, J., & Mendes, E. (2006). Usage-based statistical testing of Web applications. In *Proceedings of the ICWE 2006* (pp. 17-24). ACM Press

Heer, J., & Chi, E. H. (2002). *Separating the swarm: Categorization methods for user sessions on the Web.* ACM

Hofmann, T. (1999). Probabilistic latent semantic indexing. In *Proceedings of SIGIR 1999* (pp. 50-57).New York: ACM Press.

Jacoby, G. A., & Luqi. (2007). Intranet model and metrics. *Communications of the ACM, 50*(2), 43-50.

Jin, X., Zhou, Y., & Mobasher, B. (2004). Web usage mining based on probabilistic latent semantic analysis. *Proceedings of ACM SIGKDD 2004* (pp. 197-205).

Lee, U., Liu, Z., & Cho, J. (2005). Automatic identification of user goals in Web search. In *Proceedings of ACM WWW Conference 2005.*

Pather, S., Erwin, G., & Remenyi, D. (2003). Measuring e-commerce effectiveness: A conceptual model. In *Proceedings of SAICSIT 2003* (pp. 143-152).

Spiliopoulou, M., & Pohle, C. (2001). Data mining for measuring and improving the success of Web sites. *Journal for Data Mining & Knowledge Discovery* 5(1-2), 85-114.

Stolz, C., Viermetz, M., Skubacz, M., & Neuneier, R. (2005). Guidance performance indicator—Web metrics for information driven Web sites, *Proceedings of IEEE International. Conference Web Intelligence 2005.*

Viermetz, M., Stolz, C., Gedov, V., & Skubacz, M. (2006). Relevance and impact of tabbed browsing behavior on Web usage mining. *Web Intelligence 2006.*

Yeung, W. L., & Lu, M. (2004). Functional characteristics of commercial Web sites: A Longitudinal. *Information & Management Journal, 41*, 483-495.

Zviran, M., Glezer, C., & Avni, I. (2005). User satisfaction from commercial Web sites: The effect of design and use. *Information & Management Journal.*

ENDNOTE

1 Note a transition is an element of a session $\tau \in \sigma$, while $\sigma \subseteq T$

This work was previously published in Int. Journal of Information Technology and Web Engineering, Vol. 2, Issue 3, edited by L. Zhang, pp. 37-52, copyright 2007 by IGI Publishing (an imprint of IGI Global).

Compilation of References

Aas, K., & Eikvil, L. (1999). *Text categorization: A survey* (Tech. Rep.) Norwegian Computing Centre.

Aggarwal, R., Verma, K., Miller, J., & Milnor, W. (2004). Constraint driven Web service composition in METEOR-S. In *Proceedings of the 2004 IEEE International Conference on Services Computing* (pp. 23-30).

Agrawal, R., Gehrke, J., Gunopulos, D., and Raghavan, P. (1998). Automatic subspace clustering of high dimensional data for data mining applications. In *Proceedings of the 1998 ACM SIGMOD International Conference on Management of Data*, pages 94-105. ACM Press.

Allen, J.F. (1983). Maintaining Knowledge about Temporal Intervals. *Communications of the ACM, 26*, 832-843.

Allison, C., Cerri, S. A., Ritrovato, P., Gaeta, A. & Gaeta, M. (2005) Services, Semantics, and Standards: Elements of a Learning Grid Infrastructure. *Applied Artificial Intelligence* 19(9-10): 861-879

Allison, C., Ruddle, A. & Michaelson, A. (2002): Systems Support for Collaborative Learning. In *1st LEGE-WG International Workshop on Educational Models for GRID Based Services*. Lausanne, Switzerland. 16 September.

Al-Rashdi, A., Al-Muraikhi, H., Al-Subaiey M., Al-Ghanim, N., & Al-Misaifri, S. (2001). *Knowledge extraction and reduction system*. Senior Project, Computer Science Department, University of Qatar.

Anderson, B., & Moore, A. (2005). Active learning for hidden Markov models: Objective functions and algorithms. In *Proceedings of the ICML 2005 Conference*, Bonn, Germany.

Angell, R., & Freund, G. (1983). Automatic spelling correction using a trigram similarity measure. *Information Processing and Management, 19*(4), 255-161.

Ankerst, M. (2002). Report on the SIGKDD-2002 Panel the Perfect Data Mining Tool: Interactive or Automated? *ACM SIGKDD Explorations Newsletter, 4*(2), 110-111.

Apte, C., Damerau, F., & Weiss, S. M. (1994). Automated Learning of Decision Rules for Text Categorization. *TOIS: ACM Transactions on Information Systems, 12*(3), 233-251.

Apte, C., Damerau, F., & Weiss, S. M. (1998). Text mining with decision trees and decision rules. In *Proceedings of the Conference on Automated Learning and Discovery*, Carnegie-Mellon University (pp. 72-79).

Australian Bureau of Statistics. (2005). *8153.0 Internet Activity, Australia*, from http://www.abs.gov.au

Baldi, P., Frasconi, P., & Smyth, P.(2003). *Modeling the Internet and the Web—Probabillistic methods and algorithms*. Wiley.

Barnard, L., & Wesson, J. L. (2003). Usability issues for e-commerce in South Africa: An empirical investigation. In *Proceedings of SAICSIT 2003* (pp. 258-267).

Barth, M., Skubacz, M., & Stolz, C. (2005). Web performance indicator by implicit user feedback—Application and formal approach. *Proceedings from the LNCS International Conference (WISE 2005)*. New York: Springer.

Barth, M., Stolz, C., Viermetz, M., & Wilde, K. D. (2006). *Searchstrings revealing user intent—A better understanding of user perception*. Stanford: ICWE.

Bates, M. (1986). Subject access in online catalogs: A design model. *American Society for Information Science Journal, 37*(6), 357-376.

Bayardo, R., W, B., R, B., A, C., G, F., A, H., et al. (1997). *Semantic integration of information in open and dynamic environments*. Paper presented at the Proceedings of the 1997 ACM International Conference on the Management of Data (SIGMOD).

Bazell, D., Miller, D. J., & Borne, K. (2003). Novel approaches to semi-supervised and unsupervised learning. In *Proceedings of the ASP Conference Series, Astronomical Data Analysis Software and Systems XII* (Vol. 295).

Becker, M., Hachey, B., Alex, B., & Grover, C. (2005). Optimising selective sampling for bootstrapping named entity recognition. In *Proceedings of the ICML-2005 Workshop on Learning with Multiple Views*, Bonn, Germany.

Belkhiter, N., Bourhfir, C., Gammoudi, M., Jaoua, A., Le Thanh, N., & Reguig, M. (1994). Decomposition Rectangulaire Optimale d'une Relation Binaire: Application aux Bases de Donnees Documentaires. *Canadian Journal: INFOR, 32*(1), 33-54.

Bellavista, P., Corradi, A., Montanari, R., & Toninelli, A. (2006). Context-aware semantic discovery for next generation mobile systems. *IEEE Communications, 44*(9), 62-71.

Bellifemine, F., Caire, G., & Greenwood, D. (2007). *Developing multi-agent systems with JADE*. West Sussex: John Wiley & Sons.

Bellifemine, F., Caire, G., Trucco, T., & Rimassa, G. (2006). JADE programmer's guide. Retrieved July 7, 2007, from http://jade.cselt.it/docs

Ben Yahia, S., & Jaoua, A. (2001). Discovering knowledge from fuzzy concept lattice. In A. Kandel, M. Last, & H. Bunke (Eds.), *Data mining and computational intelligence, studies in fuzziness and soft computing* (Vol. 68, pp. 167-190), Heidelberg: Physica Verlag.

Ben Yahia, S., Arour, K., Slimani, A., & Jaoua, A. (2000). Discovery of compact rules in relational databases. *Information Journal, 3*(4), 497-511.

Benatallah, B., Hacid, M.-S., Leger, A., Rey, C., & Toumani, F. (2005). On automating Web services discovery. *The VLDB Journal — The International Journal on Very Large Data Bases, 14*(1), 84-96. Springer-Verlag New York.

Berchtold, S., Ertl, B., Keim, D. A., & Kriegel, H. P. (1998). Fast nearest neighbor search in high-dimensional space. In *Proceedings of the 14th IEEE Conference on Data Engineering (ICDE)* (pp. 209-218).

Berners-Lee, T. (2001). Keynote presentation on Web services and the future of the Web.

Berners-Lee, T., Hendler, J., & Lassila, O. (2001). The Semantic Web. *Scientific American, 284*(5), 34-43.

Bhaskar, K., & Ramon, B, & Stephen W. (2001). Distributed Constraint Satisfaction and the Bounds on Resource Allocation in Wireless Networks. Sixth International Symposium on Communications Theory & Application (ISCTA01), Ambleside, UK.

Billsus, D. and Pazzani, M. J. (1998). Learning collaborative information filters. In *Proceedings of the Fifteenth International Conference on Machine Learning*, pages 46-54. Morgan Kaufmann Publishers Inc.

Blum, A., & Mitchell, T. (1998). *Combining Labeled and Unlabeled Data with Co-Training.* Paper presented at the COLT 1998: Proceedings of the 11th Annual Conference on Computational Learning Theory, Madison, Wisconsin, United States.

Blum, A.L., & Rivest, R.L. (1992). Training a 3-node neural network is NP- complete. *Neural Networks, 5*(1), 117-127.

Boag, S., Chamberlin, D., Fernandez, M. F., Florescu, D., Robie, J., & Simeon, J. (2006). *XQuery 1.0: An XML query language.* Retrieved from http://www.w3.org/TR/xquery/

Böhm, K., Aberer, K., Neuhold, E. J., & Yang, X. (1997). Structured document storage and re?ned declarative and navigational access mechanisms in HyperStorM. *The VLDB Journal, 6*(4), 296-311.

Böhm, K., Aberer, K., Özsu, T. M., & Gayer, K. (1998). Query optimization for structured documents based on knowledge on the document type definition. In *Proceedings of IEEE International Forum on Research and Technology Advances in Digital Libraries (ADL'98)* (pp. 196-205), Santa Barbara, California, April 22-24, 1998.

Bollacker, K., Lawrence, S., and Giles, C. L. (1998). CiteSeer: An autonomous Web agent for automatic retrieval and identification of interesting publications. In Sycara, K. P. and Wooldridge, M., editors, *Proceedings of the Second International Conference on Autonomous Agents*, pages 116-123, New York. ACM Press.

Bollacker, K., Lawrence, S., and Giles, C. L. (1999). A system for automatic personalized tracking of scientific literature on the Web. In *Digital Libraries 99 - The Fourth ACM Conference on Digital Libraries*, pages 105-113, New York. ACM Press.

Boutilier, C., Brafman, R., Domshlak, C., Hoos, H., & Poole, D. (2004). Preference-based constrained optimization with CP-nets [Special issue]. *Computational Intelligence,* 20(2), 137-157.

Bozkaya, T., & Ozsoyoglu, M. (1997). Distance-based indexing for high-dimensional metric spaces. In *Proceedings of ACM Special Interest Group on Management of Data (SIGMOD)* (pp. 357-368).

Bradshaw, J.M. (1997). *Software agents*. Cambridge, MA: MIT Press.

Bradshaw, S., Scheinkman, A., and Hammond, K. J. (2000). Guiding people to information: providing an interface to a digital library using reference as a basis for indexing. In *Intelligent User Interfaces*, pages 37-43.

Breese, J. S., Heckerman, D., and Kadie, C. (1998). Empirical analysis of predictive algorithms for collaborative filtering. In *In Proceedings of the 14th Conference on Uncertainty in Artificial Intelligence*.

Breiger, R. (2004). The analysis of social networks. In *Handbook of data analysis* (pp. 505-526).

Bremer, J. M., & Gertz, M. (2003). *An efficient XML node identification and indexing scheme*. University of California at Davis. Technical Report, 2003 (http://www.db.cs.ucdavis.edu/papers/TR CSE-2003-04 BremerGertz.pdf).

Brin, S., & Page, L. (1998). The anatomy of a large-scale hypertextual Web search engine. In *Proceedings of International Conference on the World Wide Web*, Amsterdam, The Netherlands (pp. 107-117). Elsevier Science Publishers.

Broder, A. (2002). A taxonomy of Web search. *SIGIR Forum, 36*(2).

Buneman, P., Fan, W., & Weinstein, S. (1999). Query optimization for semistructured data using path constraints in a deterministic data model. In *Proceedings of DBPL Conference* (pp. 208-223).

Burges, C. J. C. (1996). Simplified support vector decision rules. In *Proceedings of the 13th International Conference on Machine Learning* (pp. 71-77).

Burges, C.J.C. (1998). A tutorial on support vector machines for pattern recognition. In *Proceedings of the Data Mining and knowledge discovery* (Vol. 2, pp. 121-167).

Burgstahler, S. & Swift, C.(1996) Enhanced Learning Through Electronic Communities: A Research Review, http://164.116.18.39/research_report.html, February

Calisti, M., & Neagu, N. (2004). Constraint Satisfaction Techniques and Software agents. Agents and Constraints Workshop, AIIA'04, Perugia, Italy.

Cardoso, J., & Sheth, A. (2003). Semantic e-Workflow Composition. *Journal of Intelligent Information Systems, 21*(3), 191-225. Kluwer Academic Publishers

Castillo, J. G., Trastour, D., & Bartolini, C. (2001). *Desciption Logics for Matchmaking of Services*. Paper presented at the Paper presented at the Workshop on Application of Description Logic.

Chaib-draa, B., & Moulin, B., & Mandiau, R., & Millot, P. (1996). Trends in Distributed Artificial Intelligence, Foundations of Distributed Artificial Intelligence. G.M.P.O' Hare and N. R. Jennings (Eds.), John Wiley & Sons Inc., 3-55.

Chakrabarti, S., Berg, M. v. d., & Dom, B. (1999). *Focused Crawling: A New Approach to Topic-Specific Web Resource Discovery*. Paper presented at the WWW 1999: In Proceedings of 8th International World Wide Web Conference, Amsterdam, Netherlands.

Chakrabarti, S., Dom, B., Agrawal, R., & Raghavan, P. (1998). Scalable Feature Selection, Classification and Signature Generation for Organizing Large Text Databases into Hierarchical Topic Taxonomies. *VLDB Journal: The International Journal on Very Large Data Bases, 7*(3), 163-178.

Chakrabarti, S., Roy, S., & Soundalgekar, M. (2003). Fast and Accurate Text Classification via Multiple Linear Discriminant Projections. *VLDB Journal: The International Journal on Very Large Data Bases, 12*(2), 170-185.

Chan, C. Y., Felber, P., Garofalakis, M., & Rastogi, R. (2002). Efficient filtering of XML documents with XPath expressions. In *Proceedings of the International Conference on Data Engineering* (pp. 235-244), San Jose, California, February 2002.

Chan, C. Y., Garofalakis, M. N., & Rastogi, R. (2002). RE-Tree: An efficient index structure for regular expressions. In *Proceedings of VLDB Conference* (pp. 263-274), Hong Kong, China, 2002.

Chang, J.-W. and Jin, D.-S. (2002). A new cell-based clustering method for large, high-dimensional data in data mining applications. In *Proceedings of the 2002 ACM symposium on Applied computing*, pages 503-507. ACM Press.

Chao, K.-M., Younas, M., Lo, C.-C., & Tan, T.-H. (2005). *Fuzzy Matchmaking for Web Services*. Paper presented at the WAMIS Workshop, Tamkang University, Taiwan.

Chavez, A., & Maes, P. (1996). Kasbah: An agent marketplace for buying and selling goods. In *Proceedings of the 1st International Conference on the Practical Applica-*

tion of Intelligent Agents and Multi-Agent Technology, London, United Kingdom.

Che, D. Accomplishing deterministic XML query optimization. *Journal of Computer Science and Technology, 20*(3), 357-366.

Che, D. Efficiently processing XML queries with support for negated containments. *International Journal of Computer & Information Science, 6*(2), 119-120.

Che, D. Implementation issues of a deterministic transformation system for structured document query optimization. In *Proceedings of the 7th International Database Engineering and Applications Symposium* (pp. 268-277), Hong Kong, July 16-18, 2003.

Che, D., Aberer, K., & Özsu, M. T. (2006). Query optimization in XML structured-document databases. *The VLDB Journal, 15*(3), 263-289.

Chen, D.-Y., & Li, X. (2004). *PLD: A Distillation Algorithm of Misclassified Documents.* Paper presented at the WAIM 2004: Advances in Web-Age Information Management: 5th International Conference, Dalien, China.

Chen, D.-Y., Li, X., Dong, Z. Y., & Chen, X. (2005). *Determining the Fitness of a Document Model by Using Conflict Instances.* Paper presented at the ADC 2005: The 16th Australasian Database Conference, Newcastle, Australia.

Chen, H., & Dumais, S. T. (2000, April 1-6). Bringing order to the Web: automatically categorizing search results. In *Procceedings of the ACM SIGCHI 2000 conference on Human factors in computing systems*, The Netherlands, (pp.145-152).

Chen, T. Y., Kuo, F., & Merkel, R. G. (2004, September 8-10). On the statistical properties of the f-measure. In *Proceedings of the Fourth International Conference on (QSIC'04)* (pp. 146-153). Braunshweig, Germany.

Cheng, C.-H., Fu, A. W., and Zhang, Y. (1999). Entropy-based subspace clustering for mining numericaldata. In *Proceedings of the fifth ACM SIGKDD International Conference on Knowledge discovery and data mining*, pages 84-93. ACM Press.

Cheung, C. M. K., & Lee, M. K. O. (2005). Consumer satisfaction with Internet shopping: A research framework and propositions for future research. *Proceedings of the ICEC 2005.* ACM Press.

Chiang, H., & Liao, Y. (2004). An agent-based architecture for impulse-induced mobile shopping, *Computer and Information Technology.*

Chickering, D. M., Heckerman, D., & Meek, C. (1997). *A Bayesian Approach to Learning Bayesian Networks with Local Structure.* Paper presented at the UAI 1997: Proceedings of 13th Conference on Uncertainty in Artificial Intelligence.

Chien, S. Y., Vagena, Z., Zhang, D., Tsotras, V. J., & Zaniolo, C. (2002). Efficient structural joins on indexed XML documents. In *Proceedings of VLDB Conference* (pp. 263-274), Hong Kong, August 20-23, 2002.

Chiueh, T. (1994). Content-based image indexing. In *Proceedings of the 20th International Conference on Very Large Data Bases (VLDB)* (pp. 582-593).

Chmiel, K., et al. (2004). Testing the efficiency of JADE agent platform. In *Proceedings of the 3rd International Symposium on Parallel and Distributed Computing* (pp. 49-57). IEEE Computer Society Press.

Chorafas, D.N. (1998). *Agent technology handbook.* New York: McGraw-Hill.

Chung, T. S., & Kim, H. J. (2002). XML query processing using document type definitions. *Journal of Systems and Software, 64*(3), 195-205.

Ciaccia, P., Patella, M., & Zezula, P. (1997). M-tree: An efficient access method for similarity search in metric spaces. In *Proceedings of the 23rd International Conference on Very Large Data Bases (VLDB)* (pp. 426-435).

Ciravegna, F. (2001, August 4th-10th). Adaptive information extraction from text by rule induction and generalization. In *Proceedings of the 17th International Joint Conference on Artificial Intelligence*, Seattle, WA (pp. 133-139).

Clancey, W.J. (1986). From GUIDON to NEOMYCIN and HERACLES (Twenty Short Lessons: ORN Final Report 1979-1985). *AI Magazine, 7*(3), 40-60.

Clark, J., & DeRose, S. (1999). *XML path language (XPath) Version 1.0.* Retrieved from http://www.w3.org/TR/1999/REC-xpath-19991116

Cockayne, W.T., & Zyda, M. (1998). *Mobile agents.* Greenwich, CT: Manning Publications.

Cohn, E. R. & Hibbitts, B. J., (2004). *Beyond the Electronic Portfolio: A Lifetime Personal Web Space.* Retrieved on December 10, from http://www.educause.edu/apps/eq/eqm04/eqm0441.asp.

Colucci, S., Noia, T.D., Sciascio, E.D., Donini, F., & Mongiello, M. (2005). Concept abduction and contraction for semantic-based discovery of matches and negotiation spaces in an e-marketplace. *Electronic Commerce Research and Applications, 4*(3), 345-361.

Consens, M., & Milo, T. (1994). Optimizing queries on files. In *Proceedings of ACM SIGMOD International Conference on Management of Data* (pp. 301-312), Minneapolis, Minnesota, May 1994.

Cooper, W. S. (1973). On Selecting a Measure of Retrieval Effectiveness. *JASIS: Journal of the American Society for Information Science, 24*, 87-100.

Corral, A., Manolopoulos, Y., Theodoridis, Y., & Vassilakopoulos, M. (2000). Closest pair queries in spatial databases. In *Proceedings of the 2000 ACM International Conference on Management of Data (SIGMOD)* (pp. 189-200).

Costa, J., & Hero, A. O. (2004, May). Manifold learning using Euclidean k-nearest neighbor graphs. In *Proceedings of the IEEE International Conference on Acoustic Speech and Signal Processing*. Montreal.

Crawford, E., Kay, J., & McCreath, E. (2002). *An Intelligent Interface for Sorting Electronic Mail.* Paper presented at the IUI 2002: Proceedings of the 7th International Conference on Intelligent User Interfaces, San Francisco, California, USA.

Cristianini, N., Shawe-Taylor, J., Elisseeff, A., & Kandola, J. (2001). On kernel-target alignment. In *Proceedings of the Neural Information Processing Systems* (*NIPS 2001*) (pp. 367-373).

Culotta, A., & McCallum, A. (2005). Reducing labeling effort for structured prediction tasks. In *Proceedings of the American Association of Artificial Intelligence* (*AAAI05*) (pp. 746-751).

Curbera, F., Duftler, M., Khalaf, R., Nagy, W., Mukhi, N., & Weerawarana, S. (2002, March-April). Unraveling the Web services Web: An introduction to SOAP, WSDL, and UDDI. *IEEE Internet Computing, 6*(2), 86-93

Cutler, M., & Sterne, J. (2000). *E-metrics business metrics for the new economy.* Retrieved from www.netgen.com/emetrics

Dagan, I., Karov, Y., & Roth, D. (1997). *Mistake-Driven Learning in Text Categorization.* Paper presented at the EMNLP 1997: Proceedings of 2nd Conference on Empirical Methods in Natural Language Processing, Providence, US.

Dasgupta, S., Tauman Kalai, A., & Monteleoni, C. (2005, June). *Analysis of perceptron-based active learning.*

Davey, B. A., & Priestley, H. A. (1990). *Introduction to lattices and order.* Cambridge Mathematical Textbooks.

Davis, R., & Smith, R. (1983). Negotiation as a Metaphor for Distributed Problem Solving. *Artificial Intelligence, 20*, 63-109.

Deerwester, S., Dumais, S. T., Furnas, G. W., Landauer, T. K., & Harshman, R. (1990). Indexing by Latent Semantic Analysis. *JASIST: Journal of the American Society for Information Science and Technology, 41*(6), 391-407.

Demiriz, A. (2001). An association mining-based product recommender. In *In NFORMS Miami 2001 Annual Meeting Cluster: Data Mining.*

Demiriz, A. (2004). Enhancing product recommender systems on sparse binary data. *Data Min. Knowl. Discov.*, 9(2):147-170.

Dempsey, M. C. (1986). *Automated guided vehicle control systems: Design application and selection.* Socicty of Manufacturing Engineers Publication.

Deshpande, M. and Karypis, G. (2004). Item-based top-n recommendation algorithms. *ACM Trans. Inf. Syst.*, 22(1):143-177.

Dhillon, I. S. and Guan, Y. (2003). Information theoretic clustering of sparse co-occurrence data. In *Proceedings of the third International Conference on Data mining.* IEEE Press.

Di Noia, T., Di Sciascio, E., Donini, F.M., & Mongiello, M. (2004). A system for principled matchmaking in an electronic marketplace. *International Journal of Electronic Commerce, 8*(4), 9-37.

Dimitrakos, T., Ritrovato, P. (2004) Progressing with a European Learning Grid. *4th International LeGE-WG Workshop - Towards a European Learning Grid Infrastructure.* Stuttgart, Germany. 27 - 28 April. BCS 2004

Duda, R., & Hart, P. (1973). *Pattern Classification and Scene Analysis.* New York: Wiley.

Duda, R.O., & Hart, P. (1973). *Pattern classification and scene analysis.* New York: John Wiley & Sons.

Dumais, S. T., Platt, J., Heckerman, D., & Sahami, M. (1998). *Inductive Learning Algorithms and Representations for Text Categorization.* Paper presented at the CIKM 1998: Proceedings of the 7th International Conference on Information and Knowledge Management, Bethesda, Maryland, United States.

Ebel, H., Mielsch, L.I., & Bornholdt, S. (2002). Scale-free topology of email networks. *Physical Review, E*(66), 035103.

ECLiPSe (2005). http://www.icparc.ic.ac.uk/eclipse/

Eirinaki, M., & Vazirgiannis, M. (2003). Web mining for Web personalization. *ACM Transactions on Internet Technology, 3,* 1-27.

Eisenstadt, M. & Komzak, J. (2005) Peer Conversations for e-Learning in the Grid. Knowledge Media Institute, The Open University, UK & Stefano A. Cerri, LIRMM, CNRS & Université Montpellier II, France

Faloutsos, M., Faloutsos, P., & Faloutsos, C. (1999). On power-law relationships of the Internet topology. In *SIGCOMM '99: Proceedings of the Conference on Applications, Technologies, Architectures, and Protocols for Computer Communication* (pp. 251-262). New York: ACM Press.

Fan, M., Tan, Y., & Whinston, A.B. (2005). Evaluation and design of online cooperative feedback mechanisms for reputation management. *IEEE Transactions on Knowledge and Data Engineering, 17*(2), 244-254.

Fensel, D. (2004). *Ontologies: A silver bullet for knowledge management and electronic commerce.* Berlin: Springer-Verlag.

Fensel, D., & Benjamins, V.R. (1998). Key issues for automated problem-solving methods reuse. In *Proceedings of the 13th European Conference on Artificial Intelligence.* John Wiley & Sons.

Ferber, J. (1999) Multi-Agent System: An Introduction to Distributed Artificial Intelligence. Harlow: Addison Wesley Longman. ISBN 0-201-36048-9

Fernandez, M. F., & Suciu, D. (1998). Optimizing regular path expressions using graph schemas. In *Proceedings of the 14th International Conference on Data Engineering* (pp. 14-23), Orlando, Florida, USA, February 23-27, 1998.

Fernandez, R., Ginzburg, J., & Lappin, S. (2005). Using machine learning for non-sentential utterance classification. In *Proceedings of the SIGdial 6*, Lisbon, Portugal (pp. 77-86).

Finin, T., & Labrou, Y., & Mayfield, J. (1997). KQML as an Agent Communication Language. In Bradshaw J.M. (Ed.), *Software Agents* (pp. 291-316), Cambridge, MA: AAA/MIT Press.

FIPA Agent Communication. (2002). Retrieved July 3, 2007, from *http://www.fipa.org/repository/aclspecs.html*

FIPA. (2006). Retrieved July 7, 2007, from http://www.fipa.org

Fonseca, S., Griss, M., & Letsinger, R. (2001). *An agent-mediator e-business environment for the mobile shopper* (HP Tech. Rep. No. HPL-20010157).

Foster, I., Kesselman, C., Nick, J. M., & Tuecke, S. (2002). Grid services for distributed system integration. *IEEE Computer, 35*(6), 37-46.

Foster, I., Kesselman, K. & Tuecke, S. (2003) : The Anatomy of the Grid: Enabling Scalable Virtual Organizations. CCGRID 2001: 6-7

Frasincar, F., Houben, G. J., & Pau, C. (2002). XAL: An algebra for XML query optimization. In *Proceedings of the 13th Australasian Database Conference, (ADC2002)* (pp. 49-56).

Freidman-Hill, E.J. (2003). *Jess in action: Java rule-based system.* Greenwich, CT: Manning Publications.

Frolund, S., & Koistinen, J. (1998). QML: A Language for Quality of Service Specification. *Technical report HPL on HP Laboratories.*

Fuhr, N. (1989). Models for Retrieval with Probabilistic Indexing. *Information Processing and Management, 25*(1), 55-72.

Fung, P., & Roth, D. (2005). Guest Editors Introduction: Machine learning in speech and language technologies. In *Proceedings of the ACM*, Numbers 1-3 (Vol. 60, pp. 5-9). The Netherlands: Springer.

Gagnes, T., Plagemann, T., & Munthe-Kaas, E. (2006). *A Conceptual Service Discovery Architecture for Semantic Web Services in Dynamic Environments.* Paper presented at the The 22nd International Conference on Data Engineering, Georgia, USA.

Ganter B., & Wille, F. (1999). *Formal concept analysis.* Springer-Verlag.

Garber, D.(2004). Growing Virtual Communities. International Review of Research in Open and Distance Learning, 3(4). August, 2004, ISSN: 1492-3831

Garfield, E. (1972). Citation analysis as a tool in journal evaluation. *Science, 178*(60), 471-479.

Garlan, D., Siewiorek, D., Smailagic, A., & Steenkiste, P. (2002). Project aura: Toward distraction-free pervasive computing. *IEEE Pervasive Computing, 1*(2), 22-31.

Garofalakis, J., Panagis, Y., Sakkopoulos, E., & Tsakalidis, A. (2004). *Web Service Discovery Mechanisms: Looking for a Needle in a Haystack?* Paper presented at the International Workshop on Web Engineering.

Genesereth, M. et al. (1998). Knowledge Interchange Format, draft proposed American National Standard (dpANS), NCITS.T2/98-004.

Getz, G., Shental, N., & Domany, E. (2005). Semi-supervised learning—A statistical physics approach. In *Proceedings of the 22nd ICML Workshop on Learning with Partially Classified Training Data*, Bonn, Germany.

Giles, C. L., Bollacker, K. D., and Lawrence, S. (1998). CiteSeer: an automatic citation indexing system. In *Proceedings of the third ACM conference on Digital libraries*, pages 89-98. ACM Press.

Goil, S., Nagesh, H., and Choudhary, A. (1999). Mafia: E±cient and scalable subspace clustering for very large data sets. Technical Report CPDC-TR-9906-010, Northwestern University, 2145 Sheridan Road, Evanston IL 60208.

Gomez-Perez, A., Gonzalez-Cabero, R., & Lama, M. (2004). A framework for design and composition of Semantic Web services. In *Proceedings of the AAAI Spring Simposyum on Semantic Web Services*. AAI Press.

Good, I. J. (1965). *The Estimation of Probabilities: An Essay on Modern Bayesian Methods*: Cambridge, Mass., M.I.T. Press.

Gottlob, G., Koch, C., & Pichler, R. (2002). Efficient algorithms for processing XPath queries. In *Proceedings of VLDB Conference* (pp. 95-106), Hong Kong, China, 2002.

Gouardères, G., Mansour, S. ,Yatchou, R. & Nkambo, R. (2005), The Grid-e-Card: Architecture for Collective Intelligence Sharing on the Grid

Graefe, G., & DeWitt, D. (1987). The EXODUS optimizer generator. In *Proceedings of ACM SIGMOD International Conference on Management of Data* (pp. 160-172), May 1987.

Graham, P. (2004). *A Plan for Spam*, from http://www.paulgraham.com/spam.html

Graham, S., & Treadwell, J. (Eds.) (2004, 10 June). *Web Services Resource Properties (WS-ResourceProperties) v1.2*. OASIS WSRF TC.

Graham, S., Karmarkar, A., Mischkinsky, J., Robinson, I., & Sedukhin, I. (2004).

Gray, R.S. (1997). Agent Tcl. *Dr. Dobb's Journal*, pp. 18-26.

Greenwood, D., & Calisti, M. (2004, October). **Engineering Web service: Agent integration.** *Proceedings of the IEEE International Conference on Systems, Man and Cybernetics, 2.*

Grust, T. (2002). Accelerating XPath location steps. In *Proceedings of ACM SIGMOD Conference* (pp. 109-120), 2002.

Guarino, N., (1998) Formal Ontology and Information Systems, In N. Guarino (ed.), *Formal Ontology in Information Systems, Proc. of the 1st International Conference*, Trento, Italy, http://www.ladseb.pd.cnr.it/infor/Ontology/Papers/FOIS98.pdf

Guha, S., Jagadish, H. V., Koudas, N., Srivastava, D., & Yu, T. (2002). Approximate XML joins. In *Proceedings of the ACM SIGMOD Conference* (pp. 287-298), 2002.

Haarslev, V., & Möller, R. (2001). *RACER System Description*. Paper presented at the the First International Joint Conference on Automated Reasoning.

Hao, J., & Mendes, E. (2006). Usage-based statistical testing of Web applications. In *Proceedings of the ICWE 2006* (pp. 17-24). ACM Press

Haruechaiyasak, C., Shyu, M.-L., Chen, S.-C., & Li, X. (2002). *Web Document Classification Based on Fuzzy Association*. Paper presented at the COMPSAC 2002: Proceedings of the 26th IEEE Computer Society International Computer Software and Applications Conference, Oxford, England.

Hashemi, R. R., Razzaghi, M., Jelovsek, F. R., & Talburt, J. R. (1992). *Conflict Resolution in Inductive Learning from Examples*. Paper presented at the SAC 1992: Proceedings of the 1992 ACM/SIGAPP Symposium on Applied computing, Kansas City, Missouri, United States.

Hayes, P. J., Andersen, P. M., Nirenburg, I. B., & Schmandt, L. M. (1990). *TCS: A Shell for Content-Based Text Categorization*. Paper presented at the CAIA 1990: Proceedings of the 6th Conference on Artificial Intelligence for Applications, Santa Barbara, California, United States.

Heb, A., Johnston, E., & Kushmerick, N. (2005, February 13-18).Machine learning techniques for annotating semantic Web services. In *Proceedings of the Dagstuhl Seminar on Machine Learning for the Semantic Web*, (pp. 77-83).

Heckerman, D. G., Dan & Chickering, David Maxwell. (1994). *Learning Bayesian Networks: The Combination of Knowledge and Statistical Data*. Paper presented at the KDD Workshop.

Heckerman, D., Chickering, D. M., Meek, C., Rounthwaite, R., and Kadie, C. (2001). Dependency networks for inference, collaborative filtering, and data visualization. *J. Mach. Learn. Res.*, 1:49-75.

Heer, J., & Chi, E. H. (2002). *Separating the swarm: Categorization methods for user sessions on the Web.* ACM

Helal, A. (1997). InfoSleuth: Agent-based Semantic Integration of Information in Open and Dynamic Environments. In M. Huhns & M. Singh (Eds.), *Readings in Agents*: Morgan Kaufman.

Hendler, J. (2001). Agents and the Semantic Web. *IEEE Intelligent Systems, 16*(2), 30-37.

Herlocker, J. L., Konstan, J. A., Terveen, L. G., and Riedl, J. T. (2004). Evaluating collaborative filtering recommender systems. *ACM Trans. Inf. Syst.*, 22(1):5-53.

Hjaltason, G. R., & Samet, H. (1999). Distance browsing in spatial databases. In *Proceedings of ACM Transactions on Database Systems, 24(2)*, 265-318.

Hofmann, T. (1999). Probabilistic latent semantic indexing. In *Proceedings of SIGIR 1999* (pp. 50-57).New York: ACM Press.

Hofmann, T. (2004). Latent semantic models for collaborative filtering. *ACM Trans. Inf. Syst.*, 22(1):89-115.

Hondo, M., & Kaler, C. (2002). Web Services Policy Framework (WSPolicy) Version 1.0. Available at http://www.verisign.com/wss/WS-Policy.pdf

Horrocks, I., Patel-Schneider, P.F., Boley, H., Tabet, S., Grosof, B., & Dean, M. (2004). SWRL: A Semantic Web rule language combining OWL and RULEML (W3C Member Submission). Retrieved July 3, 2007, from http://www.w3.org/Submission/SWRL/

Hsu, P.-Y., & Zaniolo, C. (1993). *A new User's Impressions on LDL++ and CORAL.* Paper presented at the Workshop on Programming with Logic Databases (Informal Proceedings).

Hu, Y., Li, H., Cao, Y., Meyerzon, D., & Zheng, Q. (2005, June 7-11). Automatic extraction of titles from general documents using machine learning. In *Proceedings of the 14th Joint Conference on Digital Library (ACM-JCDL'05)* Denver, CO (pp. 145-154).

Huang, C.-L., Chao, K.-M., & Lo, C.-C. (2005). *A Moderated Fuzzy Matchmaking for Web Services.* Paper presented at the The 5th International Conference on Computer and Information Technology (CIT2005), Shanghai, China.

Huang, Z., Chen, H., and Zeng, D. (2004). Applying associative retrieval techniques to alleviate the sparsity problem in collaborative filtering. *ACM Trans. Inf. Syst.*, 22(1):116-142.

Huhns, M., & Mohamed, A. (1999). Benevolent Agents, *IEEE Internet Computing, 3*(2), 96-98.

Impulse. (2006). Retrieved July 7, 2007, from http://agents.media.mit.edu/projects/impulse/

ISO 2788. (1986). *Documentation-Guidelines for the establishment and Development of monolingual Thesauri* (2nd ed.).

Jacoby, G. A., & Luqi. (2007). Intranet model and metrics. *Communications of the ACM, 50*(2), 43-50.

JADE (Java Agent DEvelopment Framework) version 3.2

Jaeger, M. C., Tang, S., & Liebetruth, C., *The TUB OWL-S Matcher.*

Jagadish, H. V., Lakshmanan, L. V. S., Srivastava, D., & Thompson, K. (2001). TAX: A tree algebra for XML. In *Proceedings of DBPL Conference* (pp. 149-164), Rome, Italy, 2001.

Jaoua A., & Elloumi S. (2002). Galois connection: Formal concepts and Galois lattice in real relations: Application in a real classifier. *The Journal of Systems and Software, 60*, 149-163.

Jaoua A., Boudriga, N., Durieux, J. L., & Mili, A. (1991). Regularity of relations a measure of uniformity. *Theoretical Computer Science, 79*, 323-339.

Jaoua A., Bsaies, K., & Consmtini, W. (1999). May reasoning be reduced to an information retrieval problem. *International Seminar in Relational Methods in Computer Science*, Quebec, Canada.

Jaoua, A., Belkhiter, N., Desharnais J., & Moukam, T. (1992). Properties of difunctional dependencies in relational database. *Canadian Journal INFOR, 30*(1), 297-315.

Jezic, G., Kusek, M., & Sinkovic, V. (2006). Teamwork coordination in large-scale mobile agent network. *Lecture Notes in Artificial Intelligence, 4251*, 236-243.

JGraph (JGraph, 2006). http://www.jgraph.com/

Jin, X., Zhou, Y., & Mobasher, B. (2004). Web usage mining based on probabilistic latent semantic analysis. *Proceedings of ACM SIGKDD 2004* (pp. 197-205).

Joachims, T. (1998). *Text Categorization with Support Vector Machines: Learning with Many Relevant Features.* Paper presented at the ECML 1998: Proceedings of 10th European Conference on Machine Learning, Chemnitz, DE.

Jøsang, A., & Ismail, R. (2002, June). The Beta Reputation System. In *Proceedings of the 15th Bled Electronic Commerce Conference*, Bled, Slovenia.

Jung, H., & Tambe, M., & Kulkarni, S. (2001). Argumentation as Distributed Constraint Satisfaction: Applications and Results. Proceedings of the fifth international conference on Autonomous agents, Montreal, Quebec, Canada, 324-331.

Jung, S., & Pramanik, S. (2002). An efficient path computation model for hierarchically structured topological road maps. In *Proceedings of IEEE Transaction on Knowledge and Data Engineering (TKDE), 14(1),* 1029-1046.

JXTA (JXTA, 2006). http://www.jxta.org/

Kawamura, T., Blasio, J. D., Hasegawa, T., Paolucci, M., & Sycara, K. (2003). *Preliminary Report of Public Experiment of Semantic Service Matchmaker with UDDI Business Register.* Paper presented at the 1st International Conference on Service Oriented Computing (ICSOC 2003), Trento, Italy.

Kawamura, T., Blasio, J. D., Hasegawa, T., Paolucci, M., & Sycara, K. (2004). *Public Deployment of Semantic Service Matchmaker with UDDI Business Registry.* Paper presented at the 3rd International Semantic Web Conference (ISWC 2004).

Keller, U., Lara, R., Lausen, H., Polleres, A., & Fensel, D. (2005). Automatic location of services. *Lecture Notes in Computer Science, 3532*, 1-16.

Khcherif, R., Gammoudi, M. N., & Jaoua, A. (2000). Using difunctional relations in information organization. *Journal of Information Sciences, 125*, 153-166, Elsevier N.H.

Kieβling, W., Hafenrichter, B., Fischer, S., & Holland, S. (2001, September). Preference XPATH: A query language for e-commerce. *In Proceedings of the 5th International Tagung WirtschaftsInformatik*, Augsburg, Germany.

Kim, J., Spraragen, M., & Gil, Y. (2004). An intelligent assistant for interactive workflow composition. In *Proceedings of the 9th International Conference on Intelligent User Interfaces*, Funchal, Madeira, Portugal (pp.125-131). New York: ACM Press,.

Klein, M., & Bernstein, A. (2004). Toward high-precision service retrieval. *IEEE Internet Computing, 8*(1), 30-36.

Kleinberg, J. (1999). Authoritative sources in a hyperlinked environment. *Journal of the ACM, 46*, 604-632.

Klimt, B., & Yang, Y. (2004). *Introducing the Enron Corpus.* Paper presented at the CEAS 2004: The 1st Conference on Email and Anti-Spam, Mountain View, CA, U.S.A.

Kolahdouzan, M., & Shahabi, C. (2004a). Continuous K nearest neighbor queries in spatial network database. In *Proceedings of the 2nd Workshop on Spatio-Temporal Database Management (STDBM).*

Kolahdouzan, M., & Shahabi, C. (2004b). Voronoi-based K nearest neighbor search for spatial network database. In *Proceedings of the 30th International Conference on Very Large Data Bases (VLDB)* (pp. 840-851).

Koller, R. D., & Wilamowski, B. M. (1995, July 17-21). A relaxation/regression algorithm for efficient training of multilayer neural networks. In *Proceedings of the World Congress of Neural Networks* Washington DC (Vol. 1, pp. 683-686).

Kollios, G., Gunopulos, D., & Tsotras, V. J. (1999). Nearest neighbor queries in a mobile environment. In *Proceedings of the International Workshop on Spatio-Temporal Database Management* (pp. 119-134).

Konstan, J. A., Miller, B. N., Maltz, D., Herlocker, J. L., Gordon, L. R., and Riedl, J. (1997). Grouplens: applying collaborative filtering to usenet news. *Commun. ACM*, 40(3):77-87.

Kopena, J., & Regli, W. (2003). DAMLJessKB: A tool for reasoning with the Semantic Web. In *Proceedings of the 2nd International Semantic Web Conference (ISWC2003)*, Sanibel Island, Florida (pp. 628-643). Berlin: Springer-Verlag. Lecture Notes in Computer Science, 2870.

Kopena, J., & Regli, W.C. (2003). DAMLJessKB: A tool for reasoning with the Semantic Web. *IEEE Intelligent Systems, 18*(3), 74-77.

Korn, F., Sidiropoulos, N., Faloutsos, C., Siegel, E., & Protopapas, Z. (1996). Fast nearest neighbor search in medical image databases. In *Proceedings of 22nd International Conference on Very Large Data Bases (VLDB)* (pp. 215-226).

Kotz, D. (2002). Future directions for mobile agent research. *IEEE Computer Science*.

Kotz, D., & Gray, R. (1999). Mobile code: The future of the Internet. In *Proceedings of Autonomous Agents'99: Workshop on Mobile Agents in the Context of Competition and Cooperation.*

Kowalczyk, R., et al. (2002). Integrating mobile and intelligent agents in advanced e-business: A survey. In *Proceedings of Agent Technologies, Infrastructures, Tools, and Applications for E-Services, NODe'2002 Agent-Related Workshops*, Erfurt, Germany.

Kurino, R., Sugisaka, M. & Shibata, K. (2004). Growing neural network with hidden neurons. In *Proceedings of the 9th International Symposium on Artificial Life and Robotics* (AROB) (Vol. 1, pp. 144-147).

Kusek, M., Lovrek, I., & Sinkovic, V. (2005). Agent team coordination in the mobile agent network. *Lecture Notes in Artificial Intelligence, 3053*, 240-246.

Kwon, O. W., & Lee, J. H. (2003). Text categorization based on k-nearest neighbor approach for Web site classification. *Information Processing & Management, 39*(1), 25-44.

Lam, W., & Han, Y.Q. (2003). Automatic textual document categorization based on generalized instance sets and a meta-model. *IEEE Transactions on Pattern Analysis and Machine Intelligence, 25*(5), 628-633.

Lange, B.D., & Oshima, M. (1998). *Programming and deploying Java mobile agents with aglets*. Addison-Wesley.

Lange, D.B., & Oshima, M. (1999). Seven good reasons for mobile agents. *Communications of the ACM.*

Larkey, L. S. (1998). *Automatic Essay Grading Using Text Categorization Techniques.* Paper presented at the SIGIR 1998: Proceedings of the 21st Annual international ACM SIGIR Conference on Research and Development in Information Retrieval, Melbourne, Australia.

Le, D. N., & Goh, A. (2005). *Matching Semantic Web Services Using Different Ontologies.* Paper presented at the ICWE 2005, Sydney, Australia.

Le, D. N., Goh, A., & Tru, C. H. (2005). *Multi-Ontology Matchmaker.* Paper presented at the 7th International conference on Information Integration and Web Based Applications and Services (iiWAS2005), Malaysia.

Le, D. N., Hang, T. M., & Goh, A. (2006). *MOD- A Multi Ontology Discovery system.* Paper presented at the International Workshop on Semantic Matchmaking and Resource Retrieval, Seoul, Korea.

Lee, P., & Necula, G. (1997). Research on proof-carrying code on mobile-code security. In *Proceedings of the Workshop on Foundations of Mobile Code Security.*

Lee, U., Liu, Z., & Cho, J. (2005). Automatic identification of user goals in Web search. In *Proceedings of ACM WWW Conference 2005.*

Leuf, B. (2006). *The Semantic Web: Crafting infrastructure for agency.* New York: Wiley.

Lewis, D. D. (1992). *An Evaluation of Phrasal and Clustered Representations on a Text Categorization Task.* Paper presented at the SIGIR 1992: Proceedings of the 15th Annual International ACM SIGIR Conference on Research and Development in Information Retrieval, Copenhagen, Denmark.

Lewis, D. D. (1995). *Evaluating and Optimizing Autonomous Text Classification Systems.* Paper presented at the SIGIR 1995: Proceedings of the 18th Annual International ACM SIGIR Conference on Research and Development in Information Retrieval, Seattle, Washington, United States.

Lewis, D. D. (2000). *Reuters Corpus (21578)*, from http://www.daviddlewis.com/resources/testcollections/reuters21578/

Li, G., Uren, V., Motta, E., Buckingham-Shum, S., and Domingue, J. (2002). Claimaker: Weaving a semantic Web of research papers. In *Proceedings of the 1st International Semantic Web Conference, Sardinia, June 2002.*

Li, L., & Horrocks, I. (2003). *A software framework for matchmaking based on semantic Web technology.* Paper presented at the 12th International World Wide Web Conference, Budapest, Hungary.

Li, Q., & Moon, B. (2001). Indexing and querying XML data for regular path expressions. In *Proceedings of VLDB Conference* (pp. 361-370), Rome, Italy, September 2001.

Li, Y., Su, S., & Yang, F. (2006). *A Peer-to-Peer Approach to Semantic Web Services Discovery.* Paper presented at the Computational Science – ICCS 2006: 6th International Conference, Reading, UK.

Liang, Q., Chakarapani, L. N., Su, S. Y. W., Chikkamagalur, R. N., & Lamr, H. (2004). A Semi-automatic approach to composite Web services discovery, description and invocation. *International Journal of Web Services Research, 1*(4), 64–89. Idea Group Publishing.

Lim, W.S., & Tang, C.S. (2006). An auction model arising from an Internet search service provider. *European Journal of Operational Research, 172*(3), 956-970.

Limthanmaphon, B., & Zhang, Y. (2003). Web service composition with case-based reasoning. In *Proceedings of the 14th Australasian Database Conference on Database Technologies* (pp. 201-208). Darlinghurst, Australia: Australian Computer Society, Inc.

Lin, C., Alvarez, S., and Ruiz, C. (2000). Collaborative recommendation via adaptive association rule

Lindberg, J., Pasman, W., Kranenborg, K.., Stegeman, J., & Neerincx, M.A. (2007). Improving service matching and selection in ubiquitous computing environments: A user study. *Personal and Ubiquitous Computing, 11*(1), 59-68.

Littlestone, N. (1988). Learning Quickly When Irrelevant Attributes Abound: A New Linear Threshold Algorithm. *Machine Learning, 2*(4), 285--318.

Littlestone, N. (1991). *Redundant Noisy Attributes, Attribute Errors, and Linear-Threshold Learning Using Winnow*. Paper presented at the Proceedings of the fourth annual workshop on Computational learning theory, Santa Cruz, California, United States.

Liu, B., Xia, Y., and Yu, P. S. (2000). Clustering through decision tree construction. In *Proceedings of the ninth International Conference on Information and Knowledge Management*, pages 20-29. ACM Press.

Liu, H., Mandvikar, A., Foschi, P., & Torkkola, K. (2003, August 9-15). Active learning with ensembles for image classification. In *Proceedings of the 18th International Joint Conference on Artificial Intelligence*, Acapulco, Mexico (pp. 1435-1436).

Liu, J., & Jing, H, & Tang, Y. (2002). Multi-agent Oriented Constraint Satisfaction. *Artificial Intelligence, 136*(1), 101-144.

Liu, W. Y., & Song, N. (2003). A Fuzzy Approach to Classification of Text Documents. *JCST: Journal of Computer Science and Technology, 18*(5), 640-647.

Lodhi, H., Saunders, C., Shawe-Taylor, J., Cristianini, N., & Watkins, C. (2002). text classification using string kernels. *Machine Learning Research Journal, 2*, 419-444.

Lopes, A., & Botelho, L. (2005). *SEA: A Semantic Web services context-aware execution agent. In Proceedings of the AAAI Fall Symposium in Agents and the Semantic Web, Arlington, Virginia.*

Luan, X. (2004). *Adaptive middle agent for service matching in the Semantic Web: A quantitive approach.* Thesis, University of Maryland, Baltimore County.

Ludwig, H. (2003). Web Service Level Agreement (WSLA) Language Specification Version 1.0. *Techincal report in IBM.*

Maddouri, M., Elloumi, S., & Jaoua, A. (1998). An incremental learning system for imprecise and uncertain knowledge discovery. *Information Science Journal, 109*, 149-164.

Makoto Yokoo, M., & Durfee, E., & Ishida, T., & Kuwabara, K. (1998). The Distributed Constraint Satisfaction Problem: Formalization and Algorithms. *IEEE Transaction on Knowledge and Data Engineering, 10*(5), 673-685.

Martin, D., Burstein, M., & *et al.* (2004). *OWL-S: Semantic markup for Web services.* W3C Member Submission by the OWL-S (formerly DAML-S) Coalition.

Mazzieri, M., & Dragoni, A. F. (2005). *A Fuzzy Semantics for Semantic Web Languages.* Paper presented at the Proceedings of the ISWC Workshop on Uncertainty Reasoning for the Semantic Web, Galway, Ireland.

McGuinness, D. L., & van Harmelen, F. (Eds.). (2004, February 10). *OWL Web ontology language overview*. W3C Recommendation.

McGuinness, D., & Pinheiro da Silva, P. (October 2004). Explaining answers from the Semantic Web: The inference Web approach. *Journal of Web Semantics, 1*(4), 397-413.

McGuinness, D., & van Harmelen, F. (2004). OWL Web ontology language overview (World Wide Web Consortium (W3C) Recommendation). Retrieved July 3, 2007, from http://www.w3.org/TR/owl-features

McHugh, J., & Widom, J. (1999). Query optimization for XML. In *Proceedings of VLDB Conference* (pp. 315-326), Edinburgh, Scotland, September 1999.

McHugh, J., Abiteboul, S., Goldman, R., Quass, D., & Widom, J. (1997). Lore: A database management system for semistructured data. *ACM SIGMOD Record, 26*(3), 54-66.

McIlraith, S., Son, T.C., & Zeng, H. (2001, March/April). Semantic Web services [Special issue]. *IEEE Intelligent Systems*, 16(2), 46-53.

McNee, S. M., Albert, I., Cosley, D., Gopalkrishnan, P., Lam, S. K., Rashid, A. M., Konstan, J. A., and Riedl, J. (2002). On the recommending of citations for research papers. In *Proceedings of the 2002 ACM Conference on Computer supported cooperative work*, pages 116-125. ACM Press.

Middleton, S. E., Shadbolt, N. R., and Roure, D. C. D. (2004). Ontological user profiling in recommender systems. *ACM Trans. Inf. Syst.*, 22(1):54-88.

Milgram, S. (1967). The small world problem. *Psychology Today, 2*, 60-67.

Milo, T., & Suciu, D. (1999). Index structures for path expressions. In *Proceedings of ICDT* (pp. 277-295).

Mineau G. W., & Godin, R. (1995). Automatic structuring of knowledge bases by conceptual clustering. *IEEE Transactions on Knowledge and Data Engineering*, *7*(5), 824-829.

mining. In *In Proceedings of the International Workshop on Web Mining for E-Commerce (WEBKDD*

Mitchell, T. M. (1997). *Machine Learning*: McGraw Hill.

Mobasher, B., Cooley, R., and Srivastava, J. (2000). Automatic personalization based on Web usage mining. *Commun. ACM*, 43(8):142-151.

Montebello, M., & Abela, C. (2003). DAML-enabled Web services and agents in the Semantic Web. In *Revised Papers from the NODe 2002 Web and Database-Related Workshops on Web, Web-Services, and Database Systems* (pp. 46-58). Berlin: Springer-Verlag.

Moore, J.D. (1995). *Participating in explanatory dialogues: Interpreting and responding to questions in context*. Cambridge, MA: MIT Press.

Moreno, et al. (2005). Using JADE-LEAP to implement agents in mobile devices. Retrieved July 7, 2007, from http://www.zdnet.de/itmanager/whitepapers

Muggleton, S. (1994). *Bayesian Inductive Logic Programming*. Paper presented at the COLT 1994: Proceedings of the 7th Annual ACM Conference on Computational Learning Theory, New York.

Narayanan, S., & McIlraith, S. (2002). Simulation, verification and automated composition of Web services. In *Proceedings of the 11th International World Wide Conference*, Hawaii (pp. 77-88).

Neuenhofen, K.A., & Thompson, M. (1998). Contemplations on a secure marketplace for mobile Java agents. In K.P. Sycara & M. Wooldridge (Eds.), *Proceedings of Autonomous Agents 98*, Minneapolis, Minnesota. New York: ACM Press.

Okabe, A., Boots, B., Sugihara, K., & Chiu, S. N. (2000). *Spatial tessellations: Concepts and applications of Voronoi diagrams* (2nd ed.). John Wiley & Sons.

Ordonez, C. (2003). Clustering binary data streams with k-means. In *Proceedings of the 8th ACM SIGMOD workshop on Research issues in data mining and knowledge discovery*, pages 12-19. ACM Press.

Osuna, E., & Girosi, F.. (1998). Reducing the run-time complexity of support vector machines. In *Proceedings of the International Conference on Pattern Recognition*.

Oundhankar, S., Verma, K., Sivashanugam, K., Sheth, A., & Miller, J. (2005). Discovery of Web serivces in a Muti-Ontologies and Federated Registry Environment. *International Journal of Web Services Research, 1*(3).

OWL-S Java API. (2004). Retrieved July 3, 2007, from http://www.mindswap.org/2004/owl-s/api/

Padovan, B., Sackmann, S., Eymann, T., & Pippow, I. (2002). A prototype for an agent-based secure electronic marketplace including reputation-tracking mechanisms. *International Journal of Electronic Commerce, 6*(4), 93-113.

Paolucci, M., Kawamura, T., Payne, T. R., & Sycara, K. (2002). *Semantic Matching of Web services Capabilities*. Paper presented at the 1st International Semantic Web Conference (ISWC 2002), Sardinia, Italy.

Paolucci, M., Kawamura, T., Payne, T., & Sycara, K. (2002). Semantic matching of Web services capabilities. In *Proceedings of the 1st International Semantic Web Conference (ISWC)*. Berlin: Springer-Verlag.

Papadias, D., Zhang, J., Mamoulis, N., & Tao, Y. (2003). Query processing in spatial network databases. In *Proceedings of 29th International Conference on Very Large Data Bases* (pp. 802-813).

Parsons, L., Haque, E., and Liu, H. (2004). Subspace clustering for high dimensional data: a review. *SIGKDD Explorations.*, 6(1):90-105.

Pather, S., Erwin, G., & Remenyi, D. (2003). Measuring e-commerce effectiveness: A conceptual model. In *Proceedings of SAICSIT 2003* (pp. 143-152).

Patil, A., Oundhakar, S., Sheth, A., & Verma, K. (2004). *METEOR-S Web service Annotation Framework*. Paper presented at the Proceeding of the World Wide Web Conference.

Patrikainen, A. and Manilla, H. (2004). Subspace clustering of high-dimensional binary data - a probabilistic approach. In *Workshop on Clustering High Dimensional Data and its Applications, SIAM International Conference on Data Mining*.

Pawlak, Z., Grzymala-Busse, J., Slowinski, R., & Ziarko, W. (1995). Rough Sets. *CACM: Communications of the ACM, 38*(11), 88-95.

Peer, J. (2004). A PDDL based tool for automatic Web service composition. In *Principles and Practice of Semantic Web Reasoning* (pp. 149-163). Berlin: Springer-Verlag.

Peters, M. and Zaki, M. J. (2005). Clicks: Clustering categorical data using k-partite maximal cliques. In *IEEE International Conference on Data Engineering*. IEEE.

Pierre J. M. (2000, 21 September). Practical issues for automatic categorization of Web sites. In *Proceedings of ECDL 2000 Workshop on the Semantic Web*, Lisbon Portugal (pp. 83-88).

Pinheiro, P., McGuinness, D., & Fikes, R. (2004). *A proof markup language for Semantic Web services* (Tech. Rep. KSL-04-01). Stanford University.

Pitkäranta, T. (2004). *Software agents in Semantic Web environment.* Thesis, Helsinki University of Technology, Finland.

Podobnik, V., Jezic, G., & Trzec, K. (2006). An agent-mediated electronic market of Semantic Web services. In *Proceedings of the AAMAS Workshop on Business Agents and the Semantic Web (BASeWEB '06)*, Hakodate, Japan (pp. 1-10).

Podobnik, V., Petric, A., & Jezic, G. (2006). The CrocodileAgent: Research for efficient agent-based cross-enterprise processes. (*LNCS, 4277)* 752-762.

Podobnik, V., Trzec, K., & Jezic, G. (2006). An auction-based semantic service discovery model for e-commerce applications. (*LNCS, 4277)*, 97-106.

Ponnekanti, S.R., & Fox, A. (2002). SWORD: A developer toolkit for Web service composition. In *Proceedings of the International Conference on the World Wide Web (WWW)*, Honolulu, Hawaii.

Porter, M. F. (1980). An Algorithm for Suffix Stripping. *Program, 14*(3), 130-137.

Procopiuc, C. M., Jones, M., Agarwal, P. K., and Murali, T. M. (2002). A monte carlo algorithm for fast projective clustering. In *Proceedings of the 2002 ACM SIGMOD International Conference on Management of Data*, pages 418-427. ACM Press.

Project JXTA (2003) v2.0: Java™ Programmer's Guide *Sun Microsystems* May 2003

Qian, G., Sural, S., Gu, Y., & Pramanik, S. (2004). Similarity between Euclidean and Cosine angle distance for nearest neighbor queries. In *Proceedings of the ASM Symposium on Applied Computing.*

Qian, J., & Luscombe, N. (2001). Protein family and fold occurrence in genomes: Power-law behaviour and evolutionary model. *Journal of Molecular Biology, 313*(4), 673-681.

Quinlan, J. R. (1996). Improved Use of Continuous Attributes in C4.5. *JAIR: Journal of Artificial Intelligence Research, 4*, 77-90.

Recuerda, F. M., & Robertson, D. (2005). *Discovery and Uncertainty in Semantic Web Services.* Paper presented at the Proceedings of the International Semantic Web Conference (ISWC 2005), Workshop 3: Uncertainty Reasoning for the Semantic Web, Galway, Ireland.

Rennie, J., et. al. (2003, August 21-24) .Tackling the poor assumptions of naive bayes text classifiers. In *Proceedings of the Twentieth International Conference on Machine Learning*, Washington (pp. 199-205).

Resnick, P. and Varian, H. R. (1997). Recommender systems. *Commun. ACM*, 40(3):56-58.

Rheingold, H. (1993) The Virtual Community: Homesteading at the Electronic Frontier. A William Patrick Book Addison-Wesley, ISBN 0-201-60870-7

Riccardi, G., & Tur, D. (2003). Active and unsupervised learning for automatic speech recognition. In *Proceedings of the Eurospeech.*

Richards, D. (2000). User-centred and driven knowledge-based systems for clinical support using ripple down rules. In *Proceedings of the 33rd Hawaii International Conference on System Sciences.*

Rigaux, P., Scholl, M., & Vorsard, A. (2001). *Spatial databases with applications to GIS.* Morgan Kaufmann, Inc.: San Francisco.

Riguet, J. (1948). Relations Binaries, Fermetures et Correspondences de Galois. *Bulletin de la Societe Mathematique de France*, 114-155.

Robertson, S. E., & Jones, K. S. (1976). Relevance Weighting of Search Terms. *JASIS: Journal of the American Society for Information Science, 27*, 129-146.

Rocchio, J. J. (1971). Relevance feedback in information retrieval. In G. Salton (Ed.), *The SMART Retrieval System: Experiments in Automatic Document Processing* (pp. 313-323): Prentice-Hall.

Roddick, J.F., Hornsby, K., & De Vries, D. (2003). A unifying semantic distance model for determining the similarity of attribute values. In *CRIPTS 03: Proceedings of the 26th Australasian Computer Science Conference in Research and Practice in Information Technology* (pp. 111-118). Darlinghurst, Australia: Australian Computer Society, Inc.

Roman, D., Lausen, H., & Keller, U. (2004). *Web Service Modeling Ontology - Standard (WSMO - Standard), WSMO deliverable D2 version 1.1.*

Rosenschein, J. S., & Zlotkin, G. (1994). Rules of Encounter, MIT Press.

Roure D. de, Jennings, N. R. & Shadbolt, N. (2003) The Semantic Grid: A future eScience infrastructure. *Int. J. of Concurrency and Computation: Practice and Experience* 15 (11)

Roussopoulos, N., Kelley, S., & Vincent, F. (1995). Nearest neighbor queries. In *Proceedings of the ACM International Conference on Management of Data (SIGMOD), 24(2)*, 71-79.

Ruiz, M. E., & Srinivasan, P. (2002). Hierarchical text categorization using neural networks. *Information Retrieval*, 5(1), 87-118. Kluwer Academic Publishers.

Safar, M. (2005). K nearest neighbor search in navigation systems. *Journal of Mobile Information Systems (MIS), 1(3)*, 1-18.

Saha, D., & Mukherjee, A. (2003). Pervasive computing: A paradigm for the 21st century. *IEEE Computer, 36*(3), 25-31.

Sahai, A., Durante, A., & Machiraju, V. (2002). Towards Automated SLA Management for Web Services. *Technical report HPL-2001-310 (R.1) on HP Laboratories*

Salminen, A., & Tompa, F. W. (1994). PAT expressions: An algebra for text search. *Acta Linguistica Hungarica, 41*(1), 277-306.

Saltenis, S., Jensen, C. S., Leutenegger, S. T., & Lopez, M. A. (2000). Indexing the positions of continuously moving objects. In *Proceedings of the ACM International Conference on Management of Data (SIGMOD)* (pp. 331-342).

Salton, G. (1988). *Automatic Text Processing: The Transformation, Analysis and Retrieval of Information by Computer*: Massachusetts.

Salton, G. (1989). Automatic text processing: The transformation, analysis, and retrieval of information by computer. Addison-Wesley.

Salton, G., Wong, A., & Yang, C. S. (1975). A Vector Space Model for Automatic Indexing. *CACM: Communications of the ACM, 18*(11), 613-620.

Sandholm, T., & Huai, Q. (2000). Nomad: Mobile agent system for an Internet-based auction house. *IEEE Internet Computing*, pp. 80-86.

Sarwar, B., Karypis, G., Konstan, J., and Reidl, J. (2001). Item-based collaborative filtering recommendation algorithms. In *Proceedings of the tenth International Conference on World Wide Web*, pages 285-295. ACM Press.

Sarwar, B., Karypis, G., Konstan, J., and Riedl, J. (2000). Analysis of recommendation algorithms for e-commerce. In *Proceedings of the 2nd ACM Conference on Electronic commerce*, pages 158-167. ACM Press.

Schafer, J. B., Konstan, J. A., and Riedl, J. (2001). E-commerce recommendation applications. *Data Mining and Knowledge Discovery*, 5(1/2):115-153.

Schein, A., Popescul, A., Ungar, L., and Penncok, D. (2002). Methods and metrics for cold-start recommendations. In *Proceedings of the 25th Annual International ACM SIGIR Conference on Research and Development in Information Retrieval (SIGIR 2002).*

Schmidt, A. R., Waas, F., Kersten, M. L., Carey, M. J., Manolescu, I., & Busse, R. (2002). XMark: A benchmark for XML data management. In *Proceedings of VLDB* (pp. 974-985), Hong Kong, China, August 2002.

Schmidt, G., & Ströhlein, S. (1989). *Relations and graphs.* Springer-Verlag.

Schollmeier., R. (2001) A definition of peer-to-peer networking for the classification of peer-to-peer architectures and applications. In IEEE, editor, *2001 International Conference on Peer-to-Peer Computing (P2P2001),* Departement of Computer and Information Science Linko ping Universität, Sweden, august 2001.

Schutze, H., Hull, D. A., & Pedersen, J. O. (1995). *A Comparison of Classifiers and Document Representations for the Routing Problem.* Paper presented at the SIGIR 1995: Proceedings of the 18th annual international ACM SIGIR conference on Research and development in information retrieval, Seattle, Washington, United States.

Schwier, R.A. (2004). Virtual learning communities. In G. Anglin (Ed.), *Critical issues in instructional technology.* Portsmouth, NH: Teacher Ideas Press.

Sebastiani, F. (2002). Machine learning in automated text categorization. *CSUR: ACM Computing Surveys, 34*(1), 1-47.

Sedukhin, I. (Ed.). (2005, March 9). *Web services distributed management: Management of Web services.* OASIS Standard.

Segal, R. B., & Kephart, J. O. (2000). *Incremental Learning in SwiftFile.* Paper presented at the ICML 2000:Proceedings of the 7th International Conference on Machine Learning, Stanford, CA, USA.

Segal, R., & Kephart, J. O. (1999). *MailCat: An Intelligent Assistant for Organizing E-Mail.* Paper presented at the AGENTS 1999: Proceedings of the 3rd International Conference on Autonomous Agents.

Seidl, T., & Kriegel, H.P. (1998). Optimal multi-step k-nearest neighbor search. In *Proceedings ACM International Conference on Management of Data (SIGMOD)* (pp. 154-165).

Selamat A., Omatu, S., & Yanagimoto, H.. (2002, August 5-7). Web news classification using neural networks based on PCA. In *Proceedings of the of SICE*, Osaka, Japan. (pp. 2388-2393).

Selinger, P. G., Astrahan, M. M., Chamberlin, D., Lorie, R., & Price, T. (1979). Access path selection in a relational database management system. In *Proceedings of ACM SIGMOD Conference* (pp. 23-34), 1979.

Shahabi, C., Kolahdouzan, M., & Sharifzadeh, M. (2002). A road network embedding technique for k-nearest neighbor search in moving object databases. In *Proceedings of the 10th ACM International Symposium on Advances in Geographic Information Systems (ACMGIS)* (pp. 94-100).

Shakshuki, E. (2002). Intelligent Agents for Open Environments. The 6th IASTED International Conference on Artificial Intelligence & Soft Computing, Banff, Alberta, Canada, 37-41.

Shakshuki, E., & Ghenniwa, H., & Kamel, M. (2003). Agent-based System Architecture for Dynamic and Open Environments. *International Journal of Information Technology and Decision Making, 2*(1), 105-133.

Shakshuki, E., & Luo, Z., & Gong, J. (2005). An Agent-based Approach to Security Service. *International Journal of Network and Computer Applications, 28*(3), Elsevier Science Journal, 183-208.

Shankar, R.D., Tu, S.W., & Musen, M.A. (1998). *A declarative explanation framework that uses a collection of visualization agents.* Stanford Medical Institute, Stanford University School of Medicine, Stanford, California.

Shardanand, U. and Maes, P. (1995). Social information filtering: algorithms for automating word of mouth. In *Proceedings of the SIGCHI Conference on Human factors in computing systems*, pages 210-217. ACM Press/Addison-Wesley Publishing Co.

Shaw, S., Foggiato-Bish, L., Garcia, I., Tillman, G., Tryon, D., Wood, W., et al. (1993). *Improving Data Quality Via LDL++.* Paper presented at the Workshop on Programming with Logic Databases (Informal Proceedings).

Siberski, W., Pan, J.Z., & Thaden, U. (2006). Querying the Semantic Web with Preferences. In *Proceedings of the 5th International Semantic Web Conference*, Athens, Greece.

Singh, P., Bhimavarapu, R., Davalcu, H., Baral, C., Kim, S., Liu, H., Bittner, M., and Ramakrishnan, I. (2005). Biolog: A browser based collaboration and resource navigation assistant for biomedical researchers. In *Proceedings of 2nd International Workshop on Data Integration in the Life Sciences (DILS'05).*

Sirin, E., Hendler, J., & Parsia, B. (2003). Semi automatic composition of Web services using semantic descriptions. In *Proceedings of the Workshop on Web Services: Modeling, Architecture and Infrastructure.*

Sirin, E., Parsia, B., & Hendler, J. (2004). Filtering and selecting Semantic Web services with interactive composition techniques. *IEEE Intelligent Systems, 19*(4), 44-51.

Sirin, E., Parsia, B., & Hendler, J. (2005, November). Template-based composition of Semantic Web services. In *Proceedings of the AAAI Fall Symposium on Agents and the Semantic Web*, Arlington, Virginia.

Sivashanmugam, K., Verma, K., Sheth, A., & Miller, J. (2003). *Adding Semantics to Web Services Standards.* Paper presented at the The 2003 International Conference on Web Services (ICWS'03), Erfurt, Germany.

Solan, Z., Horn, D., Ruppin, E., & Edelman, S. (2005, August 16). Unsupervised learning of natural languages. In *Proceedings of the National Academy of Sciences* (Vol. 102, No. 33, pp. 11629-11634).

Song, Z., & Roussopoulos, N. (2001). K-nearest neighbor search for moving query point. In *Proceedings of the 7th International Symposium on Advances in Spatial and Temporal Databases* (pp. 79-96).

Sperduti, A., & Starita, A. (1993). Speed up learning and network optimization with extended back-propagation. *Neural Networks, 6*, 365-383.

Spiliopoulou, M., & Pohle, C. (2001). Data mining for measuring and improving the success of Web sites. *Journal for Data Mining & Knowledge Discovery 5*(1-2), 85-114.

Srinivasan, N., Paolucci, M., & Sycara, K. (2004, 6-9). *Adding OWL-S to UDDI, implementation and throughput.* Paper presented at the First International Workshop on Semantic Web Services and Web Process Composition (SWSWPC 2004), San Diego, California, USA.

Srivastava, D., Al-Khalifa, S., Jagadish, H. V., Koudas, N., Patel, J. M., & Wu, Y. (2002). Structural joins: A primitive for efficient XML query pattern matching. In *Proceedings of ICDE Conference* (pp. 141-152), San Jose, CA, February 26-March 1, 2002.

Stoilos, G., Stamou, G., Tzouvaras, V., Pan, J., & Horrocks, I. (2005). *The Fuzzy Description Logic f-SHIN.* Paper presented at the Proceedings of the ISWC Workshop on Uncertainty Reasoning for the Semantic Web, Galway, Ireland.

Stolz, C., Viermetz, M., Skubacz, M., & Neuneier, R. (2005). Guidance performance indicator—Web metrics for information driven Web sites, *Proceedings of IEEE International. Conference Web Intelligence 2005.*

Sun A., Lim, E., & Ng, W. (2002). Web classification using support vector machine. In *Procceedings of ACM Workshop on Web Information and Data Management (WIDM'02)*, VA. (pp. 96-99).

Sun. (2006). Java. Retrieved July 7, 2007, from http://java.sun.com/javame/

Suri, N., et al. (2000). NOMADS: Toward a strong and safe mobile system. In *Proceedings of the 4th International Conference on Autonomous Agents* (pp. 163-164). New York: ACM Press.

Sycara, K., J. Lu, M. K., & Widoff, S. (1999a). Dynamic service matchmaking among agents in open information environments. *ACM SIGMOD Record (Special Issue on Semantic Interoperability in Global Information Systems), 28*(1), 47-53.

Sycara, K., J. Lu, M. K., & Widoff, S. (1999b). *Matchmaking among heterogeneous agents on the internet.* Paper presented at the AAAI Spring Symposium on Intelligent Agents in Cyberspace.

Sycara, K., Paolucci, M., Anolekar, A., & Srinivasan, N. (2004). Automated discovery, interaction and composition of Semantic Web services. *Journal of Web Semantics, 1*(1), 27-46.

Sycara, K., Widoff, S., & M. Klusch, J. L. (2002). *LARKS: Dynamic Matchmaking Among Heterogeneous Software Agents in Cyberspace.* Paper presented at the Autonomous Agents and Multi- Agent Systems.

Tan, A. C., Gilbert, D., & Deville, Y. (2003). Integrative machine learning approach for multi-class SCOP protein fold classification. In *Proceedings of the German Conference on Bioinformatics* (pp. 153-159).

Tang, S. (2004). *Matching of Web services specifications using DAML-S descriptions.* Thesis, Technical University of Berlin, Germany.

Tao, Y., Papadias, D., & Shen, Q. (2002). Continuous nearest neighbor search. In *Proceedings of the 28th International Conference on Very Large Data Bases (VLDB)* (pp. 287-298).

Tax, D. M. J., & Laskov, P. (2003). *Online SVM Learning: From Classification To Data Description And Back.* Paper presented at the NNSP: IEEE International Workshop on Neural Networks for Signal Processing, Toulouse France.

Thaden, U., Siberski, W., & Nejdl, W. (2003). *A Semantic Web based Peer-to-Peer Service Registry Network* (Technical Report): Learning Lab Lower Saxony.

Todd, S., Parr, F., & Conner, M. (2005). An overview of the reliable HTTP protocol. Retrieved July 7, 2007, from http://www-128.ibm.com/developerworks/Webservices/library/ws-phtt/

Trastour, D., Bartolini, C., & Gonzalez-Castillo, J. (2001). *A Semantic Web Approach to Service Description for Matchmaking of Service.* Paper presented at the 1st Semantic Web Working Symposium, CA.

Tresch, M., & Luniewski, A. (1995). *An Extensible Classifier for Semi-Structured Documents.* Paper presented at the CIKM 1995: Proceedings of the 4th International Conference on Information and Knowledge Management, Baltimore, Maryland, United States.

Trudel, A., & Zhang, H. (2005). Exploiting the Relationship between IA Networks and Finite Domain CSPs. 12th International Symposium on Temporal Representation and Reasoning (TIME'05), Burlington, Vermont, USA.

Trzec, K., & Lovrek, I. (2006). Modelling behaviour of trading agents in electronic market for communication resources. In *Proceedings of the 2nd Conference on Networking and Electronic Commerce Research (NAEC '06)*, Riva Del Garda, Italy (pp. 171-186).

Trzec, K., Lovrek, I., & Mikac, B. (2006). Agent behaviour in double auction electronic market for communication resources. *Lecture Notes in Artificial Intelligence, 4251*, 318-325.

Tur, G., Hakkani-Tür, D., & E.Schapire, R. (2005). Combining active and semi-supervised learning for spoken language understanding. *Speech Communication, 45*(2), 171-186.

Tut, M.T., & Edmond, D. (2002). The use of patterns in service composition. In *CAiSE 02/WES 02: Revised Papers from the International Workshop on Web Services, E-Business, and the Semantic Web* (pp. 28-40). Berlin: Springer-Verlag.

UDDI. (2006). Retrieved July 7, 2007, from http://www.uddi.org/

Ungar, L. H. and Foster, D. P. (1998). Clustering methods for collaborative filtering. In *In Workshop on Recommendation Systems at the 15th National Conference on Artificial Intelligence.*

van Beek, P., & Manchak, D. (1996). The Design and Experimental Analysis of Algorithms for Temporal Reasoning. *Journal of Artificial Intelligence Research*, 1-18.

Van Rijsbergen, C. J. (1979). Evaluation. In *Dept. of Computer Science, University of Glasgow*: Department of Computer Science, University of Glasgow.

Vanides, J. & Morgret, K. (2002) STEP ePortfolio Workspace: Supporting Pre-Service Teachers with Electronic Portfolio Creation, Reflection and Online Collaboration . ldt.stanford.edu/~**keri**/project/mySTEPstanford.doc

Vanides, J., (2002) A Personalized, Web-Based Learning Electronic ePortfolio Workspace, White paper. http://ldt.stanford.edu/~jvanides/eportfolio/STEP-eportfolio-workspace.pdf

Vapnik, V. (1998). *Statistical learning theory*. New York: John Wiley & Sons.

Vapnik, V. (1999). *The nature of statistical learning theory* (2nd ed.). New York: Springer-Verlag.

Viermetz, M., Stolz, C., Gedov, V., & Skubacz, M. (2006). Relevance and impact of tabbed browsing behavior on Web usage mining. *Web Intelligence 2006.*

Vlastos, G. (1980). The Socratic Elenchus. *Oxford Studies in Ancient Philosophy, 1*, 27-58.

W3C. Organization, *SOAP - Simple Object Access Protocol.*

Wahbe, R., Lucco, S., Anderson, T.E., & Graham, S.L. (1993). Efficient software-based fault isolation. In *Proceedings of the 14th ACM Symposium on Operating Systems Principles* (pp. 203-216).

Walsh, A. E. (2002). *UDDI, SOAP, and WSDL: The Web Services Specification Reference Book* (1st edition ed.) 0130857262: Pearson Education.

Wang, A.I., Sørensen, C.F., & Indal, E. (2003). **A mobile agent architecture for heterogeneous devices.** *Wireless and Optical Communications.*

Wang, G., & Liu, M. (2003). Query processing and optimization for regular path expressions. In *Proceedings of CAiSE Conference* (pp. 30-45), Klagenfurt, Austria, June16-18, 2003.

Web services resource (WS-Resource) V1.2. OASIS.

Weiser, M. (1991). The computer for the 21st century. *Scientific American, 265*(3), 94-104.

Weiser, M. (1994). The world is not a desktop. *ACM Interactions, 1*(1), 7-8.

Weiser, M., & Brown, J.S. (1997). The coming age of calm technology. In P.J. Dening, R.M. Metcalfe, & J. Burke (Eds.), *Beyond calculation: The next fifty years of computing* (pp. 75-86). New York: Springer-Verlag.

Weiss, S. M., & Indurkhya, N. (1993). Optimized Rule Induction. *IEEE Expert, 8*(6), 61-69.

Weston, J., & Watkins, C. (1999). Multi-class support vector machines. In *Proceedings of the ESANN99* Brussels (pp. 219-224).

White, J.E. (1999). Telescript technology: Mobile agents. In Mobility: Processes, computers, and agents (pp. 460-493). New York: ACM Press/Addison-Wesley.

Whittaker, S., & Sidner, C. (1996). *Email Overload: Exploring Personal Information Management of Email.* Paper presented at the CHI 1996: Proceedings of the SIGCHI conference on Human factors in computing systems, Vancouver, British Columbia, Canada.

Wishart, R., Robinson, R., Indulska, J., & Jøsang, A. (2005). SuperstringRep: Reputation-enhanced service discovery. In *Proceedings of the 28th Australasian Conference on Computer Science (ACSC'05)*, Newcastle, Australia (pp. 49-57).

Wooldridge, M., & Jennings, N. (1995). Intelligent agents: theory and practice. *The Knowledge Engineering Review, 10*(2), 115-152.

WSRF TC. (2004). *OASIS Web services resource framework (WSRF).* Retrieved from http://www.oasis-open.org/committees/tc home.php?wg abbrev=wsrf

Wu, B., Parsia, B., Sirin, E., Hendler, J., & Nau, D. (2003). Automating DAML-S Web services composition using SHOP2. In *Proceedings of the International Semantic Web Conference* (pp. 195-210).

Wu, H., Jin, H., Li, Y., & Chen, H. (2005). *An Approach for Service Discovery Based on Semantic Peer-to-Peer.* Paper presented at the Advances in Computer Science – ASIAN 2005: 10th Asian Computing Science Conference, Kunming, China.

Xiao, G., Southey, F., Holte, R. C. & Wilkinson, D. (2005, July). Software testing by active learning for commercial games. In *Proceedings of the 20th National Conference on Artificial Intelligence* (*AAAI-2005*) (pp. 898-903).

Xu, J., Cao, Y., Li, H., & Zhao, M. (2005, May 10-14). Ranking definitions with supervised learning methods. *Special interest tracks and posters of the 14th international conference on World Wide Web*, Chiba, Japan (pp. 811-819).

Yamazaki, T., & Dagan, I. (1997). *Mistake-Driven Learning with Thesaurus for Text Categorization*. Paper presented at the NLPRS 1997: Proceedings of the Natural Language Processing Pacific Rim Symposium, Phuket, TH.

Yang & Liu, X. (1999). A re-examination of text categorization methods. In *Proceedings of the 22nd Annual International ACM SIGIR Conference on Research and Development in Information Retrieval (SIGIR'99)* (pp. 42-49).

Yang, Z., Gay, R., Miao, C., Zhang, J.-B., & Shen, Z. (2005). Automating integration of manufacturing systems and services: A semantic Web services approach. In *Proceedings of the 31st Annual Conference of the IEEE Industrial Electronics Society*.

Yang, Z., Zhang, J. B., Tao, J., & Gay, R. (2005). Characterizing Services Composeability and OWL-S based services composition. In H. Zhuge & G. Fox (Eds.), *The 4th international conference on grid and cooperative computing (GCC 2005)*, Beijing, China (LNCS 3795, pp. 244-249).

Yeung, W. L., & Lu, M. (2004). Functional characteristics of commercial Web sites: A Longitudinal. *Information & Management Journal, 41*, 483-495.

Yoon, J.-L. (2007). Telco 2.0: A new role and business model. *IEEE Communications Magazine, 45*(1), 10-12.

Yu, C., Ooi, B. C., Tan, K. L., & Jagadish, H. V. (2001). Indexing the distance: An efficient method to KNN processing. In *Proceedings of the 27th International Conference on Very Large Data Bases* (pp. 421-430).

Yu, H., Han, J., & Chang, K. C. C. (2004, January). PEBL: Web page classification without negative examples. *IEEE Transactions on Knowledge and Data Engineering, 16*(1), 70-81.

Yu, H., Yang, J., & Han, J. (2003, August).Classifying large data sets using SVM with hierarchical clusters. In *Proceedings of the Ninth ACM SIGKDD '03 International Conference on Knowledge Discovery and Data Mining*, WA.

Yu, S., Liu, J., & Le, J. (2004a). *Decentralized Web Service Organization Combining Semantic Web and Peer to Peer Computing*. Paper presented at the Web Services: European Conference, ECOWS 2004, Erfurt, Germany.

Yu, S., Liu, J., & Le, J. (2004b). *Intelligent Web Service Discovery in Large Distributed System*. Paper presented at the Intelligent Data Engineering and Automated Learning – IDEAL 2004, Exeter, UK.

Zamora, E., Pollock, J., & al, e. (1981). The Use of Trigram Analysis for Spelling Error Detection. *Information Processing and Management, 6*(17), 305-316.

Zhang , Y. & Tanniru, M. (2005) An Agent-based Approach to Study Virtual Learning Communities, *Proceedings of the 38th Annual Hawaii International Conference on System Sciences (HICSS'05)* - Track 1, January 03 - 06, 2005 Big Island, Hawaii.

Zhang, C., Naughton, J. F., DeWitt, D. J., Luo, Q., & Lohman, G. M. (2001). On supporting containment queries in relational database management systems. In *Proceedings of ACM SIGMOD Conference* (pp. 425-436), Santa Barbara, CA, USA, 2001.

Zhou, C., Chia, L.-T., & Lee, B.-S. (2005a). Semantics in Service Discovery and QoS Measurement. *IEEE IT Professional Magazine, 7*(2), 29-34.

Zhou, C., Chia, L.-T., & Lee, B.-S. (2005b). Web Services Discovery with DAML-QoS Ontology. *International Journal of Web Services Research(JWSR), 2*(2), 44-67.

Zinky, J. A., Bakken, D. E., & Schantz, R. E. (1997). Architectural Support for Quality of Service for CORBA Objects. *Theory and Practice of Object Systems, 3*(1), John Wiley & Son.

Zviran, M., Glezer, C., & Avni, I. (2005). User satisfaction from commercial Web sites: The effect of design and use. *Information & Management Journal*.

Index

T

U

V

W

X

Z